Great Pies & Tarts

Great Pies & Tarts

OVER 150 RECIPES TO BAKE, SHARE, AND ENJOY

by

CAROLE WALTER

....

Foreword by
Arthur Schwartz

....

Photographs by Gentl & Hyers
Illustrations by Rodica Prato

Gramercy Books
New York

This 2006 edition is published by Gramercy Books,
an imprint of Random House Value Publishing, by arrangement
with Clarkson N. Potter/Publishers, a member of the Crown
Publishing Group, both divisions of Random House, Inc.

GRAMERCY is a registered trademark and the colophon is
a trademark of Random House, Inc.

Random House
New York • Toronto • London • Sydney • Auckland
www.randomhouse.com

Printed and bound in the United States

DESIGN BY JILL ARMUS

Library of Congress Cataloging-in-Publication Data
Walter, Carole.
Great pies & tarts : over 150 recipes to bake, share, and enjoy /
Carole Walter ; foreword by Arthur Schwartz.—2006 ed.
p. cm.
Originally published: New York : C. Potter, 1998.
Includes bibliographical references and index.
ISBN-13: 978-0-517-22807-4
ISBN-10: 0-517-22807-6
1. Pies. I. Title: Great pies and tarts. II. Title.

TX773.W323 2006
641.8'652—dc22

2006041104

10 9 8 7 6 5 4 3 2 1

To Gene,

When I couldn't find the words, you found them.

When I became discouraged, you encouraged.

When I was tired, you gave me strength.

Thank you for making this book possible.

ACKNOWLEDGMENTS

HIS ODYSSEY BEGAN in 1994 at the International Association of Culinary Professionals conference in San Francisco when master baker Nick Malgieri introduced me to my editor, Roy Finamore of Clarkson Potter/Publishers. While we only had a brief chat, there was an immediate chemistry. Roy, working with you these past years has been a privilege. Your artistic eye and creativity have contributed immeasurably to the success of this book. Most of all, Roy, thank you for listening, a rare gift that most do not possess.

My literary agent, Judith Weber, has been constantly at my side, encouraging, advising, and wisely administrating the essential business details. Judith, your accessibility has meant a great deal to me. Thank you for always being there and for going that extra mile.

Kelly Volpe, my assistant, has been an invaluable partner in the creation of this book. The Fruit and Berry Glossary exemplifies her fine work. Her dedication toward getting the job done far exceeded what was expected. Kelly, thank you for your patience, your loyalty, and for brightening my days.

Judie Levenberg, my other devoted teammate, spent hours taking notes and testing recipes as well as contributing clever text. Judie, thank you for your confidence, devotion, and friendship. Your spunk and tenacity are an inspiration to all.

Judith Moore, my faithful student with a gift for words, did fine work on the Techniques and Procedures and the Ingredients sections. Judith, thank you for being so thorough and for your ability to capture my thoughts on paper.

Andrea Gentl and Marty Hyers, my talented photographers, made every photograph shine. How fortunate I was to have "two" of you! Anne Disrude, my food stylist, meticulously translated my recipes from paper to reality. Betty Alfenito, my prop stylist, tastefully gave personality to every photo. Thank you to a superb team.

The talented network at Clarkson Potter receives "4 stars" for bringing this manuscript from my hands to yours. Thank you to my publisher, Chip Gibson, editorial director Lauren Shakely, designer Jill Armus, art director Jane Treuhaft, production editor Amy Boorstein, production manager Joan Denman, copy editor Carole Berglie, indexer Rose Grant, and publicity director Wendy Schuman. Thanks also to Steve Magnuson, Alison Gross, and Joan DeMayo for your invaluable help.

To Christopher Monte Smith, Roy Finamore's editorial assistant, my deep appreciation for your calm and cool manner in the face of fire. Your dry wit has helped me chuckle during many a crisis.

A special thank you to Arthur Schwartz for his kind words and unflagging belief in me. Arthur, I am continually awed by your incredible wealth of knowledge. Having you as a friend is truly a privilege.

Terry Ford has been an invaluable resource and never failed to extend a helping hand. Terry, your enthusiasm, dedication to the culinary profession, and twinkling eyes make it a pleasure to be in your company.

Friend and colleague Shirley Corriher was always willing to sort out the complexities of food science. Shirley, thank you for generously sharing your expertise.

Joe Volpe and Mike Waugh have been my computer wizards throughout this massive text. Many weekend hours were shared with the New York Jets to keep my equipment running smoothly. Fellas, thanks a bunch.

Thank you to the following technical advisors. Delicious Orchards, Colts Neck, N.J.: David Caldera, Ron Gassaway, George Simmons, Mike Taglietta; Ronald Fish, North Carolina Department of Agriculture; Jay Jansen, Monrovia Nursery Co., Azusa, Calif.; Sue Johnson-Langdon, Executive Director of the North Carolina Sweet Potato Commission; Chris Olsen, Cherry Central, Inc.; "Produce Pete" Napolitano, Bergenfield, N.J.; Bob Rathgeb, Tice Farms, Woodcliff Lake, N.J.; Bob Sickle, Sickles Farms, Little Silver, N.J.; Christopher Tracy, Calphalon Cookware.

No work of this size and detail would have been possible without the help of many personal and professional friends who were eager to share in this undertaking. My heartfelt thanks to: Lenny Allen, Judith Bernhaut, my brother Robert Blum, Linda Bogan, Mariette Bronstein, Mary Ann Buonocore, Donna D'Amato, Nancy D'Edwardo, Debbie DeGorges, Catherine Titus Felix, Dolores Feinswog, Lee Dicks Guice, Annellen Guth, Antoinette Hartman, Joann Hoff, Sally Kofke, Jeffrey Levenberg, Shirley Lynch, Virginia McKinley, Marla Mendelsohn, Elaine Morrison, Hilda Pearlman, Rick Rodgers, Arlene Sarappo, Kathleen Kenny Sanderson, my biased cousin Paul Schwartz, June Seligman, Anne Semmes, Joyce Stitch, and Sue Zelickson. Thanks also to my pie bird fanciers, Lillian Cole, Linda Fields, and Catherine Noyes, to Selma Yagoda, who was always willing to help wherever it was needed, and Suzen Mines-O'Rourke of Cooking by the Book for her gracious hospitality.

Susan Loden and the great staff at Kings CooKINGstudios continuously extended support and enthusiasm. Your patience when dealing with this workaholic teacher has been appreciated more than words can say.

To my "tasting committee," Lynn and Rudy Lopes, their friends and neighbors, thank you for opening your hearts and mouths. Your objectivity and input when sampling the recipes helped bring forth the cream of the crop.

To my children, Frank, Marla, Pam, and Andy, and my grandchildren, Zach, Samantha, and twins Jeffrey and Neil, thank you for sharing with me this book and for not making my guilt trip any worse than it is. You are my most precious jewels.

CONT

FOREWORD BY ARTHUR SCHWARTZ.........................xii

PREFACE xiv

INTRODUCTION xvi

1. BEFORE YOU BEGIN 1

Ingredients..2

Fruit and Berry Glossary.......................................17

Equipment..41

Techniques and Procedures 49

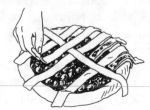

2. THE PRIMER 81

THE PASTRY PRIMER 84

Lesson 1: About Apple Pie....................................106

Lesson 2: About Lemon Meringue Pie.....................112

Lesson 3: About Open Fruit Tarts.........................118

Lesson 4: About French Fruit Tarts with Pastry Cream...124

E N T S

3. BEYOND THE PRIMER 131
Pastry Doughs & Crunchy Shells 132
From Orchards, Vines & Bushes 176
Decadent & Delicious 240
Pie & Tart Potpourri 302
Cobblers, Crisps & Crumbles 324
Out of the Deep Freeze 344
Little Tarts, Pies & Turnovers 367
Lusciously Light & Lean 393
Favorite Savory Pies & Tarts 412
Sauces, Toppings & Garnishes 437

GLOSSARY OF TERMS 457
BIBLIOGRAPHY 462
MAIL ORDER SOURCES 466
EQUIVALENTS AND SUBSTITUTIONS 468
INDEX 470

FOREWORD

NLESS YOU CAN DO IT ALREADY, it's hard to imagine how empowering it is to be able to bake the perfect apple pie. If you can't now, this book will teach you. ✳ Carole Walter never stops astounding me. If she doesn't actually know more about baking than any other living person, she certainly knows how to communicate and teach what she knows better than anyone I've ever encountered. Grown men—responsible businessmen and good cooks, guys who are not daunted by managing hundreds of people, poaching a 15-pound salmon, whipping up bouillabaisse for 20, a soufflé for their sweetheart, or de-boning a turkey so it can be stuffed with a duck—are known to cry when faced with a pastry project. But I've seen it: when Carole gets finished with them they leave class thinking they're good enough to open a bakery.

Carole is not my first baking teacher. As a newspaper food editor, cookbook writer, and broadcaster, I've been observing cooking teachers (and picking their brains) for nearly 30 years. She has the patience, meticulous mind, organizational ability, fine-tuned taste, and long experience that you need to be a truly great baker and baking teacher. *Great Pies & Tarts*—like her first book, *Great Cakes*—conveys all that. If you can't experience a Carole Walter class in person, this book is the next best thing. It's not merely a book of fabulous recipes guaranteed to work because Carole has been baking and teaching them for years. It's a teaching manual, and it's like having her in your kitchen, at your elbow, every step of the way.

Carole is my "baking guru," in the truest sense, too. For not only does she explain all the particulars—the properties and behavior of flours, eggs, leavenings, sweeteners, and shortenings . . . the real science behind baking ingredients and techniques—but she also imparts a certain spiritual calm to the proceedings. Anyone can bake beautiful, delicious desserts if they want to, she likes to say, and the reward isn't merely something good to eat. It will garner you the love that good baking always invokes. I wish I'd been the one to say "nothin' says lovin' like somethin' from the oven," but a flour company got there first. And it is Carole who knows how to make it true.

—*Arthur Schwartz*

PREFACE

HEN I TOLD my friend Selma Yagoda, a fine cook with a keen wit, that the subject of my next book would be pies and tarts, she chuckled. "Pies," she said! "Let me tell you of the first and last pie I attempted some forty years ago, when I was just married. I got only as far as the dough, and that was enough for me. My hands had bits of fat and flour stuck to my skin. I couldn't answer the phone or touch anything. There was flour all over the kitchen. What a mess! Rolling out the dough was not even a consideration. I threw everything away swearing never to venture into pie baking again." And she didn't.

My friend is not alone in this. I once had a minister's wife as a student; she took the matter so seriously that she left my classroom in tears because her pastry dough was overworked and impossible to roll.

Tales like this give some insight into why pies and tarts get such a bad rap. Doughs can be too soft or too hard. They can be too wet or too dry. They crack, they break, they shrink. They can be difficult to lift. Most people can't roll pastry into a circle; some can't roll it at all. Cooked custards don't always thicken, and if they do, they occasionally thin out. Fruit pies have puddles of juice that make crusts soggy. Meringues shrink and weep. The edges of pie crusts burn. It's no wonder that even the best cooks shy away from baking pies and tarts.

Desserts are my love, and teaching people how to make them is my profession. When it comes to sweets, I tune in to what people like. While I've never taken a full-blown census, I think pies and tarts are people's absolute favorites. Unfortunately, good ones are hard to find. Most store-bought pies and tarts are a far cry from their homemade counterparts. Too often these commercial pastries are made from overly thickened canned fruit fillings or packaged pudding mixes. If made with fresh fruit at all, the amount of fruit in the filling is skimpy and congealed with starch. And ready-made pie shells don't begin to measure up to the taste and texture of crust made from scratch.

For years I have wanted to write a teaching book on pastries and rolling pin skills because so many people are intimidated by the subject. Silly as it seems, when people are put to the test of having to combine flour, fat, and liquid to make a dough to roll out, paranoia sets in and they freeze. I view this with sadness. Pies and tarts are delicious desserts—and nothing to be afraid of.

Stories relating to this form of cookery date back to the Egyptians, where etchings on the subject were made in the tomb of Ramses II. Primitive versions of pies were made from coarsely ground meals that were moistened and molded into a dough, then filled with a variety of fruits and nuts. The art became more refined during the opulent era of the Persian kings. Sugar from India and aromatic spices and nuts from the Orient were brought to the Middle East to satisfy people's desires for lavish meals.

Through travel and trade, regions of Europe that are now Italy, France, and England were exposed to these enticing ingredients. These European pies were laden with meats or combinations of meat, game, fish, and fruits wrapped in a heavy paste. With such cooking soon recognized as a true art form, the first trade union or pastry guild was formed in Paris as early as 1270. In 1306, Chaucer made reference to pies in his Prologue to the *Canterbury Tales*.

Surely the Pilgrims brought their knowledge of pies and tarts from England to America. Here they found a wealth of new ingredients to broaden the base of this virtually endless craft. As the country developed, so did its cuisine: more refined and lighter pies were made of pumpkin, cranberry, apple, and quince.

Regions of our new country became known for styles of food and their special dishes. The Pennsylvania Dutch settlers gave us a molasses creation called shoo-fly pie, while from the pecan trees of Georgia, Louisiana, and Texas came pecan pies, rich with eggs, corn syrup, and crunchy nuts.

From nursery rhymes like "Little Jack Horner" and "Sing a Song of Sixpence," to legendary works of renowned writers, pies and tarts have given us a legacy of literary and culinary pleasures. *Great Pies & Tarts* is a cookbook written for all who enjoy the classic favorites, as well as those who like exciting new tastes.

INTRODUCTION

ROM SAVORIES TO SWEETMEATS, almost everything we eat can be wrapped or nestled in a pastry casing. Each season of the year, each favorite holidays, has a signature pie or tart to herald its arrival. What would autumn be without a cinnamon-scented apple pie? Thanksgiving conjures up visions of pastries with pumpkin, pecan, and cranberries. Mincemeat and nesselrode pies are enjoyed at Christmas, followed soon by citrus tarts and Washington's Birthday cherry pies. Strawberry-rhubarb is a harbinger of spring, and summer has glorious bounty of fruits and berries so numerous that we hardly know where to begin.

As you explore *Great Pies & Tarts* you will discover a treasury of wonderful recipes. There are delicate layers of tender pastry filled with sweet fresh fruits and crunchy crusts with lush cream fillings. But this just hints at what you will find in the pages of this book.

Part 1 will familiarize you with ingredient and equipment information. I've also included a section on procedures and techniques, with a quick overview for troubleshooting, "Pastry Problem Solving." A special feature is the "Fruit and Berry Glossary," complete with hints on shopping, storage, and seasonal availability.

Part 2, "The Primer," is a teaching section. Start with the "Pastry Primer," which contains the essential master dough recipes, featuring both hand and food processor techniques. Then in the "Pie and Tart Primer," you will learn all about making pies and tarts from four principal recipes. Basic techniques such as baking with seasonal fruits, making cooked fillings, and preparing perfect meringue toppings are explained in detail. Throughout the Primer are step-by-step illustrations to eliminate any guesswork. Once you feel comfortable with these fundamentals, you should have the confidence to move along to explore the other recipes.

Part 3, "Beyond the Primer," has myriad recipes for mouthwatering pies, tarts, cobblers, and crisps. The first chapter contains a large variety of doughs, cookie crusts, and other pastry casings, such as the Goof-Proof Puff Pastry. Also included are "no-roll" recipes like the Butter-Batter Pastry, crumb crusts, and meringue shells.

The pie and tart recipes begin with "From Orchards, Vines & Bushes," a chapter with more than two dozen all-fruit recipes that make the most of nature's bounty. These are suited for people who wish to savor delectable, freshly baked pies or tarts that are not overly rich. Such recipes as Peaches and Berries with Patchwork Linzer Crust and Autumn Pear and Grape Pie with Cheddar Pastry are tempting examples of what lies in store for you.

When a splurge is in order, refer to "Decadent & Delicious." Here are classic American favorites like Black Bottom Pie and Florida's treasure, Key Lime Pie. New ideas include Devilish Chocolate Candy Tart and Melon and Mascarpone Tart in Chocolate Crumb Crust. There are chapters on frozen ice cream and Bavarian-style pies, as well as on little pies, tartlets, and turnovers. Also included is a chapter with classic and contemporary savory tarts like Smoky Joe's Turkey Tart and Corn Custard Pie with Wild Rice.

In the "Lusciously Light & Lean" chapter, waistline watchers can satisfy sweet cravings with tasty low-fat recipes such as Stuffed Cinnamon Apple Top-Knots and Tangerine Meringue Pie. Many of the recipes in the "Cobblers, Crisps & Crumbles" chapter can also easily be adapted to special diet needs. Elsewhere, fruit pie recipes can be made crustless, while others may rely on just the natural sweetness of fruits and berries to keep calories and fat to a minimum.

Great Pies & Tarts is packed with my best recipes; there is a wealth of mouthwatering treats in store for you. But I've also relied on my years of teaching to do everything possible to take the guesswork out of making pies and tarts. So whether you're a novice or an experienced baker, head for "The Primer" and get your hands in some flour.

The Key to Success

TWO VALUABLE PORTIONS of this book should not be overlooked when preparing the recipes in this book. They are the Fruit and Berry Glossary (page 17) and the Recipe Roundups found in The Primer (pages 81–129).

The Fruit and Berry Glossary contains essential information on selecting, storing, handling, and cleaning produce. The Recipe Roundups highlight tips and techniques that will benefit even the most experienced baker.

Great PIES & TARTS

1

Before You Begin

INGREDIENTS

UNDERSTANDING YOUR INGREDIENTS is essential for achieving consistent baking results. Because so many variables exist with food products, the success of a recipe can depend on having some knowledge of the products you are working with.

Flours run the gamut from smooth and delicate to grainy. Each has their place in baking, but determining the best one for the job is not always easy. Fats can range from fluid to semisoft to solid, and they all create distinctive doughs. Sweeteners, as well, vary from light to dark, granules to syrups. While all act to flavor, the flavors they produce are quite different.

How do we choose? To help you in making your decisions, the following section gives an overview of commonly used ingredients found in the baker's pantry. Take time to review it; you will be amazed at how much there is to learn.

Flours, Meals, and Starches

N EVER BEFORE has there been such a vast selection of flours available to the consumer. While wheat flours are still the most common variety, flours made from such grains and cereals as rye, rice, corn, barley, and oats have become staples on most supermarket shelves. Even nongrain flours like buckwheat and soybean have become accessible to many of us without a visit to the health food store.

The varieties of flours grown worldwide number more than thirty thousand. Wheat flours are often referred to by their colors: white, yellow, and red. They fall into two seasonal categories. Winter wheat is sown in the fall and harvested in the spring or summer. The opposite growing season exists for spring wheat; it is planted in the spring and harvested in the fall, before severe winter weather sets in.

The most delicate flours are commonly made from winter wheat. These are the "soft" varieties. The stronger, or "hard," flours come from spring crops. But at times these classifications overlap, owing to local climate and soil conditions wherever the wheat happen to be grown.

Wheat stalks contain many small kernels, called wheat berries. Each wheat berry is composed of three parts: the outer shell or bran, the starchy center or endosperm, and the embryo or germ. All white wheat flours are made from the starchy center. Whole wheat flour is produced from the entire wheat kernel.

Once flour is milled, it is aged. This process controls liquid absorption and conditions the flour for better baking qualities. Although oxygen in the air naturally bleaches flour as it ages, some flours are chemically bleached with hydrogen gas and benzoyl peroxide or other substances. Also, white wheat flours are commonly "enriched" with ingredients such as malted barley flour, reduced iron, niacin, riboflavin, and thiamine mononitrate. As a rule, bleached and unbleached flours may be used interchangeably.

While all flours contain some form of protein, only white and whole wheat flours have the gluten-forming proteins glutenin and gliadin. Gliadin gives doughs and batters elasticity, while glutenin adds stability and strength. These are insoluble proteins that convert to gluten when they come into contact with moisture. They soak up liquid in much the same way that a sponge soaks up water. The greater the protein content of the flour, the more liquid it will absorb.

Flours that are high in protein have the stability to form an elastic mesh to entrap air for rising. This framework is developed through the kneading process. Strong flours should never be used for pie or tart doughs, however, because the gluten is easily activated and will make a tough crust. For a tender delicate crust, always use a lower protein softer flour. If you want to vary the type of flour in a dough, always use at least 50 percent wheat flour so that the pastry will hold together for rolling.

To determine how much protein is in flour, refer to the nutritional facts on the side of the bag or box. In recent years, the Food and Drug Administration changed the labeling information. Today, the protein values shown are based on a range and then rounded off, rather than the more specific calculations previously used. These updated calculations are based on a $1/4$ cup (30 gram) measurement.

With these labeling changes, the consumer is not privy to exact figures. Other than providing the amount of protein in $1/4$ cup of the flour, presently there are no regulations for labeling to differentiate one type of flour from another. High-protein bread flour and lower-protein biscuit flour can both be labeled all-purpose, yet they react quite differently if used for the same recipe.

To explain, the complexities of flours, unbleached flour has a slightly higher protein value than bleached flour. Although the difference is subtle, pastry dough made with unbleached flour could require a little more liquid than the same recipe made with bleached flour.

Cake flour, a soft wheat white flour commonly used for cakes, has the least amount of protein, with 2 grams per $1/4$ cup. The stronger hard wheat white flours (used for breads) and whole wheat flours can have up to 4 grams per $1/4$ cup. All-purpose flour falls in the middle, with 3 grams per $1/4$ cup. If the brand or variety of flour is unfamiliar to you, always check the protein quantity listed on the package.

For making pie and tart doughs, choose an all-purpose flour, either bleached or unbleached. Understanding the differences in flour protein levels and moisture absorption qualities can help you solve many baking problems commonly encountered. Also, keep in mind that bags from the same manufacturer will vary in protein strength and moisture content because of such varying factors as climate and soil conditions among different crops.

Packaged flour is very susceptible to temperature changes. If it is stored near heat, it can dry out, causing it to absorb more of the liquid in a dough. Flour stored in a humid place will pick up moisture; therefore less liquid will be needed in the dough.

Small bugs called grubs or weevils may also develop under moist storage conditions and in dark environments. While all flours are susceptible to these tiny pests, whole wheat flours are prime targets.

To keep your flour fresh, store it in an airtight container at room temperature and use it within a few weeks. Since bugs and grubs dislike light, I recommend using jumbo glass containers. For longer storage, refrigerate flour for about three months or freeze for up to a year. Because of its perishability, I always keep whole wheat flour and specialty varieties in the refrigerator or freezer. It is unnecessary to bring the flour to room temperature when making a rolled dough. Cold flour produces excellent results.

The following is a list of commonly available flours, meals, grains, and starches. However, it does not include flours produced by smaller specialty companies because their protein ranges are too variable.

WHEAT FLOURS

BLEACHED ALL-PURPOSE FLOUR (*3 grams protein per $1/4$ cup*): An enriched, pure white flour made from hard and soft wheats that is milled from the starchy center part of the wheat kernel. Bleaching is a chemical process that manufacturers use to whiten the flour and to even out the liquid absorption. Bleached all-purpose flour is recommended for pie and tart pastry.

UNBLEACHED ALL-PURPOSE FLOUR *(3 grams protein per ¼ cup flour):* An enriched unbleached all-purpose flour that is made from the starchy center of hard and soft wheat and sometimes from hard wheat only. Unbleached flour, which is slightly cream colored, is natural other than the added enrichments required by law. It does not go through a chemical bleaching process. The protein value of unbleached flour is slightly higher than bleached. Bleached and unbleached flours may be substituted for each other in recipes. Pastry doughs made with unbleached flour may need a bit more liquid.

CAKE FLOUR *(2 grams protein per ¼ cup flour):* An enriched bleached flour made from high-quality soft wheat; cake flour is milled especially for making cakes and delicate pastries. If you have trouble finding cake flour in the flour section, look for it in the cake mix section, where some stores choose to stock it. (Unbleached cake flour is sold in some specialty food shops and health food stores.) Make sure to buy *plain* cake flour, not labeled "self-rising," which contains leavening and salt. Pastry flour can be made by using a combination of one-third cake flour and two-thirds all-purpose flour.

SELF-RISING FLOUR *(2 grams protein per ¼ cup flour):* An enriched bleached soft wheat flour that contains leavening and salt and is used for biscuits, cakes, and quick breads. Self-rising flour is *not* recommended for pie or tart doughs.

INSTANT FLOUR *(3 grams protein per ¼ cup flour):* A specialty granular all-purpose flour that pours like salt and dissolves easily in cold water. Many professional chefs prefer to use instant flour for pie and tart doughs because its performance is similar to flour used in France.

PASTRY FLOUR *(approximately 2.5 grams protein per ¼ cup flour):* A specially blended flour that is less delicate than cake flour, pastry flour is softer than all-purpose flour. This flour is used for making pie and tart doughs, cookies, and sweet doughs, and also in some European recipes. It is stocked with the specialty flours and is usually sold in 2-pound bags. (Arrowhead Mills is a common brand.) To make your own pastry flour, use a ratio of two parts all-purpose flour to one part cake flour. As an example, to make 2 cups of pastry flour, use 1⅓ cups of all-purpose flour combined with ⅔ cup cake flour.

WHOLE-GRAIN (WHOLE WHEAT) PASTRY FLOUR *(4 grams protein per ⅓ cup flour):* A flavorful and nutritious soft-wheat flour, this is produced from the entire wheat kernel, the shell, the starch, and the germ. The flour should not be confused with regular whole wheat flour, which is too strong for pie or tart doughs. Although whole-grain pastry flour can be difficult to obtain, some supermarkets and specialty food stores do carry it. Arrowhead Mills, the most common brand, comes packaged in 2-pound bags. It can be purchased in 5-pound bags by mail from King Arthur Flour Company (page 467).

NON-WHEAT FLOURS AND MEALS

CORNMEAL: A meal made from either white or yellow corn kernels, cornmeal is sometimes used in small amounts with wheat flour in pie and tart pastry for added flavor and texture. Yellow cornmeal is more nutritious than white, but its baking properties are the same as for white cornmeal.

Commonly manufactured by smaller mills, stone-ground cornmeal is produced by grinding whole kernels between two huge stones, commonly propelled by water. The water keeps the meal cool during the milling process and, as a result, more of the natural nutrients are retained. Electric milled cornmeal has the hull and germ removed. Thus stone-ground cornmeal is less refined and more flavorful than the commercial variety. When making pie or tart crusts, mix it with wheat flour and use at a ratio of two parts wheat flour to one part cornmeal.

Store regular cornmeal at room temperature. Stone-ground

cornmeal should be stored in the refrigerator or freezer because it can go rancid quickly. It will keep for up to three months in the refrigerator and up to one year in the freezer.

ROLLED OATS (OATMEAL): A highly nutritious grain, oats are rich in protein and unsaturated fat. Quick-cooking rolled oats are a key ingredient in toppings for fruit crumbles. Old-fashioned rolled oats may also be used, but they will be firmer. Imported steel-cut oats from Ireland or Scotland are very chewy and not recommended for this purpose.

ARROWROOT: A costly thickening agent that comes from the dried and ground roots of the tropical arrowroot plant. Arrowroot is most commonly used for thickening puddings and sauces.

CORNSTARCH: A completely refined starch produced from the endosperm (starchy center) of the corn kernel. Cornstarch serves as a thickening agent for fillings and sauces.

POTATO FLOUR (POTATO STARCH): A flourlike substance made from cooked and dried potatoes, is used as a thickening agent in place of flour, cornstarch, arrowroot, or tapioca.

TAPIOCA: Used as a thickener in pies, cobblers, and other desserts, in addition to many savory dishes. Unlike flour and cornstarch, tapioca thickens without clouding the taste or color of the primary ingredients and is heat stable. It is a very digestible carbohydrate and adds no fat or cholesterol to a recipe. Foods thickened with tapioca characteristically have a somewhat beady texture that results from the swelling of the tiny tapioca granules.

Tapioca is produced from the roots of the cassava plant, which grows in tropical climates. The roots grow in clusters and are tapered like sweet potatoes. They are harvested, washed, peeled, pulverized, and cooked. The complete processing produces a starch that is formed and marketed as various-size pellet or "pearl" tapiocas (used in puddings), Minute or quick-cooking tapioca (which is good for thickening), and tapioca flour (see below).

When adding tapioca to a fruit filling, layer it with the fruit, then shake the bowl to distribute it. After combining with the fruit, it is essential for the mixture to stand for at least 15 minutes to dissolve the tapioca granules fully. Tapioca has the same thickening power as cornstarch.

TAPIOCA FLOUR: Made from the roots of the cassava plant, tapioca flour is more refined than quick-cooking tapioca. Used for the same thickening purposes, it can be purchased in Asian groceries and health food stores. It has all of the same qualities as quick-cooking tapioca, with the advantage of leaving a completely smooth texture. If tapioca flour is used in place of quick-cooking tapioca for thickening purposes, increase the amount by one-half. For example, if the recipe calls for 1 tablespoon of quick-cooking tapioca, use 1½ tablespoons tapioca flour.

Leavening and Stabilizers

L EAVENING WILL MAKE baked products rise. Although it is most commonly used in cake baking, leavening has some benefit in pastry doughs. A small amount of leavening added to a dough expands the layers of fat-coated flour to promote crispness.

BAKING POWDER: In pie and tart baking, the leavening of choice is baking powder. There are two types of baking powder, double- and single-acting. The most widely used is double-acting, composed of sodium bicarbonate (baking soda), cornstarch or potato starch (to prevent lumping), calcium acid phosphate, and sodium aluminum sulfate. This type of baking powder works in two stages: leavening action begins as soon as it comes in contact with moisture, followed by another, greater surge when exposed to heat. Single-acting baking powder has only one leavening action, which takes place immediately after contact with liquid. This baking powder is free of chemicals and is available at health food stores.

BAKING SODA: While infrequently used in the preparation of pies or tarts, baking soda is sometimes used for enhancing the color of chocolate doughs. A pinch of baking soda is occasionally used in fillings or sugar syrups that contain honey, maple syrup, molasses, or other acid ingredients.

CREAM OF TARTAR: This acid comes from the inner scrapings of wine casks after fermentation. It is widely used when beating egg whites, where it acts to add brightness, smoothness, and stability. It is also used to prevent crystallization of sugar syrups when cooked to the caramel stage and for making candies. Cream of tartar is a component in some commercial fast-acting baking powders and is combined with bicarbonate of soda and salt for homemade baking powder.

Sugar and Other Sweeteners

S UGAR IS a carbohydrate that is produced in the leaves, stems, and roots of plants. Sugar beets and sugarcane are the main sources of commercial sugar. If you peruse the labels of packaged foods, you will notice that sugar appears under numerous designations: sucrose, dextrose (grape sugar), lactose (milk sugar), levulose (fruit sugar), and maltose (malt sugar).

Honey, molasses, and maple and corn syrups are other forms of sweeteners. While they do add flavor, they are liquid and so are not a replacement for dry, granulated sugars.

GRANULATED SUGAR: The white crystal sugar derived from sugarcane or sugar beets, is 99.94 percent pure and can be stored indefinitely in an airtight container. A small amount of sugar is sometimes added to pastry doughs to create tenderness and enhance flavor. It is also used for sweeter, cookie-type doughs.

In pie and tart recipes, granulated sugar is used in almost every type of filling, from fruit to cooked custard and anything in between. It's also used in toppings such as streusel, whipped creams, and meringues.

SUPERFINE SUGAR: Also known as dessert or bar sugar, superfine sugar is a very fine grained sugar. It dissolves quickly, yielding high, light meringues and smooth whipped cream. It can be substituted in equal amounts for granulated sugar. When buying, squeeze the box to make sure the sugar is fresh and not hardened. To prevent lumps from forming, store in an airtight container.

BROWN SUGAR: As a mixture of refined white sugar and molasses, the flavor of brown sugar depends on the quality of molasses used. There are two types of brown sugar—light and dark—which in most cases may be used interchangeably. However, light brown sugar should be the choice when a lighter, more delicate flavor is desired. Dark brown sugar produces a more intense flavor and deeper color because it contains more molasses.

Brown sugar has a tendency to turn rock-hard upon exposure to air because its moisture quickly evaporates. When measuring this sugar for a recipe, keep it covered with plastic wrap until ready to use. To lengthen its shelf life after opening, store the sugar in an airtight container, or with some moist item (an old trick is to keep an apple slice in the bag). Newer packaging utilizes heavy plastic bags that keep the sugar fresher if well sealed. Make sure the air is pressed out of the bag before closing, and that it is securely fastened with a rubber band or twist tie. I have also found that storing the brown sugar in the refrigerator, once sealed, aids in extending the usable shelf life of this product.

Granulated brown sugar is crystallized and pours easily for measuring purposes. It may be substituted in equal amounts, however it is costly and an unnecessary investment.

CONFECTIONERS' SUGAR: Also referred to as powdered or 10x sugar, this is granulated sugar that has been processed to the point where it is ten times finer. While it contains 3 percent cornstarch to prevent lumping, it still must be strained before using to ensure a smooth consistency as well as an accurate measurement. Confectioners' sugar is used in larger quantities than granulated sugar in baking because it is not as sweet. Because of this and the difference in texture, confectioners' sugar cannot be substituted measure for measure for granulated sugar.

PEARL SUGAR: This sugar, an integral ornamental ingredient for Scandinavian pastries, has granules that are four to six times larger than granulated sugar. The oversize granules are slower to melt during baking. It may be used for decorating the surface of pastries before or after baking. While it may be purchased in either clear or opaque crystals, my preference is the clear because of its sparkling transparency. Look for it in specialty food stores and mail order catalogs.

MAPLE SYRUP: A pure, natural syrup derived from the sap of mature sugar maple trees. It takes 40 gallons of sap to produce each gallon of syrup, which means pure maple syrup is pricey, but a little goes a long way.

Pure maple syrup comes in grades identified by color. The most popular and delicately flavored is the light amber; medium amber has a fuller flavor. The dark amber, which has the strongest maple flavor, holds its own when baked with competing ingredients.

Common maple-flavored syrup found in your local grocery is a combination of corn syrup, artificial flavoring, and a small amount of pure maple syrup. It is less expensive, but lacks the full-bodied, natural flavor of pure maple syrup.

MAPLE SUGAR: A granulated sugar derived from maple sap, maple sugar is made similarly as maple syrup. The sap is boiled down until all of the water has evaporated. Because it has almost twice the sweetness of granulated sugar, maple sugar should be used in lesser quantities.

Maple sugar has a pleasing flavor that is complementary to many fruits. Use it as a sugar replacement in fruit pies or crumb toppings. Maple sugar can be purchased by mail (see page 467). An alternative is to combine 1/3 cup granulated sugar with 1/2 teaspoon imitation maple flavoring and whirl it in a food processor until well blended. Store in tightly sealed container.

MOLASSES: A thick, dark syrup, molasses results from the residue of crystals during the early stages of sugar refining. When the sugar crystals are removed from the juice of the sugarcane or beet, a brownish-black liquid remains. That liquid is boiled down to create light, dark, and blackstrap molasses. Molasses is sold in two forms, sulphured and unsulphured. Sulphured molasses contains sulphur dioxide and has a robust flavor; unsulphured molasses has a lighter, milder taste. Because molasses has a very pronounced flavor, it should be used in small quantities. Molasses adds color, moistness, and flavor to baked goods.

HONEY: Fully 99 percent sugar, honey has almost the same sweetening power as granulated sugar. The color and flavor vary according to the flower source, the most popular being orange blossom, clover, and lavender. Some supermarket brands use a blend of flavors to achieve a more consistent, if not as memorable, flavor. At times, honey can be used in place of sugar in equal amounts, but the flavor and consistency of the finished product will be altered. Honey can be stored at room temperature, but it may crystallize. To liquify the honey, place it in a hot water bath (but do not heat it over 160 degrees because the flavor will be affected). Honey can also be stored in the refrigerator, but it will need to be brought to room temperature before using; heat it briefly on the stovetop or in the microwave.

CORN SYRUP: Made from cornstarch that has been converted to a liquid, corn syrup is available in light and dark forms. Light corn syrup has been clarified, leaving it sweet but flavorless. Dark corn syrup is flavored with caramel and is used for its flavor and color. Corn syrup is stored at room temperature.

JAMS AND PRESERVES: Brushing the tops of tarts with jams and preserves helps produce a shiny glaze and seals the color and flavor of the filling. Apricot preserves and apple jelly are favorites because their mild flavor does not detract, but rather enhances, the flavors of other fruits. Strawberry or raspberry preserves and currant jelly impart both flavor and color, and should be used with fruits of similar hues. Jams and preserves can also be used as a flavor and color boost in dessert sauces. Higher quality products are a worthwhile investment because they contain less water.

Fats

F AT IS THE magic ingredient that provides flavor to myriad foods. In the world of pastry, it is an essential component for mouthwatering desserts and maintaining freshness. Pastries without fat are dry and tasteless.

Fat forms a partnership with flour to capture the steam that produces flaky, tender pastry. There are several types of fats, each with unique properties that alone, or in combination with other fats, result in particular tastes and textures.

BUTTER: Butter contains, on average, 80 percent animal fat and from 10 to 16 percent water. The remaining material is curd and minerals. While butter is produced in salted and unsalted (or "sweet") forms, unsalted butter is the best choice for baking. Not only does it contain less water but it also has a sweeter, fresher flavor unmatched by any other fat. Salted butter can usually be substituted for unsalted, but when doing so, reduce the amount of salt in the recipe. Butter should be kept refrigerated and has a limited shelf life (see the expiration date on the package); for longer storage, it can be frozen for up to 6 months. Always keep butter covered or wrapped, as it will pick up flavors and odors from other foods in your refrigerator.

MARGARINE: First used as a butter substitute in France in 1869, margarine is a blend of vegetable oils and hardened fat mixed with skim milk or water. It is softer than butter, but has the same caloric value. In addition to being less expensive than butter, it appeals to many health-conscious people who wish to reduce their dietary cholesterol. Some, although not all, margarines are either low in cholesterol or cholesterol-free. Further confusing the issue are lower-calorie (not the same as lower-cholesterol) margarines. The high moisture content of lower-calorie margarines make them unsuitable for baking. Regular stick margarine can be substituted for butter in most recipes.

HYDROGENATED VEGETABLE SHORTENING: A 100 percent fat, commonly white and flavorless, shortening is made from soybean, corn, cottonseed, palm, or peanut oil. The oils are processed with heat and hydrogen to form a solid fat that can be used alone or with butter to make flaky pastry. A new addition to the market is Butter Flavor Crisco, an artificially flavored and colored fat.

Vegetable shortening is a major contributor to pie crust and many tart pastries. Doughs made with it will be more crisp and flaky. My preference is for unflavored vegetable shortening in combination with butter. If substituting solid white or butter-flavored vegetable shortening for butter, more water may be needed to bind the pastry. Because the butter-flavored product is already flavored artificially, it is best not to combine it with real butter.

Although shortening can be stored at room temperature, I prefer to keep it refrigerated. I like to use it chilled when making pastry anyway.

LARD: Although out of fashion in many parts of the country, lard has long been accepted as the premier fat for producing blue ribbon pastry crusts and biscuits. It is richer than most other fats, with a crystalline structure that cuts readily into flour and produces an extremely flaky crust. Lard is pork fat rendered from fatback, clear plate, and the highly prized leaf kidney fat. It is this "leaf lard" that is regarded as the best quality.

When choosing lard, read the package carefully. Unprocessed lard has a strong flavor and soft texture. Processed lard is firmer and has a more delicate flavor and a longer shelf life. To substitute lard for butter, use 20 to 25 percent less lard than the amount of butter indicated in the recipe. As an example, if a recipe calls for 1 cup butter, you can substitute slightly more than 3/4 cup lard.

Lard can be stored on the shelf or in the refrigerator for 15 days to 2 months, depending on the processing method used; the package instructions specify the correct storage temperature. It can be frozen for up to 12 months.

VEGETABLE OILS: Peanut, canola/rapeseed, safflower, corn, soybean, and pure or extra-virgin olive oil can all be used in baking. Many recipes have been developed for pastry using oil as the main fat. Oils make extremely tender crusts, but doughs made with oil are softer and more difficult to roll. When selecting an oil, bear in mind that not all oils have a neutral flavor. My personal recommendation is canola or safflower for sweet pastries, and extra-virgin olive oil for savories.

CHEESE: Cheese can be used as a complementary fat in pastry dough. Cheddar cheese in the crust of a pear or apple pie is a delightful counterpoint to the sweetness of the fruit. (Remem-ber the old saying that an apple pie without the cheese is like a kiss without the squeeze?) Parmesan or Romano cheese in a savory crust adds a delightful nuance. A general rule of thumb is that harder cheeses work best in a crust because they do not upset the moisture balance.

Cream cheese, with its slightly tangy flavor, can be used to make a delicate, flaky crust or a rich, creamy filling for cheese pies or tarts. It works magic as a creamy companion with fruit as a filling. Mascarpone—its sinfully rich Italian cousin—creates unforgettably decadent fillings. Ricotta and cottage cheese are excellent in both sweet and savory fillings.

Although it may seem incongruous to mention "low fat" in the section on fats, the heightened health concerns of many bakers requires mention of high-quality, low-fat alternatives to some cheeses. Two percent cottage cheese and Neufchâtel or light cream cheese are two examples of substitutes that can work well, reducing the overall fat content of a pie or tart. Be careful when substituting, however, since the fat content of the cheese contributes to the fat balance in the recipe. With less fat, a filling is usually more watery. To compensate, add a little flour or cornstarch, or increase the amount of starch indicated in the recipe. Often, experimentation is the only way to judge whether a substitution will work.

Eggs

EGGS PERFORM many functions in baking pastries. Their versatility is endless. In fact, according to the American Egg Board, eggs have been called "the cement that holds the castle of cuisine together." For pies and tarts, eggs can be used as a binding agent in place of water when preparing dough; they act as a shield in preventing a bottom crust from becoming soggy; and they are excellent for sealing seams of pastry. Eggs are an enrichment and thickening agent for cooked cream fillings and baked custards, and they can entrap air for a meringue.

Each component of an egg performs a different function. Fat-rich egg yolks make doughs tender; the high-protein whites add strength and stability. Although eggs are extremely healthy, a whole egg is 75 percent water. White and brown eggs have the same nutritional value and flavor. The color of the shell is determined by the type of feed that the chickens are fed.

Eggs are graded AA, A, or B. The grade most commonly sold to the consumer is AA. Most recipes, unless otherwise specified, use large eggs. An average whole, unshelled large egg weighs 2 ounces. Of that 2 ounces, 25 percent is the egg shell. That leaves $1\frac{1}{2}$ ounces of egg, or about 3 tablespoons if calculated by capacity measurement. Twenty-five percent or

1 tablespoon is yolk, and 50 percent or 2 tablespoons is white. Knowing these weights, it is easy to calculate a measurement when you wish to use up leftover eggs.

Eggs must be kept refrigerated, stored in their original carton, with the pointed tip facing down. Do not use open containers or egg bins on refrigerator doors; the shell of an egg is porous, therefore the egg is subject to absorbing bacteria as well as odors from other foods. Because of the threat of salmonella food poisoning, eggs should be kept under refrigeration until shortly before they are used. Do not use eggs with cracked shells. Avoid tasting uncooked egg mixtures containing egg yolks, and above all, be scrupulously clean when handling all eggs.

Store opened eggs in the refrigerator, tightly covered, for up to 3 days. Egg yolks, if unbroken, can be covered with a little water and refrigerated for 2 to 3 days. If broken, omit the water, and tightly cover the bowl with plastic wrap. Leftover egg whites should also be tightly covered and refrigerated for up to 4 days. Egg whites can be frozen for several months, but they do pick up a little moisture. Therefore, I use them for less important preparations rather than for meringues or angel food cakes. Egg whites can be frozen in ice cube trays. After freezing, just pop them from their containers and store them in a tightly sealed plastic bag. Egg yolks can be frozen if a small amount of sugar is added to them. However, I rarely freeze them because they have a tendency to become grainy after thawing.

EGG SUBSTITUTES: These are made almost entirely from egg whites with the addition of stabilizers and food coloring. Because eggs are high in cholesterol and fat, for health purposes, you may want to replace whole fresh eggs in some of the recipes with egg substitutes. Although the directions on the cartons suggest using 1/4 cup of egg substitute per whole egg, I recommend reducing the amount to 3 tablespoons per egg, as this measurement is closer to that of a true large egg.

Liquids

L IQUID IS A critical ingredient in the formation of pie and tart dough. Ordinary tap water is the most common liquid, but bottled spring water or effervescent liquids like club soda or seltzer, might be used. Sometimes, orange juice is the liquid, or other acidic beverages like Champagne, white wine, or even small amounts of vodka or gin. The acid content of these liquids breaks down the gluten in the flour and thereby makes for a tender pastry dough. Do not break open a new bottle; rather, use wine or Champagne that has been open.

Other common moisteners are eggs; dairy products such as milk, light cream, half and half, or heavy creams; and cultured gluten tenderizers like buttermilk, sour cream, and yogurt.

Liquid can make or break a crust. Too much produces a sodden dough that is too pasty to roll. Too little creates a dry dough that breaks into a crumbly mess. The key is to strike a balance between the fluid and the particles of fat and flour, so that you can form a cohesive mass that will roll successfully.

WATER: Ice cold water is the most popular liquid used for binding pastry. It is an essential component in a dough because, when baked, it produces the steam that forces the layers of fat-coated flour to expand.

Tap water is fine to use for pie or tart pastry provided there is not excessive chlorine. If this is the case, use bottled water.

MILK: Whole or reduced-fat milk can be used in lieu of water for most pastry doughs, but the crust will not be as flaky. It can also be brushed on the top of pastry before it is baked. As the water in the milk evaporates, the lactose or milk sugar caramelizes, leaving a crust with a rich brown color and a crisp finish. In this case, the fat content is not a critical issue, so either whole milk or one of its leaner counterparts is perfectly acceptable.

Milk is also used in the preparation of cream and custard fillings. If a low-fat milk is used for these purposes, the thickening agent may have to be slightly increased. Added starch will give the filling stability and also prevent it from becoming too watery.

You can also use reconstituted powdered milk, evaporated whole milk, or evaporated skimmed milk diluted with 50 percent water for any of the usages listed above. Condensed milk, which is sweetened milk with the water removed, is *not* a suitable substitute for regular milk. It should be used only when specified, as in Key Lime Pie. By the same token, there is no substituting when condensed milk is called for; even the richest heavy cream cannot take its place.

CREAM: Heavy cream is used in cream and custard fillings, frozen desserts, sauces, and for whipping as an incomparable garnish for pies and tarts. There are two types of heavy cream produced today. A richer, pure whipping cream with a milk fat content of at least 36 percent is available mostly to commercial bakeries and restaurants. This quick whipping cream forms thick, stable mounds and is extremely smooth. If you're fortunate enough to live by a dairy, purchase some for home use. You'll love it. Heavy cream that is distributed to the consumer is a light whipping cream, with a milk fat content of between 30 and 36 percent. Light cream has between 18 and 30 percent milk fat, and half and half is a mixture of milk and cream with anywhere from a 10.5 to 18 percent milk fat content.

When a recipe specifies a particular type of cream, it is because it needs that particular fat content for proper balance and mixing. Do not attempt to interchange them, as cream with less than 30 percent milk fat will not whip.

Most store-bought cream is ultrapasteurized, which is a process of heating the cream to extend its shelf life; it also contains stabilizers and emulsifiers to give body for whipping. While the extended shelf life is of great benefit, the tradeoff is that this is not 100 percent pure cream and, at times, has a slightly cooked taste and may take longer to whip. If you have difficulty finding cream that is not ultrapasteurized, watch for it at your local grocer at holiday time, or throughout the year at specialty food markets and health food stores.

CULTURED DAIRY PRODUCTS: Sour cream, yogurt, buttermilk, and crème fraîche are cultured dairy products—that is, they are dairy products that have been treated with lactic acid or bacterial cultures. The result is a product with a tangy flavor and improved shelf life. While sour cream, yogurt, and crème fraîche are marketed in convenient 8-ounce packages, buttermilk is commonly sold in 1-quart containers. Since most recipes containing buttermilk call for only a pint or less, waste is often inevitable. To circumvent this problem, buttermilk is available in a powdered form that can be reconstituted in the necessary amount.

Chocolate

C OCOA BEANS are harvested from large pods produced by the cocoa tree. Each pod can contain as much as fifty seeds, or beans. After they are split and scraped, the beans are fermented, dried, and then roasted to develop their flavor and soften the husk. Manufacturers of fine chocolates have their own specialized, guarded blends of roasted beans, in much the same way as coffees beans are blended.

After roasting, the beans are crushed to separate the meat or "nib" from the husk and germ. These nibs are ground and then heated to make cocoa butter, a process that ultimately turns the nibs into chocolate liquor. This rich mass is about 53 to 55 percent cocoa butter and 45 to 47 percent chocolate liquor. After processing, the liquor is shaped into blocks of unsweetened chocolate or combined with sugar, milk solids, and other ingredients to make bittersweet, semisweet, or milk chocolate.

The last procedure is to "conch" the chocolate. For this, the chocolate is put through massive rollers to smooth and refine the ingredients. The more the chocolate is conched, the smoother and higher quality it will be. Finally, the chocolate is tempered to stabilize the cocoa butter crystals, giving chocolate its characteristic shiny surface.

UNSWEETENED (BITTER) CHOCOLATE: Often referred

to as baking chocolate, it contains 45 to 47 percent chocolate liquor and 53 to 55 percent cocoa butter. Because it does not contain sugar, unsweetened chocolate is not a suitable substitute for semisweet or bittersweet chocolate unless other adjustments are made in the recipe.

SEMISWEET AND BITTERSWEET CHOCOLATE: Semi- and bittersweet chocolates are made from chocolate liquor, sugar, cocoa butter, lecithin, cocoa solids, and vanilla or vanillin, with formulas that vary from manufacturer to manufacturer. These chocolates, professionally referred to as "real" chocolates, must contain a minimum of 35 percent chocolate liquor according to specifications set by the U.S. Standards of Identity.

Along with the individualized formulas used by different manufacturers, there are variations in the names given to each product. Some manufacturers label their chocolate bittersweet, when in actuality it tastes more like semisweet. Conversely, some semisweets taste like bittersweet chocolate. Unfortunately, you cannot tell the differences without tasting the products. Here are some of the more popular names for these sweetened dark chocolates: bittersweet, special dark, semisweet, extra bittersweet, Eagle sweet, dark sweet, and German sweet.

While some fine bitter and semisweet chocolates are pro-

duced in the United States, the most revered brands are made in Switzerland, Holland, Belgium, France, and England. Imported brands are Tobler Tradition, available in 3- or 13-ounce bars; Lindt Excellence, sold in 3- or 13-ounce bars; Callebaut Bittersweet, sold in 17.5-ounce bars or by mail in 5-pound blocks. Maillard Eagle Sweet Chocolate comes in 4-ounce bars, and Poulain Bittersweet is available in a 7-ounce bar.

MILK CHOCOLATE: Milk chocolate, also termed a "real" chocolate, is a light-colored, sweetened confection made from at least 10 percent chocolate liquor and 12 percent milk solids, with the addition of sugar and vanilla or vanillin. Rarely used for baking, it is the most popular eating chocolate in the United States.

WHITE CHOCOLATE: White chocolate is not a "real" chocolate, as it does not contain chocolate liquor. It is made from cocoa butter with the addition of sugar, dry or whole milk, and vanilla or vanillin. The product is extremely sweet and has a barely discernible chocolate flavor.

White chocolate is extremely perishable and must be handled with great care because it is so rich in fat and contains about 30 percent milk. Unless you use it frequently, buy it in small quantities. It should not be used as a substitute for true chocolate because it reacts differently when combined with

other ingredients. A popular brand is Lindt Swiss Confectionery bar, found in the candy department of many supermarkets in a 3-ounce bar. Another fine brand, popular with confectioners, is Merckens, available at stores specializing in candy making.

CHOCOLATE CHIPS: Bits of molded semisweet chocolate containing less cocoa butter than regular semisweet are the most common variety. Chocolate chips are also available in milk and white chocolate, as well as mint flavored. They are sold in cellophane packages with chip sizes ranging from mini to jumbo. Their reduced cocoa butter content makes melting these chips as a substitute for melted chocolate unadvisable.

UNSWEETENED COCOA POWDER: There are two types of cocoa powder available for baking: nonalkaline and Dutch-process or alkaline. Both are made from chocolate liquor that has been put under hydraulic pressure to remove at least 75 percent of the cocoa butter. From the remaining cocoa solids, a compact mass called a presscake is ground into a powder. While most of the cocoa butter has been removed, cocoa powder still contains from 8 to 24 percent fat.

Nonalkaline cocoa, such as Hershey's, Ghirardelli, or Baker's, is the most popular variety sold in the United States. This is an acidic cocoa with a heady, full-bodied flavor. When you use nonalkaline cocoa in baked goods that contain leavening, the correct leavening agent to use is baking soda in order to neutralize the acid.

Dutch-process cocoa, first introduced in Holland by Coenraad Van Houten in 1815, has the acid neutralized with alkali. This is a rich, dark powder with a delicate flavor favored by baking professionals. Since the acid is neutralized, baking powder may be used for leavening. Popular Dutch-process cocoas are Dröste, Poulain, Feodora, and Van Houten, along with Hershey's, who introduced its own Dutch-process cocoa powder, boxed in a silver tin.

For information on storing chocolate, see page 13.

HOW TO STORE SOLID CHOCOLATE: Chocolate should always be well wrapped in aluminum foil and then rewrapped in plastic wrap. Because of the cocoa butter, chocolate readily absorbs flavors from other ingredients. Store it in a cool, dry place with low humidity and *away from light*. The optimum temperature for storing chocolate is 65 degrees. A "bloom" on chocolate means that it has changed its color while in storage. A "gray bloom" is a sign of improper tempering during the manufacturing process. A milky yellow "sugar bloom" results when chocolate was not well wrapped and was subjected to extreme temperature changes and hu-

midity. This bloom also appears when chocolate has melted and resolidified; when the chocolate is melted again, the bloom will disappear.

The shelf life of chocolate is determined by the amount of cocoa butter it contains. Unsweetened, bittersweet, and semisweet chocolates have the longest shelf life. If well wrapped and stored in a cool dry place, they will keep for years. Milk and white chocolates are far more perishable. Use milk chocolate within 1 year and white chocolate within 8 months.

In a perfect world, chocolates should not be refrigerated. However, if you live in a warm, humid environment it may be unavoidable. Milk and white chocolate can be frozen. Break it into usable pieces, then wrap it well for the freezer. Thaw the chocolate while still wrapped to prevent condensation from forming on the surface.

Flavoring and Spirits

VANILLA: Vanilla can never be overlooked when it comes to desserts. While its use in baking cakes and cookies is expected, vanilla makes a major contribution to a variety of pie and tart fillings as well. Creams, custards, Bavarians, and frozen desserts all benefit from this popular yet exotic flavoring. It

can stand alone or be used to complement other flavorings such as coffee, chocolate, liqueurs, cordials, and brandies.

Vanilla has long been treasured for the aromatic nuance it lends to foods. Vanilla beans are often referred to as the fruit of the orchid. But of the thousands of orchids grown, only one produces an edible fruit. The finest quality vanilla comes from the Bourbon Islands, off the coast of Madagascar. However, in recent years, Tahitian vanilla beans have come into favor with many chefs.

Using a high-quality vanilla is essential in baking. While several types of vanilla flavorings are available, pure vanilla extract, made from vanilla beans and at least 35 percent alcohol, water, and often sugar, should be your choice. Pure vanilla flavor is lower in alcohol and not as strong as the pure, but it is a natural product. Artificial or imitation vanilla flavoring—an inferior, synthetic, commercially manufactured vanillin—is a byproduct of paper making.

Whole vanilla beans are far superior to extract for infusing hot milk or cream for crème anglaise, cream-type fillings, or sugar syrups for poaching fruits. Steep the bean for 10 to 15 minutes in the hot liquid to soften, then using a paring knife, split it lengthwise and scape out the tiny seeds, and return them to the liquid. These seeds give a peppery appearance, so they should not be used in preparations where they would detract from the food's visual appeal. The used pod of the vanilla bean can be dried and added to a jar of granulated sugar to make aromatic and flavorful vanilla sugar.

When using a vanilla bean instead of extract, use one whole vanilla bean to equal 2 to 3 teaspoons of extract. It is safe to estimate that about 2 inches of vanilla bean equals 1 teaspoon of vanilla extract.

The flavor of vanilla extract, and indeed all extracts, is highly concentrated and should be used sparingly. Because the flavor is so intense, take care to measure carefully and accurately. Also, because of their alcohol content, extracts evaporate rapidly when exposed to the air, so they should be measured out just before incorporating them into a recipe.

FLAVORED EXTRACTS: Imitation and pure extracts are available in a wide variety of flavors. Pure extracts like almond, lemon, orange, banana, spearmint, and peppermint are stocked in most groceries, as are imitation maple and coconut. If a pure extract in the flavor you are desiring is unavailable, imitation flavorings will make a passable substitute.

COFFEE AND ESPRESSO: Many dessert fans like their coffee flavor "straight up," while others appreciate the accent coffee lends to chocolate and spice creations. Most recipes call for instant freeze-dried coffee crystals or instant espresso powder, which are added to liquids in the recipe. While crystals and powders are convenient to use and store, a more intense flavor results when concentrated coffee or espresso zest is the flavoring. Coffee zest is made by combining 3 parts coffee crystals with 1 part boiling water. To make espresso zest, blend 2 parts espresso powder with 1 part boiling water. Use as you would an extract, in small amounts.

LIQUEURS (CORDIALS), BRANDIES, LIQUOR, AND WINE: Cordials and liqueurs often make a wonderful flavoring addition to pie and tart fillings, frozen desserts, and sauces. Since they are fruit alcohols, which contain sugar, they are slightly syrupy. White fruit brandies, which are made from fermented fruits with no additional sweetening, have a thinner and lighter consistency.

Among the more commonly used liqueurs and fruit brandies are Grand Marnier, Cointreau, and Triple Sec (orange); Crème de Cassis (currant); Kahlúa and Tia Maria (coffee); Amaretto (almond); Crème de Menthe (mint); Framboise (from fermented raspberries); Kirschwasser (from wild black cherries); Calvados and Applejack (from apples); and Fraise de Bois (from strawberries).

While "hard" liquor and wines are common flavoring agents for sweet fillings and sauces, they have a place in pastry making as well. Either can be used as part or all of the moistening when preparing crusts (see "Liquids," page 10), and fortified wines such as Marsala and Sauternes can add a complementary flavoring to many fruit fillings.

As always, use products of the highest quality when adding liqueurs, brandies, or other spirits to your baked goods. Inferior brands can impart a harsh or unpleasant overtone to your foods. Remember, the rule of thumb is to never cook with anything you wouldn't want to drink on its own.

Seasonings, Spices, and Herbs

SALT: Salt is vital in the preparation of pastry doughs. It adds character and brings out flavor. Always use table salt for baking rather than coarse or sea salt. Its fine crystals will dissolve more readily. A pinch of salt also brightens the flavor of cooked fillings and will help to break down the proteins when whipping egg whites. If necessary, salt can be omitted if you are on a salt-restricted diet.

PEPPER: While pepper is not commonly thought of as an ingredient in baking, don't overlook the contribution it can make to pastry, fresh fruit, and chocolate. When used sparingly, it adds a pleasant spark to these foods. All of the recipes in this book using pepper were tested with freshly ground black pepper. If using pre-ground pepper, reduce the measurement by one-third to one-half because of its finer grains.

SPICES: Fruit pies and tarts provide a natural background to showcase a variety of spices. The most common are cinnamon, nutmeg, allspice, cloves, and ginger. Ground spices should release a pleasant aroma when the lid is removed. If they do not, they are stale and should be replaced. Store spices in a dark, cool cabinet and be sure that the lids are tightly closed.

Freshly grated, whole nutmeg is far superior to pre-ground. When measuring this spice, take note of the kind of nutmeg the recipe calls for. Because pre-ground nutmeg is more compact, if it is to be substituted for freshly grated, you *must* reduce the amount. Too much nutmeg can overwhelm a recipe.

Other whole spices that might be used are cinnamon sticks, whole cloves, peppercorns, and coriander seeds. These are commonly used for steeping and are discarded once their essences have been released.

A word of caution about the use of spices. They are meant to enhance the flavor of, not dominate, your main ingredient. Striking the right balance of flavorings is a skill that you should strive for. Regardless of the amount a recipe calls for, taste is personal, so always use spices sparingly. Sample what you are

seasoning and adjust the spices accordingly.

HERBS: The use of fresh herbs with poached fruits and in pastry crusts has become more prevalent in recent years. Sturdy herbs like thyme and rosemary are well matched with fruit; while chopped chives, rosemary, thyme, sage, and parsley make flavorful additions to pastry. For pastry purposes, always be sure these herbs are thoroughly dried.

If using dried herbs in place of fresh in a savory pastry, reduce the amount by two-thirds. Dried herbs should be rubbed in your hands to enliven the oils and bring out their flavor before adding them to other ingredients.

Nuts and Seeds

NUTS: Nuts are one of the more widely used ingredients in baking. In a crust, they add flavor and an appealing crunchiness. Ground nuts act not only as a sealing layer between a crust and filling but also as a delicious addition to the filling itself. And nuts either whole or chopped, candied or toasted, are wonderful for garnishes and plate decorations.

The most common nuts used in pies, tarts, and other pastries are walnuts, pecans, hazelnuts (filberts), and almonds. Peanuts, pistachios, pine nuts (pignoli),

chestnuts, macadamias, and coconut are also frequently used. Since both walnuts and pecans are rich in oil and similar in texture, they can often be substituted for one another. Hazelnuts and almonds, which are harder nuts, are also interchangeable.

The delicious flavor of nuts comes largely from their natural oils. These oils, however, are the culprits behind why nuts often turn rancid. When purchasing nuts, select vacuum-sealed packages or cans instead of loose nuts whenever possible. If you are buying nuts in bulk from open containers, be sure to taste them for freshness before purchasing. Once you have brought them home, store them in a cool, dark place and once opened, place them in a well-sealed container. Keep nuts in the refrigerator (for up to 3 months) or in the freezer (for up to 1 year) to reduce spoilage. Refresh frozen nuts by heating in a 325 degree oven for 8 to 10 minutes.

SEEDS: Another wonderful addition to both crusts and savory pie and tart fillings are sesame, caraway, and poppy seeds. These seeds are most often sold in small jars in your grocer's spice department and, like nuts, tend to go stale rapidly. Avoid buying seeds in bulk to be assured of always having fresh ones for baking use. Store them in a cool, dark place in a well-sealed container. Refrigerate or freeze them if longer storage is desired.

Dried Fruits

TOP-QUALITY dried fruits, such as apples, apricots, cherries, cranberries, currants, pears, and raisins, make a welcome addition to a host of fruit desserts. They add intense, concentrated flavor as well as texture to pies, tarts, small pastries, and even frozen desserts. They can be used alone or in combination with fresh fruits.

Care must be taken when purchasing dried fruits to avoid stale, dried pieces whose flavor is lacking. Try to avoid pre-cut, smaller pieces as they dehydrate and lose their flavor quickly. If you wish to purchase any of the many varieties of dried fruit available in bulk, always taste before you buy to ascertain freshness.

Once the wrappings on dried fruits have been opened, reseal the package and cover tightly with plastic wrap. Plastic storage bags can also be used; press out as much air as possible from them before sealing. Bulk dried fruits should be stored in a tightly sealed glass jar. Refrigerate them if you are not planning to use them within 2 to 3 weeks. Once refrigerated, they can be kept for up to 3 months. To refresh dried fruits before baking, see "Handling Dried Fruits," page 58.

Canned and Frozen Fruit

AT TIMES canned and frozen fruits have their place in baking and can even be a better choice than fresh.

CANNED FRUITS: Canned fruits are superior to fresh when incorporated into frozen desserts. Because they are pre-cooked in sugar syrup, they will not turn as icy.

Solid-pack pumpkin is a time saver and provides a more consistent puree than one prepared from scratch.

Mandarin oranges make a tasty addition to cream-style and Bavarian pies. They are also perfect for decorating the tops of cream-based open fruit tarts. Apricot halves are perfect for garnishing tarts made with pastry cream.

Canned tart cherries ("tart" has replaced "sour" in the cherry industry) make an excellent subsitute for the short-season fresh variety, allowing you to enjoy them year-round.

Pineapple (crushed, sliced, and diced) is the smarter choice for fillings and garnishes because it has been cooked as part of the canning process. Using it with protein based foods is not a problem (see "Pineapple," page 36).

UNSWEETENED FROZEN FRUITS: Berries like blackberries, blueberries, raspberries, and strawberries, are excellent for coulis and other fruit-based sauces because they are consistent and more economical.

Frozen rhubarb makes a satisfactory substitute when fresh is unavailable.

Gelatin

PLAIN, UNFLAVORED gelatin, which is a derivative of cooked animal bones and hooves, is a colorless, odorless, and sugarless, high-protein, granular substance. It comes packaged in $1/4$-ounce envelopes (approximately $2 1/4$ teaspoons each). These envelopes typically come in boxes of four or eight, and are readily available at your local supermarket.

Unflavored gelatin is most frequently used in pie and tart fillings, such as mousses and Bavarian creams, which require refrigeration. Watery or liquid fillings depend almost entirely on gelatin to firm them. Mixtures that are thickened with starch require less gelatin because the starch does part of the work. Always measure accurately and follow your recipe instructions carefully, as too much gelatin gives as an unpleasant, rubbery consistency.

See "Working with Gelatin," page 60.

FRUIT AND BERRY GLOSSARY

APPLES

SEASON: Available year-round (cold storage). Peak season for local crops, September–November.

YIELD: 3 medium apples = approximately 1 pound.

HISTORY: Clear archaeological evidence of the apple's presence dates back to Neolithic times. They are believed to have originated in western Asia, in the form of the sour crab apple; there are now from 7,500 to 8,000 varieties of apples. Pages that could fill volumes address the role apples have played in folklore, religion, superstition, history, magic, medicine, and, of course, food. Ancient Greek and Roman myths speak of apples as symbols of beauty and love. The common phrase "the apple of one's eye" quite possibly originated in those times. This fruit has been credited with curative powers unsurpassed by other fruits and vegetables, hence, the saying "An apple a day keeps the doctor away." In fact, apples are rich in pectin, provide necessary dietary fiber, and contain substantial amounts of potassium, vitamin C, and beta-carotene. When eaten raw, they also work to promote dental health.

Apples are now grown throughout the world in cool, moist temperate climates. Cooler temperatures allow the trees time to lie dormant and gain strength for the fruit-bearing months. The first orchards for cultivating apples were planted in Virginia and Massachusetts by the colonists. John Chapman, the legendary Johnny Appleseed, was responsible for promoting the growth of apples across the nation, establishing orchards from Pennsylvania to Indiana. Currently, at least thirty-five states cultivate them in significant quantities, with the biggest producers being Washington, New York, Michigan, California, Pennsylvania, and Virginia.

HOW TO CHOOSE: Select apples that have good color for their type and appear fresh and smooth skinned. They should feel firm and be free of withered skin or bruises. This versatile fruit ranges in size from small to large. Apples can be sweet, mellow, or tart and firm, crispy, or soft-textured. Some will give off an aroma when ripe, while others don't reveal their scent until cut. Many are well formed, yet others are lumpy and misshapen. Some apple skins are shiny and bright, and others tend to be dull or mottled.

Many commercially grown apples are coated with a thin layer of a harmless, tasteless wax. Not only does this give them a more attractive sheen, but it serves to preserve flavor and retard moisture loss during cold storage.

MOST COMMON VARIETIES: The following is a listing of the more common apples found in the United States, evaluated, both raw and baked, for flavor, color, texture, and moisture content. Results are based on a comparative test of the wide range of apples available to me in the Northeast. Results for varieties not available to me are based on reliable sources and marked with an asterisk(*).

Apples can vary from crop to crop and season to season. Keep in mind that most any apple can be used in a cobbler or crisp, but only certain types will make superior pies and tarts. While everyone has his or her own favorites, the recommendations that follow are based on my personal preferences.

✦ *Baldwin*:* An "old," or heirloom, apple with limited availability. Hard flesh, crisp, tart flavor, good for sauces, jams and jellies. Recommended for baking and pies.

✦ *Braeburn:* Crisp fruit with tart flavor. Bland after cooking with fibrous flesh. Moderate moisture content. Long shelf life. Available year-round. Best for eating.

✦ *Cortland:* Tart with low to moderate moisture content. Remains snowy white after peeling. After baking, softer flesh retains shape. Best to cut in thicker slices, 3/4 inch. Highly recommended for pies.

✦ *Empire:* Moderately tart, low to moderate moisture. Soft flesh retains shape after baking. Similar to Cortland. Best cut in thick slices, 3/4 inch. Recommended for pies.

✦ *Fuji:* Pacific Coast crops most consistent in quality. Very crisp with low moisture. Recommended for cooking and baking.

✦ *Gala:* Sweet flavor with moderate to high moisture content. Retains shape well after baking, but has a dull color when cooked. Not recommended for baking.

✦ *Golden Delicious:* Superior flavor from farm-fresh fruit. Sweet and aromatic, with low moisture content. Retains shape well after baking. Best of the bunch for visual appeal, with rich, golden color when cooked. Very thin skin, peeling is optional. Resists discoloration when peeled. Short shelf life. My top choice for open fruit tarts.

✦ *Granny Smith:* Preferred for tart flavor. Moderate moisture content. Hard flesh, best used in 1/4-inch slices. Retains shape after baking, but color is dull and unappetizing. Recommended for pies and tarts, but lack of visual appeal is the tradeoff for flavor.

✦ *Gravenstein*:* "Old" apple, similar to Stayman Winesap. Tart-sweet with juicy, white flesh. Retains shape after baking. Recommended for pies (but increase thickening).

✦ *IdaRed:* Sweet-tart flavor, very aromatic. Moderate to high moisture content. Soft, white flesh, retains shape when baked. Recommended for pies (but increase thickening).

✦ *Jonagold:* Sweet-tart flavor with moderate moisture content. Soft flesh, golden color, retains shape fairly well. Best to cut in 1/2-inch slices. Recommended for pies.

✦ *Jonathon*:* Small, tart, firm and juicy. Early crop. All-purpose apple, used for cider. Hard to find. Not recommended for baking.

✦ *McIntosh:* Pungent flavor. High moisture content. White flesh, loses crispness and shape after baking. Produces soft, mushy pie fillings. Makes superior applesauce.

✦ *Macoun:* Moderately tart flavor. High moisture content. Short shelf life. Same cooking and baking properties as McIntosh.

✦ *Mutsu (Crispin):* Tart-sweet flavor. Low moisture content. Retains shape when baked, with soft, golden color. Best cut in 1/2-inch slices. Similar to Golden Delicious, but more tart with greater depth of flavor. Highly recommended, a top choice for pies.

✦ *Northern Spy:* Mildly tart, superior flavor. Crisp flesh with low moisture content. Retains shape well after baking. Short season, highly perishable. Cooked fruit softens and turns a creamy yellow with a pink overtone. Best sliced 1/2 inch thick. Highly recommended, a top choice for pies.

✦ *Newtown Pippen*:* Tart with moderate moisture content. Good for cooking, but not recommended for baking.

✦ *Opalescent:* Tart, lacks strong flavor. Moderate moisture content. Not a favorite for pies.

✦ *Red Delicious:* Sweet eating apple. High moisture content. Poor texture for cooking or baking.

✦ *Rhode Island Greening:* Very tart with moderate moisture content. Thin skinned. Extremely hard, cut in 1/4-inch slices. Excellent for pies. Limited availability.

✦ *Rome Beauty:* Bland, lacks sweetness when raw. Flavor improves with cooking. Low moisture content. Soft flesh, holds shape well when baked. Best cut in 3/4-inch slices. Highly recommended for pies, especially when combined with tart apples.

✦ *Stayman Winesap:* Tart flavor, juicy with moderate moisture content. Used widely for apple cider. Recommended for pies.

✦ *York Imperial*:* Tart-sweet flavor, moderately juicy. Recommended for cooking and baking.

STORAGE AND HANDLING: Apples are best kept refrigerated because warm temperatures lead to a loss of both crispness and flavor. However, apples can be kept unrefrigerated in a cool area of your kitchen for up to 1 week. For longer storage, place them in an open plastic bag in the refrigerator for up to 6 weeks. Always remove any decaying fruit, as one bad apple does indeed spoil the whole bushel. Wash all apples well before using. Once peeled, most varieties should be sprinkled with lemon juice to prevent discoloration.

TO PEEL AND CORE

METHOD 1: PARING KNIFE
✦ Cut the apple into quarters with a paring knife. Remove the core by cutting a V-shaped wedge from the center. Then thinly peel each quarter with the paring knife.

METHOD 2: VEGETABLE PEELER
✦ Remove the skin from a whole apple with a vegetable peeler. Cut into quarters. Remove the core by cutting a V-shaped wedge from the center with a paring knife.

METHOD 3: APPLE CORER
✦ Level the apple by removing a thin slice from the base. Stand it on a solid surface. Hold the apple as straight as possible, and insert an apple corer into the center of the fruit. A fair amount of height is needed for leverage. Push the corer down through the center to the bottom. If you meet with resistance, jiggle the corer as you are pushing down. Peel the fruit after coring, either whole or after cutting into halves or quarters.
✦ *To Freeze:* Not recommended

CAROLE'S COMMENTS ═══
On a crisp fall day, with Thanksgiving around the corner, pies made with apples fresh from the tree are truly a gift from Mother Nature. It seems that everyone remembers someone in their family whose apple pie was "the best." Although the nostalgia evoked by these memories is cherished, many of those revered favorites, in truth, can be disappointing. All too often the apples used for these pies run the gamut from the wrong variety for baking to apple filling straight from a can.

We are fortunate to have so many apple choices available to us. Where does one begin with such a vast selection of this glorious fruit? Although apples are plentiful throughout the year, when autumn is here I know it's time to make a visit to my favorite farm. When I arrive, I cannot resist the brimming bins of vibrant red, gold, and green fruit whose aroma completely seduces me. Will I be lucky enough to find some Northern Spys, a grand apple with a tart-sweet flavor? Might there be Mutzus, the newest apple to have captured my fancy? If not, I am content with IdaReds, Cortlands, Empires, Granny Smiths, Romes—oh, I could go on and on.

Whether it be for pies, tarts, crisps, or cobblers, don't limit yourself to baking with one kind of apple. Try combining different textures and flavors to come up with your own, distinctive apple pie.

In an orchard there should be enough to eat, enough to lay up, enough to be stolen, and enough to rot upon the ground.

SAMUEL MADDEN,
BOSWELL'S LIFE
OF JOHNSON

APRICOTS

SEASON: Mid-May–early August. Peak season, early July.

YIELD: 6 to 7 medium apricots = approximately 1 pound.

HISTORY: The apricot, known in Persian as "egg of the sun," is a member of the rose family and cousin to the peach, plum, and cherry. It is believed to have its origins in China and was brought to Europe by Alexander the Great. Many years later it was cultivated in the New World by Franciscan friars in California. Evidence of its infamously short shelf life can be found dating back to the time of Pliny the Elder, in the 1st century B.C., who noted, "There is no other fruit which keeps worse: the longest time it will last after being plucked is two days."

HOW TO CHOOSE: A ripe apricot is sweet, fragrant, and richly colored in tones of gold to deep rose. Because the fruit is costly and extremely fragile, choose with care. Apricots must be picked at full ripeness, for while they will continue to soften once removed from the tree, they will not become sweeter. At times, the sweetest-tasting apricot may look a little mushy and have a few small bruises or soft spots—this is okay. The fruit should feel slightly soft to the touch and the skin should have no trace of green. If it is your good fortune to happen upon a basket of plump, velvety, colorful apricots, buy them.

STORAGE AND HANDLING: A mildly underripe or hard apricot can be softened by placing it in a paper bag and leaving it at room temperature for a day or two, but remember that the flavor will never be as sweet as a tree-ripened fruit. If you are unable to use the ripe fruit immediately, store it in the refrigerator for no more than 1 to 2 days.
✦ *To Clean:* Wipe with a damp towel. Run a small knife around the fruit following the natural groove in the skin. Twist gently to separate the halves. Remove the pit with either the tip of the knife or your fingernail. For most recipes, peeling is unnecessary. However, if you wish to peel the fruit, immerse the whole fruit in boiling water for 25 to 30 seconds, then plunge into cold water. The skins will slip off easily.
✦ *To Freeze:* Remove the skins; they will become tough when frozen. Then halve and pit. Place in a single layer on a shallow pan and freeze. Package in airtight plastic bags.

CAROLE'S COMMENTS
I love to use fresh apricots for pies and tarts because of their low moisture content and distinctive flavor. Although this pleasingly tart fruit requires a lot of sweetening, its versatility makes it worth the splurge.

Fresh apricots are an excellent source of both beta-carotene and potassium.

In the winter months, you may find apricots imported from Chile, New Zealand, or Australia. Keep in mind that although they may look tempting, their flavor will be no more than a mere reminder of this luscious summer fruit.

BANANAS

SEASON: Year-round.

YIELD: 3 medium (6- to 7-inch) bananas = approximately 1 pound.

HISTORY: More bananas are consumed daily than perhaps

Testing Fruit

WHEN YOU WANT TO KNOW if a particular fresh fruit is a good candidate for a pie or tart, here is my "secret" for testing it for moisture, texture, color, and flavor.

Peel, core, and cut an apple (as an example) into 1/4-inch slices. Place the pieces in an ovenproof glass dish (about 8-ounce capacity). Sprinkle with 1 tablespoon of sugar, and bake in a 375 degree oven for 20 minutes. Remove from the oven, cover the dish loosely with aluminum foil, then continue to bake it for 15 minutes, or until the juices are bubbling. Let the fruit cool for at least 15 minutes, then invert it onto a small plate. Note the amount of liquid that is present and how well the apple slices retain their shape. If it is of importance, check their color, and, finally, taste them for flavor.

If the fruit is not too watery or mushy, use it for baking. Adjust the sweetening in the recipe to your taste, adding a touch more lemon juice if the fruit needs a lift. If the fruit is on the watery side, add a bit more thickening to the filling. I have used this method primarily for apples and pears, but you can test the waters with other fruits as well.

any other fruit in the world. Their origin is believed to be eastern Asia or Oceania, but they can now be found in just about every tropical locale. The largest exporters of bananas are the islands of the Caribbean and Central and South America. Their culinary uses are plentiful, as are the many colorful myths that can be found about them throughout recorded history.

HOW TO CHOOSE: Choose firm, greenish to greenish-yellow fruit and allow them to ripen at room temperature. A buttery yellow skin speckled with brown is an indication of a ripe and sweet fruit.

STORAGE AND HANDLING: Once ripened, bananas can be stored in the refrigerator. However, this will cause the skins to blacken. While the color is most unappealing, the fruit will remain sweet and firm, perfect for baking. Once the fruit becomes overripe and mushy, it gains an even deeper sweetness and is perfect for using in bread and cake recipes. Overripe bananas can also be wrapped tightly and frozen for later use. When slicing bananas for use in a pie or tart, always sprinkle with lemon juice to prevent any discoloration.
✦ *To Freeze:* Peel and freeze in chunks in a single layer on a shallow pan. Then package in airtight plastic bags.

CAROLE'S COMMENTS ══
Bananas are one of the more difficult fruits to use in pies and tarts. They are rarely baked or cooked because the flesh is soft and quickly discolors once peeled. Although the shelf life of a peeled banana is short, when appropriately used the sweet flavor and creamy texture make them a favorite of both young and old.

Bananas are very easily digested. They are exceptionally nutritious with high levels of vitamins B and C, potassium, iron, calcium, and fiber. They are also an invaluable tool to help ripen other fruits. If you place a ripe banana in a brown paper bag with a green tomato or a hard avocado, the ethylene gas released from the banana will hasten its ripening.

BLACKBERRIES

SEASON: May–September. Peak season, June and July.

YIELD: 1 dry pint basket = approximately 1½ cups.

HISTORY: The blackberry has been eaten, in its wild form, for thousands of years. Today, blackberries enjoy the distinction of being one of the few fruits consumed in greater quantity as a fresh-picked wild berry than as store-bought cultivated fruit. The largest commercial growing areas are in New Jersey, Michigan, and the Pacific Northwest, but wild blackberries can be found in virtually every part of the United States. In recent years, we have also seen credible cultivated berries being imported from Chile during the winter months.

HOW TO CHOOSE: Look for blackberries that are firm and glossy with a deep bluish-black color. Always check the bottom of the basket or box for any signs of moisture or staining, which indicates spoiling or rotted berries. Avoid baskets with fruit that appears at all soft, wet, or mildewed.

STORAGE AND HANDLING: Refrigerate berries in their basket or, if space permits, spread in a single layer on paper towels in a shallow pan, as soon as possible and use within 2 days. If using farm-picked berries, put them in a bowl and refrigerate, loosely covered. Do not wash until just before use.
✦ *To Wash Berries:* Fill a bowl or the sink with cool water, place the berries briefly in the water. Carefully remove them with your hands, letting the water drip through your fingers. Place the berries on a shallow pan lined with a double thickness of paper towels. Gently shake the pan back and forth to roll the berries. This will remove the excess moisture. Although it has long been said that cultivated berries do not need to be washed, because of certain health issues in recent years you may be more comfortable doing so.
✦ *To Freeze:* Clean berries as instructed above. Spread in a single layer on a shallow pan and freeze. Package in airtight plastic bags.

One of my favorite fruits to use in baking are blackberries. These tasty berries range from sweet to tart and from small to large. I find that the smaller berries, especially those grown in the Pacific Northwest, are the sweetest. For most recipes, blackberries can be combined with or subsituted for raspberries or blueberries.

BLUEBERRIES

SEASON: Early June–early September.

YIELD: 1 dry pint basket = approximately 2–2½ cups.

HISTORY: The blueberry, a true American native, grows wild throughout the United States and is commercially cultivated along the entire eastern seaboard, as well as in the Pacific Northwest and Michigan. While there is much debate as to the more delicious of the two forms, wild or cultivated, this versatile berry is excellent for baking as well as for eating out of hand. The wild, farm-picked blueberry is smaller and tarter than its larger mass-market sibling. Many cooks believe that the wild makes a tastier pie.

HOW TO CHOOSE: Look for plump, firm, deep blue berries with no wetness or mildew. A dusty bloom, which is the blueberry's form of protection from the sun, is an excellent sign of freshness.

Check the bottom of the basket for any wet spots or staining, the telltale markings of spoiled berries.

STORAGE AND HANDLING: Blueberries can be stored at room temperature for 1 to 2 days if kept in their basket. For longer storage, refrigerate for up to 10 days. Never wash blueberries until just before using.

✦ *To Wash:* Place berries in a colander and rinse with cool water. Empty onto a shallow pan lined with a double thickness of paper towels and gently shake the pan back and forth to remove excess moisture.

✦ *To Freeze:* Place cleaned berries in a single layer on a shallow baking pan. Freeze until hard, then transfer to an airtight plastic bag for up to one year. It is best to use them while still frozen.

CAROLE'S COMMENTS ===
Much can be said in praise of the blueberry. It has great flavor, beautiful color, is durable, and has a long shelf life. While blueberries make terrific pies and cobblers, they do contain a lot of moisture. For this reason, I often parcook the fruit to remove some of the liquid. A few blueberries added to most any pie or tart will be a wonderful enhancement. Blueberries are a good source of vitamin C, potassium, and dietary fiber, while being quite low in calories.

CHERRIES

SEASON: Sweet cherries, late May–August; tart cherries, few weeks in July.

YIELD: 1 quart basket = approximately 3–4 cups, pitted.

HISTORY: The cherry is believed to have originated in western Asia and the Middle East, well before the appearance of humans. Cherry pits have been found in prehistoric cave dwellings in Switzerland, Italy, and as far north as Scandinavia. Over the years, cultivation has produced two basic types of cherries, the sweet and the tart. Sweet cherries include the deep burgundy Bings, Lamberts, and the more intensely flavored Royal Annes, with their yellow to amber skin. Tart cherries are primarily used for pies. They range in color from yellow to pink to reddish. Not only is this variety of cherry extremely juicy but its extreme tartness necessitates the use of additional sugar. Unfortunately, their peak season is very short, with availability usually limited to farmer's markets and upscale produce sellers.

HOW TO CHOOSE: Take time to hand-select your cherries, and avoid fruit packaged by the grocer when possible. Pick cherries that appear plump, firm, and brightly colored with bright green, fresh-looking stems. Reject cherries with gashes, brown spots, or any trace of stickiness, which is an indicator of spoilage. When choosing Bing or Lambert cherries, select those with the deepest color for they will be the sweetest.

STORAGE AND HANDLING: Cherries will not ripen once picked. Sweet cherries, which are used primarily for eating, should be refrigerated in an uncovered bowl. They will keep for as long as 2 weeks. Tart cherries have a much shorter shelf life, so try not to purchase them more than 2 or 3 days of cooking them. As with sweet cherries, they may be stored in an uncovered bowl in your refrigerator. Do not wash cherries until just before use.

✦ *To Clean:* Remove the stems, place the cherries in a colander, and rinse under cool water. Empty the colander onto a shallow pan lined with a double thickness of paper towels, and shake gently back and forth to remove excess moisture.

✦ *To Pit Cherries:* I strongly recommend one of the readily available and inexpensive pitting tools (also useful for pitting olives). These can be found in kitchen supply shops, gourmet cookware stores, or anywhere that carries an extensive line of culinary gadgetry. Hand pitting, though messy and time consuming, is an alternative. Simply make a small slit with a paring knife down one side of the cherry, from stem end to the bottom. Then, using either the tip of the knife or your thumbnail, gently pry out the pit.

✦ *To Freeze:* Once pitted, spread cherries in a single layer on a shallow sheet pan and freeze, then package in airtight plastic bags for up to one year. Do not thaw before using.

CAROLE'S COMMENTS
I prefer to use Bing or other sweet cherries in refrigerated desserts and for poaching or for macerating. For baking, I like tart cherries because their sweet-sour flavor adds a certain character to the pastry. While using fresh cherries is a treat, I find that excellent pies can be made with high-quality canned tart cherries.

COCONUTS

SEASON: Year-round. Most plentiful October–January.

YIELD: 1 coconut = approximately 3½–4 cups shredded.

HISTORY: The variety of palm tree that gives us the coconut is one of the single most important plants in tropical regions of the world. Its name in Sanskrit, *kalpa vriksha*, translates as "the tree which gives all that is necessary for living." Most scholars believe that the tree's origin is Malaysia. Its worldwide spread is due in part to commerce and in part to its ability to germinate on newfound soil. This unique fruit has been known to survive for long periods, adrift on the ocean currents, until it washes ashore.

HOW TO CHOOSE: Select coconuts that are heavy and contain ample amounts of liquid. Shake the coconut; you should hear a sloshing sound within. Avoid coconuts that sound dry, have cracked shells, or that have any sign of mold or moisture at the eyes. Smell the eyes; there should be no odor to indicate fermentation.

STORAGE AND HANDLING: Keep coconuts at room temperature for up to 2 weeks or refrigerate for up to 1 month. Once drained and cracked open, they must be covered well with plastic wrap and refrigerated.

✦ *To Remove the Coconut Meat:* Pierce the eyes of the coconut with a sharp instrument, such as an ice pick or screwdriver. Hold the coconut with the eyes down to drain out all of the liquid. (This liquid is *not* coconut milk, but it can be reserved to moisten grated or chunks of coconut before freezing.) Next, place the drained coconut on a sheet of aluminum foil and heat in a 350 degree oven for 25 to 30 minutes. After 30 minutes, if the coconut hasn't split, remove it from the oven. Wrap it in a towel and help it along with a few smacks of a hammer. Pry the meat away from the shell with a thin screwdriver or blunt knife. Peel away the thin, outer brown skin with a paring knife or vegetable peeler. Wash and dry well with paper towels.

✦ *To Freeze:* Store clean grated or chunk coconut in an airtight container for up to 6 months.

My students often ask me, "Is all this worth it?" until they taste a dessert made with fresh coconut. "You bet it is!" they answer. Packaged coconut is far too sweet. Unsweetened, desiccated coconut from health food stores is dry and tasteless. Unfortunately, what I consider a satisfactory packaged product is not yet available to the consumer. While fresh coconut may seem bland to you when compared to the sweetened bagged product, its delicate flavor and pleasing crunch make it desirable for certain cream fillings. I save the sweetened coconut for those times when a recipe calls for toasting. Coconut is high in fat and calories, with negligible vitamin content.

CRANBERRIES

SEASON: September–January.

YIELD: 12 oz. package = approximately 3 cups.

HISTORY: Cranberries are one of many fruits native to North America. Their existence and use by the Native Americans was discovered when the Pilgrims settled in Plymouth Bay, Massachusetts. This berry has become firmly entrenched in our national folklore, associated with the celebration of Thanksgiving. Cranberries, both rich in vitamin C and blessed with a long shelf life (owing to their high acid content), were a staple of nineteenth-century American loggers and sailors to prevent scurvy. Almost half of the cranberries sold today are grown in Massachusetts, with the remainder harvested in New Jersey, Wisconsin, Washington, and Oregon.

HOW TO CHOOSE: Cranberries are sold in plastic bags and, owing to their exceptional shelf life, are usually in prime condition. Cranberries should look smooth, glossy, and brilliant in color. If you happen upon a package of dry, shriveled fruit, pass it by.

STORAGE AND HANDLING: Cranberries should be refrigerated in their original packaging for up to 4 weeks. Before use, wash them well in cool water. Pick through them, discarding any stems or soft berries, then dry thoroughly on paper towels. ✦ *To Freeze:* Cranberries can be frozen in their original packaging for up to 1 year. Do not thaw before using. If thawed, the liquid released will cause the berries to become unpleasantly soggy.

Cranberries are too sour and astringent for most palates to tolerate without sweetening, but they make a lovely addition to baked goods. While I like the flavor of cranberries, for baking purposes I use them mostly as an accent ingredient because of their extreme tartness. Keeping a bag or two in the freezer gives me the opportunity to enjoy this versatile berry all year.

CURRANTS

SEASON: Late June–early August.

YIELD: 6 ounce basket = approximately 1¼ cups.

HISTORY: Currants, a close relative of gooseberries, have a short season with limited availability. They are believed to have originated in Scandinavia where they commonly grow wild. In northern temperate regions of Europe and Asia, these berries are cultivated. In the United States, commercial growth is restricted to a few areas of the Pacific Northwest and California. Their limited cultivation is due to its propensity to play host to white pine blister rot, a disease that does not harm the berry but can be devastating to trees.

There are three varieties of fresh currants. The red berry, with its pleasantly tart flavor, is most common. The black currant, which is the basis for the liqueur Cassis, is too bitter to eat raw but makes flavorful preserves, jams, and sauces. The rarer white currant has a golden hue, a lower acid content, and is the sweetest for eating out of hand. Fresh currants should not be confused with the widely available dried currant, which is actually a dried Zante grape.

HOW TO CHOOSE: Currants are highly perishable so take care to check the berries carefully before purchasing. They should be plump, dry, and firmly attached to their stems. Avoid baskets containing shriveled or crushed berries.

STORAGE AND HANDLING: Check currants immediately upon getting them home. Remove any moldly or smashed fruit. Store them in the refrigerator, covered, for 3 to 4 days.
✦ *To Clean:* Just before using, rinse them in cool water, drain in a colander, and dry on a sheet pan lined with a double thickness of paper towels. When dry, carefully remove the berries from the stems.
✦ *To Freeze:* Wash and dry the currants and spread them in a single layer on a shallow baking pan. Freeze until hard, then transfer to an airtight plastic bag for up to one year. Do not thaw currants before cooking.

CAROLE'S COMMENTS
When you come upon fresh red currants, snap them up. When cooked, they have a vibrant color and make an exciting alternative to raspberries when you want to serve a fresh berry sauce. Fresh currants are high in both vitamin C and potassium.

FIGS

SEASON: California figs, late June–early September.

YIELD: 3 to 4 figs = approximately 1 cup.

HISTORY: Figs have played an important role throughout his-

tory. Originally from Asia Minor, not only were they Cleopatra's food of choice but the first Olympians wore figs as medals to celebrate their victories. Owing to their great expense and perishability, many people have never enjoyed the delicate, honey-sweet pleasures of a fresh fig. Ninety-nine percent of the fresh figs available in the United States are grown in California. Because of their delicate nature, transporting figs over long distances is problematic. Extremely fine figs are grown in Turkey and the Mediterranean, but are available to us only as dried fruit.

HOW TO CHOOSE: Figs come in a variety of colors, ranging from white, green, or reddish to brown and purple. The most common variety eaten in the United States is the Black Mission, with Breba and Green Kadota following in popularity. When selecting these fruits, avoid any with spots, which indicate fermentation has begun. They should be soft and plump, with just the tiniest bit of sap appearing at the opening on the base. Figs will not ripen once picked, so avoid those that appear hard.

STORAGE AND HANDLING: Figs are highly perishable and should be eaten or cooked within 2 or 3 days of purchase. For storage, the fruit should be placed on paper towels, covered with plastic wrap, and left on the bottom shelf of the refrigerator, where the air is coolest. Be-

fore using, wipe clean with a damp paper towel, and remove the dried bit of stem at the top of the fruit.
✦ *To Freeze:* Sprinkle whole figs lightly with lemon juice, wrap well, and freeze for up to 1 year.

CAROLE'S COMMENTS
I envy people who are fortunate enough to have a fig tree in their yard, for one of my newest passions in recent years has been for fresh figs. Though outwardly they appear dull, once cut, a perfectly ripe fig will have a brilliantly colored flesh and a delightful, delicate flavor. My favorite is the Black Mission, with its deep purple skin and vibrant pink meat. I love to use figs as an accent for desserts, and a pie or tart made from fresh figs is a treat for the gods. Figs are extremely healthful; they are low in fat, high in fiber, and rich with potassium, iron, magnesium, and calcium.

GOOSEBERRIES

SEASON: July.

YIELD: 1 pint = approximately 2 cups.

HISTORY: The gooseberry, a native of Europe, northern Africa, and western Asia, is cousin to the currant. Gooseberries are highly praised by the British, primarily for jams, jellies, and preserves. However, because of their extremely sour flavor, they have never been widely accepted in the United States. They are commercially cultivated in northern California and the Pacific Northwest. Gooseberries are not readily available to most American consumers; however they can be found at local farmstands.

HOW TO CHOOSE: Gooseberries may be found with coloring ranging from yellow, green, and white to pinkish-red. Look for berries that are plump, dry, and fairly firm. This fruit should be cooked when it is slightly underripe, as the pectin content will be at its highest.

STORAGE AND HANDLING: Refrigerate in a cellophane-covered basket, as purchased, or loosely covered with plastic wrap. Do not wash until ready to use.
✦ *To Clean:* Rinse in a colander, then spread on a shallow pan lined with a double thickness of paper towels. Shake pan back and forth to remove excess moisture, then pat gently with additional paper towels. Pluck off the small tail on bottom of each berry with your fingers.
✦ *To Freeze:* Clean, stem, and tail the berries. Place berries in a single layer on a shallow pan. Freeze until hard then pour into covered plastic containers and freeze for up to one year. Do not thaw before using.

CAROLE'S COMMENTS ══
Owing to the gooseberry's high moisture content, they are best used in recipes with no bottom crust, such as a crisp. Also, keep in mind that the gooseberry is extremely sour and requires abundant sweetening to make it palatable.

GRAPES

SEASON: Available year-round. California season, May–November; Chilean season, December–May.

YIELD: 1 pound = approximately 3–3½ cups.

HISTORY: Historically, the cultivation of grapes dates back at least to the ancient Egyptians. This "fruit of the vine" is mentioned frequently in the Bible and in other early writings. Grapes are treasured for their unlimited versatility. Hardly any festive occasion is without their presence in one form or another. Grapes are now grown in every part of the world except in severely cold regions. Indeed, the growing of grapes is currently the world's biggest fruit industry. The table or eating grapes that are commonly purchased in this country are harvested mostly in California and the northeastern states, with a large quantity imported from Chile. Table grapes can be found in varying shades of green, red, and purplish-black. Some are seedless, while others have small, hard seeds. All, however, share the quality of a firm, almost crisp skin with a softer, toothsome interior.

HOW TO CHOOSE: Grapes should be plump, firm, well shaped, and firmly attached to a fresh, green stem. When selecting, pick up a bunch and shake it. If many of the grapes fall off, the fruit is not as fresh as it should be. Avoid grapes whose stems are dried and withered or those that are sticky or shriveled. All grapes, regardless of variety, should be rich in color. A dusty bloom, especially on purple grapes, is a good indicator of freshness. On darker grapes, avoid those with any tinge of green. Green grapes, such as the Thompson Seedless, will prove sweetest if they show an undertone of gold or yellow. Lastly, taste the grapes before purchasing. This is the surest way to gauge their sweetness.

Some of the seedless varieties are:
✦ *Thompson:* Golden green, sweet, somewhat tender flesh. This is the most popular grape in the United States.
✦ *Red Flame:* Sweet-tart and crunchy firm. This is a relatively new variety that is gaining in popularity.
✦ *Black Beauty:* Sweet and spicy, resembling Concords in flavor. The only seedless black grape, it is relatively new to the market.

Among the seeded varieties are:
✦ *Red Emperor:* Second most popular variety in the United States. Available throughout the winter and spring. These large, round, thick-skinned grapes are less sweet, but are most attractive for garnishing.

+ *Concord:* Tart skin with sweet flesh. The Concords have the flavor we associate with jams, jellies, and juice. With a distinctive flavor all their own, they make exceptional pies if you have the patience to seed them.

STORAGE AND HANDLING: Refrigerate in a perforated plastic bag for up to 1 week. Do not wash until just before use.

+ *To Wash:* Place the bunch of grapes in a colander and rinse with cool water. For baking purposes, remove from the stem and spread on a shallow pan lined with a double thickness of paper towels. Gently shake the pan back and forth to roll the excess moisture off of the grapes. Blot any remaining moisture off with paper towels.

+ *To Freeze:* Store clean, dry grapes in an airtight container for up to 6 months. Do not thaw before using.

CAROLE'S COMMENTS ═══
The poor grape is often overlooked by bakers. We most often think of using grapes uncooked, as a garnish, or as a topping for an open fruit tart. However, we forget that grapes can and do make terrific pies, used alone or as an accent ingredient. They add color, texture, and distinctive flavor. Today, we are fortunate to have seedless varieties, which makes baking with them a pleasure. Grapes contain a fair amount of vitamin C and are high in carbohydrates.

KIWIFRUIT (CHINESE GOOSEBERRIES)

SEASON: Year-round.

YIELD: N/A. Used primarily as garnish.

HISTORY: The kiwifruit achieved its American popularity during the 1970s, heyday of nouvelle cuisine. The fruit was introduced to New Zealand in 1906 but was not commercially grown until the late 1950s. Originally known as the Chinese gooseberry, as a marketing strategy the moniker was changed to kiwi, named for the native bird of New Zealand. The name change paid off; within a decade, this tangy, sweet fruit with its beautiful green flesh and crunchy, edible seeds became the rage in North America and Europe. Today, 95 percent of the kiwis sold in the United States have been cultivated in California.

HOW TO CHOOSE: Look for fruit with light brown skins with a greenish hue, which give slightly when gently squeezed. Avoid fruits with large blemishes or rough patches. An overripe kiwi, while edible, loses its opaque lime color and becomes somewhat translucent and mushy.

STORAGE AND HANDLING: The kiwi has a remarkably long shelf life. An unripe kiwi can be stored for up to 3 months in the refrigerator. When you are ready to ripen it, leave the fruit at room temperature. To hasten the ripening process, place the kiwi in a brown paper bag with either a banana or an apple. To stop a kiwi from overripening and becoming too soft, refrigerate it for up to 1 month. A ripe kiwi that is close to being eaten can be kept at room temperature for 3 to 4 days. It is not necessary to peel the skin of the kiwi for eating out of hand. The thin skin is totally edible and not at all bitter. For garnishing purposes, however, most recipes benefit from the stunning eye appeal of a peeled kiwi.

+ *To Freeze:* Not recommended.

CAROLE'S COMMENTS ═══
To me, the primary function of a kiwi is that of a garnish. Because of its delicate, mellow flavor, I prefer to use it as an accent ingredient along with assertive fruits such as pineapple or berries. In addition, kiwis contain an enzyme called actinidin, which makes binding with gelatin impossible when used uncooked. However, if cooked, such as in a puree, this enzyme weakens and makes gelling possible. Actinidin, used in many meat tenderizers, will also cause problems when raw kiwis are combined with either whipped cream or ice cream. If used with these products, make sure the dish is served immediately or you will see a breakdown in their consistency. Kiwis are rich in vitamin C and potassium, and contain a signif-

icant amount of dietary fiber while remaining low in both fat and sodium.

LEMONS

SEASON: Year-round, but less abundant in summer. Summer lemons are more costly and have less flavor.

YIELD: 1 medium lemon = approximately 2½ tablespoons of juice; 1 medium lemon = 2–3 teaspoons of zest, depending on the grating method.

HISTORY: There is some debate regarding whether the lemon originated in Southeast Asia or in the Middle East. However, it is clear that it spread north toward the Mediterranean, where it became an integral part of that cuisine. While lemons are still cultivated widely in those regions, 80 percent of the lemons purchased in the United States are grown in California, Texas, or Florida. The lemon, prized for its versatility, acts as a flavor enhancer to many foods. Its high acidic content has many benefits in the kitchen. A few drops of lemon juice drizzled on raw fruits prevent discoloration. Lemon juice added to cooking water will keep broccoli and green beans brilliantly colored, as well as increasing the whiteness of cauliflower or rice.

HOW TO CHOOSE: Lemons can be found with both thick and thin (the slightly less acidic Meyer variety) skins. Both are delicious, but note that while thin-skinned fruits will yield more juice, the thicker-skinned variety will give more zest with greater flavor. Always choose fruit that is firm, slightly oily to the touch, has a smooth, bright skin, and feels heavy for its size. Modern technology has led to the artificial ripening of lemons; if left on the tree to ripen naturally, the fruit becomes soft and subject to spoilage. The end result guarantees firm, ripe fruit practically year-round.

STORAGE AND HANDLING: Lemons can be kept at room temperature for 2 to 3 days or refrigerated, preferably in the fruit/vegetable drawer, for 1 to 2 weeks. A partially sliced or zested lemon can be covered tightly in plastic wrap and refrigerated for up to 1 week.
✦ *To Zest or Juice:* See "Handling Citrus Fruits," page 59.
✦ *To Freeze:* Not recommended for the whole fruit. Juice and zest can be frozen for up to 3 months in airtight containers.

CAROLE'S COMMENTS In my culinary world, I cannot imagine life without the versatile lemon. When combined with sugar, the sweet and sour flavors are so complementary. The citric tang of lemon desserts is satisfying after a heavy meal and, in general, enjoys a universal popularity. This versatile fruit's contribution to the kitchen is limitless. Long known to be a replacement for salt, some of its other virtues are that it brings out flavor, brightens food, enhances chocolate, and even removes stains from cookware. If ever I'm in doubt as to what to serve for dessert, I turn to the ever reliable lemon. The absorbic acid in 1 medium lemon provides more than half of the recommended daily dose of vitamin C.

LIMES

SEASON: Persian or green limes, available year-round. Peak season for California crop is winter–late spring. Key limes (Mexican lime), available late fall–early spring.

YIELD: 1 medium lime = approximately 3 tablespoons juice; 1 medium lime = approximately 2 teaspoons zest.

HISTORY: It seems likely that the green, or Persian, lime originated in Southeast Asia, traveled west to the Middle East, and then north to the Mediterranean on its journey to worldwide usage. It has been favored for centuries for its tangy, acidic flavor, and its high vitamin C content. British sailors as far back as the 1800s were known to carry limes aboard ship for eating to aid in the prevention of scurvy (hence the slang term for British seamen, "limeys"). The Key lime, or Mexican lime, is available for a more limited season in most parts of the United States. It is noted for its tarter flavor, smaller size, and yellow-green skin.

HOW TO CHOOSE:

✦ *Persian Limes:* Choose firm, deep green fruit with shiny, unblemished skin.

✦ *Key Limes:* Commonly sold in mesh bags or small crates. A few blemishes are acceptable. Key limes will have a duller, yellow to light green surface with a thinner skin.

STORAGE AND HANDLING:

All varieties of limes may be kept at room temperature for 3 to 4 days or refrigerated for 2 to 3 weeks. Exposure to sunlight will cause a yellowing of the skin, but will not affect the flavor. To prolong the life of an aging lime, sprinkle lightly with water and refrigerate in a plastic bag. Partially zested or sliced limes may also be kept in the refrigerator, tightly covered with plastic wrap.

✦ *To Zest or Juice:* See "Handling Citrus Fruits," page 59.

✦ *To Freeze:* Not recommended for the whole fruit. Juice and zest may be frozen for up to 3 months in airtight containers.

CAROLE'S COMMENTS

Limes are not always interchangeable with their citrus relative, the lemon, because the flavor is sharper and more acidic. However, with some sweetening adjustments, at times they can make a tasty substitution. With regard to the much revered Key Lime Pie (page 264), bottled Key lime juice, such as Nellie & Joe's "Famous" Key Lime Juice, is used extensively in its preparation. If you prefer fresh lime juice over bottled, using ordinary Persian limes will work just fine. As with the lemon, limes are rich in vitamin C.

MANGOES

SEASON: January–September.

YIELD: Varies widely by type.

HISTORY: The mango, known in ancient Persian as *samarbehist,* or "fruit from heaven," has been esteemed in Asia for over 5,000 years. Its use and consumption, in more than half the world, is more common than that of apples or even bananas. This is not surprising, considering the mango's lush, sweetly fragrant, and juicy flesh. The variety of mangoes is extensive, owing to the numerous areas (India, Haiti, the Caribbean, California, Florida, and Mexico) in which they are cultivated.

HOW TO CHOOSE: Mangoes range in size from 4 ounces to 5 pounds and in colors covering the spectrum from green, to gold, to rich orange, or red. Choose fruit that yields to the pressure of a gentle squeeze. A mango should be free of large bruises or blackening and exude a sweet, rich aroma. Ideally, the fruit should weigh between 1 and 1½ pounds. I have chosen not to include information on the Indian green mango, which is commonly used in the preparation of chutneys and condiments. This variety of mango is not recommended for baking owing to its hard, fairly dry pulp and astringent flavor.

It should be noted that the skin on mangoes, especially when unripe, contains a chemical substance which can cause severe allergic skin reactions in some people. When you eat a fresh mango, *always* remove the peel first.

MOST COMMON VARIETIES:

✦ *Haitian:* Available January–September. They have a flattish shape and are colored from green to yellow when fully ripe. This variety of mango is somewhat fibrous; the fruit is fine for eating out of hand but not a top choice for baking.

✦ *Mexican:* Available March–September (peak is in May). When fully ripe, color ranges from greenish to yellow with an amber blush. Better for eating than baking.

✦ *Kent:* Available May–September. Juicy and virtually fiber-free, these mangoes have a sweet golden flesh and a skin that is green with a red blush at the sides. Generally 1 to 2 pounds. This variety is one of my favorites for baking.

✦ *Keith:* Available May–September. One of the larger mangoes, these roundish, green fruits range from 2 to 3 pounds each. They are fiber-free and have a yellow-gold flesh, with a mildly tart, citrus flavor. While not quite as sweet as Kents, they work wonderfully in pies and tarts.

✦ *Palmer:* Available May–September. These smaller (14–18 ounces) rose- and peach-colored fruits have a bit more fiber near their small pit and a slightly less robust flavor. Not my first choice for baking.

✦ *Haden:* Available May–September. Small and round, these green, yellow, and reddish mangoes have a radiant orange flesh that is packed with rich flavor. Another terrific choice for baking.

✦ *Tommy Atkins:* Available May–September. Sweet and full of juice, these are the most widely sold mangoes in the United States. Although their skin coloring runs an eye-appealing vibrant orange to red, their flesh is fibrous and not my first choice for baking.

STORAGE AND HANDLING: Mangoes can be successfully ripened at home by leaving them at room temperature. Once ripe, they should be eaten within 2 to 3 days or they will quickly soften. Never refrigerate mangoes. The chilling robs the fruit of its lush tropical flavors.

The mango has a large, somewhat flat pit that does not seperate naturally from the fruit. The flesh that is located on each side of the pit is referred to as the "cheek."

✦ *To Remove the Cheeks:* Using a chef's knife, remove a thin slice from the bottom of the mango. Hold the fruit upright. With the chef's knife, cut into the mango from top to bottom, positioning the knife slightly off-center and parallel to the flatter side of the fruit. Slice downward, cutting as close to the pit as possible. Repeat on the opposite side. Trim any large pieces of fruit that are still attached to the pit.

✦ *To Slice:* Peel the cheeks with a paring knife, removing as little of the flesh as possible. Lay the fruit, flat side down, and cut on the diagonal into 1/4-inch slices.

✦ *To Cube:* Using the tip of a sharp knife, score the flesh of the unpeeled cheeks into 3/4-inch squares. Be careful not to cut through the skin. Press the cheek, on the skin side, to push the flesh out, forming a "porcupine" of mango chunks. Remove the cubes with a paring knife, cutting as close as possible to the skin.

✦ *To Freeze:* Peel and cut into cubes and store in an airtight container for up to 3 months. For baking, use while still frozen.

CAROLE'S COMMENTS
One of my favorite fruit discoveries in recent years is the mango. It can be used in many of the same ways that peaches are, with the great benefit of not having to cope with excessive moisture. The fruit retains its shape when cooked or baked, and the delicate flavor blends well with many other fruits. A perfect mango is sweet, juicy, and aromatic, and has vibrant color and velvety flesh. The only drawback to the mango is that some types, such as the readily available Tommy Atkins, are fibrous. I much prefer the flavorful Keith or Kent varieties with their tender, fiber-free pulp. Don't be deceived by the green skin of the Keiths; the color has no bearing on its ripeness or superb flavor. Mangoes are a fine source of vitamins A and C, calcium, potassium, and phosphorous.

MELONS— CANTALOUPE AND HONEYDEW

SEASON: Cantaloupe, June–December (peak June–September); Honeydew, August–October.

YIELD: N/A.

HISTORY: Melons have been prized for centuries. They seem to have originated in the Middle East, most likely Persia. Their presence is documented as far back as the era of the Roman emperor Tiberius, and even to the pharaohs of Egypt. While many types of melon exist, the most common varieties are the cantaloupe and the honeydew. Melons are widely cultivated in the United States, with the largest crops coming from California.

HOW TO CHOOSE:
✦ *Cantaloupe:* Look for well-rounded melons with sandy gold skin and thin, close-knit webbing. The melon should have little or no trace of green. Feeling for softness at the stem end is not a reliable indicator of ripeness. Because a ripe cantaloupe easily separates from its vine, when purchasing you

should see no sign at the stem end that it was cut rather than picked. A ripe cantaloupe should have a subtle, sweet aroma

✦ **Honeydew:** These melons, one of the "winter melon" varieties, should have a creamy yellowish skin with a matte, almost sticky, surface. Select melons that give off a strong, aromatic scent. Avoid fruit that is stark white with a greenish tinge or with a high, glossy shine; these will undoubtedly be underripe. Likewise, a deep yellow skin often indicates that the melon is overripe. Often, faint spidery veins or freckles are a sign of a sweet melon with a high sugar content.

STORAGE AND HANDLING: Melons should be left at room temperature before cutting to fully appreciate the sweetness of the fruit. A very hard melon will soften over time, but will not gain further sweetness. Once cut, it should be refrigerated, covered especially well with plastic wrap. If trimmed of the skin, smaller pieces can be stored in airtight containers. Loosely covered melons can easily impart their aroma, as well as pick up those of neighboring foods.

✦ **To Freeze:** Not recommended.

CAROLE'S COMMENTS
While I appreciate the refreshing qualities of fresh melons, they do not lend themselves to cooking or baking. Save these fruits for garnishing, where they can really shine. Melons are

high in vitamin C and potassium, while being low in calories and sodium.

NECTARINES

SEASON: Late June–early October. Peak season, August–September.

YIELD: 3 medium nectarines = approximately 1 pound.

HISTORY: This fruit, whose flavor is so sweet and delectable, is named for nectar, the drink of the Greek gods. There is considerable debate over both its origin (presumably in eastern Asia) and its lineage with the peach. Some scholars argue that the nectarine is merely a fuzzless offspring of the peach. Others profess that it is its own, independent branch of the stone fruit family tree. Regardless, its wonderful perfume and sweet juicy flesh is a treat. Early-season nectarines are shipped primarily from Georgia and Florida, while the more flavorful summer fruit is mainly produced in California. Crops grown in the Northeast reach their zenith in late August through September.

HOW TO CHOOSE: Look for smooth, plump fruit with a skin that is bright yellowish-orange with a red blush. A perfectly ripe nectarine will have a fragrance that is more intoxicating than that of a peach. When choosing nectarines, it is helpful to know where the fruit was

> *Friends are like melons, shall I tell you why? To find one good one, you must fifty try.*

CLAUDE MERMET, CIRCA 1600

grown. California nectarines are superb but will be mealy if picked too late in their season. It is better to stick with crops that are locally grown.

STORAGE AND HANDLING: Since nectarines lack the protective fuzz of the peach, shipping them at peak ripeness is precarious. As a result, it is rare to purchase a nectarine that was picked when ready to eat, unless it was locally grown. To ripen a nectarine, place it in a closed brown paper bag and store it at room temperature for 2 to 3 days. Large bruiselike spots, known as brown rot, may develop after ripening; they are the result of particularly rainy weather during the growing season and, unfortunately, cannot be detected until the fruit has gone from market to consumer. When ripe, refrigerate and use within 1 to 2 days in order to savor their full flavor. Wipe with a damp paper towel before use.

✦ *To Pit a Nectarine:* Use a small paring knife and cut the fruit, from stem end to base, following the fruit's natural crease. Hold the nectarine on either side of the cut and twist gently to seperate the halves. The pit can then be removed easily with your fingernail or the tip of the paring knife.

✦ *To Freeze:* Sliced nectarines, peeled or unpeeled, may be frozen. Sprinkle fruit with a little sugar and freeze on a sheet pan. Transfer to airtight containers and keep for up to 6 months.

CAROLE'S COMMENTS ═══
Nectarines have all of the virtues of peaches with two added advantages. Their skin is thinner than that of a peach and the flesh is firmer. I particularly like to use them for open fruit tarts because peeling is unnecessary. When sliced, the peach-colored flesh tinged with shades of crimson has great visual appeal. Peaches and nectarines are interchangeable in most recipes. Nectarines are rich in vitamins A and C and are sodium free.

ORANGES

SEASON: Navel, November–April; peak season, February–April. California Valencia, May–November. Blood orange, mid-March–mid-May.

YIELD: 1 medium Navel orange = $^1/_4$ cup juice; 1 medium Navel orange = 4–5 teaspoons zest

HISTORY: A fruit native to southern China, orange seeds came to the Americas on Christopher Columbus's second voyage in 1493, along with those of the lemon and lime. Settlers in Florida began cultivation in the early 1500s. Currently, citrus fruits are grown predominantly in Florida, California, and Arizona. Florida is the largest producer, and although they grow some eating oranges, the greater share of its crops are smooth, thin-skinned juice oranges. California and Arizona growers produce mostly thicker-skinned, seedless eating varieties. These western oranges have a rough, pebbly rind that is excellent for zesting. The exotic and colorful blood orange, native to the Mediterranean, is now cultivated in California.

HOW TO CHOOSE: Navel and Valencia eating oranges, like all citrus fruits, should be firm and feel heavy for their size. By law, all oranges are picked when they are fully mature. A bright orange skin is preferable for zesting, but a slight tinge of green, caused by weather fluctuations, does not affect the sweet juice inside.

STORAGE AND HANDLING: Oranges can be kept at room temperature for up to 1 week. Refrigeration, preferably in the crisper drawer, is recommended for longer storage.

✦ *To Zest, Supreme, or Juice:* See "Handling Citrus Fruits," page 59.

✦ *To Freeze:* Not recommended for the whole fruit. Juice and zest can be frozen for up to 3 months in airtight containers.

CAROLE'S COMMENTS ═══
Oranges have long been a favorite of mine as a flavor enhancer for other foods. Unlike the lemon, whose tart juice makes its presence known, the juice of an orange adds flavor without overpowering. I often use the juice as a replacement for water when poaching fruits. It can be used as the liquid for binding pastry dough, and adds character to cooked fillings. The fragrant zest with its natural oils not only perks up pastry but also adds immeasurable flavor to most fruit and cream fillings. Oranges are high in vitamin C, fiber, and potassium, and low in sodium and calories.

PAPAYAS

SEASON: Available year-round. Peak season, February and March, October.

YIELD: 1 papaya = about 1 cup diced or puree.

HISTORY: This sweet fruit, which looks like a cross between a small melon and a rather dumpy pear, is native to the Caribbean. By the beginning of the 1100s, its seeds had spread as far as eastern Asia, the South Pacific, and South America. In Hawaii, the papaya became an integral part of the culture and was thrown into volcanic lava flows to placate Pele, goddess of fire. Today, Hawaii is the largest commercial exporter of this fruit, along with Mexico and South Africa. The fruit, whose exterior is not particularly attractive, has a breathtaking interior of creamy pinkish to orange flesh, with a central cavity filled with dozens of shiny, round black seeds. The seeds are somewhat peppery in flavor and can be dried and used to season salad dressings.

HOW TO CHOOSE: The two main varieties found in our groceries are the Hawaiian "Solo," which weighs in at about 1 pound, and the larger, slightly less sweet Mexican. Hispanic markets also sell a green papaya that is cooked and eaten as a vegetable, but is not recommended for baking. While fresh papayas have become increasingly popular in this country, at present the varieties available to us cannot be compared to those grown in the tropics.

Select large, pear-shaped fruits that yield slightly when squeezed gently between your palms. The skin of the fruit, which will ripen from the bottom to the stem end, turns from pale green to a blotchy yellow and finally orange when it is fully ripe. It is safest to choose fruit that has already begun to ripen and is at least half yellow. Lack of aroma is not a factor in choosing papayas; their wonderful scent is not evident until it is cut open. Avoid fruit that is bruised or soft and mushy at the stem end.

STORAGE AND HANDLING: To ripen a papaya, place it in a brown paper bag and leave it at room temperature for 2 to 4 days. Ripe fruit should be stored in a plastic bag, in the refrigerator, for 1 to 2 weeks. As with most ripe fruit, however, it is best to eat it as soon as possible.

✦ *To Slice a Papaya:* Wash the fruit and dry thoroughly. Slice in half lengthwise, scoop out the seeds with a spoon, then peel the skin with a paring knife. Cut into long strips.

✦ *To Freeze:* Freezing is not recommended.

CAROLE'S COMMENTS
Papaya has a coral-hued flesh that is soft, delicately scented, and sweet, but rather subtle in flavor. It invites the use of a strong flavoring such as lemon or lime juice, cayenne pepper, or vanilla to make it come alive. Papayas contain a high proportion of the enzyme papain. Because this enzyme breaks down proteins, it is widely used in the manufacture of commercial meat tenderizers. Do not combine uncooked papaya with gelatin, as the papain will prevent the mixture from setting. I prefer to use papaya as an accent fruit rather than as a primary ingredient. The fruit is especially attractive when used to garnish cream-style pies or in fresh fruit salads. It really shines when poached in a sugar syrup, alone or with other tropical fruits. Papayas are rich in vitamins C and A, and contain potassium and phosphorous.

PEACHES

SEASON: May–September. Peak season, mid-July–August.

YIELD: 3 medium or 2 large peaches = approximately 1 pound.

HISTORY: The peach is believed to have originated in China and was introduced to the New World in the sixteenth century. Long revered in the Orient as a symbol of longevity, today this fruit enjoys a popularity in the United States that is surpassed only by apples. Most of the peaches available in the United States are grown in Georgia, the Carolinas, California, and New Jersey. Many authorities consider the sweetest peaches on the market to be those cultivated in Georgia and the Carolinas. There are two major varieties of peaches, the clingstone and the freestone. The clingstones are generally early-season peaches and have a firmer, drier pulp, that clings to the pit. Freestones, which separate easily from the pit, are available later in the summer and are more flavorful and juicy. Today, the fuzzy protective covering we associate with peaches is removed mechanically on most commercially cultivated crops. Peaches purchased at local farmstands will still have their natural, furry jacket.

HOW TO CHOOSE: Select aromatic fruit that is plump, unwrinkled, free of bruises, and relatively firm—but not hard. The skin should have a golden or creamy base color with no trace of green. Green-tinged peaches, or rock-hard ones, were picked too early and will never properly ripen. Peaches with a mealy texture have remained too long on their trees before harvesting, or have been kept in cold storage for excessive periods of time. Unfortunately, the mealy texture is not apparent from the fruit's exterior. Your best bet is to buy your peaches from high-quality produce markets and local farmstands.

For baking and cooking, purchase the freestone variety; the pits in clingstone peaches are nearly impossible to remove.

STORAGE AND HANDLING: To ripen peaches, leave them at room temperature for 3 to 4 days. To hasten the process, place the fruit in a loosely closed brown paper bag for 1 to 2 days. Once fully ripe, refrigerate for no longer than 2 or 3 days. Refrigerated peaches diminish in both flavor and moisture. The large bruises, which often appear on peaches as they ripen, are referred to as brown rot and are undetectable when the fruit is first purchased. This rot is usually the result of a particularly rainy growing season. The fruit is still quite usable, and can be salvaged simply by cutting out the softened, discolored area.

✦ *To Pit a Freestone Peach:* Using a small paring knife, cut the fruit from the stem end to the base, following the fruit's natural crease. Hold the peach on either side of the cut, and gently twist in opposite directions to separate the halves. The pit can easily be removed with your fingernail or the tip of the paring knife.

✦ *To Peel a Freestone Peach:* For baking pies and tarts, wipe with damp paper towels, halve the fruit, and thinly peel the skin with a paring knife. For poaching and canning, cut an X at the base of the fruit and plunge it into boiling water for 30 seconds or longer, depending on the ripeness of the fruit. After the initial 30 seconds, test the looseness of the skin every few seconds by lifting it at the slit. If it pulls away easily, immediately remove the fruit with a slotted spoon and plunge into cold water. To prevent the peach from slipping out of your hand, it is best to halve it before removing the peel. If the peach is too hot to handle, hold it with paper towels.

✦ *To Freeze:* Peel and pit the fruit. Sprinkle fruit with a little sugar and freeze on a shallow pan. Store in freezer in airtight bags or containers for up to 6 months. Do not thaw before using.

CAROLE'S COMMENTS ═══
Almost everyone finds eating a homemade peach pie irresistible. Who can deny that biting into this juicy, golden orange flesh leaves the taste buds salivating for more? But alas, it's that flavorful juice that works against you when you want to bake a peach pie. It always amuses, as well as frustrates, me when I read recipes for peach pie whose instructions cover the information with only an inch or so of text. In reality, making a good one is a challenge that requires more direction than the reader is typically given. Peaches release an extraordinary amount of juice when cooked. In my experience, the only way to avoid a soupy filling and soggy bottom crust is to par-cook and drain the fruit before assembling the pie. I regret the extra work, but the end result will be well worth your efforts. One final reminder: Don't be tempted to bake with early season, clingstone peaches. They lack full flavor and are nearly impossible to pit. Peaches contain fairly high amounts of vitamins A and C, and are low in both sodium and calories.

PEARS

SEASON: July–May. Peak season, August–October.

YIELD: 3 medium pears = approximately 1 pound.

HISTORY: The delicate pear has been cultivated for nearly 4,000 years. This fruit is thought to have been native to western Asia and the region of the Caspian Sea. The original wild pear was a hard, sour fruit, not suitable for eating out of hand. In the eighteenth century, Belgian growers developed the sweet "butter" pear, which is the ancestor of today's full-flavored fruit with its melting texture. Available to us during a large part of the year, 95 percent of our American crops are harvested in California, parts of Oregon, and Washington State. There are a multitude of varieties, each with their own distinctive traits. The best choices for baking are the Anjou, Red Bartlett, and Bosc. The regal Comice is the most exquisite for eating. Popular varieties such as Green Bartletts, tiny Seckels, Nellis, Clapps, and Forelles also make savory snacks.

HOW TO CHOOSE: Pears are one of very few fruits that will ripen best after they are picked. Fruit that is left on the tree to full maturity develop "stone cells" that give a gritty texture; they will also become brown and watery at the core. Select fruit that is still firm and underripe. When choosing pears, neither fragrance nor color should necessarily be a deciding factor. The Anjou remains the same light green to yellow shade regardless of its level of development. Red Bartletts do change color, beginning as a deep maroon and ripening to a bright crimson red. Golden brown Boscs, with their graceful, long necks, will develop a cinnamon-toned russeting as they mature. All pears ripen from the inside out. The best way to check for readiness is to look for softening at the stem end by pressing gently with your fingers. Avoid pears that are fully mature unless you plan to use them immediately; they quickly become

overripe. Steer clear of fruit with soft bases or shriveled stem ends. Some external blemishes are acceptable, but do not purchase fruit with dark bruises, cuts, or nicks.

The most common varieties for baking are:

✦ *Anjou:* Peak season, October–May. One-third of the pear crop harvested in the United States is of this type. Anjous are spicy-sweet with lots of juice, but are firm and hold their shape well for baking.

✦ *Red Bartletts:* Peak season, August–October. This fruit has more character than the Green Bartlett. They release less liquid, have a firmer textured flesh, and will hold their shape better when baked. Red Bartletts are more robust in flavor. Their tart-sweet flesh develops a rich sweetness after baking.

✦ *Bosc:* Peak season, September–May. Although somewhat bland when raw, Boscs come into their glory when cooked. They are extremely juicy and have a velvety texture that makes them ideal for poaching. The Bosc's firm flesh holds up reasonably well for baking, but the excessive amount of liquid the fruit exudes prevents it from being a favorite for pies and tarts. It can, however, make a reasonable substitute if Anjous or Red Bartletts are not available.

STORAGE AND HANDLING: Ripening pears can take anywhere from 3 to 14 days depending on the variety and maturity of the fruit. They can be kept in a bowl at room tem-

perature or, to speed the ripening process, placed in a loosely closed brown paper bag along with a banana or apple. Do not let the fruit become overly ripe as it will turn mushy and grainy. In addition, ripe pears are extremely fragile and should not be overhandled. Once the stem end softens, use immediately or refrigerate for up to 3 to 4 days. For baking, slightly underripe pears are best. Unripe pears can be stored in the refrigerator for lengthy periods of time, up to 2 to 3 weeks for Bartletts and 2 months for Boscs and Anjous. Peeled pears must be immediately sprinkled with lemon juice as they will discolor rapidly.

✦ *To Peel and Core:* For soft pears, halve them from top to bottom, remove the core with a melon baller, and peel with a vegetable peeler. Firmer pears can be peeled whole, then halved and cored. Avoid using a a fruit corer. Pears are pricey, and with the corer there is too much waste.

✦ *To Freeze:* Not recommended.

CAROLE'S COMMENTS
Pears have long been one of my favorite fruits to use in pies and tarts. Pear desserts carry an air of elegance, yet they are equally suited for down-home baking. Cooked pears are pleasantly sweet and have a translucent beauty. Their neutral flavor makes them easy companions for stronger-flavored fruits such as apples, plums, and grapes. Pears marry splendidly with spices, herbs, caramel, and even chocolate. Never buy a ripe pear,

as it will never make it home without bruising. Frustrating as this may be, this stately fruit is worth waiting for. The skin of a pear has the most nutrition and is high in dietary fiber. The flesh contains some vitamin C and is high in carbohydrates.

PINEAPPLE

SEASON: Available year-round. Hawaiian peak, March–June; Caribbean peak, December–February/August–September.

YIELD: 1 pineapple = approximately 3 cups finely chopped or crushed.

HISTORY: Pineapple, known as the "king of fruit," has long served as a symbol of welcome by the natives of the West Indies, and of luxury by Europeans and American colonists. This prized fruit is thought to have originated in Brazil. Today, pineapples are commercially cultivated in Hawaii, Honduras, Mexico, the Dominican Republic, and Costa Rica. The two most widely available varieties in the United States have been the Red Spanish, grown in Mexico and the Caribbean, and the smooth-skinned Cayenne from Hawaii. The Caribbean variety is generally thornier, slightly drier, and not quite as sweet. The Cayenne, although considerably more expensive, is consistently sweeter and juicier. A new arrival to retail groceries has been the Del Monte Gold

pineapple, a more reasonably priced hybrid grown in Costa Rica. These full-flavored Del Monte Golds have outstanding sweetness and a flesh that is smooth textured and full of juice.

HOW TO CHOOSE: Choose firm, plump fruit that smells sweet at the base. It should feel heavy for its size and have deep green leaves. According to television's popular "Produce Pete" Napolitano, author of *Farmocopeia*, "the more scales or marks on a pineapple, the stronger the tropical taste will be. A pineapple with fewer and larger scales will have a milder but sweeter flavor and more juice." Easily pulled leaves are not an indication of ripeness, as is widely believed. A fruit that is on its way to maturity will have a yellowish-orange or reddish tint, with its richest color at the base. The fruit should show a little softness when pressed gently with your fingers. A pineapple whose bottom is green will never reach the desired sweetness and juiciness. Avoid pineapples with bruises, those that are overly soft, or any with dry, browning leaves. Until recently, a commonly asked question from my students concerned how to pick a sweet, ripe pineapple. With the introduction of the Del Monte Gold, the guesswork has all but disappeared.

STORAGE AND HANDLING: When purchasing a pineapple, it is wise to buy one that will be

used within 2 or 3 days. While refrigeration prevents fermentation, whole pineapples kept at room temperature will have the best flavor. If a pineapple has reached its prime, peel and core it, cover well with plastic wrap, and refrigerate for up to 1 week.

✦ *To Peel and Core:* Lay the pineapple on its side. Position a long, serrated knife about 1 inch below the crown and saw through, keeping the cut as straight as possible (save the crown for use as a decorative centerpiece if desired). If the pineapple gives too much resistance, roll the fruit slightly as you slice. After the crown has been removed, stand the pineapple on its base. Cut the fruit in half, from top to bottom, and then into quarters. Once again, if you have trouble moving the knife through, rock the fruit gently back and forth as you cut. Stand each quarter on its end and slice down to remove the core. To separate the skin from the flesh, use a curved, serrated grapefruit knife. Lay each quarter skin side down. Insert the knife where the skin and the flesh meet, and using a sawing motion, cut around the entire wedge. If your knife is at the right level, most of the "eyes" will be removed.

✦ *To Freeze:* Not recommended.

CAROLE'S COMMENTS
Fresh pineapple has a unique and distinctive quality. Some people have an aversion to eating fresh pineapple because of the puckering sensation it causes

inside the mouth. This is unfortunate, as they miss one of the most refreshing fruit flavors around. Fresh pineapple contains an enzyme called bromelin, which aids in the digestion of protein. It is this enzyme that prevents gelatin from setting when the two are mixed. Also, uncooked pineapple should not be used with such dairy products as whipped cream, ice cream, or cream cheese until just before serving, as their consistencies and flavors will change. Because of the above, fresh pineapple must be cooked before using; as an alternative, you can substitute canned pineapple. As for purchasing pineapple that has been cored and peeled, try my method of peeling first. It is easy to do and far more economical. Pineapple is rich in vitamin C and low in sodium.

PLUMS

SEASON: Mid-May–September, varies by type.

YIELD: 3 to 9 plums per pound, depending on variety.

HISTORY: Originally from central Asia, plums are now grown on every continent except Antarctica. More than 140 varieties of this fruit can be found in the United States alone. While California produces 90 percent of our commercial crop, locally grown fruit is abundant at farmstands during the summer.

Plums come in a rainbow of colors ranging from yellow to green, scarlet, blue, and purple. Flavor, too, varies widely from tart to mellow to sweet. All plums are descended from two original species, the European and the Japanese. Of the two, the European plum has less moisture. They are also smaller in size and have dark skins of blue, black, and purple. The colorful Japanese plums are juicier and are popular for eating. With a few exceptions, the European varieties are preferred for baking.

HOW TO CHOOSE: Select plump fruit that is fairly firm and will give slightly under gentle pressure. You should look for some softness, but avoid fruit that feels overly soft or mushy.

The most common varieties for baking are:
✦ *Black Amber:* Amber flesh with a deep blackish skin.
✦ *Black Diamond:* One of the most popular. Large, deep purple with yellow flesh.
✦ *Greengage:* Firmer, yellow flesh with a high sugar content.
✦ *Santa Rosa:* Sweet-tart flavor. Flesh radiates from red to yellow and skin is a deep purplish red.
✦ *Italian prune plums:* Small, and oval in shape. One of the most popular plums for baking.

STORAGE AND HANDLING: Allow plums to ripen at room temperature in a closed brown paper bag. Once ripe, use within 2 to 3 days or refrigerate.

Wash and dry thoroughly before use.
✦ *To Pit a Plum:* Use a small paring knife to cut the fruit from stem end to base, following the fruit's natural crease. Hold the plum on either side of the cut and twist gently, in opposite directions, to separate the two halves. The pit can then be removed with your fingernail or the tip of the paring knife.
✦ *To Freeze:* Not recommended.

CAROLE'S COMMENTS
In late summer, one of my favorite fruits for baking are plums. This is the time of the year when Black Diamond and Italian prune plums are in season. These fruits are especially easy to use because they do not release much moisture, peeling is not needed, and the firm flesh does not darken quickly. I especially like these plums for making open fruit tarts. Another terrific way to use plums is in cobblers or in pies combined with other fruits. Try adding a few purple plums to apple or peach pies. They lend an appealing hint of tartness, as well as a vibrant pink color. Plums are high in carbohydrates, but have a negligible vitamin content.

RASPBERRIES

SEASON: May–November. Peak season, June–August.

YIELD: 1 dry pint basket = approximately 1½ cups.

HISTORY: Raspberries grow wild primarily in the cooler regions of the Northern Hemisphere. In the United States, the largest cultivators of raspberries are in California, the Pacific Northwest, and in the northern states. Raspberries, like their cousins the blackberries, are members of the rose family. One notable difference between the two is that raspberries have a hollow core, which makes them more fragile. Over 95 percent of the raspberries available to us are red, but there are also purplish-black, amber, and yellow varieties. Of all raspberries grown, the reds have the highest amount of pectin. This makes them particularly desirable for pie and tart fillings as well as jams and preserves.

HOW TO CHOOSE: Look for plump, firm berries with no evidence of mildew, blackening, or softness. If the basket shows signs of staining or leakage, do not buy them.

STORAGE AND HANDLING: Raspberries have a short shelf life. Their fragile nature causes them to easily form mold and mildew. Refrigerate the berries in their original container for 1 to 2 days. If farm fresh, empty them into a bowl and refrigerate, loosely covered. Most raspberries used by professionals in restaurants and bakeries are never washed, merely picked through to remove leaves. However, recent cyclospora scares have made it prudent to wash all berries just before use. Imported berries should be avoided.

✦ *To Wash:* Fill a sink or large bowl with cool water and place the berries in it. Carefully lift the berries out, letting the water drain through your fingers. Lay them on a sheet pan lined with a double thickness of paper towels and very gently shake the pan to roll the moisture off the berries.

✦ *To Freeze:* Lay clean raspberries in a single layer on a shallow pan and flash-freeze. Once frozen, pack them in airtight containers and store for up to 6 months. Do not thaw before using.

CAROLE'S COMMENTS
The popularity of raspberries has grown enormously in recent years. While always a staple of fine European desserts, with the dawning of nouvelle cuisine and its widespread use of fruit purees, raspberry sauce (*coulis de framboise*) has become a signature item few restaurants are without. Cultivated raspberries are available to us most of the year, and although they are of decent quality, they are costly. For most baked pastries, I prefer to use berries that are locally grown. The price is right and the flavor can't be beat. Throughout the year the cultivated berries are fine to use for garnishing. For sauces, quick, economical, and tasty results can be achieved by using frozen unsweetened raspberries. Raspberries are rich in vitamin C and potassium, and low in calories.

RHUBARB

SEASON: March–July (field grown). January–June (hothouse).

YIELD: 1 pound rhubarb stalks = approximately 3 cups, chopped.

HISTORY: Rhubarb originated in northern Asia and can still be found growing wild in the Himalayas. The rhubarb available to us in the United States, both hothouse and field grown, comes primarily from Washington, Michigan, and California. Often referred to as the "pie plant," it is so exclusively used in desserts that its botanical claim to being a vegetable has been challenged. In a 1947 legal case at the U.S. Customs Court in Buffalo, New York, it was ruled that, since the rhubarb was normally prepared as a fruit, it should henceforth be classified as a fruit. Rhubarb has an extremely astringent flavor that makes it unpalatable unless sweetened substantially. This astringency comes from the high concentration of oxalic acid, which is most prevalent in the rhubarb leaf. *The leaves of the rhubarb plant are toxic and should not be eaten, either raw or cooked.*

HOW TO CHOOSE: Always choose stalks that are firm and crisp. Avoid those that appear flabby or have wilted leaves. Field-grown rhubarb is tarter and has a deep red color with green foliage. Hothouse plants are stringier, will be a much lighter shade of pink, and contain more moisture.

STORAGE AND HANDLING: Remove all leaves and discard. Refrigerate unwashed rhubarb stalks in a plastic bag for 2 to 4 weeks.

✦ *To Clean:* Wash with cool water and dry well with paper towels. The stringy outer layer of the stalks, which is much more pronounced in the hothouse-grown rhubarb, can be removed with a vegetable peeler.

✦ *To Freeze:* Wash, dry, cut into ½-inch pieces, and freeze in airtight containers for up to 6 months. Do not thaw before using.

CAROLE'S COMMENTS
Although rhubarb can be used singly, I prefer to combine it with sweeter fruits and berries to reduce the amount of sugar needed. The most common companion is the strawberry, but rhubarb can also be teamed with such fruits as apples, figs, or pears. When possible, I prefer to use field-grown rhubarb instead of the hothouse, as the latter contains too much moisture. Although some recipes call for peeling the rhubarb before it is used, I find that this is not necessary. Rhubarb has substantial amounts of vitamin C, calcium, and manganese.

STRAWBERRIES

SEASON: Available year-round. California, January–November; peak season, April–June. Locally grown, June–August.

YIELD: 1 dry pint basket = approximately 2 cups.

HISTORY: The strawberry heralds the arrival of spring, and its pleasant, sweet flavor makes it our most popular dessert berry. Strawberries grow wild in many parts of the world. In the United States, the berry we are most familiar with is a hybrid variety, cross-bred in the 1600s. In the late 1800s, a larger, more robust berry was developed. Prior to this, strawberries were a relatively rare commercial commodity. Their fragility made shipping precarious and expensive. So widely recognized was the problem that they became an issue during Martin Van Buren's 1840 presidential campaign. He was attacked on the grounds that he had used taxpayer money to finance strawberry and raspberry cultivation for his personal dining pleasure. Today, we are fortunate to have these succulent berries available to us almost year-round, with over half of the crop originating in California.

HOW TO CHOOSE: Strawberries will not continue to ripen once they have been picked, so look for vibrant red berries. Their leaflike cap should still be attached and not appear withered. There should be no signs of mildew, stains, or seepage. Size should not be a determining factor in choosing strawberries. Often, smaller berries will be the more flavorful.

STORAGE AND HANDLING: Cultivated strawberries should be refrigerated, in their original packaging, for only a few days. Farm-fresh berries should be stored in a bowl, loosely covered so they can breathe. Refrigerate for up to 2 to 3 days. Do not wash until just before use.

✦ *To Wash:* Place berries in a colander and rinse with cool water. Spread drained fruit on a shallow pan lined with a double thickness of paper towels. Gently shake the pan back and forth to roll the excess moisture off of the strawberries. Blot any remaining moisture with paper towels.

✦ *To Hull:* After the berries are washed and dried, take the tip of a paring knife or a strawberry huller and lift off the stem. Take care to remove as little of the pulp as possible.

✦ *To Freeze:* Not recommended.

CAROLE'S COMMENTS
When local strawberries are in their prime, I find myself reminiscing about the luscious berries I grew up with in Memphis, Tennessee. In recent years, I keep asking myself, "What has happened to strawberries?" Unless locally grown, these often oversized berries are mostly tasteless, are mealy textured, and have bland color. Equally disturbing is the crunching sound

I hear when I slice through a berry. The strawberry that was once a sweet, tender, juicy, vibrantly red fruit has, sadly, all but disappeared from the market. The demand for this popular fruit seems to have driven manufacturers to producing quantity rather than quality. If you have access to locally grown berries, consider it your good fortune. Because of the strawberry's soft texture and juicy flesh, they tend to become mushy when cooked. For these same reasons, I do not recommend freezing them unless they are to be used in a sauce. For baking purposes, be sure to cut the pieces large. Since they are very watery, at times additional thickening is needed. Strawberries are exceedingly high in vitamin C, have a fair amount of dietary fiber, and are low in calories.

TANGERINES

SEASON: Mid-October–March; peak season November–January.

YIELD: N/A.

HISTORY: Originally native to China, the tangerine was named for Tangiers, where the Italians first began to import it in the early 1800s. They were first cultivated in America in New Orleans in the mid-1800s, and are now commercially grown in Florida, California, Texas, and Arizona. These flattish citrus fruits are members of the rue family and have a deep orange, pebbly skin that is thinner at the stem end. They are often referred to as having a "slip" or "zipper" skin because of how easily they are peeled. Once peeled, the fruit easily separates into segments, making them ideal for snacking. Tangerines are marvelously sweet, juicy, and lower in acid than their cousin, the orange.

HOW TO CHOOSE: Look for shiny, tight-skinned fruit without excessive puffiness. Avoid fruit that doesn't feel heavy for its size or that has a mushy stem end.

STORAGE AND HANDLING: Tangerines may be kept at room temperature for 1 to 2 days, but should be refrigerated in the crisper drawer for longer storage. They are the most perishable of the citrus fruits and will only keep for about a week once refrigerated. When preparing a tangerine, always remove the bitter, thin, white webbing that covers the fruit segments before eating.

◆ *To Zest or Juice:* See "Handling Citrus Fruits," page 59.

◆ *To Freeze:* Not recommended for the whole fruit. Juice and zest may be frozen for up to 3 months in airtight containers.

CAROLE'S COMMENTS
Because tangerines are traditionally eaten out of hand, one never thinks of juicing this fruit, but they should be. Not only does the juice have an exquisite, vibrant color but it is also low in acid, is extraordinarily sweet, and makes a superb substitute for orange juice. The next time you make a recipe that calls for orange juice, switch to tangerine and see if you don't agree. Tangerines contain a fair amount of vitamin C, although not as much as is found in oranges.

EQUIPMENT

AT FIRST GLANCE, the equipment list for preparing pies and tarts looks daunting. How can so much be needed when all you remember your grandmother using to turn out those fragrant treats was a bowl and a couple of knives?

A closer look at this list reveals that many of the items are already in your kitchen and are used for regular cooking needs—like bowls, spoons, and saucepans. Other items, such as the batarde and ice pick, are used in innovative ways to facilitate some pie and tart preparations. Finally, there are some items unique to pie and tart baking that you will find helpful in your preparation and baking operations. While having all of the items listed below is an ideal goal, *the basic tools to launch you comfortably are marked with a diamond.* And when you need to make a purchase, invest in quality equipment. It will pay off in the long run.

FOR MEASURING
+ Set of four high-quality stainless steel measuring cups—$1/4$, $1/3$, $1/2$, and 1 cup—for dry ingredients
+ 8-, 16-, and 32-ounce ovenproof glass or clear plastic measuring cups, for liquids
+ Set of four high-quality measuring spoons—$1/4$, $1/2$, and 1 teaspoon and 1 tablespoon
+ Kitchen scale, ounces clearly marked

+ Thermometers, candy and oven
+ 18-inch artist's ruler, for accurate measuring of rolled dough

FOR MIXING AND SHAPING
+ 4-quart glass mixing bowl
+ 1-, 2-, 3-, and 4-quart stainless steel mixing bowls
+ Pastry blender with wires extending to the handle
+ Bench, dough, or pastry scraper
+ Large cutting board
+ Wooden pastry board, 18 × 24 inches
+ Pastry cloth and rolling pin cover or a smooth-surfaced dish towel, preferably linen
+ Ball-bearing rolling pin with a 10- or 12-inch barrel
+ Tapered French-style rolling pin with a 19- to 21-inch barrel
Pastry docker
Batarde (flat-bottomed meat pounder)
+ Fluted pastry wheel
Pizza cutter
Pie crimper
Cookie cutters in assorted shapes and sizes
Aspic cutters
+ One small rubber spatula

+ Two standard-size rubber spatulas
+ One jumbo (oversize) rubber spatula, $2^3/4 \times 4^1/4$ inches
Oversize metal spatula (approximately 3 × 6 inches)
+ Narrow offset metal spatulas, $3^1/2$ and 6 inches
+ Square metal, mini offset spatula, $2^1/4 \times 2^1/4$ inches
+ Scissors
+ 3-inch paring knife
+ 6-inch utility knife
+ 10- to 12-inch chef's knife
Pineapple or grapefruit knife (fine serrated double edges)
+ Swivel blade vegetable/fruit peeler
Melon baller
Fruit corer
+ Small, flat hand shredder (for grating) with $1/16$-inch scalloped slits
Four-sided shredder/grater
Nutmeg grater
+ Juicer
+ Slotted metal spoons
+ Wooden spoons, flat and bowl shaped
Cherry pitter
Ice pick, for breaking up blocks of chocolate
+ Can opener
+ Sifter, preferably triple screen

- Fine-mesh strainer
- Large medium-mesh strainer
- Colander
- Three wire whisks in graduated sizes of 8, 10, and 12 inches

12- to 14-inch balloon whisk

Rotary egg beater

- Portable hand-held mixer

Electric stand mixer

Food processor

FOR COOKING

- Heavy-bottomed 1-, 2-, and 3-quart saucepans

10-inch cast-iron skillet

- 12-inch fry pan

Double boiler

FOR BAKING

- 9-inch ovenproof glass pie plate

9- or 9½-inch deep-dish, ovenproof glass pie plate

- 11-inch metal tart pan with removable bottom

9-inch metal tart pan with removable bottom

11-inch flan ring

4-inch flan rings, for tartlets

- One 7 × 11 × 1½-inch ovenproof glass baking dish

8- and 10-ounce ceramic ramekins

- 10-ounce Pyrex custard cups
- Shallow baking pan, 11 × 17 × 1-inch or 12 × 18 × 1-inch
- Heavy cookie sheet

Dark baking pans

- Dried beans, baking nuggets, or pie weights for blind baking

Pizza stone

- Two pastry brushes, 1- or 1½-inch natural bristle

Feather brush

- Cooling racks
- Timer

FOR GARNISHING

Confectioners' sugar/flour shaker

Pastry or decorating comb

- Plastic-lined 14- or 16-inch canvas pastry bag
- Pastry decorating tips: #824 large open star, #805 large round, and #2 or #3 standard writing
- Coupler for small pastry tips

Plastic squeeze bottle with small opening

FOR SERVING AND OTHER USES

Extra-long flat or offset metal spatula

- 5- or 6-inch utility knife for cutting pies and tarts

Pie or tart server, triangular metal spatula with serrated edge

Ice cream scoop

- Plastic wrap
- Waxed paper
- Aluminum foil, regular and 18-inch heavy-duty
- Parchment paper
- Scotch tape
- Toothpicks

DRY AND LIQUID MEASURES

The equipment list for baking clearly distinguishes between dry and liquid measures. Keep in mind that not all measuring equipment is created equal, literally. Off brands are frequently inaccurate and can easily break. Inexpensive plastic can become distorted with frequent dishwasher cleaning.

Dry ingredients should *always* be measured in dry measures. My preference is to use heavy stainless steel cups with sturdy handles. They are available in sets of ¼-, ⅓-, ½-, and 1-cup capacities and cost about $10 in kitchen supply stores.

Spend a little extra for measuring spoons and get heavy stainless steel or best-quality plastic. They come in sets of ¼, ½, 1 teaspoon, and 1 tablespoon. Some newer sets add a ⅛ teaspoon and 1½ teaspoons (equal to ½ tablespoon) to the standard four.

The most common liquid measures are heatproof glass or plastic cups with a spout for relatively spillproof pouring. They come in 1-, 2-, or 4-cup (1-quart) capacities. Unfortunately, variations in the manufacturing process can produce inaccurately stamped measuring lines, resulting in too much or too little liquid in your mixture. This is especially true of popular brands like Pyrex and Anchor Hocking.

It is always wise to double-check the accuracy of your measuring cup before using it for the first time. To do this, fill a dry measuring cup to the *brim* with water, empty it into the new liquid measure, and see if the volumes are comparable. If not, when measuring, adjust the liquid accordingly.

KITCHEN SCALES

A good-quality spring scale is accurate enough for most kitchen tasks and is quite affordable. When weighing fruits, vegetables, nuts, and chocolate, I look for a scale with a basket that can hold up to 10 pounds without tipping when it is filled. A spring scale with a flat top (basket removed) can accommodate a larger, lightweight container for awkward produce. Be sure to adjust the dial on the scale to account for the weight of the substitute container. If the items to be weighed are just beyond the capacity of your scale, you may have to weigh in batches; be aware, however, that this is not as accurate.

THERMOMETERS

There are two essential thermometers needed for a baker's kitchen—oven and candy—each serving its own purpose. Since oven temperatures are frequently inaccurate, owning an oven thermometer will help you make any necessary minor adjustments. Candy thermometers are placed into a saucepan as a liquid cooks. In this book, they are frequently used for testing the temperature of sugar syrup.

PASTRY BLENDER

Although two knives will work and classicists can turn out a fine crust with their fingertips, a pastry blender with wires extending to the handle will make quick work of blending flour and fat to the desired consistency. This tool is inexpensive

and available in kitchen supply stores. The brand I particularly like is Androck. Its six-wire construction allows crumbs to flow freely without clogging and the handle is particularly comfortable to grasp.

BENCH, DOUGH, OR PASTRY SCRAPER

If you have trouble handling dough, this is the purchase to make. This versatile tool is used throughout the preparation of pastry doughs, from the beginning to the end. It is handy for leveling the cup when measuring dry ingredients, for piling pieces of dough into a mound, for moving pastry, for releasing pastry that is stuck to the rolling surface, for turning the dough, for cleaning the rolling surface, and for cutting. Select one that feels weighty, with a stainless steel blade and a wooden or plastic handle. Avoid those with metal handles as they are slippery, and as a result, are hard to grip.

PASTRY CLOTH AND ROLLING PIN COVER

Another inexpensive pastry miracle worker is the pastry cloth. My favorite is the canvas cloth made by Ateco, paired with a knitted rolling pin cover or "stocking." When flour is

rubbed into the weave of the cloth and stocking, a nearly nonstick surface is created. This treated surface greatly reduces the amount of flour absorbed by the dough. In addition, sticking, breaking, and tearing crusts are virtually eliminated. The pastry cloth and rolling pin cover are washed after each use and will become softer with time. They are best stored, after drying, rolled flat around a rolling pin. Do not fold as creases will form in the cloth and mark future crusts. See, "The Pastry Cloth and Rolling Pin Cover" in the Pastry Primer (page 90) for more detailed information.

ROLLING PINS AND SURFACES

Your grandmother would be amazed at the array of rolling pins available today. What used to be a nondescript barrel of wood in the baker's cupboard has evolved into many sizes, shapes, and materials.

Rolling pins may be marble, wood, Teflon coated, cold water filled, spiked, patterned, metal, and grooved horizontally or vertically. These specialty pins are designed for rolling everything from puff pastry to candy preparations such as nougat and caramel. While many of these specialty rolling pins are extremely useful, some novelty pins are pure gimmickry.

Regarding rolling surfaces, it's true that pastry can be rolled on any flat surface. However, the one you choose may help or hinder your pastry efforts. So what do you buy? Turn to "Tools for Rolling" on page 87 and "The Rolling Surfaces," page 87 in the Pastry Primer.

PASTRY DOCKER

A pastry docker is a cylinder approximately 5 inches long with sharp spikes at $1/2$-inch intervals around the entire surface. Older models are made of wood and nails while newer models are plastic. Although it resembles a medieval torture instrument, a docker is a very useful piece of equipment. Its greatest use is for piercing holes in sheets of puff pastry to cut the gluten strands. When rolling pie and tart pastry, a four-pronged table fork serves the same function.

GRATERS

There are a variety of graters on the market, the most common being the four-sided box grater/shredder. Since most of the grating called for in this book is for zesting citrus fruits, the size and shape of the cutting edges are of utmost importance. My preference for zesting is a small, flat, stainless steel shredder. Its handle makes it easy to grasp and the tiny, scalloped cutting edges are safe for your knuckles and produce an ideal size zest.

SIFTERS

There are two different styles of sifters—triple mesh and single mesh. Triple-mesh sifters are made of three layers of wire mesh through which the ingredients must pass. The advantage of this style is that the flour need only be sifted once to aerate and remove lumps and one more time to combine it with leavening and/or other dry ingredients. Using a single-mesh sifter requires that the dry ingredients be passed through the sifter's mesh up to three times to thoroughly combine them, and is therefore more time-consuming. A medium-gauge strainer can be substituted for a either type of sifter.

As opposed to strainers, sifters should never be washed because small particles of flour will stick in the mesh and turn to paste when wet. To clean a sifter, shake it well, tipping it from side to side. Then give it a few firm taps with the side of your hand to loosen any remaining flour, and wipe both the outside and inside with a dish towel or paper towels. I like to store my sifters in a plastic bag to keep my cabinet free of loose flour.

Unfortunately, most of the sifters purchased today, both single and triple mesh, are poorly made. The handles tend to break easily under the stress of sifting and the mesh layers in the triple-mesh sifters clog quite readily. Rather than risk breaking the handle through repeated squeezing, I find it better to tap the sifter with the side of my hand to shake the dry ingredients through.

STRAINERS

Strainers are essential, not only for sifting flour and straining the seeds from the juice and pulp of fruit, but also for removing the lumps in a cooked filling and for aerating confectioners' sugar and cocoa. It is wise to have an assortment of sizes and mesh densities on hand to suit varying functions. Strainers are available in all price ranges. You will find that investing in those that are well constructed is worthwhile. The mesh is easily damaged and bent out of shape on less expensive equipment.

FOOD PROCESSOR

The only thing that can be said absolutely about food processors is that there are no absolutes! Timing depends on the model and age of the machine. Motor differences from model to model (and even machine to machine in the same model) will affect the size of the crumbs when making pastry doughs. A dull blade can chop for the amount of time specified in the recipe but not achieve the desired consistency. Check your blades and return them to the manufacturer for sharpening if necessary. Food processors are indispensable for so many tasks, but like oven temperatures, you have to know your own equipment and adjust accordingly.

ELECTRIC MIXERS

Electric mixers come in two major categories— the stand mixer and the hand mixer. While electric mixers play a lesser role in pie and tart baking than in other desserts, their use and convenience cannot be minimized. They are helpful in preparing Bavarian-style fillings as well as for whipping meringues, heavy cream, and, at times, even blending pastry doughs.

The most versatile but costly unit is the KitchenAid stand mixer. Its powerful motor and paddle accessory enable the baker to perform a variety of tasks not possible with machines that have only a beater attachment. While almost all of the pastry recipes in this book call for doughs to be mixed either by hand or in a food processor, many doughs can successfully be made in this type of an electric mixer.

Other brands of stand and hand mixers that lack the power and accessories of the KitchenAid are quite suitable for mixing and whipping purposes. They perform well as long as the mixtures being combined are not too heavy.

POTS AND PANS

The importance of using high-quality cooking equipment cannot be overstated. While only a few key pieces are needed for preparing pies and tarts, the performance of well-constructed, heavy-duty cookware like that manufactured by All-Clad and Calphalon will contribute to the success of a recipe. A well-insulated fry pan ensures an even reduction of liquid when preparing a precooked fruit filling; a thick-bottomed saucepan prevents scorching of a cooked custard-type filling. Although a double boiler is recommended for heat-sensitive mixtures, this method of cooking can be improvised. Placing a covered stainless steel or heatproof glass bowl over a pot of simmering water will do in a pinch.

PIE PLATES

Ovenproof glass pie plates make the best containers for baking pies. This inexpensive type of pan has the following advantages over those made from materials such as metal or porcelain.

✦ *It is an excellent heat conductor.*

✦ *It browns bottom crusts extremely well.*

✦ *Its transparency allows you to view the progress of the browning to determine when the pie is done.*

✦ *The glass surface will not be marred by the blade of a knife when cutting.*

✦ *The nonporous surface permits long storage without perishability.*

✦ *It is easy to clean.*

The first Pyrex pans, as it happens, were pie plates, and the name Pyrex itself is a commercial pun, combining the sound of pyr *(from the Greek for* fire*) with that of* pie*, and adding the Latin* rex*, meaning "king," for good measure.*

THE COOKS
CATALOG, 1975

Many types of metal pans are sold for pie baking, but not all metals are suitable. The best metal pie plates are high-quality, professional pans made of Aluminite, a standard-gauge metal pan with a dull satin finish.

These are stain-resistant and retain heat better than pans with shinier surfaces. Many commercial bakers prefer to use these pans instead of glass because breakage is not an issue.

Dark metal pans do brown crusts well on the bottom, but their coated surface is easily damaged when the pie is sliced with a knife. When this surface is marred, the metal is prone to rust. Another metal pie plate on the market, made of tinned steel, has a perforated bottom to encourage browning.

Other widely sold metal pans, such as those made of tin, are less desirable because they do not conduct heat well. In addition, they are made from reactive metals that make them unsuitable containers for storing baked goods, especially those that contain fruit acids.

Disposable aluminum pans are handy for freezing or for giving away. Unfortunately, their thin construction makes them poor heat conductors. To compensate, place a filled disposable pan inside a glass pan or on a preheated cookie sheet to encourage browning of the bottom crust.

Porcelain and most pottery pie plates are attractive for serving, but few conduct heat well enough to brown a bottom crust.

TART PANS

The best tart pans are those made of tinned or black steel with removable bottoms. Tinned steel conducts heat well and produces a golden brown crust particularly when baked on a shallow baking pan. The dark metal version is especially desirable because its black finish makes using an underlying baking pan unnecessary for browning.

As with pie plates, tart pans made of porcelain or pottery do not brown bottom crusts because they are poor conductors of heat.

A flan ring, made of tinned or stainless steel, can be put on a cookie sheet and used to bake a tart. If you are purchasing a flan ring, choose tinned steel if it is available because it conducts heat better. Avoid using insulated cookie sheets like Cushionaire when baking this way because the bottom will not brown as well.

TARTLET PANS

Like tart pans, the best pans for these individual pastries are made of tinned or black steel and are imported from France. These smaller pans come in a variety of shapes and sizes. Larger tartlet pans have remov-

---

Standard Pie and Tart Pans

HERE IS A LIST OF THE MOST popular size pans and capacities. Since much of this type of equipment is imported from either Europe or Asia, pan sizes are not always uniform. If the measurement of your pan is not exactly the same as the one listed, a small difference in size should not alter the recipe. See "Techniques and Procedures" for Changing Pies to Tarts, Tarts to Pies, page 63.

PIE PLATES	CAPACITY
9-inch ovenproof glass (23 cm)	$4^{1}/_{2}$ cups
$9^{1}/_{2}$-inch fluted deep-dish ovenproof glass	7 cups
11-inch ovenproof glass (25 cm)	$6^{1}/_{2}$ cups
9-inch disposable aluminum	4 cups
9-inch metal	$4^{1}/_{2}$ cups

TART AND TARTLET PANS	CAPACITY
$4^{1}/_{2} \times 1$-inch round	$3/_{4}$ cup
$7^{3}/_{4} \times 1$-inch round	3 cups
$9^{1}/_{4} \times 1$-inch round	5 cups
11×1-inch round	$6^{1}/_{2}$ cups
$10 \times 1^{7}/_{8}$-inch deep round	9 cups
$14 \times 4^{1}/_{2} \times 1$-inch oblong	4 cups
$9^{1}/_{2}$-inch flan ring	about $4^{1}/_{2}$ cups
11-inch flan ring	about 6 cups

able bottoms, while others, such as boat-shaped barquettes or diamond-shaped tartlet tins, are pressed from a single sheet of metal.

RAMEKINS AND CUSTARD CUPS

White porcelain ramekins with a capacity of 8 to 10 ounces are commonly found in cookware shops and department stores. An alternative to these ramekins is the widely available oven-proof glass custard cups made by Pyrex.

OTHER BAKING PANS

SHALLOW BAKING PAN (*half sheet or jelly-roll pan*) Common sizes $10^{1}/_{2} \times 15^{1}/_{2} \times 1$-inch, $11 \times 17 \times 1$-inch, and $12 \times 18 \times 1$-inch. Used to hold pies and tarts while baking. Encourages browning, catches overflow of juices, and makes for easier handling.

COOKIE SHEET Flat pan without sides. Used to encouraging browning of bottom crusts. Select heavy-duty aluminum or, for deeper browning, use Professional Bakeware by Calphalon.

BAIN-MARIE (*shallow roaster pan*) Can be made of aluminum or stainless steel. Approximate desirable size $10^{1}/_{2} \times 15^{1}/_{2} \times 2$-inch, or similar. See "About Water Baths," page 61.

MISCELLANEOUS TOOLS

RUBBER SPATULAS (*scrapers*) These useful tools come in a variety of sizes. The small 1-inch spatula is handy for scraping out the inside of measuring cups and containers. The 2-inch spatula is useful for stirring, blending, and scraping the bottom of nonstick cookware. The $2^{3}/_{4}$-inch oversize variety is essential for folding aerated ingredients together. Its larger surface covers a wider area in fewer strokes preventing a loss of volume. I recommend those with a plastic handle made by Rubbermaid. While all rubber spatulas are supposed to be great for scraping a bowl clean, not all brands do the job well. The blades on most less expensive brands are either too stiff or too limp.

OFFSET SPATULA A thin spatula with the metal blade bent so that it is positioned lower than the handle. This enables the tool to smooth a surface that is filled lower than the lip of a pan. It is also useful for smoothing icings, whipped cream, and other toppings. The recommended sizes have $3^{1}/_{2}$-inch and 6-inch blades.

WHISKS Every kitchen should have a variety of whisks. For baking purposes the two handiest styles are the longer, tapered sauce whisk and the rounder, balloon style. Sauce whisks quickly remove lumps from cooked fillings with just a few brisk zigzag motions and are useful for blending and stirring, combining dry ingredients, and numerous other tasks.

The fullness of balloon whisks draws in air, making them ideal for whipping eggs, cream, and other light mixtures. These whisks are not the best choice for smoothing fillings as they create too many air bubbles. Look for graduated sizes in the sauce whisks and an 11- to 13-inch for whipping purposes.

PASTRY AND GOOSEFEATHER BRUSHES Brushes are indispensable accessories for making pastry. They are used for greasing a pan, for brushing excess flour from dough, and most important, for painting a glaze on the bottom and/or top crust of pies and tarts. I recommend flat, natural bristle brushes with tight ferrules, or metal bands, to prevent bristles from straying into your food. Brushes in widths of 1, $1^{1}/_{2}$, and 2 inches are the most practical and commonly used. Be sure to soak used brushes in very hot soapy water, changing the liquid a few times if greasy. After a thorough rinsing, reshape the bristles.

Goosefeather brushes, made from a tightly wrapped cluster of five feathers, are used for more delicate work. They are very desirable for removing excess flour from puff pastry and for applying thin layers of glaze. As with natural bristle brushes, they should be thoroughly cleaned, especially if they were used for an eggwash.

PASTRY CRIMPER A small, stainless steel tweezer with serrated tips. Used to either tightly seal the top and bottom crust of a pie together or to decoratively finish the edge of a single-crust pie or tart pastry shell. Pastry crimp-ers can be purchased at specialty cookware shops.

PASTRY CUTTING WHEELS *(also called jaggers)* There are two styles of pastry wheels: one with a straight blade and the other with a jagged or fluted edge. While both can be used for the same purpose, I prefer the look of the fluted wheel. It makes an attractive zigzag edge, similar to the finish of pinking shears, that is hard to surpass when making a lattice-topped crust. Look for a stainless steel pastry cutter with a sturdy wheel that is firmly secured to the handle to prevent wobbling.

DECORATING EQUIPMENT When creating decorative garnishes and designs for the pies and tarts in this book, I purposely limited the amount of equipment to a few basic but versatile pieces. This equipment is available in most upscale cookware shops or stores where cake decorating supplies are sold. The brand that I recommend is Ateco.

✦ *14- or 16-inch plastic-coated canvas pastry bag*

✦ *#824 large open star tip for making borders, lattices, and rosettes*

✦ *#805 large round tip for making borders, lattices, and lines*

✦ *#2 or #3 standard writing tip for making fine lines*

✦ *2-piece plastic coupler for attaching writing tips onto the pastry bag*

✦ *Pastry or decorating comb*

To care for decorating equipment, wash thoroughly in hot soapy water, then rinse well. Hand dry all pieces with a cloth towel, however the pastry bag should be air dried.

OVENS— CONVENTIONAL, CONVECTION, AND MICROWAVE

The question I am most frequently asked by my students is what kind of oven I recommend. If your budget permits, the optimum arrangement is a gas cooktop with an electric oven. Most professional cooks agree that gas burners produce more intense heat and are easier to adjust than electric. Yet electric ovens are preferred for their even baking.

Stoves fueled by both gas and electric are more widely available today than ever. If this arrangement is out of your price range, a good gas stove is fine. Always be selective about the insulation of the oven and the size of the cavity. Oven space varies from brand to brand.

In recent years, stove technology has drastically changed, and for the better. Today, it is possible to purchase heavy-duty, commercial-type stoves that are designed for home use. This type of equipment is well insulated and equipped with oversize burners that can accommodate professional cookware. Other new designs have a three-way combination—a traditional oven that converts to convection baking, with a microwave oven set over the burners. These "all in one" packages are okay for small spaces, but they are not always well designed or convenient to use.

Convection ovens are fine to use for baking pies and tarts because these pastries are not as delicate as cakes. However, owing to the circulating air from the oven fan, the temperature must be reduced by 25 degrees to prevent overbrowning. Be sure to check the baking time as well. Your pastry will often be finished sooner than if baked in a standard oven.

Microwaves ovens serve little purpose for pastry baking. I much prefer them for smaller jobs like melting chocolate or butter, for heating liquids, or for thawing frozen foods. All of the heating and melting procedures in this book were tested in a 700 watt microwave.

Even with the many innovative pieces of baking equipment available now, I'm still old-fashioned at heart. Although large strides have been made, classic conventional baking continues to be my preference. Still, you should choose the appliance that works best for your situation. Whatever the decision, research your options thoroughly before making a final purchase.

TECHNIQUES AND PROCEDURES

DON'T OVERLOOK THIS SECTION OF the book. It is my personal diary where I share a multitude of basic techniques plus many secrets that I have learned over years of baking. While numerous approaches exist for achieving successful baking results, what follows are the tips and tricks that have worked for me.

Here is where you will find directions on how to measure flour and fats accurately, how to beat eggs, to work with chocolates and dried fruits, to chop nuts and clarify butter. Guidance on rolling and shaping doughs, making lattice and decorative cutouts, crimping and fluting—all are addressed. Also to follow are useful hints for creating pretty garnishes with a pastry bag along with how to slice, serve, and store your pastries.

Handling Flour and Other Dry Ingredients

PASTRY IS far more forgiving than cakes when it comes to precise measurements. No matter how many times you make the same recipe, the ratio of flour to liquid can change, owing to variables beyond your control. Some flours are drier than others, hotter people will have hotter hands, some days are dry and other days are wet and humid. Dealing with the cards that Mother Nature hands out, you should have as many stacked on your side as possible. Handfuls of flour may have worked for grandma, but if you are looking for consistency, bring out the dry measures.

The most accurate method of measuring is with the metric system, measuring by weight. This is the way it is done throughout most of the world. However, though not as precise, Americans are more comfortable using volume measurements. So here are some tips for using our less precise style of measuring.

MEASURING DRY INGREDIENTS

Always use dry measuring cups. The flour is always sifted before measuring, unless the dough is being made in a food processor. It should be spooned into the container, then leveled with a straight-edged knife, straight metal spatula, or scraper. Do not bang or shake the container, as this will pack the flour.

Some people are "shakers"—individuals who cannot break the habit of shaking the cup as they measure. If that's you, remove the temptation by placing the cup on the counter first, then spoon your ingredients in without holding the cup. Do not measure with the "dip-and-sweep" method—that is, by dipping the measuring cup into the container. This packs too much flour into the cup, at times up to 2 tablespoons or more. Excessive flour throws the balance of the ingredients out of proportion.

When measuring dry ingredients under ¹/₄ cup, use measuring spoons. For smaller quantities, dipping is okay, because there is little risk of packing.

SIFTING AND STRAINING

Sifting aerates flour, smooths lumps, and combines ingredients. Since flours compact as they stand, sifting ensures a more consistent measurement. *Note:* Sifting can be omitted when using whole-grain flours because of their texture.

I always recommend sifting flour before measuring, regardless of package labeling, which might indicate that it has been "pre-sifted." Whether you use a single or triple-sifter, or a medium-gauge strainer, the job will be done as long as the flour passes through a mesh. For convenience, I do my initial sifting over a square of waxed paper, then measure as directed above. Any unused flour can then easily be picked up and poured back into its original container. When combining flour with other dry ingredients such as leavening, sift the pre-measured ingredients together two or three times to ensure thorough blending.

When using a food processor, sifting can be omitted because the processor does the work. *Note:* If a pastry dough recipe is adapted from hand to a food processor method, start with slightly less flour. For example, if the recipe calls for 2 cups of *sifted* flour, when a food processor is used, reduce the amount to 1³/₄ cups of *unsifted* flour. After the flour is aerated in the food processor, the final volume is about the same.

Confectioners' sugar and cocoa powder should always be passed through a strainer (before measuring). Confectioners' sugar is very heavy and easily clogs a sifter. By the same token, since a sifter is never washed, cocoa powder will discolor it for future use.

Handling Sugars and Thick Syrups

S UGAR PLAYS a vital role in making pies and tarts. Its obvious function is to sweeten doughs and their fillings, but it also contributes moistness, tenderizes, and promotes browning. A small amount—up to 1 teaspoon per cup of flour—can safely be added to most regular pie dough recipes. Sweet tart pastry, on the other hand, usually contains a higher ratio of sugar. This dough makes extremely delicate crusts, but they are often difficult to roll. For this reason, cookie-style doughs are sometimes pressed into the pan instead of being rolled.

Take notice of the size of the crystals of your granulated sugar. If they are especially coarse, use them for fruit pies and cooked fillings, where they can easily be dissolved. In contrast, meringues and sugar syrups often benefit from using superfine sugar; this quick-dissolving sugar can be used in equal amounts for ordinary sugar. You can also grind coarse granulated sugar in a food processor or blender. Brown sugar, both light and dark, is best used when it is not rock-hard (see "Brown Sugar," page 6).

Sugar substitutes are best used in recipes that are written for these products. They are not recommended for the recipes in this book.

MEASURING WHITE SUGARS

Always use a dry measuring cup to measure sugar. The cup should be filled to the brim, either by spooning the sugar in with a large spoon or by using the dip-and-sweep method. Level it with a straight blade knife. Confectioners' sugar, which is consistently lumpy, must be strained before it is measured and used.

MEASURING BROWN SUGAR

Brown sugar should also be measured in a dry measuring cups. Before measuring, empty the approximate amount needed on a sheet of waxed paper. Crumble any hard pieces with your fingers, then pack the sugar into the measuring cup. Sometimes the recipe specifies "lightly packed" and at other times "firmly packed." The packing is determined by how hard you press the sugar into the cup. Lightly packed sugar will hold its shape when inverted but will have some open spaces; firmly packed sugar is more compact. Never leave brown sugar exposed after measuring, as the surface will crust soon upon exposure to air. Cover the measured sugar with a piece of plastic wrap until ready to use.

MEASURING THICK SYRUPS

For thick syrups like honey, corn syrup, molasses, and maple syrup, use a dry measuring cup, not only for accuracy but also to remove the syrup easily from the container. Always grease the cup lightly with vegetable oil or nonstick cooking spray before measuring, and when pouring, hold the cup directly over the mixture to avoid spillage. Any remaining syrup can be scraped out with a rubber spatula.

Handling Fats

T HE FATS commonly used in pastries are butter, margarine, vegetable shortening, oil, and lard. The two most popu-

lar are unsalted butter and vegetable shortening. Oil is sometimes used because it is unsaturated and considered healthier by some. Many bakers prefer lard because it makes a very flaky dough. Margarine is occasionally used by those who observe dietary laws and still want the flavor of butter without the presence of dairy products.

Butter and other semisolid fats like margarine, lard, and vegetable shortening are classified as plastic fats. When these fats come in contact with flour, they shorten or cut the gluten strands by wrapping themselves around the starch granules. Because they hold air, these plastic fats can also be worked or kneaded until malleable. On the other hand, oils, which are liquid fats, immediately lubricate the starch granules because of their fluidity. When making a pastry, you need to clearly understand the different effects that plastic and liquid fats have on flour.

THE CORRECT TEMPERATURE

The success of many pie and tart doughs greatly depends on using fats at the proper temperature. When butter or margarine is to be cut into dry ingredients, the fat should be firm enough to remain in pieces, rather than melt into the flour. A stick of butter should be hard enough so that you cannot press an indentation into it without force. If the butter is to be

creamed, the indentation should be less difficult to make. But for either procedure, the butter should never be too soft.

While chilling vegetable shortening is not essential, it's a good idea to do so because the dough is less likely to be overworked. If you are a baker who favors lard, chill it as well. The temperature of oils is not relevant.

MEASURING BUTTER OR MARGARINE

Most butter and margarine is wrapped in marked $1/4$-pound sticks. Bear in mind that the paper covering is not always positioned correctly; when dividing a stick, make allowances as necessary. Sometimes butter is packaged in 1-pound blocks. In this case, first divide it into quarters and then make your measurements. Lard, also sold in blocks, should be divided in the same manner.

MEASURING VEGETABLE SHORTENINGS AND OILS

Vegetable shortenings are commonly packaged in cans. However, in recent years Crisco has been packed in easy-to-measure 1-cup sticks. Convenient as these sticks are, a 1-cup stick of Crisco *does not weigh* the same as 1 cup of butter. This is because vegetable shortening is 100 percent fat while butter and margarine have 80 percent fat and 20 percent water. *If you are substituting butter for shortening, reduce the amount of liquid in the recipe by 1 tablespoon per ½ cup (4 ounces) of fat.*

To measure vegetable shortening from a can, use a dry measuring cup, not a liquid one. I find it easier to pack the shortening to the very top of the container and level it straight across. The measuring line on a fluid measuring cup is below the top of the container, therefore it is more difficult to determine an accurate measurement.

Another way to measure vegetable shortening is with the displacement method. For example, if you need ½ cup of shortening, fill a liquid measuring cup with ½ cup water. Add enough vegetable shortening to make the water level reach 1 cup.

CLARIFYING BUTTER

Clarified, or drawn, butter is commonly used for such baking purposes as making pastries with phyllo. It is easy to prepare and can be stored for months in the refrigerator or freezer. When butter is clarified, it first must be heated until it separates into layers; a heavy-bottomed saucepan is essential. The foamy top layer contains whey proteins, or milk solids; this must be removed and discarded. This leaves a center layer of clear, golden liquid that is 100 percent fat and free of impurities. The remaining, bottom layer is a watery substance of milk proteins and salts, which should also be discarded. The melted butterfat can either be poured off or allowed to cook until the water evaporates, leaving behind a brown sediment. Butter cooked to this point has a stronger, more pronounced flavor.

Keep in mind that the volume of the butter you clarify will be reduced by 20 to 25 percent. For this reason, clarify a full pound of butter at a time. What isn't used immediately can be stored for later use.

STOVETOP METHOD Cook 1 pound of unsalted butter over very low heat in a medium heavy-bottomed saucepan until white foam (the milk solids) accumulates on the surface. Carefully remove the foam with a skimmer or large spoon, repeating the process until no more foam appears. Keep cooking the butter over very low heat until the butterfat is clear and the milk proteins have settled at the bottom of the saucepan. For a full pound of butter, this could take 30 to 40 minutes. Cool until tepid. Allow the butterfat to remain undisturbed in the saucepan. Then, place a fine-mesh strainer over a jar or bowl. Pour butterfat through the strainer, taking care to keep any of the sediment from slipping through into the clear fat.

MICROWAVE METHOD The clarified butter this method will produce is not as flavorful or pure as that made on the stovetop but will suffice if a small amount is needed in a hurry. Put unsalted butter in an oven-proof glass dish and microwave on medium power until melted. Carefully skim off the foam (milk solids) that have accumulated on the top. Let the dish sit at room temperature for 2 to 3 minutes to allow the milk proteins to sink to the bottom of the dish. Strain through a fine-mesh strainer into a dish, being careful to not let any milk solids slip through. Remember that the butter's volume will decrease by 20 to 25 percent after clarifying. If you need 6 tablespoons of clarified butter, begin the process with 8 tablespoons.

MAKING BROWNED BUTTER To make browned butter (*beurre noisette*), follow instructions for clarifying butter but allow the butter to cook even further until the golden fat begins to brown, at which point it will develop a nutty flavor. Care should be taken not to overcook the fat, as it will ultimately burn.

Handling Eggs

E GGS ARE an essential ingredient for a variety of pies and tarts. They contribute color, flavor, texture, and stability to both doughs and fillings.

Eggs, whether whole or separated, make an excellent binder for pastry doughs. The yolk imparts fat and tenderness, while the high-protein white adds moisture and strength. Beaten egg whites, when combined with sugar, transform into billowy meringue toppings.

Eggs are highly perishable and if not properly cared for have been known to transmit salmonella food poisoning. Whether this is the fault of breeding, poor storage, or unsanitary conditions remains unclear. To avoid any problem, always keep eggs refrigerated and stored in their original cartons.

Eggs are best used at room temperature, however, because warmer eggs blend more readily with other ingredients and achieve more volume when beaten. They should be removed from the refrigerator 20 to 30 minutes before using. For a quicker warm-up, place them in a bowl of tepid water to stand for a minute or two.

SEPARATING EGGS

When separating eggs, choose those that are closer to their expiration date. Aged eggs separate more easily, as do eggs that are still chilled.

Always use the "three-bowl method": one to crack the egg over, one to empty the whites into, and one to hold the yolks. To crack the shell, use the blade of a knife to give a firm tap across the center of the egg.

Hold the egg upright, then separate the top from the bottom, letting the white flow over the side. Pour the yolk from shell to shell, removing as much of the white as possible. If the yolk breaks, avoid letting any droplets contaminate the whites. The fatty yolk, no matter how small an amount, will reduce the volume if the whites are to be beaten.

If the chalazae (the cordlike threads that cling to the yolk) are large, remove them with your fingertips as they harden when heated. Any bits of broken shell that may have dropped into the egg can be removed with a spoon. Using a piece of eggshell to do the job is not sanitary.

BEATING EGGS

Pie and tart fillings rarely require heavily beaten eggs. Eggs most commonly are an addition to doughs or the base for a filling. As a general rule, when eggs are added to other ingredients, gently whisk them in a bowl before combining them.

Egg yolks that must be beaten to the ribbon stage need to be well whipped. My preference is to beat them by hand with a whisk in a large stainless steel bowl, allowing enough room for the movement of the whisk. An alternative is to use a hand-held mixer, but be careful not to overbeat the yolks. Too many air bubbles will result in a foamy filling.

TEMPERING EGGS

When eggs are to be added to hot mixtures, you must first raise the temperature of the eggs to make them compatible. Whisk about $1/4$ of the hot mixture into the eggs, then return the warmed eggs to the base mixture. This tempering prevents the eggs from curdling and/or forming lumps.

BEATING EGG WHITES

The primary functions of beaten egg whites in pie and tart cookery are to "lighten" fillings, to make soft meringue toppings, and to form baked meringue shells. Most people overbeat egg whites for fear that they will collapse. In fact, the reverse is the case. Less is better because egg whites continue to expand in the oven if they have not been overbeaten. On the other hand, egg whites that are overly whipped have reached their maximum air capacity and will not expand further.

When properly beaten, egg whites should be shiny and moist. If excessively whipped, the whites become dull, lumpy, dry, and will not combine smoothly with other mixtures. Sometimes, a small amount of sugar is added to beaten egg whites to stabilize them. This sugar prevents the egg whites from overbeating because it slows the beating process, buying you time.

For the best volume, always have the whites at room temperature. Be sure the bowl is thoroughly clean, with no oils on the surface. A wiping of white vinegar or lemon juice will eliminate this film. While a copper bowl is always best to use for whipping, a stainless steel bowl will work just fine. Glass and pottery are okay, but these materials do not create much friction for generating air cells. Avoid bowls made of reactive metal (like aluminum) or of plastic.

Many cookbooks refer to egg whites as being beaten in three stages: frothy, soft peak, and stiff peak. For the sake of clarity, I add a fourth stage, "firm peak," which falls between soft peak and stiff peak. In the beating instructions that follow, these stages are numbered:

✦ STAGE 1—*frothy*
✦ STAGE 2—*soft peak*
✦ STAGE 3—*firm peak*
✦ STAGE 4—*stiff peak*

Using a stand mixer or hand-held beater, begin beating the egg whites on medium-low speed, adding salt and cream of tartar when the whites are at Stage 1, frothy. The salt breaks the albumin of the whites, while the cream of tartar stabilizes and whitens them. Gradually increase the mixer speed to medium-high. The whites will have a stronger structure if they are not beaten too rapidly in the beginning. Starting them on high speed will result in unstable air cells that can easily pop, similar to a balloon that is overblown.

When beaten egg whites are used to lighten a filling, they are whipped only to Stage 2, *soft* peaks. I call this the "bird beak" stage. If the beater is lifted, the point of the whites should droop slightly, resembling a bird's beak.

Note: To salvage egg whites that have been overbeaten, add one unbeaten egg white. Whip briefly, just until you reach the desired consistency.

MAKING MERINGUES

Meringues are made with whipped egg whites and sugar. The amount of sugar used, when it is added, and the length of time the egg whites and sugar are beaten all determine whether the meringue will be soft or hard.

Soft meringues are made with less sugar than hard meringues. With the exception of a meringue topping, most soft meringues have the sugar added at Stage 2, soft peaks. However, to make a soft meringue for a topping, the sugar should be added to the whites just as they enter Stage 3, firm peaks. To determine this stage, watch for the ridges that form on the surface. As they become defined, stop the beating to check them. The moment they stand in shiny, firm peaks, they are ready for the sugar to be added. Determining this stage takes a watchful eye, as the whites can pass from Stage 3, firm peaks, to Stage 4, stiff peaks, in a matter of seconds.

Egg whites for hard meringues contain more sugar and require longer beating. The sugar is added when the ridges in the whites are *well* defined and still shiny—toward the end of Stage 3. Then the meringue is beaten to Stage 4, when the peaks will be stiff and glossy. Only with this addition of sugar can egg whites safely be beaten to Stage 4, stiff peaks, without deflating. Whether making soft or hard meringues, the goal is to achieve a smooth and shiny final result.

For more on Meringue, see "The Primer," Lesson 2, page 112.

Measuring Liquids

L IQUIDS SHOULD always be measured in fluid (liquid) measuring cups. Ovenproof glass is the easiest to use because of the "easy-to-read" measurements on the side. For accuracy, always check your measurement at eye level—that is, bend down to the counter; don't lift the cup —and fill the liquid exactly to the line. It is always best to use a cup size closest to the amount you need. If you are measuring under 1/2 cup, do not use a 2-cup measure.

Handling Chocolate

WORKING with chocolate is serious business. This exotic ingredient is sensitive to high and low temperatures, to moisture, to overmixing, and to odors. When exposed to any of the above, no amount of coaxing can rectify the wrongs. Overheating chocolate impairs the flavor, cold temperatures cause it to look chalky, too little liquid ruins its velvety texture, overmixing results in streaking, and if exposed to garlic, chocolate will taste like it. Because working with chocolate has so many pitfalls, it must be treated with tender, loving care.

In the "old days," when the American chocolate vocabulary consisted of unsweetened chocolate, occasionally semisweet chocolate, chocolate chips, and cocoa powder, nobody paid much attention to how chocolate was melted. My, how things have changed. Today, we are obsessed with the luxurious premium imports that have come to our shores. It's no wonder; they have a velvety, melt-in-your-mouth texture and a depth of flavor that is hard to surpass. Although we do have a few fine domestic chocolates, the crème de la crème is manufactured in Europe.

HOW TO CHOP CHOCOLATE

When working with chocolate, the key to melting it is slow and even heat. To achieve this, the chocolate must be cut into small pieces. Dark chocolates can be left larger than milk and white chocolates, but all must be reduced in size. Indeed, milk and white chocolates should be very finely chopped. Smaller pieces of chocolate receive more surface heat, especially if they are melted in a proper-size utensil. Larger pieces become too hot on the outside before the heat can penetrate the center.

I like to use an ice pick (available in most hardware stores) to break large chunks of chocolate. Here is my quick trick for chopping or breaking packaged chocolates, such as paper-wrapped 1-ounce squares of dark chocolate and aluminum foil-wrapped bars: without unwrapping the chocolate, pierce the bar several times with the ice pick; remove the wrapping and the chocolate is in pieces and bits, ready for melting. To cut larger chunks of chocolate, use a chef's knife and a clean cutting board, and shave the chocolate into thin slivers.

Dark chocolate can also be chopped in a food processor. For even chopping and to avoid damage to the machine, first break the chocolate into pieces no larger than 1 inch. Milk and white chocolate are too soft to be chopped in the food processor.

If you are melting a large amount of chocolate, use the "seeding" method: reserve a portion of the chocolate to be melted. As the first part melts, gradually add the remaining chocolate. The unmelted chocolate prevents the earlier batch from overheating.

HOW TO MELT DARK CHOCOLATE
(unsweetened, bittersweet, and semisweet)

IN A WATER BATH *(bain-marie)* Use a wide pan such as a 10-inch skillet. Fill the pan with ½ inch of hot water. Turn the heat on very low; the water should only simmer. Place the chopped chocolate in a heatproof bowl large enough to protect the chocolate from coming in contact with water or steam. Stir the chocolate from time to time with a rubber spatula. As the chocolate starts to melt, turn the heat off and let the chocolate continue to melt slowly, stirring it occasionally.

IN A DOUBLE BOILER Fill the bottom of a double boiler with 1 to 2 inches of water. The liquid should not touch the bottom of the inserted pot. Bring the water to a boil, then reduce to a simmer. Add the chopped chocolate to the double boiler top and place it over the simmering water. Turn off the heat and let the chocolate melt slowly, stirring it occasionally to ensure even melting. Do not let steam escape from the bottom of the pot and *do not cover* the saucepan.

IN A MICROWAVE OVEN Place the chopped chocolate in an ovenproof glass container. Heat the chocolate on medium power for 1 minute. Stir with a rubber spatula, then heat again for 30 seconds, stir, then heat for another 15 seconds. The chocolate does not have to melt completely; it will continue to melt at room temperature. The melting time of the chocolate will depend on the wattage of your microwave and the quantity in the container. Watch carefully—the chocolate will hold its shape even though it is melted. If the chocolate is not completely melted when you are ready to use it, return it to the microwave oven for a few seconds.

IN AN OVEN Preheat the oven to 225 degrees. Place the chopped chocolate in a shallow heatproof container. Melt slowly, stirring every so often. When the chocolate is almost melted, turn the oven off and let the chocolate stand in the unlit oven until melted.

HOW TO MELT MILK AND WHITE CHOCOLATES

Milk and white chocolates require much less heat to melt than dark chocolates. For this reason, you need to oversee the complete melting process.

Cut the chocolate into very small pieces, about $1/4$ to $1/2$ inch. Place the chocolate in a stainless steel bowl and set in a skillet filled with $1/2$ inch of warm, *not hot,* water. Stir slowly and constantly with a rubber spatula until the chocolate is melted. Watch carefully, as these soft chocolates only take a few minutes.

HOW TO MELT CHOCOLATE IN LIQUIDS

Many people believe that chocolate cannot be melted with a liquid. This is not true. As long as enough liquid is present, combining the two is not a problem.

The following ratio is a good guideline:

✦ *For each ounce of bittersweet or semisweet chocolate, use no less than $1^1/2$ teaspoons of liquid.*

✦ *For each ounce of unsweetened chocolate, use no less than 2 tablespoons of liquid.*

To prevent lumping or "seizing" when combining melted chocolate with a liquid, always add the chocolate to the liquid, *not* the liquid to the chocolate.

Melted chocolate should always be warm when adding it to liquid, otherwise it will not blend smoothly. If small flecks or pieces appear, heat the mixture slowly, stirring it constantly, until the chocolate is melted.

Here are a few additional tips for melting chocolate:

✦ *Always use equipment that is completely free of moisture. Not one drop of water should be present.*

✦ *To ensure even melting, stir the chocolate frequently with a rubber spatula.*

✦ *Never cover melting or melted chocolate; it will pick up condensation.*

✦ *Never use boiling water near chocolate as the steam will cause the chocolate to "seize" (become gritty).*

✦ *When melting dark chocolate, never allow the temperature to reach more than 120 degrees. The temperature for milk and white chocolates should never exceed 110 degrees. These delicate chocolates contain milk, which burns quickly.*

About Nuts

TO TOAST NUTS

Nuts benefit greatly from toasting—the heat brings out their flavor and adds a pleasurable crunch. If nuts are to be chopped, always toast them first.

OVEN TOASTING Because nuts are high in fat, they burn easily and so should always be toasted on a heavy-gauge metal pan in a low to moderate oven—no more than 325 degrees. To ensure even baking, spread them in a single layer on a shallow baking pan. The toasting time depends on the amount of nuts in the pan, their oil content, and their size. For example, toasting only a few nuts takes considerably less time than doing a panful. Sliced or slivered almonds toast quicker than whole pieces.

Nuts that are high in oil, like pine nuts, take the least amount of time to toast, about 5 to 6 minutes, while larger nuts such as pecans and walnuts take 8 to 10 minutes. Less oily nuts such as whole almonds or hazelnuts (filberts) can take 12 minutes or more to turn a light golden brown. Unskinned nuts like whole almonds and hazelnuts do not show color, but when toasted they will look dry and have a slightly cracked surface. With so many variables to deal with, the safest test for doneness is to check the nuts as soon as a pleasant toasted aroma emanates from the oven.

SKILLET TOASTING A quick method for toasting nuts is to brown them on top of the stove in an ungreased skillet. This works especially well for toasting small amounts of pine nuts or sliced and slivered almonds. Use medium-low heat and stir them frequently. Although this method is okay for spur-of-the-moment needs, oven toasting gives the best flavor and ensures the most even browning.

TO SKIN TOASTED HAZELNUTS

As soon as the nuts are toasted, pour them onto a double thickness of paper towels. Cover them with a top layer and rub the nuts between the towels un-

til the skins peel off. This procedure must be done while the nuts are still hot. It's okay if a few pieces of skin remain.

TO SKIN ALMONDS AND PISTACHIOS

Blanch the nuts in boiling water, testing one or two nuts every few minutes to see if the skins have loosened—pistachios will shed their skins sooner than almonds. When the nuts are ready, drain them and immediately rinse with cold water to stop the cooking. Dry well on a sheet pan lined with a double thickness of paper towels. Remove the skins as directed for hazelnuts, then spread the nuts on a shallow baking pan, and bake in a 325 degree oven until they are dry.

All nuts should be cooled before using to allow the oils to reabsorb into the nuts. If nuts are chopped when they are too hot, the oily surface can cause them to become pasty.

TO CHOP NUTS

Chopping nuts by hand ensures more uniform pieces than those chopped in a food processor. High-fat nuts like macadamias and cashews should always be chopped by hand. Recipes that call for coarsely chopped nuts should also be cut by hand into large, pea-size pieces. To hand-cut nuts, place the nuts on a cutting board and chop to the desired size with a chef's knife.

A quick way to chop nuts without soiling equipment is to crush them while in a ziplock plastic bag. Place them in the bag, press out the air, and seal. Pound the nuts into the desired size using a batarde (page 457) or the bottom of a small, heavy saucepan.

Food processors can sometimes be used to chop nuts. Processors do not chop the nuts evenly, but they can be efficient when the following measures are taken:

✦ *Use the steel blade.*

✦ *Do not overfill the processor bowl. It's better to chop the nuts in small batches—no more than 1½ to 2 cups at a time, depending upon the size of your processor.*

✦ *Add a tablespoon or two of sugar or flour from your recipe to the processor bowl with the nuts. Either of these dry ingredients will help absorb the oils released during chopping. Likewise, if the nuts become too oily during processing, pulse them with 1 to 2 tablespoons of flour.*

✦ *To achieve more evenly chopped nuts, use the pulse button.*

✦ *An alternative to chopping medium-size nuts is cut them with a processor shredding disk instead of the steel blade.*

✦ *Soft nuts like pecans and walnuts take less time to chop than harder varieties like almonds and hazelnuts.*

✦ *Stop the food processor frequently to check the size of the nuts. The processor works so swiftly, and nuts can easily become overchopped.*

TO MEASURE NUTS

Whether a recipe calls for "1 cup of nuts, chopped," or "1 cup of chopped nuts" dictates when they should be measured. Since nuts reduce in volume after chopping, 1 measured cup of nuts that is then chopped will yield less than 1 cup chopped nuts. Therefore, if you want 1 cup of chopped nuts, start with a brimming *full* cup of nuts. This is why weight measures are more precise: if the amount of nuts is weighed, when the nuts are chopped is irrelevant—4 ounces of nuts, chopped or whole, still weigh 4 ounces.

About Coconut

T HE MOST common kind of coconut used in this country is the packaged shredded or angel flake variety that is sold in supermarkets. It is cloyingly sweet but its flaky texture and high sugar content lends itself to toasting. Fresh coconut, on the other hand, has a delicate, rather bland flavor, is somewhat moist, with a coarse texture. When paired with custards, pastry creams, and frostings, this natural product truly shines. Refer to the Fruit and Berry Glossary (page 17) for instructions on how to remove fresh coconut from its shell.

Frozen unsweetened coconut is also available in many supermarkets. It is finely grated and quite moist, but also bland. If the size of the coconut shred is unimportant, frozen coconut is a suitable alternative to fresh. Fresh and frozen coconut do not toast as well as sweetened.

Another form of unsweetened coconut is desiccated, which is often sold in health food stores. This coconut has a dry, powdery grain and little taste.

HOW TO TOAST COCONUT
Spread sweetened coconut on shallow baking pan. Bake in a 325 degree oven for 8 to 10 minutes. Turn the coconut with a fork every so often for even browning. The coconut will crisp as it cools.

HOW TO SHRED FRESH COCONUT Cut the cleaned coconut in 1-inch pieces and place in the feeder tube of a food processor fitted with the medium shredding disk. Shred the coconut using little or no pressure on the plunger. Change to the steel blade, and process until the shreds of coconut are cut into small pieces, about 1/4 inch. Shredded fresh coconut can be stored in a tightly covered container in the refrigerator for 5 to 7 days or in the freezer for up to 6 months.

TO MAKE COCONUT RIBBONS
Reserve one of the larger pieces of fresh coconut, at least 2 inches in length. Run a vegetable peeler down its length, making the slices as thin as possible.

Spread the ribbons on an aluminum foil–lined cookie sheet and sprinkle with granulated sugar, using 1 teaspoon for each 1/4 cup of loosely packed ribbons. Toss the shreds to coat with sugar.

Bake in a 325 degree oven for 10 to 12 minutes or until golden brown. Turn with a spatula every so often for even browning. The ribbons will crisp as they cool. Coconut ribbons are best stored, loosely covered, at room temperature. They should be used within 1 to 2 days.

Handling Dried Fruits

D RIED FRUITS come alive when they are "plumped," or reconstituted. Plumping enhances flavor, tenderizes the fruit, and brings out color. The fruit is either submerged in boiling water or steamed. If the fruit is very dry and hard, the boiling water method is recommended.

Sometimes the fruit is steeped or macerated in a liqueur after plumping. For better absorption, steep while the fruit is still warm.

WATER METHOD Place the fruit in a bowl and cover it with boiling water. Let stand 1 to 2 minutes, depending on the size and hardness of the fruit. Discard the water, then empty the fruit onto a double layer of paper towels. Blot the top with additional paper towels to remove as much moisture as possible.

STEAMING METHOD Place the fruit in a steamer basket and set it over simmering water. Steam for 1 to 2 minutes, depending on the size and hardness of the fruit. Empty the fruit onto a double layer of paper towels. Blot with additional paper towels to remove as much moisture as possible.

HOW TO CUT DRIED FRUIT

Cut dried fruits that do not require plumping with scissors. Cut fruits that have been plumped on a cutting board with a chef's knife.

Handling Citrus Fruits

C ITRUS FRUITS are a magic ingredient in pies and tarts. They have an almost magnetic ability to pull flavors together. At times, their subtle presence is barely detectable, but they can also make a powerful statement. The beauty of citrus fruits is that the entire fruit—zest, pulp, and juice—makes a major contribution to baking.

TO ZEST CITRUS FRUITS

The zest is the colorful, outermost layer of skin on all citrus fruits. The oils contained in the skin can make a flavorful contribution to many recipes. To remove the zest, use a fine shredder for grating and a vegetable peeler for cutting long strips. But when removing the zest, take care not to include any of the bitter white pith that lies just below the zest. If your recipe calls for grated zest and you have used a vegetable peeler to remove the skin, mince the strips with a chef's knife. Although the classic "zester" tool produces lovely, long strips that are ideal for a garnish, they cannot be used for flavoring unless finely minced.

The manner in which the zest has been cut will determine the intensity of its flavor. Zest that has been finely grated will be more pungent than zest that has been minced. This is because the texture of grated zest can at times be almost pulpy, producing a flavor that is highly concentrated. Too much zest can be overpowering, therefore adjust the measurement according to the equipment used.

The zest measurements used in this book are based on zest that was grated to a consistency midway between mashed and minced (see "Graters," page 44). Zest can be frozen in a tightly covered container, with the bottom lined with aluminum foil, for up to 3 months.

TO JUICE CITRUS FRUITS

To get the maximum amount of juice, roll the room-temperature fruit with the palm of your hand back and forth on a counter. An alternative is to heat the whole fruit briefly in a microwave oven on low power. The juice can be extracted with either an electric or a hand juicer, or simply by squeezing it in your hand. Take care to strain out all the seeds and bits of pulp. If only a small amount of juice is needed, cut the fruit in half, insert a fork into the pulp, and twist the fork while squeezing the fruit. Freshly squeezed juice can be frozen in a well-sealed plastic container for up to 6 months.

TO SUPREME CITRUS FRUITS

Supreming a citrus fruit is to remove all of the fruit's sections from the skin and membrane without damaging the individual wedges. A thin-bladed, very sharp knife is essential for this procedure.

Place the fruit on a cutting board and cut off the top and bottom. Using a sharp 6-inch utility knife, expose the flesh by cutting down the side of the fruit, curving the knife along the contour of the fruit. Be careful not to remove too much of the flesh. Then cut on either side of the membrane and lift out the wedge of fruit. Continue around the entire fruit until all of the wedges have been removed. The remaining membrane can be squeezed to extract any juice.

About Whipped Cream

ALTHOUGH WHIPPING cream is a seemingly simple procedure, there are many refinements that help ensure perfect results. Bear in mind that heavy cream, when whipped, slightly more than doubles in volume.

Here are some tips:

✦ *Aged cream—closer to the expiration date—will whip better than very fresh cream.*

✦ *Pure cream, which has not been ultrapasteurized, has better beating properties.*

✦ *Always start with a well-chilled bowl, beaters, and cream. A quick 10- to 15-minute chill in the freezer is sufficient.*

✦ *When using an electric mixer, start whipping on medium-low speed. Increase the speed gradually to medium. Unless you are whipping cream in amounts of over 2 cups, this speed should be sufficient.*

✦ *Whipping cream on lower speeds makes for a more stable product and prevents the air cells from bursting. The whipped cream will have a longer life with less risk of becoming watery.*

✦ *Sweeten and flavor the cream as it starts to thicken. If added too early, the cream will take longer to thicken.*

✦ *Chocolate tends to make whipped cream thicken more rapidly. Watch it carefully.*

✦ *To increase the life of whipped cream for decorating, stabilize it with a small amount of gelatin (see "Stabilized Whipped Cream," page 450).*

✦ *When whipping cream for lightening and folding purposes, beat it only to soft mounds.*

✦ *Whipped cream should be beaten just until it is smooth, creamy, and holds its shape. When beaten too stiffly, it loses its gloss and starts to look lumpy. When overbeaten, it "breaks" or separates, at which point it can turn to butter.*

✦ *When whipped cream is piped through a pastry bag, it will stiffen slightly as it is forced through the pastry tip. For this reason, cream to be piped should not be beaten too stiffly (see "Garnishing," page 74).*

✦ *Heavy cream whipped with an electric mixer should be finished with a wire whisk to lessen the risk of overbeating and ensure proper consistency.*

✦ *To salvage whipped cream that has been too stiffly beaten but has not yet "broken," add a small amount of heavy cream and beat until the desired consistency is reached.*

✦ *The ultimate way to whip cream is over ice with a wire whisk. For those with a KitchenAid electric mixer, an ice-bowl attachment is manufactured for this purpose. It attaches below the standard mixing bowl.*

Working with Gelatin

PROPERLY USED, gelatin is a terrific stabilizer for pie and tart fillings and for whipped cream. However, care must be taken to dissolve gelatin properly, and it is essential that gelatin be at the correct temperature when added to other ingredients. If gelatin is too cool when added to a mixture, it will not blend in smoothly. Cool gelatin added to a cool base creates gelled lumps and strings, while *tepid to warm* gelatin will incorporate smoothly.

Using gelatin with high concentrations of sugar, alcohol, or very acidic fruits can retard its thickening ability. When these ingredients are present, the amount of gelatin used must be increased. Avoid overmixing foods stabilized with gelatin, especially after the gel has begun to set. Too much action will cause the gelatin to thin and its thickening power will never return.

Working with gelatin is a threefold process. The first step is to dissolve it in liquid, a procedure referred to professionally as "blooming." Next, the gelatin must be heated in order to melt it. Finally, the gelatin is cooled down to a point where it easily combines with other ingredients.

Here are the two methods I prefer for blooming and dissolving packaged unflavored gelatin.

STOVETOP METHOD Place the liquid being used, most often water, in a small heatproof container and sprinkle the gelatin over the surface. Do not stir. Let the mixture stand for 5 minutes. Then place the container in a skillet filled with ½ inch of simmering water. Heat in the water bath for 3 to 5 minutes or until the gelatin is dissolved and the liquid is clear.

MICROWAVE OVEN METHOD Proceed as above through letting the mixture stand for 5 minutes. Then heat in a microwave oven, on medium power, for 45 to 60 seconds or until the gelatin is dissolved and the liquid is clear.

About Lightening and Folding

L IGHTENING and folding are mixing techniques done together: first you lighten and then you fold.

"Lightening" a mixture means to take a portion of an airy, whipped substance and blend it into a heavier one to loosen the denseness. This prevents loss of air, as well as ensures even blending. Once the base has been lightened, the remaining whipped ingredient can be folded in.

The airy mixture should always be whipped to soft peaks or mounds, *never* stiffly beaten.

Overwhipped egg whites or heavy cream will not blend smoothly into a base (see "Handling Eggs," page 52, and "About Whipped Cream," page 60).

Folding is commonly used to combine two or more substances of different densities without deflating the lighter or aerated one. It is always done by hand, never with an electrical appliance. In pie and tart fillings, folding usually applies to beaten egg whites or whipped cream that must be combined with a cream-style filling. Foods such as chocolate, nuts, and fruits are also sometimes folded into a mixture.

To lighten a base, use a small whisk to stir in one-fourth to one-third of the whipped product. **1** Switch to a rubber spatula and fold in the remaining aerated ingredient. If necessary, transfer the mixture to a large bowl to allow for the folding movement.

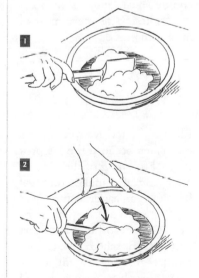

Hold the spatula with the curved side facing down. **2** Cut through the center of the filling with the spatula, then move it under the filling, scraping the bottom of the bowl.

3 Bring the spatula up the side, over the top, and cut through the center again. The bowl should be turned as you fold to ensure even blending. Every so often, clean around the entire bowl.

About Water Baths (Bain-Maries)

U SING A water bath is one of the more versatile techniques in anyone's culinary arsenal. Water baths can be useful to both heat and cool mixtures. Since proper temperature plays such a vital role in dessert preparation, the importance of water baths cannot be minimized.

In the oven, a hot water bath is used for preventing delicate mixtures from overbaking. It creates a humid environment that keep foods moist, reduces surface cracking, and makes removal from the pan easier. In stovetop cookery, the hot water bath also has many uses, including gentle melting of chocolate or dissolving of gelatin.

Cold water baths are used to hasten the cooling of foods. In this book, they are used primarily for reducing the temperature of cooked fillings and for speeding the thickening of gelatin mixtures.

HOT WATER BATH FOR THE OVEN Place your baking pan into a larger pan with fairly deep sides, such as an open roaster with a depth of 2 to 2½ inches. Set the empty, larger pan on the oven shelf, then carefully pour boiling water into the larger pan to a depth of about 1 inch. Add the boiling water close to the sides of the larger pan to avoid splattering.

HOT WATER BATH FOR THE STOVE The mixture to be heated must be in a heatproof container large enough to protect it from steam or splashing water. Fill a skillet with about ½ inch of water, place the container into the skillet, and bring the water to a simmer. Keep the water simmering until your mixture has reached the desired consistency and/or temperature. At times, the heat can be turned off, allowing the food to warm even more gently.

COLD WATER BATHS A cold water bath is a mixture of ice cubes and cold water (ice cubes alone will not cool as efficiently), in either an oversize bowl or the kitchen sink. Keep in mind that foods will cool faster if placed in a larger bowl. Fill the sink or bowl with enough cold water and ice cubes to reach about ¼ up the side of the container. Place the container with the warm ingredients into the ice water. Using a rubber spatula, gently stir the mixture from time to time to promote even chilling.

About Baking Pans

T HERE IS such a tempting array of pie, tart, and tartlet pans on the market that making a choice can be dizzying. However, most pies and tarts call for straightforward equipment. Give me a plain Pyrex glass pie plate, a French tin tart pan, and a heavy-duty cookie sheet, and I'm in business. These pans serve most of my baking needs.

PREPARING PANS FOR BAKING

I like to butter ovenproof glass pie plates because the fat promotes browning of the bottom crust and also makes removal from the pan easier. A thin layer applied with a pastry brush is fine. On the other hand, tart pans, except when new, do not require greasing. Again, use a pastry brush to ensure that all of the scalloped grooves are well coated. After baking one or two tarts, the pans will become seasoned, making removal a breeze.

For those of you who are trying to lower your fat intake, a nonstick cooking spray, such as Pam or Baker's Joy, can be used. While these sprays answer a need, doughs have a tendency to slip when fitted into pans so coated.

Crumb crusts are prone to sticking, especially to ovenproof glass pie plates. To resolve this, not only must the plates be *heavily* greased but they should be dusted with a light coating of either flour or cocoa (for chocolate crusts).

When I make free-form tarts, I always bake them on a cookie sheet. Because this pan has no sides, the tart is easy to slide off after baking. Baking parchment is excellent for lining pans. Although I secure it at the corners with some dabs of butter, it sometimes moves about. For those times when I roll pastry directly on the pan, I prefer to line it with aluminum foil instead of using baking parchment. I tuck the ends of the aluminum foil underneath the sides of the pan, so it won't slide as I roll. Most of the time, the pastry does not stick, but if you're concerned about the possibility, spray the surface with nonstick cooking spray.

SPECIALTY PANS

Occasionally I use specialty tart pans, such as daisies, squares, rectangles, oblongs, and hearts. When I do, it is sometimes necessary to make some changes in the recipe to accommodate their size. Another consideration is that unusual shaped tart pans require unusual-shaped serving pieces. There is no point in making a unique shape, no matter how pretty, if the tart has to be cut in the kitchen for lack of an appropriate serving plate.

Tarts can also be baked in a flan ring—a bottomless piece of tinned or stainless steel metal than is set on a cookie sheet. To avoid leaks, these hoop-shaped rings are best used with fruit fillings, or with fillings that do not have much liquid. The advantage of baking in a flan ring is that after lifting the ring off, all you do is slide the tart from the pan onto a serving platter. The disadvantage is that these rings are not as high as the classic two-piece fluted tart pans, so you may have to use less filling. Also, they require some skill to assure a well-formed shape.

Personally, I don't mind if the form is a bit irregular; it can lend the tart a rustic look that I find appealing.

CHANGING PIES TO TARTS, TARTS TO PIES

One of the best features of pies and tarts is their versatility. Unlike cake batters, which are so precise in measurement and pan sizes, pie and tart recipes can be adjusted and interchanged with good results.

Many pie fillings can be used for tarts. Some that work best are those made with fruits and berries and those that are precooked, such as a pastry creams or lemon fillings.

For example, a filling for a 9-inch pie can be used to fill an 11-inch tart, but it will not be as deep because the surface area of a tart pan is wider. If you wish to have a more generous filling, increase the recipe for a 9-inch pie by $1/3$ to $1/2$ (you will need to make $1 1/3$ or $1 1/2$ times the recipe). This same formula will also work when you want to convert an 11-inch tart into two 8-inch tarts.

To enlarge the size of a pie from a 9-inch to a $10 1/2$-inch, the filling again must be increased by between $1/3$ to $1/2$. To enlarge a cobbler or crisp from a 7×11-inch to a 9×13-inch, make $1 1/2$ times the recipe. This same quantity will also make two smaller, 8×8-inch cobblers.

Although the baking time may have to be adjusted when pan sizes change, judging doneness is easy. For pies, watch for the crust to brown on the bottom. For tarts, look for a browned edge. For cobblers and crisps, only the top need be checked for color. For all fruit pies, tarts, or cobblers, bubbling juices are one of the sure signs of doneness.

Dough quantities are given with each pastry recipe in this book. When using a tart dough for a pie, the recipe has to be increased, since it takes more dough to line a pie plate owing to its depth. Many tart dough recipes are difficult to halve, so it is easiest to double the recipe; I then use the extra dough to line small tart shells. For a $4 1/2$-inch single-serving tart, allow about 2 ounces of dough. Keep the tarts well wrapped in the freezer, ready for use—they are great to have on hand. (Refer to "Freezing Pastry Dough," page 78.)

Converting a filling for a tart to one for a pie can be risky, because pie plates are so much deeper than tart pans. Also, many tart fillings bake best when the filling is spread over a wide, shallow area. This is especially true of fresh fruit tarts, which use less fruit and thickening than a pie. Cooked fillings, such as pastry creams, or frozen desserts, are good conversion candidates.

An extremely rich filling will be delicious when made into a tart, but it may be overpowering as a pie. A high-calorie filling works successfully when it is in correct proportion to a crust, with enough pastry to offset the richness. An example of this is the Colossal Cashew Cluster (page 306). While addicting as a tart, it would be overwhelming as a pie.

Working with Phyllo

A MAGICAL PRE-MADE dough, phyllo can perform wonders. The dough can be purchased in the freezer section of most supermarkets, at specialty food stores, and at Greek and Middle Eastern groceries. My preference is to buy it at specialty stores where it has not been frozen.

Unfortunately, phyllo gets a bad rap, primarily because most people purchase it at the supermarket in its frozen form. Supermarkets have a bad habit of allowing their inventory to thaw while stocking their freezer shelves. Phyllo that has been partially thawed and then refrozen is a nightmare to work with. When completely thawed, the sheets stick together, break, and are often gummy. If supermarkets are your only source for phyllo, buy an extra box or two in case you have problems.

While you will find directions for handling phyllo on the package, here are some tips and techniques to help you along.

✦ *Frozen phyllo must be thawed overnight in the refrigerator.*

✦ *Assemble the necessary equipment and filling ingredients before opening the package of phyllo.*

✦ *Always work with well-chilled fillings that are not overly moist.*

✦ *Lay a long sheet of waxed paper on your work surface. Remove the phyllo from the package and carefully unroll. Estimate the number of sheet you think you will need and rewrap the remainder.*

✦ *Lay a second sheet of waxed paper on top of the phyllo sheets. Dampen a dish towel or a double thickness of paper towels and lay it over the waxed paper. This will prevent the dough from drying and cracking.*

✦ *Always recover the phyllo as the sheets are removed.*

✦ *Melted clarified butter and/or oil should first be applied around the edges of each sheet. The edges are prone to drying sooner than the center of the dough.*

✦ *An oversize pastry brush is helpful for moistening the phyllo with butter or oil. Its larger size will cover the dough's surface more quickly.*

✦ *The final, shaped sheet of phyllo should always be brushed with butter and/or oil.*

✦ *Unused phyllo can be rerolled, covered with plastic wrap, and placed back in its original package. Store in the refrigerator for up to 1 week. I do not recommend refreezing phyllo.*

Making Lattice Crusts

A LATTICE-TOPPED pie or tart is a work of art, which is not as intimidating to make as you might think. While you can make a lattice top on a tart, these crusts work the best on pies because the baking pan has a rim that secures the crust. To make the most of a lattice topping, use it to show off a colorful fruit filling. The woven lattice gives the prettiest effect, but if you lack the time and patience, it's perfectly alright to make an unwoven top.

For a traditional pie lattice, use twelve 3/4-inch strips, cut with a fluted or straight-edge pastry wheel. You can also create a pretty effect with a few very wide strips or lots of narrow strips placed close together. The wide strips can be cut up to 1½ inches across, but the narrow pieces should be cut no less than ½ inch wide (otherwise, they will be too difficult to handle). Likewise, the strips of dough can be positioned wide apart or close together. If you choose to make a closely woven lattice, you will need plenty of dough—make 1½ times the recipe of your favorite double-crust pastry.

It is best to use a lattice for pre-cooked fruit fillings or for fruit fillings that will not shrink too much during baking. I do not recommend a lattice on apple pies made with raw fruit or for other fruits where the filling is piled high above the rim of the pan. The fruit will shrink during baking, and the beautiful lattice work will be for naught.

HOW TO WEAVE A TRADITIONAL LATTICE TOP

1. Roll the second half of your pastry into a 13-inch circle. Using a fluted or straight-edge pastry wheel, cut twelve 3/4-inch strips.

2. Start with the two longest strips of pastry. Place them slightly off center on top of the pie, leaving a 3/4-inch space between each strip.

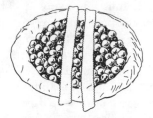

3. Take two more strips of dough, graduating the sizes, and place one on either side of the first two strips, again leaving a 3/4-inch space between the strips.

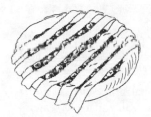

4. Take two of the smaller strips, and place them on either side of the last two strips. You should have six graduated strips.

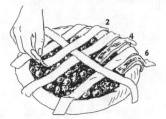

5. To weave the dough, fold strips 2, 4, and 6 back slightly more than halfway. Starting with the largest strip of dough, place it slightly off center on top of the pie filling. Carefully return the folded strips to the edge of the pie.

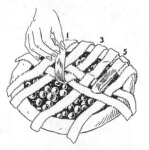

6. Now fold strips 1, 3, and 5 back. Use the next graduated strip of dough, and place it on top of the pie, leaving a 3/4-inch space between it and the preceding row. Then return the strips to the edge. Repeat with the smallest strip, folding strips 2, 4, and 6 back. One side of the pie should now be woven.

7. Turn the pie around. Weave the opposite side of the pie as you did the first side using the remaining three strips of pastry.

8. Trim the pastry strips, leaving a 1-inch overhang around the pie. Fold the pastry strips under the bottom pastry. Press the two layers together, forming a wall. Use the selvage to build up the thinner parts of the edge, then flute. Proceed with the baking directions in your recipe.

HOW TO MAKE A DIAGONAL LATTICE TOP

1. Follow the directions for the traditional lattice top through step 4. Weaving is optional.

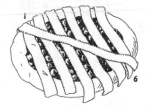

2. Turn the pie slightly, about one-eighth of a turn. Position the first lattice strip on the top of strip 1 and extend it to the bottom of strip 6.

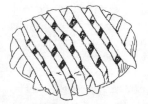

3. Continue with the remaining 5 strips, keeping them parallel and at equal distances. Repeat until all the pieces of pastry

have been used. When you are done, the holes should be diamond shaped.

4. Continue with step 8 of traditional lattice top.

HOW TO MAKE AN UNWOVEN LATTICE TOP

1. Roll the second half of dough into a 13-inch circle. Using a fluted pastry wheel, cut the pastry into twelve 3/4-inch graduated strips.

2. Place half of the strips on top of the pie, using the longest pieces in the middle. Arrange all the pieces in the same direction.

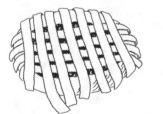

3. Give the pie a one-quarter turn (90 degrees), and lay the remaining pastry strips perpendicular to the first layer, spacing them as you did before.

4. Trim the pastry, leaving a 1-inch overhang around the pie. Fold the pastry strips under the bottom pastry. Press the two layers together, forming a wall. Use the selvage to build up the thinner parts of the edge, then flute. Proceed with the baking directions in your recipe.

HOW TO MAKE AN UNWOVEN SPIRAL LATTICE TOP

Spiral lattices are very attractive, but you must pay extra attention to the temperature of the dough. If the pastry is too cold or too warm, it will break as it is twirled. Do not attempt a spiral top on a woven lattice.

1. Follow step 1 of the directions for unwoven lattice.

2. To form the spirals, take each strip of dough, hold at both ends, and gently twist a few times in opposite directions. Do not twist too tightly or the strips of dough will break.

3. Complete using steps 2–4 for unwoven lattice.

Making Decorative Edges

W HEN I MAKE a pie crust, my first concern is that it be tender and flaky, and have good flavor. Pictures of pies with beautiful, sculptured edges are pretty to look at, but they often aren't worth the trouble. A flavorful pie crust must contain an adequate amount of butter and vegetable shortening. Fat makes crusts tender and taste good, but at the same time it makes them lose their shape and easily crumble. The richer the dough, the more fragile it will be.

If you want a fancy edge, the quality of the pastry will have to be sacrificed. More flour and liquid have to be added to reduce the percentage of fat. This makes the dough stronger. While it will hold its shape better, it will be tough and tasteless.

To help decide what style of edge to make, keep in mind the type of filling you plan to use. For a double-crust fruit pie, choose an edge that seals well, so there is less risk of the juices leaking. (A lattice crust does not require a sealed edge because so much filling is exposed. The juices evaporate readily, so overflow is not as great a problem.) When making a single crust, use a "built-up" fluted edge. A high wall can hold more filling and also guard against spillage with more fluid mixtures.

Since pies are less formal desserts, keep it simple. Forget about the braids—a homemade look is just fine. Here are some good choices for attractive edges that are easy to make.

The spacing measurements below are approximate and may vary with your finger size.

ANGLED FLUTE
Using one hand, pinch the dough at a 45 degree angle between your thumb and forefinger while twisting slightly outward. Repeat at 1-inch intervals.

POINTED FLUTE

Pinch the dough between your thumb and forefinger. With your opposite hand, using your forefinger in a bent position, push into the dough to form a point. Repeat at 1-inch intervals. *Note:* Fingertips can be used in lieu of a bent forefinger.

SCALLOPED

Spread thumb and forefinger 1 inch apart and place on the inner edge of the crust. With the other forefinger, pull the dough toward the outer edge to form a scallop. Repeat at regular intervals.

POLKA-DOT SCALLOP

Repeat above procedure for a scalloped edge. Make 24 pea-size balls from scraps of dough. Moisten the bottom of the balls with egg wash and press into the scallops.

DECORATIVE SCALLOPED

Repeat above procedure for a scalloped edge. When complete, press into the scallops with a floured four-prong fork.

FORKED EDGE

Press a floured four-pronged fork into the dough at regular intervals. With each movement of the fork, support the dough with the forefinger of the opposite hand.

CROSSHATCH

Press a floured four-pronged fork into the dough at a 45 degree angle. Then repeat, reversing the angle of the fork. With each movement of the fork, support the dough with the forefinger of the opposite hand.

There are far fewer choices for finishing the edge of a tart than there are for a pie. The straight-sided, thin-edged metal pans that tarts are usually baked in do not lend themselves to a decorative edge. As a rule, tarts have only a bottom crust, leaving less pastry to work with. Because the surface of a tart is usually decorative, the fancy edge is not missed.

Many tarts with a shallow filling require no edge at all. For these, the rolling pin is run over the surface of the pan to cut the dough, leaving a clean, flush edge. Tarts that require deeper shells have edges that are built up. The pastry has a 1/2-inch overhang that is folded over to the inside edge of the pan, leaving a double thickness of dough. The pastry is pressed against the side, which pushes it upward—about 1/4 inch higher than the edge of the pan. The dough can either be left plain, pinched with a pastry crimper, or notched with the tip of a knife, as illustrated below.

CRIMPED EDGE

Starting with a built-up edge, press a floured pastry crimper into the dough at a 45 degree angle. Repeat, inserting the crimper into the impression left by the previous crimp. Each time you crimp, support the inner edge of the dough with the fingertips of your opposite hand.

NOTCHED EDGE

Starting with a built-up edge, press into the dough with the tip of closed scissors or the dull side of a table knife at each scallop of the tart pan.

Making Ornamental Pastry Cutouts

PASTRY CUTOUTS are easy finishing touches, transforming an ordinary pie or tart into something special. Cutouts are a great alternative to the decorative pie edges that are so hard to achieve with a delicate pastry. And the best part is that you won't have to compromise the quality of your pastry to make them.

Cutouts are made in the same manner as rolled cookies, except that pastry dough is used. They can be made ahead and stored in the refrigerator or freezer, either baked or unbaked. Just before serving, arrange them in a design or at random on top of the pie or tart. They can also be set into whipped cream rosettes or into ice cream atop individual portions.

Pastry trimmings are fine to use for a few spur-of-the-moment cutouts, but if you know you need the decorations in quantity, make extra dough. An additional half-recipe should be adequate for most needs. I use ordinary cookie cutters, no smaller than 1½ inches— dough shrinks when it bakes. Hearts, diamonds, triangles, and circles make great decorations. Leaves are pretty, too, but avoid shapes with too many curves. They break easily.

If you are artistic, try creating your own free-form designs. You can make apples, pears, and leaves in all sorts of sizes and shapes to lay on top of a baked pie. You can even make a jumbo cutout, such as a single pumpkin. Imagine how impressive this is when set on top of a pumpkin or sweet potato pie.

TO MAKE CUTOUTS WITH A COOKIE CUTTER

Roll the pastry to a ⅛-inch thickness. Cut the forms and place them on an ungreased cookie sheet. Chill for at least 30 minutes. *Note:* If the pastry becomes too soft to cut, carefully wrap it around a rolling pin; transfer it to a cookie sheet and chill it for a few minutes.

TO MAKE LEAF-SHAPED CUTOUTS

If you make leaves, it's nice to score impressions in the dough to simulate the veins. To do this, chill the cutouts for about 10 minutes to partially firm them.

Then, using a paring knife, cut *halfway* into the dough to make the grooves. By chilling the pastry first, the indentations are easier to make and the impressions will be more defined after baking. Then return the cookie sheet to the refrigerator for 20 minutes longer.

TO MAKE FREE-FORM CUTOUTS

Draw your design on a thin piece of cardboard. Cut it out and set the form on top of the rolled dough. Use a thin paring knife to cut around the template. Lift the cutout onto the cookie sheet, and chill it for about 30 minutes.

TO MAKE A PUMPKIN OR OTHER BIG SHAPE

Roll the pastry slightly thicker than ⅛ inch. After the form has been cut, chill it for 10 minutes to firm the dough. Then, if the cutout needs additional detail work, such as the vertical lines on a pumpkin, make the ridges or other lines with a paring knife. Chill the cutout again for at least 30 minutes.

To Bake the Cutouts

Preheat the oven to 375 degrees. Lightly brush the tops of the cutouts with 1 large egg white lightly beaten with 1 teaspoon water. Sprinkle the tops generously with granulated sugar—they will sparkle after baking. (A great-looking finish can be made with pearl sugar, but do not sprinkle it as heavily.) Bake the cutouts until lightly brown. Watch carefully; smaller ones will brown quickly. The time will vary from 10 to 15 minutes, according to size.

Fraisage

F RAISAGE COMES from the French verb *frasier,* which means "to knead." The term is commonly used for a procedure where the butter and flour crumbs for pastry dough are smeared with the heel of the hand to incorporate them together. This technique is especially desirable when making doughs that have a high fat content. Since electrical appliances easily overwork doughs, pastry finished by hand using the fraisage method ensures a tender pastry.

Lightly flour a clean, cool surface such as a marble or granite slab or countertop. Form the flour-butter crumb mixture into a mound. With the heel of your hand, smear 2 to 3 tablespoons of the mixture outward against the surface, making 6- to 8-inch-long sweeps. Continue the procedure until all of the mixture

has been worked into a dough. Repeat the process two or three times until the dough is fairly smooth. *Be careful not to overwork the dough or it will become too soft and impossible to mold into the pan.*

Rolling and Shaping Cookie-Style Doughs for Pies and Tarts

C OOKIE-STYLE DOUGHS are very fragile and do not hold together when transferred from the rolling surface to the pan. When a pastry dough is this buttery and soft, roll the dough either on plastic wrap or directly on the bottom portion of the tart pan.

Note: The following technique can also be used by those who have difficulty with traditional rolling methods or who have very warm hands.

These instructions are for rolling and shaping dough to fit metal tart pans. The pastry should be rolled 4 inches larger than the pan you are using.

Method 1

1. Tear two sheets of plastic wrap, 18 inches long. Overlap the sheets to make an 18-inch square.

2. Lightly flour the plastic wrap. Place the dough in the center. Sprinkle the top of the dough lightly with flour.

3. Tear two more sheets, and overlap them on top of the dough. Roll the pastry into the desired size. Turn the dough clockwise frequently to ensure even thickness. In addition, turn the dough over a few times when rolling.

4. Remove the top sheets of wrap and invert the dough over the tart pan.

5. Without removing the plastic wrap, gently press the dough into the pan. Be sure to mold it against the crease and into the grooves. Place the tart shell on a baking sheet. Chill the dough for 5 to 7 minutes, *no longer.*

6. Carefully peel off the plastic wrap. Run the rolling pin over the top of the pan to trim the edge. If the dough tears as the wrap is removed, or if the pastry has bare spots, repair them by pressing some of the selvage into the open spaces. Then chill the shaped dough for at least 30 minutes before baking. Proceed with directions for "Baking Blind," page 95.

Note: Method 1 can also be applied to pie plates. Follow the directions through step 5. Complete the edge by rolling the overhang under, then flute.

Method 2

1. Remove the wrapping from the pastry and place the dough in the center of the bottom portion of the metal tart pan, which has been anchored on a damp towel.

2. Lightly flour the surface, and lay a sheet of plastic wrap on

top of the dough. Roll the pastry to the edge of the metal. Lift the bottom portion with the pastry into the rim section of the pan. Do not remove the plastic wrap.

3. Place your hand flat on the pastry, with your thumb against the outer edge. With your hand, push the dough against the side, working your hand around the edge of the pan. Continue around the pan several times until you have pushed the pastry to the top of the rim.

4. Set the tart pan on a shallow pan and refrigerate the dough for 5 minutes. Carefully peel off the plastic wrap. If there are bare spots or areas where the dough is too thick, cover it again with the plastic wrap, and gently press.

5. Trim the edge of the dough by running a rolling pin over the edge. Remove any excess dough. Chill the pastry at least 30 minutes before baking. Proceed with directions for "Baking Blind," page 95.

Lining Tartlet and Other Small Pans

T HE SPECTRUM of tartlet pans available makes it necessary to give more than one method for lining the pans with pastry. Pans with removable bottoms are done differently from those with stationary bottoms. In addition, some doughs are more fragile than others. Refer to the various methods, and choose the one that is best suited for your recipe.

COOKIE-TYPE DOUGHS IN TARTLET PANS WITH REMOVABLE BOTTOMS

Cookie-type doughs make superb tart crusts, but the dough softens quickly and is difficult to roll. After baking, these shells must be handled with great care because they are so fragile.

For $4\frac{1}{2}$-inch tartlet pans, divide the pastry dough into 2-ounce pieces (adjust the amount for smaller pans). With lightly floured hands, roll each piece into a ball, then flatten it into a 2- to 3-inch disk.

METHOD 1—ROLLING PIN
Place the disk between two sheets of lightly floured plastic wrap. Roll the dough into a $5\frac{1}{2}$- to 6-inch circle. Remove the top piece of wrap, and invert the pastry onto the tartlet pan. Do not remove the plastic wrap. Press the pastry gently into the pan, molding it into the crease and grooves. Remove plastic wrap, place on a shallow pan with sides, and chill for at least 5 minutes.

METHOD 2—HAND
Place the disk in the center of the pan. With floured fingers, press the pastry dough against the bottom of the pan, gradually working it toward the side. Place your forefinger at the crease and ease the dough up the side, pushing it until it reaches the rim. Rotate the pan as you work. To even the bottom, place a sheet of plastic wrap against the dough. Using a batarde or a smooth-bottomed glass, press against the crease and then across the bottom. Remove plastic wrap, place on a shallow pan, and chill for at least 5 minutes.

TO BLIND BAKE
1. Preheat the oven to 375 degrees (for miniature tartlets, set the oven for 350 degrees). Position the oven shelf to the lower third of the oven.

2. Prick the pastry dough in several places with a fork.

3. Cut 6×6-inch pieces of aluminum foil. Butter or spray with nonstick coating, a 5-inch circle on each piece of foil. Place the foil, greased side down, into the tartlet pan. Mold it into the crease. Line with dried beans. For easier handling, keep the tartlet shells on the shallow pan when baking.

4. Bake for 16 to 18 minutes. Remove the foil and beans, and continue baking for 2 minutes longer. If the aluminum foil sticks, bake the shell another 1 to 2 minutes. The crust will crisp as it cools.

CLASSIC TART PASTRY IN TARTLET PANS WITHOUT REMOVABLE BOTTOMS

Classic tart pastry is more durable than cookie-style dough. The double pan method outlined here ensures a well-shaped tartlet shell and eliminates the need for baking beans, but more baking tins are needed. These tartlet shells are also very fragile.

1. On a lightly floured pastry cloth or a rolling surface, roll dough to slightly less than 1/8 inch thick. Prick well with a fork. Invert one of the pans you plan to use on top of the pastry, placing it on the upper right side of the pastry. With a pastry wheel, using the pan as a guide, cut around the pan allowing a 1/2-inch margin.

2. Turn the mold right side up and butter the inside. Lay the cut piece of dough over the top of the mold and gently press it in. Prick again with a fork. Let the dough rest a few minutes.

3. Butter the bottom of the second mold and insert it into the pastry-lined pan. Press the two together like a sandwich. Trim the edge with your fingers or a small knife. Place the double pans, inverted, on a shallow sheet pan.

4. Continue making shells until all of the dough is used. Chill the tartlets 30 minutes to relax the gluten

5. Preheat the oven to 425 degrees. Position the shelf in the lower third of the oven.

6. Bake the tartlet shells for 8 to 10 minutes or until the edge of the dough starts to brown. With the tip of a paring knife, remove the top molds.

7. Reduce the oven to 375 degrees. Lightly prick the tartlet shells again and return them to the oven. Bake for 4 to 5 minutes longer, or until the shells are golden brown. Let stand about 5 minutes, then gently lift the shells from the molds and place them on a rack to cool.

Shaping and Baking Free-Form Tart Shells

F REE-FORM TARTS are baked directly on a cookie sheet. The biggest advantage, other than not needing a tart pan, is that they can be made in any shape or size. The most common forms are rectangles and squares, however you can make hearts, diamonds, triangles, ovals, or any creative shapes you like.

Be sure to use a cookie-style pastry dough as the crumb is strong enough to support a filling when baked free-form. Some of the best choices are: Sweet Tart Pastry, Shortbread Tart Pastry, and Golden Cornmeal Pastry.

Do not use a pan with sides; large tarts will be easiest to remove by sliding them from the pan instead of lifting

1. Cut a piece of 18-inch wide heavy-duty aluminum foil measuring about 6 inches larger than the width of a cookie sheet.

2. Place the aluminum foil over the pan so that the ends extend over the sides. Tuck the ends under and smooth the surface.

3. Sprinkle the pan with 1 tablespoon of flour (use cornmeal for the Golden Cornmeal Pastry).

4. Place the pastry in the center of the pan. Sprinkle the top of the dough with a little flour.

5. Roll the dough, preferably with a tapered rolling pin, into a large circle, rectangle, or other shape. The dough should be rolled 2 inches larger than the desired finished size.

6. Fold the edge of the pastry under, about 1 inch, giving it a double thickness. Press the doubled layers together to form a wall. Finish with a pointed, fluted edge or one that is scalloped.

POINTED FLUTE (FREE-FORM)
Pinch the dough between your thumb and forefinger at 1-inch intervals.

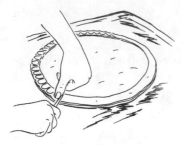

SCALLOPED EDGE
(FREE-FORM)

Spread thumb and forefinger 1 inch apart and place on inner edge of crust. With the opposite forefinger, pull the dough toward the outer edge, forming a scallop. Repeat at regular intervals.

Prick the center lightly with a fork (omit this step if baking with a filling). Chill for 30 minutes.

Preheat the oven to 375 degrees (use 350 degrees for smaller pastry shells). Position the oven shelf to the lower third of the oven. Bake the pastry until lightly browned. *The baking time will vary according to the type of dough used and the size of the pastry shell.* An average 11-inch tart shell will take approximately 18 to 20 minutes. If the center puffs up, tap it gently with the bottom of a fork to expel the air.

Cool the pastry shell before filling.

To remove the tart from the pan, run an oversize, long spatula under the pastry, and gently slide it on to a serving platter.

For directions on shaping and baking puff pastry, refer to pages 170–171.

Using Sealers and Glazes

EGGS

An egg wash plays many roles in the world of pastry. Not only can it be a protective coating (page 96) but it also is an excellent "glue" to seal pastry pieces together. A light brushing of egg wash along the edge of a turnover before sealing, when building an edge on a piece of puff pastry, or along the folds of a free-form tart all help keep the dough from separating during baking.

Dough can also be glazed with an egg wash to add color and gloss to your finished pastry. An egg yolk gives the deepest color, a whole egg imparts moderate color, and egg white leaves a pleasant sheen. If you wish to top your pastry with a sprinkling of sugar, chopped nuts, or even seeds, an egg wash is the surest way of keeping these finishing touches in place. Egg wash is also the best way to secure decorative pastry cutouts.

Note: While an egg wash is my preference, if you are not planning to use one for the top glazing of your pastry, or you would prefer to not use an egg at all, ice water can be used as an alternative for securing pieces of dough together.

MILK AND CREAM

A rustic glazing finish can be obtained from whole milk, heavy cream, or anything in between. Simply place 2 or 3 teaspoons of the liquid in a small dish and lightly brush the surface of the dough. Do not brush the edge of pies that require aluminum foil bands for baking; brush the top only, otherwise the foil will stick to the pastry.

Note: If glazing the surface of a pie or tart is done solely for esthetic reasons, and not for securing purposes, the top pastry can be left unglazed. Glazing is an option, not a rule.

Keeping the Juice from Running Out

THE PROBLEM OF A JUICY filling running over the top and the sides of a pie was just as great in the olden days as it is today, and the old cookbooks offered the following idea.

A splendid way to fix any juicy pie so it will not run out while baking: tear off a strip of cloth one-half inch wide and long enough to go around your plate or tin. Let half the width lap on your pie, and be sure to lap it good at the ends. Wet the cloth a little and squeeze it out dry.

—Gertrude Wilkinson, *The Attic Cookbook*

PRESERVES AND JELLIES

Apricot is the most popular preserve used in home kitchens for sealing and glazing pies and tarts. Its flavor complements, rather than overpowers, most fruit fillings. Next in line is currant jelly, followed by apple and quince. Feel free to experiment with these or other flavors and see which you like the best.

My preferred sealer is apricot because the preserve is more fruity and thicker than any jelly. I often brush strained preserves on the bottom of the pastry shell before the filling is added to prevent the crust from absorbing juices during baking. At times, I brush the preserves onto the surface of a baked pastry shell to retain crispness. For an even stronger sealer, the glazed baked shell can be returned to the oven to dry the surface. The flavor remains, but the moisture evaporates.

For glazing the tops of baked fruit tarts, apply the glaze shortly after removing the tarts from the oven. Not only does the glaze leave a mirrorlike sheen but it also seals the surface to preserve freshness and prevent the fruit from discoloring.

Tarts topped with fruit or berries that do not require baking are treated the opposite of baked fruit tarts. The glaze is applied shortly before serving, or no more than an hour or two ahead. While a glaze enhances color and provides flavor, once it is applied to fresh fruits and berries, the fruit begins to deteriorate and becomes soggy.

APRICOT GLAZE

While this recipe is adequate for 1 large (11-inch) tart, I often prepare a whole jar to keep on hand in the refrigerator. Since preserves have a long shelf life, it will save you time—just heat up what you need. When purchasing, be sure to buy good quality preserves; less expensive brands contain too much water. If your preserves are thin, cook the preserves longer to evaporate some of the liquid.

Place 3 tablespoons thick apricot preserves and 1 teaspoon water in an ovenproof glass container. Heat in a microwave on medium setting for 15 to 20 seconds or until bubbly. *Pass through a fine-gauge mesh strainer. Brush on while still warm. Makes enough for an 11-inch tart.

JELLY GLAZE

Place 3 tablespoons jelly in an ovenproof glass container. Heat in a microwave on medium setting for 15 to 20 seconds or until it is melted. *Brush on while still warm. Makes enough for an 11-inch tart.

*Note: Alternatively, cook in a small saucepan on direct heat until bubbly.

VANILLA GLAZE

Combine 1 cup strained confectioners' sugar, 4 teaspoons boiling water, 1 1/2 teaspoons corn syrup, and 1/2 teaspoon vanilla extract in a small bowl. Blend the ingredients with a wire whisk, mixing until smooth. Dip a fork into the glaze and drizzle over the pastry. Makes enough for an 11-inch pie or tart or 12 turnovers.

Helping a Bottom Crust to Brown

THE NEMESIS of pies is an underbaked, soggy bottom crust. The most common victims are pies made from fresh fruits and berries and those with fluid fillings, such as custards. Tarts can be affected, too, but pies are the greater problem. This is because a pie plate is considerably deeper than a tart pan. It holds much more filling, and there is less air surface in which the liquid can evaporate.

While all of the recipes in this book have been written to eliminate as much liquid as possible, there are times when Mother Nature takes over. No matter what precautions you take, she may win out. Listed here are a few measures to encourage the browning of the bottom crust.

◆ *Wipe pieces of fresh fruit with damp towels instead of dousing them* with water. Submerge fresh berries briefly in water; don't let them sit. For further cleaning instructions, refer to the Fruit and Berry Glossary (page 17).

✦ Pre-cook the fillings of very juicy fresh fruits, then drain off some of the liquid before placing them in pastry shells. Some of the juiciest offenders are peaches, blueberries, blackberries, raspberries, strawberries, and rhubarb.

✦ Sprinkle a layer of finely chopped nuts or dry bread crumbs, zwieback, or other less rich cookie crumbs on the bottom of the pastry shell before adding the filling.

✦ Patch any cracks or holes in the pastry dough.

✦ Place the unbaked pie or tart on a preheated shiny metal cookie sheet.

✦ Place the unbaked pie or tart on a heavy-duty, dark metal cookie sheet, such as one made by Calphalon. Do not preheat.

✦ Place the unbaked pie or tart on a preheated pizza stone. Clay tiles can also be used, but be sure to allow enough air to circulate in the oven.

✦ Avoid baking in aluminum foil pans; they are poor conductors of heat. If you must use these, place the pan on a preheated light or dark metal cookie sheet. You can also insert the pie into a second, larger pie plate, preferably made of ovenproof glass.

✦ It is wise to place the baked pie or tart on a cooling rack. This allows the air to circulate underneath the pastry to prevent the buildup of condensation.

Garnishing and Decorating

F INISHING THE top of a pie or tart with an ornamental flourish from a pastry bag or the zigzag of a pastry comb transforms an ordinary dessert into a showpiece. Such touches as abstract squiggles and streaks of a brightly colored coulis under a tartlet can bring drama to a table.

To create these beautiful garnishes takes only a small investment in decorating equipment (page 48) and a little patience and creativity. In this book, all of the designs for decorated pies and tarts are detailed in the individual recipes. You can follow the directions for my suggested designs or use your imagination and create your own.

In this book, the primary mediums for decorating are whipped cream, cream-based fillings, and meringue. Always use large pastry tips, never small ones, for lightened mixtures such as these. Openings on smaller tips will cause the air cells to burst. Small pastry tips are used with a coupler for line or detail work.

What follows are helpful hints and techniques to guide you through the fundamentals of decorating.

USING A PASTRY BAG

Holding the pastry bag in one hand, form a cuff by folding the edge of the bag, about one-fourth to one-third down the length of the bag. Insert the pastry tip. Using a large rubber spatula, fill the pastry bag about one-third to one-half full with whipped cream or other mixture to be piped. Do not overfill the bag. Turn up the cuff and twist the top of the pastry bag to gently push the filling toward the tip.

Using your thumb and forefinger, grasp the pastry bag at the level of the filling. Wrap your fingers around the front of the bag and position your thumb across the twisted opening. Press your fingers and thumb directly on the bag to force the filling out. Your opposite hand should be placed underneath the bag and only be used to steer the movement of the bag. Do not squeeze the pastry bag with both hands. Use only your dominant hand or the filling will overflow from the top.

As you begin to form your design, tilt the pastry bag slightly so you are holding it at a 90 degree angle (almost straight up). The decorating tip should almost touch the top of the pie or tart, about $1/2$ inch above the surface. When you complete each decoration, dip the bag down, then lift it up. This will break or stop the flow.

SPACING A DESIGN

With the aid of toothpicks, your design can be evenly spaced. My handy rule of thumb is to imagine the face of a clock. Insert toothpicks at 12 o'clock and 6 o'clock. This divides the surface in half. Now place toothpicks at 3 o'clock and 9 o'clock, dividing your surface into quarters.

The spaces can be further divided by placing 2 toothpicks, at equal distances, in each quarter. You will now have 12 design points, one for each number on the face of the clock. If more or fewer points are desired, adjust the markings accordingly.

DECORATING WITH A SQUEEZE BOTTLE

Plastic squeeze bottles have become a popular tool for garnishing plated desserts. They are filled with a slightly thick, smooth mixture that will flow from the tip without excessive dripping. Colorful free-form designs can be done on the surface of a plate or over a shallow pool of crème anglaise. If using the crème anglaise, run the point of a toothpick or the tip of a knife lightly through the pattern to bleed the mixtures together.

Good candidates are raspberry and mango coulis. Thick sauces like butterscotch and chocolate ganache are also recommended, but they must first be warmed. Test the flow of the sauce before you completely fill the bottle. Achieving the proper consistency may take a little practice.

Releasing a Tart From Its Pan

R EMOVING A TART from its pan is not as difficult as it may appear. In fact, it's easy. Place the tart pan on top of a coffee can or a can of similar size. The rim will drop to the counter. Run a long, thin spatula between the crust and the bottom metal disk. Carefully lift the tart off the can. Position the serving plate on the counter, toward the upper right-hand corner of the tart (use the opposite side if you are left-handed). Use the spatula to ease it gently off the metal disk and onto the serving platter.

Cutting and Serving Pies and Tarts

T HERE IS NO way to state an exact time that a pie or tart must stand before it is cut. However, a good thing to remember is that heat expands while cold contracts.

Every filling has its own requirements. Tarts can always be cut sooner than pies because, as a rule, they contain less filling. A shallow fruit tart can usually be cut within 30 minutes of baking. Tarts that have deeper fruit fillings should stand 2 to 3 hours to allow the juices to reabsorb. Fruit pies must stand a minimum of 4 hours. But these times will fluctuate with the moisture content of the fruit. A pie that is cut 1 hour after baking will gush with liquid, while the same pie cut 6 hours later will release just a little. If left uncut overnight, it will release none.

Other pies such as pecan and pumpkin have to cool down long enough to set; 2 to 3 hours is usually sufficient. Savory pies should stand 15 to 20 minutes before slicing. Cream and cooked custard fillings, and those with gelatin bases, will set as they cool. Those that require refrigeration will have to stand at least several hours. Test the firmness by jiggling the pan slightly to see if the filling is still loose or by tapping the surface lightly with your finger. Cobblers are meant to be juicy and can be cut soon after baking.

Here are some tips on cutting and serving the pastries.

✦ *When cutting pies or tarts, always use a sharp knife with a blade of about 6 inches.*

✦ *Pies will cut better if the knife is first dipped in warm water.*

◆ Be sure to release the pie from the edge of the plate before you attempt to remove the slices. To do this, run a sharp knife around the edge.

◆ Because pies can be difficult to remove from the pan, the first slice is for the cook!

◆ For many pies, a short, square spatula is more efficient than a wedge-shaped server. After the first piece is removed, lift the slices from the side instead of the outer edge.

Storing Pies, Tarts, and Cobblers

M OST FRUIT PIES, tarts, cobblers, and other pastries that do not contain dairy products can be kept at room temperature the day they are baked. But pastries made with eggs, cream, or other highly perishable ingredients should be refrigerated as soon as possible after preparing.

While storage and wrapping instructions have been given with each recipe, the following is a brief roundup.

◆ If the pastry contains a fruit filling, wrap first with a sheet of waxed paper, then cover with aluminum foil. This will prevent contact between the acidic filling and the aluminum foil.

◆ A plastic wrap covering is not recommended for pastries with moist fillings. This type of airtight covering causes condensation and will result in a soggy crust. Very few pies, tarts, or other such pastries should be wrapped airtight unless they are to be frozen. Remember, pastries need to breathe.

Reheating Pies, Tarts, and Cobblers

O THER THAN refrigerated whipped cream–style pastries, most pies, tarts, and cobblers benefit from a brief freshening in the oven. As pastries age, flaky crusts often turn soft and limp. This is especially true of those with fruit fillings. Reheating pies, tarts, and cobblers brings the pastry back to life and greatly enhances the taste of the filling as well.

For best results, heat pies, tarts, and cobblers in a conventional oven. A toaster oven will do for smaller pieces, but *never* reheat pastry in a microwave oven—this type of heat is a disaster for crusts because it makes them soggy.

Individual or small pieces of pastry can be left uncovered for reheating. When reheating a whole pie, lay a sheet of aluminum foil loosely over the top to prevent it from drying out. Remove the foil covering during the last 5 to 10 minutes for a fi-

Using "At a Glance"

THE "AT A GLANCE" BOXES throughout the book were written to give the baker a quick overview of key information in each recipe.

◆ They list the number of people a recipe serves—rather than the number of servings. For example, a pie that serves 6 to 8 people allows enough for some second helpings.

◆ The pan size lists the primary pan used in each recipe. Auxiliary pans such as shallow baking pans that might be used to set a pie or tart pan on during baking, are not included here.

◆ Pastry Prep indicates the state of the dough when you *begin* the recipe.

◆ The oven temperature and baking time are self explanatory but could vary according to individual oven.

◆ The level of difficulty ranges from 1 to 3 pie symbols. It is based on the length of time needed for preparation and/or the intricacy of the recipe.

◆ Uses for pastry doughs and crunchy shells are my recommendations, but feel free to experiment.

nal crisping. Bake in a low to moderate (325 to 350 degrees) oven until heated through

The reheating time will depend on whether you are warming a single piece or a whole pie. The estimated time for an individual serving is 5 to 7 minutes, while a whole pie or tart could take 20 to 30 minutes, depending upon size, density, and height.

Freezing Pies, Tarts, and Cobblers

MOST FRUIT PIES and tarts can be frozen before or after baking. If freezing them after assembling, but unbaked, the tradeoff is a better crust at the time of baking but a wet filling. If freezing after baking, the pastry loses some of its crispness but the filling will not be wet. Cobblers and crisps freeze very well before they are baked. A soupy bottom is irrelevant when there is no underlying crust. The extra juices are wonderful spooned over ice cream.

While no pie, tart, or cobbler is ever quite as good after it has been frozen, freezing is a great time-saver and is necessary on occasion. When this is the case, my preference is to freeze pies and tarts after they have been baked, while cobblers and crisps are best frozen before baking. Whatever method you choose, your final result is still far better than store-bought pastry.

WRAPPING PASTRIES FOR FREEZING

I partially freeze my filled pastry (unbaked or baked and cooled) before I wrap it to protect the surface from being mashed or damaged. For easier handling, place the pastry on a shallow baking pan and put it in the freezer until the surface is hard. After it is firm, cover it.

To wrap the pastry, tear off a long sheet of 18-inch-wide heavy-duty aluminum foil and set the container in the middle. Bring the ends to the center and make a butcher or drugstore fold. Press the air from the side openings, fold the ends, and tuck the tabs underneath. Press the foil gently against the container to remove any excess air.

Label with the name of the pastry and the date. Put the wrapped pastry in a plastic bag, press out the air, secure it with a twist tie, and freeze.

PREPARING FROZEN PASTRIES

PRE-BAKED PASTRIES Remove the outer plastic wrapping from the frozen pastry. Loosen the foil slightly by pulling up the tabs from under the pan. *Do not remove the foil.* The wrapping protects the pastry from over-browning on the outside before it can thaw on the inside.

Place the wrapped frozen pastry in a preheated 325 to 350 degree oven and bake until it is heated through. Test by inserting a toothpick through the aluminum foil. Thawing could take up to 1 hour, depending on the size of the pastry. When the toothpick slides in easily and feels warm to the touch, open the aluminum foil and continue to bake until the crust is crisp.

Note: If a pie or cobbler was frozen in an overproof glass container, begin the baking in a cold oven. Then heat the oven to 350 degrees and proceed with the baking directions. Starting the pie in an unlit oven prevents the glass from cracking. (Tempered glass should not break if it is not exposed to sudden, extreme heat; and if moisture from the bottom of the pan does not come in contact with the hot metal shelf. Placing the plate on a sheet of aluminum foil provides a barrier between the oven shelf and the glass plate.)

Alternatively, a frozen pie or tart can be slowly thawed in the refrigerator for a day or two. When completely thawed, remove the wrapping. Preheat the oven to 350 degrees. If using heatproof glass, place the container on a sheet of aluminum foil before baking. Warm the pie until it is heated through. The time will depend upon its size, height, and the density of the filling. If the top starts to brown too quickly, lay a sheet of aluminum foil loosely over the surface.

BAVARIAN CREAM AND MOUSSE-TYPE FILLINGS Remove all of the plastic and foil wrappings. Place a sheet of aluminum foil loosely over the pastry, tucking the sides in. This will prevent the surface of the pie from discoloring or drying out. Refrigerate the pastry until thawed. This will take anywhere from 12 to 24 hours depending upon its size and the height and density of the filling.

UNBAKED PASTRIES Remove the plastic and aluminum foil wrapping from the pie or tart. Place the frozen pastry on a shallow baking pan. To prevent the edges from burning, make aluminum foil bands. Cut two 3-inch-wide strips of 18-inch heavy-duty aluminum foil. Fold 1 inch of each strip to the center, making a double-thick foil. Mold the foil around the edge of the pie keeping the double fold on top of the dough. Secure the bands with tape.

Preheat the oven to 350 degrees. Position the oven shelf to the lower third of the oven. Bake the frozen pie or tart on a shallow baking pan for 25 to 30 minutes, or until a toothpick can be inserted through the center. If it shows resistance, the filling is not completely thawed. The thawing time is determined by the size, density, and height of the filling.

Note: If the pie was frozen in heatproof glass, set the plate on a sheet of aluminum foil, then on the baking pan. Place the pie in an unlit oven, then heat the oven and bake the pie for 30 to 35 minutes, or until a toothpick can be inserted through the center.

When the pastry is thawed, increase the oven temperature to 400 degrees. Continue baking until the filling begins to bubble and the crust is browned. If the top is browning too quickly, lay a sheet of aluminum foil loosely over the surface.

Freezing Pastry Doughs

M OST OF THE pastry doughs in this book can be frozen before or after rolling and shaping.

✦ *Sweet Cream Biscuit Dough, page 140*

✦ *Vegetable Oil Pastry and variations, page 140*

✦ *Press-On Butter Pastry, page 158*

Some pastry doughs can only be frozen *after* shaping. Those are:

✦ *All-Nut Pastry Shell, page 163*

✦ *Crumb Crusts, pages 164–169*

Meringue shells of any sort can be frozen but their crispy texture may suffer.

Thawing shaped crusts before filling is optional, depending on the nature of the filling.

UNSHAPED PASTRY DOUGHS

Shape the pastry dough into disks as directed in the recipe.

Place the disks in a labeled and dated plastic bag. Press to remove all the air, secure with a twist tie, and freeze.

To thaw the dough, remove the disks from the freezer and thaw in the refrigerator for several hours, or preferably overnight. Before shaping, let stand at room temperature about 30 minutes or until soft enough to roll.

ROLLED AND SHAPED PASTRY DOUGHS

After the pastry dough has been rolled and shaped, place the pie or tart shell on a shallow sheet pan and freeze until hard. Remove it from the shallow pan. Cover the pastry shell with plastic wrap, pressing well to remove all of the air. Place the wrapped shell in a large plastic bag. Press to remove all the air, secure with a twist tie, and freeze.

Individual tartlet shells are treated in the same manner. Wrap each separately, and after they are frozen, nest them in an airtight plastic bag.

When ready to bake the pastry shell, remove the wrapping and place it on a shallow baking pan. Proceed with the baking directions given for each individual recipe. The pastry shell does not have to be thawed before baking, however the baking time will have to be increased by 5 to 10 minutes.

Pastry Problem Solving

IF THE PASTRY IS NOT SMOOTH . . .

✦ The flour was lumpy.

✦ The board and rolling pin were not kept clean.

✦ Fresh flour was not used for rolling.

IF THE PASTRY IS TOO STICKY TO HANDLE . . .

✦ Too much liquid was added.

✦ The dough was handled too much.

✦ The baker's hands are too hot—wash often in cold water.

✦ The baker's hands are sticky—wash them.

✦ The rolling surface was not kept clean.

IF THE PASTRY FALLS APART WHEN SHAPING . . .

✦ Not enough liquid was added.

✦ The liquid was not evenly distributed through the flour.

IF THE PASTRY STICKS TO THE ROLLING SURFACE . . .

✦ There was not enough flour on the rolling surface.

✦ The pastry was overworked.

✦ The rolling surface was not smooth.

✦ The pastry was not rotated.

IF THE PASTRY CRACKS WHEN ROLLED . . .

✦ The pastry was too cold.

✦ The pastry did not have enough liquid in it.

✦ The pastry needed more time to absorb the liquid.

✦ The pastry disk was improperly shaped.

IF THE PASTRY DOES NOT SPREAD WHEN ROLLED . . .

✦ The dough was too cold.

✦ The dough has stuck onto the rolling surface.

✦ The rolling surface was not floured enough.

✦ Not enough pressure was applied to the middle of the dough.

✦ Too much pressure was applied to the ends of the dough.

IF YOU HAVE TROUBLE ROLLING LENGTH . . .

✦ After making dough, it should be molded in the same shape that it will be rolled into.

✦ Too much pressure was applied at the edge of the dough.

✦ Not enough pressure was applied in the center of the dough.

✦ Width of the dough was not established before length.

IF YOUR PASTRY CIRCLE HAS AN IRREGULAR SHAPE . . .

✦ Pastry disk was improperly shaped.

✦ Pastry was not given a quarter turn periodically when rolled.

✦ There is not enough attention paid to shape while rolling.

✦ There was too much rolling-pin pressure at the edge of the dough.

✦ There was not enough pressure applied in the center of the dough.

IF PASTRY SHELL IS POORLY SHAPED OR SHRUNK TOO MUCH . . .

✦ Pastry was stretched in pan.

✦ Pastry was not chilled long enough.

✦ Pastry was not pressed firmly against the crease of the pan.

✦ Pastry was not pressed firmly against the side of the pan.

✦ Pastry was not pricked enough on bottom and side.

✦ Aluminum foil was not molded well against the crease of the pan.

IF BOTTOM CRUST IS SOGGY . . .

✦ Filling is too wet.

✦ Filling did not contain enough thickening.

✦ Pie or tart was cut when too hot.

✦ Improper baking pan was used.

✦ Not enough heat reached bottom crust during baking.

IF BOTTOM CRUST DOES NOT BROWN . . .

✦ Crust was not baked long enough.

✦ Improper baking pan was used.

✦ Not enough heat reached bottom crust during baking.

✦ Incorrect oven temperature.

IF THERE IS A LARGE SPACE BETWEEN THE TOP CRUST AND FILLING . . .

✦ The top pastry was stretched.

✦ The pastry was too thick.

2

The Primer

HEN I SET OUT to write a book on pies and tarts, I wanted to share everything I knew about making them with anyone who expressed even the slightest interest. ✳ Teaching baking and cooking has brought me pleasure for more than 25 years. During this time, I have come in contact with thousands of students who, like myself, love to bake. But, all too often, the mere suggestion of attempting a pie or tart from scratch has been met with a look of terror from these students. Why should the anticipation of making and rolling out a pastry dough signal such panic? You would think I was asking them to rocket to the moon, solo. ✳ In 1995, when I attended a pie baking event at a public school in San Antonio, Texas, one

THE PRIMER

hundred fourth-grade students made apple pies from scratch. It was a thrill to see the pride and satisfaction in their faces. No fear, just joy. Unlike adults, these girls and boys didn't know that they were supposed to be afraid. No one had told them; they were just having a good time. The old adage ignorance is bliss certainly held true.

In light of this, I decided to create a "primer," or teaching section, as part of this book. It is divided into two parts. The first zeros in on how to make and roll out two foundation doughs: an American-style pie pastry and a French-style tart pastry. Both recipes give directions for preparation by hand and in a food processor.

The second part is devoted to making four of the most popular kinds of pies and tarts. There are recipes for two American classics: a terrific apple pie and a fail-proof lemon meringue. For the tarts, I have a traditional European-style pear tart and a refreshing French fruit tart filled with pastry cream. These are foundation, or "mother," recipes upon which countless variations can be built. You'll find the principles will remain the same; only the ingredients change.

The detailed instructions and illustrations in The Primer are designed to eliminate guesswork. I have tried to share all my tips, techniques, and tricks to help you bridge the gap from fear to fun. Keep practicing these recipes until you have them down pat. They will lead you to an unlimited repertoire of new and delicious sweet and savory pastries.

Remember, baking pies and tarts is a timeless art and one that can be so pleasurable. Forget about those silly old wives' tales about rolling out dough. You might find that this step really is fun.

The PASTRY PRIMER

 WO ALL-PURPOSE DOUGHS will cover most of your pastry needs: American-style pie pastry and French-style tart pastry. Both crusts are equally delicious. ∗ The American-style dough, Flaky Pie Pastry, is the more delicate of the two. Flaky Pie Pastry is best to use for pies because pies are served directly from the pan in which they are baked. Since the pan supports the crust, its fragile nature does not pose

a problem. Conversely, the French-style dough, Classic Tart Pastry, bakes into a sturdier crust that can successfully be unmolded. This makes it the best choice for tarts, which are commonly removed from the pan.

WHAT MAKES
DOUGH DOUGH?

PIE OR TART PASTRY is made from one or a combination of flours or meals that are blended with fat and worked into crumbs. The fat "shortens" or cuts the flour proteins and prevents them from becoming elastic. When a liquid is added, the crumbs bind together and form a mass. That mass is called "dough."

The liquid in dough, which is most commonly water, forms steam in the oven. Steam forces the layers of fat-coated flour to expand and separate. As the dough bakes, the moisture evaporates, the dough dries and leaves a multitude of layered flakes that form a casing called "crust."

HOW DO THESE
TWO DOUGHS DIFFER?

FLAKY PIE PASTRY and Classic Tart Pastry are both made from the same ingredients. While there are subtle differences in the quantities used, of greater significance is the manner in which the fats are incorporated and the size and shape of the final fat-flour particles.

Both pastries start with a combination of butter and vegetable shortening that is either rubbed or cut into the flour. Flaky Pie Pastry has larger pea-size particles of fat, which form larger flakes after baking. Classic Tart Pastry is worked into smaller meallike bits that

What Is the Difference
Between a Pie and a Tart?

ALTHOUGH PIES AND TARTS may seem similar, each has unique qualities. The greatest difference is that a pie is always served from the container it is baked in, and a tart is always unmolded from the pan. Pies are more homey and tarts more formal. Pies are higher than tarts, and usually double-crusted or have their fillings covered. The fillings of tarts are commonly left exposed, with surfaces that are often decorative and colorful.

form smaller flakes. Though still delicate, the smaller flakes in the tart pastry bake into more compact layers, and thus are stronger.

THE HAND VS. THE FOOD PROCESSOR

IN YEARS PAST, pastry dough was primarily made by hand. This timeless method did, and still can, produce some of the finest pastry you will ever taste. Generally, when you use hands you have more control working fats into flour to form crumbs. Also, you are less likely to add too much liquid or overwork the dough. Overworked dough becomes too soft, is difficult to roll, and turns tough after baking. Bakers with cool hands and a light touch will have less trouble making pastry by hand than those who have warmer hands or lack a gentler touch. For those who have the time and enjoy the art of doing hands-on pastry, this is the method for you.

Today, with the aid of a food processor, cutting the fats into the flour can be accomplished successfully. The drawback, however, is that the crumbs can bind into a sticky ball in a matter of seconds, before any or sufficient liquid is added. In addition, the dough can form a wet mass around the steel blade before all of the particles have been absorbed. This can be troublesome since an even distribution of liquid throughout the dough is crucial to a tender pastry. For these reasons, after the fats are cut into the flour, I recommend emptying the crumb mixture into a large bowl and adding the liquid by hand. However, if this intimidates you, with careful timing you can add the liquid to the crumbs in the processor.

WHAT IS MEANT BY OVERWORKING THE DOUGH?

WHEN PASTRY DOUGH is overworked by hand or machine, the layers of flour-coated fat mash together. Not only does this destroy the layers of crumbs but also the pasty mass cannot absorb enough water. Without water, little or no steam can form in the oven to expand the layers.

WHEN IS A DOUGH READY TO ROLL?

PASTRY SHOULD BE chilled in the refrigerator at least 30 to 45 minutes before rolling. This allows the liquid to permeate through the dough, the fats to firm, and the gluten to relax.

Pastry that chills for longer periods will be too hard to roll. Remove it from refrigerator and let it rest 30 to 45 minutes or until soft enough for you to make a slight indentation on the surface of the dough.

Frozen dough should be removed from the freezer and thawed overnight in the refrigerator. Then let it stand at room temperature for 45 to 60 minutes or until soft enough for you to make a slight indentation on the surface of the dough.

TOOLS FOR ROLLING

MY FORMULA FOR ROLLING doughs is to keep it simple. All you need is the proper rolling pin and a suitable surface. Avoid equipment with unnecessary gimmickry and stick to the well- made, higher-quality basics.

While many types of rolling pins are available, each serves a different function. The following four types are the ones I most frequently use:

AMERICAN BALL BEARING PIN *(cylinder size: 12 inches)*: Two-handled, multipurpose, heavyweight, made from hardwood. Ball bearings facilitate longer, smoother rolling strokes. More expensive than the French pins, but the best for home bakers. In my opinion, it's the easiest to use for most rolling needs.

AMERICAN-STYLE BALL BEARING, HEAVY-DUTY PIN *(15 inches)*: Same advantages as the 12-inch ball-bearing pin. The extra weight aids in stretching larger pieces of dough. This is recommended for puff pastry and other butter-layered doughs. Most expensive.

STRAIGHT FRENCH PIN *(17 to 19 inches)*: Medium weight, barrel shaped, well balanced, inexpensive. This is the most popular with professional pastry chefs. With experience, it gives the most even, controlled roll.

TAPERED FRENCH PIN *(19 to 21 inches)*: Lighter in weight than the straight French rolling pin, inexpensive. Recommended for rolling thinner doughs or doughs that must be stretched. This pin is also good for rolling pastry into circles and ovals.

THE ROLLING SURFACE

ONE OF THE MOST asked questions from my students is, "Don't I have to roll my dough on marble?" My answer: "Absolutely *not!*" While marble has its place in rolling pastry, almost any flat, hard

What is a roofless cathedral compared to a well-built pie?

WILLIAM MAGINN, *1793–1842*

surface will work. Besides marble, such surfaces as granite, Corian, Formica, and wood can be used. My favorite rolling surface is a large wooden pastry board covered with a canvas cloth or linen dish towel. To keep any movable board from sliding, I always anchor it by placing it on top of a damp linen towel or several layers of moistened paper towels.

While all of The Primer doughs can be rolled on the surfaces just mentioned, some bakers who have difficulty rolling pastry feel more comfortable rolling it between two sheets of plastic wrap. This method is more commonly used for fragile doughs, however if you can't master the rolling techniques in The Primer, by all means use plastic wrap. For more information, refer to "Rolling and Shaping Cookie-Style Doughs" (page 69). The same techniques can be used for most basic pastry doughs.

"Roll Around the Clock"
The Key to a Perfect Circle

WHEN YOU BEGIN TO ROLL the dough, imagine that the pastry disk is the face of the clock. Start from the center and roll toward 12 o'clock. Then roll in the opposite direction to 6 o'clock, then to 3 o'clock, and finally to 9 o'clock.

Each time you roll, the starting position of the rolling pin should be from the center.

Roll around the clock again, beginning at 12 o'clock. This time roll to 1 o'clock, 2 o'clock, and so on until you roll full circle. Repeat the procedure 2 or 3 times, always starting at the center. Roll until the desired size has been reached.

✦ Always relax the rolling pressure as you reach the edge of the dough, otherwise the edge will be too thin.

✦ Do not roll the pin back and forth over the pastry.

✦ Do not turn the pastry over.

✦ For even thickness, give the pastry a quarter-turn frequently. (Most people apply more pressure on their dominant side.)

✦ To resolve irregular shaping of dough, see opposite.

Rolling and Shaping Tips

✦ Don't attempt to roll pastry when it is too cold—it will crack.

✦ Keep a pile of clean flour for rolling dough in the upper right-hand corner of your rolling surface (opposite side if you are left-handed).

✦ The rolling surface *must* be kept clean of dough particles. Scrape and re-flour as needed. For easy clean-up, use a sheet of waxed paper at the end of the board to catch scrapings.

✦ *Always work from clean to dirty.* Assuming you are right-handed, fresh flour to your right, scrapings to your left. *The center should be clean for rolling.*

✦ Do *not* continue to roll dough if it doesn't spread. This is an indication that the pastry is stuck to the rolling surface. Carefully release the pastry with a dough scraper, draping it over the rolling pin. Then re-flour the surface and continue.

✦ To resolve irregular shaping of dough, such as uneven circles, squares, or rectangles, angle the end of the rolling pin toward the area that needs filling, then roll. This movement will ease the dough toward the precise spot where it is needed. Repeat the motion until the dough is properly shaped **1**.

✦ Cracks in dough can easily be repaired with a piece of pastry trimmed from the edge. Lay the patching dough over the split, then re-flour your rolling pin and lightly roll over the patched surface **2**.

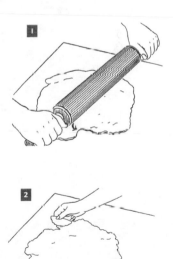

✦ Don't discard pastry scraps or gather them together until after the pie or tart is completed. Put them aside. You may need these pieces for patching damaged crust.

✦ Recycle unused dough for decorations. Place scraps on a sheet of plastic wrap, pull the corners up, and gently squeeze the pieces together. Avoid touching dough directly with your hands. After wrapping, chill until firm enough to roll.

For additional tips on rolling, see "Pastry Problem Solving" (page 79).

THE PASTRY CLOTH
AND ROLLING PIN COVER

A PASTRY CLOTH is a large rectangular piece of canvas that covers a rolling surface. It is specially treated to prevent dough from sticking. The rolling pin cover is a stocking that fits over the barrel of a rolling pin. By rubbing a generous amount of flour into the weave of the cloth and rolling pin cover, you create a nonstick coating, enabling you to roll dough more easily than you've ever been able to before.

The benefits of the pastry cloth and rolling pin cover are:

✦ *Less flour is absorbed into the dough.*

✦ *Pastry will not stick as readily to the rolling surface.*

✦ *Pastry can be rotated freely. This allows you to turn the dough so that its thickness will be uniform.*

✦ *When moving the dough from the rolling surface to the baking pan, the cloth supports the dough as you wrap it over the rolling pin.*

The cloth and cover can be used two or three times before washing, depending on how soiled they become. Be sure to use both sides. If you plan on using the cloth and sleeve within a few days after the initial use, unless very soiled, shake the excess flour from the cloth and scrape any dough from the surface. Roll the covered rolling pin into the canvas, place in a plastic bag, and store in the refrigerator to prevent bacteria from forming.

While many brands are available, I highly recommend the canvas cloth and rolling pin cover set made by Ateco. It is easy to care for—simply put it in the washing machine and dryer along with your dish towels. No special handling is necessary, but after drying, *do not fold* it because the creases will leave an imprint on your pastry. To store, place the rolling pin cover inside the cloth and wrap it around the rolling pin. With proper care, this equipment will last for years.

Although the pastry cloth can be used on any flat surface, it is best to place it on a nonslippery surface like a pastry board or large cutting board. This will prevent the cloth from sliding when you roll the dough. If the cloth is large enough, tuck the ends under the edge of the cutting board. Otherwise, just lay it on the board.

Rub 3 to 4 tablespoons of all-purpose flour *very well* into the weave of the canvas, covering at least a 16-inch area. Then rub about 2 tablespoons of flour into the rolling pin cover. You are now ready to roll.

How to Line the Pie Plate with Pastry

1. Thoroughly butter the bottom, sides, and rim of an oven-proof glass pie plate.

2. Position the rolling pin 4 inches from the *top* of the pastry. Lift the dough over the top of the rolling pin and gently roll the dough toward you.

3. Lift the pastry up. Be sure to keep a finger pressed against the barrel of the rolling pin to keep it from slipping. Position the pastry, leaving about 2 inches of dough hanging over the edge of the pan on the side closest to you. Then unroll the pastry over the pie plate, moving the pin away from you **1**.

4. Drape the dough loosely into the pan, molding it into the crease. To do this, place your fingers against the side of the pan, and gently push the dough down toward the crease. **2** Do this around the entire pan. *Be careful not to stretch the dough.*

5. Trim the edge with scissors leaving a $^1/_4$- to 1-inch overhang. The size is determined by the type of finished edge you plan to use (see "Sealing the Edge," page 92).

Note: If the pie shell is to be filled before baking, be sure to leave some additional dough around the edge because the weight of the filling will cause the dough to "draw in" or contract.

✦ IF MAKING A SINGLE-CRUST PIE, BAKED WITHOUT A FILLING (*Baking Blind*) After the dough is shaped, *lightly* prick the bottom and sides with a fork at $^1/_2$- to 1-inch intervals. Do not pierce too deeply or the filling may seep through the crust. Place the pie plate on a half-sheet or jelly-roll pan and refrigerate at least 15 minutes. Proceed with directions for "Baking Blind" (page 95).

MAKING A TOP CRUST
FOR A DOUBLE-CRUST PIE

1. Re-flour the rolling surface and rolling pin. Roll pastry using the same procedure as for the bottom crust.

2. Place the pastry on top of the filling. If using uncooked fruit that is mounded higher than the level of the pan, gently push the dough up toward the center, placing your hands on top of the pastry and easing it toward the middle. **1** This eliminates the open pocket that can form if the top crust does not drop with the fruit as it reduces during baking.

3. Trim the edge of the dough with scissors leaving a ¹/₂- to ₁-inch overhang, depending on the finished edge you plan to use.

4. Tuck the top dough under the bottom, crimping the layers together to form a solid edge. **2** This will prevent the juices from overflowing during baking. Finish the edge according to the recipe directions.

5. Proceed with the recipe directions for making steam vents and for garnishing the top of the pie.

SEALING THE EDGE

THE DIFFERENCE BETWEEN crimping and fluting is a subject of much debate. Although dictionaries define crimping as a form of sealing and fluting as a decorative finish, in the world of pastry the terms appear to be used interchangeably. Crimping or fluting dough usually applies to pies; tarts are baked in different-shaped pans, so the information that follows is not applicable.

Whether a dough is crimped or fluted, the edge of the pastry, be it for a double- or single-crusted pie, is raised. This raised edge acts either as a wall to prevent the filling from overflowing or as a seal to keep the juices contained within the pie.

As a rule, the top pastry in a double-crust pie is turned under the bottom pastry to make it airtight. Because of this, the dough is not trimmed flush to the pie plate. The bottom should have an overhang of from ¹/₄ to ¹/₂ inch while the top needs to be larger, ¹/₂ to ₁ inch. How much of a pastry overhang you will need depends on the type of edge you choose to make. For the novice, the simplest method for a double-crust pie is to seal the edges with a fork dipped in flour. For this finish, the smaller overhang is sufficient. If you wish to tackle decorative crimping and fluting, see page 66.

Single-crust pies always require the maximum overhang to give you enough pastry to fold over and form a double thickness of dough for height and extra support at the lip. Single-crust pies are commonly fluted or crimped. However, this step can be omitted if you wish.

STEAM VENTS

DOUBLE-CRUSTED PASTRIES *must* be given steam vents to release hot air and moisture as the pastry bakes. Filled pastry that is not vented will retain too much liquid; the filling will overflow and the crust will be soggy.

The venting can be done as simply as with the tip of a knife, the prongs of a fork, or with a few slashes across the top. Small cookie or canapé cutters can be used for more ornamental venting. Pie birds are discussed on page 239.

HOW TO LINE A
TART PAN WITH PASTRY

There are two ways to transfer the dough to the pan.

METHOD 1
1. After the dough has been rolled, position the rolling pin 4 inches from the top of the pastry. Lift the dough over the top of the rolling pin and gently roll the dough toward you.

2. Lift the pastry up. Be sure to keep a finger pressed against the barrel of the rolling in to keep it from slipping. Position the pastry, leaving about 1½ inches of dough hanging over the edge of the pan on the side closest to you. Then unroll the pastry over an ungreased tart pan, moving the pin away from you. *Immediately* lift the overhang into the tart pan to prevent the sharp edge of the pan from cutting the dough.

METHOD 2
1. After the dough has been rolled, carefully fold it into quarters.

2. Lift the pastry up. Position the point of the folded dough in the center of an ungreased tart pan. Carefully unfold the pastry. *Immediately* lift the overhang into the tart pan to prevent the sharp edge of the pan from cutting the dough.

3. Once the dough has been transferred, you need to mold the pastry to the pan. Working a small portion of dough at a time, mold it into the crease of the pan. Place your fingers against the side of the pan and gently push the dough down toward the crease.  Do this around the entire pan. Be careful not to stretch the dough.

✦ FOR A FLUSH EDGE, trim off excess pastry by running the rolling pin across the top edge of the pan.

✦ FOR A RAISED EDGE, trim pastry with scissors, leaving a ¹/₂-inch overhang. Fold the overhang to the inside of the pan, making a double thickness of dough.  Press your forefinger against the dough to seal the two layers together. Press firmly until the dough rises about ¹/₄ inch above the rim of the pan. The pastry can be used as formed or finished decoratively (see "Making Decorative Edges," page 66).

✦ IF MAKING A TART USING UNBAKED PASTRY: Add filling to pastry-lined pan. Proceed with directions for baking.

✦ IF MAKING A TART BAKED WITHOUT A FILLING (*Baking Blind*): After the dough is shaped, prick the bottom and side *lightly* with a fork at ¹/₂- to 1-inch intervals. Do not pierce too deeply or the filling may seep underneath the crust. Place the tart pan on a half-sheet or jelly-roll pan and refrigerate for at least 15 minutes. See next section.

CHILLING SHAPED PASTRY BEFORE BAKING

ALL PASTRIES BENEFIT from chilling. Whether they have been filled or are to be baked blind, chilling the dough relaxes the gluten, which helps the pastry maintain its form. Pastry that has not been chilled has a mind of its own, and no amount of coaxing will keep it in shape.

Here are a few tips:

✦ For easier handling, place the pie plate or tart pan on a shallow baking pan. Be sure to choose one with sides to prevent the pan from sliding off the edge.

✦ Pastry can be chilled in either the refrigerator or the freezer. This will take anywhere from 10 minutes in the freezer to up to 30 minutes in the refrigerator.

✦ When the pastry begins to firm, redefine any fluting, crimping, or decorative edging. This will give the finished crust a more pronounced design. In addition, if the edge is to be covered with aluminum foil bands, chilling will prevent the bands from mashing the pastry.

How to Make a Baked Pie or Tart Shell: Blind Baking

A PASTRY SHELL baked without a filling is "blind baked" (pre-baked). Blind baking is done when a recipe uses a refrigerated cream-style filling. It is also used to prevent a soggy bottom crust and to promote browning with recipes made with fruit or loose custard fillings. These fillings give off a lot of moisture and the crust will benefit greatly from this procedure.

Since the shape of a crust is difficult to maintain when it is baked without a filling, three steps are essential. The shell must be pricked lightly with a fork at 3/4- to 1-inch intervals, the shaped pastry must be thoroughly chilled before baking, and it must be weighted during baking to prevent it from puffing up.

1. Tear an 18-inch square of heavy-duty aluminum foil. Make a buttered circle in the center of the foil 2 inches larger than the size of the pan. Place the foil buttered side down, centering it into the baking pan. Using your hand, press the foil completely flush against the sides.

Should a Blind-Baked Pie or Tart Shell Be Par-Baked or Fully Baked?

I ALWAYS USED TO PAR-BAKE most crusts, which is the traditional method for promoting a crispier bottom crust. While this works up to a point, once the filling is added and the pie is baked, the crust does not remain crisp. The filling can actually prevent a par-baked crust from ever fully baking.

After testing dozens of recipes for this book, I came to the conclusion that a fully baked pastry shell is the way to go. My reasoning is this: when a filling, be it fruit or custard, is placed in a fully baked shell, the uncooked filling becomes an insulator, keeping the crust cool enough to prevent overbaking. By the time the filling completes baking, both the crust and the filling are properly done.

If the edges of the crust appear to be browning too much, simply lay a square of aluminum foil loosely over the top and let the pie or tart finish baking.

2. Preheat the oven to 425 degrees. Position the shelf in the lower third of the oven. Fill the pan with enough ordinary dried beans (any kind or size will do) or baking nuggets to *just* cover the surface of the pan. Do not overfill. For easier handling, bake the pastry shell on a shallow pan with sides.

3. Bake the crust for 15 to 18 minutes or until the sides begin to brown. Remove the pan from the oven. Let stand about 30 seconds, then gently remove the foil and the beans.

4. Reduce the oven to 375 degrees. Continue to bake the crust for 3 to 5 minutes, or until it is golden brown. If the bottom of the pastry shell puffs up, tap it very gently with the bottom of a fork to expel the air. This must be done carefully so that the pastry crust doesn't break. When the crust is done, cool completely before filling.

Note: If any splits or breaks have developed, they must be patched with leftover pastry scraps before the final baking. Simply place a small piece of raw dough over the opening and gently tap it with your finger until it adheres. Then continue baking the shell.

Always bake pastry shells on a half-sheet or jelly-roll pan as they are extremely fragile. Once baked, *handle with care.*

PROTECTIVE COATINGS AND SEALERS

SEALERS CREATE A barrier between filling and an unbaked crust, protecting the shell from moisture. A sealer is especially needed when the pie or tart is made with an extremely juicy fruit or a filling that has a tendency to soak into the crust while baking.

An egg wash is particularly suited for this job. The whole egg can be used, or the yolk or white alone. My preference is a white beaten lightly with a teaspoon of water and a pinch of salt or sugar to thin the albumen and make brushing easier. For sweet pastries, another protective coating is 3 to 4 teaspoons of strained fruit preserves (such as apricot); for savories, 3 to 4 teaspoons Dijon mustard.

Sometimes, a thin layer of crushed cookie crumbs, finely chopped nuts, or dried bread crumbs can be used. Add these to an unbaked shell or after the pastry is finished baking. Just sprinkle 2 to 3 tablespoons over the pastry shell before adding the filling.

When assembling most fruit-filled pies and tarts, apply a thin coating of sealer before adding the filling. However, when sealing a blind-baked shell, add the coating *after* the aluminum foil and beans have been removed. Return the shell to the oven to bake the coating and finish the browning.

Before You Begin

✦ Assemble all of your ingredients.

✦ If pastry is made by hand, always sift or strain flour before measuring. If pastry is made by processor, sifting is unnecessary because the machine aerates and eliminates all lumps.

✦ Always spoon flour into a measuring cup used for dry ingredients, then level with a straight-edged utensil (page 49).

✦ In exceptionally hot, muggy weather, chill dry ingredients after measuring and proceeding with recipe.

✦ Keep measured and diced butter and shortening well chilled until ready to use.

✦ Before you work fats into flour, first toss the two to coat the fat pieces.

✦ When cutting fats into flour with a pastry blender, *do not* turn or twist your wrist. Always keep the wire or blades of the pastry blender in the same position, rotating the bowl, not the blender. This prevents the mixture from becoming pasty.

✦ To keep ice water cold, don't measure it until just before using. Have ready a container filled with water and ice cubes to measure when needed. Never include bits of ice with your measured water.

✦ If making dough in a food processor, use a liquid measuring cup with a spout for adding liquids.

✦ For accuracy, always fill tablespoons to the brim when measuring liquids.

✦ Use a large bowl—at least 3 quarts—for making pastry by hand or when tossing water into a flour-fat mixture.

✦ For even distribution, don't pour all your liquids into one area. Pour around the side of the bowl so that they will trickle into the flour-fat mixture.

✦ For a flaky pastry, don't stir or mash dough when adding liquid; the delicate layers of fat and flour will be flattened. It is best to toss the mixture lightly with a fork.

✦ If dough sticks to your hands, wash them in cool water, dry, and coat lightly with flour before proceeding.

✦ Don't overwork the dough when forming into disks.

✦ For storing dough, use an airtight covering such as plastic wrap to prevent the surface of the pastry from drying out.

Flaky Pie Pastry I

THIS IS AN EXCELLENT all-purpose American-style pastry with measurements given for both a small and large pie crust. Although the smaller recipe contains equal portions of butter and vegetable shortening, for the sake of measuring convenience, the larger recipe uses a bit more butter. Both crusts are equally delicious. Be sure to look at the step-by-step photographs in the color section.

At a Glance

SMALL RECIPE:
1 double crust for
a 9-inch pie

LARGE RECIPE:
1 double crust for
a 10-inch pie

METHOD: Hand

SMALL	LARGE	
$2^{1}/_{2}$	3	cups sifted all-purpose flour
3	4	teaspoons sugar
$3/_{4}$	1	teaspoon salt
$1/_{2}$	$3/_{4}$	cup firm, unsalted butter, cut into $1/_{2}$-inch cubes
$1/_{2}$	$1/_{2}$	cup chilled vegetable shortening, cut into small pieces
5 to 6	6 to 8	tablespoons ice water, or more as needed

1. Sift together the flour, sugar, and salt in a large mixing bowl. Add the butter and shortening and toss to coat the fats with flour.

2. Using a pastry blender, cut the fats into the flour until the mixture resembles coarse meal with some pea-size particles. Position your hand at the far side of the bowl. Draw the blender toward the center while scraping it along the bottom of the bowl.

Rotate the bowl with your free hand to keep the pastry blender in the same position. *Do not turn or twist your wrist* or the crumbs will become too sticky. Scrape the blender clean every so often.

Break up larger particles of fat by pressing the blender straight down on them.

3. Add the ice water, 1 *tablespoon* at a time, drizzling it around the rim of the bowl. Use a kitchen fork to push the mixture toward the center with each addition. Do this around the entire bowl. As more water is added, clumps of dough will form. They will become larger with each addition. Add the final tablespoon of water, a teaspoon at a time. Now feel the dough with your hand; it should feel cool and slightly moist.

To determine if the mixture has enough water, gather some in your hand and press it against the bowl to see if it will hold together. If not, add more water *sparingly*, about 1 teaspoon at a time, adding only enough for it to form a mass. *Too much liquid and/or overworking the dough will toughen it* (see color insert).

4. With floured hands, press the dough against the side of the bowl, forming 2 balls. All of the crumbs should adhere to the balls and clean the bowl. If not, add a few drops of water. Flatten the balls into two 4- to 5-inch disks (see color insert).

5. Dust the disks generously with flour, then score with the side of your hand to relax the gluten. Cover with plastic wrap. Chill 30 minutes or longer before using.

STORAGE

The dough will keep for up to 3 days in the refrigerator or 6 months in the freezer. To thaw, remove from the freezer to refrigerator. Thaw overnight or at least 12 hours.

The Art of the Pastry Cook...

It is a most important branch of the culinary science; unceasingly occupied with flattering the sight as much as the taste, it raises graceful monuments, delicious fortresses, seductive ramparts, which as soon as they are on all sides attacked, totter, crumble, and no longer present anything but glorious and ephemeral ruins, like every other work of man—all pass away whether they be temples, columns, pyramids or pies.

ALEXIS SOYER, *The Pantropheon, or A History of Food and Its Preparation in Ancient Times*, 1853

Flaky Pie Pastry II

THE INGREDIENTS FOR this recipe have been adjusted for the food processor. Since the processor aerates the flour and eliminates any lumps, sifting is unneccesary. However, when a processor is used, the cup measurement of flour is reduced and the butter and vegetable shortening should be partially frozen. In addition, I add a touch of baking powder for extra flakiness. Again, see the photographs in the color section.

At a Glance

SMALL RECIPE:
1 double crust for
a 9-inch pie

LARGE RECIPE:
1 double crust for
a 10-inch pie

METHOD: Food Processor

SMALL	LARGE	
2 1/3	2 3/4	cups unsifted all-purpose flour
3	4	teaspoons sugar
3/4	1	teaspoon salt
1/2	1/2	teaspoon baking powder
1/2	3/4	cup partially frozen unsalted butter, cut into 1/2-inch cubes
1/2	1/2	cup partially frozen vegetable shortening, cut into small pieces
5 to 6	6 to 8	tablespoons ice water (see Note)

1. Place the dry ingredients in the bowl of a food processor. If time permits, place the flour-filled processor bowl in the freezer for 20 to 30 minutes to chill the dry ingredients. Process for 5 seconds to blend.

2. Add half of the butter and shortening. Toss to coat with flour. Pulse 4 or 5 times, then process for 4 to 5 seconds. Add the remaining fats and pulse again 4 to 5 times, then process about 4 to 5 seconds. The mixture should have the texture of coarse meal and still contain some larger pieces of fat.

3. Empty the mixture into a large bowl. Add the ice water, 1 tablespoon at a time, drizzling it around the side of the bowl. Use a kitchen fork to push the mixture toward the center with each addition. Do this around the entire bowl. As more water is added, clumps of dough will form. They will become larger with each addition. Add the remaining tablespoon of water, a teaspoon at a time. Feel the dough with your hand; it should feel cool and moist.

4. With floured hands, form the mixture into two 4- to 5-inch disks by pressing the dough against the side of the bowl. All of the crumbs should adhere and clean the bowl. If not, add a few more drops of water. Dust the disks generously with flour, score with the side of your hand to relax the gluten, and wrap in plastic wrap. Refrigerate for 30 minutes or longer before rolling.

NOTE
If adding liquid in the food processor, measure $1/3$ cup ice water in a container with a spout. Start the processor. *Immediately* pour in the ice water through the feeder tube. *Stop* the machine as soon as the water is added. *Do not let the dough form a mass.* Empty the mixture into a large bowl. Then proceed with step 4.

STORAGE

The dough will keep for 3 days in the refrigerator or for up to 6 months in the freezer. To thaw, remove from the freezer to the refrigerator. Thaw overnight or for at least 12 hours.

VARIATIONS

Flaky Pie Pastry with Citrus Zest

Add $1 1/2$ teaspoons grated lemon zest and $1/2$ teaspoon grated navel or Valencia orange zest to the mixing or processor bowl with the dry ingredients and blend. Proceed with the master recipe.

Use with fruit and berry pies.

Sesame Pastry

Add 2 tablespoons unhulled sesame seeds to the mixing or processor bowl with the dry ingredients and blend. Add $1/2$ teaspoon light sesame oil to the ice water. Proceed with the master recipe.

Use with fruit and berry pies. Also recommended for savory pastries, with the sugar omitted.

Classic Tart Pastry I

PÂTE BRISÉE

CLASSIC TART PASTRY is a basic European-style all-purpose dough that can be used for most sweet and savory tarts, as well as for pies.

At a Glance

MAKES: 1 9- or
11-inch shell

METHOD: Hand

1½ cups sifted all-purpose flour
½ teaspoon salt
*⅓ cup firm unsalted butter, cut
into ½-inch pieces*
*2 tablespoons chilled vegetable
shortening*
*4 tablespoons ice water, or more as
needed*

1. In a large bowl, sift together the flour and salt. Add the butter and vegetable shortening. Toss the mixture with your hands to coat the fats with flour. Then rub the flour-coated fats between your fingertips to form flat, flakelike crumbs.

As the pieces become smaller, with floured hands, take a handful of crumbs and gently let them roll from between your hands into the bowl, while moving your hands in one direction. *Do not move them back and forth or you will mash the flakes. The tips of your fingers should always point down into the bowl.* Each time the crumbs fall from your hands, pick up another handful. After 6 to 8 times, alternate the rubbing movement with the rolling movement.

Continue until the flour-coated fats are the size of coarse meal with some larger pea-size pieces. The crumb mixture will change color from off-white to pale yellowish.

2. Add 3 tablespoons ice water, 1 *tablespoon at a time,* drizzling it around the rim of the bowl. Using a kitchen fork, push the mixture toward the center with each addition. Do this around the entire bowl. As more water is added, clumps of dough will form. They will become larger with each addition. Add the remaining 1 tablespoon water, a teaspoon at a time. Feel the dough with your hand; it should feel cool and slightly moist.

THE PRIMER

To determine if the mixture has enough water, gather some in your hand and press it against the side of the bowl to see if it will hold together. If not, add more water *sparingly*, about 1 teaspoon at a time, adding only enough for it to form a mass. *Too much liquid and/or overworking the dough will toughen it* (see color insert).

3. With floured hands, press the dough against the side of the bowl to form a ball. All of the crumbs should adhere to the ball and clean the bowl. If not, add a few drops of water. Flatten the ball into a 5-inch disk (see color insert). Dust with flour and score with the side of your hand to relax the gluten. Cover with plastic wrap. Chill 30 minutes or longer before using.

STORAGE

The dough will keep for up to 3 days in the refrigerator or 6 months in the freezer. To thaw, remove from the freezer to the refrigerator. Thaw overnight or at least 12 hours.

Early American Pie and Tart Lore

THE FIRST PIES MADE BY the settlers were of pumpkin or "pompions," as they were called. Originally, pumpkins were baked whole, tops sliced off and seeds removed, filled with sweeteners, milk, and spices, then baked on hot ashes. The cooked filling was scooped out of the shell.

In later years the pumpkin shell was abandoned and replaced by a form of English open pie known as a "trap." Eventually, a deeper, rectangular pie with a lid evolved, referred to as a "coffin." Lattice-topped pies were known before the American Revolution as "grated," because of their weblike surface.

"Coffins" were deep and required a substantial amount of filling, so a shallow version without a lid came into being thanks to the frugality of the New England women. This new variation was called a tart, in all likelihood from the original English "trap." These flat, open pastries became a favored form for enjoying the native apples, quince, and pears.

Classic Tart Pastry II

PÂTE BRISÉE

THE INGREDIENTS FOR this Classic Tart Pastry have been adjusted for the food processor. Since the processor aerates the flour and eliminates any lumps, sifting is unneccesary. However, when a processor is used, the cup measurement of flour is reduced and the butter and vegetable shortening should be partially frozen. A touch of baking powder adds extra flakiness.

At a Glance

MAKES: 1 9- or
11-inch shell

METHOD: Food Processor

1 1/2 cups less 2 tablespoons
   unsifted all-purpose flour
1/2 teaspoon salt
1/4 teaspoon baking powder
1/3 cup partially frozen unsalted
   butter, cut into 1/2-inch cubes
2 tablespoons partially frozen
   vegetable shortening, cut into
   small pieces
4 tablespoons ice water, or more as
   needed (see Note)

1. Place the flour, salt, and baking powder into the bowl of a food processor. If time permits, place the flour-filled processor bowl in the freezer for 20 to 30 minutes to chill the dry ingredients. Process 5 seconds to blend.

2. Add half of the butter and shortening. Toss to coat with flour. Pulse 4 or 5 times, then process for 4 to 5 seconds. Add the remaining fats and pulse again 4 or 5 times, then process 4 to 5 seconds. The mixture should have the texture of fine meal with some small, pea-size pieces. *Stop the machine.*

3. Empty the mixture into a large bowl. Add 3 tablespoons ice water, *1 tablespoon at a time*, drizzling it around the rim of the bowl. Use a kitchen fork to push the mixture toward the center with each addition. Do this around the entire bowl. As more water is added, clumps of dough will form and become larger with each addition. Add the remaining tablespoon of water a teaspoon at a time. Feel the dough with your hand; it should feel cool and slightly moist. To

determine if the mixture has enough water, gather some in your hand and press it against the bowl to see if it will hold together. If not, add more water *sparingly*, about 1 teaspoon at a time. Add only enough for it to form a mass.

4. With floured hands, press the dough against the side of the bowl to form a ball. All of the crumbs should adhere to the ball and clean the bowl. If not, add a few drops of water. Flatten the ball into a 5-inch disk. Dust the disk generously with flour, score with the side of your hand to relax the gluten, and cover with plastic wrap. Refrigerate for 30 minutes or longer.

NOTE

If adding liquid in the food processor, measure the ice water in a container with a spout. Start the processor, and *immediately* add the ice water through the feeder tube. As soon as all of the water is added, *stop the machine. Do not wait for the mixture to form a ball or it will be overprocessed.* Then proceed with step 4.

STORAGE

The dough will keep for up to 3 days in the refrigerator or 6 months in the freezer. To thaw, remove from the freezer to the refrigerator. Thaw overnight or for at least 12 hours.

VARIATION

Rosemary Chive Tart Pastry

Using the food processor method for Classic Tart Pastry, add 1 tablespoon finely chopped fresh rosemary and 1 tablespoon of finely chopped chives to the dry ingredients. Pulse to blend and proceed with master recipe.

Recommended for savory tarts.

LESSON 1

ABOUT

Apple Pie

HE MOST popular pie made in the United States is undoubtedly apple. Recipes for this pastry number in the hundreds, most carbon copies of each other. The variables are subtle, but in these subtleties lies the difference between a poor pie and a great one. The type of apples, the kind of pastry, what sweeteners and thickeners are used—all play a role in making a delicious pie. Spicing the pie with cinnamon, nutmeg, allspice, or clove is personal taste and doesn't affect the quality of this favorite.

When you are ready to make an apple pie, choose the type and quality of the apple with thought. My two favorite pie apples are Mutzu and Northern Spy. Both varieties have a short season and are not available in all parts of the country. The Cortland apple, which has a longer season, would be another top choice.

If these varieties are not available, my backups are Rome and Granny Smith. These two apples are available most of the year. While their flavor is not as evocative of autumn as the seasonal fruit, they allow you to enjoy apple pies most any time. Rather than use Cortlands or Romes alone, combine them with the tarter Granny Smiths. All of these apples hold their shape during baking and create a pleasant balance of flavors.

Not every apple is suitable for baking pies, so make sure you buy an appropriate variety. The Fruit and Berry Glossary (page 17) discusses the major varieties, but if you know of a local apple that it good for pie baking, by all means take advantage of it.

Because I like my apples to retain their shape during baking and not become mushy, I slice them according to their texture. Cortlands and Romes are soft-fleshed, so I cut them into thick slices of about 3/4 inch. Granny Smiths are harder and crisper, so they are cut into thinner 1/4-inch slices.

The best choice for pastry dough is an American-style Flaky Pie Pastry. Always make the pastry first, so it can rest in the refrigerator while you peel the apples and make the filling.

After the pie is baked, it must stand several hours before serving to give the juices a chance to be reabsorbed by the fruit. Pies that are cut too soon will have a puddle of juice at the bottom of the pan. So during holiday season or for company dinners, make your pie a day or two in advance—in fact, I prefer it that way. Before serving, place the pie in the oven for a few minutes to refresh it, bring out the vanilla ice cream, and enjoy.

Evan Jones quotes from the nineteenth-century memoir of a Michigan woman in his *American Food: The Gastronomic Story.*

My mother's pie was beyond description. The crust was flaky, crisp, and tender. She used lard, and she mixed this with flour until it felt right. She poured in water with a teacup, or the dipper, or whatever was at hand, but she never poured too much or too little. She laid on to the lower crust a bed of sliced apples to exactly the right height for proper thickness when the pie was done. It was never so thick that it felt like biting into a feather bed, nor so thin that your teeth clicked. It never ran over, and it had just the proper amount of juice. She sprinkled sugar over it with neither mete nor measure, and allspice and cinnamon from a can. But when the pie was done (crimped around the edges and golden brown on the humps, with an "A" slashed in the top crust) it was a masterpiece of culinary art. With the edge of the oven's heat taken off, but never allowed to chill, and a goodly piece of cheese from the neighboring factory alongside, here was a dish which the average citizen of any country rarely meets.

Old-Fashioned American Apple Pie

THERE IS NO better time to get started than now. Read the recipe through, then organize your ingredients in the order they are listed. Remember, apples pies are a cinch to make once you have a little know-how.

At a Glance

SERVES: 6 to 8

PAN: 9-inch ovenproof glass

PASTRY PREP: Unbaked

OVEN TEMP: 400 degrees

BAKING TIME: 55 to 60 minutes

DIFFICULTY: 👟 👟

1 recipe Flaky Pie Pastry (pages 98, 100)

FILLING
1 1/2 to 2 pounds Cortland or Rome apples (about 4 large)
1 pound Granny Smith apples (about 3 medium)
2 teaspoons fresh lemon juice
3/4 cup lightly packed light brown sugar
1/4 cup granulated sugar
3 tablespoons cornstarch
1 teaspoon ground cinnamon
1/8 teaspoon grated nutmeg (optional)
1 tablespoon unsalted butter

EGG WASH
1 large egg white
1 teaspoon water

GARNISH
1 teaspoon granulated sugar
1/8 teaspoon ground cinnamon, optional

1. START THE FILLING: Cut the apples into quarters. Remove the core and peel. Cut the Cortland or Rome apples into 3/4-inch slices and the Granny Smith apples into 1/4-inch slices. Place in a large bowl, sprinkle with lemon juice, and toss.

2. MAKE THE FILLING: Combine the sugars, cornstarch, cinnamon, and nutmeg in a small bowl. Set aside. Do not add to the fruit; the sugar draws moisture from the apples and will make the filling too watery.

3. ASSEMBLE THE PIE: Preheat the oven to 400 degrees. Position the oven rack in the lower third of the oven. Butter a 9-inch ovenproof glass pie plate.

4. Roll one pastry disk into a 13-inch circle. Line the pie plate with the dough.

5. Use a fork to lightly beat the egg white with water in a small bowl. Brush a thin layer of egg wash onto the bottom and sides of the dough.

6. Toss the sugar mixture through the apples. Empty the filling into the pie plate, forming the apples into a snug mound with your hands. Fill in spaces with apple wedges. Dot the pie with butter. Trim the dough with scissors, leaving a ¼-inch overhang.

7. Roll out the other pastry disk into a 13-inch circle and place it on top of the apples. With your hands, 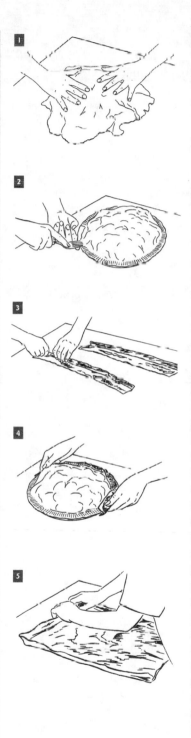 push the dough gently toward the center to allow the dough to drop during baking. Then press the top and bottom layers of pastry together with your fingers.

8. With a small knife, trim the dough flush against the rim of the pie plate. To seal the edge, dip a 4-prong fork into flour, and press the fork gently into the edge of the dough, going completely around the rim of the pie **2**.

Note: If you wish to finish the pie with a fluted edge, you will have to leave extra dough around the edge of the pie. Leave a ½-inch overhang on the bottom and a 1-inch overhang for the top. Tuck the top dough under the bottom and press the two together to form a solid edge. Refer to directions for "Sealing the Edge," page 92.

9. Prick the top of the pastry in several places with the fork to allow steam to escape during baking. Lightly brush the top of the pie with egg wash. To garnish, sprinkle with sugar and a few dashes of cinnamon.

10. To prevent the edge from burning, make aluminum foil bands. Cut two 3-inch-wide strips of 18-inch heavy-duty aluminum foil. **3** Fold 1 inch of each strip to the center, making a double thickness of foil on one side. **4** Cover the edge of the pie with the bands, keeping the double fold on top of the dough. Be careful not to mash the edge of the pastry. Seal the bands together with tape.

11. Make an aluminum foil drip pan to place on the oven rack below the pie to catch any juices that may overflow during baking. Cut an 18-inch square of heavy-duty aluminum foil. **5** Double-fold each edge (about 1-inch per fold), turning the foil up at the second fold, forming a rim.

12. Set the pie in the oven. Halfway through the baking, place the drip pan on the rack below. Bake the pie for 45 to 50 minutes. Remove the foil bands from the edge, and continue to bake 5 to 10 minutes longer. The pie is done when the juices begin to bubble through the top crust and the edge and bottom crust are golden brown. Cool at least 4 hours before serving.

STORAGE

This pie will keep for 1 day at room temperature. For longer storage, cover with aluminum foil and refrigerate for up to 5 days. Before serving, warm in a 350 degree oven for 15 to 20 minutes. This pie can be frozen (see page 77).

Recipe Roundup

✦ After cutting or peeling the fruit, do not put it in lemon water to prevent discoloration, as the fruit will absorb too much moisture. Plain lemon juice drizzled on top will do the trick. After baking, any minor discoloration won't be noticed. In addition, if the recipe contains spices or brown sugar, as many fruit pies do, these ingredients will cause the fruit to darken anyway.

✦ Slice fruits according to their texture because they will become tender at different times during cooking. Soft-fleshed fruit should be cut into thick pieces, while firm-fleshed fruit should be sliced into thin pieces.

✦ Soft-fleshed apples, such as McIntosh, and other soft-fiber fruits, such as Bartlett pears, are not the best choices for making pies because these fruits do not keep their shape during baking. This results in a mushy filling.

✦ It's okay to combine different kinds of fruits in a filling as long as they complement each other.

✦ Taste fruits before you add sugar to determine sweetness. You can adjust the amount of sugar to your own taste.

✦ Starch for thickening a filling can be adjusted according to how moist or dry the fruit is. The sooner fruits are used after picking, the juicier they will be. Adding an extra tablespoon of thickening is recommended for very juicy fruit. Older fruit, which is often dry and mealy, will contain less moisture and therefore need less thickening.

✦ Always mix the starch with the sugar before adding it to the fruit. It will dissolve more thoroughly.

✦ Don't mix sugar through the fruit until the pie is ready to be filled. The sugar will draw out too much of the fruit's natural juices.

✦ Don't trim the pastry to the edge of the pan until the filling is added. The bottom pastry may draw in from the weight of the filling.

✦ Brushing the bottom of the pie shell with beaten egg white will help keep the dough from becoming soggy.

✦ When a fruit filling dome is higher than the top of the pie plate, the dough must have plenty of slack so it will drop as the fruit shrinks after baking. Pushing the top layer of dough toward the center before baking will eliminate the space between crust and filling in the finished pie.

✦ Buttering the pie plate before lining it with pastry holds the pastry in place, helps the dough retain its shape, and promotes browning on the bottom.

✦ Pierce airholes in the top of double-crusted pies to allow the steam to be released during baking. This keeps the fruit from overcooking and helps the liquid evaporate, preventing spillage from the fruit juices.

✦ Pies must bake long enough for the thickening and fruit to come to a boil. If the pie is removed from the oven too soon, the juices will not thicken and they will be cloudy. That is why the filling of fruit pies must bubble—that is, come to a boil—before the pie is removed from the oven.

✦ Pastry on the edge of a pie plate must be protected with aluminum foil bands during baking to prevent it from scorching. If left uncovered, the pastry on the edge may overbake before the center of the pie has had a chance to cook.

✦ A disposable drip pan keeps the inside of the oven clean. Oozing fruit juices with sugars easily burn and smoke. They are also difficult to clean off the oven floor.

✦ After baking, fruit pies must stand several hours to allow the juices to reabsorb into the fruit. Then they will cut like a charm. If a fruit pie is cut too soon, the filling will be soupy; the pie will be difficult to slice and will have a soggy bottom crust.

✦ Leftover fruit pies always taste better when they are reheated. The crust will recrisp and warm fruit is more flavorful.

✦ Most fruit pies can stand at room temperature for up to 1 day as long as the filling does not contain eggs or other dairy products. For longer storage, or in very warm weather, it is best to refrigerate the pie because fruit attracts bacteria and mold. Just refresh the pie in the oven before serving.

✦ Fruit pies freeze very well. I prefer to freeze my fruit pies fully baked. Freezing pies with uncooked fresh fruits often results in watery fillings.

LESSON 2

ABOUT

Lemon Meringue Pie

 Y STUDENTS have expressed more frustrations about lemon meringue pies than about almost any other kind of pastry. This was one of the foremost reasons that prompted me to write this primer. Soggy crusts, runny fillings, and weeping meringues are the nemesis of lemon meringue. ✳ To have a bottom crust remain crisp after the pie is finished, you must lay the groundwork almost from the beginning. The pastry must be correctly fitted into the pan, and it must be well shaped. It must

have enough slack to expand while baking, then shrink without the crust cracking as it cools.

Most important, the crust cannot have any holes or tears. Any splits in the dough will only get larger during baking. It takes only a single crack to attract moisture that the filling and topping release as the pie cools. Once the liquid finds this escape hatch, it runs out and makes its home underneath the crust—and bingo! a soggy crust.

Loose fillings can result from undercooking, overcooking, or overmixing. Although making a cooked filling is not difficult, it can be tricky. Most people make the mistake of removing the filling from the heat at the first sign of a bubble, for fear of overcooking it. Wrong! A filling must continue to cook for at least a minute or two after it has come to a gentle boil so the starch granules can bond. If the filling is removed from the heat too soon, the starch will not fully develop and the filling will thin as it cools.

Additionally, a perfectly thickened filling will turn to soup if it is stirred too often as it cools. Excessive mixing weakens the structure, causing the starch granules to separate and the filling to liquefy.

Making a foolproof meringue is another matter. Because they are made with a high level of sugar, meringues are sensitive to humidity. Sugar attracts the moisture in the air, and moisture makes meringues loose their volume and become sticky.

Meringues also must be whipped to the proper consistency—not too little, not too much. If they are underbeaten, the bubbles will not bond into a strong enough structure to hold air. The egg foam will reduce, and the volume will be poor. Conversely, overbeating causes proteins in the egg whites to pop and lose their water. The meringue will reduce in volume, and the foam will be dry and lumpy.

To try to resolve the complexities of this pie, I researched dozens of recipes and did comparative tests using various theories. In the end, I remained loyal to the bag of tricks that have stood by me for years.

The pie is an English institution which, planted on American soil, forthwith ran rampant and burst forth into an untold variety of genera and species.

HARRIET BEECHER STOWE

Lemon Meringue Pie

THE RECIPE THAT follows is one that I made for my children, Frank and Pam, when they were growing up. It was their favorite then, and still is today. The pastry remains dry and flaky, the sweet and tart lemon filling will cut like a charm, and the velvety meringue will not weep. The pie is impossible to resist, especially when freshly made. It's a slice of heaven!

At a Glance

SERVES: 6 to 8

PAN: 9-inch ovenproof glass

PASTRY PREP: Baked

OVEN TEMP: 325 degrees

BAKING TIME: 15 to 18 minutes

DIFFICULTY: 🥧🥧

1 9-inch *Flaky Pie Pastry* crust (*pages 98, 100*), baked
3 ginger snaps, finely crushed

FILLING
1 1/4 cups granulated sugar
6 tablespoons cornstarch
1/4 teaspoon salt
1 1/2 cups cold water
5 large egg yolks
2 tablespoons unsalted butter
1 tablespoon grated lemon zest
1/3 cup fresh lemon juice

MERINGUE
7 tablespoons sugar, preferably superfine
3 tablespoons strained confectioners' sugar
Pinch of salt
5 large egg whites, at room temperature
1/2 teaspoon cream of tartar
1/2 teaspoon vanilla extract

1. MAKE THE FILLING: Combine the granulated sugar, cornstarch, and salt in a medium, heavy, nonreactive saucepan. Stir in about 1/4 cup of the water, mixing until smooth. Blend in the remaining water.

2. Cook over medium-low heat, stirring constantly, until the mixture comes to a boil, 4 to 5 minutes. Reduce the heat to low and cook for 1 minute longer, stirring occasionally to prevent scorching on the bottom of the pan.

3. Lightly beat the eggs yolks in a small bowl. Off the heat, stir a small amount of filling into the egg yolks to temper, or warm, them. Pour the yolk mixture into the pot. Gently mix with a whisk.

4. Cook the filling over low heat until it comes to a slow boil. Continue to simmer for a minute longer to thicken the filling and cook the yolks. Stir slowly to prevent scorching, but *do not overmix*. Remove the saucepan from the heat, blend in the butter, lemon zest, and juice, and set aside.

5. Position the oven rack to the lower third of the oven. Preheat the oven to 325 degrees.

6. **MAKE THE MERINGUE:** Whisk together the sugars and salt in a small bowl, until thoroughly combined.

7. In the large bowl of an electric mixer fitted with beaters or the whip attachment, beat the egg whites on medium speed until frothy. Add the cream of tartar and increase the mixer speed to medium-high. Beat the egg whites until they form firm peaks but are not dry. Add the sugar mixture, 1 tablespoon at a time, taking about 1 minute. Add the vanilla and beat the whites until thick and glossy, 30 to 45 seconds longer.

8. **ASSEMBLE THE PIE:** Sprinkle the ginger snap crumbs over the baked crust. Warm the filling briefly over very low heat. Again, *do not overmix*. Immediately pour the filling into the pie shell.

9. With a tablespoon, drop mounds of meringue in a ring around the edge of the filling, then fill in the center. 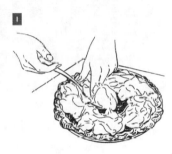 With the back of a tablespoon, spread the meringue to cover the filling *completely*. Swirl the meringue with the back of the tablespoon to form peaks.

10. Bake the pie for 15 to 18 minutes, or until golden brown. Cool the pie on a rack away from drafts to prevent the meringue from weeping. When cool, serve at once, or refrigerate until ready to use.

STORAGE

Any leftover pie will keep for up to 3 days in the refrigerator, loosely covered with an aluminum foil tent. *Never* cover with plastic wrap; too much condensation will form under the wrapping. Freezing is not recommended.

Hints for Making "Weep-Proof" Meringue

+ It is essential that the baked pie shell have no cracks or holes in it.

+ Blend the granulated and confectioners' sugars thoroughly.

+ Beat the sugars into the whipped egg whites slowly.

+ Spread the meringue onto the filling while the filling is hot.

+ Use a large tablespoon to drop mounds of meringue around the outer part of the pie filling first, then cover the center. Gently press down on the meringue to fill in any air pockets.

+ Be sure that the filling is *completely* covered. The meringue must touch the edge of the pie crust.

+ Cool away from drafts.

Recipe Roundup

✦ Baked pastry shells that contain cooked fillings with baked meringue toppings must always be well formed and free of cracks and holes to prevent a soggy bottom crust.

✦ A prebaked pastry shell should cool before you add a filling. Although very fragile, the pastry will stabilize and firm as it cools.

✦ When cornstarch or flour is to be added to liquid, always premix all or part of the sugar with the starch. This will prevent a filling from forming lumps when the starch is added to liquid.

✦ When making a cooked filling, always choose a heavy saucepan. Avoid thin pots—the filling will burn.

✦ A cooked filling should continue to cook at a gentle boil for about a minute so that the starch granules can bond. If the filling is removed from the heat too soon, the starch will lose its thickening ability and the filling will liquefy.

✦ Cooled fillings that are overmixed after they have come to a boil will liquefy. When starch comes to a boil, the granules swell and link together. Overmixing weakens the bond, causing the starch granules to separate.

✦ High-acid ingredients like lemon juice prevent the bonding of starch granules. Therefore, these kinds of ingredients should be added to cooked fillings *after* the fillings have thickened. It is preferable to do this off the heat.

✦ Always add about one-quarter of the hot mixture to beaten egg yolks before adding the yolks to the saucepan. Tempering prevents egg yolks from curdling.

✦ A layer of crushed cookies like ginger snaps or graham crackers placed between the baked crust and the hot filling will absorb excess moisture and help keep the bottom crust crispy.

✦ Beating speed for whipped egg whites should begin on medium, and then be increased to medium-high when the sugar is added. Starting the beating process on high speed results in large, unstable air cells. These cells will eventually break, resulting in loss of volume, lack of smoothness with a watery consistency.

✦ Superfine sugar is used in a meringue because it dissolves more quickly than granulated sugar.

✦ Confectioners' sugar contains a small amount of cornstarch. A combination of one part confectioners' sugar to two parts superfine sugar will help to prevent meringues from weeping.

✦ When making a meringue, add the sugar gradually to the beaten egg white, about 1 tablespoon at a time. It should be added when the egg whites *begin* to stand in firm peaks.

✦ Meringue will become firmer and have more body if it is beaten for 45 to 60 seconds after all of the sugar has been added. Conversely, beating meringue too long will result in a loss of volume.

✦ Meringue toppings should be dropped by spoonfuls around the edge of the pie or tart first, and then spooned into the center. The topping should be spread from the outside to the center.

✦ Toppings should never be emptied all at once onto a filling because they will not cover it properly. Too many spaces are left and sealing the edge becomes difficult.

✦ Meringue toppings should be pressed with a spoon to remove pockets of air underneath the filling. These spaces cause weeping or beads of moisture to form under the filling.

✦ Meringue toppings should be pressed onto the outer edge of the crust to completely cover a cooked filling before the pie or tart is baked.

✦ Meringue toppings should be placed on a *hot* cooked filling and be thoroughly baked to avoid salmonella bacteria from forming.

✦ Pies and tarts with baked meringue toppings should be cooled away from drafts to prevent the baked meringue from shrinking and weeping.

✦ Never cover baked meringue with plastic wrap—too much moisture forms under the wrapping.

LESSON 3

ABOUT

Open Fruit Tarts

PEN FRUIT TARTS are to the French what fruit pies are to Americans. These tarts are not complicated to make—usually no more than a crust topped with a thin layer of sweetened, seasonal fruit. Simple, yes. But achieving a good one is another matter. The pastry should be well shaped and crisp on the bottom. The fruit should be tender but not mushy. It should be pleasantly sweet, yet have a touch of tartness. It should shine with moistness, but not be runny. * There are several types

of crusts that can be used for making tarts, along with numerous methods, each giving a different result. The crust can be a classic tart pastry, a sweet cookielike pastry, or a multilayered puff pastry. The pastry can be used unbaked, parbaked, or completely baked before it receives its covering of fruit. Some like to cook the fruit first, while others start with it uncooked. Often, the bottom crust is coated with warm preserves or egg wash to shield it.

The fruit can be placed directly on the pastry, on a puree of dried fruits, or on one made of thickly cooked fresh fruit, such as apple sauce. It can also be placed on a layer of frangipane, that mixture of almond paste, eggs, and flour. This flavorful mixture catches the juices of the fruit, thus protecting the bottom crust from becoming too wet. Other flavored nut pastes, such as those made from walnuts or pecans, can also be used to shield the undercrust from moisture.

Unlike pies, open fruit tarts can be eaten shortly after baking. These tarts are very shallow and contain much less fruit, so there is less juice to worry about. Tarts are always removed from their pans before serving. They can be easily sliced and are visually beautiful. While fruit pies do not make good candidates for a buffet table because slicing can be messy, open fruit tarts are ideal.

I tested numerous methods for making fruit tarts before I determined the best technique for this primer. While all of the methods I discussed above will work under certain circumstances, the one I chose to use here will give you consistent results. Follow the recipe carefully and you, too, will be able to master a terrific yet simple fruit tart.

A Simple Pear Tart

HERE IS A FRUIT TART that will make a novice look like a pro. It is quick to prepare, pretty, and tastes wonderful.

At a Glance

SERVES: 8 to 10

PAN: 11-inch metal tart

PASTRY PREP: Baked

OVEN TEMP: 375 degrees

BAKING TIME:
55 to 60 minutes

DIFFICULTY: 🥄🥄

---

1 11-inch Classic Tart Pastry shell
(pages 102, 104), baked

GLAZE
1/3 cup apricot preserves
2 teaspoons water

FILLING
6 or 7 medium Anjou or Bartlett
    pears, slightly underripe
    (2 1/2 pounds)
1 tablespoon fresh lemon juice
1/2 cup sugar
2 tablespoons cornstarch
1 to 2 tablespoons unsalted butter,
    at room temperature

1. MAKE THE GLAZE: Combine the apricot preserves and water in a small bowl. Heat in a microwave oven on medium power for 20 to 30 seconds or until bubbly. Alternatively, cook in a small saucepan over direct heat until bubbly. Brush the bottom of the tart shell with a thin layer of the glaze. Save the remainder for glazing the top of the tart.

2. PREPARE THE PEARS: Peel the pears with a potato peeler. Cut the pears in half from top to bottom and core with a melon baller. Immediately place the pears in a large nonreactive bowl, and sprinkle them with the lemon juice to prevent them from turning brown. Do not slice pears until you are ready to fill the tart shell.

3. ASSEMBLE THE TART: Preheat the oven to 375 degrees. Position the oven rack in the lower third of the oven.

4. Combine the sugar and cornstarch in a small bowl. Set aside.

5. Place the pears cut side down on a cutting board. Using a thin sharp knife with a 4- to 5-inch blade, cut the pear halves lengthwise in 1/4-inch slices. 1

6. Return the sliced pears to the large bowl with the lemon juice. Add the sugar and cornstarch mixture, and gently toss the fruit with the dry ingredients to coat the slices.

7. Fill the tart shell with the pears making 2 layers of pears. 2 Use the smaller pieces for the bottom layer, arranging them in overlapping slices with the widest side of the pears placed against the edge of the tart pan.

8. Arrange the inside row of pears perpendicular to the first,

with the rounded side facing parallel to the edge of the pan. Overlap the slices to form a large rosette in the center. Tuck leftover slices into the already arranged slices (see color insert).

9. Using a rubber spatula, scrape remaining juices from the bottom of the bowl onto the pears. Dot the fruit with butter.

10. Bake the tart for 50 minutes. Lay a square of aluminum foil loosely over the top of the tart, and continue baking for another 5 to 10 minutes, or until the juices begin to bubble.

11. Place the tart on a cooling rack and glaze while it is still warm. Starting with the outer edge of the pears, brush the top of the fruit lightly with warm apricot preserves. Serve the tart slightly warm with vanilla ice cream.

STORAGE

Store any leftover tart, covered loosely with waxed paper then aluminum foil, in the refrigerator for up to 3 days. This tart can be frozen (see page 77).

VARIATION

A Simple Apple Tart

Follow the preceding recipe for the Simple Pear Tart, making the following changes:

✦ *Substitute 5 to 6 Golden Delicious or Granny Smith apples (about 2 1/2 pounds).*

✦ *Reduce the sugar to 6 tablespoons.*

✦ *Reduce the cornstarch to 1 tablespoon.*

✦ *Add 1/2 teaspoon ground cinnamon to the sugar and cornstarch mixture.*

✦ *Peel the apples with a potato peeler. Cut the fruit in half from top to bottom, then core. Lay the apples cut side down on a cutting board. Using a thin, sharp knife with a 4- to 5-inch blade, cut the apple halves into 1/4-inch slices. Cut across the fruit instead of from top to bottom.*

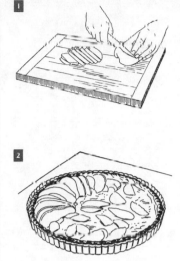

Recipe Roundup

✦ Prebaking a pastry shell will ensure a crisp bottom crust when using a moist fruit filling.

✦ If you want a dry bottom crust, be sure there are no cracks or holes in the dough.

✦ Coating and baking an un-filled pastry shell with melted preserves seals the pastry and prevents fruit juices from penetrating the crust.

✦ Use a melon baller to remove the core of a pear with the least amount of waste.

✦ Fruit for tart shells should be cut according to its contour. Because pears are tapered, slice them lengthwise, starting from the stem end. Apples and most other round fruit fit better in the shell if sliced the opposite way.

✦ It is best not to slice pears ahead of time because the flesh deteriorates quickly.

✦ After fruit is cut, sprinkle the surface with lemon juice to prevent discoloring. *Do not soak the fruit in lemon water;* it will pick up too much moisture.

✦ Combine cornstarch or flour with sugar before adding it to the fruit to prevent lumping.

✦ Starch will dissolve better during baking if the fruit is first sprinkled with lemon juice. The juice moistens the surface of the fruit, which helps the cornstarch dissolve.

✦ Fruit used for open tarts is rarely cut thick because it would take too long to soften during baking.

✦ Less fruit is used for tarts than for pies because most tarts are baked in shallow pans without a top crust.

✦ When arranging fruit in a tart shell, use the ends and irregular pieces for the bottom layer. Save the more uniform pieces for the top layer.

✦ When arranging sliced fruit in a pastry shell, use the larger pieces for the outer ring and the smaller ones for the center. Since the dimension of a circle is graduated, always place the widest pieces near the edge.

✦ The fruit on open tarts is usually artfully placed. The slices can be positioned lengthwise or with the rounded side against the edge.

◆ If the top of a tart is browning too quickly, lay a strip of aluminum foil loosely over the top.

◆ To tell if a fruit tart is done, watch for the juices to bubble.

◆ Glaze the top of the baked tart while it is still hot. This will seal the surface.

◆ Unlike pies, most fruit tarts can be served soon after baking.

LESSON 4

ABOUT

French Fruit Tarts with Pastry Cream

 CRISP CRUST, COLORFUL fruit, and silky pastry cream are the tastes and textures that have made this European-style dessert a classic favorite. Its popularity has never wavered, and it continues to be a staple in pastry shops and on dessert menus in fine restaurants. ✳ Although fruit tarts with pastry cream may seem similar to fresh fruit tarts, there are three distinct differences that set them apart: (1) the pastry shell is almost always

completely baked before it is filled; (2) some form of cream filling is always used with the fruit; and (3) the filled tart is rarely baked.

Pastry cream (*crème patissière*) made from scratch is far superior to artificially flavored, packaged vanilla pudding. It is even better when it includes the tiny seeds of a vanilla bean. *Crème patissière* is a mainstay in the making of a multitude of desserts. While numerous recipes for fine pastry creams exist, there are slight variations in ingredients and somewhat different methods of incorporating them. What is important is that the cream be the desirable consistency and that it be smooth.

You'll be happy to master a pastry cream because of its versatility— it lends itself to a variety of flavors. For example, if I want to lighten the custard, I fold lightly whipped cream into it. With the addition of the whipped cream and unflavored gelatin, pastry cream becomes a Bavarian cream. The only drawback to pastry cream is that, because it is made with fresh eggs, it is highly perishable and should be used within 2 or 3 days.

The best fruits to use for these tarts are berries or soft-flesh varieties that do not discolor or require cooking. Strawberries, raspberries, blackberries, and blueberries are obvious choices. Other candidates are plums, mangoes, green and purple grapes, and sliced kiwi. Canned fruits such as apricots, cling peaches, pears, pineapple, and mandarin oranges also work extremely well—either singly or in combination with fresh fruits. Avoid hard, uncooked fruits such as apples and pears. If you wish to use these, they should be poached first.

A great advantage to these tarts is that they are quick to assemble. While the crust will be at its prime if the tart is put together shortly before serving, it can be made early in the day. Just leave the glaze off until the end because, if it is applied too soon, it makes the fruit soggy.

Toujours strawberries and cream.

SAMUEL JOHNSON

French Fruit Tart with Pastry Cream

I CAN'T THINK of a more handsome dessert to serve for unexpected company than this glistening fruit-topped pastry.

At a Glance

SERVES: 8 to 10

PAN: 11-inch metal tart

PASTRY PREP: Baked

DIFFICULTY: 🥿🥿

1 11-inch *Classic Tart Pastry* crust (pages 102, 104), baked

PASTRY CREAM
2½ cups milk
½ cup sugar
3-inch piece vanilla bean or 1½ teaspoons vanilla extract
5 large egg yolks
3 tablespoons unsifted all-purpose flour
2 tablespoons cornstarch
¼ teaspoon salt
1 to 2 tablespoons unsalted butter, at room temperature

GARNISH
1 pint strawberries, preferably uniform, medium berries
6 to 8 shelled pistachio nuts, skinned and coarsely chopped (optional)

GLAZE
⅓ cup apricot preserves
2 teaspoons water

1. MAKE THE PASTRY CREAM: Place the milk and ¼ cup of the sugar in a large nonreactive saucepan. Stir to combine. Split the vanilla bean in half lengthwise and add it to the milk. Cook over low heat without stirring until the milk forms a skin on the surface.

2. Whisk the egg yolks well in a large bowl. Gradually whisk in the remaining ¼ cup sugar, beating until the mixture is slightly thickened.

3. Remove the vanilla bean from the milk. With a paring knife, scrape the seeds from the pod. Whisk the seeds into the yolks, reserving the pod. Sift the flour, cornstarch, and salt together, and stir into the yolks. Whisk until smooth.

4. Stir one-third of the hot milk into the yolks to temper them. Then pour the yolk mixture into the remaining milk, stirring well. Add the vanilla pod. Over low heat, bring the mixture to a boil, stirring constantly with a whisk. After it comes to the boil, continue to simmer the pastry cream for at least 1 minute.

5. Remove the pastry cream from the heat. Discard the vanilla bean. Dot the top with butter. *Note:* If using vanilla extract, add it now. Stir briefly to blend in the butter.

6. Empty the pastry cream into a medium bowl. Tear a square of plastic wrap, and butter a circle in the center, about the same size as the top of the pastry cream bowl. Lay the plastic wrap, buttered side down, against the pastry cream. This will prevent a skin from forming on the surface. Let cool in the refrigerator until ready to use.

7. Spoon the pastry cream into the pastry shell. Smooth the surface with a small offset spatula. Press a square of buttered plastic wrap against the top of the pastry cream. Refrigerate until ready to garnish with strawberries.

8. **COMPLETE THE TART:** Wash, thoroughly dry, and hull the strawberries. Cut the berries in half lengthwise, and lay them out on a pan in a single layer to prevent bruising.

9. Arrange the strawberries in concentric circles on top of the pastry cream (see color insert). Choose the larger berries for the outer circle, and place them with the widest side against the edge of the pan. Refrigerate.

10. **MAKE THE GLAZE:** Combine the apricot preserves with the water in an ovenproof glass container. Heat in a microwave oven on medium power for 30 seconds. Alternatively, cook in a small saucepan over direct heat until bubbly. Pass through a strainer. Gently brush the warm preserves on the strawberries. Garnish the center with pistachios. Serve at once. This tart is best eaten the day it is made.

STORAGE

Lay a square of waxed paper over the top of any leftover tart. Then cover loosely with aluminum foil and refrigerate for up to 3 days. Freezing is not recommended.

Enriched Pastry Cream

FOLLOW THE RECIPE FOR PASTRY CREAM, increasing the cornstarch to 3 tablespoons. When the pastry cream is tepid, whip 1/2 cup heavy cream to *soft peaks*. Fold about 1/2 cup of the pastry cream into the whipped cream to temper it, then fold the whipped cream mixture into the remaining pastry cream. The whipped cream will blend more smoothly into the pastry cream if combined before the pastry cream becomes too firm.

Recipe Roundup

✦ Pastry cream is highly perishable because it is made with fresh eggs and dairy products. Always use immaculately clean equipment, and keep the finished cream refrigerated until ready for use.

✦ Always make pastry cream in a heavy, nonreactive saucepan such as stainless steel or heavy-bottomed enamel. Avoid aluminum and thin metal pots.

✦ Milk burns easily. Never scald or heat it in a thin pot or over high heat. Heating milk with some sugar will help prevent burning.

✦ When combining liquid and dry ingredients, start by adding only enough liquid to dissolve the dry. Adding too much liquid at once promotes lumping.

✦ Avoid adding starch directly to liquid unless the starch is combined with some sugar. The sugar helps bridge the starch to the liquid to prevent immediate lumping.

✦ When cooking a pastry cream, always scrape around the bend of the saucepan to release any starch that may adhere.

✦ As the filling reaches the boiling point, whisk it rapidly. This will ensure a smoother filling. However, once the filling boils for a few seconds, cease mixing vigorously.

✦ Pastry cream should continue to cook at a gentle boil for about a minute after the boiling point so that the starch granules can swell and bond. If the filling is removed from the heat too soon, the starch will lose its thickening ability and the filling will liquefy.

✦ Avoid overmixing a cooked filling. Overmixing weakens the bonding of the starch, causing the granules to separate.

✦ If a cooked filling forms lumps after it thickens, whisk it briefly. If it is still not smooth, strain it while it is still hot. Do not beat or overmix it.

✦ If butter is to be added to a cooked filling, distribute the butter pieces on top of the hot filling. Wait a few seconds for it to melt, then stir it in gently.

✦ For the best flavor, add extracts and/or liqueur off the heat, after the filling is cooked.

✦ If using a vanilla bean, don't discard the pod after removing it from the filling. It can be used again (see page 13).

✦ Completed pastry cream should be removed from the saucepan immediately after cooking to promote fast cooling.

✦ A hot, cooked filling should always be covered with a piece of buttered plastic wrap to prevent a skin from forming.

✦ A prebaked pastry shell should always be cool before it is filled with pastry cream.

✦ For the optimum crisp pastry shell, it should be topped with the pastry cream shortly before serving. However, for convenience, the shell can be filled up to 1 day ahead.

✦ Fruits and berries can be arranged on the tart several hours before serving; however they should not be glazed until shortly before serving. Once the glaze is applied, the surface of the tart becomes watery and the fruits turn soggy.

✦ If garnishing the tart with nuts, do this just before serving. Otherwise, they will become too soft.

Beyond the Primer

Pastry Doughs & Crunchy Shells

 HE PRIMER HAS given you the foundation you need for making basic pie and tart doughs. Now here is the playground for expanding your repertoire of pastry doughs. This chapter includes a broad variety of contemporary recipes, along with many old-time favorites. ✳ In The Primer, I was reluctant to recommend using the food processor for adding liquid

to the dry ingredients. This is because experience is needed to develop the sense of timing necessary to avoid overprocessing the dough. But now that you have mastered the basics and are familiar with how dough should look and feel, you can move on to adding the liquid by machine.

Before you start, take time to go back to The Primer, and read "Before You Begin" on the following page. Both the novice and the experienced baker can benefit from the many invaluable tips you will find there. Now you can move forward and explore myriad mouthwatering crusts.

LOOK IN THE PRIMER to find recipes for most widely used pastry doughs and variations.

◆ Flaky Pie Pastry I (page 98)

◆ Flaky Pie Pastry II (page 100)

◆ Classic Tart Pastry I (page 102)

◆ Classic Tart Pastry II (page 104)

Before You Begin

✦ You can substitute up to 50 percent whole wheat flour for all-purpose flour in most pastry dough recipes. However, the higher the percentage of whole wheat flour, the more water the dough will absorb.

✦ On warm, humid days, chill the flour for 10 minutes in the freezer before you make pastry dough. This will prevent the fat from becoming too soft, which would make a pasty dough.

✦ A small amount (up to 1 tablespoon) of sesame, poppy, or other tiny seeds can be added to pastry dough for added flavor. Just stir the seeds into the dry ingredients before you incorporate the fat.

✦ When fat is incorporated into the flour, there should be some large crumbs and some small ones, rather than a uniform texture. Large crumbs give flakiness and small crumbs give tenderness.

✦ Remember that the amount of liquid needed for a pastry dough can differ with every new bag of flour, even those of the same brand.

✦ While bleached and unbleached flour can be used interchangeably, unbleached flour may require more liquid.

✦ To determine if pastry dough contains enough liquid, press it against the side and bottom of the bowl with your hand. If its particles form a mass, it is ready.

✦ Never use a spoon to blend the liquid into pastry crumbs as it mashes the dough and makes it tough. Use a fork and toss the mixture rather than stir.

✦ Pastry dough should always be refrigerated for at least 30 minutes before it is rolled. This allows the liquid to be absorbed evenly through the dough and the gluten to relax.

✦ Avoid rolling dough that is chilled to the point where it is hardened. Cold dough is difficult to roll and cracks at the edges. To overcome this, remove the dough from the refrigerator 15 to 30 minutes before rolling depending upon climate conditions.

✦ Dough should frequently be given a quarter turn, clockwise, during the rolling process. This will ensure an even surface.

✦ Lifting pastry periodically during rolling helps prevent stretching of the dough.

✦ Buttering the pie plate helps brown the pastry on the bottom and reduces shrinkage.

✦ All pie and tart doughs benefit if chilled briefly after fluting or crimping. This will help maintain the decorative edge.

✦ Lightly pricking the pastry dough with a fork is essential when baking blind. This cuts the gluten strands and gives the crust better shape and less shrinkage.

✦ When baking blind, it is *essential* to chill the shaped pie or tart shell before baking.

✦ When baking an unfilled pastry shell, always reserve some scraps of dough for patching if it splits during baking. It's better to patch than to risk having the filling leak through a hole.

✦ Most pastry doughs can be prepared in advance and refrigerated for up to 3 days. For longer storage, they may be frozen. Those I do not recommend making ahead or freezing are biscuit-style doughs and doughs made with vegetable or other oils.

Cheddar Pastry

TRY THIS PASTRY WITH PIES made from apples, pears, or grapes. There is no second-guessing when it comes to pairing fruit and cheese; they make a marvelous marriage.

2 1/3 cups unsifted all-purpose flour
3/4 teaspoon salt
1/2 teaspoon baking powder
1/2 cup partially frozen unsalted butter, cut into 1/2-inch cubes
1/2 cup partially frozen vegetable shortening, cut into small pieces
2/3 to 3/4 cup lightly packed grated Cheddar cheese (2 ounces)
4 tablespoons ice water, or more as needed

1. Place the dry ingredients in the bowl of a food processor. Process for 5 seconds to blend.

2. Add half of the butter and shortening and all of the cheese. Toss with a spatula to coat with flour. Pulse 4 or 5 times, then process for 5 seconds. Add the remaining fats, pulse again 4 or 5 times, then process about 5 seconds. The mixture should have the texture of coarse meal and still contain some larger pieces of fat.

3. Empty the mixture into a large bowl. Pass the crumbs through your fingers to break up any very large clumps. Add the ice water, 1 tablespoon at a time, tossing the crumbs with a fork between each addition. Take a handful of crumbs and squeeze gently to see if they will stick together. If not, add additional ice water as needed.

4. Form into two 4- to 5-inch disks by pressing the mixture against the side of the bowl. All of the crumbs should adhere and clean the bowl. If not, add a few more drops of water. Dust the disks generously with flour and cover with plastic wrap. Refrigerate for 30 minutes or longer before rolling. Shape as directed in recipe or refer to The Pastry Primer, pages 84–105.

At a Glance

MAKES: 1 double crust for a 9- or 10-inch pie

METHOD: Food Processor and Hand

USE FOR: Pies and cobblers

Toasted Coconut Pie Pastry

TOASTED COCONUT GIVES FLAVOR AND CRUNCH to this pastry. For this dough, the water is added while the food processor is in motion. You must work quickly after the coconut and water have been added so that the coconut will not be too finely ground and the pastry will not become sticky.

At a Glance

MAKES: 1 9-inch pie shell

METHOD: Food Processor

USE FOR: Pies

1/3 cup sweetened flaked coconut
1 cup plus 2 tablespoons unsifted all-purpose flour
1/4 teaspoon baking powder
3/8 teaspoon salt
1/4 cup well-chilled unsalted butter, cut into 1/2-inch cubes
1/4 cup well-chilled vegetable shortening, cut into 1/2-inch cubes
2 tablespoons ice water

1. Preheat the oven to 325 degrees. Place the coconut in a shallow pan and bake for 8 to 10 minutes or until golden brown. For even browning, stir occasionally and watch carefully, as it burns quickly. Cool before using.

2. Place the flour, baking powder, and salt in the bowl of a food processor fitted with the steel blade. Pulse until well blended. Add half the butter and shortening. Using a rubber spatula—never your fingers—toss to coat with flour. Pulse 6 to 8 times, then add the remaining fat. Pulse 4 or 5 times, then process for 10 to 15 seconds, or until the crumbs are the size of coarse meal with some larger pieces of fat.

3. Remove the processor lid and add the toasted coconut, distributing it around the bowl. Start the processor. *Immediately* pour in the ice water through the feeder tube using a container with a spout. Stop the machine as soon as the water is added. *Do not allow the dough to form a mass.*

4. Empty the contents of the processor into a large mixing bowl. With floured hands, press the crumbs against the side of the bowl, working the mixture until it forms a mass. All the crumbs should adhere, forming a dough that cleans the bowl. If it doesn't, add a few more drops of water. Shape into a 4- to 5-inch disk. Dust generously with flour, score with the side of your hand, and cover with plastic wrap. Chill in the refrigerator for at least 30 minutes. Shape as directed in recipe or see pages 91–96.

Super Tender Pie Pastry

THIS RECIPE WAS INSPIRED BY AN American pastry master, Monroe Boston Strause, from his book *Pie Marches On*, published in 1939. The butter and vegetable shortening are blended together before they are added to the flour. The end result is an extremely tender, delicate pastry that is one of my favorites.

¹/₂ cup unsalted butter, at room temperature
¹/₂ cup vegetable shortening, at room temperature
2¹/₂ cups sifted all-purpose flour
1 tablespoon sugar
3/4 teaspoon salt
4 tablespoons ice water, or more as needed

1. Blend the butter and vegetable shortening together, mixing until the two are thoroughly combined. Shape into a log, wrap in plastic, and chill until firm. Cut into ¹/₂-inch pieces.

2. Using a whisk or fork, blend the flour and sugar together. Add the pieces of fat and toss to coat with flour. Cut the fats into the flour with a pastry blender until the mixture resembles coarse meal. Scrape the blender clean every so often.

3. Dissolve the salt in the water. Add the liquid, 1 tablespoon at a time, tossing with a fork to blend. Press the dough with your fingertips to see if it will hold together. If not, add more water, 1 teaspoon at a time.

4. With floured hands, form into two 4- to 5-inch flat disks by pressing the mixture against the side of the bowl. All of the crumbs should adhere to the dough and clean the bowl. If not, add a few more drops of water. Dust the disks generously with flour, and score with the side of your hand. Cover with plastic wrap and chill 30 minutes or longer before using. Shape as directed in recipe or see pages 91–96.

At a Glance

MAKES: 1 double crust for a 9-inch pie

METHOD: Hand

USE FOR: Pies and cobblers

1940s All-Butter Pie Pastry

THIS ALL-BUTTER PASTRY MAKES a less flaky but very tender crust that is especially nice to use for juicy fruit pies.

2 1/4 cups unsifted all-purpose flour
1 tablespoon sugar
1 teaspoon baking powder
1/2 pound (2 sticks) well-chilled
    unsalted butter, cut into
    1/2-inch pieces
1/2 teaspoon salt
2 teaspoons white vinegar or
    lemon juice
3 tablespoons ice water
1 large egg, lightly beaten

1. Put the flour, sugar, and baking powder in the bowl of a food processor. Pulse 5 times to blend. Add the butter and process 10 seconds, then pulse 5 times.

2. Empty the processor bowl onto a lightly floured work surface. Make a well in the center.

3. Dissolve the salt in the vinegar. Pour into the well.

4. Add water and egg to the center of the well and beat with a fork. Draw the flour-butter mixture to the center with a fork, creating large clumps.

5. Fraisage (see page 69) 3 times. Form into two 4- to 5-inch disks, dust lightly with flour, score, cover with plastic wrap, and chill for 30 minutes. Shape as directed in recipe or see pages 91–96.

Short Pastry Dough for Cobblers

PASTRY REFERRED TO AS "SHORT" is one that usually has a high ratio of fat to flour. For easier handling, the manner in which the liquid is added to the crumbs here is slightly different from other doughs. I like to use this dough for cobblers because it is especially flaky.

1½ cups sifted all-purpose flour
½ teaspoon salt
¼ teaspoon baking powder
½ cup well-chilled vegetable shortening, cut into small bits
3 tablespoons well-chilled unsalted butter, cut into small bits
3 tablespoons ice water

1. Sift the flour, salt, and baking powder together into a large bowl. Add the shortening and butter, and toss to coat the pieces of fat with flour. With a pastry blender, cut the fats into the flour until the mixture resembles coarse meal. Scrape the blender clean every so often.

2. Place the ice water into a small bowl. Stir in ¼ cup of the crumb mixture with a fork. Then sprinkle the water mixture over all of the remaining crumbs and toss with a fork. *Do not mash —toss.* Gradually the crumbs will form into clumps.

3. With floured hands, form dough into a mass by pressing the mixture against the side of the bowl. All of the crumbs should adhere to the dough and clean the bowl. If not, add a few more drops of water. Form the dough into a flat rectangle (if you are using an oblong dish) or shape into a flat disk. Dust the dough generously with flour, score with the side of your hand, and cover with plastic wrap. Chill in the refrigerator for 1 hour or longer. Roll as directed in recipe.

At a Glance

MAKES: Crust for 7 × 11 × 2-inch cobbler

METHOD: Hand

USE FOR: Cobblers

Sweet Cream Biscuit Dough

SWEET CREAM IS THE SECRET INGREDIENT that makes this tender biscuit topping melt in your mouth. Whether you use it as a crust for a cobbler or cut it into biscuits for shortcake, you are in for a treat.

SMALL	LARGE	
1/2	3/4	teaspoon vanilla extract
2/3	1	cup heavy cream
1 1/3	2	cups unsifted all-purpose flour
3	4	tablespoons sugar
2	3	teaspoons baking powder
1/4	3/8	teaspoon salt
3/4	1	teaspoon grated navel or Valencia orange zest
1/2	3/4	teaspoon grated lemon zest
4	6	tablespoons cold unsalted butter, cut into 1/2-inch cubes

1. Stir the vanilla into the cream. Set aside.

2. Place the flour, sugar, baking powder, salt, and orange and lemon zest into the bowl of a food processor. Pulse the ingredients to blend. Distribute the butter around the bowl. Pulse 4 or 5 times, then process until the mixture forms fine crumbs, 8 to 10 seconds. Then pulse 4 or 5 more times.

3. Pour the cream into the bowl. Pulse 6 to 8 times or until the mixture begins to form a mass. *Do not overprocess.*

4. Empty the dough onto a well-floured surface. The dough will be wet. With the help of a dough scraper, turn the dough a few times to coat it with flour. Then flour your hands and knead the dough 4 or 5 times, just until the surface is smooth. Flatten the dough into a rectangle, and roll into the desired size. *Do not overwork.* Roll as directed in recipe. This dough should be baked soon after making.

**Fresh Coconut Tart
with Buttermilk Custard**
Page 378

Flaky Pie Pastry

Page 98. **1.** Sift the dry ingredients into a large mixing bowl. **2.** Use a pastry blender to cut the fats into the flour. **3.** Drizzle ice water around the rim of the bowl and use a kitchen fork to push the mixture toward the center. **4.** The dough should feel moist and clean the bowl. **5.** Form the dough into 2 balls. **6.** Flatten each ball into a disk. **7.** Smooth the edges of the disk.

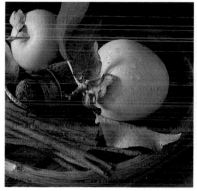

**Old-Fashioned
Apple Pie**
Page 108

(opposite)
Lemon Meringue Pie
Page 114

(opposite)
French Fruit Tart with Pastry Cream
Page 126.

A Simple Pear Tart
Page 120

**Strawberry Fig
Cobbler with Quilted
Biscuit Topping**
Page 340

Plum Rosettes on Shortbread
Page 392

Smashing Sweet Potato Pie
Page 316

(top to bottom)
**Summer Raspberry Pie
with Wine Pastry**
Page 226

**Flourless Macaroon Tart
in Almond Nut Pastry**
Page 308

**Orange Scented Middle
Eastern Nut Swirl**
Page 322

(above)
**Shaker Citrus Pie in a
Cookie Crust**
Page 250

(clockwise, from top)
**Petite Meringue Shells
and Meringue Shell**
Page 160

Chocolate Crumb Crust
Page 168

All-Nut Pastry Shell
Page 168

(top to bottom)
Blueberry Crumb Pie with Warm Blueberry Sauce
Page 192

Banana Cream Pie with Pecan Brittle
Page 246

Black Forest Cherry Tart
Page 280

(far left)
All-Fruit Mincemeat Jalousie
Page 202

(left)
Fresh Apricot Pie
Page 184

(below)
White Chocolate Caffe Tart
Page 284 and **Devilish Chocolate Candy Tart**
Page 252

(left)
Tutti-Frutti Amaretti Tart
Page 362 and **Sorbet Frosted Lemon Bavarian Tart**
Page 350

**Smoky Joe's
Turkey Tart**
Page 434

**Tomato, Pesto, and
Goat Cheese Galette**
Page 436

Sinfully Rich Pecan Pastry

THIS EXCELLENT PASTRY RECIPE COMES from caterer Marcia Germanow of Saddle River, New Jersey. Not only is it great with her pumpkin pie (page 318) but I also recommend it for chocolate cream pie, as well as most fruit pies. If you want a top and bottom crust, double the recipe.

1 1/2 cups unsifted all-purpose flour
2 tablespoons strained
    confectioners' sugar
1/2 teaspoon salt
1/2 cup well-chilled unsalted
    butter, cut into 1/2-inch dice
4 tablespoons well-chilled
    vegetable shortening, cut into
    small dice
1/2 cup medium chopped pecans
3 to 4 tablespoon ice water

1. Whisk together the flour, confectioners' sugar, and salt in a large bowl. Add the butter and vegetable shortening. Using 2 table knives or your fingertips, cut or work the fats into the dry ingredients until the mixture resembles coarse meal. Add the pecans and toss with a fork to incorporate.

2. Add the ice water, 1 tablespoon at a time, drizzling it around the edge of the bowl. Stir with the fork until moist clumps form.

3. With lightly floured hands, shape the dough into a 5-inch disk. Score the pastry with the side of your hand to relax the gluten, cover the dough with plastic wrap, and refrigerate for 1 hour. Roll as directed in recipe or see pages 91–96.

Roll as directed in recipe or see pages 91–96.

At a Glance

MAKES: 1 9-inch pie crust
METHOD: Hand
USE FOR: Pies

Whole Wheat Pastry

WHOLE WHEAT PASTRY FLOUR IS MORE refined and has a lower gluten content than most regular whole wheat flour. Do *not* try to use high-gluten stone-ground whole wheat flour; the crust will be tough, dry, and difficult to roll. Whole wheat pastry flour can be purchased at specialty food stores, upscale supermarkets, and health food stores.

At a Glance

MAKES: 1 double crust for a 9- or 10-inch pie

METHOD: Food Processor and Hand

USE FOR: Pies and cobblers

1¼ cups unsifted all-purpose flour
1¼ cups whole wheat pastry flour
1 tablespoon sugar (optional)
3/4 teaspoon salt
1/2 teaspoon baking powder
1/2 cup partially frozen unsalted butter, cut into 1/2-inch cubes
1/2 cup partially frozen vegetable shortening, cut into small pieces
6 to 7 tablespoons ice water

1. Place the dry ingredients into the bowl of a food processor. Process for 5 seconds to blend.

2. Add half of the butter and shortening. Toss to coat with flour. Pulse 4 or 5 times, then process for 5 seconds. Add the remaining fats and pulse again 4 or 5 times, then process another 5 seconds. The mixture should have the texture of coarse meal with some larger pieces of fat.

3. Empty the crumbs into a large bowl. Add the ice water, 1 tablespoon at a time, drizzling it around the side of the bowl. Toss the crumbs with a fork with each addition. Do not mash.

4. With floured hands, form into two 4- to 5-inch disks by pressing the mixture against the side of the bowl. All of the crumbs should adhere and clean the bowl. If not, add a few more drops of water.

5. Dust the disks generously with flour, score with the side of your hand to relax the gluten, and cover with plastic wrap. Refrigerate for 30 minutes or longer before rolling. Roll as directed in recipe or as desired.

Wine Pastry

USING WHITE WINE AS THE MOISTENER in pie crust is a suggestion from Verene Cohn Walsh of Escondido, California. Verene, a venerable pie baker, has a reputation for making very flaky pastry. The secret, of course, is the alcohol she uses in her dough.

Verene sometimes uses vodka or gin for her pastry, too. However, when she does, she has to open the oven door for a few seconds to let the fumes escape. If you don't have an open bottle of wine, a less risky alternative to hard alcohol is dry vermouth.

1³/4 cups sifted all-purpose flour
¹/2 cup sifted cake flour
1 tablespoon sugar
³/4 teaspoon salt
²/3 cup well-chilled vegetable
    shortening, cut into small
    pieces
3 tablespoons cold unsalted butter,
    cut into ¹/2-inch pieces
5 to 6 tablespoons well-chilled
    white wine

1. Sift together the flours, sugar, and salt in a large bowl. Add the shortening and butter, and toss to coat the pieces of fat with flour. With a pastry blender, cut the fats into the flour until the mixture resembles coarse meal. Scrape the blender clean every so often.

2. Add the wine, 1 tablespoon at a time, tossing the mixture with a fork to blend. After 5 tablespoons have been added, press the dough with your fingertips to see if it will hold together. If not, add the remaining tablespoon of wine. Do not overmix.

3. With floured hands, form into two 4- to 5-inch flat disks by pressing the mixture against the side of the bowl. All of the crumbs should adhere to the dough and clean the bowl. If not, add a few more drops of wine.

4. Dust the disks generously with flour, and score the dough with side of your hand. Cover with plastic wrap and chill 30 minutes or longer before using. Roll as directed in recipe or as desired.

VARIATION
Black Pepper Wine Pastry

Add 1 teaspoon freshly ground black pepper to the dry ingredients before sifting. Then proceed with the recipe.

Vegetable Oil Pastry

THE AMOUNT OF OIL HERE has been kept to a minimum for heart-healthy reasons. However, for an even more tender dough, you can increase the oil in the recipe by 1 tablespoon. If you miss the flavor of butter, try adding 1 tablespoon melted clarified butter along with the vegetable oil. Another enhancement is to give a touch of sweetness to the dough by adding 2 teaspoons of sugar to the flour.

At a Glance

MAKES: 1 single crust for a 9- or 10-inch pie or 9- or 11-inch tart

METHOD: Hand

USE FOR: Pies and tarts

For easier rolling, I like to chill the pastry about 15 to 20 minutes, but avoid letting it harden. If you are making a double-crust pie, double up on the recipe.

1¹/₂ cups sifted all-purpose flour
3/4 teaspoon baking powder
¹/₂ teaspoon salt
¹/₄ cup boiling water
¹/₃ cup vegetable oil (canola or safflower)

1. Sift the flour, baking powder, and salt together 3 times.

2. Place the boiling water in a large bowl. Whisk in the vegetable oil, adding it by droplets, then in a slow stream. The mixture will emulsify.

3. Add the dry ingredients all at once, blending the ingredients with a rubber spatula. Be sure to scrape around the bowl with the spatula. Gather the mixture with your hand, and knead it lightly 6 or 7 times to form a smooth dough.

4. With well-floured hands, form the dough into a 5-inch disk. Dust the disk with flour and cover with plastic wrap. Chill 15 to 20 minutes before using.

NOTE

If making a pie crust, spray the pie plate with nonstick coating. Wipe the excess with a paper towel. Tart pans do not require greasing.

5. SHAPE THE PASTRY: Roll the pastry to a ¹/₈-inch thickness between sheets of plastic wrap, making a circle that is 3 to 4 inches larger than your pan. Remove the top layer of plastic wrap. Place the pie or tart pan on the far side of the pastry. Lift the 2 corners of plastic wrap closest to you, and invert the dough into the pan. Press against the plastic wrap to mold the dough into the crease of the pan. *Do not stretch*. Peel off the plastic wrap, and flute the edge.

If making a tart, trim the pastry by running the rolling pin over the top of the pan.

6. Place the pastry shell on a shallow pan, and chill at least 30 minutes. Prick well with a fork, then bake blind (page 95).

(page 95)

NOTE ═══

The baking time must be increased for pastry doughs made with oil. Blind-bake at 425 degrees for 20 minutes. Remove beans, reduce oven temperature to 375 degrees, and bake an additional 8 to 10 minutes or until the bottom is well browned. This pastry must be thoroughly baked for a crisp crust.

VARIATIONS ═══

Nut-Flavored Pastry

Replace about half of the vegetable oil with an equal amount of walnut or hazelnut oil. Proceed with recipe.

Whole Wheat Pastry with Vegetable Oil

Replace 3/4 cup of the all-purpose flour with 3/4 cup whole wheat pastry flour. Proceed with recipe. If the dough seems a bit dry, add 1 to 2 teaspoons of water.

Savory Olive Oil Pastry

Substitute extra-virgin olive oil for the vegetable oil.

Stir 2 to 3 tablespoons finely chopped fresh herbs into the flour. Use 1 to 2 teaspoons finely chopped thyme or rosemary, 1 tablespoon minced parsley, and 1 tablespoon snipped chives.

Vegetable Oil Pastry

VEGETABLE OIL PASTRY DOUGHS offer a very pleasant alternative to doughs made with butter and vegetable shortening when cholesterol and fat are a concern. They are easy to prepare: instead of cutting the fat into the flour you stir it in.

This type of dough should be made by hand, never in a food processor. When it is assembled, the pastry does not look or feel like one made with solid or semisolid fats—the texture is somewhat oily and extremely soft. Because of this, it is best to roll the pastry between sheets of plastic wrap or waxed paper. While the pastry holds a fluted edge very well, I do not recommend using it for a lattice top because the strips are too limp to handle.

Sweet Tart Pastry

PÂTE SUCRÉE

THIS DELICATE DOUGH PAIRS ESPECIALLY well with fruit tarts because of its fine cookielike crumb and rich, buttery flavor. While I like to use a food processor to cut the butter into the flour, the procedure can also be done with a pastry blender or by rubbing the fat in with your fingertips.

1 1/2 cups unsifted all-purpose flour
3 tablespoons superfine sugar
1/4 teaspoon salt
2/3 cup cool unsalted butter, cut into 1/2-inch cubes (see Note)
1 large egg, lightly beaten
1/2 teaspoon vanilla extract

1. **HAND METHOD:** Sift dry ingredients into a large bowl.

2. Toss the butter through the flour mixture to coat the pieces. Using your fingertips, rub the fat into the flour, working it until you have created a coarse meal with a few pea-size particles of fat.

1. **FOOD PROCESSOR METHOD:** Place the flour, sugar, and salt into the bowl of a food processor fitted with the steel blade. Pulse 3 to 4 times to blend.

2. Distribute the butter around the bowl and pulse 6 to 7 times. Then process for 6 to 8 seconds. The crumbs should be about the size of coarse meal with a few pea-size particles of fat.

3. Empty the crumbs onto a cool surface, such as marble or a chilled counter. Form the mixture into a mound. Make a 4- to 5-inch well in the center of the mound. Combine the egg and vanilla, and pour the mixture into the well.

4. Using a fork, draw the crumbs into the egg mixture, about 1 to 2 tablespoons at a time. When all of the crumbs are added, toss the mixture a few times with a pastry blender to form large clumps, then scrape into a mound.

5. Using the heel of your hand, push 2 to 3 tablespoons of the dough at a time, outward in 6- to 8-inch sweeps. This will blend the fat and flour and give the crust a delicate texture. If your hand becomes sticky, flour it as needed. Repeat the process until all of the dough has been worked. Gather the dough into a mound again, then repeat the entire procedure 2 additional times (see Fraisage, page 69).

6. After the third fraisage, flour your hands and gently knead the dough 5 or 6 times to make it smooth. Shape into a 5-inch disk. Dust the disk lightly with flour, score with the side of your hand, cover with plastic wrap, and refrigerate for 20 minutes before shaping.

Do not let the dough become too hard or it will be difficult to roll. If it does, let the pastry soften at room temperature. Roll as directed in recipe or see How to Line a Tart Pan with Pastry, page 93.

page 93.

NOTE

When the fat is cut into the flour in a food processor, the correct temperature of the butter is extremely important because it can be easily overworked. Unlike Classic Tart Pastry, where the particles of fat are usually visible, Sweet Tart Pastry is more like a cookie dough. The butter should be firm enough to make crumbs without becoming pasty, yet soft enough to blend into a smooth dough. If you press the butter with your finger, it should feel firm, but not as hard as it would feel if it were extremely cold or frozen.

A Word About Substituting Doughs

TART DOUGHS CAN BE SUBSTITUTED for most pie doughs, but it's best not to substitute pie doughs for tart doughs. This is because a pie dough is more fragile and may not be able to support a filling when the tart is unmolded. Because pie and tart doughs are not entirely interchangeable, be sure to refer to the At a Glance box for the recommended use.

All the pastry doughs and fillings in this book were paired according to my personal taste. This does not mean that you are limited to these pairings. One of the reasons I have given you a variety of pastry recipes is to allow you to explore different combinations. When swapping one dough for another, keep in mind compatibility of flavors.

Chocolate Tart Pastry

I ESPECIALLY LIKE THIS CRISP cookie-style pastry with creamy fillings and frozen desserts. Because the dough is chocolate, it is one of the trickier ones to handle. Do not overmix the dough when you make it, and do take the time to chill it as needed.

1 cup sifted all-purpose flour
1/3 cup strained Dutch-process cocoa powder
1/8 teaspoon salt
2/3 cup unsalted butter, at room temperature
1/2 cup superfine sugar
1 large egg yolk
1/2 teaspoon vanilla extract

1. Strain the flour, cocoa, and salt together 3 times. Set aside.

2. Place the butter in the large bowl of an electric mixer fitted with the paddle attachment. On medium-low speed, cream the butter until smooth, then add the sugar in 3 additions.

3. Combine the egg yolk and vanilla in a small bowl, then add it to the butter-sugar mixture.

4. On low speed, add the dry ingredients in 2 additions, mixing only until smooth.

5. With floured hands, form the dough into a 5-inch disk. Cover it with plastic wrap, and refrigerate for 45 to 50 minutes. If it becomes too hard to roll, let it stand at room temperature for a few minutes.

6. For shaping directions, refer to "Rolling and Shaping Cookie-Style Doughs" (page 69), chilling it as directed.

7. Preheat the oven to 375 degrees, and position the rack in the lower third of the oven.

8. Place the tart shell on a shallow pan, and blind bake (page 95) it for 18 to 20 minutes. Test for doneness by gently easing the aluminum foil from the side. If it sticks to the pastry, bake it for 2 or 3 minutes longer.

Let it rest 1 to 2 minutes out of the oven before removing the aluminum foil and baking beans. Be especially careful—this pastry is very fragile. Then return the pastry to the oven and bake it for 2 minutes longer to firm the surface. Cool completely before using.

Free-Form Shortbread Tart Pastry

THIS DELICATE PASTRY IS A PLAY on Scottish shortbread. The secret to its tender crumb comes from the rice flour in the dough; rice flour can be purchased at Asian and health food stores. For easier handling when rolling the pastry for an 11-inch tart, roll it directly on the cookie sheet on which it will be baked (see "Shaping and Baking Free-Form Tart Shells," page 71) It is best to bake the shortbread in a moderate oven temperature of 350 to 375 degrees. Any higher heat may cause this dough to overbake.

SMALL	LARGE	
1⅓	2	cups sifted all-purpose flour
4	6	tablespoons rice flour
6	6	tablespoons superfine sugar
⅔	1	cup firm, unsalted butter, cut into ½-inch cubes

1. HAND METHOD: Sift dry ingredients together into a large bowl.

2. Add the butter to the flour mixture. Using a pastry blender, cut the butter into the dry ingredients, forming small crumbs. Then, with your fingertips, continue to rub the fat into the flour. As the mixture becomes cohesive, knead it a few times until it is smooth and forms a mass.

3. With floured hands, shape into a 6- to 7-inch disk, cover with plastic wrap, and refrigerate for 15 to 20 minutes before shaping. This dough is best when used shortly after it is made. Roll as directed in recipe or see pages 91–96.

1. ELECTRIC MIXER METHOD: On low speed, cream the butter until soft. Add the sugar, 1 tablespoon at a time. Cream until light in color, about 1 minute. Blend in ½ the flour.

2. Remove bowl from the mixer and, using a wooden spoon, stir in the remaining flour. Mix *just* until mixture starts to form a mass. Empty on to a floured surface and, with floured hands, knead it 6 to 8 times or *just* until smooth.

3. Shape dough into a 6- to 7-inch disk, cover with plastic wrap, and refrigerate for 15 to 20 minutes before shaping. This dough is best when used shortly after it is made. Roll as directed in recipe or see pages 91–96.

At a Glance

SMALL RECIPE MAKES:
1 11-inch tart shell

LARGE RECIPE MAKES:
8 4-inch tarts

METHOD: Hand or Electric Mixer

USE FOR: Tarts

Golden Cornmeal Pastry

THE FLAVOR AND TEXTURE OF stone-ground cornmeal is what makes this pastry so special. High-quality cornmeal can be purchased at most health food stores and upscale supermarkets. I especially like this crust with savory tarts and those made with stone fruits and berries.

At a Glance

MAKES: 1 11-inch tart shell

METHOD: Food Processor

USE FOR: Tarts–Shaped or Free-Form

1 cup unsifted all-purpose flour
1/2 cup yellow cornmeal, preferably stone-ground
1 teaspoon sugar
1/2 teaspoon salt
2/3 cup firm unsalted butter, cut into 1/2-inch cubes
1 large egg white

1. Place the flour, cornmeal, sugar, and salt in the bowl of a food processor. Pulse to blend.

2. Add the butter, and pulse 4 or 5 times, then process for 8 to 10 seconds. Stop the machine, remove the cover, and add the egg white. Pulse 4 or 5 times, then process for 5 to 8 seconds, just until a dough is formed.

3. With lightly floured hands, form the dough into a 5- to 6-inch disk. Dust with flour, score with the side of your hand, and cover with plastic wrap. Chill for at least 30 minutes before using. Roll as directed in recipe or see How to Line a Tart Pan, page 92, or Shaping and Baking Free-Form Tart Shells, page 71.

VARIATION
Cornmeal Pepper Pastry

Add 2 to 3 teaspoons of finely minced jalapeño pepper and 1/2 teaspoon ground cumin along with the dry ingredients. Proceed with recipe.

Almond Nut Pastry

THIS PASTRY CAN BE USED FOR most fruit tarts, as well as for cream-style or cheese fillings.

$^{1}/_{2}$ cup sliced almonds
1 large egg white
1 teaspoon vanilla extract
1$^{1}/_{4}$ cups plus 2 tablespoons
    unsifted all-purpose flour
$^{1}/_{4}$ cup superfine sugar
$^{1}/_{2}$ teaspoon grated navel or
    Valencia orange zest
$^{2}/_{3}$ cup partially frozen unsalted
    butter, cut into $^{1}/_{2}$-inch cubes

1. Preheat the oven to 325 degrees. Toast the almonds in a shallow pan for 8 to 10 minutes or until lightly brown. Cool thoroughly before using.

2. Lightly beat the egg white and vanilla with a fork in a small bowl. Set aside.

3. Place the almonds, 1$^{1}/_{4}$ cups flour, sugar, and zest in a food processor bowl. Process about 20 seconds, pulse 4 or 5 times, then process 15 seconds more, or until the nuts are finely chopped.

4. Add the butter to the nut mixture. Pulse 6 to 8 times, then process 10 seconds, or until the butter is cut into tiny pieces and the mixture resembles fine meal.

5. With the processor running, pour the egg white through the feeder tube. When the mixture just begins to form a mass, *stop the processor*. Heavily coat a work surface with the 2 tablespoons of flour. Empty the dough from the bowl onto the floured surface and, with floured hands, knead several times until smooth.

6. Shape the pastry into a 5- to 6-inch disk. Score, lightly dust with flour, and cover with plastic wrap. Chill for at least 30 minutes. Roll as directed in recipe or see pages 91–96.

At a Glance

MAKES: 1 9- or 11-inch tart shell or 1 9- or 10$^{1}/_{2}$-inch pie plate

METHOD: Food Processor

USE FOR: Tarts or pies

Pine Nut Pastry

BE CAREFUL WHEN YOU TOAST the nuts. They are rich in fat and can over-brown quickly. Because the dough is soft, it is hard to handle after rolling. If it breaks, just press it together as you would a cookie dough. When the shell is filled, no one will know the difference. Try this Pine Nut Pastry with creamy pie or tart fillings. Pine nuts impart a delicate flavor and crunch that complement smooth-textured desserts.

At a Glance

MAKES: 1 9-inch pie crust or 1 9- or 11-inch tart crust

METHOD: Food Processor

USE FOR: Tarts or pies

$^1/_2$ cup pine nuts
1 cup unsifted all-purpose flour
3 tablespoons sugar
1 tablespoon cornmeal, preferably stone-ground
$^1/_4$ teaspoon salt
$^1/_2$ teaspoon grated lemon zest
$^1/_3$ cup well-chilled unsalted butter, cut into $^1/_2$-inch dice
1 large egg white, lightly beaten

1. Preheat the oven to 325 degrees. Toast the pine nuts in a shallow pan for 5 to 7 minutes, or until lightly browned. *Cool thoroughly before using.*

2. Place the pine nuts, flour, sugar, cornmeal, salt, and lemon zest in a food processor. Pulse 5 or 6 times, then process 10 seconds, or until the nuts are finely chopped and the mixture looks grainy.

3. Add the butter to the dry ingredients. Pulse again 5 or 6 times, then process 10 seconds, or until the butter is cut into fine pieces and the mixture is mealy.

4. Remove the processor cover and add the egg white. Pulse 5 or 6 times, then process 8 to 10 seconds, or until the mixture begins to stick together. *Do not overprocess.* Empty the bowl onto a lightly floured work surface and knead 3 or 4 times to form a mass. With floured hands, shape into a disk, score lightly with the side of your hand to relax the gluten, and cover with plastic wrap. Chill 1 hour. *Note:* This is a very soft dough.

5. When ready to roll, spray the baking container well with non-stick coating. Lightly flour the pastry disk, and place in the center of an 18-inch sheet of plastic wrap. Cover with a second sheet of plastic wrap cut to the same size. Using a thin rolling pin, roll the pastry into a 12-inch circle.

6. Remove the top sheet of plastic wrap and invert the pastry over the baking container. Peel off the remaining sheet of plastic film. Mold the pastry into the pan without stretching it. Press any cracks together. If using a pie plate, make a pastry wall on the outer rim. (For easier handling, set the dish on a shallow baking pan and chill for 5 to 10 minutes.) Then flute the edges (see page 66) and pierce in several places with a fork. Chill the pastry again for 20 minutes.

Nutty Cornmeal Crust

TRY THIS CRUNCHY CRUST MADE with a mixture of walnuts and pecans. A hint of cornmeal adds extra texture to this flavorful pastry.

At a Glance

SMALL RECIPE: 1 11-inch tart shell or 8 4½-inch tartlet shells

LARGE RECIPE: 1 double crust for a 9-inch pie

METHOD: Food Processor

USE FOR: Tarts or tartlets

SMALL	LARGE	
1 cup plus 2 tablespoons	1½	cups unsifted all-purpose flour
¾	1	cup mixed walnuts and pecans
¼	⅓	cup sugar
3	4	teaspoons stone-ground cornmeal
9 tablespoons	¾	cup well-chilled unsalted butter, cut into ½-inch cubes
1	1	large egg
	1	large egg yolk
⅛	¼	teaspoon salt

1. Place the flour, nuts, sugar, and cornmeal in the bowl of a processor fitted with the steel blade. Pulse 5 or 6 times. Add the butter and pulse 10 to 12 times, then process for 8 to 10 seconds, until mixture forms fine crumbs.

2. Lightly beat the egg (and yolk, if using) and salt in a small bowl. Remove the processor cover and add the egg. Pulse 6 to 8 times, just until the mixture begins to hold together.

3. Lightly flour a rolling surface and empty the contents of the processor onto the surface. Gather the mixture into a pile and smear the dough against the surface with the heel of your hand, pushing out about 2 or 3 tablespoons with each sweep. Repeat the procedure a second time (see Fraisage, page 69). Lightly flour your hand and form the dough into a flat disk(s). Score and dust lightly with flour. Cover with plastic wrap and chill for at least one hour before rolling. Roll as directed in recipe or see pages 91–96.

Chef's Cookie Dough for Tartlets

I WAS INTRODUCED TO THIS tart pastry at the Culinary Institute of America in Hyde Park, New York. This buttery dough is simple to make and will complement any type of sweet filling.

1 cup unsalted butter, at room
    temperature
1/2 cup sugar
1 large egg
1 teaspoon vanilla extract
3 cups cake flour, sifted

1. TO MAKE DOUGH BY HAND: Using a wooden spoon, cream the butter and sugar together in a large bowl until the sugar is incorporated. Blend in the egg and vanilla. Add the flour, 1/3 cup at a time.

2. When the mixture is too difficult to handle with a spoon, knead lightly with lightly floured hands until a dough is formed. Shape into two 6-inch disks and dust with flour. Cover with plastic wrap and chill for at least 15 minutes before using. Roll as directed in recipe or see pages 370–371.

1. TO MAKE DOUGH WITH A HEAVY-DUTY ELECTRIC MIXER: Cream the butter and sugar on medium-low speed in the large bowl of an electric mixer fitted with the paddle attachment until the sugar is just incorporated. Blend in the egg and vanilla. Then add the flour all at once, mixing only until mixture begins to form a mass.

2. Using lightly floured hands, shape the dough into two 6-inch disks. Dust lightly with flour and cover with plastic wrap. Chill for at least 15 minutes before using. Roll as directed in recipe or see pages 370–371.

At a Glance

MAKES: 16 4½-inch tartlets or 2 11-inch tart shells

METHOD: Hand or Electric Mixer

USE FOR: Tartlets

Danish Nut Dough for Tartlets

USE THIS COOKIELIKE nut crust with any kind of fruit or cream filling. Just roll the dough into balls and press them into the tart pans. No fuss to make and fabulous to eat.

At a Glance

MAKES: 12 4½-inch tartlets

METHOD: Hand

USE FOR: Tartlets

⅔ cup sliced almonds
1½ cups unsifted all-purpose flour
¾ cup unsalted butter, at room temperature
6 tablespoons sugar
3 large egg yolks

1. Preheat the oven to 325 degrees. Spread the nuts in a shallow pan with sides, and bake for 8 to 10 minutes or until lightly brown. Cool completely before using.

2. Place the nuts and flour in the bowl of a food processor. Process until the nuts are finely ground. The mixture should be powdery.

3. In a large bowl, cream the butter and sugar with a wooden spoon until the sugar is incorporated. Blend in the egg yolks, mixing until well incorporated and color lightens.

4. Stir in the flour-nut mixture in 3 additions. Do not overwork. With floured hands, shape it into a 6-inch disk. Cover the dough with plastic wrap, and refrigerate for 1 hour before using.

5. Divide the dough into 12 pieces. With floured hands, roll each into a ball. Place the ball in the tart pan. Press the dough across the bottom and up the side of the pan, shaping it as best you can. Trim excess dough with a dough scraper. Fill as desired.

Cream Cheese Pastry

THIS PASTRY IS ONE OF THE easiest to prepare; however, to improve the flakiness, be sure that the butter and cream cheese are very soft so that they can be blended smoothly.

1 cup unsalted butter, at room temperature
8 ounces cream cheese, at room temperature
2 cups unsifted all-purpose flour

1. Cream the butter and cream cheese with a wooden spoon in a large bowl until thoroughly blended together.

2. Add 1 cup of the flour and blend into the butter–cream cheese mixture with the wooden spoon. Add the remaining flour. Cut in the flour with the spoon, working it only until the flour is incorporated. Then knead the mixture briefly and form a ball. Do not overwork.

3. With lightly floured hands, divide the dough in half and form two 4- to 5-inch disks. Dust the disks lightly with flour, score with the side of your hand, and cover with plastic wrap. Chill for at least 4 hours. Let dough stand at room temperature for 30 minutes before rolling. Roll as directed in recipe or see pages 91–96.

Press-On Butter Pastry

IF THE THOUGHT OF ROLLING PIE PASTRY is intimidating, this is the crust for you. The end result is soft and cakelike, quite unlike pie pastry. I recommend using it for fruit pies when the filling has been par-cooked.

At a Glance

MAKES: 1 9$^{1}/_{2}$-inch deep-dish crust

METHOD: Food Processor

USE FOR: Pies

1$^{1}/_{4}$ cups unsifted all-purpose flour
2 tablespoons sugar
1 teaspoon baking powder
$^{1}/_{4}$ teaspoon salt
$^{1}/_{2}$ cup partially frozen unsalted butter, cut into $^{1}/_{2}$-inch cubes
1 large egg yolk
2 tablespoons orange juice
$^{1}/_{2}$ teaspoon vanilla extract

1. Place the dry ingredients in the bowl of a food processor fitted with the steel blade. Pulse 3 or 4 times to combine. Add the butter, pulse 4 or 5 times, then process 4 to 5 seconds, or until the mixture forms meallike crumbs.

2. Use a fork to beat together the egg yolk, orange juice, and vanilla. With the processor off, pour the liquids into the crumb mixture. Pulse 4 or 5 times, or until the mixture *begins* to stick together.

3. Lightly flour a flat surface. Empty the dough onto the floured surface and, with floured hands, shape into a 5- to 6-inch flat disk.

4. Butter a 9$^{1}/_{2}$-inch deep-dish ovenproof glass pie plate. Place the disk into the pan. With floured hands, press the pastry into the dish, working it up the sides first, then smoothing out the middle. Re-flour hands as needed.

Krispie Meringue Crust

THIS CRUST IS HIGHLY RECOMMENDED FOR frozen pies. Its crunchy texture really complements ice creams and sorbets. If you're looking for a twist, don't overlook the pistachio variation. Any nut can be substituted if you wish.

1 large egg white
¹/₄ cup superfine sugar
¹/₂ teaspoon vanilla extract
2 cups Rice Krispies cereal

1. Spray a 9-inch ovenproof glass pie plate very well with nonstick coating, then dust with flour. Tap out excess flour. Preheat the oven to 300 degrees. Position the oven rack in the lower third of the oven.

2. In an electric mixer, beat the egg white until firm peaks form. Gradually add the sugar, 1 tablespoon at a time. Add the vanilla and continue to beat until a stiff and glossy meringue is formed.

3. Using a rubber spatula, fold the cereal into the meringue. Empty the mixture into the pie plate. Using the back of a tablespoon, push the meringue up the side of the pie plate and across the bottom.

4. Lay a square of plastic wrap on top of the meringue mixture. Using a batarde or a smooth-bottomed glass, press the meringue into place, smoothing it as best you can.

5. Remove the plastic wrap and bake the shell for 18 to 20 minutes, or until the top feels set. It will harden as it cooks. Cool completely before filling.

VARIATION

Krispie Pistachio Crust

Fold ¹/₄ cup of finely chopped pistachios into the meringue. Proceed with step 3 of the recipe.

At a Glance

MAKES: 1 9-inch shell

METHOD: Electric Mixer and Hand

USE FOR: Pies

Meringue Shell

MERINGUE SHELLS MAKE IDEAL CASES for a variety of fillings. You might try serving them with fresh or poached fruit, cream fillings, ice creams, or sorbets. A word of caution: Although meringues have a long shelf life (up to 1 week), you should not fill them until shortly before eating—they'll become soggy. The good news is that they are totally fat free.

$^1/_3$ cup superfine sugar
3 tablespoons strained
    confectioners' sugar
2 egg whites
Pinch of salt
$^1/_4$ teaspoon fresh lemon juice
$^1/_2$ teaspoon vanilla extract

1. Preheat the oven to 225 degrees. Position the oven rack in the lower third of the oven. Spray a 9-inch ovenproof glass pie plate with nonstick coating, then dust lightly with flour. Tap lightly to release excess flour.

2. Strain together the superfine and confectioners' sugar.

3. With an electric mixer, beat the egg whites until frothy. Add the salt and lemon juice. Beat until very stiff. Add the sugars, 1 tablespoon at a time, over about 30 seconds. Add the vanilla and continue beating until stiff and glossy, 1 to 2 minutes.

4. Spoon the mixture into the prepared pan and spread with the back of a tablespoon. Cover the sides of the pan first, then the bottom. Make sure to form a distinct crease where the sides and bottom of the pan meet.

5. Bake for 60 to 70 minutes. The shell will have just started to brown lightly. Turn off the oven. Leave the shell in the unlit oven for about 1$^1/_2$ hours or until crisp and dry in the center.

VARIATION
Petite Meringue Shells

1. Double the recipe for the Meringue Shell. Line a cookie sheet with heavy-duty aluminum foil, wrapping the ends underneath to prevent it from slipping.

2. Fit a 16-inch pastry bag with a #825 star tip. Fill the bag one-third full with the meringue mixture. Pipe the meringue in concentric circles, starting in the center. Work outward until the circle measures 3$^1/_2$ inches. **1**

3. Build the sides by going around the circle 3 times in a continuous flow. **2** This will create the sides of the shell.

4. Bake at 225 degrees for 50 to 60 minutes or until slightly browned. Turn off the oven. Leave the shells in the unlit oven for about 1½ hours or until crisp and dry in the center. Makes six 3½-inch shells.

Baked meringue shells should be wrapped loosely with aluminum foil. Do not use plastic wrap or any other airtight container. They will stay crisp only if they can breathe.

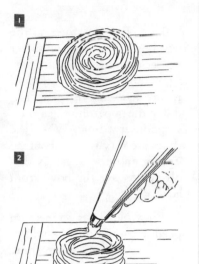

Coco-Nutty Meringue Shell

ALMONDS AND COCONUT ARE GROUND into a nut flour and then folded into meringue. This crispy shell is excellent for frozen pies and cream fillings.

$^1/_2$ cup sliced almonds
$^1/_2$ cup shredded sweetened
   coconut
2 tablespoons cornstarch
1 tablespoon granulated sugar
3 egg whites
Pinch of cream of tartar
$^1/_4$ cup superfine sugar

1. Preheat the oven to 325 degrees. Place the sliced almonds and coconut in a shallow baking pan. Toast in the oven for 8 to 10 minutes or until golden brown. Cool completely.

2. Place the almonds and coconut in a food processor with the cornstarch and granulated sugar. Process until the mixture is finely ground into a nut flour.

3. Reduce the oven to 250 degrees. Butter a 9-inch ovenproof glass pie plate very well, and sprinkle it with flour. Tap it to remove the excess flour.

4. Place the egg whites in the large bowl of an electric mixer and set the bowl over simmering water. Beat the whites and cream of tartar with a whisk, adding the superfine sugar, 1 tablespoon at a time. When the whites are very warm, about 120 degrees and the sugar is dissolved, remove the bowl from the heat.

5. Whip the whites on medium speed, beating until the whites are cool and form a firm shiny meringue. Using a large rubber spatula, fold the nut flour into the meringue.

6. Empty the nut meringue into the pie plate. Using the back of a tablespoon, spread the meringue up the sides and on the bottom of the pie plate. Make sure to form a distinct crease where sides and bottom meet. Bake the pie shell for 55 to 60 minutes, or until the surface feels set. The shell will harden as it cools.

All-Nut Pastry Shell

IF YOU ARE A LOVER OF NUTS, this is the crust for you. It's best paired with refrigerated or frozen desserts, and great with the Prickly Fudge-Nut Tart (page 163).

13/4 cups walnuts or pecans
2 1/2 tablespoons sugar
3 tablespoons soft unsalted butter

1. Preheat the oven to 350 degrees. Position the oven rack in the lower third of the oven. Butter a 9-inch ovenproof glass pie plate very well, then dust with flour. Invert the pan and tap out excess flour.

2. Place the nuts and sugar in the bowl of a food processor fitted with the steel blade. Pulse 5 times, then process for 3 to 4 seconds. If any very coarse pieces remain, pulse 1 or 2 times more. The nuts should not be too finely ground.

3. Empty the nut mixture into a large bowl, add the butter, and work the ingredients together with your fingertips. Gather the mixture together, and empty it into the pan.

4. Using the back of a tablespoon, press the mixture into the bottom and up the sides of the pan.

5. Lay a square of plastic wrap on top of the nut mixture. Using a batarde (see page 457), or a smooth-bottomed glass, even out the nut mixture as best as you can. It will be somewhat chunky. Remove the plastic wrap, and bake for 15 to 20 minutes, or until the edge of the crust *begins* to brown. Do not overbake. The shell will harden and crisp as it cools.

At a Glance

MAKES: 1 9-inch pie shell

METHOD: Food Processor and Hand

USE FOR: Pies and tarts

Master Crumb Crust

CHOOSE PLAIN COOKIES, WITHOUT FROSTING, for crumb crusts. Good choices are vanilla wafers, plain or honey graham crackers, ginger snaps, or zwieback, preferably not pre-ground. If you feel like splurging, try such premium cookies as Pepperidge Farm Lemon Nut Crunch cookies, imported butter cookies, Swedish ginger snaps, amaretti, or biscotti. These quality cookies create interesting, flavorful crusts.

At a Glance

SMALL RECIPE:
1 9-inch crust

LARGE RECIPE: 1 10-inch pie crust or 11-inch tart shell

METHOD: Food Processor

USE FOR: Pies and tarts

Many possibilities exist for the final taste of a crumb crust. When a cookie is very buttery or intensely flavored, add zwieback crumbs, which have a neutral taste, if you wish to off-set the richness and mellow the flavor. Another way to vary a crust is to add grated lemon or orange zest to the melted butter you will add to your crumbs. Allow 1/2 teaspoon for the small recipe and 3/4 teaspoon for the larger one. Sugar quantities are always variable. You can decrease, increase, or omit it as you wish. If a little more butter is needed to bind the crumbs, add it sparingly. A little goes a long way.

SMALL	LARGE	
5	6	tablespoons unsalted butter
1¼	1½	cups cookie crumbs
2	2 to 2½	tablespoons sugar

1. Preheat the oven to 350 degrees. Position the oven rack in the lower third of the oven. Butter the pie or tart pan very well. Dust the pan with flour and shake out any excess.

2. Melt the butter in a medium saucepan over low heat, then set aside to cool.

3. Place the cookies in the bowl of a food processor. If large cookies are used, break them into smaller pieces. Process until the cookies are finely chopped, then measure the crumbs in dry measuring cups without shaking or packing.

4. Add the measured crumbs and sugar to the cooled butter, stirring around the saucepan with a fork to blend.

5. Empty the crumbs into the baking pan. Using a tablespoon, press firmly against the sides of the pan, working the crumbs up to the rim, forming a 1/4-inch-

thick edge. Smooth the bottom with a spoon.

6. Lay a square of plastic wrap over the crumbs. Using a batarde (see page 457) or a glass with a smooth bottom, press firmly against the plastic to even the crumbs on the bottom. Also press firmly at the bend of the pan because the crumbs are always thicker there. Remove the plastic wrap.

7. Place the pie plate on a shallow pan and bake for 8 to 10 minutes, or until you smell the crust. The surface should feel set, but the bottom will not firm until the shell cools. Alternatively, the shell can be chilled in the refrigerator or freezer until firm.

About Crumb Crusts

✦ Simplest of all crusts to make, crumb crusts have their own personalities and idiosyncrasies, as do crusts made from pastry, owing to the variables in manufactured cookies. Cookies such as graham crackers or chocolate wafers contain different quantities of fat and sugar. Zwieback are drier and less sweet than vanilla wafers, and the intensity of spices in ginger snaps varies according to the brand.

✦ While the above differences affect the taste, of greater consequence is the amount of fat used to bind the crumbs. If a crust has too little butter, it will not hold together. And when too much fat is added, the crust will lose its shape during baking and slip down the side of the pan.

✦ Take care when measuring the cookie crumbs as they have a tendency to settle or pack when spooned into a container. Always use dry measures and, above all, do not shake the container. Packaged crumbs are fine, but they become stale quickly. Seal the unused portion well and refrigerate or freeze.

✦ Crumb crusts can be firmed by either chilling or baking. My preference is to bake the crust because baking makes it crispier. However, chilled crusts are quicker to make and easier to remove from their molds. I do use unbaked crusts for frozen pies and tarts.

✦ To resolve the problem of removing a crumb crust from the pan, dust the greased pan with flour. For a chocolate crumb crust, use a light coating of strained cocoa powder, either nonalkaline or alkaline. Nonstick coating is recommended for crusts that are not baked.

The recipes that follow can be adjusted as the need arises. Refer to the introduction to the Master Crumb Crust (opposite) for additional information. Whatever crumb crust you choose to make, take the time to do a thorough job in preparing your pan. When you serve your pie, you'll be happy you did.

Nut Crumb Crusts

FOLLOW THE RECIPE FOR THE Master Crumb Crust (page 164), adding toasted pecans, walnuts, sliced almonds, or hazelnuts to the processor bowl with the cookie crumbs. While you can use any combination of cookies and nuts, I have listed a few of my favorites. Be sure to toast the nuts first; the flavor of the crust will be so much better.

GRAHAM CRACKERS WITH PECANS OR WALNUTS
Baking time: 10 to 12 minutes

	CRUMBS	SUGAR	BUTTER	NUTS
SMALL	1 cup	2 tablespoons	4 tablespoons	1/3 cup
LARGE	1 1/4 cups	2 1/2 tablespoons	5 tablespoons	1/2 cup

VANILLA WAFERS WITH TOASTED ALMONDS
Baking time: 10 to 12 minutes

	CRUMBS	SUGAR	BUTTER	NUTS
SMALL	1 cup	1 tablespoon	4 tablespoons	1/2 cup
LARGE	1 1/4 cups	1 1/2 tablespoons	5 tablespoons	2/3 cup

GINGER SNAPS WITH PECANS
Baking time: 12 to 14 minutes

	CRUMBS	SUGAR	BUTTER	NUTS
SMALL	1 cup	2 tablespoons	4 tablespoons	1/3 cup
LARGE	1 1/4 cups	2 1/2 tablespoons	5 tablespoons	1/2 cup

BUTTER COOKIES WITH PECANS, WALNUTS, OR ALMONDS
Baking time: 10 to 12 minutes

	CRUMBS	SUGAR	BUTTER	NUTS
SMALL	1 cup	1 tablespoon	3 tablespoons	1/2 cup
LARGE	1 1/4 cups	1 1/2 tablespoons	4 tablespoons	2/3 cup

ZWIEBACK WITH ALMONDS OR HAZELNUTS
Baking time: 12 to 14 minutes

	CRUMBS	SUGAR	BUTTER	NUTS
SMALL	1 cup	2 tablespoons	4 tablespoons	1/3 cup
LARGE	1 1/4 cups	2 1/2 tablespoons	5 tablespoons	1/2 cup

BISCOTTI WITH ALMONDS OR HAZELNUTS
Baking time: 12 to 14 minutes

	CRUMBS	SUGAR	BUTTER	NUTS
SMALL	1 cup	1 tablespoon	4 tablespoons	1/3 cup
LARGE	1 1/4 cups	1 1/2 tablespoons	5 tablespoons	1/2 cup

LEMON COOKIES WITH WALNUTS, PECANS, OR ALMONDS
Baking time: 10 to 12 minutes

	CRUMBS	SUGAR	BUTTER	NUTS
SMALL	2/3 cup	2 teaspoons	3 tablespoons	1/3 cup
LARGE	3/4 cup	1 tablespoon	4 tablespoons	1/2 cup

NOTE

For a less rich crust, substitute zwieback crumbs for 1/3 cup lemon cookie crumbs in the small recipe, and 1/2 cup for the lemon cookie crumbs in the large recipe.

AMARETTI COOKIES WITH ALMONDS OR HAZELNUTS
Baking time: 12 to 14 minutes

	CRUMBS	SUGAR	BUTTER	NUTS
SMALL	3/4 cup	2 teaspoons	4 tablespoons	1/3 cup
LARGE	1 cup	1 tablespoon	1/3 cup	1/2 cup

NOTE

For a less rich crust, substitute zwieback crumbs for 1/4 cup amaretti cookie crumbs in the small recipe, and 1/3 cup for the amaretti cookie crumbs in the large recipe.

Chocolate Crumb Crust

FOR CHOCOLATE CRUMB CRUSTS, I especially like to use the packaged ground chocolate Oreo cookie crumbs (not to be confused with the cookies) or the black chocolate "Famous" wafers, both manufactured by Nabisco. These have an intense chocolate flavor and are not too sweet. Other choices are chocolate graham crackers or Keebler's low-fat chocolate wafers.

At a Glance

SMALL RECIPE:
1 9-inch pie crust

LARGE RECIPE:
1 10-inch pie crust or
1 11-inch tart shell

METHOD: Food Processor

USE FOR: Pies and tarts

SMALL	LARGE	
4	4 to 5	teaspoons strained cocoa powder
1 cup plus 2 tablespoons	1½	cups chocolate cookie crumbs
2	3	tablespoons dark brown sugar
4	6	tablespoons unsalted butter, melted and cooled

1. Preheat the oven to 350 degrees. Position the oven rack in the lower third of the oven. Butter the baking pan very well. Dust the pan with the cocoa and shake out any excess.

2. Place the crumbs and brown sugar in a food processor bowl. Process 20 to 30 seconds to combine. Pour the crumb mixture into the melted butter and combine with a fork.

3. Empty the crumb mixture into the pan. Using a tablespoon, press the crumbs firmly against the sides of the pan, working them up to the rim to form an edge. Smooth the bottom with the spoon.

4. Lay a square of plastic wrap over the crumbs. Using a batarde (page 457) or a smooth-bottomed glass, press firmly against the plastic to smooth the crumbs on the bottom. Press firmly at the bend because the crumbs accumulate there. Remove the plastic wrap.

5. Place the pie plate on a sheet pan and bake for 10 to 12 minutes, or until the crumbs begin to smell. The surface should feel set, but the bottom will not firm until the shell cools. Let shell cool completely before filling.

Reduced-Cholesterol Graham Cracker Crust

FOR THOSE WHO DESIRE A LOWER cholesterol crumb crust, here is a modified version of a classic Graham Cracker Crumb Crust.

1½ cups graham cracker crumbs
1 large egg white
1 tablespoon sugar (optional)
4 tablespoons margarine, melted
    and cooled

1. Preheat the oven to 325 degrees. Position the oven rack in the lower third of the oven. Spray a 9-inch ovenproof glass pie plate with nonstick cooking spray.

2. Place the cracker crumbs in the bowl of a food processor.

3. Using a fork, lightly beat the egg white until frothy. Discard about 1 tablespoon of the egg white. Add the sugar to the remaining egg white and beat with a fork until blended. Empty the egg white into the processor along with the melted margarine. Pulse briefly to coat the crumbs.

4. Empty the crumb mixture into the prepared pan. Using a tablespoon, press firmly against the sides of the pan, working the crumbs up to the rim, forming a ¼-inch-thick edge. Smooth the bottom with the back of the spoon.

5. Lay a square of plastic wrap over the crumbs. Using a batarde (see page 457) or a glass with a smooth bottom, press firmly against the plastic to smooth the crumbs on the bottom. Press firmly at the bend because the crumbs accumulate there. Remove the plastic wrap.

6. Place the pie plate on a shallow pan and bake for 12 to 14 minutes or until the crumbs begin to brown. The surface should feel set, but the bottom will not firm until the shell cools. Let crust cool completely before filling.

At a Glance

MAKES: 1 9-inch pie crust

METHOD: Food Processor

USE FOR: Pies

About Puff Pastry (Pâte Feuilletée)

WHENEVER PUFF pastry is mentioned in a repertoire of desserts, eyes roll in anticipation of a heavenly treat. And why not? This luxurious multilayered pastry, a cornerstone of French pastry, has been prized for centuries. It is relished for its crisp, gossamer layers and buttery flavor. When elaborate pastries were in vogue, puff pastry was used to build ethereal casings several inches in height. Today, puff pastry is more commonly used as a base for such sweets as napoleons, tarts, or turnovers, where volume is not a requirement.

There are two kinds of puff pastry—the classic and the quick (*rapide*). Both doughs are made from a traditional French formula of equal parts, by weight, of flour and butter with half as much liquid. The primary difference between the two doughs lies the manner in which these ingredients are combined.

Classic puff pastry is made with a large malleable block of butter that is encased in an enriched flour-water dough. Quick puff pastry is made from butter that is cut into chunks, tossed through the flour, and then moistened. Both doughs are rolled and folded many times, a procedure that is known as "turning" the dough. The number of "turns" the dough receives, along with the particular technique used to encase the butter, determines how high the finished product will be. When the pastry is baked, the heat of the oven causes the moisture in the butter to release steam. This forces the layers to separate and rise. Ultimately, the steam evaporates, leaving extremely fragile, flaky sheets of pastry that can number close to a thousand layers.

In recent years, especially with the advent of food processors and electric mixers, pastry chefs have striven to shorten the procedure. While a base dough can be done by machine, once the butter has been incorporated into the dough, the rolling and folding must be performed by hand. Though both doughs produce satisfactory results, the finished texture of the classic technique is consistently flakier—and actually simpler to make. To me, rolling a smooth dough made with a large mass of butter is easier than working a bumpy one that contains chunks.

Note: If making puff pastry by hand is not your passion, or if time is of the essence, don't let these limitations prevent you from making the terrific puff pastry pastries in this book. Ready-made puff pastry is the answer for you. Two very fine brands to consider are Dufour and Pennant. They are available in the freezer cases of many supermarkets.

Some Puff Pastry Tips

✦ Although puff pastry can be made in any weather, it is best to make it on a dry day.

✦ In warm weather, chill the dry ingredients first.

✦ The butter should be neither too hard, nor too soft. Hard butter is difficult to roll, and soft butter is too oily. Try the "thumb test." Hold a wrapped bar of butter in your hand—it should be firm, but not hard. You should be able to make a slight imprint with your thumb.

✦ Cool surfaces such as marble, granite, or a countertop are the best for rolling the dough.

✦ A rolling surface can be further chilled by placing a couple of ice-filled sheet pans on the area for at least 15 minutes.

✦ Always pay attention to the dough measurements. A ruler is an essential tool.

✦ When rolling the pastry, avoid pressing hard on the ends. Too much pressure will cause the butter to burst through the seams of the dough.

✦ If the butter breaks through the dough during the rolling process, brush the area with flour.

✦ Always roll the dough from the center to the edge. Avoid rolling back and forth.

✦ Keep a feather brush or one with fine bristles handy for patching spots and for removing excess flour from the dough surface.

✦ Turn dough over periodically to check for sticking and uneven edges.

✦ Use a dough scraper frequently to even the edges of the dough and to keep it symmetrical.

✦ If dough becomes too elastic during rolling, let it rest for a minute or two.

✦ If the dough becomes too soft, chill it for a few minutes.

✦ Chilling the dough after shaping is essential for maintaining its form.

✦ When refrigerating the dough, *always* cover it to prevent the surface from drying.

✦ When shaping the dough, secure ends that have to be joined with egg wash or ice water to prevent them from opening.

✦ To prevent a soggy crust, avoid using overly moist fruit or loose custard-style fillings.

✦ If re-rolling leftover pastry, to maintain the layers, align the scraps in the same direction.

✦ Never rush the chilling process. Insufficient chilling results in uneven shapes.

✦ Don't be heavy-handed with egg wash. A light covering is all that is necessary. Always brush up so the wash doesn't drip on the pan.

Goof-Proof Puff Pastry

KEEP A WATCHFUL EYE ON THE temperature of the butter, and bring out the ruler when you roll. Before you know it, your pastry will be "goof-proof" and you'll be turning your "turns" like a pro.

3 sticks (3/4 pound) unsalted butter, firm but not hard
2 1/2 cups unsifted all-purpose flour
1 1/2 cups unsifted cake flour
2 teaspoons salt
1 stick (1/4 pound) soft unsalted butter
1 cup plus 2 tablespoons ice water
1 tablespoon freshly squeezed lemon juice

1. Cut the butter into 1-inch chunks and place it in a large bowl, preferably stainless steel. Set aside.

2. **PREPARE THE DOUGH:** Place the all-purpose flour, cake flour, and salt in a processor bowl. Pulse 5 or 6 times, then process for 6 to 8 seconds.

3. Cut the soft butter into 1/2-inch slices. Add it to the flour, distributing it around the processor bowl. Pulse 5 to 6 times, then process for 8 to 10 seconds or until the mixture resembles fine meal.

4. Put the ice water in a container with a spout. Add the lemon juice to the water. With the processor running, add the water to the flour. *Immediately stop the processor.* Pulse 4 to 5 times. If the mixture has not be-gun to form a ball, pulse 2 to 3 times but do not overprocess.

5. Empty the dough onto a well-floured surface. It will be sticky. Coat your hands with flour and gather it into a mound. Knead gently, about 6 to 8 times or just until the surface is smooth and no longer sticky, flouring the kneading surface as needed. Shape the dough into a 6- to 7-inch disk and set it on a cookie sheet. Cover with plastic wrap and refrigerate it for 25 to 30 minutes.

6. **PREPARE THE BUTTER:** While the dough is chilling, knead the butter. To do this, make a fist and press your knuckles into the butter and twist your wrist at the same time. If the butter is too hard, break it up with your fingertips and then press with your knuckles. Make a "claw" with your hand, spread your fingers apart, and rake your fingertips through the butter. Alternate pressing your knuckles into the butter and raking the butter until you no longer feel lumps and it is smooth and malleable. *Do not overwork it, the butter should not stick to your hands.*

7. Using a rubber spatula, scrape the butter onto a piece of plastic wrap. Cover it with a second sheet of plastic wrap. Flatten the butter with either a rolling pin or your hand, and form it into a 7-inch square. Remove the top sheet of plastic wrap and use a dough scraper to even the sides and smooth the top. Cover the butter with plastic wrap and chill it for 15 to 20 minutes.

8. ENCLOSE THE BUTTER IN THE DOUGH: On a cool, lightly floured surface, with a floured rolling pin, roll pastry into a 14-inch circle. Check the bottom to make sure it is not sticking to the rolling surface. Unwrap the square of butter and invert it onto the center of the dough.

NOTE

The butter and the pastry should be about the same consistency so they will blend smoothly when rolled. If the butter is too hard, let it stand at room temperature for a few minutes before you enclose it in the dough.

Starting at the lower part of the circle (A), lift the dough up and fold it to the center, stretching it as needed. ■ Press it down lightly. Then move to the right (B), then the top (C), and finish with the left side (D). Each time you make a fold, press the dough at the corners to ensure that the butter is completely tucked in. **2** Pinch all the seams together very well. When completed, you will have a square package measuring approximately 8 × 8 inches.

9. Scrape the rolling surface clean, then re-flour the surface. Roll the pastry into a long strip, measuring 20 × 10 inches.

NOTE

Always start rolling from the center. Roll away from you, and then toward you, as if you are rowing a boat. Do not press on the ends, or the butter will burst through the seams. Flip the dough over once or twice during rolling. This ensures even rolling and will prevent sticking.

10. Fold the dough into thirds. To help you space evenly, make two slight indentations with a dough scraper or the dull side of a knife at one-third intervals. **3**

Starting with the end closest to you, make your first fold. Press the edge of the dough gently with a rolling pin to flatten it slightly. This will make the following fold of dough lie smoother.

As you fold the dough, be sure to stretch the ends to make all the seams even. **4** Brush the dough often with a pastry brush to prevent any accumulation of flour. This folding procedure is known as "booking."

11. Make a one-quarter turn of the dough clockwise so the seam of the book will be on your right. **5** Roll the pastry again into a long strip, this time measuring 22 × 10 inches.

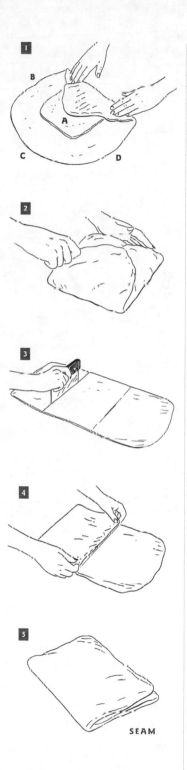

SEAM

Each time you roll and book the dough, it is called a "turn."

Fold the dough into thirds as before, then cover it with plastic wrap, and refrigerate for 30 minutes. You have now made 2 "turns."

12. After 30 minutes, make a third turn, this time rolling the pastry to 24 × 10 inches. When you start to roll, always position the dough with the seam to your right. Chill again for 30 minutes.

13. Give the dough a fourth and final "turn," rolling it to 28 × 10 inches. Fold it into 3 layers. Press the top gently until the dough is approximately 7 × 9 inches. Even the sides with a pastry scraper. Seal well in plastic wrap and refrigerate. The dough must chill for a minimum of 1 hour.

STORAGE

Store dough in the refrigerator for up to 3 days. This dough may be frozen for 4 to 6 months (page 78).

How to Blind-Bake a Puff Pastry Shell

1. Preheat the oven to 425 degrees. Position the rack in the lower third of the oven. Cut a 12-inch strip of aluminum foil. Butter one side of the foil and lay it, buttered side down, onto the pastry. Press the foil into the bottom, molding it where the border and bottom meet. Weight the pastry down with a pan, such as a layer cake tin, approximately the same size and shape as the opening of the tart.

2. Bake the shell for 20 minutes. Then reduce the oven temperature to 375 degrees and continue to bake the crust for 10 to 15 minutes longer. *Gently* press on the weighting pan every so often to release the steam and to prevent the pastry from rising too high. This will give the pastry a better shape.

3. When the sides of the pastry are golden brown, remove the tart shell from the oven. Let it stand for a few seconds, then carefully remove the weighting pan and aluminum foil. If the foil sticks to the sides, the shell needs to be baked longer. After the weighting pan and foil have been removed, return the shell to the oven and bake for 5 minutes longer or until the center is golden brown. Cool before filling.

How to Shape a Round Free-Form Puff Pastry

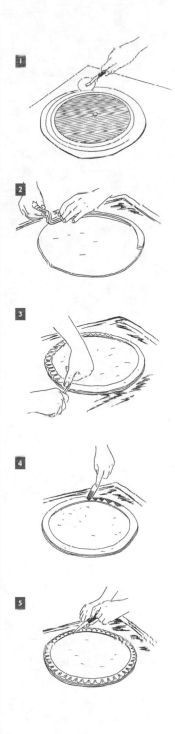

1. Line a cookie sheet with a piece of heavy-duty aluminum foil. Sprinkle a few drops of water onto the foil.

2. On a lightly floured surface and with floured hands, tuck the corners of the puff pastry block under to round it out. Roll the pastry into a 14-inch circle. To prevent the dough from shrinking, pierce the dough, at ½-inch intervals, using a fork.

3. To trace a round circle, use an 11-inch lid from a pot, an 11-inch flan ring, or the removable bottom of an 11-inch tart pan. If using the bottom of a tart pan, cut ½ inch larger than the edge of the disk. Using a smooth-edged pizza cutter or a small knife, cut deeply into the dough to make an 11-inch circle. Then cut a second ring ¾ inch *larger* than the first to use as a border, using the edge of the first circle as a guide. **1**

4. Wrap the circle of dough around the rolling pin, and unroll it onto the cookie sheet. Moisten a ¾-inch edge around the circle with ice water. Fold the ¾-inch ring of dough into quarters. Then carefully unfold the strip onto the moistened edge of pastry, working one-quarter of the dough at a time. **2** If the pastry ring is too large, trim it leaving ½ inch extra so you can overlap the ends. Seal the 2 ends together with a little water. Press the 2 layers together gently and chill for 10 minutes.

5. To make a scalloped edge: Press your thumb into the edge of the pastry. **3** Make a deep cut next to your thumb with the dull side of a paring knife. Repeat the process until the entire circle has been completed. You will have a scalloped effect.

To make a crosshatch edge: **4** Press the edge of the dough firmly with the back of a fork, creating a crisscross pattern.

6. Using the dull side of a paring knife, cut *halfway* through the pastry, tracing the inside of the circle where the border meets the bottom dough. **5** This will help the sides to rise, giving the shell a more defined shape after baking. Prick the inside of the pastry case at 1-inch intervals with a fork. Chill for ½ hour or longer. Use unbaked or baked as the recipe directs.

From
Orchards,
Vines
& Bushes

RUIT PIES AND TARTS have long been favored by dessert lovers. Today more than ever, with the emphasis on healthy eating, sweet foods from nature's bounty are on the cutting edge of contemporary cuisines. This chapter is directed to just that. Here we have an array of recipes whose primary ingredients come from the lushness of nature. ＊ In this chapter, the

key ingredient in all of the recipes is fruit—fruit and cream combinations have been saved for "Decadent & Delicious." Some of the recipes you will find here are American and European classics like peach or cherry pie, and apple or pear tarte Tatin. There is a traditional strawberry rhubarb pie and a terrific linzer tart.

While well-loved standards are not neglected here, the greater part of this chapter is devoted to a timely and fresh approach to the age-old art of combining fruits and berries with pastry, either wrapped in or resting on lovely layers of flaky or tender crusts.

One of my favorite newcomers is the Tart of Strawberries in Raspberry Puree. It has an all-fruit filling made from sliced strawberries which are folded into a puree of fresh raspberries. Another favorite is the Crimson Appleberry Pie: chunks of apples, baked with homemade cranberry sauce, are nestled in Nutty Cornmeal Crust. The combination is memorable. My new love, the mango, is used with terrific results in both the Black and Blue Mango Pie and the Mango Tart with Blackberries. These are but a few of the tempting pastries that lie ahead in this chapter.

As appealing as these desserts may be, baking with fruits and berries is not without its frustrations. Try as you will, there is no sure way to determine the amount of moisture in fresh produce. Food chemists, who work with professional bakers, have developed ways to resolve this problem. Commercial pastries may be free of excess liquid and cut like a dream, but the gels and thickeners they are made with are not always palatable.

Simply put, there is a tradeoff. Appearance is important, but a pleasing texture and good taste should always win out. There is no mistaking the appeal of home-baked, fruit-laden pies and tarts. Don't be concerned if you can't always have a picture-perfect slice; when a pie or tart is made in your kitchen, with your hands, it will taste mighty good.

If fruits had mouths, they would eat themselves.

TOBIAS SMOLLETT

Big Easy Apple Tart

THIS RUSTIC TART IS MADE with sliced apples and fresh cranberries encased in a cookie crust and baked free-form on a sheet pan. Although simple to make, the delicate pastry commonly splits during baking, causing the fruit juices to run onto the pan. This makes removal of the tart to a serving platter a frustrating task.

At a Glance

SERVES: 8 to 10

PAN: 14 × 17-inch cookie sheet and bottom disk of 9-inch metal tart pan

PASTRY PREP: Unbaked

OVEN TEMP: 375 degrees

BAKING TIME: 50 to 55 minutes

DIFFICULTY:

I have two tricks to overcome this. First, before rolling the dough, set the bottom metal disk of the tart pan on a cookie sheet under the pastry for added support and to shield the bottom from the juices. My second trick is to brush the syrupy juices onto the tart, coating the fruit and crust as well. Using the juices helps prevent the crust from sticking to the pan and gives the tart a pretty, caramelized surface.

Be sure to loosen the hot tart with a long, thin spatula before the juices have a chance to cool, and use a cookie sheet without sides so you can slide the tart from the pan.

PASTRY

2 cups sifted all-purpose flour
2/3 cup strained confectioners' sugar
1/4 teaspoon salt
2/3 cup unsalted butter, cut into 1/2-inch cubes
1/2 teaspoon grated lemon zest
1 large egg
1 tablespoon cold water
1/2 teaspoon vanilla extract

FILLING

4 Golden Delicious apples (about 2 pounds)
1/2 cup fresh cranberries
2 teaspoons fresh lemon juice
1/3 cup granulated sugar
1/3 cup lightly packed dark brown sugar
1 tablespoon cornstarch
1 teaspoon ground cinnamon
1 large egg
1 teaspoon water
1 to 2 tablespoons unsalted butter

1. MAKE THE PASTRY: Place the flour, confectioners' sugar, and salt in a large bowl. Stir thoroughly with a whisk to combine. Add the butter and lemon zest, then using your fingertips, rub the butter into the dry ingredients until the mixture resembles coarse meal.

2. In a small bowl, combine the egg, water, and vanilla. Make a well in the crumb mixture and pour in the liquid. Using a fork, draw the crumb mixture into the liquid, tossing it with the fork until large clumps form. It will not be smooth.

3. Gather the mixture into a mound. Using the heel of your hand, push the dough outward making 8- to 10-inch sweeps (see "Fraisage," page 69). Gather up the dough again and push out a second time. If the dough is still rough, fraisage a third time. Shape the dough into a disk, dust with flour, cover with plastic wrap, and chill for 1 hour.

4. ASSEMBLE THE TART: Preheat the oven to 375 degrees. Position the oven rack in the upper third of the oven.

5. Line a large cookie sheet with baking parchment. Dab butter under the corners of the paper to secure it. Center the bottom disk of a tart pan on the cookie sheet, then coat the surface of both the disk and the pan with nonstick vegetable spray and dust well with confectioners' sugar.

6. Place the pastry in the center of the metal disk. Dust with confectioners' sugar and roll into a 14-inch circle, using the disk to help guide you. Refrigerate while preparing the filling.

7. MAKE THE FILLING: Peel the apples, cut into quarters, remove the cores (page 17), and cut into 1/4-inch slices. Rinse the cranberries, dry on paper towels, and coarsely chop. Place the fruit in a large bowl and drizzle the lemon juice over the top. In a small bowl, combine the sugars, cornstarch, and cinnamon. Add to the fruit and shake the bowl to distribute.

8. Remove the pastry from the refrigerator. Lightly beat the egg and water in a small bowl with a fork. Brush the egg wash on the pastry. Mound the fruit mixture in the center of the pastry, forming a 9-inch circle of fruit. Dot with butter.

9. Using a pastry scraper or your fingers, lift the pastry over the edge of the fruit, folding it in pleats as needed. The fruit will be exposed in the center. If the pastry cracks, it is too cold—let it stand a few minutes to soften. Lightly brush the outside of the pastry with egg wash, sealing the pleats. Bake for 50 to 55 minutes or until the juices begin to bubble and the crust is golden brown. *Note:* If the tart exudes a lot of juice, brush this syrup on the fruit and crust. This will create a lovely caramelized shine.

10. Remove the tart from the oven and cool on a rack. Let stand 10 minutes. Slip a long, thin spatula under the metal disk and carefully loosen the tart from the parchment to prevent it from sticking. When the tart is cool enough to handle, slide it onto a serving platter. Serve warm with crème anglaise or cinnamon ice cream.

STORAGE
Cover any leftover tart with a sheet of waxed paper, then aluminum foil, and refrigerate for up to 3 days. Reheat before serving. This tart can be frozen.

Crimson Appleberry Pie

HERE IS A PIE THAT is in keeping with traditional holiday flavors. The apples are bound with a sauce made of fresh cranberries flavored with orange juice, with plump raisins added for sweetness. When baked, the pie filling has a glorious crimson color with a sensational blend of flavors. Because cranberries contain so much pectin—a natural thickener—2 tablespoons of cornstarch is usually sufficient for the filling. However, increase the cornstarch to 3 tablespoons if you plan on eating the pie within 4 hours of baking. Served warm with vanilla ice cream or frozen yogurt, this pie is a real holiday winner.

At a Glance

SERVES: 6 to 8

PAN: 9-inch ovenproof glass

PASTRY PREP: Unbaked

OVEN TEMP: 400 degrees

BAKING TIME:
55 to 60 minutes

DIFFICULTY: 🍪 🍪

1 large recipe Nutty Cornmeal Crust pastry (page 154)

FILLING
1 (12-ounce) package fresh cranberries, rinsed and well drained (page 24)
1/2 cup fresh orange juice
1 cup granulated sugar
1/2 cup lightly packed dark brown sugar
1/2 cup golden raisins (optional)
1 teaspoon grated navel or Valencia orange zest
2 to 3 tablespoons cornstarch
1 teaspoon ground cinnamon
2 tablespoons unsalted butter
1 1/2 teaspoons fresh lemon juice
2 1/2 to 3 pounds Cortland or Rome apples (about 6 to 8 apples)

GLAZE
1 large egg white
1 teaspoon granulated sugar
1 teaspoon pearl sugar, for garnish

1. Preheat the oven to 400 degrees. Position the oven rack in the lower third of the oven. Butter a 9-inch ovenproof glass pie plate.

2. On a floured pastry cloth, roll half the pastry into a 13-inch circle. Line the pie plate with the pastry. Trim edge, leaving a 1/4-inch overhang.

3. MAKE THE FILLING: Place the cranberries, orange juice, 1/2 cup granulated sugar, and the brown sugar in a large nonreactive saucepan. Stir and bring to a boil. Simmer over low heat for 10 minutes, stirring occasionally to break up the cranberries. Mix in the raisins and orange zest.

4. Combine the remaining ¹/₂ cup granulated sugar, cornstarch, and cinnamon in a small bowl. Add to the cranberries, stirring constantly to prevent lumping. Bring the mixture to a boil, then reduce the heat and simmer 1 minute. Blend in the butter and lemon juice. Set aside to cool.

5. Quarter the apples, remove the cores, and peel (page 17). Cut into 3/4-inch-thick slices. Fold the apples into the cranberry mixture. Set aside to cool.

6. ASSEMBLE THE PIE: Empty the fruit filling into the pastry shell, mounding the fruit in the center. Fill in spaces as needed around the side with pieces of apple.

7. Roll the remaining pastry into a 13-inch circle and place it over the fruit. With your hands, push the dough gently toward the center to prevent it from stretching during baking.

8. Trim the edges with scissors leaving a 3/4-inch overhang. Tuck the top dough under the bottom and press together. Crimp the edge with a fork dipped in flour. Prick the top of the pie in several places with a fork to allow the steam to escape. Lightly beat together the egg white and the granulated sugar and brush over the top of the pie with a pastry brush. Sprinkle with pearl sugar.

9. To prevent the edge from burning, make aluminum foil bands. Cut two 3-inch-wide strips of 18-inch heavy-duty aluminum foil. Fold 1 inch of each strip to the center, making a double thickness on one side. Mold the foil around the edge of the pie, keeping the double fold on top of the dough. Secure the bands with tape, and place the pie in the oven.

10. Make an aluminum foil drip pan to place on the rack below the pie halfway through the baking. Cut an 18-inch square of heavy-duty aluminum foil. Fold each edge twice (about 1 inch per fold) standing the folded edges upright to form a 4-sided pan.

11. Bake the pie for 50 minutes. Remove the aluminum foil bands and bake for 10 minutes longer, or until the top and bottom crusts are golden brown and the juices begin to bubble. Remove the pie from the oven and cool on a rack. Let stand at least 4 hours before serving.

STORAGE
Cover any leftover pie with a sheet of waxed paper then aluminum foil and refrigerate for up to 3 days. Reheat before serving. This pie can be frozen.

Apple Walnut Tart in Sweet Tart Pastry

THIS TART HAS BEEN A FAVORITE with my students for years.

1 11-inch Sweet Tart Pastry crust (page 146), baked
2 tablespoons strained apricot preserves, warmed

FILLING
4 or 5 Granny Smith or Golden Delicious apples (about $1\frac{1}{2}$ to 2 pounds)
2 teaspoons fresh lemon juice
$\frac{1}{2}$ cup broken or coarsely cut walnuts
$\frac{2}{3}$ cup sugar
$\frac{1}{4}$ cup unsifted all-purpose flour
$\frac{1}{2}$ teaspoon ground cinnamon
3 to 4 tablespoons soft unsalted butter

1. Brush the baked pastry shell with apricot preserves while it is still warm.

2. Position the oven rack in the lower third of the oven. Preheat the oven to 400 degrees.

3. **PREPARE THE FRUIT:** Peel, core and halve the apples (page 17). Then slice them $\frac{1}{4}$ inch thick, *across the core*. Keep slices from each apple half pressed together so they appear intact; place on a sheet pan and sprinkle with lemon juice.

4. **ASSEMBLE THE TART:** Remove the 2 smaller slices of apple from the ends of each half. Coarsely chop them and spread evenly on the bottom of the baked pastry shell. Arrange the remaining slices, fanning them around the pastry shell. Start at the top of the pan and point the apple slices toward the center. On the second row, place the apples in the opposite direction. Fill in the center as best you can with a few smaller apple slices placed perpendicular to the first 2 layers. You will have 3 circles of apples. Scatter the walnuts over the fruit.

5. Combine the sugar, flour, and cinnamon in a small bowl. Add 3 tablespoons of the butter and work the mixture with your fingertips to form a crumb topping. If the mixture seems too dry, add a little more butter. Sprinkle the crumb topping over the apples.

6. Place the tart on a cookie sheet and bake for 40 to 45 minutes, or until the top is golden brown. Lay a piece of aluminum foil loosely over the top if it is browning too quickly. Serve while still warm with cinnamon ice cream.

STORAGE
Cover any leftover tart with a sheet of waxed paper, then aluminum foil, and refrigerate for up to 4 days. Reheat before serving. This tart can be frozen after baking.

How to Fan Fruit

SOME FRUITS FOR TARTS are often "fanned," or arranged in uniform, overlapping slices. Those that are commonly used for fanning are firm-fleshed fruits such as apples, pears, nectarines, and plums. Mangoes can also be used but are more difficult to slice evenly.

The most important thing to remember when fanning fruits is to keep them in larger pieces, generally beginning with halved, pitted fruit. Then the fruit is cut either parallel or perpendicular to the cavity.

+ Use a very sharp, thin-bladed knife and a cutting board.

+ Cut in $1/8$- to $1/4$-inch slices.

+ Keep each half stacked together after it is cut.

+ Lift stacks of fruit onto a clean, flat pan, taking care to keep them intact.

+ Drizzle with lemon juice when applicable.

To arrange the fans, remove the smaller end pieces from either side of the stacks. These can be scattered on the bottom of the pastry-lined pan or discarded. Using one stack of fruit at a time, fan the slices at the top while holding the bottom together, much as you would when spreading a hand of cards.

Place the fanned fruit into the pastry shell, starting with the outer edge and working toward the center. When making a circular tart, select the larger stacks for the outer circle. Spread the wider, top edge of the fan toward the edge of the pastry shell, repeating the process until all of the fruit is used.

Fresh Apricot Pie with Apricot Rum Sauce

IF YOU WANT A SUMMER fruit pie that is a little out of the ordinary, try one made with fresh apricots. This luxurious sweet and tart fruit makes a great pie. Be sure to serve it with the sauce, and don't forget the ice cream. When it melts into the sauce, it's absolutely wonderful.

At a Glance

SERVES: 6 to 8

PAN: 9-inch ovenproof glass

PASTRY PREP: Unbaked

OVEN TEMP: 400 degrees

BAKING TIME:
50 to 55 minutes

DIFFICULTY: 🥄 🥄

---

1 small recipe Flaky Pie Pastry
  (pages 98, 100)
1 large egg white
1 teaspoon water

FILLING
2 pounds fresh apricots
3/4 cup plus 1 teaspoon granulated
  sugar
1/3 cup lightly packed light brown
  sugar
2 to 3 tablespoons cornstarch
1 teaspoon grated navel or
  Valencia orange zest
1/2 teaspoon grated lemon zest
1/2 teaspoon ground cinnamon
Scant 1/4 teaspoon ground ginger
2 tablespoons light rum
1 tablespoon unsalted butter

1 recipe Apricot Rum Sauce
  (page 443)

1. START THE FILLING: Clean and pit the apricots (page 19). Cut each half into 3 wedges and place the fruit in a large bowl.

2. Preheat the oven to 400 degrees. Position the oven rack in the lower third of the oven. Butter a 9-inch ovenproof glass pie plate.

3. MAKE THE PIE: On a floured pastry cloth, roll 1 disk of pastry into a circle measuring approximately 13 inches. Fit loosely into the pie plate. Trim the edges with scissors, leaving a 1/2-inch overhang. Beat the egg white and water together with a fork. Using a pastry brush, brush the dough with the egg white, reserving the remainder for glazing the top.

4. Combine 3/4 cup granulated sugar with the brown sugar, cornstarch, orange, and lemon zest, cinnamon, and ginger in a small bowl. Sprinkle 2 tablespoons of the dry mixture over the bottom of the pastry shell. Toss the remaining sugar mixture with the apricots. Mound the fruit in the pie plate, sprinkle with rum, and dot with butter.

5. Roll the second disk of dough into a 13-inch circle. Place the dough on top of the filling. With your hands, push the dough gently toward the center to prevent it from stretching during baking. Trim excess with scissors leaving a 1-inch overhang. Tuck the top edge of the dough under the bottom, pressing the 2 layers together. Crimp or flute the edge (page 66). Make steam vents in the top of the pastry. Brush the top of the pastry with the remaining egg white and sprinkle with 1 teaspoon of sugar.

6. To prevent the edges from burning, make aluminum foil bands. Cut two 3-inch-wide strips of 18-inch heavy-duty aluminum foil. Fold 1 inch of each strip to the center, making a double thickness of foil. Mold the foil around the edge of the pie, keeping the double fold on top of the dough. Be careful not to crush the edge of the pastry. Secure the bands with tape, and place it in the oven.

7. Make an aluminum foil drip pan to place on the rack below the pie halfway through the baking. Cut an 18-inch square of heavy-duty aluminum foil. Fold each edge twice (about 1 inch per fold) standing the folded edges upright to form a 4-sided pan.

8. Bake the pie for 45 minutes. Remove the foil bands and bake for 5 to 10 minutes longer, or until the juice begins to bubble and the crust is golden brown on the top and bottom. Remove the pie from the oven and cool on a rack. Let stand for 3 to 4 hours before cutting. Serve with vanilla ice cream or yogurt and warmed Apricot Rum Sauce.

STORAGE

Cover any leftover pie with a sheet of waxed paper then aluminum foil and refrigerate for up to 3 days. Reheat before serving. This pie may be frozen.

The apricot exists on the brink of viability.

WAVERLY ROOT,
FOOD

Roy's Apricot Cherry Pie with Almond Crunch Topping

THE PIQUANT COMBINATION OF FRESH apricots and tart cherries was inspired by my editor, Roy Finamore. Roy's talents go beyond that of a fine editor; he's a terrific baker as well. For this pie, crunchy crumbs made from sweetened ground and sliced almonds top the colorful fruit filling. Indeed, opposite flavors do attract.

At a Glance

SERVES: 6 to 8

PAN: 9-inch ovenproof glass

PASTRY PREP: Unbaked

OVEN TEMP: 400 degrees

BAKING TIME:
60 to 65 minutes

DIFFICULTY: 🍪 🍪

½ small recipe Flaky Pie Pastry
(pages 98, 100)

TOPPING
³/4 cup sliced unblanched almonds
4 tablespoons unsalted butter
2 tablespoon honey
²/3 cup unsifted all-purpose flour
¹/3 cup sugar
¹/4 teaspoon baking powder
¹/4 teaspoon ground cinnamon
¹/4 teaspoon vanilla extract

FILLING
1½ pounds fresh apricots
1 pound fresh tart cherries (canned
tart red cherries may be
substituted)
1 tablespoon instant tapioca
1 cup sugar
3 tablespoons cornstarch
1 teaspoon fresh lemon juice

1. MAKE THE TOPPING: Preheat the oven to 325 degrees. Spread the almonds in a shallow baking pan. Toast for 8 to 10 minutes or until lightly browned. Cool completely.

2. Melt the butter in a medium saucepan. Stir in the honey and set aside to cool.

3. Place the flour, sugar, baking powder, cinnamon, vanilla, and half the almonds in a processor bowl fitted with the steel blade. Process until the nuts are finely chopped.

4. Use a table fork to stir the flour mixture into the cool butter, mixing until large and small crumbs form. Stir the remaining sliced almonds into the topping. Set aside to dry for at least 15 minutes.

5. START THE FILLING: Clean and pit the apricots (page 19). Cut each half into 3 wedges and place the fruit in a large bowl.

6. Wash and thoroughly dry the cherries (page 22). Remove the pits with a cherry pitter, then place the cherries in the bowl with the apricots.

7. Sprinkle the tapioca over the fruit, shaking the bowl to distribute well. Set aside for 15 minutes.

8. **MAKE THE PIE:** Increase the oven temperature to 400 degrees. Position the oven rack in the lower third of the oven. Butter a 9-inch ovenproof glass pie plate.

9. On a floured pastry cloth, roll the pastry into a 13-inch circle. Line the pie plate with the pastry. Trim the edge, leaving a 1-inch overhang. Tuck the overhanging dough under itself to form a thicker edge and flute. Chill until ready to fill.

10. In a small bowl, combine the sugar and cornstarch. Sprinkle about 1 tablespoon of this mixture over the bottom of the pastry-lined plate.

11. Toss the remaining sugar mixture through the fruit and empty it into the pie plate, filling in the spaces as best you can. Drizzle the lemon juice over the top, then cover with the topping.

12. To prevent the edges from burning, make aluminum foil bands. Cut two 3-inch-wide strips of 18-inch heavy-duty aluminum foil. Fold 1 inch of each strip to the center, making a double thickness of foil on one side. Cover the edge of the pie with the bands, keeping the double fold on top of the dough. Be careful not to crush the edge of the pastry. Seal the bands together with tape.

13. Make an aluminum foil drip pan to place on the rack below the pie halfway through the baking. Cut an 18-inch square of heavy-duty aluminum foil. Fold each edge twice (about 1 inch per fold) standing the folded edges upright to form a 4-sided pan.

14. Bake the pie for 30 minutes. Then lay a square of aluminum foil loosely over the top to prevent the crumbs from overbrowning. Continue to bake 30 to 35 minutes longer, or until the fruit is bubbly and the bottom of the crust is golden brown.

NOTE
Remove the aluminum foil bands the last 5 to 10 minutes of baking, but keep the top of the pie covered

15. Remove the pie from the oven and cool on a rack. Let stand for at least 4 hours before serving.

STORAGE
Cover any leftover pie with a sheet of waxed paper then aluminum foil and refrigerate for up to 3 days. Reheat before serving to crisp the crumb topping. This pie may be frozen.

Steven Santoro's Glazed Banana Lemon Tart

ONE OF THE MOST GIFTED CHEFS I have ever met is Steven Santoro. During his professional career, Steve has worked at some of New York and New Jersey's finest dining establishments. Not only is his food extraordinary but his magnificent desserts are awesome.

At a Glance

SERVES: 8 to 10

PAN: 14 × 17-inch cookie sheet

PASTRY PREP: Baked

BROILING TIME: 4 to 6 minutes

DIFFICULTY: 🥐 🥐 🥐

When I sampled this Glazed Banana Lemon Tart, I knew I had to include the recipe in this book. It has a puff pastry tart shell that is covered with lemon curd, chopped macadamia nuts, and glazed sliced bananas. Steve served the tart with homemade chocolate ice cream. High-quality store-bought is fine, but try the unique combination of bananas, lemon, and chocolate. It's memorable.

1/2 recipe Goof-Proof Puff Pastry (page 172), shaped into a round free-form 11-inch shell (page 175), baked

FILLING

4 large egg yolks
2/3 cup plus 3 to 4 teaspoons sugar
1/4 cup plus 2 to 3 teaspoons fresh lemon juice
2 teaspoons finely grated lemon zest
4 tablespoons unsalted butter, cut into 1/2-inch slices
1/3 cup coarsely chopped macadamia nuts (do not use a food processor)
3 firm medium bananas

1. MAKE THE LEMON CURD: Using a whisk, lightly beat the yolks until well blended in the top of a double boiler or medium stainless steel bowl. Stir in 3/4 cup sugar, 1/4 cup of lemon juice, lemon zest, and butter.

2. Fill the bottom of the double boiler with about 1 inch of water (if using a metal bowl, select a saucepan that will allow the bowl to set above the water). Bring the water to a boil, then reduce to a simmer.

3. Place the mixture over the water and cook 25 to 30 minutes, stirring occasionally. When the mixture reaches the consistency of thick mayonnaise, it is done. Remove it from the heat and set the bowl in a sink filled with about 2 inches of cold water and ice cubes. Stir occasionally until cold.

4. ASSEMBLE THE TART: Use a small offset spatula to spread about 2/3 cup lemon curd over the pastry shell. Reserve the rest for topping the bananas. Sprinkle the macadamia nuts over the lemon curd.

5. Peel the bananas, and cut them on a slight diagonal into ⅛-inch slices. Arrange the pieces, slightly overlapping on the lemon curd, starting on the outer edge, making 3 concentric circles.

6. Thin the remaining lemon curd with about 2 teaspoons of lemon juice. Using a pastry brush, lightly glaze the banana slices with the lemon curd. This will prevent them from turning brown. If the curd is still too thick to use with a pastry brush, add a bit more juice. At this point, the tart will keep for up to 12 hours. Store in the refrigerator until ready to broil and serve.

7. GLAZE THE TART: Preheat the broiler. Position the shelf so the tart will be 4 to 5 inches from the heat. Sprinkle the top of the bananas with 3 to 4 teaspoons sugar.

8. To prevent the crust from burning, make an aluminum foil shield. Measure across the surface of the exposed fruit. It should be about 8½ inches. Using the bottom of a layer pan as a guide, trace a circle on the foil and cut it out with scissors.

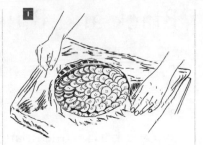

Lay the foil over the fruit. If the opening is too large, make a tuck or fold in the foil to adjust the size. **1**

9. Place the tart under the broiler. Broil the tart until the bananas are caramelized and charred on the edges. This should take about 4 to 6 minutes. *Watch carefully.* Before unmolding, let the tart stand about 5 minutes. Serve while warm.

STORAGE
This tart should be eaten on the day it is made. Freezing is not recommended.

Black and Blue Mango Pie

THE LUSCIOUS COMBINATION OF BLACKBERRIES, blueberries, and mangoes is one that came about by chance. After days of testing recipes, I had some leftover berries and mango in the refrigerator. Rather than waste them, I put the fruit together for a pie. It turned out to be one of my favorite recipes in this book. Try this, and see if you don't agree.

At a Glance

SERVES: 6 to 8

PAN: 9-inch ovenproof glass

PASTRY PREP: Unbaked

OVEN TEMP: 400 degrees

BAKING TIME:
50 to 60 minutes

DIFFICULTY: 🥖 🥖

1 small recipe Flaky Pie Pastry
   (pages 98, 100)

FILLING
2 large or 3 medium mangoes
2 cups (1 pint) fresh blueberries
1 1/2 cups (6-ounce basket) fresh
   blackberries
2/3 cup plus 1 teaspoon sugar
3 tablespoons cornstarch
2 teaspoons fresh lemon juice
2 tablespoons unsalted butter

1. START THE FILLING: Remove the cheeks from the mangoes. Score the flesh for 3/4-inch squares and remove from the skin. Trim flesh from the pit area and dice (page 29).

2. Wash and thoroughly dry the blueberries and blackberries (pages 21 and 22). Cut the larger blackberries in half.

3. MAKE THE PIE: Preheat the oven to 400 degrees. Position the oven rack in the lower third of the oven. Butter a 9-inch ovenproof glass pie plate.

4. Roll half the pastry into a 13-inch circle. Line the pie plate with the pastry. Trim the edge, leaving a 1/2-inch overhang.

5. Place the diced mangoes and berries in a large bowl. Combine 2/3 cup sugar and the cornstarch in a small bowl. Sprinkle 2 tablespoons of this mixture on the bottom of the pastry shell. Add the remaining dry ingredients to the fruit and shake the bowl to distribute. *Do not stir; you will crush the fruit.*

6. Empty the mixture into the pie plate, mounding the fruit in the center. Sprinkle with lemon juice and dot with butter.

7. Make a lattice top with the remaining pastry as follows: Roll the pastry into a 13-inch circle. Using a pastry wheel, divide pastry into twelve 3/4 inch strips. Evenly space the pastry, starting with 2 longer strips placed to the left and right of the center, about 3/4 inch apart. Continue, using 2 more strips on either side, keeping the shortest strips toward the outer edge. Rotate the pie 90 degrees and repeat the process, weaving new strips over and under the initial 6 strips (see "Making Woven Crusts," page 65). Trim, leaving a 1-inch overhang.

8. Seal the edges by folding the pastry strips under the bottom layer of dough. Flute the edge of the pastry (page 66). Sprinkle the lattice with 1 teaspoon sugar.

9. To prevent the edges from burning, make aluminum foil bands. Cut two 3-inch-wide strips of 18-inch heavy-duty aluminum foil. Fold 1 inch of each strip to the center, making a double thickness of foil. Mold the foil around the edge of the pie, keeping the double fold on top of the dough. Be careful not to crush the edge of the pastry. Secure the bands with tape.

10. Make an aluminum foil drip pan to place on the rack below the pie halfway through the baking. Cut an 18-inch square of heavy-duty aluminum foil. Fold each edge twice (about 1 inch per fold) standing the folded edges upright to form a 4-sided pan.

11. Bake the pie for 45 minutes. Remove the aluminum foil bands. Continue baking for 10 minutes longer or until the crust is golden brown and the juices begin to bubble. Remove the pie from the oven and cool on a rack. Let stand at least 4 hours before serving.

STORAGE

Cover any leftover pie with a sheet of waxed paper then aluminum foil and refrigerate for up to 4 days. This pie can be frozen.

Blueberry Crumb Pie with Warm Blueberry Sauce

IT'S NO SURPRISE THAT BLUEBERRY PIE is a Fourth of July favorite. This sweet, succulent berry—native to our country—is in its prime at that time of year, and it makes sensational pies. When I make blueberry pie, I always par-cook the filling first, removing some of the juice before filling the pie shell. This helps to prevent the bottom crust from becoming soggy.

At a Glance

SERVES: 6 to 8

PAN: 9-inch ovenproof glass

PASTRY PREP: Unbaked

OVEN TEMP: 400 degrees

BAKING TIME:
50 to 55 minutes

DIFFICULTY:

$^1/_2$ small recipe Flaky Pie Pastry
   (pages 98, 100)
1 large egg white
1 teaspoon water

FILLING
$^3/_4$ cup granulated sugar
2 tablespoons cornstarch
$^1/_2$ teaspoon ground cinnamon
$^1/_4$ cup water
6 to 7 cups blueberries, washed
   and dried (3 pint baskets)
   (page 22)
1 tablespoon instant tapioca
1 tablespoon unsalted butter
$1^1/_2$ to 2 teaspoons fresh lemon
   juice

STREUSEL CRUMB TOPPING
1 cup unsifted all-purpose flour
$^1/_4$ cup finely chopped walnuts
$^1/_4$ cup granulated sugar
$^1/_4$ cup lightly packed light brown
   sugar
$^1/_2$ teaspoon ground cinnamon
$^1/_4$ teaspoon baking powder
$^1/_8$ teaspoon salt
$^1/_3$ cup unsalted butter, melted
   and cooled to tepid

WARM BLUEBERRY SYRUP
Reserved syrup from filling
$^1/_2$ cup water
1 to 2 tablespoons crème de cassis
   or Kirschwasser
1 teaspoon fresh lemon juice

1. Preheat the oven to 400 degrees. Position the oven rack in the lower third of the oven. Butter a 9-inch ovenproof glass pie plate.

2. On a floured pastry cloth, roll the pastry into a circle measuring approximately 13 inches. Fit loosely into the pie plate. Trim the edge with scissors, leaving a 1-inch overhang. Fold over and flute or crimp the edge (see page 66). In a small bowl, lightly beat the egg white and water. Brush the dough with a thin layer of egg white to seal the surface.

3. MAKE THE FILLING: Whisk together the sugar, cornstarch, and cinnamon in a large skillet. Stir in the water. Add the blueberries and stir gently. Bring to a slow boil, then cook over low

heat, stirring occasionally with a rubber spatula, for about 5 minutes, or *just* until mixture thickens. *Avoid mashing the blueberries.* Be careful not to overcook the blueberries.

4. Using a slotted spoon, empty blueberries into a large shallow container about $1/3$ at a time, sprinkling each layer with tapioca. Let stand for 15 minutes to soften the tapioca. Reserve the syrup for the blueberry sauce. Empty the filling into the pie plate. Dot with butter and sprinkle with lemon juice.

5. **MAKE THE STREUSEL CRUMB TOPPING:** Combine the flour, walnuts, sugars, cinnamon, baking powder, and salt in a medium bowl. Add to the cooled melted butter and toss with a fork to make crumbs. Take a clump of the crumb mixture in your hand and squeeze gently to form a larger clump. Then break the large clump apart over the blueberry filling. Repeat using all of the crumbs. Do not press the crumbs into the filling.

6. To prevent the edges from burning, make aluminum foil bands. Cut two 3-inch-wide strips of 18-inch heavy-duty aluminum foil. Fold 1 inch of each strip to the center, making a double thickness of foil. Mold the foil around the edge of the pie, keeping the double fold on top of the dough. Be careful not to crush the edge of the pastry. Secure the bands with tape.

7. Make an aluminum foil drip pan to place on the rack below the pie halfway through the baking. Cut an 18-inch square of heavy-duty aluminum foil. Fold each edge twice (about 1 inch per fold) standing the folded edges upright to form a 4-sided pan.

To prevent the crumbs from overbrowning, cover the pie loosely with a sheet of aluminum foil.

8. Bake for 40 minutes. Remove the foil bands and the foil from the top and continue baking for 10 to 15 minutes, or until bottom crust and crumbs are golden brown. Cool on a rack for 4 hours before cutting. Serve with vanilla ice cream or frozen yogurt and Warm Blueberry Sauce.

9. **MAKE WARM BLUEBERRY SYRUP:** Place the reserved blueberry syrup and water in a medium, heavy saucepan. Bring to a slow boil, stirring constantly. Off the heat, stir in the cassis, then return to the boil, and cook for 30 seconds longer. If the sauce is too thick, add a little more water. Stir in the lemon juice and empty into a container. This sauce can be made ahead and reheated as needed.

STORAGE
Store any leftover pie, loosely covered with a sheet of waxed paper then aluminum foil, and refrigerate for up to 2 days. This pie can be frozen.

Fresh Tart Cherry Pie in Black Pepper Wine Pastry

FROM EARLY TO MID-JULY, FRESH tart cherries can be found in farmer's markets and at local supermarkets. Pies made with this short-season fruit are a special treat. I like to make this pie with Black Pepper Wine Pastry, as the zing of the pepper complements the tartness of the cherries.

At a Glance

SERVES: 6 to 8

PAN: 9-inch ovenproof glass

PASTRY PREP: Unbaked

OVEN TEMP: 400 degrees

BAKING TIME:
40 to 45 minutes

DIFFICULTY: 🥟🥟

Pitting cherries is no longer a chore with the newer cherry pitters available. I especially like a brand called Westmark, made in Germany and sold at the Williams-Sonoma stores. If you bake cherry pies in quantity, I recommend purchasing the larger device. Using this tool makes cherry pitting a breeze.

1 recipe Black Pepper Wine Pastry (page 143)

FILLING
4 cups fresh red tart cherries (1 quart basket)
1 tablespoon instant tapioca
1 to 1 1/4 cups plus 1 teaspoon sugar
2 tablespoons cornstarch
1/2 teaspoon ground cinnamon
1/8 teaspoon fresh black pepper
1 teaspoon freshly squeezed lemon juice
1/4 teaspoon almond extract
1 tablespoon unsalted butter

1. **START THE FILLING:** Wash and thoroughly dry the cherries (page 22). Remove the pits with a cherry pitter and place the fruit in a large bowl.

2. Sprinkle the tapioca over the cherries, shaking the bowl to distribute well. Set aside for 15 minutes.

3. **PREPARE THE CRUST:** Preheat the oven to 400 degrees. Position the oven rack in the lower third of the oven. Butter a 9-inch ovenproof glass pie plate.

4. On a floured pastry cloth, roll half the pastry into a 13-inch circle. Line the pie plate with the pastry. Trim the edge, leaving a 1/2-inch overhang.

5. **ASSEMBLE THE PIE:** Combine 1 cup sugar, the cornstarch, cinnamon, and black pepper in a small bowl; whisk together well. Sprinkle about 1 tablespoon of this mixture over the bottom of the pastry-lined plate.

6. Toss the remaining dry ingredients through the cherries. Taste, and add ¼ cup of sugar if necessary. Pile the fruit into the pie plate, mounding the cherries in the center. Sprinkle the lemon juice and almond extract over the top and dot the surface with butter.

7. Make a lattice top with the remaining pastry as follows: Roll the pastry into a 13-inch circle. Using a pastry wheel, divide the pastry into twelve ¾-inch strips. Evenly space the pastry, starting with 2 longer strips, placed to the left and right of the center, about ¾ inch apart. Continue using 2 more strips on either side, keeping the shortest strips toward the outer edge. Rotate the pie 90 degrees. Repeat the process, weaving new strips over and under the initial 6 strips (see "Making Woven Crusts," page 65). Trim, leaving a 1-inch overhang.

8. Seal the edges by folding the pastry strips under the bottom layer of dough. Flute the edge of the pastry (see page 66). Sprinkle the lattice with 1 teaspoon sugar.

9. To prevent the edges from burning, make aluminum foil bands. Cut two 3-inch-wide strips of 18-inch heavy-duty aluminum foil. Fold 1 inch of each strip to the center, making a double thickness of foil. Mold the foil around the edge of the pie, keeping the double fold on top of the dough. Be careful not to crush the edge of the pastry. Secure the bands with tape.

10. Make an aluminum foil drip pan to place on the rack below the pie halfway through the baking. Cut an 18-inch square of heavy-duty aluminum foil. Fold each edge twice (about 1 inch per fold) standing the folded edges upright to form a 4-sided pan.

11. Bake the pie for 30 minutes. Remove the aluminum foil bands. Continue baking for 10 minutes longer or until the crust is golden brown and the juices begin to bubble. Remove the pie from the oven and cool on a rack. Let stand for at least 4 hours before serving.

STORAGE

Cover any leftover pie with a sheet of waxed paper then aluminum foil and refrigerate for up to 3 days. Reheat before serving. This pie can be frozen.

Cheese-Layered Tart Cherry Pie in Almond Nut Pastry

HERE IS AN OLD-FASHIONED cherry pie with a thin cream cheese layer between the bottom crust and the cherry filling. The cheese mellows the tartness of the cherries and helps to keep the bottom of the pastry crisp. You can omit the cheese layer if you wish.

At a Glance

SERVES: 6 to 8

PAN: 9-inch ovenproof glass

PASTRY PREP: Unbaked

OVEN TEMP: 400 degrees

BAKING TIME:
55 to 50 minutes

DIFFICULTY: 🍪 🍪

This pie can be enjoyed all year because it is made with canned cherries; but be sure to buy water-packed tart cherries, not those in syrup.

1 recipe Almond Nut Pastry
    (page 151)

FILLING
2 (1-pound) cans water-packed
    tart cherries
1 cup sugar
$^1/_4$ cup cornstarch
1 teaspoon fresh lemon juice
$^1/_2$ teaspoon almond extract
$^1/_2$ teaspoon red food coloring
    (optional; see Note)
2 tablespoons soft unsalted butter

CREAM CHEESE LAYER
1 (3-ounce) package cream cheese,
    at room temperature
4 teaspoons sugar
1 teaspoon unsifted all-purpose
    flour
1 large egg yolk
$^1/_4$ teaspoon vanilla extract

GLAZE
1 large egg white
1 teaspoon water
1 teaspoon sugar

1. MAKE THE FILLING: Set a colander in a large bowl. Empty the cherries into the colander and drain thoroughly. Reserve 1$^1/_4$ cups of the juice. Line a large sheet pan with a double thickness of paper towels and spread the cherries on the pan to dry.

2. Combine the sugar and cornstarch in a large saucepan. Gradually add the reserved cherry juice, stirring until smooth. Place the saucepan over low heat and cook, stirring constantly, until the mixture comes to a boil and is thickened. Simmer for 1 minute, stirring occasionally. Do not overmix. Remove from the heat and blend in the lemon juice, almond extract, red food coloring, and butter. Gently fold in the drained cherries. Set aside to cool.

3. MAKE THE CREAM CHEESE LAYER: Blend the cream cheese, sugar, and flour in a small bowl. Stir in the egg yolk and vanilla. Whisk to smooth any lumps. Set aside.

4. **ASSEMBLE THE PIE.** Preheat the oven to 400 degrees. Position the oven rack in the lower third of the oven. Butter a 9-inch ovenproof glass pie plate.

5. On a floured board, roll half of the pastry into a 13-inch circle. Line the pie plate with the pastry. Trim the edges, leaving a 1/2-inch overhang.

6. Spread the cheese layer smoothly on the bottom of the pastry. Spoon the cherry filling over the cheese, starting from the edge and working to the center. Smooth the top.

7. Make a lattice top with the remaining pastry as follows: Roll the remaining pastry into a 13-inch circle. Using a pastry wheel, divide the pastry into twelve 3/4-inch strips. Evenly space the pastry, starting with the 2 longer strips to the left and right of center, about 3/4 inch apart. Continue, using 2 more strips on either side, keeping the shortest strips toward the outer edge. Rotate the pie 90 degrees. Repeat the process, weaving new strips over and under the initial 6 strips (see "Making Lattice Crusts," page 65). Trim, leaving a 1-inch overhang.

8. Seal the edges by folding the pastry strips under the bottom layer. Flute the edge of the pastry (see page 66).

9. To glaze the top of the pastry, lightly beat the egg white and water with a fork. Gently brush over the lattice top, then sprinkle with sugar.

10. To prevent the edges from burning, make aluminum foil bands. Cut two 3-inch-wide strips of 18-inch heavy-duty aluminum foil. Fold 1 inch of each strip toward the center, making a double thickness of foil. Mold the foil around the edge of the pie, keeping the double thickness on top of the pastry. Be careful not to crush the pastry. Secure the strips together with tape.

11. Make an aluminum foil drip pan to place on the rack below the pie halfway through the baking. Cut an 18-inch square of heavy-duty aluminum foil. Fold each edge twice (about 1 inch per fold) standing the folded edges upright to form a 4-sided pan.

12. Bake the pie for 45 minutes. Remove the aluminum foil bands. Continue baking 10 minutes longer or until the top of the pie is golden brown, the juices start to bubble, and the crust is brown on the bottom. Cool on a rack at least 4 hours before serving.

NOTE
The color of water-packed canned cherries is drab, but if you are finicky about using red food coloring, omit it.

STORAGE
Cover any leftover pie with a sheet of waxed paper then aluminum foil and refrigerate for up to 3 days. Reheat before serving. This pie can be frozen.

Terry Ford's Green Tomato Pie

RIPLEY, TENNESSEE, IS THE HOME of Terry Ford, owner of *The Lauderdale County Enterprise,* a local newspaper his family started in 1885. Imagine my surprise when I learned that Terry has one of the largest private cookbook collections in the United States.

Terry loves to cook and bake. Through his media contacts, he has amassed an incredible amount of culinary knowledge. So who better to ask when I needed a recipe for a green tomato pie? Of course, he had one!

His version of this Pennsylvania Dutch pie is made with chopped green tomatoes, golden raisins, and pecans and is flavored with balsamic vinegar, sugar, and spices. The mixture is bound with lots of tapioca and has a texture similar to mincemeat. If you prefer a looser filling, reduce the tapioca to 2 to 3 tablespoons.

Terry suggests using this versatile filling for crepes; if you're into home canning, it's great for gift-giving as well.

1 9-inch *Flaky Pie Pastry crust (pages 98, 100), baked*

FILLING
4 cups diced green tomatoes, in 3/8-inch pieces (do not remove the skins or seeds)
4 to 6 tablespoons instant tapioca
1 cup golden raisins
1 cup pecans, coarsely chopped
1 cup granulated sugar
$1/4$ cup firmly packed dark brown sugar
2 tablespoons unsalted butter, softened
2 tablespoons balsamic vinegar
1 teaspoon ground cinnamon
$1/2$ teaspoon freshly grated nutmeg
$1/4$ teaspoon ground allspice

1 START THE FILLING: Layer the tomatoes and tapioca in a large, nonreactive bowl. Toss with your hands to distribute the tapioca. Let stand for 15 minutes.

2. Preheat the oven to 350 degrees. Position the rack in the lower third of the oven. Lightly butter a 2-quart casserole dish.

3. MAKE THE PIE: Add the remaining ingredients to the tomatoes, then empty the mixture into the casserole. Bake the mixture, uncovered, for 45 to 55 minutes. Stir 2 or 3 times as it bakes. The filling is cooked when it is very bubbly and all the tapioca seems dissolved.

4. Remove the casserole from the oven and let stand about 15 minutes. It will become very thick. Empty the filling into the pastry shell. Smooth the top, and let stand at room temperature for several hours, until set. Serve the pie with a dollop of lightly whipped cream or vanilla ice cream.

STORAGE

Cover any leftover pie loosely with a sheet of waxed paper then aluminum foil, and keep at room temperature for up to 1 week. Freezing is not recommended.

Mango Tart with Blackberries

TANGY BLACKBERRIES SPRINKLED ON A BUTTERY tart pastry are topped with fanned slices of sweet mangoes. This pairing of fruits is not only a dynamite flavor combination, but when sliced, the contrasting colors of apricot and purple make this tart an eye-appealing beauty. Because this tart is not rich, it is especially nice to serve after a heavy meal or for the diet-conscious.

At a Glance

SERVES: 8 to 10

PAN: 11-inch metal tart

PASTRY PREP: Baked

OVEN TEMP: 375 degrees

BAKING TIME:
45 to 50 minutes

DIFFICULTY: 🍪 🍪

---

1 11-inch *Sweet Tart Pastry crust (page 146), baked*
2 tablespoons *strained apricot preserves, warmed*

Brush the bottom and sides of the baked pastry crust with apricot preserves while it is still warm. Set aside to cool while you prepare the filling.

FILLING
2 large or 3 medium mangoes
1 1/2 to 2 cups blackberries
   (8–10 ounces)
3 tablespoons cornstarch
5 tablespoons sugar
1 1/2 teaspoons fresh lemon juice
1/2 teaspoon ground cinnamon

GLAZE
1/2 cup apricot preserves
1 tablespoon water

---

1. START THE FILLING: Cut the cheeks from the mangoes and peel. Place the mango flat side down on a cutting board and cut lengthwise into 1/4-inch pieces (page 29). Trim flesh from the sides of the pit and cut into 1-inch pieces. Set aside.

2. Wash and thoroughly dry the blackberries (page 21). Cut larger berries in half.

3. Preheat the oven to 375 degrees. Position the oven rack in the lower third of the oven.

4. ASSEMBLE THE PIE: Combine the cornstarch and 3 tablespoons sugar in a large bowl. Add the blackberries and shake the bowl to coat the berries with the dry ingredients. Empty the mixture into the pastry shell.

5. Use smaller pieces of mango to fill in gaps around the blackberries. Cover the berry mixture with the sliced mango, fanning the slices on the outer edge and tapering them toward the middle. Make a second, smaller row to fill in the center. Tuck less uniform pieces under the even slices.

6. Drizzle the lemon juice over the top. Combine the remaining 2 tablespoons sugar with the cinnamon, and sprinkle the mixture over the fruit.

7. Place the tart on a cookie sheet and bake for 45 to 50 minutes or until the juices begin to bubble and the edge of the crust is golden brown. Remove the tart from the oven, lift from the cookie sheet, and cool on a rack.

8. MAKE THE GLAZE: Place the apricot preserves and water in a heatproof glass container. Heat in a microwave oven on medium power for 20 to 30 seconds, until bubbling. Alternatively, cook in a small saucepan over direct heat until bubbly Pass through a strainer. Gently brush the warm apricot glaze on the top of the hot tart. Let tart stand 1 hour before cutting. This tart is best when served warm.

STORAGE

Cover any leftover tart with a sheet of waxed paper then aluminum foil and refrigerate for up to 3 days. Reheat before serving. Freezing is not recommended.

All-Fruit Mincemeat Jalousie

A JALOUSIE, FRENCH FOR "venetian blinds," is also a pastry with thin open slats that expose the filling beneath. It is traditionally made with puff pastry and is filled with jam or fruit.

For this recipe, I blended sautéed apples with rum, raisins, nuts, and spices. You are in for a treat when you taste this flavorful fruit mixture. The combination of chewy fruit and crisp flaky pastry layers is unbeatable.

This filling is also ideal for individual mincemeat tarts (see page 385). Both the jalousie and the mincemeat tarts freeze extremely well, a plus at holiday time when do-ahead desserts are a blessing. For this reason, the recipe makes two.

2/3 block Goof-Proof Puff Pastry (page 172) (1 3/4 pounds)

FILLING
3 Granny Smith apples (about 1 pound)
3 tablespoons unsalted butter
1/4 cup dark rum
2/3 cup lightly packed dark brown sugar
1/3 cup dark raisins
1/3 cup golden raisins
3/4 teaspoon ground cinnamon
1/2 teaspoon freshly grated nutmeg
1/8 teaspoon ground cloves
1 tablespoon fresh lemon juice
1 teaspoon grated navel or Valencia orange zest

1/2 teaspoon grated lemon zest
1/4 teaspoon salt
1 cup coarsely chopped walnuts, lightly toasted (see pages 56 and 57)
2 tablespoons apricot preserves

EGG WASH
1 large egg
1 teaspoon water
Sugar, for garnish

1. MAKE THE FILLING: Peel the apples, then cut in quarters, remove the cores, and cut into 1-inch chunks (page 17). Place in the bowl of a food processor fitted with the steel blade and pulse to chop the apples into 1/4-inch pieces.

2. Melt the butter in a heavy 12-inch nonreactive skillet. Add the apples and cook over medium heat until soft and transparent, 5 to 6 minutes. Off the heat, add the rum. Return to the heat and cook until the rum has almost evaporated. Stir in the brown sugar, raisins, spices, lemon juice, orange and lemon zests, and salt. Cook over low heat for 4 to 5 minutes. Off the heat, add the walnuts and apricot preserves. Empty into a container and chill until ready to use.

3. SHAPE THE JALOUSIE: Line a large sheet pan with aluminum foil or parchment. Sprinkle the paper lightly with cold water. Set aside.

4. Use half of the pastry at a time. On a lightly floured board, roll the pastry into a rectangle 12 inches wide and 16 inches long (see "Rolling and Shaping Tips," page 89). Trim the edges with a dough scraper. Prick the pastry in several places with a fork to prevent shrinking.

5. Divide the pastry in half lengthwise, making 2 strips measuring 6 × 16 inches. Invert one strip on the baking pan, straightening the dough into a perfect rectangle. Spread half of the fruit filling in a 4-inch strip down the center of the pastry.

6. MAKE THE EGG WASH: Lightly beat the egg and water in a small bowl with a fork. Brush the edges of the pastry with the egg wash.

7. Fold the remaining strip of puff pastry in half lengthwise. **1** Using the dough scraper, make slashes at 1/4-inch intervals, at the folded side leaving a 1-inch margin on 3 sides. Lift the strip carefully over the fruit filling, positioning it to the upper corner of the pastry. Then match the straight edges all the way down the strip. **2** Gently open the pastry, and stretch it to the opposite side, again matching the straight edges all the way down. Press all the edges to seal the strip well.

Make a second jalousie with the remaining dough and filling. Chill jalousies for 10 minutes.

8. Preheat the oven to 425 degrees. Position the oven rack in the upper third of the oven.

9. Remove pastry from the refrigerator and crimp edges with a 4-prong fork. Brush pastry lightly with egg wash, and sprinkle with a little sugar. Refrigerate for 20 minutes longer.

10. Bake in 425 degree oven for 20 minutes, then reduce oven to 375 degrees and bake 10 to 15 minutes longer, or until golden brown.

STORAGE
Wrap any leftover jalousie in aluminum foil and store in a cool place for up to 5 days. Reheat in a 325 degree oven for 6 to 8 minutes before serving. This pastry can be frozen.

Catherine Alexandrou's Tart of Blood Oranges, Rhubarb, and Dried Fruit

DINING WITH MY FRIEND Chef Catherine Alexandrou, of Chez Catherine Restaurant in Westfield, New Jersey, is always stimulating. She has her finger on the pulse of what's new or different in food. Catherine told me of an orange tart she had made using a unique combination of fresh and dried fruits. It was made with overlapping slices of blood oranges on a pink puree of rhubarb with figs and dates. I loved the idea because the selection of fresh fruit is so limited during mid-winter. Serve the tart with Orange Crème Anglaise. It's the best!

At a Glance

SERVES: 8 to 10

PAN: 11-inch metal tart

PASTRY PREP: Baked

OVEN TEMP: 350 degrees

BAKING TIME:
50 to 55 minutes

DIFFICULTY: 🥄 🥄

1 11-inch *Sweet Tart Pastry crust (page 146), baked*

FILLING
6 *8-inch stalks rhubarb, cleaned* (1¹⁄₂ *pounds*) (*page 38*)
6 *dried figs, cut into* ¹⁄₄-*inch dice*
6 *dates, cut into* ¹⁄₄-*inch dice*
3/4 *cup pecans, toasted*
6 to 8 *tablespoons sugar*
¹⁄₃ *cup apricot preserves*
2 *teaspoons water*
6 to 7 *large blood oranges*
Orange Crème Anglaise (page 442)
Candied Pecans (page 453)

1. START THE FILLING: Cut the rhubarb into ¹⁄₂-inch pieces and place in a large saucepan with the figs and dates. Cover, bring to a slow boil, and simmer 20 to 30 minutes, or until the fruits are very tender. (The time will vary according to the freshness of the dried fruit.)

2. Remove the fruit from the heat. Use a fork to whip the mixture into a puree. Set aside and cool until tepid.

3. MAKE THE PIE: Preheat the oven to 350 degrees. Position the rack in the lower third of the oven.

4. Place the pecans in a food processor with the sugar. Process until the pecans are very finely chopped. Stir them into the rhubarb puree.

5. Heat the apricot preserves and water in a microwave glass container in the microwave oven on medium power for 20 seconds or until bubbly. Alternatively, cook in a small saucepan over direct heat until bubbly. Pass through a strainer and discard the pulp. Brush the bottom of the tart shell with a

thin layer of preserves. Save the remainder for glazing the top.

6. Using a small offset spatula, spread the rhubarb mixture on the bottom of the baked pastry shell.

7. **PREPARE THE ORANGES:** Slice off the ends of the oranges. Turn each orange onto one of its flat sides. 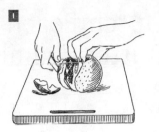 Using a very sharp knife, remove the rind by cutting deep enough into the skin to expose the flesh. When cutting, be sure to follow the contour of the fruit. Trim any bits of white pith and discard. Cut the fruit in *very thin* slices—less than 1/4 inch.

8. Arrange the slices in overlapping concentric circles on top of the rhubarb puree. Place the tart on a cookie sheet and bake for 50 to 55 minutes, or until the filling shows signs of bubbling around the edge.

9. Remove the tart from the oven and set it on a rack to cool. After 5 to 10 minutes, heat the remaining apricot puree and brush it gently over the top of the hot tart. Serve with Orange Crème Anglaise and Candied Pecans.

STORAGE

Lay a piece of waxed paper on top of any leftover tart, then cover loosely with a sheet of aluminum foil. Store in the refrigerator for up to 3 days. Freezing is not recommended.

Dutch Peach Pie with Butter-Crumb Topping

MY AUNT BLANCHE WAS A superb cook and baker. She loved to cook, but baking was her forte. No meal in her home was complete unless it was served with at least two desserts, and always homemade. This recipe dates back to when I was a child. She knew I loved this pie and always had it for me when I visited her in the summer.

The crust was made from a buttery, cakelike dough. It was filled with lots of sweet, thick-sliced peaches and topped with crunchy streusel. If you like peach pie as much as I do, this is one recipe you won't want to miss.

1 recipe Press-On Butter Pastry (page 158)

FILLING
3 to 3 1/2 pounds ripe peaches, peeled, pitted, and cut into 1-inch slices (page 33)
1 tablespoon fresh lemon juice
1/2 cup granulated sugar
1/4 cup lightly packed light brown sugar
3 tablespoons cornstarch
1/2 teaspoon ground cinnamon

TOPPING
1 1/3 cups unsifted all-purpose flour
1/2 cup granulated sugar
3/4 teaspoon ground cinnamon
1/4 teaspoon baking powder
6 tablespoons unsalted butter, melted and cooled

1. Preheat the oven to 375 degrees. Position the oven rack in the lower third of the oven. Butter a 9 1/2-inch deep-dish oven-proof glass pie plate.

2. With floured hands, press the dough into the prepared pie plate, working the pastry up the sides. Re-flour your hands as needed.

3. **MAKE THE FILLING:** Place the peach slices in a large skillet. Sprinkle with lemon juice.

4. Combine the sugars, corn-starch, and cinnamon in a small bowl. Sprinkle the sugar mixture over the peaches and stir gently to distribute through the fruit. Cover the skillet and bring the peaches to a slow boil. Gently stir the fruit to prevent it from sticking to the bottom. When the peaches begin to exude their liquid, cook about 2 minutes longer. Uncover the skillet and remove the pan from the heat.

5. Use a slotted spoon to transfer the peaches to the pastry shell. *Do not add the liquid in the skillet.*

6. MAKE THE TOPPING: Whisk together the flour, sugar, cinnamon, and baking powder in a medium bowl. Add the butter and toss with a fork to form crumbs. Take a clump of the crumb mixture in your hand and squeeze gently to form a larger clump. Then break the large clump apart over the peaches. Repeat using all of the crumb mixture. Do not press the crumbs into the fruit.

7. Bake for 40 to 45 minutes, or until the top is golden brown and the juices begin to bubble. Cool on a rack. Let stand 3 to 4 hours before cutting. Serve with ice cream or frozen yogurt.

STORAGE

Store any leftover pie in the refrigerator, loosely covered with a sheet of waxed paper, then aluminum foil, for 2 to 3 days. Reheat before serving. This pie can be frozen.

Peaches and Berries with Patchwork Linzer Crust

NESTLED UNDER STRIPS OF CRISSCROSSED nutty pastry are sweet summer peaches, raspberries, and blackberries. The patchwork effect gives this luscious tart great visual appeal. While the tart is still warm, remove the outer rim of the tart pan and loosen the bottom with a long spatula. The juices may run, making the tart difficult to remove from the pan if the tart becomes too cool. If you wish to give the tart support, wash the outer rim and replace it. Serve this tart slightly warm (see jacket).

At a Glance

SERVES: 8 to 10

PAN: 11-inch metal tart

PASTRY PREP: Unbaked

OVEN TEMP: 375 degrees

BAKING TIME: 50 to 60 minutes

DIFFICULTY: 🍪 🍪 🍪

COOKIE DOUGH
1 cup unblanched almonds
1/2 cup unblanched hazelnuts
1 1/2 cups unsifted all-purpose flour
1/4 teaspoon salt
3/4 teaspoon ground cinnamon
3/4 cup unsalted butter, at room temperature
1/2 cup granulated sugar
1/2 teaspoon grated lemon zest
2 hard-boiled egg yolks, finely sieved
1 teaspoon vanilla extract

FILLING
8 large ripe peaches (about 3 pounds)
1 tablespoon fresh lemon juice
1 1/2 cups mixed fresh blackberries and raspberries, washed and thoroughly dried (pages 21 and 37)
1/2 cup granulated sugar
1/4 cup lightly packed light brown sugar
1/4 cup cornstarch
1/2 teaspoon ground cinnamon
1 large egg white
1 teaspoon water
2 tablespoons unsalted butter

1. MAKE THE COOKIE DOUGH: Preheat the oven to 325 degrees. Place the almonds and hazelnuts in a shallow pan with sides and lightly toast for 10 to 12 minutes. Cool completely.

2. Place the nuts and ½ cup flour in the bowl of a food processor fitted with the steel blade. Process until the nuts are finely ground and the mixture starts to clump. Add the remaining flour, the salt, and cinnamon. Process until cakey and well blended.

3. Place the butter, sugar, and lemon zest in the large bowl of an electric mixer fitted with the paddle. Mix on medium-low speed until blended. Add the yolks and vanilla, and mix again. On low speed, blend in the flour-nut mixture, one-half at a time. Mix just until it forms a dough.

4. Remove one-third of the dough and shape it into a disk. Shape the remaining dough into a larger disk. Dust the disks with flour, cover with plastic wrap, and chill for 15 to 20 minutes.

5. Generously butter an 11-inch tart pan with a removable bottom. Remove the bottom of the pan from the outer ring and place it on a flat surface. Place the larger piece of pastry in the center of the metal disk. Sprinkle with flour, and cover the dough with plastic wrap. Roll the pastry into an 11-inch circle using the metal disk as a guide. Remove the plastic wrap, and set the pastry-lined disk into the outer ring.

6. Flour the outer edge of your thumb up to your wrist. Using this floured part of your hand, press the pastry toward the edge of the pan. Push the dough up the sides until it reaches the top of the rim. Keep rotating the pan so the pastry will spread evenly, dipping your hand in flour as needed. Lay a piece of plastic wrap over the dough. Using a batarde (see page 457) or a smooth-bottomed glass, press firmly against the plastic to smooth the dough on the bottom and at the bend. Remove the plastic wrap and chill for 15 to 20 minutes.

7. Lightly flour a sheet of waxed paper. Place the smaller pastry disk on the paper, sprinkle with flour, and top with a second sheet of waxed paper. Roll the smaller pastry disk into an 11-inch circle. Place the pastry on a cookie sheet without removing the paper and chill at least 15 minutes.

8. Preheat the oven to 375 degrees. Position the oven rack in the lower third of the oven. Place a large jelly-roll pan in the oven to preheat.

9. MAKE THE FILLING: Peel and pit the peaches (page 33), slice them into 1-inch pieces, and place them in a large bowl. Sprinkle with the lemon juice. Add the berries.

The peaches here leave behind a warm, rich and delicious taste, that I can only liken in its effects to that which you call the bouquet of a glass of Romanee.

JAMES FENIMORE COOPER, THE TRAVELING BACHELOR

10. Set aside 1 tablespoon granulated sugar to glaze the tart. Mix the remaining sugar with the light brown sugar, cornstarch, and cinnamon. Toss through the fruit.

11. Lightly beat the egg white and water together with a fork, and brush the bottom of the pastry shell with egg white. Reserve the remaining egg white for glazing.

12. Empty the fruit mixture into the tart pan, arranging the fruit so that the empty spaces are filled. Pack the fruit down, molding it higher in the center. Dot with butter.

13. Remove the pastry circle from the refrigerator and peel off the top sheet of waxed paper. Using a pastry wheel or pizza cutter, cut the pastry into ten 1-inch strips. Cover the dough again with waxed paper and invert it. Remove the top sheet of waxed paper. (Inverting the pastry onto fresh waxed paper will prevent it from sticking.) Cut each strip into 3 short pieces. Lift up each strip with a thin spatula and arrange over the top of the fruit, crisscrossing the dough at random. The fruit should not be completely covered.

14. Brush the pastry strips with the remaining egg wash. Sprinkle with the reserved tablespoon of granulated sugar. Set the tart on an 18-inch square of heavy-duty aluminum foil. Bring the sides of the foil up to the edge of the tart pan.

15. Place the tart on the jelly-roll pan in the oven and bake for 50 to 60 minutes, or until golden brown. Remove from the oven and cool on a rack. As soon as the tart is cool enough to handle, remove the outer ring to prevent the crust from sticking. Cool for at least 4 hours before cutting.

STORAGE

Lightly cover any leftover tart with a sheet of waxed paper, then aluminum foil and refrigerate for up to 4 days. Reheat before serving. Freezing is not recommended.

Nectarine Galette

FLAKY LAYERS OF PUFF PASTRY ARE topped with overlapping slices of unpeeled nectarines. The contrast of the vibrant magenta skin with the nectarine flesh makes this pastry an eye-catching dessert.

¹/₂ recipe Goof-Proof Puff Pastry (page 172), shaped into a free form 11-inch pastry shell (page 175)

FILLING
4 to 5 nectarines (about 1¹/₂ pounds)
1 teaspoon fresh lemon juice
2 tablespoons sugar
¹/₄ cup apricot preserves
1 teaspoon water

1. Preheat the oven to 425 degrees. Position the oven rack in the lower third of the oven.

2. **FILL THE PASTRY:** Clean, halve, and pit the nectarines (page 31). Do not peel. Slice the nectarine halves into ¹/₄-inch wedges.

3. Starting at the outer edge of the pastry shell, arrange the fruit in concentric circles, overlapping each slice slightly. You should have 2 circles.

4. Sprinkle the fruit with the lemon juice and sugar. Bake for 25 to 30 minutes, or until the crust is well browned and fruit begins to bubble.

5. Remove the tart from the oven. Set the oven to broil. To prevent the crust from burning, cover the edge of the tart with a sheet of aluminum foil. Cut a hole in the center of a square of the foil (see "Glaze the Tart," page 189), and lay the foil over the tart, positioning it so the fruit is exposed. Caramelize the fruit under the broiler for 15 to 20 seconds or until the edges of the nectarines begin to singe. Watch constantly, this only takes a few moments.

6. Remove the tart from the oven. In a small microwave-safe dish, heat the apricot preserves and water in a microwave oven on medium power for 20 to 30 seconds. Alternatively, cook in a small saucepan over direct heat until bubbly. Brush the tart with apricot glaze. Serve shortly after baking.

STORAGE

Any leftover tart can be covered loosely with a sheet of waxed paper then aluminum foil and stored in the refrigerator. Freezing is not recommended.

At a Glance

SERVES: 8 to 10

PAN: 14 × 17-inch cookie sheet

PASTRY PREP: Unbaked

STARTING OVEN TEMP: 425 degrees

BAKING TIME: 25 to 30 minutes

DIFFICULTY: 🥄 🥄

Southern Peach Pie in Nutty Cornmeal Crust

ONE OF SUMMER'S GREATEST GIFTS has to be fresh peaches with their suedelike skins in brilliant colors of blush pink, crimson, magenta, and amber. Mounds of these colorful fruits perfume the air at farmstands and supermarkets when peach season hits its peak in early August.

These succulent fruits make luscious pies, but the abundant juices they exude when baked are the pie baker's nemesis. To overcome this, I like to par-cook the peach filling. This way, I can remove the excess liquid before I empty the fruit into the pie plate.

1 large recipe Nutty Cornmeal
   Crust pastry (page 154)

FILLING
8 medium to large ripe peaches
   (about 3 pounds)
2 tablespoons water
1/2 cup lightly packed light brown
   sugar
1/2 cup granulated sugar
2 to 2 1/2 tablespoons cornstarch
1/2 teaspoon ground cinnamon
1 tablespoon instant tapioca
1 tablespoon fresh lemon juice
1 tablespoon unsalted butter

GLAZE
2 tablespoons milk
2 teaspoons sugar

1. Preheat the oven to 400 degrees. Position the oven rack in the lower third of the oven. Butter a 9-inch ovenproof glass pie plate.

2. On a floured pastry cloth, roll half the pastry into a 13-inch circle. Line the pie plate with the pastry. Trim the edge, leaving a 1/4-inch overhang.

3. MAKE THE FILLING: Wipe the peaches with damp paper towels. Cut the fruit in half and remove the pits (page 33). Peel if the skins are thick. Cut peaches into 1-inch wedges.

4. Place the water and brown sugar in a large skillet. Heat slowly, stirring until the sugar is melted. Combine the granulated sugar, cornstarch, and cinnamon and add to the peaches. Shake the bowl to distribute the dry ingredients through the fruit.

5. Empty the mixture into the skillet and stir gently to combine with the brown sugar. Cover the skillet and bring to a slow boil. Simmer for 1 to 2 minutes, or until the fruit begins to exude juices.

6. Use a slotted spoon to remove the peaches from the skillet, leaving the liquid behind. Place them in a large bowl, about a third at a time, sprinkling each layer with the tapioca. Let stand 15 mintues.

7. ASSEMBLE THE PIE: Again use a slotted spoon to transfer the peaches to the pie plate. Sprinkle the fruit with lemon juice and dot with butter.

8. Roll the remaining pastry into a 13-inch circle. Top the peaches with the pastry, then trim the edges, leaving a 3/4-inch overhang. Fold and flute the edges (page 66). Prick the pastry with a fork. Brush the pastry lightly with milk, then sprinkle with sugar.

9. To prevent the edges from burning, make aluminum foil bands. Cut two 3-inch-wide strips of 18-inch heavy-duty aluminum foil. Fold 1 inch of each strip to the center, making a double thickness of foil. Mold the foil around the edge of the pie, keeping the double fold on top of the dough. Be careful not to crush the edge of the pastry. Secure the bands with tape.

10. Make an aluminum foil drip pan to place on the rack below the pie halfway through the baking. Cut an 18-inch square of heavy-duty aluminum foil. Fold each edge twice (about 1 inch per fold) standing the folded edges upright to form a 4-sided pan.

11. Bake the pie for 45 minutes. Remove the aluminum foil bands. Continue baking the pie for 10 minutes longer or until the crust is golden brown and the juices begin to bubble. Remove the pie from the oven and cool on a rack. Let stand at least 3 hours before serving.

STORAGE

Cover any leftover pie with a sheet of waxed paper then aluminum foil and refrigerate for up to 3 days. Reheat before serving. This pie can be frozen.

Pair of Pears Tart

THE DELICATE FLAVOR OF sweet pears is enlivened by pear lekvar—cooked dried pears whipped with butter. The lekvar is spread under pears poached in a light syrup made with quince jelly. The jelly is also used to glaze the baked tart, giving it a subtle pink glow.

At a Glance

SERVES: 8 to 10

PAN: 14 × 17-inch cookie sheet and 11-inch round flan or daisy ring

PASTRY PREP: Unbaked

OVEN TEMP: 400 degrees

BAKING TIME: 50 to 55 minutes

DIFFICULTY:

1 recipe Sweet Tart Pastry (page 146)

PEAR LEKVAR
1 cup water
3 tablespoons sugar
4 ounces dried pears, quartered
1/8-inch slice of lemon
2 tablespoons cold unsalted butter

FILLING
3 tablespoons plus 1 teaspoon fresh lemon juice
8 cups water
5 large, firm Anjou pears (about 2 1/2 pounds)
6 tablespoons quince jelly
1 cup sugar
1 tablespoon unsalted butter, melted
1 tablespoon chopped skinned pistachios (optional)
Sauce Anglaise flavored with Poire William (page 442)

1. MAKE THE LEKVAR: Place the water and sugar in a small, heavy saucepan. Add the dried pears and lemon slice. Cover the pot and bring to a boil over medium-high heat. Reduce the heat and simmer the pears for 45 to 50 minutes, or until about 2 tablespoons liquid remains and the pears are fork-tender. Remove the lemon slice. Off the heat, whip with a fork to form a puree. Let stand 5 minutes, then swirl in the butter. Cool to tepid.

2. MAKE THE FILLING: Combine 3 tablespoons lemon juice and water in a large bowl. Peel, halve, and core the pears (page 34), placing them in the acidulated water as you go.

3. Pour 3 cups of the acidulated water into a 12-inch skillet. Add 4 tablespoons quince jelly and the sugar, then bring the liquid to a boil over medium heat. Arrange the pears in the liquid with the rounded side down. Add enough acidulated water to barely cover the pears. Place a parchment circle on top of the

pears Bring the pears to a slow boil, and poach 20 to 30 minutes or until transparent and *just* tender. The time will depend on how ripe the pears were before cooking.

4. Carefully turn the pears over during the last 3 to 5 minutes of cooking. Do not let pears get too soft. Remove the pears from the liquid with a slotted spoon and drain on a sheet pan lined with a double layer of paper towels. Set aside.

5. **ASSEMBLE THE TART**: Preheat the oven to 400 degrees. Position the oven rack in the upper third of the oven. Line a large cookie sheet with baking parchment. Dab butter under the corners of the paper to secure it. Set the flan ring in the center of the pan.

6. On a well-floured pastry cloth, roll the pastry into a 13-inch circle. Fold the pastry into quarters. Place it into the flan ring, positioning it so the point is in the center. Gently open the pastry and fit it loosely into the pan. With your forefinger, press the dough into the seam of the ring, letting the edge of the pastry extend over the pan. Do not stretch the dough. Trim the dough by running the rolling pin over the flan ring. Chill pastry 10 minutes.

7. Working one piece at a time, place pear cut side down on a board. With a thin, sharp knife, slice each pear lengthwise into ¼-inch strips, starting from the wider side and keeping the narrow end intact. Do not separate the slices.

8. Spread the tepid lekvar on the pastry with an offset spatula. Arrange the pear halves in the pan as follows: Press down on each half of pear with your fingers to fan it, then lift the fruit up with a metal spatula and place the wide side at the outer edge of the pan.  Press the pear again to further spread it. After the outer ring is filled with fruit, make a second, smaller circle, filling in the center. Sprinkle with 1 teaspoon lemon juice, then brush the pears with melted butter.

9. Bake the tart for 40 to 45 minutes or until the edge of the crust is golden brown. Set on a cooling rack. After 10 minutes, melt the remaining 2 tablespoons quince jelly. Brush the jelly on the pears. Sprinkle the center with chopped pistachio nuts. Unmold the tart when it is cool enough to handle. Serve with Sauce Anglaise flavored with Poire William liqueur.

NOTE ═══════════
To use the daisy ring, follow the directions above; however, reduce the number of pears to 4. No other changes are necessary.

STORAGE ═══════════
Cover any leftover tart with a sheet of waxed paper then aluminum foil. Store at room temperature for 1 day or refrigerated for up to 3 days. Freezing is not recommended.

Pear and Apricot Strudel Pie

THIS PASTRY IS REMINISCENT OF a huge fruit strudel. Layers of crisp phyllo encase chunks of sautéed pears and dried apricots, all baked in a pie plate. The tissue-thin strips of dough are brushed with butter, then sprinkled with sweetened chopped almonds. The top is finished with a confetti of shredded phyllo that is heavily dusted with confectioners' sugar. A word of caution: this pie is good only when served warm, as it loses its crispness when cold.

At a Glance

SERVES: 6 to 8

PAN: 9-inch ovenproof glass

PASTRY PREP: None

OVEN TEMP: 375 degrees

BAKING TIME:
40 to 45 minutes

DIFFICULTY: 🍥

---

7 sheets phyllo pastry, preferably not frozen

FILLING
1/2 cup plus 2 tablespoons unsalted butter
3/4 cup unblanched almonds, lightly toasted
2 tablespoons plain dry bread crumbs
6 tablespoons granulated sugar
1/2 teaspoon ground cinnamon
3 pounds ripe but firm Red Bartlett or Anjou pears
6 ounces dried apricots, halved (about 1 cup)
1 teaspoon grated lemon zest
6 tablespoons lightly packed dark brown sugar
2 tablespoons cornstarch
1/8 teaspoon ground allspice
1 tablespoon fresh lemon juice
2 tablespoons confectioners' sugar, for garnish

---

1. MAKE THE FILLING: Place 1/2 cup butter in a heavy, medium saucepan. Melt over low heat. Remove the white foam as it forms on the surface (see "Clarifying Butter," page 52). Continue to skim the surface until no more foam is present. Cook the butter slowly until a brown sediment begins to form on the bottom of the pot, about 10 minutes. Remove from heat. Let stand until ready to use.

2. Place the almonds, bread crumbs, 2 tablespoons of the granulated sugar, and cinnamon in the bowl of a food processor. Process until nuts are finely chopped. Add 2 tablespoons of the melted butter. Pulse 3 or 4 times to combine. Set aside.

3. PREPARE THE FRUIT: Peel and core the pears (page 34), then cut them lengthwise into ½-inch slices.

4. Melt the remaining 2 tablespoons butter in a 12-inch skillet. Add the pears, apricots, lemon zest, and the remaining 4 tablespoons granulated sugar. Turn the fruit with a large spatula to coat the pears with sugar. Over medium-high heat, sauté the fruit for 8 to 10 minutes, turning occasionally with the spatula. Drain the mixture in a large colander and discard the juices.

Mix the dark brown sugar, cornstarch, and allspice in a small bowl.

5. ASSEMBLE THE PIE: Preheat the oven to 375 degrees. Position the oven rack in the lower third of the oven. Butter a 9-inch ovenproof glass pie plate.

6. Arrange 6 phyllo sheets in the pie plate in the following manner: Center a double sheet of phyllo over the pie plate and press it in. Brush the phyllo with the melted butter and sprinkle with 2 tablespoons of the ground nut mixture. Repeat the above procedure, crisscrossing 1 sheet at a time until all 6 sheets are used. Reserve 2 tablespoons of the nut mixture to garnish the top.

7. Fill the pie plate by layering the pears in 3 additions alternating with the brown sugar mixture in 2 additions, starting and ending with the fruit. Drizzle the lemon juice over the top. Finish the pie by folding the edges of the phyllo over the filling, brushing each layer with butter, and sprinkling each layer again with the nut mixture.

8. Brush the top of the pie with more butter. Roll the remaining sheet of phyllo into a cylinder. Using a sharp knife, shred the phyllo into ¼-inch slices. Sprinkle the shredded phyllo over the pie. Drizzle with any remaining butter. Scatter the reserved nut mixture over the top.

9. Bake for 40 to 45 minutes or until the pie is well browned. Let stand at least 30 minutes before cutting. Put confectioners' sugar in a strainer and sprinkle it over the top. This pie must be served warm.

STORAGE

Cover any leftover pie with a sheet of waxed paper then aluminum foil and store in the refrigerator for up to 4 days. Reheat before serving. This pie can be frozen before or after baking.

Autumn Pear and Grape Pie in Cheddar Pastry

PEARS AND GRAPES BAKED IN a pie. I like to use whole black seedless grapes because they are so succulent. While most any pastry can be used, the savory sharp cheese pastry truly complements the spiced fruit.

At a Glance

SERVES: 8 to 10

PAN: 9-inch ovenproof glass

PASTRY PREP: Unbaked

OVEN TEMP: 400 degrees

BAKING TIME:
55 to 60 minutes

DIFFICULTY: 🥐 🥐

---

1 recipe Cheddar Pastry (page 135)
1 large egg white
1 teaspoon water
1 teaspoon sugar, for garnish

FILLING
3 pounds firm Red Bartlett or Bosc
    pears (about 7 pears), peeled,
    cored, and cut lengthwise into
    sixths (page 34)
1/2 pound dark purple seedless
    grapes (about 1 1/2 cups),
    washed and dried (page 26)
4 teaspoons fresh lemon juice
1 tablespoon instant tapioca
3/4 cup sugar
2 tablespoons cornstarch
3/4 teaspoon ground cinnamon
1/2 teaspoon ground ginger
Pinch of ground cloves (optional)
2 tablespoons unsalted butter

1. Preheat the oven to 400 degrees. Position the oven rack in the lower third of the oven. Butter a 9-inch ovenproof glass pie plate.

2. MAKE THE PIE: On a floured pastry cloth, roll 1 disk of pastry into a circle measuring approximately 13 inches. Fit loosely into the pie plate. Trim the edges with scissors, leaving a 1/2-inch overhang. Beat the egg white and water with a fork. Brush the pastry with the egg wash and reserve the remainder for glazing the top of the pie.

3. Combine the pears and grapes in a large bowl. Sprinkle the fruit with lemon juice and tapioca. Shake the bowl to distribute. Let stand 15 minutes.

4. Blend the sugar, cornstarch, cinnamon, ginger, and cloves in a small bowl. Just before filling the shell, combine the dry ingredients with the fruits and shake the bowl to distribute them well.

5. Empty the fruit into the shell, mounding the fruit in the center and making sure that there are no empty spaces. Dot the top of the filling with butter.

6. Roll the second disk of dough into a 13-inch circle. Place the dough on top of the filling. With your hands, push the dough gently toward the center to prevent it from stretching during baking. Trim excess with scissors, leaving a 1-inch overhang. Tuck the top edge of dough under the bottom, pressing the 2 layers together to form a wall. Crimp or flute the edge (see page 66). Make steam vents on top of the pastry. Brush the top with the remaining egg wash, and sprinkle with sugar.

7. To prevent the edges from burning, make aluminum foil bands. Cut two 3-inch-wide strips of 18-inch heavy-duty aluminum foil. Fold 1 inch of each strip to the center, making a double thickness of foil. Mold the foil around the edge of the pie keeping the double fold on top of the dough. Be careful not to crush the edge of the pastry. Secure the bands with tape.

8. Make an aluminum foil drip pan to place on the rack below the pie halfway through the baking. Cut an 18-inch square of heavy-duty aluminum foil. Fold each edge twice (about 1 inch per fold) standing the folded edges upright to form a 4-sided pan.

9. Bake the pie for 55 to 60 minutes. Remove the aluminum foil bands the last 5 to 20 minutes of baking. The pie is done when the top and bottom crusts are golden brown and the juices begin to bubble. Cool on a rack for at least 4 hours before serving.

STORAGE

Cover any leftover pie with a sheet of waxed paper and then loosely cover with aluminum foil for 1 day at room temperature or up to 5 days in the refrigerator. Reheat before serving. This pie can be frozen.

Tropical Pineapple Pie

SOME YEARS AGO, WHENEVER I ran out of ideas as to what kind of dessert to make my husband would say, "Pineapple pie." The truth is, this was a pie that I had never made, nor ever eaten, because quite frankly it didn't appeal to me. One day I broke down, pulled a can of crushed pineapple off the shelf, and went to work. Much to my surprise, the pie turned out great. I more than liked it—I loved it.

At a Glance

SERVES: 6 to 8

PAN: 9-inch ovenproof glass

PASTRY PREP: Unbaked

OVEN TEMP: 400 degrees

BAKING TIME:
45 to 50 minutes

DIFFICULTY: 🐚

Don't bother making this with fresh pineapple. Canned crushed pineapple packed in unsweetened juice works just fine. If you can handle the calories, keep the amount of the butter as is. The flavors of pineapple and butter are extremely complementary.

1 small recipe Flaky Pie Pastry
    (pages 98, 100)
1 large egg white
1 teaspoon water
1 teaspoon sugar, for garnish

FILLING
1 (1-pound 4-ounce) can plus
    1 (8-ounce) can crushed
    pineapple, packed in
    unsweetened pineapple juice
1/2 cup sugar
3 tablespoons cornstarch
1/4 teaspoon salt
3 to 4 tablespoons unsalted butter,
    cut into pieces
1 1/2 teaspoons grated lemon zest
3/4 teaspoon grated navel or
    Valencia orange zest
1 tablespoon fresh lemon juice

1. Preheat the oven to 400 degrees. Position the oven rack in the lower third of the oven. Butter a 9-inch ovenproof glass pie plate.

2. MAKE THE PIE: On a floured pastry cloth, roll 1 disk of pastry into a circle measuring approximately 13 inches. Fit loosely into the pie plate. Trim the edge with scissors, leaving a 1/2-inch overhang. Beat the egg white and water lightly with a fork. Brush the dough with the egg white. Reserve the remaining white for glazing the top of the pie. Chill the shell while preparing the filling.

3. MAKE THE FILLING: Drain the pineapple well in a strainer placed over a bowl. Reserve 1 1/3 cups of the pineapple juice.

Whisk together the sugar, cornstarch, and salt in a 3-quart saucepan. Slowly whisk in the reserved pineapple juice, mixing until smooth. Bring the mixture to a slow boil over medium-low heat, stirring constantly with a wooden spoon, until it is smooth and thickened. Simmer for 1 minute longer.

4. Remove from the heat and add the crushed pineapple, butter, lemon and orange zests, and lemon juice. Stir gently until the butter is melted. Let cool before filling the pie shell.

5. Empty the filling into the pie shell, smoothing the top with the back of a tablespoon. Roll the second half of the pastry into a 13-inch circle. Place the dough on top of the filling. Trim excess with scissors, leaving a 1-inch overhang. Tuck the top edge of dough under the bottom, pressing the 2 layers together to form a wall. Crimp or flute the edge (see page 66). Make steam vents on top of the pastry. Brush the top with the remaining egg white and sprinkle with 1 teaspoon of sugar.

6. To prevent the edges from burning, make aluminum foil bands. Cut two 3-inch-wide strips of 18-inch heavy-duty aluminum foil. Fold 1 inch of each strip to the center, making a double thickness of foil. Mold the foil around the edge of the pie, keeping the double fold on top of the dough. Be careful not to crush the edge of the pastry. Secure bands with tape, and place it in the oven.

7. Make an aluminum foil drip pan to place on the rack below the pie halfway through the baking. Cut an 18-inch square of heavy-duty aluminum foil. Fold each edge twice (about 1 inch per fold) standing the folded edges upright to form a 4-sided pan.

8. Bake the pie for 35 minutes. Remove the foil band, and bake for 5 to 10 minutes longer or until the crust is golden brown on the top and bottom. Cool on a rack. Let stand 3 to 4 hours before serving.

STORAGE
Any leftover pie should be refrigerated loosely covered with waxed paper and then aluminum foil for up to 4 days. Reheat before serving. This pie may be frozen.

Italian Frangipane Plum Tart

THIS VERSATILE TART CAN BE MADE with a variety of fruits, but the two that I prefer are plums and nectarines. These fruits make a stunning presentation, with the wedges of fruit arranged skin side down to fully expose the colorful flesh. Frangipane, a sweet, almond-flavored paste, is spread on the crust and acts as a shield to prevent the fruit juices from penetrating the pastry.

1 11-inch *Sweet Tart Pastry crust* (page 146), baked

FRANGIPANE
2 ounces almond paste (about 2 tablespoons)
2 tablespoons sugar
2 tablespoons soft unsalted butter
$1/2$ teaspoon grated lemon zest
1 tablespoon unsifted all-purpose flour
1 large egg white
$1/2$ cup sliced almonds, lightly toasted and finely chopped

FRUIT TOPPING
$1^1/2$ pounds Italian prune plums or other dark purple plums, pitted and quartered (page 37)
Note: Larger plums like Santa Rosas, Black Ambers, or Black Diamonds should be cut into one-sixths.
2 teaspoons fresh lemon juice
$1/4$ cup sugar
2 tablespoons cornstarch

GLAZE
$1/2$ cup apricot preserves
2 tablespoons water

1. MAKE THE FRANGIPANE: Place the almond paste, sugar, butter, and lemon zest in a small bowl. (If almond paste is too hard, soften it in the microwave on defrost setting for 30 to 40 seconds.) Mash the ingredients together with a pastry blender or fork. Blend in the flour. Add the egg white and mix with a small whisk, making the mixture as smooth as possible.

2. Reserve 2 tablespoons of the toasted almonds. Stir the remaining nuts into the paste mixture. Spread the frangipane smoothly over the cooled tart shell.

3. ASSEMBLE THE TART: Preheat the oven to 375 degrees. Position the oven rack in the lower third of oven.

Place the plums in a large bowl and sprinkle with the lemon juice. Combine the sugar and cornstarch in a small bowl. Sprinkle the mixture over the plums and shake the bowl to distribute throughout the fruit.

4. Starting with the outer edge, arrange the plums, skin side down, on top of the frangipane in concentric circles, placing the slices close together. The points of the plums should be wedged high against the side of the tart pan. For the second circle, again position the points of the plums higher, wedging them against, and slightly overlapping, the first row of plums. Fill in the center with the remaining plums.

5. Place the tart on a shallow pan lined with aluminum foil. Bake for 55 to 60 minutes or until the fruit starts to bubble. Remove from the oven and cool on a rack.

6. GLAZE THE TART: Place the apricot preserves and water in a small, heavy saucepan and bring to a slow boil. Reduce the heat and simmer for 1 minute. Strain and let cool briefly. Using a pastry brush, dab the warm apricot glaze on the fruit. Garnish with the reserved almonds.

STORAGE

Store any leftover tart in the refrigerator loosely covered with a sheet of waxed paper then aluminum foil, for up to 3 days. This tart can be frozen.

VARIATION

Nectarine Tart

Substitute 2 pounds (5 to 6) ripe nectarines for the plums. The fruit does not have to be peeled unless the skins are very thick. Cut the nectarines in $1/4$-inch slices and arrange in concentric circles.

Prune and Apricot Crackle Tart

HERE IS A TART THAT IS shaped like a round jalousie. The slits in the top crust allow a glimpse of the Armagnac-flavored prunes, resting on a layer of tangy apricot lekvar. The tart is garnished with crisp almond brittle. Be sure to take advantage of these do-ahead components.

At a Glance

SERVES: 8 to 10

PAN: 11-inch metal tart

PASTRY PREP: Unbaked

FRUIT PREP: Begin the day before

STARTING OVEN TEMP: 425 degrees

BAKING TIME: 40 to 45 minutes

DIFFICULTY: 🥿 🥿 🥿

---

¹/₂ recipe Goof-Proof Puff Pastry (page 172)
1 small recipe Nut Brittle (page 452), made with sliced almonds

STEWED PRUNES
18 prunes (about 1 cup)
1 cup water
2 tablespoons Armagnac brandy

APRICOT LEKVAR
3/4 cup (6 ounces) dried apricots
1¹/₂ cups water
3 tablespoons sugar
1 to 2 tablespoons unsalted butter

FILLING
Stewed prunes
Apricot Lekvar
2 tablespoons sugar
2 tablespoons unsalted butter

EGG WASH
1 large egg
1 tablespoon water
¹/₄ cup apricot preserves, for glazing

1. MAKE THE PRUNES: The day before, place the prunes and water in a small, heavy saucepan. Cover and bring to a slow boil. Simmer 2 minutes. Remove from the heat and add the Armagnac. Transfer to a covered container and refrigerate overnight or longer.

2. MAKE THE LEKVAR: The day before, place the apricots in a medium bowl. Add the water, cover, and let stand overnight at room temperature.

3. The next day, place the apricots, water, and sugar in a small, heavy saucepan. Cover and bring to a slow boil. Simmer 30 to 35 minutes or until apricots are very soft. Stir vigorously with a fork to form a thick puree. Remove from the heat, let stand about 5 minutes, then blend in the butter.

4. ASSEMBLE THE TART: Divide the pastry in half. On a lightly floured surface, roll half the pastry into a 15-inch circle. Line the tart pan with the pastry, inverting it so that the top side of the dough is down. Fit the dough loosely into the pan, paying particular attention at the bend. It should have plenty of slack with no stretching. Run the rolling pin across the top of the tart pan to trim excess pastry. Refrigerate pastry for 15 to 20 minutes.

5. Make an egg wash by lightly beating together the egg and 2 teaspoons of the water with a fork. Brush a thin coat of the egg wash on the bottom of the tart shell. With a small offset spatula, spread the apricot lekvar smoothly on the pastry. Drain the prunes on paper towels. Arrange the prunes on top of the lekvar as follows: 11 prunes around the outer edge; 6 prunes in a second, smaller circle; 1 prune in the center. Press the prunes slightly into the lekvar.

6. Sprinkle the top of the fruit with sugar and dot with butter. **1** Fold the side of the dough over the fruit to form a 3/4-inch edge. Brush the pastry lightly with the egg wash.

7. Roll the remaining pastry into a 13-inch circle. Cut the dough into a 10½-inch circle. **2** To measure this accurately, set the removable bottom of the tart pan on top of the rolled pastry and cut a circle using the disk as a guide. Reserve pastry cuttings for another use (see page 171).

8. **3** Fold the pastry in half. Using a pastry scraper, slash the pastry at ¼-inch intervals, starting at the fold and leaving a 1-inch border at the rounded edge. Lay the pastry on top of the fruit, positioning it so the straight side of the dough is exactly in the center of the pan. Carefully open the pastry and stretch it gently to the edge of the pan. Press the 2 layers firmly together.

9. **4** To seal the edge well and make a decorative finish, press deeply into the pastry at ¼-inch intervals using the dull side of a paring knife. If the pastry becomes too soft to handle, chill for 5 to 10 minutes, then proceed with the design. Brush the top lightly with egg wash. Chill at least 30 minutes.

10. Preheat the oven to 425 degrees. Place the oven rack in the upper third of the oven.

11. Bake the tart for 25 minutes. *Reduce* the oven temperature to 375 degrees, and bake for another 15 to 20 minutes or until well browned.

12. Remove the tart from the oven. Let stand 5 minutes. Combine the apricot preserves with the remaining 1 teaspoon water. Heat in the microwave oven or on top of the stove. Brush the top of the tart with the hot apricot glaze.

13. Place the Nut Brittle on a cutting board. Using a sharp knife, chop the brittle into ¼-inch pieces. Sprinkle over the top of the tart before the apricot glaze has set. This tart is at its best when served within 1 to 6 hours after baking.

STORAGE

Cover any leftover tart with aluminum foil and store in a cool place for up to 3 days. Reheat in a 325 degree oven for 8 to 10 minutes before serving. This tart can be frozen.

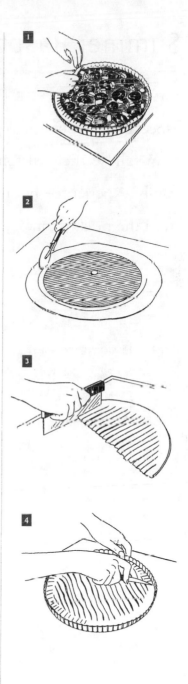

Summer Raspberry Pie with Wine Pastry

SAVORING A PIECE OF RASPBERRY PIE is an unforgettable experience, especially if you're lucky enough to find berries fresh from the bush. Many farms allow their customers to hand-pick their berries, which can be a great family experience—but be sure to wear gardening gloves to protect your hands from the prickly canes.

Farm-fresh berries are especially delicate and easily bruise, so use care in handling them. It's okay to make the pie with store-bought berries if local ones are unavailable.

Lattice crusts are especially pretty on fresh berry pies. For this pie, I like to cut the pastry into very wide strips.

1 recipe Wine Pastry (page 143)

FILLING
*6 cups (4 6-ounce baskets) fresh
    raspberries*
1 tablespoon instant tapioca
3/4 cup sugar, or to taste
2 to 2¹/₂ tablespoons cornstarch
*1 teaspoon grated navel or
    Valencia orange zest*
2 teaspoons fresh lemon juice
2 tablespoons unsalted butter

GLAZE
2 tablespoons milk
*2 teaspoons pearl sugar
    (granulated sugar can be
    substituted)*

1. Preheat the oven to 400 degrees. Position the oven rack in the lower third of the oven. Butter a 9-inch ovenproof glass pie plate.

2. **MAKE THE PIE:** Wash and thoroughly dry the raspberries (page 37). Place the berries in a large bowl and sprinkle with tapioca. Shake bowl to distribute. Let stand 15 minutes.

3. On a floured pastry cloth, roll half the dough into a 13-inch circle. Line the pie plate with the pastry. Trim the edge, leaving a ¹/₂-inch overhang.

4. Combine the sugar, cornstarch, and orange zest in a small bowl. Sprinkle 2 tablespoons of this mixture over the pastry shell.

5. Place half the raspberries in the pie plate. Sprinkle half the sugar mixture over the berries. Top with the remaining raspberries, then sprinkle with the remaining sugar mixture. Drizzle with lemon juice and dot with butter.

6. Make a lattice top with the remaining pastry as follows: Roll the pastry into a 13-inch circle. Using a pastry wheel, divide the pastry into six 2-inch-wide strips. Center 1 of the longer strips on the fruit. Place 1 shorter strip on either side, then rotate the pie 90 degrees. Center another longer strip over the top, weaving it over and under the first 3 strips (see "Making Lattice Crusts," page 65). Complete the weaving with the 2 remaining strips. Trim strips leaving a 1-inch overhang.

7. Seal the edges by folding the pastry strips under the bottom layer of dough. Flute the edge of the pastry (see page 66). Brush the lattice lightly with milk and sprinkle with pearl sugar.

8. To prevent the edges from burning, make aluminum foil bands. Cut two 3-inch-wide strips of 18-inch heavy-duty aluminum foil. Fold 1 inch of each strip to the center, making a double thickness of foil. Mold the foil around the edge of the pie, keeping the double fold on top of the dough. Be careful not to crush the edge of the pastry. Secure the bands with tape.

9. Make an aluminum foil drip pan to place on the rack below the pie halfway through the baking. Cut an 18-inch square of heavy-duty aluminum foil. Fold each edge twice (about 1 inch per fold) standing the folded edges upright to form a 4-sided pan.

NOTE

Remove the aluminum foil bands the last 5 to 10 minutes of baking.

10. Bake the pie for 45 minutes. Remove the aluminum foil bands. Continue baking the pie for 10 minutes longer or until the crust is golden brown and the juices begin to bubble. Remove the pie from the oven and cool on a rack. Let stand at least 3 hours before serving.

STORAGE

Cover any leftover pie with a sheet of waxed paper then aluminum foil and refrigerate for up to 4 days. Reheat before serving. This pie can be frozen.

> *There is something in the red of a raspberry pie that looks as good to man as the red in a sheep looks to a wolf.*
>
> EDGAR WATSON HOWE, SINNER SERMONS

Apple Tarte Tatin

THIS CLASSIC DESSERT, KNOWN AS *La Tarte des Demoiselles Tatin,* takes its name from two sisters who were hotel proprietors in the Loire Valley in France. The Tatin sisters created a tart of caramelized apples made with only a top crust. After baking, the tart was inverted, which allowed the caramelized juices to flow over the apples onto the crust beneath. The tart is at its best when served shortly after it is inverted. Try it with crème fraîche as it was served in France.

So popular was this tart that a deep, round, copper baking utensil, called a Tatin pan, was named for this dessert. This copper pan conducts heat extremely well, essential for caramelizing the fruit. However, a heavy 10-inch Dutch sauté pan or even an ordinary black cast-iron skillet will perform well. Be wary of letting the tart stand too long in an iron pan, as the metal is corrosive and can give the fruit a metallic flavor.

1 recipe Sweet Tart Pastry (page 146)

FILLING
6 tablespoons unsalted butter, at room temperature
6 Granny Smith or Golden Delicious apples (about 2 1/2 pounds)
3/4 cup sugar

1. **MAKE THE FILLING:** Place the butter in a heavy Dutch sauté pan or black cast-iron skillet. Butter the sides, then using a small offset spatula, spread a thick layer of butter evenly across the bottom of the pan. Place all but 2 tablespoons of the sugar in a fine-mesh strainer and sprinkle it evenly across the bottom of the pan.

2. Peel, then core the apples (page 17). Cut into quarters. Starting at the outer edge of the pan, arrange the apples on their sides in a circle. Pack them as tightly as you can. Then press the remaining apples in the center. Sprinkle the remaining 2 tablespoons sugar over the top.

3. On the stovetop, cook apples over medium-high heat for 15 to 17 minutes. Shake the skillet occasionally to prevent the apples from sticking and to ensure even browning. As the apples begin to soften and shrink, press the top of the fruit with a metal spatula to flatten the apples so that the rounded side will be on the bottom. When the juices turn deep golden brown and are caramelized, remove the pan from the heat. *Do not let the syrup become too dark or it will taste bitter.* As the apples stand, shake the pan occasionally because they will continue to cook. Cool 10 to 15 minutes before assembling.

4. **ASSEMBLE THE TART:** Preheat the oven to 425 degrees. Position the oven rack in the lower third of the oven.

5. On a well-floured pastry cloth, roll the pastry into an 11- to 12-inch circle. Using the bottom of a 10-inch springform pan or a 10-inch pot cover as a guide, cut a 10½-inch circle of dough with a pastry wheel. Roll the pastry onto the rolling pin, center it over the apples, and unroll. Fold the edges of the dough over toward the center to form a ½-inch lip. Using a fork, press the edges against the pan and make a few steam holes in the top.

6. Bake the tart for 25 to 30 minutes or until the crust is golden brown and the juices begin to bubble. Cool on a rack. Let stand 15 to 20 minutes. Run a thin knife around the edge, invert the pan onto a platter, and unmold. If any fruit sticks to the bottom of the pan, remove it with a metal spatula and place it on the tart. Serve warm with crème fraîche, sweetened whipped cream, or vanilla ice cream.

STORAGE
Cover any leftover tart with a sheet of waxed paper then aluminum foil and refrigerate for up to 3 days. Reheat before serving. Freezing is not recommended.

Pear Tarte Tatin

THIS RECIPE FOR PEAR TARTE TATIN is a variation of the one made with apples. Since pears are sweeter than apples, I have reduced the sugar and added some additional flavors to enhance the elusive flavor of the pear.

At a Glance

SERVES: 6 to 8

PAN: 10-inch heavy Dutch sauté pan or black cast-iron skillet

PASTRY PREP: Unbaked

OVEN TEMP: 425 degrees

BAKING TIME: 25 to 30 minutes

DIFFICULTY: 🥄🥄

1 recipe Sweet Tart Pastry (page 146)

FILLING
4 tablespoons unsalted butter, at room temperature
1/2 teaspoon grated navel or Valencia orange zest
1/2 cup sugar
6 or 7 firm Anjou pears (2 1/2 to 3 pounds), slightly underripe
2 tablespoons fresh lemon juice
1/4 teaspoon freshly grated nutmeg

1. **MAKE THE FILLING:** Combine the butter and orange zest and place in a heavy Dutch sauté pan or black cast-iron skillet. Spread the mixture on the sides, then using a small offset spatula, spread a thick layer evenly across the bottom. Place all but 2 tablespoons of the sugar in a fine-mesh strainer and sprinkle it evenly across the bottom of the skillet.

2. Peel, core, and quarter the pears (page 34). Place them immediately into a large bowl and sprinkle with lemon juice.

3. Starting at the outer edge of the pan, arrange the pears on their sides in a circle. Pack them as tightly as you can. Then arrange the remaining pears in the center. Combine the remaining sugar with the nutmeg and sprinkle over the top.

4. On the stovetop, cook over medium-high heat for 12 to 13 minutes. Shake the skillet occasionally to prevent the pears from sticking and to ensure even browning. As the pears begin to soften and shrink, press the top of the fruit with a metal spatula to flatten the pears so the rounded side will be on the bottom. When the juices turn deep golden brown and are caramelized, remove the pan from the heat. *Do not let the syrup become too dark or it will taste bitter.* As the pears stand, shake the pan occasionally because they will continue to cook. Cool 10 to 15 minutes before assembling.

5. **ASSEMBLE THE TART.** Preheat the oven to 425 degrees. Position the oven rack in the lower third of the oven.

6. On a well-floured pastry cloth, roll the pastry into an 11- to 12-inch circle. Using the bottom of a 10-inch springform pan or a 10-inch pot cover as a guide, cut an 11-inch circle of dough with a pastry wheel. Roll the pastry onto the rolling pin, center it over the pears, and unroll. Fold the edges of the dough over toward the center to form a $1/2$-inch lip. Using a fork, press the edges against the pan, and make a few steam holes in the top.

7. Bake the tart for 25 to 30 minutes or until the crust is golden brown and the juices begin to bubble. Cool on a rack. Let stand 15 to 20 minutes. Run a thin knife around the edge, invert the pan onto a platter, and unmold.

If any fruit sticks to the bottom of the pan, remove it with a metal spatula and place it on the tart. Serve warm with crème fraîche, sweetened whipped cream, or vanilla ice cream.

STORAGE

Cover any leftover tart with a sheet of waxed paper then aluminum foil and refrigerate for up to 3 days. Reheat before serving. Freezing is not recommended.

As it is, in my view, the duty of an apple to be crisp and crunchable, a pear should have such a texture as leads to quiet comsumption.

EDWARD
BUNYARD

Tart of Strawberries in Raspberry Puree

I HAVE THE PERFECT EXCUSE FOR making this fresh berry tart in mid-summer, because the strawberry and raspberry seasons are at their peak. The ruby red filling is made almost entirely of sliced strawberry rounds bound with a thick raspberry puree. There are lots of berries here, so make this when you want an outstanding dessert that is not too rich.

At a Glance

SERVES: 8 to 10

PAN: 11-inch metal tart

PASTRY PREP: Baked

CHILLING TIME: 3 hours

DIFFICULTY: 🍥 🍥

1 11-inch Classic Tart Pastry crust (pages 102, 104), baked

FILLING
1 quart (2 pint baskets) fresh strawberries
3 cups (2 to 2½ 6-ounce baskets) fresh raspberries
¼ cup fresh orange juice
1 package unflavored gelatin
¾ cup granulated sugar
2 tablespoons seedless blackberry jam
1½ teaspoons fresh lemon juice

TOPPING
1 cup heavy cream, well chilled
2 tablespoons strained confectioners' sugar
½ teaspoon vanilla extract
1 to 2 tablespoons sliced almonds, lightly toasted, for garnish

1. MAKE THE FILLING: Wash and thoroughly dry the berries (pages 37 and 39). Hull the strawberries.

2. Puree the raspberries in a food processor or blender and pass the pulp through a very fine mesh strainer to remove the seeds. Discard the seeds and set the puree aside.

3. Place the orange juice in a small heatproof container and sprinkle the gelatin over the surface. Do not stir. Let the mixture stand 3 to 5 minutes to soften the gelatin. Set the container in a small skillet filled with ½ inch of simmering water. Heat in the water bath until the gelatin is clear and dissolved.

4. Place the puree, sugar, and blackberry jam in a medium saucepan over low heat. Stir with a whisk until the jam dissolves and the mixture comes to a boil. Simmer for 8 to 10 minutes, stirring occasionally. Stir in the dissolved gelatin. Remove from the heat and add the lemon juice. Empty the puree into a medium bowl and refrigerate until the mixture begins to gel. This will take 45 to 60 minutes, depending on how cold your refrigerator is. If you wish to hasten the thickening, place the bowl in a larger one filled with ice water.

5. Cut the strawberries crosswise into 1/4-inch rounds and gently fold into the slightly thickened puree. Pour the berry mixture into the baked tart shell and refrigerate until the filling is firm, about 3 hours.

6 GARNISH THE TART: In a medium chilled bowl with chilled beaters, beat the cream until it starts to thicken. Add the confectioners' sugar and vanilla. Whip just until the cream holds its shape. Do not overbeat.

7. Fit a large 16-inch pastry bag with a #824 open star tip. Fill with the whipped cream and pipe a scroll pattern around the edge of the tart. Refrigerate the tart, uncovered, until ready to serve. Sprinkle with toasted almonds just before serving.

STORAGE

Cover any leftover tart with a sheet of waxed paper then aluminum foil and refrigerate for up to 2 days. Freezing is not recommended.

Doubtless God could have made a better berry, but doubtless God never did.

WILLIAM BUTLER, CIRCA 1600

Strawberry Rhubarb Pie
with Lattice Crust

WHEN PRODUCE BINS ARE STOCKED with spears of pink rhubarb and baskets of strawberries, it's a sure sign that warmer days are heading our way. The tart rhubarb complements the sweet berries, making this a favorite fruit combination. Although I've chosen to top this pie with a lattice crust to show the pretty pink color of the fruits after baking, a simple pastry covering is okay to use.

At a Glance

SERVES: 6 to 8

PAN: 9-inch ovenproof glass

PASTRY PREP: Unbaked

OVEN TEMP: 400 degrees

BAKING TIME:
45 to 50 minutes

DIFFICULTY: 🥧 🥧

To retain the character of the strawberries, I like to keep them in large chunks because if cut too small, the delicate berries become mushy when baked. Peeling the stringy surface of the rhubarb is unnecessary since it softens when cooked, but *don't forget to remove the leafy parts of the rhubarb.* The stalks are perfectly safe, *but the leaves are toxic.*

1 small recipe Flaky Pie Pastry
(pages 98, 100)

FILLING
3/4 cup sugar
3 tablespoons cornstarch
1/2 teaspoon ground cinnamon
1/2 teaspoon grated navel or
Valencia orange zest
3 cups (1 1/2 pints) fresh
strawberries, cleaned, hulled,
and cut into 1 1/2-inch chunks
(page 39)

3 cups fresh rhubarb, cleaned and
sliced into 1/2-inch pieces
(about 1 pound) (page 39)
1 teaspoon fresh lemon juice
2 tablespoons unsalted butter

GLAZE
2 tablespoons milk
2 teaspoons sugar (optional)

1. Preheat the oven to 400 degrees. Position the oven rack in the lower third of the oven. Butter a 9-inch ovenproof glass pie plate.

2. On a floured pastry cloth, roll half the pastry into a 13-inch circle. Line the pie plate with the pastry. Trim the edge, leaving a 1/2-inch overhang.

3. MAKE THE PIE: Combine the sugar, cornstarch, cinnamon, and orange zest in a small bowl, using a whisk to combine well. Sprinkle 2 tablespoons of this mixture over the pastry shell.

4. Place the strawberries and rhubarb in a large bowl. Pour the remaining sugar-cornstarch mixture over the fruit. Shake the bowl briskly to distribute the dry ingredients through the fruit.

5. Empty the fruit into the pie plate, making sure that filling is evenly spread. Sprinkle with lemon juice, and dot with butter.

6. Make a diagonal lattice top with the remaining pastry as follows: Roll the remaining pastry into a 13-inch circle. Using a pastry wheel, divide pastry into twelve 3/4-inch strips. Evenly space the pastry, starting with 2 longer strips, placed to the left and right of the center, about 3/4 inch apart. Continue, using 2 more strips on either side, keeping the shortest strips toward the outer edge. Rotate pie about an eighth of a turn. Repeat the process, weaving new strips over and under the initial 6 strips (see "Making Diagonal Lattice Crusts," page 65). Trim, leaving a 1-inch overhang.

7. Seal the edges by folding the pastry strips under the bottom layer of dough. Flute the edge of the pastry (see page 66). Brush the lattice lightly with milk and sprinkle with sugar.

8. To prevent the edges from burning, make aluminum foil bands. Cut two 3-inch-wide strips of 18-inch heavy-duty aluminum foil. Fold 1 inch of each strip to the center, making a double thickness of foil. Mold the foil around the edge of the pie, keeping the double fold on top of the dough. Be careful not to crush the edge of the pastry. Secure the bands with tape.

9. Make an aluminum foil drip pan to place on the rack below the pie halfway through the baking. Cut an 18-inch square of heavy-duty aluminum foil. Fold each edge twice (about 1 inch per fold) standing the folded edges upright to form a 4-sided pan.

10. Bake the pie for 35 minutes. Remove the aluminum foil bands. Continue baking for 10 minutes longer or until the crust is golden brown and the juices begin to bubble. Remove the pie from the oven and cool on a rack. Let stand at least 3 hours before serving.

STORAGE

Cover any leftover pie with a sheet of waxed paper then aluminum foil and refrigerate for up to 3 days. Reheat before serving. This pie can be frozen.

Fruity Viennese Linzer Tart

MY RECIPE FOR THIS MIDDLE EUROPEAN specialty has long been a favorite with my students. What made this tart such a hit was the filling of cooked frozen raspberries mixed with raspberry preserves. It is more fruity and less sweet than the classic jam filled Linzertorte.

At a Glance

SERVES: 8 to 10

PAN: 10-inch extra-deep metal tart

PASTRY PREP: Unbaked

OVEN TEMP: 350 degrees

BAKING TIME: 45 to 50 minutes

DIFFICULTY: 🥐🥐🥐

The crumbly texture of the crust comes from sieved hard-boiled egg yolks and lots of ground nuts. Be sure to use unblanched nuts. The skin imparts a rich nutty taste. Because the dough is fragile, it is best to form the lattice top by shaping balls of pastry into ropes with your hands. These balls are also used to trim the edge of the pan. The dough will spread during baking, creating an eye-appealing top.

FILLING
1 (10-ounce) package frozen
    unsweetened raspberries
1/3 cup granulated sugar
Raspberry preserves
1/2 teaspoon fresh lemon juice

PASTRY
1 cup unblanched almonds
1/2 cup unblanched hazelnuts
1 1/2 cups unsifted all-purpose flour
1/4 teaspoon salt
3/4 teaspoon ground cinnamon
1/8 teaspoon ground cloves
1/2 pound unsalted butter, at room
    temperature
1/2 teaspoon grated lemon zest
2/3 cup granulated sugar
2 hard-boiled large egg yolks

1 large egg
1 teaspoon fresh lemon juice
1 tablespoon confectioners' sugar,
    for garnish

1. MAKE THE FILLING: Place the frozen raspberries and sugar in a small, heavy saucepan. Bring to a slow boil over medium-low heat. Reduce heat and simmer for 15 to 20 minutes, or until most of the liquid has evaporated. *Watch carefully* to avoid burning. Empty the raspberries into a liquid measuring cup. You should have about 1 cup. Add enough preserves to equal 1 1/3 cups of filling. Stir in the lemon juice. Set aside to cool.

2. MAKE THE PASTRY: Place almonds, hazelnuts, and 1/2 cup flour in the bowl of a food processor fitted with the steel blade. Process until the mixture resembles very fine meal. Add the remaining flour, the salt, cinnamon, and cloves. Pulse until well blended. Set aside.

3. Fit an electric mixer with the paddle attachment and blend the butter, lemon zest, and sugar on low speed. Sieve the yolks through a medium-gauge strainer and add to the butter mixture along with ¹/₂ cup of the nut-flour mixture. Lightly beat together the egg and lemon juice and add to the butter mixture. Blend in remaining nut-flour, forming a soft dough. *Do not overmix.*

4. Butter a 10 × 1³/₄-inch extra-deep tart pan with a removable bottom. With floured hands, press slightly more than half of the dough into the bottom of the tart pan. Chill while preparing the lattice top.

5. **MAKE THE LATTICE:** Make 10 graduated balls from the remaining dough. The first 2 should be the size of large walnuts, the next 4 should be slightly smaller, and the final 4 should be a bit smaller still. The rest of the pastry will be used to complete the edge. Chill the dough balls and remaining pastry for 10 to 15 minutes or until firm enough to handle without sticking to your hands.

6. **ASSEMBLE THE TART:** Preheat the oven to 350 degrees. Position the oven rack in the lower third of the oven.

7. Spread the raspberry filling on the pastry-lined tart pan, leaving a ¹/₂-inch border of dough. Take one of the largest balls of dough, and roll it back and forth on a lightly floured surface with floured hands to form a rope approximately 10 inches long. Position the rope down the center of the pan. Make two 9-inch ropes using 2 medium balls of dough. Position them to the left and right of the center rope, approximately 1¹/₄ inches apart. Make two 8-inch ropes from the smallest balls of pastry. Position them 1¹/₄ inches to the left and right of the medium length ropes.

8. Rotate the pan about an eighth of a turn and, starting at the center, repeat with the remaining balls of dough, forming a lattice

9. Shape 32 equal-size balls from the remaining dough. Place each ball into a groove in the pan. There will be 32 grooves. Bake for 45 to 50 minutes or until golden brown. Cool at least 4 hours before cutting. Dust the edge with confectioners' sugar before serving.

STORAGE

Any leftover tart should be refrigerated loosely covered with a sheet of waxed paper then aluminum foil for up to 5 days. Warm briefly before serving. This tart can be frozen.

Walnut-Topped Blueberry Tart

THIS TART IS INSTANT LOVE for those who like the combination of berries and nuts. Buttery pastry cradles plump, juicy blueberries topped with loads of crunchy walnuts. Serve this tart slightly warm with French vanilla ice cream.

1 11-inch *Sweet Tart Pastry crust* (page 146), *baked*

FILLING
4 cups fresh blueberries, washed and dried (1 quart basket) (page 22)
1 cup granulated sugar
2 tablespoons cornstarch
1/2 teaspoon ground cinnamon
1/4 cup fresh orange juice
1 tablespoon freshly squeezed lemon juice
3/4 teaspoon grated navel or Valencia orange zest
1 teaspoon vanilla extract
2 tablespoons unsalted butter, softened (optional)
2 cups walnuts, coarsely chopped
2 tablespoons confectioners' sugar

1. Preheat the oven to 375 degrees. Position the oven rack in the lower third of the oven.

2. **MAKE THE FILLING:** Coarsely chop 2 cups of the blueberries; reserve the remaining 2 cups.

3. Place the granulated sugar, cornstarch, and cinnamon in a medium saucepan. Using a whisk, blend thoroughly. Stir in the orange juice. Add the chopped blueberries and cook the mixture over low heat until it comes to a boil. Reduce the heat and simmer for 30 to 45 seconds, stirring every 10 to 15 seconds.

4. Remove from the heat and blend in the lemon juice, orange zest, vanilla, and butter. Fold in the whole blueberries. Empty the mixture into the pastry shell, smoothing the surface. Cover the top evenly with the walnuts.

5. Place the tart on a cookie sheet. Bake for 30 to 35 minutes or until the juices begin to bubble and the nuts start to brown. Remove from the oven and cool on a rack.

6. Just before serving, dust the tart heavily with confectioners' sugar.

STORAGE
Cover any leftover tart with a sheet of waxed paper then aluminum foil and refrigerate for up to 4 days. Reheat before serving. Freezing is not recommended.

About Pie Birds

WOULD YOU BELIEVE THAT IN this age of computer technology and explorations to Mars, a small pottery funnel, commonly molded in the shape of a bird, has attracted the attention of several hundred fanciers? An organization called Pie Bird Collectors meets every other year in Paris, Tennessee, to "show, tell, and trade." Its members travel to this Dixie antique center from all parts of our vast nation and abroad.

I visited with Lillian Cole in Flemington, New Jersey, editor of *Piebirds Unlimited*, the organization newsletter. To my astonishment, Lillian owns a vast collection of several hundred pie birds, ranging from a valuable Walt Disney Donald Duck to a miniature pottery chef. According to Lillian's historical research, there are references of pie funnels dating back to the reign of George III (1738–1820). Originally used in England in the baking of meat pies, it is thought that this little tool took its name and shape from the nursery rhyme, "Four and Twenty Blackbirds Baked in a Pie."

An authentic pie bird is made of a lead-free pottery material that is glazed inside and out, is approximately 3 to 5 inches tall, and has arches at the base to allow the steam to enter. At the top is a "beak" or exit hole to release the steam and prevents the fruit juices from overflowing. Some pie birds have "shoulders" to keep the top crust from sinking into the filling and becoming soggy. I tested a few pies using this charming gadget, and, yes indeed, it does reduce the spillage.

To use a pie bird, stand it in the center of an unfilled, pastry-lined pie plate. Distribute the fruit filling around the bird. After the top crust is rolled, cut a 1-inch X in the center of the pastry. Roll the pastry around the rolling pin, then unroll it carefully over the top of the pie, positioning the slit portion at the head of the bird. Pinch the pastry at the opening to seal it and bake. When serving, slice the pie around the bird and watch your guests eyes light up with delight!

For information on where to purchase pie birds, see Mail Order Sources, page 466.

Decadent & Delicious

ELCOME TO THE LAND OF the rich and creamy, the forbidden territory that every so often we all must visit. ✻ As we enter this chapter of heavenly pies and tarts, many tastes from the past will surface. Treats like banana, chocolate, and coconut cream pies are reminders of the comfort desserts that Mom and Grandma used to whip up—often simply with a package of My-T-Fine pudding mix and a graham

cracker crust. As a child they tasted mighty good. As maturity set in, and my palate became more refined, I began my quest for the ultimate in rich and sinful desserts.

Here, for your pleasure, is a roundup of enticing recipes. There are, of course, classic favorites like Key Lime Pie and Black Bottom Cream Pie. Others were gathered through my travels; some are specialties of baking professionals and good friends; and many are the products of my own inspiration and imagination.

The Hall of Fame Raspberry Streusel Tart was influenced by a visit to Carl Schumacher's Oberlaa, a huge pastry emporium in the suburbs of Vienna, Austria. There I had the pleasure of experiencing the pinnacle of fine pastries. The Melon and Mascarpone Tart in Chocolate Crumb Crust is my adaptation of a miniature tartlet that I first tasted in a class taught by pastry chef Peter Greweling at the Culinary Institute of America in Hyde Park, New York. It's wonderful! Some of the other exciting new creations you will find here are Devilish Chocolate Candy Tart, Java Eggnog Pie, and Sweet Risotto and Orange Tart.

Fortunately, these pies and tarts are not difficult to prepare. Unlike baking with fresh fruits, cream, custard, and chiffon fillings are a joy to make because their ingredients perform with predictability. Bavarian fillings offer great versatility as many can be transformed into frozen desserts.

True enough, these are pastries that should be eaten with prudence. But when that special occasion arises, it's time to indulge. After all, what is life without a little sin once in a while?

If my old nose don't tell me lies, It 'pears like I smell custard pies.

JAMES WHITCOMB RILEY

✳

About Custards and Creams

A WIDE VARIETY OF PASTRIES are made with custards, pastry creams (*crème pâsissière*), and similar cooked fillings. Both custards and pastry creams are the foundation for myriad open-faced pies and tarts. Although these two types of fillings share the base ingredients of eggs, milk and/or cream, and sugar, the similarities end there.

Custard fillings thicken in the oven. They are made without starch and are fluid until they are baked. The proteins in the eggs coagulate during baking and form smooth, velvety fillings. Custard fillings are the root of more foods than you may realize. Flans, crème caramels, and their savory sister, quiche—all are made from custards.

These preparations must be baked on low heat to prevent them from becoming watery or curdling, yet the pastry shells require higher temperatures to bake and brown them. Herein lies the problem: filling and crust do not arrive at home base at the same time. This often leads to soggy bottom crusts.

On the other hand, fillings made with pastry cream are thickened on top of the stove and do contain starch—usually flour or cornstarch, or a combination of the two. Unlike custard fillings, cream fillings are generally not baked, and therefore are used with prebaked pastry shells.

Pastry cream and custard fillings are easy to make, but there are a few tricks that will help to guarantee your success. Many of these hints can be found in The Primer. But refer also to the Recipe Roundups for Lemon Meringue Pie (page 116) and French Fruit Tarts with Pastry Cream (page 128). The tips below are specific to the recipes in this chapter.

✦ *Avoid high oven temperatures because they cause custards to become watery.*

✦ *Never boil custards because they are made without flour and will curdle.*

✦ *Custards can be baked with or without a pastry shell.*

✦ *Custards baked without a pastry shell will form their own golden crust during baking.*

✦ *For a velvety, crustless texture, bake custards made without a pastry shell in a water bath. The moist oven air ensures a silky finish.*

✦ To prevent a soggy bottom crust, prebake the pastry shell before filling, or bake the pie or tart on a preheated pizza stone or baking sheet, preferably one made of dark metal, or brush the pastry shell with an egg wash or other sealer.

✦ Don't use cookie crumbs or finely chopped nuts as a sealer for a bottom crust when baking custard pies; they will float to the top.

✦ Place larger, heavier ingredients—such as fresh or dried fruits, coarsely chopped nuts, or sautéed vegetables and meats for savories—on the bottom of the pastry shell before adding the custard.

✦ When making pastry cream, always use a heavy nonreactive saucepan, such as stainless steel or heavy-bottomed enamel.

✦ Temper egg yolks before adding them to a cooked pastry cream by adding a small amount of the hot mixture to the yolks to elevate their temperature. Warming the yolks gradually helps them blend smoothly into the cooked base.

✦ When the pastry cream comes to a boil, whisk it rapidly to prevent lumps from forming. Once it is smooth, mix only occasionally. Overmixing can cause some fillings to become thin.

✦ Pastry cream and other starch-thickened, cooked fillings must simmer for 1 to 2 minutes after the boil to prevent thinning.

✦ To prevent a skin from forming on the surface of a cooked filling as it cools, cover it with a sheet of buttered plastic wrap.

✦ Pastry creams lend themselves to a variety of flavors. Mocha, coffee, butterscotch, and praline are some choices you may wish to consider.

✦ Baked Meringue Topping (page 115), can be substituted for whipped cream on most pies made with ordinary pastry cream fillings.

✦ Many baked custard pies and tarts have a short life. The sooner they are eaten, the better. This also applies to meringue toppings.

✦ Since custard and cream fillings are made with eggs, they are susceptible to bacteria and are very perishable. Refrigeration and cleanliness are essential.

Sour Cream Apple Crunch Pie with Dried Fruits

THIS UNUSUAL PIE IS MADE WITH chopped tart apples, dried apricots, and golden raisins mixed with a sour cream filling. After the fruit mixture sets in the oven, cinnamon-flavored crumbs are scattered on top. The pie is returned to the oven to bake until the crumbs become crunchy and golden brown.

At a Glance

SERVES: 6 to 8

PAN: 9-inch ovenproof glass

PASTRY PREP: Baked

OVEN TEMP: 425 degrees

BAKING TIME: 40 minutes

DIFFICULTY: 🥐 🥐

1 9-inch *Flaky Pie Pastry (pages 98, 100) or Super Tender Pie Pastry crust (page 137), baked*

FILLING
1/4 *cup golden raisins*
1/4 *cup diced dried apricots, in* 1/4-*inch pieces*
6 *tablespoons sugar*
4 *teaspoons unsifted all-purpose flour*
1/4 *teaspoon salt*
1 *cup sour cream*
1 *large egg*
3/4 *teaspoon vanilla extract*
1/2 *teaspoon grated navel or Valencia orange zest*
1/2 *teaspoon grated lemon zest*
3 *Granny Smith apples (about* 1 1/2 *pounds)*

TOPPING
1/2 *cup unsifted all-purpose flour*
6 *tablespoons sugar*
3/4 *teaspoon ground cinnamon*
1/4 *cup unsalted butter, melted and cooled to tepid*

1. Preheat the oven to 425 degrees. Position the oven rack in the lower third of the oven.

2. **MAKE THE FILLING:** Place the raisins and apricots in a small bowl. Add enough boiling water to cover the fruit by at least 1 inch. Let stand about 2 minutes. Drain and place fruit on a double thickness of paper towels. Blot dry with more towels.

3. Blend the sugar, flour, and salt.

4. Stir together the sour cream, egg, vanilla, and orange and lemon zests in a medium bowl. Blend in the dry ingredients, stirring with a whisk until smooth. Set aside.

5. Peel and core the apples (page 17), cut into eighths, and add to a food processor bowl fitted with the steel blade. Pulse 8 to 10 times, or until the apples are chopped into 1/4- to 3/8-inch

pieces. *Do not overprocess.* Stir the apples into the sour cream mixture with the dried fruit, then empty the filling into the pastry shell. Smooth the surface.

6. To prevent the edges from burning, make aluminum foil bands. Cut two 3-inch-wide strips of 18-inch heavy-duty aluminum foil. Fold 1 inch of each strip to the center, making a double thickness of foil. Mold the foil around the edge of the pie, keeping the double fold on top of the dough. Be careful not to crush the edge of the pastry. Secure the bands with tape.

7. Bake for 30 minutes or until the top has just set.

8. PREPARE THE TOPPING: While the pie is baking, combine the flour, sugar, and cinnamon in a small bowl. Add the butter and toss with a fork to form crumbs. Take a clump of the crumb mixture in your hands and squeeze gently to form a larger clump. Then, break the larger clump apart into smaller crumbs.

9. After 30 minutes, remove the pie from the oven and let stand for 5 minutes. Do not remove aluminum foil bands. Sprinkle the crumbs on top of the pie. Return the pie to the oven and bake for 10 to 12 minutes or until the crumbs turn golden brown. Set the pie on a rack to cool. Remove the foil bands. Cool at least 1 hour before serving.

STORAGE

Cover any leftover pie with an aluminum foil tent and store in the refrigerator for up to 3 days. This pie tastes best if reheated briefly before serving, in a 325 degree oven, for 15 minutes or just until slightly warm. This pie can be frozen.

Banana Cream Pie with Pecan Brittle

HERE IS A SOPHISTICATED VERSION OF banana cream pie. The rum-flavored pastry cream is topped with mirrorlike bits of crunchy caramelized pecans. If you prefer a more traditional banana cream pie, omit the rum, the rum extract, and the caramelized pecans. Whatever you choose, I am sure you will have an appreciative audience.

1 9-inch *Flaky Pie Pastry* crust (pages 98, 100), baked

FILLING
2¹/₂ cups milk
¹/₂ cup granulated sugar
4 large egg yolks
3 tablespoons unsifted all-purpose flour
2 tablespoons cornstarch
¹/₄ teaspoon salt
2 tablespoons dark Jamaican rum
1¹/₂ teaspoons vanilla extract
1 to 1¹/₂ teaspoons rum extract
1 tablespoon soft unsalted butter
2 to 3 firm, ripe medium bananas
2 teaspoons fresh lemon juice

GARNISH
3/4 cup heavy cream, well chilled
1 tablespoon strained confectioners' sugar
¹/₄ teaspoon vanilla extract
1 small recipe *Nut Brittle* (page 452), made with pecans, coarsely chopped

1. **MAKE THE FILLING:** Place the milk and ¹/₄ cup of the sugar in a large saucepan and stir to blend. Cook over low heat without stirring until the mixture is just under the boil or until a skin forms on the surface. Remove from the heat and set aside.

2. Beat the yolks in a large bowl with a hand mixer or whisk until light in color, about 1 minute. Add the remaining sugar, 1 tablespoon at a time, and beat until thick and very light. Combine the flour, cornstarch, and salt, and stir into the yolk mixture.

3. Temper the egg mixture by adding one-quarter of the hot milk to the yolks, stirring well to blend. Pour the yolk mixture back into the saucepan and, using a whisk, blend the mixtures.

4. Bring the mixture to a boil over low heat, stirring constantly with a whisk. As it begins to thicken, stir more vigorously, mixing until smooth. Be sure to reach into the bend of the saucepan. After it reaches the boil, continue to cook the pastry cream for about 1 minute, stirring gently to prevent the cream from scorching on the bottom of the saucepan. Do not overmix.

5. Remove the filling from the heat. Stir in the rum, vanilla, and rum extract. Dot the top of the filling with butter and set aside to cool until tepid. (To hasten the cooling, half-fill a large bowl with ice cubes. Add only enough water to float the cubes. Set the saucepan in the ice water. *Gently* stir the pastry cream every few minutes to prevent it from forming lumps on the bottom of the pot where the temperature is the coldest.)

6. While the filling is cooling, cut the bananas in 1/4-inch slices. Drizzle with lemon juice and set aside.

7. ASSEMBLE THE PIE: Gently fold the sliced bananas into the cooled pastry cream. Empty the mixture into the baked shell and smooth the top as best you can with the back of a large tablespoon. Refrigerate the pie at least 4 hours before serving.

8. GARNISH THE PIE: In a chilled bowl with chilled beaters, whip the cream, confectioners' sugar, and vanilla on medium speed until the cream is thick. Empty the cream into a 16-inch pastry bag fitted with a #824 large open star tip. Pipe the cream in a lattice design. When ready to serve, sprinkle the top with the chopped pecan brittle. This tart is best eaten the day it is made.

STORAGE
Cover any leftover pie with aluminum foil and store in the refrigerator for up to 1 day. Freezing is not recommended.

Anne Semmes' Lemon Chess Pie

ANNE SEMMES, FORMER RESTAURANT reviewer for the New Jersey section of the *New York Times,* gave me her recipe for chess pie, a dessert that has its roots in the Deep South. Anne grew up in Baton Rouge, Louisiana, and has a fine palate; I knew her offering would be special.

At a Glance

SERVES: 6 to 8

PAN: 9-inch ovenproof glass

PASTRY PREP: Baked

OVEN TEMP: 350 degrees

BAKING TIME: 40 to 45 minutes

DIFFICULTY: 🍪

Much has been written about chess pies, but their history is somewhat vague. According to Anne, "Nobody seems to be sure how it got its name. It has been attributed to the British, since many settlers of the middle South came from England, where similar cheese pies and custard pies were known."

Anne has two stories that relate to the origin of the name. The pie may have been called "chest" pie to indicate that it held up well when stored in the pie safe or chest, an old piece of furniture with perforated tin panels. The second tale suggests that a southern housewife came up with the recipe, and when her delighted husband asked her what kind it was, she replied, "Oh, I don't know, it's jes' pie."

Here is Anne's version of jes' pie.

1 9-inch Pine Nut Pastry crust (page 152), baked

FILLING
1/2 cup unsalted butter, softened
Finely grated zest of 2 large lemons (about 2 1/2 teaspoons)
1 1/2 cups sugar
2 large eggs
3 large egg yolks
1/3 cup milk
1/4 cup fresh lemon juice
1 teaspoon vanilla extract
2 tablespoons stone-ground cornmeal
4 teaspoons unsifted all-purpose flour

1. Preheat the oven to 350 degrees. Position the oven rack in the lower third of the oven.

2. MAKE THE FILLING: Place the butter and lemon zest in the large bowl of an electric mixer fitted with beaters or paddle attachment. Cream together on medium-low speed until light. Add the sugar gradually over 3 to 4 minutes. Blend in the eggs 1 at a time, then beat in the yolks. Continue beating about 2 minutes. Gradually add the milk, then the lemon juice and vanilla. Reduce the mixer speed to low. Combine the cornmeal and flour and add all at once to the batter.

3. Place the pie shell on a jelly roll pan. Pour the batter into the pastry shell. Bake 40 to 45 minutes. The pie is done when the top is puffy and the center quivers just slightly when moved. Set the pie on a rack to cool. Cool at least 3 hours before serving.

NOTE

If the top is browning too quickly, spray a square of aluminum foil with nonstick coating and lay gently over the surface during the last 5 minutes of baking.

STORAGE

Cover any leftover pie with an aluminum foil tent and refrigerate for up to 3 days. Freezing is not recommended.

Shaker Citrus Pie in a Cookie Crust

THE SHAKERS, A SMALL RELIGIOUS sect from England, settled in the eastern part of America in about 1706. The Shaker communities cultivated some of the finest farmlands in America. They were advocates of healthful, natural foods, making them centuries ahead of their time.

At a Glance

SERVES: 6 to 8

PAN: 9-inch ovenproof glass

PASTRY PREP: Unbaked

OVEN TEMP: 375 degrees

BAKING TIME:
45 to 50 minutes

DIFFICULTY: 🍪

This pie was inspired by a classic Shaker recipe made with thinly sliced whole lemons macerated in sugar, then bound with eggs and baked in a crust. For a twist, I used a combination of navel oranges and lemons. Instead of using a traditional pie pastry, this pie is made with a buttery sweet tart pastry—a melt-in-your-mouth, cookielike crust. You must double the recipe to have enough for a top and bottom crust. The result is "oh-so-good" and guaranteed to make you a believer.

When you make this pie, allow yourself ample time. The citrus fruits must macerate in sugar for no less than 4 hours, and are even better if left overnight.

2 recipes Sweet Tart Pastry
  (page 146), shaped into 2 disks

FILLING
1 medium navel orange (about
  7 ounces)
1 large lemon (about 4 ounces)
1 1/2 cups granulated sugar
4 large eggs

EGG WASH
1 large egg
1 teaspoon water

1 to 2 tablespoons confectioners'
  sugar, for garnish

1. MACERATE THE FRUIT: Wash and dry the orange and lemon. Be sure to scrub off the produce label. Cut the fruits in half lengthwise, from the stem end to the tip, with a serrated knife. Lay the fruit, cut side down, on the cutting board, and cut into *very* thin slices, no more than 1/8 inch. Layer the fruit and sugar in a medium bowl. Cover and let stand at room temperature for a minimum of 4 hours to tenderize the rinds and extract the juices.

2. **MAKE THE PIE:** Preheat the oven to 375 degrees. Position the oven rack in the lower third of the oven. Butter a 9-inch oven-proof glass pie plate.

3. On a floured pastry cloth, roll 1 disk of the pastry into a 13-inch circle. Line the pie plate with the pastry. Trim the edge, leaving a ¼-inch overhang.

4. Strain the fruit over a bowl, pressing out excess liquid. Reserve the juices.

5. Layer the sliced fruit in the pie plate and set aside.

6. In the large bowl of an electric mixer fitted with the whisk attachment, beat the eggs on medium speed for about 4 minutes or until thick and very light in color. Slowly beat in the reserved citrus liquid. Pour the egg mixture over the fruit.

7. Roll the remaining pastry into a 13-inch circle. Top the pie with the pastry, then trim the edge, leaving a ¾-inch overhang. Flute the edge (see page 66). Prick the pastry with a fork. Reserve the pastry scraps for cutout decorations.

8. Beat the egg and water together with a fork in a small bowl. Lightly brush the top of the pie with the egg wash. Gather the pastry scraps and roll into an ⅛-inch-thick layer. Using a decorative cutter, make cutouts (see page 68). Space them evenly around the perimeter of the pie, then brush with egg wash.

9. To prevent the edge of the pie from burning, make aluminum foil bands. Cut two 3-inch-wide strips of 18-inch heavy-duty aluminum foil. Fold 1 inch of each strip to the center, making a double thickness of foil. Mold the foil around the edge of the pie, keeping the double fold on top of the dough. Be careful not to crush the edge of the pastry. Secure the bands with tape.

10. Bake the pie for 45 to 50 minutes or until the top and bottom crusts are golden brown. Let cool on a rack at least 3 hours before cutting. Just before serving, strain confectioners' sugar heavily over the top.

STORAGE
Cover any leftover pie loosely with a sheet of waxed paper then aluminum foil and refrigerate for up to 4 days. Reheat before serving. Freezing is not recommended.

Devilish Chocolate Candy Tart

IF YOU CRAVE CHOCOLATE, this double-decker chocolate tart will be your Pandora's box. One bite, and you're in big trouble. The chocolate pastry holds a layer of intense chocolate custard covered with a crunchy chocolate candy topping. For this recipe, I used Hershey's Skor candy bars, but other brands of chocolate-covered toffee will do fine. Cut this tart in small pieces—it's sinfully rich.

At a Glance

SERVES: 8 to 10

PAN: 11-inch metal tart

PASTRY PREP: Baked

DIFFICULTY:

---

1 11-inch Chocolate Tart Pastry crust (page 148), baked

CHOCOLATE CUSTARD
1 1/2 cups milk
1 cup light cream
2 large egg yolks
1 large egg
1/2 cup sugar
1/8 teaspoon salt
2 tablespoons cornstarch
2 tablespoons unsifted all-purpose flour
4 ounces bittersweet chocolate, finely chopped
1 ounce unsweetened chocolate, finely chopped
2 teaspoons vanilla extract

CHOCOLATE CANDY TOPPING
1 cup heavy cream, well chilled
3/4 cup chopped chocolate-covered toffee candy, in 1/8-inch pieces (3 bars)
1 teaspoon vanilla extract

---

1. MAKE THE CHOCOLATE CUSTARD: Scald the milk and cream in a medium saucepan and set aside. Whisk the egg yolks and whole egg together in a large bowl. Gradually add the sugar, beating until the mixture is thick and light in color. Whisk in the salt, cornstarch, and flour. Temper the egg mixture by adding about a third of the hot milk to the eggs, then pour the egg mixture back into the saucepan. Stir continuously over low heat until the mixture comes to a boil and thickens. At the boiling point, whisk until smooth. Be sure to reach into the bend of the saucepan. Simmer the custard for about 1 minute.

2. Remove from the heat and stir in the chocolates. Let stand for a few minutes to melt the chocolate, add the vanilla, and gently mix. Remove 3/4 cup custard and place into a large bowl. Cover the custard in the bowl with a piece of buttered plastic wrap. Do not refrigerate. Pour the remaining hot custard into the pastry shell and smooth the top. Refrigerate until almost cool, about 45 minutes.

3. MAKE THE CHOCOLATE CANDY TOPPING: Using a chilled bowl and chilled beaters, whip the cream to soft peaks. Using a whisk, blend a third of the whipped cream into the reserved chocolate custard. Fold in the remaining cream, 1/2 cup candy, and vanilla. Spoon over the custard layer. Smooth the top. Using a decorator's pastry comb or the tines of a fork, make zigzag lines across the top of the tart .

4. Chill the tart for 3 to 4 hours. Just before serving, garnish the top of the tart with the remaining candy.

STORAGE

Cover any leftover tart with an aluminum foil tent and refrigerate for up to 3 days. Freezing is not recommended.

Chocolate Cream Pie in a Nutty Cornmeal Crust

WHEN MY CHILDREN WERE GROWING UP, one of their biggest treats was Mom's chocolate cream pie, piled high with whipped cream and chocolate shavings. It seems this kind of comfort food never goes out of style as it's number one with my grandchildren as well.

Although I used to make this pie with a graham cracker crumb crust, my 1990s version has a crispy cornmeal and nut pastry. Whatever your preference, this timeless favorite is one that appeals to all ages.

1 9-inch Nutty Cornmeal Crust (page 154), baked

FILLING
2½ cups milk
¼ cup heavy cream
⅔ cup granulated sugar
4 large egg yolks
3 tablespoons unsifted all-purpose flour
2 tablespoons cornstarch
¼ teaspoon salt
3 ounces bittersweet chocolate, finely chopped
1 ounce unsweetened chocolate, finely chopped
1 tablespoon unsalted butter, at room temperature
1½ teaspoons vanilla extract

GARNISH
1 cup heavy cream, well chilled
1 tablespoon strained confectioners' sugar
½ teaspoon vanilla extract
Chocolate shavings (see page 455)

1. **MAKE THE FILLING:** Place the milk, cream, and ⅓ cup of the sugar in a large saucepan and stir to blend. Cook over low heat without stirring until the mixture is just under the boil or until a skin forms on the surface. Remove from the heat and set aside.

2. Beat the yolks in a large bowl with a hand mixer or whisk until light in color, about 1 minute. Add the remaining ⅓ cup sugar, 1 tablespoon at a time, and beat until thick and light. Combine the flour, cornstarch, and salt, and stir into the yolk mixture.

3. Temper the egg mixture by adding about a quarter of the hot milk-cream to the yolks, stirring well to blend. Pour the yolk mixture into the saucepan and, using a whisk, blend the mixtures.

4. Bring the mixture to a boil over low heat, stirring constantly with a whisk. As it begins to thicken, stir more vigorously, mixing until smooth. Be sure to reach into the bend of the saucepan. After it reaches the boil, continue to cook the pastry cream for about 1 minute, mixing *gently* to prevent the cream from scorching on the bottom of the saucepan. Do not overmix after the boil.

5. Remove from the heat. Add the chocolates. Let stand about 1 minute to melt the chocolate. Then stir gently until thoroughly blended and smooth. Strain the pastry cream through a fine-mesh strainer into a bowl. Blend in the butter and vanilla.

6. Empty the warm filling into the baked pie shell. Smooth the surface with an offset spatula. Butter a round of plastic wrap and invert it on top of the chocolate pastry cream, pressing it against the surface. Refrigerate for at least 4 hours.

7. GARNISH THE PIE: With a chilled bowl and chilled beaters, whip the cream, confectioners' sugar, and vanilla on medium speed until the cream is thick. Empty the whipped cream into a 16-inch pastry bag fitted with a #824 large open star tip. Remove the plastic wrap from the top of the pie. Pipe overlapping rosettes in rows on top of the pie, completely covering the filling. Garnish with chocolate shavings. Chill until ready to serve.

STORAGE
Cover any leftover pie with an aluminum foil tent and store in the refrigerator for up to 3 days. Freezing is not recommended.

Meringue-Topped Coconut Pie in Coconut Crust

I WAS FIRST INTRODUCED TO this pie by a neighbor of mine, Joyce Stitch, when I lived in Red Bank, New Jersey. Joyce was always a very fine baker. In later years, she turned to catering and baked her outstanding pies for local restaurants.

Joyce's recipe for coconut pie was a favorite of mine then and still is today. While I prefer to make the pastry cream with a vanilla bean, you can substitute vanilla extract if you wish. The crust and filling can be made ahead, but because I love to eat this pie when the filling is slightly warm, I usually make the meringue topping close to eating time.

1 9-inch Toasted Coconut Pie
    Pastry crust (page 136), baked

FILLING

1¹/₂ cups milk
1 cup light cream
¹/₂ cup granulated sugar
4-inch piece of vanilla bean, split
    down the middle, or 1¹/₂
    teaspoons vanilla extraxt
4 large egg yolks
3 tablespoons unsifted all-purpose
    flour
2 tablespoons cornstarch
¹/₄ teaspoon salt
1 tablespoon unsalted butter, at
    room temperature
1 cup sweetened flaked coconut,
    chopped into ¹/₄-inch pieces

MERINGUE

¹/₃ cup superfine sugar
2 tablespoons plus 2 teaspoons
    strained confectioners' sugar
4 large egg whites
¹/₂ teaspoon cream of tartar

1. MAKE THE FILLING: Place the milk, cream, ¹/₄ cup sugar, and the vanilla bean in a large saucepan. Heat without stirring until a skin forms on the surface. Remove the vanilla bean. Split the bean in half lengthwise and use a small knife to scrape out the seeds. Whisk the seeds into the hot milk-cream mixture.

2. Beat the yolks in a large bowl with a hand mixer or whisk until light in color, about 1 minute. Add the remaining ¹/₄ cup sugar, 1 tablespoon at a time, and beat until thick and light in color. Combine the flour, cornstarch, and salt, and stir into the yolk mixture.

3. Temper the egg mixture by adding about a quarter of the hot milk to the yolks, stirring well to blend. Pour the yolk mixture into the saucepan, and using a whisk, blend the mixtures.

4. Bring the mixture to a boil over low heat, stirring constantly with a whisk. As it begins to thicken, stir more vigorously, mixing until smooth. Be sure to reach into the bend of the saucepan. After it reaches the boil, continue to cook the pastry cream for about 1 minute, mixing *gently* to prevent the cream from scorching on the bottom of the saucepan. Do not overmix after the boil. Remove from the heat. Dot the top of the pastry cream with butter and set aside for 15 minutes.

5. Reserve 2 tablespoons of coconut for a garnish. Fold the remaining coconut into the pastry cream. If using extract, add it now. Pour the filling into the pastry shell and smooth the top with a back of a tablespoon. Refrigerate for at least 1 hour or until you are ready to make the meringue.

6. MAKE THE MERINGUE: Preheat the oven to 350 degrees. Position the oven rack in the lower third of the oven. Strain the superfine and confectioners' sugar together 4 times.

7. In the large bowl of an electric mixer fitted with beaters or whip attachment, beat the egg whites on medium speed until frothy. Add the cream of tartar and increase the mixer speed to medium-high. Beat until the egg whites form firm peaks. Add the sugars, 1 tablespoon at a time, taking about 1 minute. Continue to beat the whites about 30 seconds longer, or until thick and glossy.

8. Using a large tablespoon, drop mounds of meringue in a ring around the edge of the filling. Then fill in the center. With the back of a tablespoon, spread the meringue to cover the filling completely. Swirl the meringue with the back of the tablespoon to form peaks. Sprinkle the top with the reserved toasted coconut, pressing it gently into the meringue. Bake the pie for 12 to 15 minutes, or until the meringue is lightly brown. Cool away from drafts.

STORAGE
Cover any leftover pie with an aluminum foil tent and refrigerate for up to 2 days. Freezing is not recommended.

He who plants a coconut tree, plants vessels and clothing, food and drink, a habitation for himself and a heritage for his children.

SOUTH SEAS
SAYING

Fluted Cream Cheese Flan
with Fresh Berries

HERE IS AN UPSIDE-DOWN, crustless cheese tart that resembles a flan. The filling is made with a combination of cream cheese and crème fraîche, a thick, slightly cultured heavy cream available in some gourmet shops and upscale supermarkets. The moist, velvety texture comes from baking the tart in a water bath. Be careful not to overbeat the filling, as too much air may cause it to crack during baking.

When I'm ready to serve the flan, I mound lots of fresh berries in the center and top them with raspberry coulis. I like the sauce to drip down the scalloped edge of the tart. The presentation is gorgeous, and it's sheer heaven to eat.

FILLING
1 pound cream cheese, at room temperature
2/3 cup superfine sugar
4 large eggs, separated
2/3 cup crème fraîche (1/3 cup heavy cream plus 1/3 cup sour cream can be substituted)
1 teaspoon vanilla extract

TOPPING
3 to 4 cups mixed berries, washed and thoroughly dried
1 recipe Raspberry Coulis (page 448)
A few fresh mint leaves, for garnish

1. MAKE THE FILLING: Preheat the oven to 325 degrees. Position the oven rack in the lower third of the oven. Generously butter a deep 10-inch tart pan. Line the bottom of the pan with baking parchment. Butter the parchment. Have some boiling water ready in a tea kettle.

2. Place the cream cheese and sugar in the large bowl of an electric mixer fitted with the paddle attachment. Cream the cheese and sugar on low speed until light. Blend in the egg yolks, 2 at a time. Add the crème fraîche and vanilla, mixing just until smooth. Empty the batter into a large bowl.

3. In a separate, clean bowl, whip the egg whites until they stand in firm peaks. Fold the whites into the cheese mixture. Pour the batter into the prepared pan.

4. Set the pan on an 18-inch square of aluminum foil. Trim the corners of the foil with scissors, then mold it around the pan. Be careful not to tear the foil. Set the tart pan into a roasting pan about 2 1/2 inches deep. Place both in the oven. Fill the roasting pan with 1 inch of boiling water.

5. Bake the tart for 45 to 50 minutes, until set around the edges. It is okay if it is somewhat soft in the center. It will firm as it cools. Turn the oven off. Wedge a wooden spoon handle in the door of the oven and then close the door. This will allow some of the hot air to escape and let the tart cool down slowly.

6. After 1 hour, remove the tart from the oven and set on a rack to cool further. When it is completely cool, invert it onto a serving plate. Shake gently to release it from the pan (see Note). Peel off the parchment liner. If necessary, smooth the top with an offset spatula dipped in hot water. Cover with plastic wrap and refrigerate until ready to serve. This tart can be made up to 4 days ahead.

7. PREPARE THE TOPPING: When ready to serve, mound the berries in the center of the tart, leaving a 1 1/2-inch border. Spoon the raspberry coulis at random over the berries. Garnish with mint leaves and serve at once.

NOTE

If the tart is difficult to release from the pan, mold a piece of heavy-duty aluminum foil tightly around the bottom of the pan, then place it in a sink filled with 1 inch of warm water for 1 to 2 minutes, and try again. Repeat if necessary.

STORAGE

Cover any leftover tart with waxed paper then aluminum foil and refrigerate for up to 1 day. This tart can be frozen, without the berries and coulis.

Creamy Green Grape Pie

MANY YEARS AGO, I JUDGED a pie-baking contest for Steinbach's Department Store in Asbury Park, New Jersey. The grand prize entry was an unusual grape pie made with canned green grapes. While delicious, it was extremely sweet. My variation uses fresh green grapes and less sugar. The final result has received rave reviews from my students. This pie has an attractive lattice top that is sprinkled with sliced almonds. However, if you wish, it can be made in a regular double-crust.

At a Glance

SERVES: 6 to 8

PAN: 9-inch
ovenproof glass

PASTRY PREP: Unbaked

OVEN TEMP: 400 degrees

BAKING TIME:
45 to 50 minutes

DIFFICULTY: 🥧

1 small recipe Flaky Pie Pastry
    (pages 98, 100)
1 large egg white
1 teaspoon water

FILLING
2 1/2 cups (3/4 pound) seedless green
    grapes
1/2 cup sugar
1/4 cup unsifted all-purpose flour
1 cup heavy cream
1/2 teaspoon vanilla extract

TOPPING
2 tablespoons sliced almonds
1 to 2 teaspoons sugar

1. Preheat the oven to 400 degrees. Position the oven rack in the lower third of the oven. Butter a 9-inch ovenproof glass pie plate.

2. MAKE THE PIE: On a floured pastry cloth, roll 1 disk of pastry into a circle measuring approximately 13 inches. Fit loosely into the pie plate. Trim the edge, leaving a 1/2-inch overhang. Beat the egg white and water lightly with a fork. Brush the dough with the egg white. Reserve the remaining white for glazing the top crust.

3. Wash and thoroughly dry the grapes (page 26).

4. Combine the sugar and flour in a small mixing bowl. Slowly add the cream, blending until smooth. Mix in the vanilla. Arrange the grapes in the bottom of the prepared pie plate. Pour the cream mixture over the fruit.

5. Make a lattice top with the remaining pastry as follows: Roll the remaining pastry into a 13-inch circle. Using a pastry wheel, divide the pastry into twelve 3/4-inch strips. Evenly space the pastry, starting with the 2 longer strips placed to the left and right of the center, about 3/4 inch apart. Continue, using 2 more strips on either side, saving the shortest strips for the outer edge. Rotate the pie 90 degrees. Repeat the process, weaving new strips over and under the initial strips (see "Making Lattice Crusts," page 65). Trim, leaving a 1-inch overhang. Fold the ends under. Press with your fingers to seal, then flute the edge (see page 66).

6. Brush the top with the remaining egg white, then sprinkle almonds and sugar over the top.

7. To prevent the edges from burning, make aluminum foil bands. Cut two 3-inch-wide strips of 18-inch heavy-duty aluminum foil. Fold 1 inch of each strip to the center, making a double thickness of foil. Mold the foil around the edge of the pie keeping the double fold on top of the dough. Be careful not to crush the edge of the pastry. Secure the bands with tape, and place it in the oven.

8. Bake the pie for 35 minutes and remove the aluminum foil bands. Bake 10 to 15 minutes longer or until the bottom and top crusts are golden brown. Cool on a rack. Let stand at least 3 hours before serving.

STORAGE
Cover any leftover pie with an aluminum foil tent and refrigerate for up to 3 days. Freezing is not recommended.

Lemon Cream Tart with Candied Peel

IF YOU WANT TO IMPRESS your guests with an exquisite dessert, place this tart on your priority list. A piquant lemon filling, lightened with whipped cream, rests on a delicate sweet tart pastry. The decorated top has whipped cream piped into a lattice design and is finished with glittering candied lemon peel.

At a Glance

SERVES: 8 to 10

PAN: 11-inch metal tart

PASTRY PREP: Baked

DIFFICULTY: 🥿🥿

---

1 11-inch *Sweet Tart Pastry crust (page 146), baked*

CANDIED PEEL
Zest of 2 lemons, cut into tiny slivers
1/2 cup water
2 tablespoons plus 2 teaspoons granulated sugar

LEMON FILLING
6 large egg yolks
3/4 cup granulated sugar
1/4 teaspoon salt
1/2 cup fresh lemon juice
1 tablespoon water
1/2 teaspoon unflavored gelatin
1 cup heavy cream, well chilled
1/2 teaspoon vanilla extract

GARNISH
2/3 cup heavy cream, well chilled
2 tablespoons strained confectioners' sugar
1/2 teaspoon vanilla extract

---

1. **MAKE THE CANDIED PEEL:** Boil the water and blanch the lemon slivers for 4 to 5 minutes. Pour off the water into a measuring cup. Measure 1/4 cup liquid and return it to the saucepan. Add 2 tablespoons of sugar, bring to a boil, and simmer 5 minutes. Add the lemon slivers to the sugar syrup and simmer until glazed and transparent, about 5 minutes.

2. Use a fork to remove the peel from the syrup and place on several layers of paper towels to dry, separating them as best you can. Reserve the lemon syrup. Sprinkle the slivers with the remaining 2 teaspoons sugar, tossing them lightly with a fork to coat on all sides. Set aside to dry.

3. MAKE THE FILLING: Whisk the egg yolks in the top of a double boiler. Add the sugar gradually, then the salt. Stir in the lemon juice. Place over boiling water. Cook slowly, stirring constantly, until thickened. Remove from the heat, cover with a sheet of buttered plastic wrap or waxed paper, and set aside to cool. Refrigerate for 30 minutes.

4. Place the tablespoon of water in a small heatproof dish. Sprinkle the gelatin over the surface. Do not stir. Let stand 5 minutes to soften. Set the dish in a small skillet filled with ½ inch of simmering water. Heat the gelatin in the water bath until it is clear and dissolved. Cool to *tepid*.

5. In a chilled bowl with chilled beaters, beat the cream on medium speed. When it begins to thicken, pour in the gelatin and vanilla. Beat until it is thick. Fold the cream into the lemon filling along with the reserved lemon syrup. Spoon into the baked tart shell. Smooth the top with the back of the spoon and refrigerate for at least 4 hours.

6. MAKE THE GARNISH: In a chilled bowl with chilled beaters, beat the cream on medium speed. When it starts to thicken, add the confectioners' sugar and vanilla. Continue beating until the cream is firm. *Do not overbeat.*

7. Spoon the whipped cream into a 16-inch pastry bag fitted with a large #824 large open star tip. Pipe the cream in a lattice design. Just before serving, sprinkle the top of the tart with the candied lemon peel.

STORAGE

Store any leftover tart in the refrigerator covered with a piece of waxed paper topped with aluminum foil for up to 2 days. Freezing is not recommended.

The lemon has flavor power. It sharpens the sweet, perks up the bland and enlivens the pallid.

THE BUYING GUIDE FOR FRESH FRUITS, VEGETABLES, HERBS AND NUTS

Key Lime Pie

SURELY KEY LIME PIE IS HIGH on the list of classic American pies. After researching more than a dozen sources, I find that the origin of this recipe remains a mystery. Many tales exist, but I cannot vouch for their authenticity.

One thing is fact: The pie is made with a graham cracker cookie crust and the filling from only three ingredients—Key lime juice, egg yolks, and sweetened condensed milk—used in varying amounts according to the source. Some recipes call for leaving the filling uncooked—just chilling it until the custard is set. I don't care for this method because the filling is very soft, which makes the pie difficult to slice. Others suggest baking the pie for a few minutes to firm the filling.

Joe's Stone Crab restaurant in Miami Beach, Florida, renowned for its Key lime pie, partially freezes the pie, which makes it easier to cut and gives it a pleasant frosty texture.

The following recipe is adapted from those I researched along with my own practical approach. While partially freezing the pie is an alternative, baking the filling before chilling is the method that wins hands down in my book. If fresh Key limes are not available, do what most professional bakers do: buy the juice. Look for a widely available brand called Nellie and Joe's "Famous" Key West Lime Juice. If this juice is difficult to find, regular Persian lime juice can be substituted.

Key lime pie can be finished with whipped cream or topped with meringue. The whipped cream can be made up to 2 days in advance, while a baked meringue should be made within 2 to 3 hours of serving.

1 9-inch Master Crumb Crust made with graham cracker crumbs (page 164), baked

FILLING

3 large egg yolks

1 (14-ounce) can sweetened condensed milk

1/2 cup fresh or bottled Key lime juice

2 teaspoons grated lime zest

TOPPING

1 cup heavy cream, well chilled

2 tablespoons strained confectioners' sugar

1/4 teaspoon vanilla extract

1 Persian lime, for garnish

1. **MAKE THE FILLING:** Preheat the oven to 325 degrees. Position the oven rack in the lower third of the oven.

2. Place the yolks in the large bowl of an electric mixer. Using the whip attachment, beat the yolks on medium speed until light in color.

3. Increase the speed to medium high. Slowly add the condensed milk and beat the mixture for 4 to 5 minutes. Reduce the speed to medium. Add the lime juice and zest and continue to beat until well blended.

4. Pour the filling into the crumb shell. Bake for 15 minutes, or until the center of the filling feels set when touched with your finger. Cool on a rack, then refrigerate. (The pie can be made up to this point up to 3 days in advance.)

5. **MAKE THE TOPPING:** In a chilled bowl with chilled beaters, whip the cream on medium speed until it starts to thicken. Add the confectioners' sugar and vanilla. Beat until firm peaks are formed.

6. Empty the cream into a 16-inch pastry bag fitted with a #824 large open star tip. Starting at the edge of the filling, pipe 1-inch rosettes, making a circle around the plate. Pipe a second row of rosettes, having them touch the first row, then pipe a third row, continuing until the entire surface is covered with rosettes. Insert small wedges of lime, peel side up, into the rosettes at random on top of the pie. Refrigerate until ready to use.

STORAGE

Cover any leftover pie with an aluminum foil tent and refrigerate for up to 5 days. This pie can be frozen for up to 3 months.

Melon and Mascarpone Tart in Chocolate Crumb Crust

WHEN I TOOK A BAKING COURSE at the Culinary Institute of America a few summers ago, my instructor, Chef Peter Greweling, taught a recipe for an unusual individual pastry that had a filling made from mascarpone, an Italian-style cream cheese, and whipped cream. It was covered with cantaloupe and honeydew balls that were topped with a cream sherry jelly. My version of this elegant dessert is a tart with a chocolate crumb crust. The result is terrific. The tart can be made a day ahead, which is a great advantage when entertaining.

At a Glance

SERVES: 8 to 10

PAN: 11-inch metal tart

PASTRY PREP: Baked

DIFFICULTY: 🥄 🥄

1 11-inch Chocolate Crumb Crust (page 168), baked

FILLING
9 ounces mascarpone cheese (see Note)
1/3 cup strained confectioners' sugar
3/4 cup heavy cream, well chilled
1 teaspoon vanilla extract

TOPPING
1 small ripe cantaloupe
1/2 firm honeydew
2 tablespoons water
1 1/4 teaspoons unflavored gelatin
1/2 cup cream sherry
3 tablespoons sliced almonds, toasted and crushed
Fresh mint leaves, for garnish

1. MAKE THE FILLING: Place the mascarpone cheese in a medium bowl. Gently blend in the confectioners' sugar.

2. In a chilled bowl with chilled beaters, beat the cream with the vanilla until soft mounds form. Do not overbeat.

3. Using a rubber spatula, slowly fold the cream into the mascarpone, blending until the mixture is smooth. Be careful not to overmix or the mixture will separate. Empty into the cooled pie shell and smooth the surface with the back of a tablespoon. Chill while preparing the topping.

4. PREPARING THE TOPPING:
Line a jelly-roll pan with a double thickness of paper towels. Using a 7/8- to 1-inch melon baller, make about 50 cantaloupe and 50 honeydew melon balls. Place them on the paper towels to remove excess moisture. The balls do not have to be completely round. Before using, blot the tops of the balls with additional paper towels.

5. Starting at the outer edge of the tart pan, arrange the melon balls in rings over the mascarpone filling. Place the balls with the rounded side on top.

6. Put the water in a small heatproof container. Sprinkle the gelatin over the surface. Do not stir. Let stand for 3 to 5 minutes to soften. Place the container in a small skillet filled with 1/2 inch simmering water. Heat in the water bath until the gelatin is clear and dissolved. Stir in the sherry.

7. Set the bowl with the gelatin in an ice-water bath. Stir the gelatin until it begins to set, about 5 minutes. Spoon the gelatin evenly over the melon balls. If the gelatin becomes too congealed, reheat for a few seconds in the microwave or a warm water bath.

8. While the gelatin is still soft, garnish the tart with a 1-inch border of crushed toasted almonds around the edge, then refrigerate for 3 to 4 hours. When ready to serve, trim with a few sprigs of fresh mint leaves.

NOTE
Mascarpone can be purchased at most upscale Italian grocery stores, cheese stores, or specialty food shops.

STORAGE
Lay a strip of aluminum foil or waxed paper loosely over the top of any leftover tart. Store in the refrigerator for up to 3 days. Freezing is not recommended.

Cinnamon Crumbs and Plums Tart

THIS TART HAS AN IRRESISTIBLE COMBINATION of flavors and textures—sweet pastry cream with tart plums, topped with crunchy, baked-cinnamon-flavored crumbs. The skin and flesh of the plums marble the creamy custard with a rosy pink hue.

1 11-inch *Sweet Tart Pastry crust*
    (page 146)

PASTRY CREAM
1^1/$_2$ cups milk
4 tablespoons granulated sugar
1 large egg
1 large egg yolk
3 tablespoons cornstarch
1 tablespoon unsalted butter, at
    room temperature
1 teaspoon vanilla extract

FILLING
1^1/$_4$ pounds Black Diamond or
    other dark purple plums
    (about 5 or 6)
2 tablespoons granulated sugar

CINNAMON CRUMB TOPPING
^{1}/$_4$ cup unsalted butter
1 cup unsifted cake flour
^{1}/$_8$ teaspoon baking powder
^{1}/$_3$ cup granulated sugar
3 tablespoons lightly packed light
    brown sugar
^{1}/$_2$ teaspoon ground cinnamon

1 tablespoon confectioners' sugar;
    for garnish

1. **MAKE THE PASTRY CREAM:** Place the milk and 2 tablespoons of the sugar in a medium saucepan and stir to blend. Cook over low heat without stirring until the mixture is just under the boil or until a skin forms on the surface. Remove from the heat and set aside.

2. Whisk the whole egg and the yolk in a large bowl until light in color. Add the remaining 2 tablespoons sugar, 1 tablespoon at a time, and beat until thick and light in color. Stir the cornstarch into the egg-sugar mixture.

3. Temper the egg mixture by adding about a quarter of the hot milk to the eggs, stirring well to blend. Pour the egg mixture into the saucepan and, using a whisk, blend the mixtures.

4. Bring the mixture to a boil over low heat, stirring constantly with a whisk. As it begins to thicken, stir more vigorously, mixing until smooth. Be sure to reach into the bend of the saucepan. After it reaches a boil, continue to simmer the pastry cream for about 1 minute,

mixing *gently* to prevent the cream from scorching on the bottom of the saucepan. Do not overmix after the boil.

5. Remove from the heat. Stir in the butter and vanilla. Cover the pastry cream with buttered plastic wrap. Set in an ice-water bath to cool. Empty into the pastry shell and spread evenly. Set aside while preparing the plums.

6. ASSEMBLE THE TART: Preheat the oven to 375 degrees. Position the oven rack in the lower third of the oven. Have a pastry-lined 11-inch tart pan ready.

7. Wash the plums and dry thoroughly. Cut in half and remove the pits. Lay the plums on a cutting board, cut side down. Using a sharp knife, cut the plums lengthwise in even ¼-inch slices. To arrange the plums in the tart pan, push the plums into the pastry cream, standing the slices with the skin side up. ■ Place them about ¼ inch apart and arrange them in a large circle around the outer edge of the pan. Then make a smaller circle. Fill in the center as needed. Sprinkle 2 tablespoons sugar over the top of the plums.

■

8. MAKE THE CRUMB TOPPING: Melt the butter in a large saucepan. Let stand until tepid. Add the flour, baking powder, sugars, and cinnamon to the cooled butter. Combine with a pastry blender or fork. Take a clump of the crumb mixture in your hand and squeeze gently to form a larger clump. Then break apart over the plums. Repeat, using all the crumb mixture. (The tart can be made up to this point up to 24 hours in advance. Lightly cover with aluminum foil or waxed paper and store in the refrigerator until ready to bake. The baking time may need to be increased by 5 to 10 minutes.)

9. Set the tart on an aluminum foil–lined cookie sheet and bake for 40 to 45 minutes, or until the crust and crumbs are golden brown and the filling is bubbly. If crumbs are browning too quickly, lay a piece of aluminum foil loosely over the top. When the tart is done, set on a rack and cool for 3 to 4 hours.

10. Just before serving, place the confectioners' sugar in a fine strainer and sprinkle it over the top of the tart.

STORAGE
Cover any leftover tart with an aluminum foil tent and store in the refrigerator for up to 3 days. Freezing is not recommended.

Little Jack Horner sat in the corner, eating a Christmas pie. He put in his thumb, and pulled out a plum, And said, "What a good boy am I!"

Hall of Fame Raspberry Streusel Tart

WHEN I WAS IN VIENNA, AUSTRIA, I visited Oberlaa, one of the most extraordinary pastry factories in the world. I had never seen desserts of such quality mass-produced. One of the pastries that intrigued me most was a raspberry tart topped with crunchy streusel. Instead of the berries covering a cold pastry cream, they were placed on top of hot custard. The berries on the bottom melted into the custard, cooking them slightly. Mounded over the berries was a prebaked buttery streusel topping. The combination of flavors and textures sent my taste buds into orbit. This tart has been inducted into my personal "Hall of Fame: The Ten Best Desserts."

At a Glance

SERVES: 8 to 10

PAN: 11-inch metal tart

PASTRY PREP: Baked

OVEN TEMP: 375 degrees

BAKING TIME: 20 to 25 minutes

DIFFICULTY: 🥄 🥄

1 11-inch *Sweet Tart Pastry crust (page 146), baked*

STREUSEL
6 tablespoons unsalted butter
1¼ cups unsifted all-purpose flour
6 tablespoons granulated sugar
¼ teaspoon ground cinnamon
⅛ teaspoon salt

CUSTARD FILLING
1¾ cups light cream
⅓ cup granulated sugar
4 teaspoons cornstarch
1 tablespoon all-purpose flour
4 large egg yolks
1 tablespoon unsalted butter
1 teaspoon vanilla extract
1 tablespoon framboise or kirschwasser

GLAZE
⅔ cup thick currant, apricot, or seedless raspberry preserves
1 to 2 tablespoons water
2 to 3 pints fresh raspberries washed and dried (page 37) (about 3 cups)

2 to 3 tablespoons strained confectioners' sugar, for garnish

1. **MAKE THE STREUSEL:** Preheat the oven to 350 degrees. Place the butter in a medium saucepan and slowly melt. Cool until tepid. Combine the flour, sugar, cinnamon, and salt and add to the melted butter. Toss with a fork until crumbs are formed. Take a clump of the crumb mixture in your hand and squeeze gently to form a larger clump. Then break the larger clump apart, and sprinkle

the crumbs onto a large shallow pan. Repeat until all the mixture has been made into crumbs.

2. Place the crumbs in the oven and bake for 15 to 18 minutes or until they turn light brown. Set aside to cool and harden.

3. MAKE THE CUSTARD. Heat the cream in a 2-quart saucepan until just under the boil.

4. In a medium-size mixing bowl, using a wire whisk, whip the egg yolks until slightly thickened. Whisk in the sugar, 1 tablespoon at a time. Stir in the cornstarch and flour. Stir in $\frac{1}{3}$ of the scalded cream, blend well, then add the remaining cream. Pour the mixture back into the saucepan, and heat slowly, stirring constantly with a wooden spoon until the mixture begins to thicken and come to a boil. Be sure to reach into the bend of the pot to release any custard that may stick. When the custard begins to boil, *immediately* stir it vigorously with a whisk to smooth any lumps, then simmer about 1 minute. Remove from the heat. Stir in the butter, vanilla, and framboise. Cover with a piece of buttered plastic wrap. Cool about 10 minutes.

5. *Increase the oven temperature to 375 degrees.* Spread the custard in the pastry shell and bake for 20 to 25 minutes or until bubbly. Remove it from the oven and let it stand on a rack for 10 minutes to set.

6. MAKE THE GLAZE: Combine the preserves and water in a small saucepan and heat until the mixture comes to a boil. Pass through a fine-mesh strainer. Discard pulp.

7. ASSEMBLE THE TART: Gently brush the top of the custard with half of the *hot* preserves. Sprinkle the berries generously over the hot custard. Lightly brush the tops of the berries with the remaining preserves, then sprinkle the tart generously with the streusel, pressing the crumbs gently into the berries so they will adhere. Chill the tart, uncovered, for about 2 hours to set. Just before serving, dust the streusel generously with confectioners' sugar.

STORAGE
Cover any leftover tart lightly with an aluminum foil tent and refrigerate for up to 2 days. Freezing is not recommended.

Chocolate Ripple Ricotta Tart

THIS ATTRACTIVE TART HAS A LAYER of bittersweet chocolate rippling through a creamy ricotta filling. It is decorated with an eye-catching border of shaved chocolate, candied orange rind, and toasted almonds.

The filling for this tart is somewhat thin. Because of this, the layer of shaved chocolate will tend to float to the surface. The secret to covering the bits of chocolate is to pour the batter over the chocolate using a container with a spout (a 1-quart measuring cup works perfectly). As you pour, work from the outer edge to the center.

1 11-inch Almond Nut Pastry crust (page 151), baked

FILLING
1 pound whole-milk ricotta cheese
4 ounces cream cheese, at room temperature
3/4 cup sugar
1 tablespoon grated navel or Valencia orange zest
1 1/2 teaspoons grated lemon zest
3/4 cup sour cream
3 large eggs
1 tablespoon Grand Marnier liqueur
1 teaspoon vanilla extract
1 1/2 ounces bittersweet chocolate, shaved

GARNISH
1/2 recipe Candied Citrus Zest, made with orange (page 456)
1/2 ounce bittersweet chocolate, thinly shaved
2 tablespoons sliced almonds, lightly toasted

1. MAKE THE FILLING: To drain the ricotta cheese, spread the cheese to 1/4-inch thickness on a double layer of high-quality paper towels. Lay another double thickness of paper towels over the ricotta and pat gently. Let stand 15 minutes to absorb excess moisture.

2. Preheat the oven to 350 degrees. Position the oven rack in the lower third of the oven.

3. Place the cream cheese, sugar, and the orange and lemon zests in the large bowl of an electric mixer fitted with the paddle attachment. On low speed, cream the mixture until smooth. Add the drained ricotta and sour cream. Mix just until smooth. Add the eggs, 1 at a time, mixing just until incorporated. Flavor with the Grand Marnier and vanilla.

4. Empty the mixture into a 1-quart measuring cup or a water pitcher. Place the pastry shell on a cookie sheet. Pour about half of the batter into the pastry shell. Sprinkle the shaved chocolate over the batter. Pour the remaining batter over the chocolate, starting around the edge of the pan. Go completely around the outer perimeter of the tart pan, then fill in the center. It's okay if some of the chocolate peeks through.

5. Bake the tart for 30 minutes. Do not overbake or it will become too dry. Turn off the oven. Wedge a wooden spoon handle into the oven door to allow some of the hot air to escape and let the tart cool down slowly. After 1 hour, remove the tart from the oven and place it on a rack to finish cooling.

6. GARNISH THE TART; Sprinkle the outer edge of the tart with the candied orange rind, shaved chocolate, and sliced almonds, forming a 1-inch border.

STORAGE

Cover any leftover tart with an aluminum foil tent and refrigerate for up to 4 days. If you wish to freeze this tart, do so before garnishing.

Sweet Risotto and Orange Tart

IMAGINE CREAMY RICE PUDDING BLENDED with bits of orange flesh on a crunchy almond crust. That's what we have here. This is a new twist on an old favorite, and is it delicious.

Be sure to use arborio rice. This high-starch Italian rice is essential to the creamy texture of the pudding. It is available in most supermarkets where ethnic ingredients are stocked or in an Italian specialty food store. Although this tart can be garnished with whipped cream, I like it best served slightly warm with a meringue topping.

1 11-inch Almond Nut Pastry crust (page 151), baked
2 tablespoons orange marmalade, warmed

FILLING
1¹/4 cups water
Pinch of salt
¹/2 cup arborio rice
2¹/2 cups milk
3 4-inch strips of orange zest
¹/2 cup granulated sugar
3 large egg yolks
¹/4 cup cornstarch
1¹/2 teaspoons vanilla extract
1 tablespoon unsalted butter
2 small navel oranges, supremed (page 59)

MERINGUE
4 tablespoons superfine sugar
2 tablespoons strained confectioners' sugar
3 large egg whites, at room temperature
¹/4 teaspoon cream of tartar
¹/2 teaspoon vanilla extract

1. Brush the baked pastry shell with marmalade while it is still warm.

2. MAKE THE FILLING: Place water and salt in a small, heavy saucepan. Stir in the rice. Bring to a slow boil and simmer uncovered, stirring frequently, for 16 to 18 minutes or until the rice is tender and the liquid has been absorbed.

3. In a separate medium saucepan, heat the milk with the orange zest and ¹/4 cup of the sugar until a skin forms on the surface. Place the egg yolks in a large bowl, and gradually whisk in the remaining ¹/4 cup sugar, beating until the mixture thickens and lightens in color. Blend in the cornstarch.

4. Remove the orange zest from the milk. Gradually add the hot milk to the yolks, and stir with a whisk until blended. Return the mixture to the saucepan. Bring to a slow boil over medium-low heat, stirring constantly with a wooden spoon. When the pastry cream begins to thicken, whisk until thick and smooth. Blend in the rice and cook 2 to 3 minutes, stirring gently. Remove from the heat; blend in the vanilla and butter.

5. Dice the orange flesh into 1/4-inch pieces and fold into the rice. Spoon the mixture into the pastry shell.

NOTE
If using whipped cream, chill pie until set. Prepare Whipped Cream (page 450) and, if desired, garnish top with 2 tablespoons of lightly toasted sliced almonds.

6. MAKE THE MERINGUE: Preheat the oven to 350 degrees. Position the oven rack in the lower third of the oven.

7. Sift the superfine and confectioners' sugars together 3 times through a fine-mesh strainer.

8. Place the egg whites in the large bowl of an electric mixer fitted with beaters or whip attachment. Beat on medium speed until the whites are frothy. Add the cream of tartar. Increase the speed to medium-high and continue to beat until the whites form firm moist peaks but are not dry. Add the sugars, 1 tablespoon at a time, over about 1 minute. Add the vanilla and beat until thick and glossy, about 30 seconds.

9. Drop mounds of meringue in a ring around the edge of the filling, then fill in the center. Using the back of a tablespoon, spread the meringue to cover the filling completely. Swirl the meringue with the back of the spoon to form peaks on the surface.

10. Bake the tart for 10 to 12 minutes or until the meringue is lightly browned. Place on a cooling rack away from drafts.

STORAGE
The tart will keep for up to 2 hours at room temperature. For longer storage, cover loosely with an aluminum foil tent and refrigerate for up to 3 days. Freezing is not recommended.

About Chiffons, Bavarians, and Mousses

CHIFFON, BAVARIAN, AND MOUSSE FILLINGS are light dessert fare that are never baked, only chilled. They form the base for a vast array of enticing pies and tarts. The magic ingredient that distinguishes these fillings from custards and pastry creams is air. It can come from whipped egg whites, whipped cream, or both. Another major player that sets these desserts apart is unflavored gelatin. Gelatin stabilizes refrigerated fillings and makes for neat slicing; it prevents fillings from deteriorating in warm environments; and it increases shelf life when do-ahead desserts are desired.

Chiffon fillings begin with a cooked custard containing gelatin, which is then lightened with beaten egg whites. Under refrigeration the gelatin stabilizes the cooked custard and airy egg whites. Classically, Bavarian creams are thickened custards fortified with gelatin and lightened with whipped cream. These fillings are very firm and hold their shape when unmolded or sliced. Bavarians can also be piled into straight-sided molds with paper collars and presented as cold soufflés.

In this era of lighter foods, I have crossed boundaries in some recipes and introduced whipped egg whites as a replacement for some of the whipped cream. Although not used in classic Bavarian preparations, the beaten egg whites allow me to reduce the richness of a filling without sacrificing flavor or volume.

Mousse preparations are variations of chiffon and Bavarian fillings, but are usually made without gelatin. All mousses contain whipped cream, and at times they are further lightened with beaten egg whites.

While chiffon fillings cannot be frozen, both Bavarian and mousse-style fillings freeze extremely well. They can be served either thawed in the refrigerator overnight or as a frozen dessert.

Though these fillings are not difficult to prepare, take care when working with the ingredients, as all of these mixtures are temperature sensitive. Here are some hints to guide you:

◆ *Temper egg yolks by adding a small amount of the hot mixture to the yolks to elevate their temperature. Warming the yolks gradually makes them blend smoothly into the cooked base.*

◆ *When separating eggs for chiffon fillings, always be sure there are no traces of egg yolk in the whites.*

✦ When beating egg whites for chiffon fillings, the whites should be whipped only to soft peaks. If they are too stiffly beaten, they will not blend smoothly into the custard.

✦ Whipped egg whites should be folded into tepid custard. If the custard is too cold, the whites will not incorporate smoothly.

✦ Gelatin should always be properly dissolved and used at the temperature indicated in the recipe.

✦ If dissolved gelatin becomes too cool and hardens, reheat it until it reaches the desired temperature.

✦ If gelatin is too cold when added to a cooked filling or whipped cream, it will bead or form strings. This is because the gelatin immediately solidifies when it comes in contact with another cool mixture. Gelatin must be warmer than the base mixture, so the two substances can bind smoothly.

✦ To cool a Bavarian base, quickly place the mixture in a bowl and set it into a larger bowl or sink partially filled with ice water.

✦ When stirring a Bavarian base, use a jumbo rubber spatula instead of a spoon. This ensures that the mixture along the bottom will be thoroughly incorporated.

✦ It is important that whipped cream be added to the Bavarian base when the base begins to thicken.

✦ When folding whipped egg whites and whipped cream into cooked fillings and Bavarian or mousse bases, it is essential that the whites and cream be the same consistency so that they will blend in smoothly. They should be whipped only to soft peaks.

✦ When beaten egg whites and whipped cream are both folded into cooked fillings and Bavarian bases, it is essential that the egg whites be folded in first, followed by the cream. Beads of gelatin can form when the cream is added first.

✦ If freezing Bavarian cream and mousse-type pies or tarts, do not decorate until just before serving.

Black Bottom Cream Pie

HERE IS A GRAND AMERICAN PIE with its roots ensconced in the Deep South. According to James Beard's *American Cookery*, the recipe first began to appear around the turn of the century.

Traditionally, black bottom pie has a double-layered custard filling. The bottom layer, made of chocolate pastry cream, is supposed to signify the black, swampy lowlands commonly found along the Mississippi River. My recipe has a chocolate crumb crust with a layer of dark chocolate custard covered with a rum-flavored chiffon-style topping. It is garnished with whipped cream and chocolate shavings.

1 9-inch Chocolate Crumb Crust (page 168), baked

CHOCOLATE PASTRY CREAM
4 large egg yolks
6 tablespoons sugar
4 teaspoons cornstarch
1 tablespoon all-purpose flour
2 cups milk, scalded
1 tablespoon dark rum
1 teaspoon vanilla extract
1 1/2 ounces semisweet chocolate, melted
1/2 ounce unsweetened chocolate, melted

CHIFFON TOPPING
2 tablespoons water
1 1/2 teaspoons unflavored gelatin
2 tablespoons dark rum
1 teaspoon vanilla extract
3 egg whites
1/4 teaspoon cream of tartar
6 tablespoons sugar
1/4 cup heavy cream, whipped to soft peaks

GARNISH
1/2 cup heavy cream, well chilled
1 ounce semisweet chocolate, shaved

1. MAKE THE PASTRY CREAM: Place the egg yolks in a large mixing bowl. Beat with a whisk. Gradually add the sugar, 1 tablespoon at a time, whisking until the mixture is thick and light in color. Blend in the cornstarch and flour, mixing until smooth. Stir in the hot milk. Cook the mixture in a heavy saucepan over medium-low heat, stirring constantly until mixture comes to a boil and is thickened. Remove from the heat and stir in the rum and vanilla.

2. Measure 1¼ cups of pastry cream and place it in a bowl. Keep the remaining pastry cream in the saucepan to use for the chiffon topping. Blend the melted chocolates into the 1¼ cups pastry cream, then empty the mixture into the cooled crust. Chill while preparing the chiffon topping.

3. MAKE THE CHIFFON TOPPING: Place the water in a small heatproof container. Sprinkle the gelatin over the top, and let stand about 5 minutes to soften. Do not stir. Then place container in a skillet filled with ½ inch of simmering water for 3 to 5 minutes, until the gelatin is clear and dissolved.

4. Over low heat, warm the remaining pastry cream. Off the heat, stir in the dissolved gelatin and blend well. Blend in the rum and vanilla.

5. Empty the pastry cream into a large mixing bowl. Set the bowl in an ice-water bath to cool the mixture. Stir occasionally. As the pastry cream cools, it will start to thicken and is ready to use. Remove the bowl from the ice while you make the meringue. *Do not let the mixture become too cold or it will overgel.*

6. Place the egg whites in the large bowl of an electric mixer fitted with beaters or whip attachment. Whip on medium speed until frothy. Add the cream of tartar. When the whites form soft peaks, add the sugar, 1 tablespoon at a time, taking about 30 seconds. Increase the speed to medium-high, and beat for 10 seconds longer, forming a soft meringue. *Do not overbeat.*

7. Fold a quarter of the meringue into the pastry cream to lighten it. Then fold in the remaining meringue and the whipped cream. Spoon the mixture on top of the chocolate layer and smooth the top as best you can, forming a mound in the center. Refrigerate for 6 to 8 hours or overnight before serving.

8. GARNISH THE PIE: In a chilled bowl with chilled beaters, whip the cream until firm peaks form. Empty into a 14-inch pastry bag fitted with a #822 large open star tip. Make a lattice design across the top. Sprinkle with the shaved chocolate.

STORAGE

Cover any leftover pie with an aluminum foil tent and refrigerate for up to 3 days. This pie cannot be frozen.

Black bottom pie is so delicate, so luscious, that I hope to be propped up on my dying bed and fed a generous portion. Then I think I should refuse outright to die, for life would be too good to relinquish.

MARJORIE KINNAN
RAWLINGS,
CROSS CREEK
COOKERY

Black Forest Cherry Tart

WHEN I WAS GROWING UP, my mother used to rave about a Black Forest Bing Cherry Tart that was the specialty of a friend of hers. I never tasted it, nor saw a recipe for it, so this is my interpretation of the dessert that she adored.

At a Glance

SERVES: 8 to 10

PAN: 11-inch metal tart

PASTRY PREP: Baked

DIFFICULTY: 🥄🥄

Traditionally, desserts named for the Black Forest region in Germany are made with chocolate, tart Morello cherries, and kirschwasser (cherry brandy). Instead of using Morello cherries, I substitute fresh Bing cherries, which I marinate in wine and sugar and then cook until thick and pulpy. The cherry pulp is folded into whipped cream and meringue and put into a chocolate pastry tart shell.

To garnish the tart, I trim the pretty pink filling with whipped cream and chocolate shavings. Mom, this one is for you.

1 11-inch Chocolate Tart Pastry crust (page 148), baked

MACERATED CHERRIES
1¼ pounds Bing cherries
½ cup medium-dry white or red wine
6 tablespoons granulated sugar

FILLING
1 tablespoon cornstarch
¼ cup water
1 (¼-ounce) package unflavored gelatin
2 tablespoons kirschwasser or Cherry Heering liqueur
1 teaspoon vanilla extract
2 large egg whites
¼ teaspoon cream of tartar
¼ cup superfine sugar
1 cup heavy cream, well chilled

GARNISH
1 ounce bittersweet chocolate, shaved
½ cup heavy cream, whipped to firm peaks
12 reserved Bing cherries with stems

1. **MACERATE THE CHERRIES:** Rinse and thoroughly dry the cherries. Remove 12 cherries with stems for garnish and set aside. Using a cherry pitter, remove the pits. Place the cherries and wine in the bowl of a food processor. Pulse cherries 4 or 5 times or until *coarsely* chopped. Empty the mixture into a bowl. Stir in the sugar, cover, and let stand about 1 hour to macerate. Strain the cherries, reserving ⅔ cup of the juice.

2. MAKE THE FILLING: Place the macerated cherries and ½ cup of the cherry juice in a medium saucepan. Cover the pot and cook over low heat until the cherries come to a slow boil. Simmer with the cover askew for 6 to 8 minutes or until the cherries are tender.

3. Dissolve the cornstarch in the remaining cherry juice. Stir into the cherries and cook the mixture over low heat, stirring constantly until it comes to a boil and thickens. Simmer 30 to 45 seconds after the boil. Empty the mixture into a large mixing bowl, preferably stainless steel.

4. Place ¼ cup water in a small heatproof dish. Sprinkle the gelatin over the surface to soften. Do not stir. Let stand 5 minutes. Set the bowl in a small skillet filled with ½ inch simmering water. Heat the gelatin in the water bath until it is clear and dissolved. Stir the gelatin into the cherry mixture. Add the kirschwasser and vanilla.

5. To quickly cool the mixture, set the bowl with the cherries in a ice-water bath. Stir occasionally with a large rubber spatula to cool evenly. When cherry mixture shows signs of thickening, immediately remove from the water bath and set aside. *Watch carefully* and do not allow the mixture to congeal.

6. Place the egg whites in the large bowl of an electric mixer fitted with beaters or whip attachment. Whip on medium speed until frothy. Add the cream of tartar. When the whites form soft peaks, add the superfine sugar, 1 tablespoon at a time, taking about 15 seconds. Increase the speed to medium-high and beat for 10 seconds longer, forming a soft meringue. *Do not overbeat.*

7. Using a chilled bowl and beaters or whip attachment, whip the cream only until it forms soft peaks.

8. Gently fold the meringue into the cherries. Then fold in the whipped cream. Spoon the mixture into the baked pastry shell, mounding it slightly. Smooth the top and chill 3 to 4 hours until set.

9. GARNISH THE TART: Unmold the tart (see page 75). Trim the edge of the tart with a 2-inch border of chocolate shavings. Pipe 12 large whipped cream rosettes on top of the shavings using a 14-inch pastry bag fitted with a #804 large round tip. Set a Bing cherry in the center of each rosette.

STORAGE

Cover any leftover tart with an aluminum foil tent and refrigerate for up to 3 days. This tart can be frozen.

Chocolate Pecan Mousse Tart

CHOCOLATE AND PECANS ARE THE SEDUCING flavors that make this tart so special. Unlike classical mousse recipes, which are bound with lots of egg yolks, this recipe uses fewer yolks and relies on gelatin to set the velvety filling. Make sure you use a fine-quality chocolate. Waistline watchers, beware! This one is hard to resist.

At a Glance

SERVES: 8 to 10

PAN: 11-inch metal tart

PASTRY PREP: Baked

DIFFICULTY: 🥄 🥄

---

1 11-inch Chocolate Tart Pastry crust (page 148), baked

FILLING
6 ounces imported bittersweet chocolate, coarsely chopped
1/2 cup milk
3 tablespoons granulated sugar
2 large eggs, separated
1 large egg yolk
2 tablespoons water
1 teaspoon unflavored gelatin
2 tablespoons Kahlúa liqueur
1 teaspoon vanilla extract
1 1/4 cups heavy cream, well chilled
2/3 cup toasted pecans, chopped medium

GARNISH
3/4 cup heavy cream, well chilled
2 tablespoons strained confectioners' sugar
1/2 teaspoon vanilla extract
1/3 cup toasted pecans, chopped medium
12 to 16 whole toasted pecans

---

1. MAKE THE FILLING: Place the chocolate, milk, and sugar in a small, heavy saucepan. Cook over low heat, stirring constantly, until the chocolate is melted and the mixture is smooth.

2. Lightly beat the 3 egg yolks with a fork. Add a third of the chocolate mixture to the yolks to temper them, then stir the yolks into the chocolate mixture. Stir constantly over low heat for 1 to 2 minutes to heat the yolks thoroughly. At the first sign of the mixture bubbling, *immediately* remove the saucepan from the heat. Whisk thoroughly to remove any lumps that may have formed around the edge.

3. Place the water in a small, heatproof dish and sprinkle gelatin over the top. Do not stir. Let the mixture stand for 3 to 5 minutes to soften, then place the dish in a skillet filled with ½ inch of simmering water. Heat in the water bath until the gelatin is dissolved and the liquid is clear. Stir the gelatin into the melted chocolate mixture along with the Kahlúa and vanilla. Empty into a large bowl to cool until *tepid*.

4. In a chilled bowl with chilled beaters, whip the cream until soft peaks form. Set aside. In a separate, clean bowl, whip the egg whites to soft peaks. Fold the whites into the chocolate mixture, then fold in the whipped cream.

5. Sprinkle the bottom of the tart shell with ⅔ cup chopped pecans. Spoon the mousse filling on top of the nuts, smoothing the surface with an offset spatula. Chill for 2 to 3 hours or until set.

6. GARNISH THE TART: When ready to serve, whip the cream to soft peaks. Add the confectioners' sugar and vanilla, and whip until firm enough to hold its shape for decorating.

7. Empty the whipped cream into a 16-inch pastry bag fitted with a #824 large open star pastry tip. Sprinkle ⅓ cup chopped pecans in a 5-inch circle in the center of the filling.  Space 12 to 16 toothpicks evenly around the edge of the circle to use as markers.

8. Using a marker as a guide, pipe 3 joining shells by moving the bag back and forth toward the center until you reach the circle of nuts. You should have 3 graduated shells. Repeat this at each toothpick marker.

9. To finish, wedge a whole pecan at the end of each strip of shells, facing it toward the center. **2**

STORAGE

Cover any leftover tart with an aluminum foil tent and refrigerate for up to 3 days. This tart can be frozen.

White Chocolate Caffe Tart

HERE IS A TART FOR WHITE chocolate fanatics. A ganache-glazed chocolate pastry shell holds a heavenly Kahlúa-scented Bavarian-style cream filling with chopped chocolate–covered coffee beans sprinkled throughout. There are two ideas for garnishing the tart here. The lacey Chocolate Ganache finish is more challenging; the whipped cream rosettes are a snap.

1 11-inch Chocolate Tart Pastry crust (page 148), baked, or Almond Nut Pastry (page 151), baked

GANACHE
8 ounces fine-quality bittersweet chocolate
1 cup heavy cream
1 teaspoon vanilla extract

FILLING
1 cup plus 6 tablespoons heavy cream
8 ounces white chocolate, shaved (page 455)
2 tablespoons Kahlúa liqueur
1 teaspoon espresso powder
1/2 teaspoon boiling water
1 teaspoon vanilla extract
3 tablespoons cold water
1 1/2 teaspoons unflavored gelatin
3 large egg whites
1/4 cup superfine sugar
1/2 cup (2 ounces) chocolate-covered coffee beans, coarsely chopped

OPTIONAL GARNISH
1/2 cup heavy cream, well chilled
16 whole chocolate-covered coffee beans

1. MAKE THE GANACHE: Break the chocolate into 1-inch pieces. Place in a food processor and process until the chocolate is very finely chopped. Bring the cream to a boil in a small saucepan over low heat. With the processor off, pour the hot cream over the chocolate. Let stand about 1 minute. Pulse 4 or 5 times to blend; rest again. Add the vanilla and pulse 2 or 3 times.

2. Empty the ganache into a medium bowl. Place in a cold-water bath and cool until it is spreading consistency, 3 to 5 minutes. Stir frequently with a large rubber spatula, scraping the bottom of the bowl to ensure even chilling. Do not let it become too hard. Cooling time can vary in warm or humid environments. Adding ice to the water bath will speed the process when needed.

3. Using a small offset spatula, spread about 1/2 cup of the ganache on the bottom of the

baked pastry shell. Save the remaining ganache for decorating the top of the tart.

4. MAKE THE FILLING: Place 6 tablespoons of heavy cream in a medium saucepan and bring to a slow boil. Remove from the heat and add the shaved white chocolate and Kahlúa. Swirl the saucepan with your hand to circulate the cream, then let stand about 1 minute. Stir gently until the chocolate is melted and the mixture is smooth. Dissolve the espresso powder in the boiling water and blend it into the white chocolate with the vanilla. Set aside.

5. Place the water in a small heatproof container and sprinkle the gelatin over the surface. Do not stir. Let the mixture stand 5 minutes to soften, then place the container in a small skillet filled with ½ inch simmering water. Heat in the water bath until the gelatin is clear and dissolved. Cool to *tepid*.

6. Combine the egg whites and sugar in an electric mixer bowl. Place the bowl over a saucepan filled with 2 inches of simmering water. Heat the whites, whisking constantly, until the mixture is very foamy and the sugar is dissolved (about 110 to 120 degrees). Remove the bowl from the water. Whip the whites on medium speed until a soft meringue forms. Set aside.

7. In a separate bowl, beat the remaining 1 cup of heavy cream until it starts to thicken. Pour in

the tepid gelatin, then continue to whip the cream, beating *only* until soft peaks form. Do not overwhip.

8. Empty the white chocolate into a large bowl. Using a whisk, gently stir in about a third of the meringue to lighten the mixture. Using a jumbo rubber spatula, fold in the remaining meringue, then fold in the whipped cream and chopped coffee beans.

9. Empty the mixture into the tart shell, and smooth the surface with an offset spatula. Chill at least 4 hours before serving.

10. GARNISH THE TART: Warm the reserved ganache to the consistency of a thick sauce. Place in a 14-inch pastry bag fitted with coupler (page 74) and a #2 or #3 standard writing pastry tip. Pipe wiggly lines in a lacy design over the entire top of the tart. The filling should be exposed, and some of the lines should touch the crust.

11. MAKE THE OPTIONAL GARNISH: Using an electric mixer on medium speed, whip the cream until firm enough to hold its shape. Empty into a 14-inch pastry bag fitted with a #824 large open star tip. Pipe 16 rosettes around the edge of the tart. Garnish each with a chocolate-covered coffee bean.

STORAGE
Cover any leftover tart loosely with an aluminum foil tent and refrigerate for up to 3 days. This tart can be frozen.

The "Real" Tavern Toasted Coconut Cream Pie

IN LOOKING THROUGH MY RECIPE FILES, I came across an index card written in childish script with a recipe for "The Tavern Toasted Coconut Cream Pie." The handwriting was mine. I could not have been more than twelve years old when I wrote it. When I was nine, my family moved from Elizabeth, New Jersey, to Memphis, Tennessee. My summer vacations were spent visiting family in the suburbs of Newark, New Jersey.

At a Glance

SERVES: 6 to 8

PAN: 9-inch ovenproof glass

PASTRY PREP: Baked

DIFFICULTY: 🍴

Desserts were my passion for as long as I can remember. A meal at the Tavern, a landmark restaurant in Newark, was quite a treat, especially since the restaurant was known for its heavenly desserts. At one particular dinner, I asked our waiter if I could have the recipe for my favorite pie, a Bavarian-style coconut cream topped with a thick layer of crunchy toasted coconut. Eager to please the young visitor from down South, he returned from the kitchen with recipe in hand.

Years later, after the restaurant had closed, the Bauman brothers, owners of the Weequahic Diner in Newark, opened the showy Claremont Diner in Verona, New Jersey, and supposedly hired the former pastry chef of the Tavern. Hence, the Claremont Diner became renowned for their desserts, the most popular being, you guessed it, "The Tavern's Coconut Cream Pie."

Having tasted the pie in both restaurants, my childhood memories of the original from the Tavern remain the most unforgettable. To this day, I believe this recipe to be the real McCoy.

1 9-inch Flaky Pie Pastry crust (pages 98, 100), baked

FILLING
1 1/2 cups sweetened flaked coconut
1 tablespoon water
1 1/2 teaspoons unflavored gelatin
3 large eggs, separated
1/2 cup sugar
1 cup hot milk
1 teaspoon vanilla extract
1 cup heavy cream, well chilled

1. Preheat the oven to 325 degrees. Position the oven rack in the lower third of the oven.

2. MAKE THE FILLING: Sprinkle the coconut on a large, shallow baking pan and toast for 8 to 10 minutes or until golden brown. Watch carefully. Since the coconut browns around the edges of the pan first, occasionally stir it with a fork. When evenly brown, remove from the oven. The coconut will crisp as it cools.

3. Place the water in a small heatproof container and sprinkle the gelatin over the surface. Let stand 3 to 5 minutes to soften. Do not stir. Place the container in a small skillet filled with 1/2 inch simmering water. Heat in the water bath until the gelatin is clear and dissolved. Set aside to cool to tepid.

4. Put the egg yolks in a large bowl and whisk until light in color. Gradually whisk in the sugar and beat until thickened. Pour about a quarter of the hot milk into the yolks to temper them. Stir in the remaining milk, then pour the mixture into a heavy medium saucepan.

5. Cook over low heat, stirring constantly, until the mixture forms a thin custard the consistency of heavy cream, about 3 to 5 minutes. Do not boil or it will curdle. Immediately pour the custard into a large stainless steel bowl. Stir in the dissolved gelatin and the vanilla extract. Set the bowl in a sink filled with 2 inches of ice-cold water. Cool to tepid, stirring frequently to keep the consistency smooth. Do not beat. When the custard begins to gel, remove the bowl from the ice water to prevent the mixture from becoming too firm.

6. In a chilled bowl with chilled beaters or whisk, whip the cream until it forms soft peaks and set aside.

7. Place the egg whites in the large bowl of an electric mixer. Using beaters or whip attachment, whip the whites on medium speed until frothy. Increase speed to medium-high and whip until whites form soft peaks. *Do not overbeat.*

8. Using a balloon whisk, stir about a third of the whites into the custard. With an oversize rubber spatula, fold in the remaining whites, then immediately fold in the whipped cream.

9. ASSEMBLE THE PIE: Spoon the filling into the pie shell, mounding it in the center. Sprinkle the top with half of the toasted coconut. Refrigerate the pie for at least 4 hours before cutting. When ready to serve, garnish with the remaining toasted coconut.

STORAGE
Cover any leftover pie loosely with an aluminum foil tent and refrigerate for up to 3 days. Freezing is not recommended.

Java Eggnog Pie

IF YOU WANT TO IMPRESS GUESTS at holiday time, try this luscious Bavarian cream–style filling. The eggnog with espresso is a winning combination. While most stores stock ready-made eggnog, take the time to hunt down one that is of top quality.

At a Glance

SERVES: 6 to 8

PAN: 9-inch ovenproof glass

PASTRY PREP: Baked

DIFFICULTY: 🥧 🥧

1 9-inch Chocolate Crumb Crust (page 168), baked

FILLING
3 tablespoons water
1 1/2 teaspoons unflavored gelatin
2 large eggs, separated
4 tablespoons granulated sugar
2 tablespoons cornstarch
2 cups eggnog
1 tablespoon espresso powder
1 teaspoon boiling water
1 cup heavy cream, well chilled
1 tablespoon strained confectioners' sugar
1/4 teaspoon vanilla extract
1 ounce bittersweet or semisweet chocolate, shaved (see page 455)

1. MAKE THE FILLING: Place the water in a small heatproof bowl. Sprinkle the gelatin over the top. Let stand 3 to 5 minutes to soften. Do not stir. Place the container in a small skillet filled with 1/2 inch of simmering water. Heat in the water bath until the gelatin is clear and dissolved. Set aside to cool to tepid.

2. Place the egg yolks in a medium bowl and beat with a whisk. Gradually whisk in 2 tablespoons of the sugar, beating until thick and light in color. Stir in the cornstarch and mix until completely smooth.

3. Bring the eggnog to a slow boil in a medium saucepan. While the eggnog is heating, dissolve the espresso powder in the boiling water, then stir it into the eggnog. Take a few spoonfuls of the hot eggnog and stir it into the yolk mixture. Then add the yolk mixture to the remaining hot eggnog. Cook the mixture, stirring constantly, until it comes to a slow boil and forms a thickened custard. Be sure to reach into the bend of the saucepan. Simmer 1 to 2 minutes, stirring occasionally to prevent scorching.

4. Remove from the heat and stir the gelatin into the eggnog custard. Transfer to a large bowl and set the bowl over ice. Stir occasionally until cold, 8 to 10 minutes. While the custard is cooling, complete steps 5 and 6.

5. In a chilled bowl with chilled beaters, whip ½ cup of the cream until it forms *soft* mounds. Do not let it become too stiff. Set aside.

6. In a clean mixer bowl, whip the egg whites until they form soft peaks. Gradually whip in the remaining 2 tablespoons sugar, beating for 10 to 15 seconds.

7. When the eggnog custard shows signs of gelling, gently whisk about a quarter of the whites into the custard to lighten the mixture. With a large rubber spatula, fold in the remaining whites, and then the whipped cream. Empty into the pie shell, smooth the top, and refrigerate for 3 to 4 hours or until firm.

8. GARNISH THE PIE. Whip the remaining ½ cup heavy cream to soft peaks. Add the confectioners' sugar and vanilla. Beat until firm. Place in a 14-inch pastry bag fitted with a #824 large open star tip. Make a pattern of long and short spokes around the edge of the pie by going up and down with alternating 3-inch and 1½-inch lines pointed toward the center. Decorate with shaved chocolate.

STORAGE
Refrigerate any leftover pie covered loosely with an aluminum foil tent for up to 3 days. Freezing is not recommended.

I think if I were a woman I'd wear coffee as a perfume.

JOHN
VAN DRUTEN

Lemon Chiffon Pie

"LIGHT AND LUSCIOUS" BEST DESCRIBES this airy pie. The sweet-tart lemon filling and nutty vanilla wafer crust are a very complementary twosome.

At a Glance

SERVES: 6 to 8

PAN: 9-inch ovenproof glass

PASTRY PREP: Baked

DIFFICULTY: 🍪

1 9-inch Vanilla Nut Crust (page 166), baked

FILLING
4 large eggs, separated
10 tablespoons granulated sugar
$1/4$ cup fresh lemon juice
$1^1/2$ teaspoons grated lemon zest
$1/3$ cup water
$1^1/2$ teaspoons unflavored gelatin

GARNISH
$1/2$ cup heavy cream, well chilled
2 teaspoons strained confectioners' sugar
$1/2$ teaspoon vanilla extract
Candied violets (optional)

1. MAKE THE FILLING: Place the egg yolks in the top of a double boiler. Using a whisk, beat in 6 tablespoons of the sugar, 1 tablespoon at a time. Stir in the lemon juice and zest. Cook over simmering water until thickened, 8 to 10 minutes. Stir the mixture every 2 to 3 minutes. Remove from the heat. Whisk briefly to smooth the mixture.

2. Place the water in a small heatproof container and sprinkle the gelatin over the surface. Do not stir. Let the mixture stand 5 minutes to soften, then place the container in a small skillet filled with $1/2$ inch simmering water. Heat in the water bath until the gelatin is clear and dissolved.

3. Stir the *hot* gelatin into the lemon custard. Empty the mixture into a large bowl and set it in an ice-water bath. Stir occasionally and gently to cool the mixture. When it starts to thicken, *immediately* remove the bowl from the bath.

4. Place the egg whites in the large bowl of an electric mixer. Using the whip attachment, beat on medium speed until the whites form soft peaks. Increase the speed to medium-high. Add the remaining 4 tablespoons sugar, 1 tablespoon at a time. Whip until the whites are shiny and have formed a soft meringue.

5. Stir about a quarter of the whites into the lemon custard. Using an oversize rubber spatula, fold in the remaining whites. Empty the lemon filling into the pie crust. Smooth the top with an offset spatula or the back of a tablespoon, mounding the filling in the center. Chill for 3 to 4 hours or until set.

6. MAKE THE GARNISH: In a chilled bowl with chilled beaters, beat the cream on medium speed. When it begins to thicken, add the confectioners' sugar and vanilla. Continue beating until the cream is firm enough to pipe from a pastry bag. *Do not overbeat.*

7. Spoon the whipped cream into a 14- or 16-inch pastry bag fitted with a #805 large round tip. Pipe twelve 3-inch spirals, making them widest at the edge of the pie and smaller toward the center. Decorate with candied violets.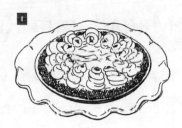

STORAGE
Cover any leftover pie loosely with an aluminum foil tent and refrigerate for up to 2 days. Freezing is not recommended.

Macadamia Rum Soufflé Tart

MANY YEARS AGO, MY HUSBAND and I belonged to a gourmet club. The theme of each dinner party was regional American food, ethnic cuisine, or foods of a foreign country. Since desserts were my forte, they were my assignment. One of the most memorable desserts I made during those 6 years of gastronomical feasts was a macadamia chiffon pie. The recipe came from the *Pacific and Southeast Asian Cooking* volume of the Time-Life Foods of the World series. The following recipe was inspired by that unforgettable pie. When you make this tart be sure to chop the macadamia nuts with a chef's knife. Macadamia nuts are very oily and, if chopped in a food processor, can quickly turn to paste.

At a Glance

SERVES: 8 to 10

PAN: 11-inch metal tart

PASTRY PREP: Baked

DIFFICULTY: 🥄 🥄

1 11-inch Classic Tart Pastry crust (pages 102, 104), baked

FILLING
1/4 cup water
2 teaspoons unflavored gelatin
4 large egg yolks
1/4 cup lightly packed dark brown sugar
3/4 cup milk
1 cup heavy cream, well chilled
4 tablespoons superfine sugar
2 tablespoons dark Jamaican rum
1 teaspoon vanilla extract
2 large egg whites
1 cup plus 2 tablespoons chopped macadamia nuts

1. MAKE THE FILLING: Place the water in a small heatproof container and sprinkle the gelatin over the surface. Let stand 3 to 5 minutes to soften. Do not stir. Set the container in a small skillet filled with 1/2 inch simmering water. Heat in the water bath until the gelatin is clear and dissolved. Turn off the heat, but do not remove the gelatin from the water bath.

2. Place the egg yolks in a medium bowl and whisk until they begin to lighten. Gradually whisk in the brown sugar, beating until thick and light in color. Scald the milk in a medium saucepan. Gradually blend it into the yolk mixture to temper it. Return the mixture to the saucepan, and cook over low heat to just *under* a boil. Remove from the heat and stir in the warm gelatin. Empty the custard into a large bowl.

3. Cool the custard by placing it in an ice-water bath. Stir frequently with a rubber spatula to keep the custard smooth. When the mixture thickens to the consistency of thick cream, remove from the water bath, and immediately prepare the egg whites and whipped cream.

4. In a chilled bowl with chilled beaters, whip ½ cup of the cream until it starts to thicken. Add 1 tablespoon superfine sugar, the rum, and vanilla. Beat until soft peaks form. Set aside.

5. In a separate mixing bowl, whip the egg whites on medium speed until soft peaks form. Add the remaining 3 tablespoons of the superfine sugar, 1 tablespoon at a time over 15 seconds, increase the speed to medium-high, and beat 5 to 10 seconds longer, until smooth and shiny.

6. Gently stir about a quarter of the whites into the custard, mixing with a whisk until smooth. Use a rubber spatula to fold in the remaining whites, then the whipped cream, and 1 cup of the chopped macadamia nuts.

7. Empty the filling into the pastry shell and smooth the top with an offset spatula or the back of a tablespoon. Refrigerate 3 to 4 hours, or until firm.

8. DECORATE THE PIE: On medium speed, whip the remaining ½ cup heavy cream until firm. Empty the cream into a 14-inch pastry bag fitted with a #824 large open star tip.

9. Starting at the top center of the pie, pipe a strip of 2-inch-wide zigzag lines from the top to the bottom. Then make another zigzag line on each side. Sprinkle the top with 2 tablespoons chopped macadamia nuts. Chill until ready to serve.

STORAGE
Cover any leftover pie loosely with an aluminum foil tent and refrigerate for up to 3 days. Freezing is not recommended.

Snappy Mango Madness

HERE IS A BAVARIAN-STYLE cream filling made with a puree of mango folded into an orange-scented English custard (crème anglaise). The coconut ginger snap crust lends a lively accent to the sweet, peachlike flavor of the creamy mango filling. Tommy Atkins mangoes are the most common variety sold, but if you see a Hayden, Keitt, or Kent, buy it. These varieties are less fibrous and especially sweet.

At a Glance

SERVES: 6 to 8

PAN: 9-inch ovenproof glass and shallow baking pan

PASTRY PREP: Unbaked

DIFFICULTY: 🥄🥄

COCONUT GINGER SNAP CRUST
3/4 cup sweetened flaked coconut, lightly packed
5 tablespoons unsalted butter
1 cup ginger snap crumbs

MANGO PUREE
1/2 cup granulated sugar
1/2 cup water
2 ripe mangoes, peeled and cut into 3/4-inch chunks (about 3 1/2 cups) (page 29)
1 tablespoon fresh lemon juice

FILLING
3 tablespoons water
1 1/2 teaspoons unflavored gelatin
1/2 cup milk
1/4 cup plus 1/3 cup heavy cream
2 4-inch strips orange zest
3 large egg yolks
6 tablespoons sugar
3/4 teaspoon vanilla extract
2 tablespoons Grand Marnier

GARNISH
2/3 cup heavy cream, well chilled
1 to 2 tablespoons strained confectioners' sugar
1/2 teaspoon vanilla extract

1. **MAKE THE CRUST:** Preheat the oven to 325 degrees. Spread the coconut in a shallow pan. Bake for 8 to 10 minutes or until golden brown. Stir occasionally for even toasting. Cool before using.

2. Melt the butter slowly in a medium saucepan. Cool to tepid. Finely crush the coconut with your hands. Add it to the butter along with the ginger snap crumbs. Stir with a fork until blended.

3. Spray a 9-inch ovenproof glass pie plate with nonstick coating. Empty the crumbs into the pan. Using the back of a tablespoon, press firmly around the side of the pan, working the crumbs up to the rim, forming a 1/4-inch-thick edge. Smooth the bottom with a spoon.

4. Lay a square of plastic wrap over the crumbs. Using a batarde (page 457) or a smooth-bottomed glass, press firmly against the plastic to smooth the

crumbs on the bottom. Press firmly at the crease as the crumbs tend to accumulate there. Remove the plastic wrap and chill until ready to fill.

5. MAKE THE MANGO PUREE: Bring the sugar and water to a slow boil in a large saucepan. Stir to dissolve. Add the cubed mango, cover, and bring to a boil. Simmer about 3 minutes or until the mango is translucent. Strain the fruit, reserving 1/3 cup of the liquid. Puree the mango and the reserved liquid in a food processor or blender, then pass it through a fine-mesh strainer. Stir in the lemon juice. You should have about 1 1/2 to 1 3/4 cups of puree. Measure 1 1/4 cups puree for the filling. Set aside the remaining puree for garnishing the pie.

6. MAKE THE FILLING: Place the water in a small heatproof dish. Sprinkle the gelatin over the water. Do not stir. Let stand 5 minutes to soften. Set the dish in a skillet filled with 1/2 inch of simmering water. Heat the gelatin in the water bath until the gelatin is dissolved and the liquid is clear. Stir the hot gelatin into the 1 1/4 cups mango puree and set aside.

7. Heat the milk, 1/4 cup of the cream, and orange zest together in a medium saucepan. Have ready a large mixing bowl and a fine strainer. In a large bowl, whisk the egg yolks until light in color. Then whisk in the sugar, 1 tablespoon at a time, whisking until thick and ribbony. Pour about a quarter of the milk into

the yolks to temper them, then return to the saucepan. Cook over medium-low heat until the mixture coats the back of a spoon. This should be *just* under the boiling point. *Do not boil.*

8. Pass the custard through a fine strainer into a large mixing bowl. Discard the orange zest. Then stir in the mango mixture. Set the bowl of mango custard into an ice-water bath. Stir occasionally with an oversize rubber spatula until it cools and *starts* to thicken. Watch carefully; it must not congeal.

9. In a chilled bowl with chilled beaters, whip the remaining 1/3 cup cream to soft peaks. Add the whipped cream to the custard, folding the two together until smooth. Add the vanilla and Grand Marnier. Pour the filling into the pie shell. Refrigerate for at least 5 to 6 hours or until the top has set.

10. GARNISH THE PIE: Drizzle the reserved mango puree on top of the pie in a zigzag design. In a chilled bowl with chilled beaters, whip the heavy cream with the confectioners' sugar and vanilla until it holds its shape. Empty the cream into a 14-inch pastry bag fitted with a #824 large open star tip. Pipe rosettes around the edge.

STORAGE

Any leftover pie should be loosely covered with an aluminum foil tent and refrigerated for up to 3 days. Freezing is not recommended.

New York Nesselrode Pie

AFTER A RADIO INTERVIEW WITH Arthur Schwartz on WOR'S "Food Talk" in New York City, I happened to ask Arthur if he knew anything about nesselrode pie, a dessert made with pureed chestnuts and candied fruits. His eyes gleamed as he told me that he had in his files an article on nesselrode pie that he had written some years back for his "Gourmet Club Newsletter."

Nesselrode pie, according to Arthur's source, *Larousse Gastronomique*, was named in honor of Count Nesselrode, a nineteenth-century Russian diplomat. This legendary French food encyclopedia doesn't explain why chestnuts are associated with the count, but it does tell us that when he negotiated the Treaty of Paris, after the Crimean War, an iced dessert called nesselrode pudding was created for him by his chef, M. Mouy.

Nesselrode pie was popularized in New York City before World War II by a Mrs. Hortense Spier, a professional baker. Over the years, the pie lost its popularity until, in 1983, when an acquaintance of Arthur's, food consultant Ruth Epstein, revived the pie and contemporized the recipe for the Assembly Restaurant in New York City. Sadly, the restaurant, now under different management, no longer serves it. We, however, can still enjoy it at home with the help of Ruth's marvelous recipe.

1 *9-inch Flaky Pie Pastry crust (pages 98, 100), baked*

FILLING

1 *(10-ounce) jar Raffetto "Nesselro" fruit topping (see Note)*
3 *tablespoons dark rum*
1 *tablespoon water*
1 *envelope (2¼ teaspoons) unflavored gelatin*
1½ *cups heavy cream, well chilled*
½ *cup milk*
2 *large eggs, separated*
6 *tablespoons sugar*
Pinch of salt
1 *ounce semisweet chocolate shavings (see page 455), for garnish*

1. **MAKE THE FILLING:** Place the fruits in a fine-mesh strainer set over a bowl. Press gently to remove syrup. (Syrup can be used to flavor puddings or fruit beverages.)

2. Place the rum and water in a small heatproof bowl. Sprinkle the gelatin over the top. Let stand 3 to 5 minutes to soften. Do not stir. Place the container in a small skillet filled with ½ inch simmering water. Heat in the water bath until the gelatin dissolves and the liquid is clear. Set aside.

3. Scald the cream and milk together in a medium saucepan.

4. Place the egg yolks in a medium bowl and beat with a whisk. Gradually whisk in 2 tablespoons of the sugar and the salt, beating until thick and light in color. Stir in the scalded cream. Pour into the top of a double boiler. Set over simmering water and cook, stirring, until thickened to the consistency of heavy cream, 8 to 10 minutes. Do not overcook or mixture will curdle.

5. Off the heat, stir in the gelatin, then transfer the mixture to a large bowl. Place in an ice-water bath and stir occasionally until cold, 8 to 10 minutes. When the custard begins to thicken, remove the bowl from the bath. While the custard is cooling, complete step 6.

6. In a mixer bowl, beat the egg whites with the whip attachment until they form soft peaks. Gradually whip in the remaining 4 tablespoons sugar, beating for 15 to 20 seconds.

7. Use a large rubber spatula to fold about a quarter of the beaten whites into the custard, along with the drained fruit. Gently fold in the remaining whites. Chill the filling for 5 minutes.

8. **ASSEMBLE THE PIE:** Pile the mixture into the pastry shell. Swirl the top with the back of a large tablespoon. Refrigerate the pie for at least 4 hours before cutting. When ready to serve, garnish the top with chocolate shavings.

NOTE

Raffetto fruit topping is distributed by Romanoff International, Inc., of Charlotte, North Carolina. It is available at Italian markets and other specialty food stores.

STORAGE

Cover any leftover pie loosely with an aluminum foil tent and refrigerate for up to 3 days. Freezing is not recommended.

Sam's Favorite Peanutty Tart

MY GRANDAUGHTER SAMANTHA'S INSATIABLE sweet tooth worked overtime when she ate this tart. The yummy tart has a creamy filling made from peanut butter, a peanut butter candy bar, fluffy egg whites, and whipped cream. The filling rests on a chocolate crumb crust covered with a crunchy layer of chocolate-coated peanuts. While most kids will love this tart, after tasting it you'll discover that there is a little bit of "kid" in all of us.

At a Glance

SERVES: 8 to 10

PAN: 11-inch metal tart

PASTRY PREP: Baked

DIFFICULTY: 🍪 🍪

1 11-inch Chocolate Crumb Crust (page 168), baked

FILLING
1 (3.7-ounce) chocolate-covered peanut butter candy bar
3/4 cup creamy peanut butter
3/4 cup milk
2 tablespoons water
1 teaspoon unflavored gelatin
2 teaspoons vanilla extract
1 1/2 cups heavy cream, well chilled
6 tablespoons superfine sugar
3 large egg whites
1/8 teaspoon salt
4 ounces bittersweet chocolate, coarsely chopped
1 cup salted Spanish peanuts, coarsely chopped

1. MAKE THE FILLING: Break the peanut butter candy bar into pieces and finely chop it in a food processor. Place the peanut butter and milk in a medium saucepan. Add the chopped candy and mix with a whisk until the ingredients are blended. Cook the mixture over low heat, stirring constantly with the whisk until the candy is melted and the mixture is thickened. It will look oily.

2. Place the water in a small heatproof bowl and sprinkle the gelatin over the surface. Do not stir. Let stand 3 to 5 minutes to soften. Place the container in a small skillet filled with 1/2 inch simmering water and heat until it dissolves and the liquid is clear. Add the gelatin to the peanut butter mixture and stir until smooth. Blend in the vanilla, then empty the mixture into a large bowl.

3. In a chilled bowl with chilled beaters, beat 1 cup of the cream on medium speed. When it begins to thicken, add 2 tablespoons of the superfine sugar and continue beating until the cream forms soft peaks.

4. Place the egg whites in a separate bowl of an electric mixer. Beat on medium speed until frothy. Add the salt, then increase the speed to medium-high. Add the remaining 4 tablespoons sugar, 1 tablespoon at a time, taking about 15 seconds, then beat for 5 to 10 seconds longer. *Do not overbeat.*

5. Stir about a quarter of the whites into the peanut butter mixture to lighten it. Fold the whipped cream into the peanut butter filling, then fold in the remaining whipped egg whites. Set the filling aside while making the chocolate-covered peanuts.

6. Place the chocolate in a medium bowl or in the top of a double boiler and heat slowly over simmering water until the chocolate is melted. Stir in the nuts, mixing with a fork until they are well coated.

7. Using a small offset spatula, spread the chocolate-coated nuts as best you can on the bottom of the pastry shell, reserving ¼ cup for garnish. Since the mixture is chunky, the nuts will not spread smoothly. *Note:* Keep any remaining coated nuts in the warm-water bath to prevent the chocolate from hardening.

8. Empty the peanut butter filling into the crust and smooth the top with a large offset spatula.

9. GARNISH THE TART: In a chilled bowl with chilled beaters, beat the remaining ½ cup cream until it forms firm peaks. Place the cream in a 14-inch pastry bag fitted with a #824 large open star tip.

10. Starting 1¼ inches from the edge of the crust, make twelve 1¼-inch circles spaced evenly around the edge of the tart as illustrated (see "Spacing a Design," page 75). Then fill in the center with 4 more circles. Place a scant ½ teaspoon of chocolate-coated peanuts in the center of each circle. ■ Refrigerate the tart uncovered for at least 4 hours before serving.

STORAGE

Cover any leftover tart loosely with an aluminum foil tent and refrigerate for up to 3 days. This pie can be frozen.

Pumpkin-Apple Chiffon Pie in a Chocolate Crumb Crust

SEVERAL YEARS AGO, THIS RECIPE WAS featured in an article written by Joanna Pruess for the *New York Times* magazine. Joanna has a keen sense of taste, and when she suggested that I use a chocolate crumb crust with pumpkin, I took her advice.

What we have here is a unique combination of pureed pumpkin and caramelized apples, lightened with meringue. The flavor is heightened with a tasteful blend of spices and a bit of crunch added by toasted pecans.

If you want to perk up your holiday dinners with a pumpkin pie that has some panache, give this one a try.

1 9-inch Chocolate Crumb Crust (page 168), baked (see Note)

FILLING
2 tablespoons unsalted butter
2 medium apples (Cortland, McIntosh, or other soft-fleshed apples), peeled, cored, and cut into $1/2$-inch pieces (about 2 cups) (page 17)
$1/3$ cup granulated sugar
$1/3$ cup firmly packed light brown sugar
$1/2$ teaspoon ground cinnamon
$1/4$ teaspoon ground ginger
$1/4$ teaspoon freshly grated nutmeg
$1/4$ teaspoon grated lemon zest

$1 1/4$ cups canned solid-pack pumpkin (not pumpkin pie mix)
1 package unflavored gelatin
$1/4$ teaspoon salt
3 large eggs, separated
$1/2$ cup half-and-half
6 tablespoons superfine sugar
$1/2$ cup coarsely chopped pecans, lightly toasted

GARNISH
$3/4$ cup heavy cream, well chilled
1 tablespoon strained confectioners' sugar.
$3/4$ teaspoon vanilla extract

1. MAKE THE FILLING: Melt the butter in a heavy 3-quart saucepan over low heat. Stir in the apples, sugars, spices, and lemon zest. Bring to a slow boil, cover, and simmer for 5 minutes. Remove the lid and raise the heat slightly. Continue to cook the apples for 6 to 8 minutes or until the syrup turns to caramel and forms a 6- to 8-inch thread when dropped from the tip of a spoon. Watch carefully: if syrup overcooks, it will taste bitter.

2. Immediately remove the pot from the heat. Stir in the pumpkin, gelatin, and salt. Blend well and return to heat. Cook over low heat until mixture is very hot, stirring constantly.

3. Blend the egg yolks into the half-and-half. Gradually whisk into the filling. Heat slowly to just under boiling, $1\frac{1}{2}$ to 2 minutes.

4. Empty the filling into a food processor. Process for 45 seconds to puree. Pour into a large bowl and place in an ice-water bath for 5 minutes to cool to room temperature. Stir occasionally. The filling can also be chilled in the refrigerator.

5. In the large bowl of an electric mixer, beat the egg whites on medium speed until soft peaks form. Add the superfine sugar, 1 tablespoon at a time. Beat 30 seconds longer to form a soft meringue. Stir about a quarter of the whites into the filling. Fold in the remaining whites along with the toasted pecans, reserving 1 tablespoon nuts for garnish. Mound the filling into the pie shell. Smooth the surface with the back of a large spoon. Chill until set, about 6 hours or longer.

6. MAKE THE GARNISH: In a chilled bowl with chilled beaters, whip the cream. As it starts to thicken, add the confectioners' sugar and vanilla. Beat until fairly thick. Place the whipped cream in a 14-inch pastry bag fitted with a #825 large open star tip. Pipe 12 large rosettes around the edge of the pie. Sprinkle the rosettes and the center of the pie with reserved chocolate crumbs and nuts.

NOTE

Reserve 1 tablespoon unbaked crumb mixture for garnish.

STORAGE

Cover any leftover pie loosely with an aluminum foil tent and refrigerate for up to 3 days. This pie can be frozen.

Pie & Tart Potpourri

ERE IS A CATCH-ALL col-
lection of recipes. They have
their own, distinctive qualities
that set them apart from topics covered in
other chapters. Some are traditional favorites, while others are inspired from
tastes I especially love. ✳ This chapter
is the home of such oldies as pumpkin
and sweet potato pies, two pastries that
have their roots in America's culinary history. Pumpkin and sweet potato are two
foods that are basically quite different: the
pumpkin is a gourd and the sweet potato

is a tuber. But when prepared in a pie, the velvety, spice-laden fillings taste similar. Also in this chapter is another mainstay, this one from the American South: pecan pie. In spite of its sweetness, you can't help but succumb to this buttery, toasted-nut creation with its gooey filling.

Colossal Cashew Cluster is a play on a candy turtle. The tart is made with the three big "cee's"—cashews, caramel, and chocolate— baked in a crisp cookie shell. For chocolate addicts, there are Mississippi Mud Pie and a Prickly Fudge-Nut Tart. The Main Attraction Chocolate Chip Cookie Pie, a recipe that I happened upon in Vermont at a quick stopover lunch, is absolutely yummy.

Sweet and toothsome is the theme of this chapter. When you need a sugar fix, start here. You'll get your high in no time.

Before You Begin

Here is an overview of tips and tricks for making great candy-style, batter-based, and chewy pies and tarts.

◆ Avoid making pastries with caramel in damp or humid weather.

◆ When making caramel, always use a heavy saucepan so the sugar can melt slowly without burning.

◆ The amount of time it takes to caramelize sugar is determined by the quality of the saucepan.

◆ The saucepan used for making caramel should be large enough to allow for bubbling up if additional liquid is added.

◆ Avoid overbaking pumpkin and sweet potato pies. The center of these pies should quiver slightly when they are removed from the oven. The fillings will set as they cool.

◆ To encourage the bottom crust to brown, bake pumpkin and sweet potato pies on a preheated cookie sheet or shallow baking pan.

◆ Dense fudge or cookie-style fillings should not be overbaked. They are done when a toothpick inserted into the center has moist crumbs clinging to it.

◆ Always let pies and tarts made with thick, dense fillings stand until cool. The center of these pies will continue to cook for a brief time after they are removed from the oven.

◆ Use an aluminum foil drip pan for pies that are rich in butter to prevent smoking from splattering fat.

◆ Pastries made with a high quantity of sugar have a long shelf life and freeze well.

Prickly Fudge-Nut Tart

BROWNIE FANS WILL LOVE THIS transformation of their beloved chocolate snack. The tart has a moist, fudgy filling sandwiched between a nut crust and a nut topping. It is finished with chocolate ganache drizzled over the top. Freshly ground black pepper adds spark to the batter, but it can be omitted.

At a Glance

SERVES: 8 to 10

PAN: 11-inch metal tart

PASTRY PREP: Unbaked

OVEN TEMP: 350 degrees

BAKING TIME:
25 to 28 minutes

DIFFICULTY:

---

1 recipe All-Nut Pastry shell
(page 163)

FILLING
$^1/_2$ cup sifted all-purpose flour
$^1/_2$ to $^3/_4$ teaspoon finely ground
   black pepper, preferably freshly
   ground
$^1/_8$ teaspoon salt
2 ounces semisweet chocolate,
   coarsely chopped
1 ounce unsweetened chocolate,
   coarsely chopped
$^1/_2$ cup unsalted butter
1 tablespoon honey
2 large eggs
$^3/_4$ cup granulated sugar
$^1/_4$ cup lightly packed dark brown
   sugar
1 teaspoon vanilla extract
$^1/_2$ cup walnuts, coarsely chopped

$^1/_2$ recipe Chocolate Ganache
   Sauce (page 447)

1. Preheat the oven to 350 degrees. Position the oven rack in the lower third of the oven. Butter *very well* an 11-inch metal tart pan. Dust lightly with flour, invert over the sink, and tap to remove excess.

2. **LINE THE TART PAN:** Empty the pastry mixture into the tart pan. Using the back of a tablespoon, spread the nuts as evenly as you can across the bottom of the pan. Cover with a sheet of plastic wrap, and using a batarde (page 457) or a smooth-bottomed glass, press the mixture to form a solid layer. It *should cover the bottom only* of the pan, not go up the side.

3. **MAKE THE FILLING:** Whisk the flour, pepper, and salt together in a bowl. Set aside.

4. Melt the chocolates and butter in the top of a double boiler, stirring occasionally until the chocolates are melted and the mixture is smooth. Stir in the honey.

5. In the large bowl of an electric mixer fitted with beaters or whip attachment, beat the eggs on medium speed until very foamy. Add the granulated sugar in 4 additions, then beat in the brown sugar. Add the vanilla and beat about 1 minute longer, until light and fluffy.

6. Reduce the mixer speed to low. Pour in the warm chocolate mixture, scraping the side of the bowl as needed. Add the dry ingredients all at once and mix only until incorporated. Empty the batter into the tart pan and smooth the surface with the back of a tablespoon. Sprinkle the top of the batter with the chopped walnuts.

7. Cut an 18-inch square of aluminum foil and set the tart in the center. Bring the foil up to frame the tart and fold the corners down. Place on the oven rack and bake for 25 minutes or until a toothpick inserted into the center comes out *almost* clean. A few of the crumbs should adhere to the toothpick.

NOTE ===========
Chocolate fillings can overbake very quickly, so watch carefully; a minute or two makes a big difference. The center of the tart should be slightly moist. As the tart cools, the center will firm.

8. Set the tart on a rack. When cool enough to handle, remove the aluminum foil and unmold from the pan. This tart is best if it stands several hours or overnight before serving.

9. GARNISH THE TART: Using the tip of a teaspoon, drizzle the ganache in thin lines across the top of the tart, moving in one direction and then the opposite to create a crisscross design. The ganache works best when it is slightly thick but still pourable; if you find that your ganache is not fluid enough to pour, warm it slightly. After garnishing, let the tart stand 1 hour to set the ganache. Slice into wedges and serve with vanilla ice cream.

STORAGE ===========
Cover any leftover tart with an aluminum foil tent and store at room temperature for up to 5 days. This tart can be frozen, but apply the glaze after thawing.

Research tells us that fourteen out of any ten individuals like chocolate.

SANDRA
BOYNTON,
CHOCOLATE:
THE CONSUMING
PASSION

Colossal Cashew Cluster

THIS TART IS MADE FROM MY favorite candy combination—cashews, caramel, and dark chocolate. It is sinfully rich, so dole out the slices with care. Be sure to make this tart on a day when the humidity is low, otherwise the caramel will not set. Although the caramel and ganache will lose their sheen after the first day, the good news is that the tart has a long shelf life. The bad news is that it's so delicious, it probably won't stay around too long.

At a Glance

SERVES: 8 to 10

PAN: 11-inch metal tart

PASTRY PREP: Baked

DIFFICULTY: 🥧 🥧 🥧

---

1 11-inch *Sweet Tart Pastry crust (page 146), baked*

GANACHE
2 ounces bittersweet chocolate, broken into pieces
1/4 cup heavy cream
1 teaspoon light corn syrup
1/2 teaspoon vanilla extract

CARAMEL-NUT FILLING
2 1/2 cups cashew nuts
1/2 cup water
3/4 cup superfine sugar
2 tablespoons honey
Pinch of baking soda
1/2 cup heavy cream, heated
3 tablespoons cold unsalted butter, cut into 1/2-inch dice
1 teaspoon vanilla extract

1. **MAKE THE GANACHE:** Place the chocolate in the bowl of a food processor and pulse until it is finely chopped. Bring the cream and corn syrup to a boil in a small, heavy saucepan. Pour it over the chocolate. Let it stand for 2 or 3 minutes, then *pulse* again 2 or 3 times. The chocolate should be melted and the mix-ture smooth. Blend in the vanilla. If it appears oily, stir in a few drops of hot water. Set the ganache aside to cool and thicken. This can take an hour or more, depending on the room temperature.

2. **MAKE THE CARAMEL-NUT FILLING:** Preheat the oven to 325 degrees. Place the cashews in a shallow baking pan. Bake the nuts for 5 to 7 minutes or until they start to brown. Cool before using.

3. Place the water in a lightly buttered 1 1/2- to 2-quart, heavy saucepan. Add the sugar and honey. Stir slowly to blend. Bring the mixture to a boil over low heat, stirring once or twice. Add the baking soda (the liquid will rise and bubble briefly). *Do not stir after the boil.*

Cook over low heat, brushing the sides of the pot occasionally with cold water to prevent sugar crystals from forming. Use a ta-blespoon to skim any foam that forms on the surface. Continue to cook the sugar syrup until it reaches 260 degrees on a candy thermometer and turns golden brown. This could take up to 20 to 25 minutes, depending on the size and weight of the saucepan.

4. Remove the saucepan from the heat and immediately add the hot heavy cream and butter. The caramel syrup will bubble up. If it hardens, stir it until it softens and is dissolved. Return the saucepan to the heat and cook the caramel syrup to 220 degrees (about 3 minutes longer). Remove from the heat and add the vanilla.

5. Set the saucepan in a sink filled with 1 inch of ice water. Stir the caramel until it cools and thickens.

6. ASSEMBLE THE TART: Using an offset spatula, spread 2 to 3 tablespoons of ganache on the bottom of the pastry shell. (If it becomes too hard to spread, warm it briefly.) Then refrigerate the shell for a few minutes to set the chocolate.

7. Gently fold the cashews into the caramel. The nuts do not have to be completely coated with caramel. Empty the nut mixture into the tart shell, spreading it as best you can. It should be somewhat chunky.

8. Drizzle the remaining ganache over the filling (warm it briefly if it is too firm to drizzle). Let the tart stand at room temperature. The ganache will set in about 1 hour. *Do not refrigerate* as the chocolate will lose its shine.

STORAGE
Cover any leftover tart with plastic wrap and store at room temperature for up to 1 week. Freezing is not recommended.

Flourless Macaroon Tart in Almond Nut Pastry

SIMPLE, DELICATE, AND DELECTABLE is how best to describe this tart. The lovely almond flavor comes from a nut flour made from pulverized almonds and confectioners' sugar. I prefer unblanched almonds here because I think they are tastier. This tart can be served simply with freshly cut fruit or elegantly plated on a pool of orange-flavored crème anglaise, garnished with fresh berries.

At a Glance

SERVES: 8 to 10

PAN: 11-inch metal tart

PASTRY PREP: Baked

OVEN TEMP: 325 degrees

BAKING TIME:
30 to 35 minutes

DIFFICULTY:

---

1 11-inch Almond Nut Pastry crust (page 151), baked
^{1}/$_4$ cup apricot preserves
1 teaspoon water

FILLING
1^1/$_2$ cups sliced almonds, with skins
1^1/$_2$ cups strained confectioners' sugar
3 large eggs
1 teaspoon vanilla extract
1 teaspoon pure almond extract
Confectioners' sugar, for garnish

1. PREPARE THE PASTRY SEALER: Place the apricot preserves and water in a small saucepan. Bring to a slow boil, then reduce the heat and simmer for a few seconds. Strain the preserves into a small dish and cool to tepid. Brush the preserves on the top and side of the pastry shell.

2. Preheat the oven to 325 degrees. Position the oven rack in the lower third of the oven.

3. MAKE THE FILLING: To make the nut flour, place the almonds and 1 cup of the confectioners' sugar in the bowl of a food processor. Pulse 5 times, then process for 15 seconds; pulse again 5 times, then process again for 15 seconds or until the nuts are very finely ground and the mixture begins to clump together around the sides of the bowl. To test the texture, take a small amount and squeeze it in the palm of your hand. If it holds together, it is ready.

4. In the large bowl of an electric mixer fitted with beaters or whip attachment, beat the eggs on medium until they are foamy. Increase the speed to medium-high and add the remaining confectioners' sugar in 3 additions. Add the vanilla and almond extracts, and beat for 30 seconds longer, until light and fluffy.

5. Remove the bowl from the mixer. Using an oversize rubber spatula, fold 1 to 2 tablespoons of the nut flour at a time into the egg foam. Be sure to sprinkle the nut flour over the eggs, do not drop it in. When all of the nut flour is incorporated, pour the batter into the tart pan. Smooth the surface and bake for 30 to 35 minutes, or until the tart is lightly browned and the surface feels set and bouncy when tapped with your fingertips. Place the tart on a rack to cool. When tepid, unmold onto a platter and cool completely.

6. GARNISH THE TART: Center a very open, lace paper doily on top of the tart. Place 1 to 2 tablespoons of confectioners' sugar in a fine-mesh strainer. Sprinkle a thick layer of the sugar over the top of the tart, leaving a 1 inch border around the edge unsugared. Carefully lift the doily without spilling any sugar. You should have a pretty floral design.

STORAGE
Cover any leftover tart with plastic wrap and store at room temperature for up to 5 days. This tart can be frozen.

Caramelized Walnut Tart

THOSE WHO KNOW ME WELL will attest to my insatiable passion for nuts. Here we have a crunchy, chewy tart that hits the jackpot for me. It is made with lots of caramelized walnuts that are baked in a buttery cookie crust. If you're nuts about nuts the way I am, you must try this tart.

At a Glance

SERVES: 8 to 10

PAN: 11-inch metal tart

PASTRY PREP: Baked

OVEN TEMP: 350 degrees

BAKING TIME:
25 to 30 minutes

DIFFICULTY: 🥿 🥿

---

1 11-inch *Sweet Tart Pastry crust (page 146), baked*

FILLING
$^2/_3$ *cup water*
1 *cup sugar*
2 *tablespoons honey*
Pinch of baking soda
$^2/_3$ *cup heavy cream, heated*
4 *tablespoons cold unsalted butter, cut into* $^1/_2$-*inch dice*
1 *teaspoon vanilla extract*
1 *tablespoon bourbon*
3 *cups walnuts, coarsely chopped*

1. Preheat the oven to 350 degrees. Position the oven rack in the lower third of the oven.

2. **MAKE THE FILLING:** Place the water in a lightly buttered 2-quart, heavy saucepan. Add the sugar and honey. Stir slowly to blend. Bring the mixture to a boil over low heat, stirring once or twice. Add the baking soda (the liquid will rise and bubble briefly). *Do not stir* after the boil. Cook over low heat, brushing the sides of the pot occasionally with cold water to prevent sugar crystals from forming. Use a tablespoon to skim any foam that forms on the surface. Continue to cook the sugar syrup until it reaches 260 degrees on a candy thermometer and turns golden brown. This could take up to 20 or 25 minutes, depending on the size and weight of the saucepan.

3. Remove the saucepan from the heat and immediately add the hot cream and 3 tablespoons of the butter. The caramel syrup will bubble up and harden, but will dissolve and soften as it is stirred. Return the saucepan to the heat and cook the caramel syrup to 220 degrees (about 3 minutes longer). Remove from the heat and stir in the vanilla extract and bourbon.

4. Set the saucepan in a sink filled with 1 inch of ice water. Stir the caramel until it cools and thickens. Add the remaining tablespoon butter and beat with a spoon until thick and creamy.

5. ASSEMBLE THE TART: Gently fold the walnuts into the caramel and spread in the baked shell, smoothing the surface as best as you can with a small offset spatula.

6. Cut an 18-inch square of aluminum foil and set the tart in the center. Bring the foil up to frame the tart and fold the corners down. This will catch any seepage from the tart. Place on the oven rack and bake the tart for 25 to 30 minutes, or until the filling is bubbly and begins to brown. Set the tart on a rack to cool. Let the tart stand for 30 minutes, then unmold from the pan while it is still warm. Serve while slightly warm.

STORAGE

Cover any leftover tart with aluminum foil and store at room temperature for up to 1 week. Refresh in the oven before serving. This tart can be frozen.

Mississippi Mud Pie
with Fudge Candy Icing

THE ORIGIN OF MISSISSIPPI MUD PIE remains a mystery to me. Although I researched dozens of cookbooks, none shed any light as to the recipe's origin. Furthermore, the few recipes I found had little in common.

At a Glance

SERVES: 10 to 12

PAN: 11-inch
ovenproof glass

OVEN TEMP: 325 degrees

BAKING TIME:
38 to 40 minutes

DIFFICULTY:

Having grown up in Memphis, Tennessee, I surely thought I would have no problem getting to the source. I was wrong. Even Craig Claiborne, a native Mississippian and author of *Southern Cooking*, states "It is conceivable that Mississippi Mud Pies existed, but no amount of research has revealed to me whether they did." The only information that has any consistency is that the dessert—sometimes referred to as a cake—is chocolate and very rich; its name refers to the muddy banks of the Mississippi River.

So I let my imagination go to work when I developed this recipe. What I came up with is a very chewy, brownielike pie jam-packed with pecans and coconut. Take care not to overbake the batter—it must remain moist. The top is finished with a crunchy pecan fudge frosting. This wonderful pie is especially delicious when eaten slightly warm.

FILLING
1 cup unsifted all-purpose flour
6 tablespoons strained cocoa
    (nonalkaline) powder
$1/4$ teaspoon salt
1 cup unsalted butter, at room
    temperature
$1^1/4$ cups granulated sugar
3 large eggs
$1^1/2$ teaspoons vanilla extract
1 cup firmly packed sweetened
    flaked coconut chopped
    medium
$2/3$ cup toasted pecans, coarsely
    chopped

FUDGE CANDY ICING
6 tablespoons unsalted butter
6 tablespoons strained cocoa
    (nonalkaline) powder
2 cups strained confectioners' sugar
6 tablespoons sweetened condensed milk
1 tablespoon light corn syrup
1 teaspoon vanilla extract
$2/3$ cup plus 2 tablespoons toasted
    pecans, coarsely chopped

1. Preheat the oven to 325 degrees. Position the oven rack in the lower third of the oven. Butter an 11-inch ovenproof glass pie plate.

2. **MAKE THE FILLING:** Strain together the flour, cocoa, and salt. Set aside.

3. In the large bowl of an electric mixer fitted with beaters or paddle attachment, cream the butter and sugar until light in color, 2 to 3 minutes. Add the eggs, 1 at a time, at 30-second intervals. On low speed, add the vanilla, then the flour mixture, mixing only until blended.

4. Stir in the coconut and pecans. Pour the batter into the pie plate and smooth the top with the back of the spoon.

5. Bake for 38 to 40 minutes, until a toothpick inserted into the center comes out slightly moist. *Do not overbake.*

6. **MAKE THE ICING:** Melt the butter over low heat in a heavy, 2-quart saucepan. Remove from the heat and blend in the cocoa, confectioners' sugar, condensed milk, and corn syrup. Mix until smooth. The mixture will be quite thick.

7. Place the saucepan back over low heat and stir constantly until the mixture becomes shiny and thin enough to spread. Remove from the heat and stir in the vanilla and ²/₃ cup of the pecans. Spread over the pie while it is still warm. Sprinkle the remaining 2 tablespoons pecans around the edge of the pie. Serve at room temperature.

STORAGE
Store any leftover pie lightly covered with aluminum foil at room temperature for up to 5 days. This pie can be frozen.

Southern Pecan Pie

W HEN I WAS A TEENAGER GROWING up in the South, I used to wonder what people loved about pecan pies. They held absolutely no appeal for me, as most of those I had eaten were either store-bought or poorly made. Years later, on a visit to Memphis, I sampled one made by a former schoolmate, Shirley Roberts, and instantly changed my opinion. Shirley shared her recipe with me, and since then pecan pie has become one of my favorites. I love to eat it warm, topped with a glob of bourbon-flavored whipped cream. It's so sinful and so good!

At a Glance

SERVES: 6 to 8

PAN: 9-inch ovenproof glass

PASTRY PREP: Unbaked

OVEN TEMP: 325 degrees

BAKING TIME:
75 to 90 minutes

DIFFICULTY: 🍪

$^1/_2$ small recipe Flaky Pie Pastry (pages 98, 100)

FILLING
4 large eggs, slightly beaten
2 tablespoons heavy cream
$^1/_2$ cup granulated sugar
$^1/_2$ cup lightly packed light brown sugar
4 teaspoons unsifted all-purpose flour
$^1/_8$ teaspoon salt
$1^1/_3$ cups light corn syrup
5 tablespoons unsalted butter, melted
$1^1/_2$ teaspoons vanilla extract
1 tablespoon bourbon (optional)
$1^1/_2$ cups broken pecans, lightly toasted

1. Preheat the oven to 325 degrees. Position the oven rack in the lower third of the oven. Spray a 9-inch ovenproof glass pie plate with nonstick coating.

2. On a floured pastry cloth, roll out the pastry into a circle measuring approximately 13 inches. Fit loosely into the pie plate. Trim the edge with scissors, leaving a 1-inch overhang. Roll the edges of the dough under, forming a wall around the outer rim of the pie plate. Flute the edges (see page 66) and chill the pastry while preparing the filling.

3. MAKE THE FILLING: Blend the eggs and the cream in a medium bowl. Combine the sugars, flour, and salt. Stir the flour mixture into the eggs along with the corn syrup and 3 tablespoons of the melted butter. *Do not overmix.* Blend in the vanilla and bourbon.

4. Pour the mixture into the pastry shell. Sprinkle the pecans over the top, then drizzle the remaining 2 tablespoons melted butter over the nuts.

5. BAKE THE PIE: To prevent the edges of the pie crust from burning, make aluminum foil bands. Cut two 3-inch-wide strips of 18-inch heavy-duty aluminum foil. Fold 1 inch of each strip to the center, making a double thickness of foil. Mold the foil around the edge of the pie, keeping the double fold on top of the dough. Be careful not to crush the edge of the pastry. Secure the bands with tape.

6. Make an aluminum foil drip pan to place on the rack below the pie halfway through the baking. Cut an 18-inch square of heavy-duty aluminum foil. Fold each edge twice (about 1 inch per fold) standing the folded edges upright to form a 4-sided pan.

7. Bake the pie for 75 to 90 minutes. Remove the foil bands during the last 10 minutes of baking. If the top is browning too quickly, lay a piece of aluminum foil loosely over the surface. The pie is done when the bottom crust is golden brown. The center of the pie should quiver slightly when the pie is moved. It will firm as it cools. The pie should stand at least 3 hours before cutting. Serve slightly warm with bourbon flavored whipped cream or vanilla ice cream.

STORAGE
Cover any leftover pie with aluminum foil and refrigerate for up to 3 days. This pie can be frozen.

VARIATION
Chocolate Pecan Pie

Blend 6 tablespoons of strained nonalkaline cocoa powder, such as Hershey's, into the egg mixture. Reduce the vanilla to 1 teaspoon and increase the bourbon to 2 tablespoons.

Smashing Sweet Potato Pie

THIS RECIPE FOR SWEET POTATO PIE comes from Viola Henderson of Ridgewood, New Jersey. Viola, a native of Camden, South Carolina, left home when she was a young girl. She settled in Ridgewood, where she worked for many years as head cook for a prominent family. Today, she still cooks and bakes for special events, as well as for friends and family.

Viola prefers using the deep orange-skinned sweet potatoes for her pie because she finds them sweeter (see sidebar). To retain the moist flavor, she likes to boil them in their jackets. While the pie may be frozen after baking, to avoid a possible soggy crust, Viola often freezes just the prepared filling. When she is ready to make her pie, the filling is thawed and poured into the prepared curst.

If you've never tasted sweet potato pie, you are in for a treat. Thank you, Viola, for sharing your special recipe with us.

1/2 small recipe Flaky Pie Pastry (pages 98, 100)

FILLING
3/4 cup sugar
1 tablespoon unsifted all-purpose flour
1/2 teaspoon baking powder
1/4 teaspoon salt
1 teaspoon ground cinnamon
1/2 teaspoon freshly grated nutmeg
1/4 teaspoon ground allspice
2 cups hot mashed cooked sweet potatoes (about 1 3/4 pounds)

1/4 cup unsalted butter, cut into 1-inch pieces
1 tablespoon fresh lemon juice
1 teaspoon vanilla extract
1 teaspoon lemon extract
1 large egg
1 cup half-and-half

1. Preheat the oven to 425 degrees. Position the oven rack in the lower third of the oven. Place a sheet pan or a pizza stone on the rack to preheat. Butter a 9-inch ovenproof glass pie plate.

2. On a floured pastry cloth, roll out the pastry into a circle measuring approximately 13 inches. Fit loosely into the pie plate. Trim the edge with scissors, leaving a 1-inch overhang. Roll the edges of the dough under, forming a wall around the outer rim of the pie plate. Flute the edge (see page 66) and chill while preparing the filling.

3. MAKE THE FILLING: Whisk together the sugar, flour, baking powder, salt, cinnamon, nutmeg, and allspice.

4. Place the hot potatoes in a large bowl. Add the butter and gently stir with a spoon. Blend in the dry ingredients and mix until smooth. Add the lemon juice and the vanilla and lemon extracts.

5. Lightly beat the egg in a small bowl. Stir in the half-and-half, then blend the mixture into the potatoes. Pour the filling into the pastry shell and smooth the surface with the back of a tablespoon.

6. BAKE THE PIE: Make aluminum foil bands to prevent the edges from burning. Cut two 3-inch-wide strips of 18-inch heavy-duty aluminum foil. Fold 1 inch of each strip to the center, making a double thickness of foil. Mold the foil around the edge of the pie, keeping the double fold on top of the dough. Be careful not to crush the edge of the pastry. Secure the bands with tape.

7. Set the pie on the preheated sheet pan. Bake for 15 minutes. Reduce the oven temperature to 375 degrees and bake for 40 to 45 minutes, or until the top is puffy and the bottom crust is golden brown. Cool on a rack. This pie is best eaten warm. Serve with lightly sweetened whipped cream.

STORAGE

Cover any leftover pie with a sheet of waxed paper then aluminum foil and refrigerate for up to 4 days. Reheat before serving. This pie can be frozen, see headnote.

Sweet Potatoes or Yams, What's the Difference?

MUCH CONTROVERSY EXISTS about the relationship between the sweet potato and the yam, two vegetables that actually belong to different families. Sweet potatoes are root vegetables and are members of the *Convolvulaceae*, or morning glory, family, while yams are "tubers" and belong to the botanical *Dioscoreaceae* family.

Sweet potatoes are native to tropical America and are considered to be a true North American food. In Peru, documentation of their cultivation can be found in archaeological data that dates back to 750 B.C. When Christopher Columbus discovered the New World, sweet potatoes were introduced to Europe and Asia.

True yams are grown in the Caribbean, Asia, and Africa, and are not readily available in this country. The name yam is believed to have come from the African word *Nyami*, which means "to eat." Yams have skins that are brown and very scaly and grow much larger than sweet potatoes, with some weighing over one hundred pounds.

One theory regarding the difference between sweet potatoes and yams comes to us from the knowledgeable staff at Delicious Orchards in Colts Neck, New Jersey. According to a spokesperson, what are referred to as yams in this country are really a variety of sweet potato. During the 1920s in the state of North Carolina, a new breed of sweet potato was developed. It had a brighter orange skin with a moist orange flesh and was sweeter than the "whites," its pale yellow predecessor. The potato was cured in a humid environment that not only sealed the skin for better shelf life, but also enhanced the sweetness. Wanting to give this new strain a name, the commission dubbed it a "yam."

North Carolina is the largest producer of sweet potatoes in the United States. Sue Johnson-Langdon, the executive director of the North Carolina Sweet Potato Commission, says, "All sweet potatoes may be used interchangeably, and no one really knows how the confusion came about."

The major varieties of sweet potatoes currently sold in this country are the whites, the Jewel, and the Beauregard. Delicious Orchards recommends using the whites for pie baking because they have less moisture and more starch. Sweet potatoes, which are extremely nutritious, are rich in beta carotene and are an excellent source of vitamins A and C.

Marcia's Pumpkin Pie in Sinfully Rich Pecan Pastry

MARCIA GERMANOW, A PARTY PLANNER and caterer from northern New Jersey, has a treasury of superb recipes acquired through years of orchestrating fantastic events. Her southern heritage accounts for her talent as a terrific pie baker. What makes this pie so special is the tasteful blend of spices in the creamy filling combined with her Sinfully Rich Pecan Pastry.

At a Glance

SERVES: 6 to 8

PAN: 9-inch ovenproof glass

PASTRY PREP: Baked

OVEN TEMP: 350 degrees

BAKING TIME:
60 to 65 minutes

DIFFICULTY: 🥧

To prevent the bottom crust from becoming soggy, fully bake the shell before filling. Also, avoid overmixing the filling or the top of the pie will crack. Pumpkin pie is best when served slightly warm. Marcia serves it with a dollop of whipped cream topped with some broken toasted pecans.

1 9-inch Sinfully Rich Pecan Pastry crust (page 141), baked

FILLING
3 large eggs
1 (15-ounce) can solid-pack pumpkin
1/2 cup granulated sugar
1/4 cup firmly packed light brown sugar
1/4 cup firmly packed dark brown sugar
1/2 teaspoon salt
1 teaspoon ground cinnamon
1/2 teaspoon ground ginger
1/4 teaspoon freshly grated nutmeg
1/8 teaspoon ground cloves
3/4 cup milk
1/2 cup heavy cream

1. Preheat the oven to 350 degrees. Position the oven rack in the lower third of the oven. Place a sheet pan or pizza stone in the oven to preheat.

2. MAKE THE FILLING: Beat the eggs lightly with a whisk in a large bowl. Stir in the pumpkin.

3. Combine the sugars, salt, and spices, then blend them into the pumpkin mixture. Slowly stir in the milk and cream, mixing just until smooth. *Do not overmix.* Pour all but about 1 cup of the pumpkin mixture into the pastry shell.

4. BAKE THE PIE: To prevent the edges from burning, make aluminum foil bands. Cut two 3-inch-wide strips of 18-inch heavy-duty aluminum foil. Fold 1 inch of each strip to the center, making a double thickness of foil. Mold the foil around the edge of the pie, keeping the double fold on top of the dough. Be careful not to crush the edge of

the pastry. Secure the bands with tape.

5. Set the pie on the preheated sheet pan. Pour in the remaining pumpkin filling. Bake for 50 minutes. Remove the foil bands and continue to bake for 10 to 15 minutes longer, or until the center is set. Do not insert a knife into the pie as the cut may cause the surface to split. It's okay if the center of the pie quivers slightly. Place on a rack and cool for 2 to 3 hours before cutting. Serve slightly warm with lightly whipped cream and broken toasted pecans.

STORAGE

Cover any leftover pie with a sheet of waxed paper then aluminum foil and refrigerate for up to 3 days. Reheat before serving. This pie can be frozen.

What moistens the lip/
And what brightens the eye;/
What calls back the past/
Like the rich pumpkin pie?

WHITTIER,
"THE PUMPKIN"

Main Attraction Chocolate Chip Cookie Pie

ON A RECENT TRIP TO MANCHESTER, Vermont, my husband and I stopped for lunch in Bennington, a rustic town in the Green Mountains. We ate at a restaurant called the Main Attraction. I thought I was in heaven when I took a bite of my dessert: a pie so special that I had to include the recipe for it in my book. The waitress was kind enough to get me a copy from the kitchen staff.

At a Glance

SERVES: 6 to 8

PAN: 9-inch ovenproof glass

PASTRY PREP: Baked

OVEN TEMP: 350 degrees

BAKING TIME: 35 to 37 minutes

DIFFICULTY: 🍪

When you prepare the pie shell, be sure to make a fluted edge so the filling will have enough room to rise in the pan. The pie should not be cut when it is fresh out of the oven, as the center will be too wet. The filling needs at least 4 hours to set, but be sure to reheat the pie before serving. Lovers of warm and chewy chocolate chip cookies will find this pie absolutely scrumptious.

1 9-inch *Flaky Pie Pastry crust (pages 98, 100), baked*

FILLING
1¼ cups sifted all-purpose flour
½ teaspoon salt
¼ teaspoon baking soda
½ cup unsalted butter, melted and cooled

½ cup lightly packed light brown sugar
⅓ cup granulated sugar
2 large eggs, lightly beaten
1 teaspoon vanilla extract
1 cup semisweet chocolate chips (1 6-ounce package)
¾ cup walnuts, coarsely chopped

1. Preheat the oven to 350 degrees. Position the oven rack in the lower third of the oven.

2. MAKE THE PIE: Sift together the flour, salt, and baking soda. Set aside.

3. Place the melted butter in a large bowl. Using a wire whisk, gradually blend in the brown and granulated sugars. Stir in the eggs, then the vanilla. Stir in the dry ingredients, one ½ cup at a time. Add the chocolate chips and ½ cup of the walnuts.

4. Pour the batter into the baked pastry shell. Sprinkle the remaining ¼ cup walnuts over the top. Bake for 35 to 37 minutes, or until top of the pie is lightly browned and the center is *just* set—a toothpick inserted into the center should remain slightly moist. *Do not overbake.* The filling will set as it cools. Cool for at least 4 hours.

5. Before slicing, reheat the pie in a 325 degree oven for 8 to 10 minutes and serve with vanilla ice cream and Warm Fudge Sauce (page 446).

STORAGE

Cover any leftover pie with aluminum foil and refrigerate for up to 5 days. Reheat for a few minutes before serving. This pie can be frozen.

Orange-Scented Middle Eastern Nut Swirl

RINGS OF NUT-FILLED PHYLLO are snuggled in a pie plate and saturated with a tasty orange- and coriander-flavored syrup. It's perfect to serve at brunches, for light meals, or when you want a nice chewy pastry to eat while sipping a cup of coffee or tea. This is one of those nibbling kind of desserts. One bite and you're hooked.

At a Glance

SERVES: 6 to 8

PAN: 9-inch ovenproof glass

OVEN TEMP: 350 degrees

BAKING TIME:
35 to 40 minutes

DIFFICULTY: 🥟 🥟

1/2 pound phyllo sheets
(#4 thickness)
1/2 pound unsalted butter, clarified
(see page 52)

FILLING
3/4 cup whole almonds
1 cup walnuts
2 tablespoons sugar
1/2 teaspoon ground cinnamon

ORANGE SYRUP
1/2 cup water
1 cup sugar
1 teaspoon honey
2 1/4-inch slices navel orange
1 1/4-inch slice lemon
3 tablespoons fresh orange juice
1 teaspoon fresh lemon juice
1/2 teaspoon vanilla extract
1 teaspoon whole coriander seeds
6 black peppercorns

1. Preheat the oven to 350 degrees. Position the oven rack in the lower third of the oven. Brush a 9-inch ovenproof glass pie plate with clarified butter.

2. MAKE THE FILLING: Place the almonds in the bowl of a food processor fitted with the stainless steel blade. Process for 10 seconds. Add the walnuts, sugar, and cinnamon. *Pulse* 5 times, then process for 3 to 4 seconds. You will have a nut mixture that ranges from finely ground to medium-coarse. Empty into a large bowl and set aside.

3. MAKE THE SYRUP: Combine all of the syrup ingredients in a medium, heavy saucepan. Bring the mixture to a boil over medium heat. Reduce the heat and simmer for 2 to 3 minutes. Remove from the heat and set aside.

4. ASSEMBLE THE PIE: Starting with 1 sheet of phyllo dough (see "Working with Phyllo," page 64), brush the pastry lightly with warm clarified butter, coating the outer edges first to prevent the dough from splitting. Lay a second sheet on top of the first, brush with butter, then sprinkle with 2 tablespoons of the nut mixture. Cover with a third sheet, brush with butter, and sprinkle with another 2 tablespoons of nut mixture. Top with a fourth sheet of phyllo, brush with butter, then sprinkle with 4 tablespoons of the nut mixture.

5. Cut the stacked phyllo sheets in half lengthwise, making 2 long pieces. Working one piece at a time, fold the ends and the edge closest to you over, about 3/4 inch, and brush with clarified butter to seal them. Then roll the phyllo lengthwise, forming a tube 1 to 1¼ inches thick. Brush the tube with clarified butter.

6. Shape the tube into a tight coil, and center it in the middle of the pie plate. It's okay if it splits; just continue. Start the second tube where the first ended.

7. Make 4 more coils by repeating steps 4 and 5 two additional times. You will have 6 coils altogether. As each tube is formed, place it where the last one ended, and continue to wrap it around the plate. The last 2 tubes will be slightly raised at the rim. Push them into the plate as best you can. If there are any spaces, press the coils gently to fill the gaps.

8. Brush the top of the pie with clarified butter, and sprinkle with the remaining nut mixture. Bake for 35 to 40 minutes, or until golden brown. It should be well baked (see color insert).

9. When the pie is removed from the oven, *immediately* spoon the cool orange syrup over the top of the pie, saturating the entire surface. Let the pie stand at least 2 to 3 hours before cutting so it can absorb the syrup.

STORAGE
Cover any leftover pie with plastic wrap and store in the refrigerator. It will keep for up to 2 weeks. Freezing is unnecessary as this pie has a long shelf life.

Cobblers, Crisps & Crumbles

OBBLERS, CRISPS, AND crumbles are desserts that can be whipped up in no time. Filled with fruit and/or berries they have only a top crust or crumb covering. This eliminates most of the problems that arise with pastries prone to soggy bottom crusts. The baking dish is the beneficiary of the juices that cause such woe to bakers.

At summer's end, I like to take advantage of the great buys at farmstands. Don't be concerned about purchasing slightly damaged or overripe fruit, they may be too juicy for pies, but that is not an issue here. Cobblers, crisps, and crumbles all freeze extremely well, allowing you to stock up and savor the tastes of summer on a snowy winter's eve.

Most any variety of fruits and berries work for these pastries, creating a wide palate of possibilities. While I do suggest mixing various kinds of fruits and berries, don't make a hodgepodge. You can elevate an ordinary cobbler, crisp, or crumble into an extraordinary dessert if you give some thought to flavor combinations.

I like to make desserts of this kind with generous toppings. The abundant amount of fruit in the fillings can usually support a substantial covering. Cobblers, according to Maida Heatter, earned their name from the term "cobble up," or to throw together in a hurry. These desserts have a pastry topping, while crisps are covered with a mix of sweet buttery crumbs that usually contain chopped nuts. This mixture is commonly called streusel, the German word for "sprinkle." While similar to crisps, a typical crumble has a streusel-like topping made denser by the addition of oatmeal. If you want a really great crumb topping, don't push the crumbs into the fruit. The warm air in the oven will circulate around them, making them irresistably crisp.

Unless you are freezing these desserts, use ovenproof glass or porcelain dishes. Since cobblers and their cousins are acidic, have no bottom crust, and are stored in their baking container, it is best not to use metal. However, if you plan on freezing, a disposable aluminum foil baking pan is your best bet.

In this chapter you will find a variety of desserts that ranges from the simplicity of the Peachy Peach Cobbler to the sophistication of the Strawberry Fig Cobbler with Quilted Biscuit Topping. Three

Berry Crisp with Butter-Nut Crumb Topping is a showcase for summer berries, while the Autumn Fruit Crumble highlights the flavors of fall—apples, pears, and cranberries.

If you were to ask me to choose a favorite from this chapter, I honestly couldn't say. Since I'm partial to warm fruit desserts laden with juice, these recipes all have special appeal for me. I love them with ice cream melting into their sweet syrup or topped with freshly whipped cream. Try some for yourself and see if you don't agree.

Before You Begin

Here is an overview of tips and tricks for making great cobblers, crisps, and crumbles.

✦ Soft-fleshed fruits (like kiwi and banana) and citrus fruits are not the best candidates for a cobbler. Use them only in small amounts as an accent ingredient.

✦ A small amount of dried fruits—such as dried cherries, cranberries, currants, or raisins can be added to any cobbler or crisp. Always plump the dried fruits before using.

✦ Both fresh and dried fruits or berries can be macerated in liqueurs before using. The steeping liquid can be added along with the fruit or reserved and used to flavor a topping.

✦ It's okay to add extra fruit to these desserts, but take care not to overload the baking dish. The juices will bubble up and overflow into the oven. To be safe, place an aluminum foil drip pan on the rack below when baking.

✦ To reduce the butter in a crumb topping, try adding a fresh egg or egg substitute for some of the fat.

✦ As a replacement for nuts, try Grape-Nuts cereal.

✦ Rolled oats can be substituted for part of the flour in most crumb toppings.

✦ While whole wheat flour can be used in place of some of the all-purpose flour, more fat will be needed to form the crumbs.

✦ For a crumb topping, never use hot melted butter. It should be *tepid*. Otherwise the crumbs will be too oily and will not form as well.

✦ The best way to form streusel crumbs is to stir the tepid butter and dry ingredients together with a table fork, not a spoon.

✦ Crumb toppings will be crispier if the crumbs are not pressed into the fruit. Sprinkle them over the fruit instead.

✦ Crumb toppings are best if allowed to stand for 10 to 15 minutes after the melted butter has been added. This gives them time to absorb the fat. The surface of the crumb will be less oily and will form better crumbs.

✦ Desserts made with crumb toppings have a shorter life than those made with a crust.

✦ Never cover a crumb topping with plastic wrap because the crumbs will become soggy. A loose covering of aluminum foil works best.

✦ Because cobblers are single-crusted, the top crust can be rolled slightly thicker than you would for a pie.

✦ For a pretty cobbler topping, make a lattice crust over a top crust.

✦ Always serve crisps, cobblers, and similar desserts warm.

Maple Pecan Apple Crisp

THIS APPLE CRISP SCORED ESPECIALLY high with my team of recipe testers. The captivating flavor comes from the sweetness of maple. When combined with apples, pecans, and browned butter, it's a real winner. I originally tested this recipe with maple sugar that I purchased while visiting the Taftsvillle Country Store in Taftsville, Vermont. Maple sugar is available through their mail order catalog, but imitation maple flavor blended with granulated sugar in a food processor is an acceptable alternative.

At a Glance

SERVES: 6 to 8

PAN: 7 × 11 × 1½-inch ovenproof glass

OVEN TEMP: 350 degrees

BAKING TIME: 40 to 45 minutes

DIFFICULTY:

FILLING

2½ pounds Granny Smith apples peeled, cored, and cut into ¼-inch slices (page 17) (about 6 apples)
1 tablespoon fresh lemon juice
4 tablespoons maple syrup

TOPPING

⅓ cup unsalted butter
2 tablespoons maple syrup
⅓ cup sugar
¾ teaspoon imitation maple flavor
1⅓ cups unsifted all-purpose flour
½ teaspoon baking powder
⅛ teaspoon salt
¾ cup broken pecans

1. Preheat the oven to 350 degrees. Position the oven rack in the lower third of the oven. Butter a 7 × 11 × 1½-inch ovenproof glass pan.

2. MAKE THE FILLING: Place the sliced apples in the pan, then drizzle with lemon juice and maple syrup.

3. MAKE THE TOPPING: Melt the butter in a medium-size heavy saucepan. When it starts to brown, remove it from the heat and cool until tepid. Stir in the maple syrup.

4. Place the sugar in a medium-size bowl and stir in the imitation maple flavor, mixing until thoroughly blended. Add the flour, baking powder, and salt and mix well to combine. Empty the mixture into the butter-syrup in the saucepan along with ¼ cup of the broken pecans. Toss with a fork to form crumbs. Take a clump of the crumb mixture in your hand and squeeze gently to form a larger clump. Break the larger clump apart over the apples. Repeat, using all of the crumb mix-

ture. Sprinkle the remaining $1/2$ cup pecans over the top. *Do not press the surface.*

5. Bake for 40 to 45 minutes, or until the fruit juices are bubbling. If the nuts are browning too quickly, cover loosely with a sheet of aluminum foil for the final 5 to 10 minutes of baking. Serve warm.

STORAGE

Cover any leftover crisp with a sheet of waxed paper then aluminum foil. Refrigerate for up to 2 days. Reheat before serving. This crisp can be frozen.

Double-Crust Blackberry Cobbler

THIS RECIPE COMES FROM A southern friend, Carolyn Beck, who is an outstanding cook and baker. She was raised in Mississippi, where her family owned a fruit orchard. Her mother made cobblers in a most unusual manner: she layered the fruits and pastry, baking one layer at a time. The berries are cooked first with lots of butter, creating a flavor that is memorable and a syrup with a gorgeous deep indigo color. While Carolyn makes her cobbler without thickening, I prefer to add a bit of cornstarch to bind the juices.

At a Glance

SERVES: 6 to 8

PAN: 7 × 11 × 1 1/2-inch ovenproof glass

PASTRY PREP: Unbaked

OVEN TEMP: 350 degrees

BAKING TIME: 60 to 70 minutes

DIFFICULTY: 🍪 🍪

This cobbler is richer than most, but well worth the treat. If you can't get blackberries, try substituting raspberries, black raspberries, or blueberries. Be sure to sample the berries for sweetness and adjust the sugar according to your own taste.

PASTRY
2 3/4 cups sifted all-purpose flour
3/4 teaspoon salt
3/4 cup well-chilled vegetable shortening, cut into 1/2-inch pieces
6 to 8 tablespoons ice water

FILLING
5 to 6 cups fresh blackberries (about 4 or 5 6-ounce baskets)
3/4 cup unsalted butter
1 1/4 cups sugar
4 teaspoons cornstarch (optional)
1 teaspoon fresh lemon juice

1. **MAKE THE PASTRY:** Sift the flour and salt into a large bowl. Add the shortening and shake the bowl to coat the fat with flour. Using a pastry blender, cut the fat into the flour until the mixture resembles coarse meal.

2. Add the ice water, 1 tablespoon at a time, using a fork to blend. The dough has enough water when it will form a mass when pressed against the side of the bowl. If it fails to adhere, add more water sparingly.

3. With floured hands, form the dough into 2 flat rectangles. Dust with flour and wrap in plastic wrap. Chill 1 hour or longer. (The dough will keep for 3 days in the refrigerator or up to 6 months in the freezer. To thaw, remove from the freezer to the refrigerator. Thaw overnight or for at least 12 hours.)

4. **MAKE THE FILLING:** Wash and throroughly dry the blackberries (page 21).

5. Place ½ cup of the butter in a large skillet. Combine 1 cup sugar and the cornstarch in a small bowl. Add to the skillet and melt over low heat. Add the berries and heat the mixture over low heat until the berries release their juices and the mixture comes to a gentle boil and thickens. Remove from the heat, and stir in the lemon juice. Set aside.

6. Preheat the oven to 350 degrees. Position the oven rack in the lower third of the oven. Spray a 7 × 11 × 1½-inch ovenproof glass pan with nonstick coating.

7. **ASSEMBLE THE COBBLER:** Using a slotted spoon, place half the berries in the pan. Ladle in about ½ cup of the berry juice. Do not add all of the juice.

8. On a lightly floured surface, roll one piece of pastry into a rectangle measuring about 8 × 12 inches. Lay the pastry loosely over the berries and prick the surface 10 to 12 times with a fork to allow the steam to escape. Dot the top of the pastry with 2 tablespoons of butter and sprinkle with 2 tablespoons of sugar. Bake for 30 to 35 minutes or until the top is golden brown. Remove from the oven.

9. With a slotted spoon, place the remaining berries on top of the baked pastry. Empty the remaining berry juice into a small, heavy saucepan.

10. Roll the remaining pastry into a rectangle measuring 8 × 12 inches and place it on top of the second layer of berries. Prick the surface with a fork. Dot the top of the dough with the remaining butter and sprinkle with the remaining sugar.

11. Return the cobbler to the oven and bake for 30 to 35 minutes, or until the top is golden brown and the juices bubble at the sides. Remove from the oven and cool 1 hour or longer before serving.

12. Bring the reserved syrup to a boil over medium heat. Reduce the heat and simmer until it reduces slightly. Cut the cobbler in squares and serve while still warm in bowls with the heated sauce and vanilla ice cream or with whipped cream.

STORAGE

Cover any leftover cobbler with a sheet of waxed paper then aluminum foil and refrigerate for up to 3 days. Reheat before serving. This cobbler can be frozen.

Autumn Fruit Crumble with Oatmeal Crunch Topping

MAKE THE MOST OF AUTUMN'S bounty with this fruit crumble made of apples, pears, and cranberries. You may want to make this dessert for Thanksgiving dinner. It's quick to make, do-aheadable, and a perfect choice for a home-style family supper.

At a Glance

SERVES: 6 to 8

PAN: 7 × 11 × 1 1/2-inch ovenproof glass

OVEN TEMP: 350 degrees

BAKING TIME: 50 to 55 minutes

DIFFICULTY: 🍳

TOPPING

3/4 cup unsifted all-purpose flour
3/4 cup whole wheat pastry flour
1/2 cup quick rolled oats
1/2 cup walnuts
1/4 cup granulated sugar
1/4 cup lightly packed light brown sugar
1/4 teaspoon baking powder
1/4 teaspoon salt
1/4 teaspoon ground cinnamon
2/3 to 3/4 cup unsalted butter, melted and cooled

FILLING

3 Cortland apples (or Empire, Macoun, or Granny Smith)
4 firm Red Bartlett or Anjou pears
1 1/2 cups fresh cranberries, washed and dried (page 24)
2 teaspoons fresh lemon juice
1/2 cup granulated sugar
1 1/2 tablespoons cornstarch
1/2 teaspoon ground cinnamon
1 teaspoon grated navel or Valencia orange zest

1. Preheat the oven to 350 degrees. Position the oven rack in the lower third of the oven. Butter generously a 7 × 11 × 1 1/2-inch ovenproof glass baking dish.

2. **MAKE THE TOPPING:** Place the flours, oats, walnuts, sugars, baking powder, salt, and cinnamon in the bowl of a food processor fitted with the steel blade. Pulse until blended and the nuts are finely chopped. Empty the contents into a large bowl.

3. Pour the melted butter over the flour mixture and toss with a fork to form crumbs. Set aside.

4. **PREPARE THE FRUIT:** Cut the apples into quarters, core, peel, and cut into 3/4-inch-thick pieces (page 17). If using apples other than Cortlands, cut into 1/2-inch-thick pieces.

5. Cut the pears in half, core, peel, and cut into 1-inch chunks (page 34).

6. Place the apples, pears, and cranberries in a large bowl. Drizzle with the lemon juice. Combine the sugar, cornstarch, cinnamon, and orange zest. Sprinkle over the fruit, then shake the bowl to distribute. Empty the mixture into the prepared baking dish. Sprinkle the crumb mixture over the fruit. Do not press.

7. **BAKE THE CRUMBLE:** Bake for 50 to 55 minutes, or until the top is golden brown and the juices are bubbly. Serve warm with ice cream, frozen yogurt, or whipped cream.

STORAGE ═══════════
Any leftover crumble can be stored in the refrigerator loosely covered with a sheet of waxed paper then aluminum foil for up to 2 days. Reheat before serving. This crumble can be frozen.

VARIATION ═══════════

Prune Plum Crumble

Make the Autumn Fruit Crumble with the following changes: Substitute 2½ pounds ripe Italian prune plums for the apples, pears, and cranberries. Decrease the sugar in the fruit filling to ⅓ cup. Decrease the cornstarch to 4 teaspoons. Omit the cinnamon.

To prepare the fruit, wipe the plums with damp paper towels. Cut each in half and remove the pit (page 37). Cut into 1-inch pieces.

Gooseberry Crumble

IF YOU HAPPEN TO SEE ROUND green or pink berries with translucent thin veins at your farmer's market in early July, you have stumbled upon gooseberries. For baking purposes, it is best to use them for cobbler-style desserts because they release a lot of moisture. In this recipe, the sweet and crunchy crumbs are the perfect complement for the tartness of the berries. Be sure to use a drip pan underneath the crumble—these berries are very juicy.

At a Glance

SERVES: 6 to 8

PAN: 7 × 11 × 1 ½-inch ovenproof glass

OVEN TEMP: 375 degrees

BAKING TIME: 50 to 55 minutes

DIFFICULTY:

FILLING
4 cups gooseberries (2 pint baskets), tips and tails removed, rinsed and well dried (page 25)
2 tablespoons instant tapioca
1 cup granulated sugar
½ cup lightly packed light brown sugar
⅓ cup cornstarch
¼ teaspoon ground cinnamon

TOPPING
6 tablespoons unsalted butter
2 tablespoons honey
1½ cups unsifted all-purpose flour
¼ teaspoon baking powder
½ cup granulated sugar
¼ cup lightly packed light or dark brown sugar
½ cup quick rolled oats
1 teaspoon grated navel or Valencia orange zest
½ teaspoon ground cinnamon

1. **START THE FILLING:** Place the gooseberries in a large bowl. Sprinkle with the tapioca, shaking the bowl to distribute it through the berries. Let stand 15 minutes.

2. Preheat the oven to 375 degrees. Position the oven rack in the lower third of the oven. Butter a 7 × 11 × 1½-inch ovenproof glass dish.

3. **MAKE THE TOPPING:** Melt the butter in a large saucepan. Remove from the heat and stir in the honey. Cool to tepid.

4. Whisk together the flour, baking powder, sugars, oats, orange zest, and cinnamon. Using a fork, stir the mixture into the butter, mixing until crumbs form.

5. **ASSEMBLE THE CRUMBLE:** Empty the gooseberries into the baking dish. Combine the sugars, cornstarch, and cinnamon with a whisk. Sprinkle the mixture over the fruit.

6. Take a handful of the crumb mixture and squeeze to form a large clump. Then break the clump apart over the fruit, making smaller clumps and crumbs. Repeat until all of the crumb mixture has been used.

7. Make an aluminum foil drip pan to place on the rack below the pie halfway through the baking. Cut an 18-inch square of heavy-duty aluminum foil. Fold each edge twice (about 1 inch per fold) standing the folded edges upright to form a 4-sided pan.

8. Bake the crumble for 50 to 55 minutes or until the juices begin to bubble. If the top of the crumble browns too quickly, lay a sheet of aluminum foil loosely over the top. Remove from the oven and cool on a rack. Serve warm with ice cream.

STORAGE

Cover any leftover crumble with waxed paper then a sheet of aluminum foil. Refrigerate for up to 2 days. This crumble can be frozen.

For when I eat gooseberry pudding or tart zig-zag goes my brain, and away whirls my heart.

H. E. PALMER

Peachy Peach Cobbler

I CAN'T THINK OF A BETTER dessert to savor at the end of a warm summer evening's meal than a homemade peach cobbler. The thickly cut slices of golden-orange fruit with their succulent sweet juices are surely one of the gastronomical treasures of the season. While excessively juicy fruits like peaches can be challenging to use in pies, the juices work in your favor in cobblers. Since I always eat my cobblers à la mode, I like to spoon these juices over the top of the ice cream and fruit. What could be better?

At a Glance

SERVES: 6 to 8

PAN: 7 × 11 × 1 1/2-inch ovenproof glass

PASTRY PREP: Unbaked

OVEN TEMP: 425 degrees

BAKING TIME:
40 to 45 minutes

DIFFICULTY:

---

1 recipe Short Pastry Dough for Cobblers (page 139), shaped into a rectangle for rolling

FILLING
8 to 9 cups fresh peaches, wiped (about 3 1/2 pounds) (page 33)
3/4 cup plus 1 teaspoon sugar
1/4 cup cornstarch
1/2 teaspoon ground cinnamon
1 tablespoon fresh lemon juice
2 tablespoons unsalted butter, cut into pieces

1. Preheat the oven to 425 degrees. Position the oven rack in the lower third of the oven. Butter a 7 × 11 × 1 1/2-inch ovenproof dish.

2. MAKE THE FILLING: Cut the peaches into 1-inch slices and place them into a large bowl.

3. Combine 3/4 cup of the sugar, the cornstarch, and cinnamon. Add to the peaches, then toss gently to coat with the sugar mixture. Empty the mixture into the baking dish, spreading the fruit evenly. Sprinkle with lemon juice and dot with butter.

4. ASSEMBLE THE COBBLER: On a floured pastry cloth, roll the pastry into a rectangle measuring 8 × 12 inches. Place the pastry loosely over the fruit. Turn the edges under and press the dough against the side of the baking dish with a fork. Prick the top in several places with a fork to make steam vents. Sprinkle the top with the remaining 1 teaspoon sugar.

5. Make an aluminum foil drip pan to place on the rack below the pie halfway through the baking. Cut an 18-inch square of heavy-duty aluminum foil. Fold each edge twice (about 1 inch per fold) standing the folded edges upright to form a 4-sided pan.

Remove the aluminum foil bands the last 5 to 10 minutes of baking.

6. Bake the cobbler for 40 to 45 minutes or until the juices begin to bubble and the top is golden brown. Serve the cobbler warm with ice cream or whipped cream.

STORAGE

Cover any leftover cobbler with a sheet of waxed paper then aluminum foil and refrigerate for up to 4 days. Reheat before serving. Freezing is recommended.

VARIATION

Peach and Blueberry Cobbler

Add $1\frac{1}{2}$ cups blueberries, washed and well dried (page 22), to the peaches. Proceed with the recipe.

Double-Crust Lattice Top for Cobblers

WHEN I WANT TO MAKE a more decorative finish for cobblers, I place a lattice over the regular top crust. To do this, you need $1\frac{1}{2}$ recipes of the Short Pastry Dough for Cobblers (page 139).

Divide the dough in half. Roll the first half of the dough into a rectangle measuring 8 × 12 inches. It will be thinner than usual. Place it loosely on the fruit. Trim the edge flush with the inside of the baking dish.

Roll the second piece of dough into a rectangle measuring 9 × 12 inches. Using a fluted pastry wheel trim the edges, then cut the dough lengthwise into 12 strips, $\frac{3}{4}$ inch wide. Lay 4 strips diagonally over the bottom crust, spacing them evenly. Weave the remaining 4 strips with the first 4 pieces to form a lattice. Trim the strips of dough flush with the inside of the baking dish, as you did with the bottom layer of pastry.

Lightly beat 1 egg white with 1 teaspoon water. Brush the top of the cobbler with the egg white. Arrange the remaining 4 strips of dough around the edge of the pan to frame the crust and give it a neat finish. Brush these edge strips with the egg wash. Sprinkle the top of the cobbler with 1 teaspoon of pearl or granulated sugar. Bake as the cobbler recipe directs.

Pear 'n' Plum Cobbler

THE LITTLE OVAL PLUMS often known as "prune plums" come into season in early September. In this cobbler, their slightly tart flavor complements the delicate sweetness of pears.

1 recipe Short Pastry Dough for Cobblers (page 139), shaped into a rectangle for rolling

FILLING
⅔ cup plus 1 teaspoon sugar
3 tablespoons cornstarch
1 teaspoon ground cinnamon
Scant ¼ teaspoon ground cloves
2 pounds large firm Anjou, Red Bartlett, or Bosc pears (about 6 or 7)
1½ pounds purple Italian (prune) plums
1 tablespoon fresh lemon juice
2 tablespoons unsalted butter, cut into bits

1. Preheat the oven to 425 degrees. Position the oven rack in the lower third of the oven. Butter a 7 × 11 × 1½-inch ovenproof glass pan.

2. MAKE THE COBBLER: Combine ⅔ cup of the sugar with the cornstarch, cinnamon, and cloves. Set aside.

3. Wipe the pears and plums with damp paper towels. Peel, core, and cut the pears into eighths (page 34). Cut the plums in half, remove the pits, and divide each piece in half (page 37). Sprinkle the lemon juice over the fruit. Empty the mixture into the baking dish, spreading the fruit evenly. Sprinkle the dry ingredients over the fruit and dot the surface with the butter.

4. On a floured pastry cloth, roll the pastry into a rectangle measuring 8 × 12 inches. Place the pastry loosely over the fruit. Turn the edges under and press the dough against the side of the baking dish with a fork. Prick the top in several places with a fork to make steam vents. Sprinkle with 1 teaspoon sugar.

5. Make an aluminum foil drip pan to place on the rack below the pie halfway through the baking. Cut an 18-inch square of heavy-duty aluminum foil. Fold each edge twice standing the folded edges upright to form a 4-sided pan.

6. Bake the cobbler for 35 to 40 minutes, or until the juices begin to bubble and the top is golden brown. Serve warm.

STORAGE

Cover any leftover cobbler with a sheet of waxed paper then aluminum foil and refrigerate for up to 4 days. Reheat before serving. This cobbler can be frozen.

Three Berry Crisp with Butter-Nut Crumb Topping

THIS CRISP MADE FROM RASPBERRIES, blackberries, and blueberries is a treat. Walnuts add a crunchy contrast to the melt-in-your-mouth texture of the topping.

FRUIT FILLING
3 cups raspberries (2 6-ounce baskets), washed and dried (page 37)
1¹/₂ cups blackberries (1 6-ounce basket), washed and dried (page 21)
2 cups blueberries (1 pint basket), washed and dried (page 22)
¹/₂ cup granulated sugar
2 tablespoons cornstarch
2 teaspoons fresh lemon juice

BUTTER-NUT CRUMB TOPPING
1³/₄ cups unsifted all-purpose flour
¹/₂ teaspoon baking powder
¹/₂ cup granulated sugar
¹/₄ cup strained confectioners' sugar
¹/₂ teaspoon ground cinnamon
1 cup broken walnuts
²/₃ cup unsalted butter, melted and cooled

1. Preheat the oven to 375 degrees. Position the oven rack in the lower third of the oven. Butter a 7 × 11 × 1¹/₂-inch ovenproof glass pan.

2. MAKE THE FILLING: Place the berries in the baking pan. Strain the sugar and cornstarch together. Sprinkle the mixture over the berries along with the lemon juice. Toss the berries gently in the pan. *Do not stir or the berries will get crushed.*

3. MAKE THE CRUMB TOPPING: Strain the flour, baking powder, sugars, and cinnamon together into a large bowl. Add the walnuts.

4. Pour in the butter and toss with a fork to form crumbs. Take a clump of the crumb mixture in your hands and squeeze gently to form a larger clump. Break the larger clump apart over the fruit. Repeat, using all of the crumb mixture. *Do not press the crumbs into the berries.*

5. BAKE THE CRISP: Bake for 30 to 35 minutes, or until the crumbs begin to brown and the fruit juices are bubbling. Serve warm with ice cream or frozen yogurt.

STORAGE
Store any leftover crisp in the refrigerator, lightly covered with a sheet of waxed paper then aluminum foil for up to 2 days. Reheat before serving. This crisp can be frozen.

At a Glance

SERVES: 6 to 8

PAN: 7 × 11 × 1¹/₂-inch ovenproof glass

OVEN TEMP: 375 degrees

BAKING TIME: 30 to 35 minutes

DIFFICULTY:

Strawberry Fig Cobbler with Quilted Biscuit Topping

IN THIS HOME-STYLE DESSERT, the piquant flavor of fresh figs offsets the sweetness of strawberries, creating an unusual and delicious combination. The fruit is topped with a crusty sweet cream biscuit dough woven into a lattice. When baked, the topping resembles the puffy surface of a comforter. Serve the cobbler while still warm in deep bowls with spoons to savor all the sweet juices. For a splurge, pass a pitcher of heavy cream to pour over the top.

At a Glance

SERVES: 6 to 8

PAN: 7 × 11 × 1½-inch ovenproof glass

PASTRY PREP: Unbaked

OVEN TEMP: 400 degrees

BAKING TIME: 30 to 35 minutes

DIFFICULTY: 🥟 🥟

Don't be tempted to overload this cobbler with strawberries. They are very watery, so the cornstarch would have to be increased. If you wish, you can omit the figs; see the variation at the end of this recipe. Whatever your choice, this fast, delicious, and eye-appealing dessert has all the components to become a family favorite.

1 small recipe *Sweet Cream Biscuit Dough* (page 140)

FILLING
3 cups strawberries (1½ pint baskets), cleaned (page 39) and cut into 1-inch chunks
3 cups fresh green or purple figs, cut into 1-inch wedges (page 25) (10 to 12 figs)
½ cup sugar
3 tablespoons cornstarch
¾ teaspoon ground cinnamon
¼ teaspoon ground allspice
½ teaspoon grated navel or Valencia orange zest
2 teaspoons fresh lemon juice
1 to 2 tablespoons unsalted butter, cut into pieces

GLAZE
1 large egg white
1 teaspoon water
1 tablespoon sugar

1. **MAKE THE FILLING:** Place the berries and figs in a large bowl. Combine the sugar, cornstarch, cinnamon, allspice, and orange zest in a bowl. Set aside.

2. Preheat the oven to 400 degrees. Position the oven rack in the lower third of the oven. Butter a 7 × 11 × 1½-inch ovenproof glass dish.

3. Pour the sugar mixture over the fruit. Shake the bowl to distribute the dry ingredients. Empty into the baking dish, arranging the fruit to fill in any empty spaces. Be sure the fruit is level on the top. Drizzle with lemon juice and dot with butter.

4. ASSEMBLE THE COBBLER: On a well-floured surface, roll out the dough into a 10 × 14-inch rectangle. With a pastry scraper or sharp knife (not a pastry wheel), divide the pastry lengthwise into 7 strips. Cut 3 of the strips in half across the middle. You should have 6 strips measuring about 7 inches long, and 4 strips about 14 inches long.

5. Space the 4 long strips evenly over the fruit. Starting slightly off center, work the 6 shorter strips into a lattice top (see page 65). You should have spaces between the strips.

6. MAKE THE GLAZE: Place the egg white and water in a small bowl. Lightly beat with a fork. Brush the surface of the dough with the egg wash, then sprinkle with sugar. Bake the cobbler for 30 to 35 minutes, or until the juices are bubbly and the top is golden brown. Serve warm or at least within 3 to 4 hours after baking.

STORAGE

Cover any leftover cobbler with a sheet of waxed paper then aluminum foil and refrigerate for up to 2 days. Reheat before serving. Freezing is not recommended.

VARIATION

Strawberry Cobbler

Follow the directions for Strawberry Fig Cobbler, but omit the figs. Increase the strawberries to 6 cups and the cornstarch to 6 tablespoons. No other changes are necessary.

Shaped like a gourd, purple and leathery/ It fits the palm, it magnetizes the touch./ What flesh designed as fruit can this fruit be?

MARY SARTON,
"THE FIG"

Double-Header Pear Cobbler

JEFFREY AND NEIL, MY TWIN grandsons, have opposite likes and dislikes. Jeff is the chocolate kid, while Neil loves the taste of butterscotch. This double-header recipe covers both bases. Jeff's cobbler has pears baked in a fudge sauce, nestled under delicate flaky pastry. Neil's is made with pears in a pool of butterscotch, covered with a biscuit topping. Mix or match the crusts, however you choose. I guarantee that spoons will be licked clean, especially when the cobbler is served with a scoop of vanilla ice cream, topped with warm fudge or butterscotch sauce.

At a Glance

SERVES: 6 to 8

PAN: 7 × 11 × 1 1/2-inch ovenproof glass

PASTRY PREP: Unbaked

OVEN TEMP: 400 degrees

BAKING TIME:
with Short Dough:
35 to 40 minutes
with Biscuit Dough:
25 to 30 minutes

DIFFICULTY: 🥄🥄

---

1 recipe Short Pastry Dough for Cobblers (page 139), shaped into a rectangle for rolling or 1 small recipe Sweet Cream Biscuit Dough (page 140)

FILLING
1 tablespoon unsalted butter
9 to 10 Anjou pears, peeled, cored, and cut into sixths (page 34) (about 4 pounds)
2/3 cup sugar
1 1/2 tablespoons cornstarch
1 1/2 tablespoons fresh lemon juice
1 teaspoon grated navel or Valencia orange zest

1 recipe Warm Fudge Sauce (page 446) or Butterscotch Sauce (page 444)

GLAZE
1 large egg white
2 teaspoons sugar

---

1. MAKE THE PEAR FILLING: Melt the butter in a large, heavy sauté pan. Add the pears, cover, and cook over medium-high heat for 5 minutes. Drain fruit in a colander. Discard the juices.

2. In a small bowl, combine the sugar and cornstarch.

3. Return the pears to the sauté pan and stir in the sugar and cornstarch, lemon juice, and orange zest. Bring to a boil, then reduce the heat to medium-low and cook, stirring occasionally, until the juices come to a boil and thicken. Remove from the heat and set aside.

4. Preheat the oven to 400 degrees. Position the oven rack in the lower third of the oven. Butter a 7 × 11 × 1 1/2-inch ovenproof glass dish.

5. ASSEMBLE THE COBBLER:
Spoon half of the Warm Fudge Sauce or Butterscotch Sauce into the baking dish. Use a slotted spoon to transfer the pears to the dish. Discard excess liquid. Press the fruit gently into the sauce, making an even surface. Cool to tepid.

6. FOR SHORT COBBLER PASTRY: On a floured surface, roll out the pastry into a 8×12-inch rectangle. Cover the cobbler with the pastry, tucking the edges under. Prick the top in several places with a fork.

FOR SWEET CREAM BISCUIT DOUGH: On a floured surface, roll out the dough into a 8×12-inch rectangle. Cut the pastry into 15 rectangular pieces with a scraper or knife. Arrange dough over the fruit, 3 pieces across and 5 down. They should not touch.

7. GLAZE THE PASTRY: Using a fork, lightly beat the egg white with 1 teaspoon sugar. Brush lightly on the top of either dough, and sprinkle the top with the remaining sugar.

8. Make an aluminum foil drip pan to place on the rack below the pie halfway through the baking. Cut an 18-inch square of heavy-duty aluminum foil. Fold each edge twice (about 1 inch per fold) standing the folded edges upright to form a 4-sided pan.

10. For the short pastry, bake the cobbler for 35 to 40 minutes. For the biscuit dough, bake for 25 to 30 minutes. Bake the cobbler until the fruit juices begin to bubble and the top is golden brown. Let stand at least 30 minutes before serving. Serve in bowls with vanilla ice cream and the remaining sauce spooned over the top.

STORAGE
Cover any leftover cobbler loosely with waxed paper then aluminum foil and refrigerate for up to 3 days. Reheat before serving. This cobbler can be frozen.

Out of the Deep Freeze

ROZEN PIES AND TARTS are excellent choices when do-ahead desserts are in your plans. These composed sundaes are suitable to serve at almost any occasion, from "down-home" cookouts to parties with panache. ❋ My crust preference for frozen pies and tarts are those made from cookie crumbs or that have lots of crunch. The contrast in textures created by the smooth and creamy filling played against a crisp, chewy shell is most appealing. In addition, these kinds of crusts are very sturdy and are able to survive the bumps and knocks that often occur with foods in the freezer. Although I occasionally use rolled cookie-style pastry doughs for frozen desserts, they are not as tasty when cold, and they always require careful handling.

In this chapter you will find fillings made from scratch as well as those prepared with ready made ice cream. "Scratch" recipes give me the opportunity to showcase flavors that are hard to find. One of my favorites is a combination of chocolate and nougatine. Choco-Nouga Chew Chew Tart addresses my craving for something different, with its marriage of crackling caramel bits and a light chocolate Bavarian filling. Another special treat is the Pineapple Zabaghone in Coconut Almond Meringue. The filling is made with fresh, sugar-sweet pineapple folded through a creamy rum-flavored filling.

Premade ice creams, yogurts, and sorbets offer lots of ideas for creativity. Tutti-Frutti Amaretti Tart has layers of coffee and vanilla ice cream that mingle with crushed cookies, flecks of chocolate, toasted almonds, and brandied dried fruit. It's a grand combination. Triple Strawberry Ice Cream Pie makes the most of this beloved berry. Macerated fresh strawberries are studded throughout strawberry ice cream that is enriched with whipped cream and flavorful strawberry preserves.

While this chapter contains an exciting selection of frozen pies and tarts, do check elsewhere for more ideas. Many of the Bavarian and mousse recipes from the Decadent & Delicious chapter are adaptable for freezing. Whether you create your own "fixins" or use one of the recipes in this book, don't be shy about making frozen desserts. They are refreshing and convenient. Those who pass on pastries will usually yield to a bite or two of these cooling treats.

Before You Begin

Here is an overview of tips and tricks for making great frozen pies and tarts.

✦ When preparing frozen desserts, use well-chilled bowls and utensils. This will buy you a little extra time to combine the ingredients before melting occurs.

✦ Always soften ice cream, frozen yogurt, or sherbets before mixing them with whipped cream, meringue, or other ingredients. While the microwave will do in a pinch, it is better to soften these products slowly in the refrigerator. This can take from 30 to 90 minutes, depending on the weather and the type of product. Rich ice creams will take longer than sherbets and ices because they are higher in fat. If you can squeeze the carton, it is ready.

✦ When preparing a frozen pie or tart, always oil the pan lightly before filling it. Then wipe the pan lightly with a paper towel to remove any excess. This will enable you to release the dessert easily.

✦ Baked pastry crusts are not the best choices for frozen pies and tarts. They rarely taste as good when cold and break easily if jarred in the freezer.

✦ If using an ice cream maker, it is best to thoroughly chill the prepared mixture at least 12 hours before freezing.

✦ When using an ice cream maker, the product you are freezing does not have to become too firm. It will harden once frozen.

✦ It's okay to substitute reduced-fat ingredients in the recipe, but remember that the less fat in the product, the more icy textured it will be.

✦ If whipped cream is mixed into a filling that is to be frozen, the cream should be whipped only to soft peaks.

✦ Raw fruit to be added to ice creams or other bases must be macerated in sugar or poached in sugar syrup before using. Although fresh fruit will always become somewhat icy, sugaring it will reduce the crystallization. Do consider using canned fruit. It works well for freezing.

◆ Do not add too much alcohol to pie or tart fillings that are to be frozen. Excess alcohol will prevent the mixture from freezing.

◆ If you don't have an ice cream machine, freeze the mixture for the filling in a shallow nonreactive metal pan. As the mixture freezes, mix it and freeze again. Do this several times until it becomes solid enough to hold its shape. This procedure prevents the filling from becoming too icy.

◆ To protect the surface of a pie or tart, freeze it first, then cover it. You want to be sure the top is firm before it is wrapped.

◆ Frozen pies and tarts will have better flavor and texture if they are allowed to mature for several hours before using. Overnight is best.

◆ Allow ice creams and other frozen desserts "thaw time" in the refrigerator before cutting or removing them from their pans. This can take anywhere from 30 minutes to 90 minutes, depending on the coolness of the refrigerator and the outdoor temperature.

◆ To remove the outer ring from a tart pan with a removable bottom, gradually push up from underneath, easing the ring away from the side. Push hard, it will release. You should *not* dip the pan in water.

◆ Use a sharp knife that has been dipped in warm water to slice frozen pies or tarts.

◆ Tarts are easier to slice than pies because the side of the pan is usually removed first. Also, tart fillings are not as high as pie fillings because the pans are not as deep.

◆ When serving frozen pies, use a short spatula to release the edge of the pie *before slicing.* After the wedge of pie is cut, use the spatula to release the crust from underneath.

◆ Once a frozen pie or tart has thawed, if the leftovers are refrozen the storage time is shortened dramatically. This is because refrozen desserts usually form ice crystals.

◆ To protect a pie or tart for long storage, freeze it first. Cover it well with plastic wrap then place it in a plastic storage bag and seal tightly.

Choco-Nouga Chew Chew Tart

MILK CHOCOLATE AND PRALINE paste make up the irresistible flavors of this tart. The creamy filling is flecked with a crunchy nut brittle called nougatine, made with caramelized almonds. Praline paste, a hazelnut butter, contributes extraordinary flavor to pastries, desserts, and confections. Some food specialty stores stock praline paste, but if you are unable to find it it is easy to make your own (page 452), though it is not as refined as the commercial product. You can also mail-order praline paste from Maison Glass, a specialty food mail order source (page 466). The paste keeps indefinitely, and is well worth the investment. Thank you to my husband, Gene, who came up with the clever name for this tart.

At a Glance

SERVES: 8 to 10

PAN: 11-inch metal tart

PASTRY PREP: Baked

OVEN TEMP: 350 degrees

BAKING TIME:
10 to 12 minutes

DIFFICULTY: 👞 👞 👞

1 11-inch Chocolate Crumb Crust
   (page 168), baked
1 small recipe Nut Brittle (page
   452), made with sliced almonds

FILLING
1/2 cup milk
3/4 cup heavy cream
2 ounces milk chocolate, chopped
2 tablespoons praline paste
3 large egg yolks
3 tablespoons granulated sugar
3 tablespoons water
1 1/2 teaspoons unflavored gelatin
1 tablespoon Frangelico or Kahlúa
   liqueur
1 teaspoon vanilla extract
2 large egg whites
1/4 cup superfine sugar

GARNISH
1 cup heavy cream, well chilled
2 tablespoons strained
   confectioners' sugar
1/2 teaspoon vanilla extract

1. Chop the brittle into small pieces.

2. Sprinkle 1/4 cup of the brittle onto the cooled crust. Reserve 1/2 cup brittle for the filling. The remaining brittle can be used for a garnish or saved for a future use.

3. **MAKE THE FILLING:** Place the milk, ¼ cup cream, the chocolate, and praline paste in a heavy saucepan. Stir over low heat until the chocolate is melted and the praline paste is dissolved. If necessary, whisk the mixture until it is smooth.

4. Beat the egg yolks with a whisk. Add the granulated sugar gradually, whipping until the yolks are light in color.

5. Stir about a quarter of the chocolate mixture into the yolks to temper them. Then add the egg mixture to the saucepan, and stir the mixtures together. Cook over very low heat until just under the boil. Stir constantly with a rubber spatula, scraping the bottom of the saucepan to keep the filling from sticking.

6. Place the water in a small heatproof container and sprinkle the gelatin over the top. *Do not stir.* Let stand for 5 minutes to soften. Place the container in a skillet filled with ½ inch of simmering water and heat until the gelatin is clear and dissolved, 3 to 5 minutes. Add the gelatin to the filling along with the liqueur and vanilla.

7. Using a whisk, beat the egg whites until soft peaks form. Gradually whisk in the superfine sugar, beating until the whites form a soft meringue and are shiny and smooth. In a separate chilled bowl with chilled beaters, whip the remaining ½ cup cream to soft peaks.

8. Empty the filling into a large bowl. It should be *tepid.* Stir a quarter of the meringue into the filling, gently mixing to lighten the mixture. Using an oversize rubber spatula, fold in the remaining meringue, then fold in the whipped cream and the reserved ½ cup brittle.

9. Spoon the filling into the crumb crust and smooth the top. Freeze the tart until the top is set, about 1 hour. Cover the tart with plastic wrap and store in the freezer for at least 12 hours before serving (This pie can be frozen for up to 1 month before serving.)

10. **SERVE THE TART:** Remove the tart from the freezer, uncover, and refrigerate for 30 minutes before serving. To garnish the tart, whip the cream to soft peaks. Add the confectioners' sugar and vanilla. Whip the cream just until it holds its shape.

11. Fit a 16-inch pastry bag with a #824 large open star tip. Fill the bag with whipped cream. Pipe 24 rosettes around the edge of the tart, then pipe 12 lines, starting at every other rosette and continuing to the center. When the 12 lines are made, pipe a large rosette in the center to complete the design. It should look like a wheel with spokes.

STORAGE
Cover any leftover tart with plastic wrap and freeze for up to 3 days.

Sorbet-Frosted Lemon Bavarian Tart

HERE IS A TART THAT is as pretty to look at as it is refreshing to eat. This cooling dessert has a graham cracker crumb crust that is topped with a velvety lemon Bavarian cream. The tart is frosted with a thin layer of raspberry sorbet or sherbet. I can't think of a nicer dessert to make for your guests on the sultry summer days.

1 small recipe Master Crumb
   Crust (page 164), made with
   graham crackers

FILLING

1/4 cup fresh orange juice
1 package unflavored gelatin
3/4 cup water
1/4 cup fresh lemon juice
1/2 cup sugar
4 large egg yolks
1 teaspoon vanilla extract
1 cup heavy cream, well chilled
1 pint raspberry sorbet or sherbet,
   slightly softened

1. Lightly oil the bottom and sides of the tart pan. Dab the pan with a paper towel to remove excess oil. Press the crumb crust over the *bottom* of the tart pan. Do not push crumbs up the sides of the pan. Chill while preparing the filling.

2. **MAKE THE FILLING:** Place the orange juice in a small heat-proof bowl. Sprinkle the gelatin over the top. *Do not stir.* Let the gelatin stand for 5 minutes to soften. Place the container in a small skillet filled with 1/2 inch

of simmering water. Heat in the water bath for 3 to 5 minutes or until the liquid is clear and the gelatin is dissolved.

3. Simmer the water, lemon juice, and sugar in a small saucepan until the sugar is completely dissolved. Lightly beat the egg yolks with a fork. Stir about a quarter of the hot lemon mixture into the yolks to temper them. Then add the yolks to the saucepan. Over low heat, stir constantly until the mixture thickens. Do not boil.

4. Pour the mixture through a fine strainer into a large stainless steel mixing bowl. Add the dissolved gelatin and the vanilla. Fill the kitchen sink with about 2 inches of cold water and ice cubes. Set the bowl in the ice-water bath. Stir gently and frequently with a rubber spatula until it starts to thicken. *Watch carefully. Remove the filling from the ice-water bath if it is congealing too quickly.* It is ready when it looks like thick soup.

5. While the lemon mixture is cooling, whip the cream in a chilled bowl with chilled beaters until it forms soft peaks. Using an oversize rubber spatula, fold a quarter of the cream into the lemon filling to lighten the mixture, then fold in the remaining cream. Pour the filling into the crumb crust, smooth the top with an offset spatula, and bang the tart on the counter to remove any air pockets. Set the tart on a shallow pan and place it in the freezer for 3 to 4 hours.

6. When the filling is hard, remove the tart from the freezer. Using a small offset spatula, spread small amounts of sorbet over the top, covering the edge first, then working toward the middle. You will need almost the whole pint of sorbet. When you are done, run a long spatula over the top to smooth the surface. Clean the edge of the pan with paper towels to remove any melted sorbet.

7. Decorate the top of the tart by pressing a slight indentation into the sorbet using the rounded tip of the spatula. Do this in rows across the entire top. Freeze the tart for at least 1 hour before serving. (For longer storage, cover with plastic wrap and store in the freezer for up to 1 month. See page 75 for unmolding instructions.)

STORAGE
Cover any leftover tart with plastic wrap and freeze for up to 3 days.

Key Lime Pie with a Twist

THIS ADAPTATION OF KEY LIME pie has much more pizzazz than the classic recipe. Its light, mousse-type filling imparts a pleasing, delicate flavor. If you want to dazzle your guests, take the time to pipe the filling through a pastry bag. The rippled effect makes a stunning showcase for the creamy topping.

At a Glance

SERVES: 6 to 8

PAN: 9-inch ovenproof glass

PASTRY PREP: Unbaked

DIFFICULTY: 🍪 🍪

---

1 9-inch Coconut Ginger Crust
(page 294)

FILLING
1 cup granulated sugar
3 tablespoons all-purpose flour
1/8 teaspoon salt
2/3 cup Key lime juice, fresh or
   bottled (see headnote, page 264)
2 large eggs, lightly beaten
1/2 cup water
2 tablespoons unsalted butter, cut
   into 1/2-inch pieces
1 teaspoon grated lime zest
1 teaspoon vanilla extract
1 1/2 cups heavy cream, well chilled
1/4 cup strained confectioners'
   sugar
1/4 cup sweetened flaked coconut,
   toasted
1 fresh lime, for garnish

1. MAKE THE FILLING: Whisk the granulated sugar, flour, and salt together in the top of a double boiler. Gradually add the lime juice, stirring until the mixture is smooth. Blend in the eggs and water.

2. Place the pot over boiling water and cook, stirring constantly, until the mixture is thickened, 5 to 10 minutes, depending on the weight of the double boiler. When the mixture is thick, pass it through a fine-mesh strainer into a large bowl. Stir in the butter, lime zest, and vanilla. Cool in a cold water bath until tepid.

3. In a chilled bowl with chilled beaters, whip the cream on medium speed. When it starts to thicken, add the confectioners' sugar and continue to beat just until it is firm enough to hold its shape. *Do not overbeat.*

4. Stir a quarter of the cream into the filling, then fold in the remaining cream. You can empty the filling into the pie shell and smooth it with a spatula, or pipe the filling through a pastry bag.

5. To pipe the filling, fit a 16-inch pastry bag with a #828 large open star tip. Pipe lines of overlapping shells, from top to bottom, using firm pressure on the bag to squeeze out the filling. Continue making rows of shells until the cavity is filled. You should have about 9 rows altogether.

6. Place the pie in the freezer, uncovered, and chill until the top is firm. Then cover the pie with plastic wrap and freeze for at least 6 hours. (This pie can be frozen for up to 1 month before serving.)

7. Remove the pie from the freezer 1 hour before serving and refrigerate until ready to garnish and serve.

8. GARNISH THE PIE. Make a 2-inch border of toasted coconut around the edge of the pie. Place a twist of lime in the center.

STORAGE ======
Cover any leftover pie with plastic wrap and freeze for up to 3 days.

Pistachio 'n Peach Ice Cream Pie in Krispie Meringue

A CRUNCHY MERINGUE SHELL MADE with Rice Krispies holds a filling of homemade pistachio ice cream with chunks of peaches throughout. It's okay if you wish to substitute a ready-made pistachio ice cream, but it lacks the delicate flavor and natural color of one made from scratch.

At a Glance

SERVES: 6 to 8

PAN: 9-inch ovenproof glass

PASTRY PREP: Baked

OVEN TEMP: 325 degrees

BAKING TIME: 20 minutes

DIFFICULTY:

Look for imported pistachios in Middle Eastern stores, as they are better than the ones grown in California. After the nuts are shelled, blanch them to remove the skins and salt.

1 3/4 cups shelled pistachio nuts

PIE SHELL
1 large egg white
1/4 cup superfine sugar
1/2 teaspoon vanilla extract
2 cups Rice Krispies cereal

ICE CREAM BASE
2 cups milk
2 cups heavy cream
1 6-inch vanilla bean, split lengthwise
8 large egg yolks
1/2 cup granulated sugar
2 tablespoons Amaretto liqueur
5 or 6 drops green vegetable food coloring
1 (29-ounce) can sliced cling peaches, well drained

1. PREPARE THE PISTACHIOS: Place the pistachios in a medium saucepan. Fill the pot with cold water and bring to a boil. Remove from the heat, drain, and rinse with cold water. Place the nuts on several layers of paper towels, then cover with more paper towels. Rub the nuts between the towels to loosen the skins. Remove any stubborn skins with a paring knife.

2. Reserve 1 cup of the nuts for the ice cream base. Place the remaining pistachios in a shallow baking pan. Lightly toast in a 325 degree oven for 6 to 8 minutes or until dry but not brown. Let cool. Chop the toasted nuts into medium pieces and reserve for the pie shell and ice cream.

3. MAKE THE PIE SHELL:
Preheat the oven to 325 degrees. Position the oven rack in the lower third of the oven. Spray a 9-inch ovenproof glass pie plate *very well* with nonstick coating, then dust with flour. Tap out excess.

4. Beat the egg white on medium speed with an electric mixer until it reaches firm peaks. Add the superfine sugar, 1 tablespoon at a time, taking about 1 minute. Add the vanilla. Increase the speed to medium-high and beat for 45 to 60 seconds longer to form a stiff meringue.

5. Using an oversize rubber spatula, fold the Rice Krispies and ¼ cup chopped toasted pistachios into the meringue. Empty the mixture into the pan. Spread the meringue on the bottom and sides using the back of a large tablespoon. Spray a 10-inch circle of nonstick coating on a sheet of plastic wrap. Invert the plastic wrap onto the meringue. Using a batarde (page 457) or a smooth-bottomed glass, press the meringue firmly and evenly across the bottom of the pan. Then press the sides into place with the side of your thumb.

6. Bake the shell for 20 minutes or until the sides begin to brown. The meringue will feel slightly soft, but it will harden as it cools. Remove from the oven and set on a rack. Cool completely.

7. MAKE THE ICE CREAM BASE: Place the milk, cream, and vanilla bean in a large saucepan. Heat without stirring until a skin forms on top, then remove from the heat. Using a food processor or blender, puree the 1 cup of untoasted pistachios with 1 cup of the hot milk.

8. Empty the pureed nut mixture into the saucepan with the remaining milk. Scald again, then remove the saucepan from the heat. Using a paring knife, scrape the tiny seeds from the vanilla bean. Add the seeds and the empty pod to the hot mixture. Let steep for at least 30 minutes.

9. Place the egg yolks into a large stainless steel bowl. Beat with a whisk until thoroughly blended. Add the granulated sugar, 1 tablespoon at a time, and whip until the mixture is thick and light in color. Reheat the milk mixture. Stir about a quarter of the hot milk into the egg yolks, then blend in the remaining liquid. Return the yolk mixture to the saucepan.

10. Stirring constantly with a wooden spoon, heat the mixture until just under the boiling point. The sauce will thicken slightly. Test by running your finger down the back of the spoon. If the line created by your finger remains, the custard is ready.

11. *Immediately* pour the mixture through a very fine-mesh strainer into a clean bowl. Discard the vanilla pod. Stir in the liqueur, then tint the custard to a soft green with the food coloring. Cover with a sheet of buttered plastic wrap and refrigerate several hours until very cold.

12. **ASSEMBLE THE PIE:** Dice the peaches into ½-inch pieces, reserving 5 uniform slices for garnishing. Set aside.

13. Freeze the custard in an ice cream maker according to the manufacturer's directions. When the ice cream is thick and almost frozen, fold in the peaches and ¼ cup of the chopped, toasted pistachios. Mix just to combine. Empty the mixture into the crust, mounding it on top. Smooth the surface with an offset spatula dipped in warm water.

14. Arrange the 5 reserved peach slices in a star pattern on top of the pie, pressing them slightly into the ice cream. Trim the edge of the pie with the remaining chopped toasted pistachios. Cover with plastic wrap and freeze for at least 24 hours. (This pie can be frozen for up to 1 month before serving.) Remove pie from the freezer 30 minutes before serving and place in the refrigerator to soften.

STORAGE

Cover any leftover pie with plastic wrap and freeze for up to 3 days.

Fudge Walnut Sundae Pie

A NUT CRUST HOLDS LAYERS OF vanilla and coffee ice creams, separated by a Kahlúa-flavored fudge walnut filling. When the pie is sliced, the pieces have an attractive ribbon effect made from the alternating layers.

1 9-inch All-Nut Pastry Shell
(page 163), baked

FILLING
1 recipe Warm Fudge Sauce
(page 446)
1 cup walnuts, toasted and cooled
2 tablespoons Kahlúa liqueur
1 pint French vanilla ice cream,
slightly softened
1 pint coffee ice cream, slightly
softened

1. MAKE THE FILLING: Measure 1 cup fudge sauce and place it in a bowl. Save the remaining sauce to use when serving the pie. Chop the walnuts into medium pieces. Stir the walnuts and Kahlúa into the fudge sauce. Remove ¼ cup for garnishing the pie.

2. Empty the vanilla ice cream into the pastry shell, spreading it as best you can with an offset spatula. Place the pie in the freezer and freeze for 15 minutes, or until the surface is set. Spread the sauce in an even layer (it should be tepid) over the vanilla ice cream. Freeze the pie again until the fudge is set, but not hard, 5 to 10 minutes. Finally, spread the coffee ice cream over the fudge layer, mounding it slightly in the center. Warm the

blade of the spatula in hot water, and smooth the surface of the pie. Freeze for 1 hour.

3. Heat the remaining ¼ cup fudge-nut mixture to tepid. Using the tip of a teaspoon, drop the fudge in small mounds (about ½ teaspoon each) around the edge of the pie. Spread the mounds slightly with the spoon so that they will join together, forming a ring around the edge of the pie. Place the pie in the freezer for 30 minutes or until the ice cream is set.

4. Cover the pie with plastic wrap and store in the freezer for at least 3 hours or until ready to serve. (This pie may be frozen for up to 1 month before serving.)

5. SERVE THE PIE: Remove the pie from the freezer. Remove the wrapping, then place the pie in the refrigerator for 30 minutes to thaw slightly. Reheat the reserved fudge sauce. Cut the pie into wedges and drizzle the sauce over the top.

STORAGE
Cover any leftover pie with plastic wrap and store in the freezer for up to 1 week.

At a Glance

SERVES: 6 to 8

PAN: 9-inch ovenproof glass

PASTRY PREP: Baked

DIFFICULTY: 🥄

Chocolate-Crusted Raspberry Soufflé Pie

CHOCOLATE CRUMBS ON THE TOP and bottom of this pie encase a frozen raspberry soufflé filling. The crunch of the crumbs is great paired with the creamy center. If you wish, this pie can be eaten without freezing, just refrigerate for at least 6 hours or until the filling has set.

At a Glance

SERVES: 8 to 10

PAN: 9½-inch deep-dish ovenproof glass

PASTRY PREP: Baked

OVEN TEMP: 350 degrees

BAKING TIME: 10 to 12 minutes

DIFFICULTY: 🥄 🥄

CRUST

2 tablespoons strained cocoa powder
1¾ cups packaged chocolate cookie crumbs (preferably Oreo)
¼ cup firmly packed dark brown sugar
7 tablespoons unsalted butter, melted and cooled

FILLING

1 (10-ounce) package frozen raspberries, thawed
¾ cup superfine sugar
¼ cup water
1 (¼-ounce) package unflavored gelatin
2 large egg whites
1 cup heavy cream, whipped to soft peaks
2 tablespoons framboise liqueur or kirschwasser
1 teaspoon vanilla extract

1. MAKE THE CRUST: Preheat the oven to 350 degrees. Position the oven rack in the lower third of the oven. Generously butter a 9½-inch deep-dish ovenproof pie plate. Dust the pan with the cocoa powder and shake out excess.

2. Place the cookie crumbs and brown sugar in a food processor bowl. Process for 20 to 30 seconds to combine.

3. Empty the crumb mixture into a bowl with the butter and combine with a fork.

4. Remove ¾ cup of the mixture and set aside. Empty the remaining crumbs into the pan. Using a tablespoon, press the crumbs firmly against the sides of the pan, working them up to the rim to form an edge. Smooth the bottom with the spoon or smooth-bottomed glass.

5. Lay a sheet of plastic wrap over the crumbs. Using a batarde (page 457) or a smooth-bottomed glass, press firmly against the plastic to smooth the crumbs on the bottom. Press firmly at the bend because the crumbs accumulate there. Remove the plastic wrap.

6. Bake for 10 to 12 minutes or until the crumbs begin to smell. The surface should feel set, but the bottom will not firm until the shell cools. Let shell cool completely on a rack before filling.

7. MAKE THE FILLING: Place the raspberries in the bowl of a food processor. Puree the berries, then pass the mixture through a fine-mesh strainer into a saucepan.

8. Add ½ cup sugar and place over medium heat. When the puree comes to a boil, simmer for 1 to 2 minutes. Set aside.

9. Place the water in a small heatproof container and sprinkle the gelatin over the top. *Do not stir.* Let stand for 5 minutes to soften. Place the container in a skillet filled with ½ inch of simmering water and heat until gelatin is clear and dissolved, 3 to 5 minutes. Stir the dissolved gelatin into the raspberry puree.

10. Empty the puree into a large bowl. Set the bowl in ice water to hasten the cooling, and stir occasionally. When it starts to gel, *immediately* remove the bowl from the water.

11. While the puree is cooling, place the egg whites in the large bowl of an electric mixer and set the bowl over simmering water. Beat the whites with a whisk, adding the remaining ¼ cup sugar, a little at a time. When the whites are hot to the touch and the sugar is dissolved, remove the bowl from the heat.

Whip the whites on medium speed, beating until they are cool and form a firm, shiny meringue.

12. Stir about a third of the meringue into the raspberry puree to lighten the mixture. Fold in the remaining meringue, then fold in the whipped cream, framboise, and vanilla. Empty the soufflé mixture into the crumb shell. Smooth the top with the back of a tablespoon.

13. Sprinkle the reserved crumbs over the top of the pie, smoothing them with a small offset spatula. When the surface of the pie is firm, cover with aluminum foil. Freeze for at least 12 hours before serving, or refrigerate for 6 hours, until filling is set. Serve pie with fresh raspberries. (This pie can be frozen for up to 1 month before serving.)

STORAGE
Freeze any leftover pie covered with plastic wrap for up to 3 days.

Triple Strawberry Ice Cream Pie

PLUMP RED STRAWBERRIES ARE MACERATED in liqueur, then combined with strawberry ice cream, whipped cream, and fruity strawberry preserves. For the most aromatic and intense flavor, visit your local farms to take advantage of fresh berries in season.

When you make this pie, be sure to let the ice cream soften in the refrigerator for about 30 minutes, so it will blend smoothly and quickly with the other ingredients. You should be able to squeeze the container. While this pie is easy to make, it is helpful to have all of your utensils well chilled.

1 9-inch Master Crumb Crust
  (page 164), made with lemon
  cookies or vanilla wafers

FILLING
3 cups (1½ pints) fresh
  strawberries
3 to 4 tablespoons superfine sugar
2 tablespoons fraise de bois liqueur
  or kirschwasser
3/4 teaspoon unflavored gelatin
1 tablespoon fresh lemon juice
½ cup heavy cream, well chilled
3 tablespoons strained
  confectioners' sugar
1 teaspoon vanilla extract
1½ pints strawberry ice cream,
  softened
6 tablespoons thick strawberry
  preserves

GARNISH
½ cup heavy cream, well chilled
  (optional)
1 recipe Strawberry Topping
  (page 449)

1. START THE BERRIES: Wash and hull the strawberries; dry well on paper towels (page 39). Cut the berries into ⅛-inch slices and place them in a large bowl. Sprinkle the superfine sugar over the berries, drizzle with the liqueur, and shake the bowl to distribute. Cover and macerate for 1 hour.

2. Place the macerated strawberries in a strainer set over a bowl and drain for at least 15 minutes.

3. Place a large shallow pan in the freezer to chill while preparing the filling.

4. MAKE THE FILLING: Place 2 tablespoons of the juice from the strawberries in a small heat-proof bowl. Sprinkle the gelatin over the top. *Do not stir.* Let the gelatin stand for 5 minutes to soften. Place the container in a small skillet filled with ½ inch simmering water. Heat in the water bath for 3 to 5 minutes, until the liquid is clear and the gelatin is dissolved.

5. Put the strawberries in a shallow bowl and mash them a few times with a potato masher or a fork to make a coarse puree. Stir in the lemon juice and set aside.

6. Whip the cream in a large chilled bowl with chilled beaters on medium speed until it starts to thicken. Add the confectioners' sugar and vanilla. On medium-low speed, drizzle the gelatin into the cream, mixing only until soft peaks form.

7. Using a large mixing spoon, blend about a quarter of the soft ice cream into the whipped cream. Fold in the strawberry preserves, then add the remaining ice cream and the pureed strawberries. (If additional juice has formed, discard it.)

8. Quickly combine all the ingredients, then spoon the mixture into the chilled shallow metal pan. Place in the freezer for 30 minutes, then gently stir with a rubber spatula. Chill again. Stir every 15 to 20 minutes. The mixture is ready when it holds its shape and is firm enough to mold.

9. Spoon the filling into the crumb crust. Pack it down, mounding it in the center. Place the pie in the freezer, and chill for 1 hour or until the top is set. Then cover the pie with plastic wrap and freeze for at least 8 hours, or up to 3 days. (This pie can be frozen for up to 1 week before serving.)

10. GARNISH THE PIE: Whip the cream in a chilled bowl with chilled beaters until it is thick enough to pipe from a pastry bag. Empty the cream into a 14-inch pastry bag fitted with a #824 large open star tip. Pipe rosettes around the edge of the pie. Return to the freezer, unwrapped.

11. Remove pie from the freezer and refrigerate until it is soft enough to slice, about 30 minutes. Cut the pie into wedges and spoon Strawberry Topping over each serving.

STORAGE

Cover any leftover pie with plastic wrap and freeze for up to 3 days.

Tutti-Frutti Amaretti Tart

THIS TART IS A KALEIDOSCOPE of colors and flavors. It has an amaretti crumb crust that is layered with coffee and vanilla ice cream and brandied dried apricots and cherries. I use more coffee ice cream than vanilla, but you can divide it as you wish. Bits of chocolate, toasted almonds (slivered are best), and crushed amaretti cookies add crunch and texture.

At a Glance

SERVES: 8 to 10

PAN: 9¹/₂-inch deep-dish metal tart *or* 9¹/₂-inch deep-dish ovenproof glass

PASTRY PREP: Unbaked

DIFFICULTY: 🥄 🥄

I prefer to make this dessert in a fluted deep-dish tart pan. When it is unmolded, the fluted edge makes an attractive presentation. If you don't have this pan, substitute a deep ovenproof glass pie plate. Either way, after one bite of this tart I guarantee that you'll be back for more.

1 large recipe Amaretti Nut
    Crumb Crust (page 167)

FILLING
¹/₂ cup water
¹/₄ cup sugar
¹/₂ cup diced dried apricots, cut in
    ¹/₂-inch pieces
¹/₂ cup dried cherries
2 tablespoons brandy or Amaretto
    liqueur
1 quart coffee ice cream, softened
1 pint vanilla ice cream, softened
4 amaretti cookies, broken into
    coarse crumbs (about ¹/₃ cup)
¹/₄ cup slivered almonds, toasted
    and coarsely chopped
2 ounces bittersweet chocolate,
    coarsely chopped

1. **START THE FRUIT:** Place the water and sugar in a small saucepan and bring to a boil. Reduce the heat and simmer for 2 to 3 minutes. Remove from the heat and add the apricots, cherries, and brandy. Cover and let macerate at room temperature for at least 6 hours.

2. **SHAPE THE CRUMB CRUST:** Spray the pan with nonstick coating. Press the crumbs firmly into the bottom of the pan and about 3/4 of the way up the sides. Smooth the bottom with a batarde (page 457) or a smooth-bottomed glass. (Use your forefinger to press the crumbs into the grooves of the tart pan.) It's okay if some of the metal is not completely covered around the side. Chill for at least 15 minutes.

3. **ASSEMBLE THE PIE:** Drain the brandied fruit in a strainer set over a bowl. Discard the liquid.

4. Using a large mixing spoon, make a layer of alternating spoonfuls of coffee and vanilla ice creams in the crust.

5. Sprinkle the ice cream with half each of the dried fruits, amaretti crumbs, slivered almonds, and chopped chocolate. Use a spoon to push these ingredients slightly into the ice cream. Repeat with a second layer of ice cream. Top with the remaining brandied fruits, amaretti crumbs, slivered almonds, and chopped chocolate, pushing them lightly into the ice cream. Finish with a top layer of ice cream, mounding it in the center.

6. To give the tart a finished look, use the tip of a small knife to scrape the crumbs from above the level of the ice cream onto the edge of the filling.

7. Place the tart in the freezer for 1 hour or until the top is frozen. Cover the tart tightly with plastic wrap and freeze for at least 6 hours. (This tart can be frozen for up to 1 month before serving.)

8. SERVE THE TART: Remove the tart from the freezer and place it in the refrigerator for 45 to 60 minutes to soften. Remove the plastic wrap and set the tart on a wide tin can. To remove the rim, push up from underneath, moving your fingers around the bottom of the pan. The rim will drop away from the side. Cut into wedges and serve.

STORAGE
Any leftover pie should be covered with plastic wrap and stored in the freezer for up to 3 days.

Frozen Honey Yogurt Tart with Pine Nut Crust

THE SWEETNESS OF HONEY IS PAIRED with the tang of yogurt for a distinctive flavor. On the bottom of this tart is a crust made with lots of toasted pine nuts mingled with crushed lemon cookies. While the tart can be made with a low-fat yogurt, the texture will be much creamier if whole-milk yogurt is used. Serve this tart with a simple garnish of sliced nectarines or peaches. It's light, refreshing, and delightful.

At a Glance

SERVES: 8 to 10

PAN: 11-inch metal tart

PASTRY PREP: Unbaked

DIFFICULTY: 🍪

CRUST
2 tablespoons unsalted butter
1/2 teaspoon grated lemon zest
1/2 cup Lemon Nut Crunch Cookie crumbs (Pepperidge Farm)
1/4 cup zwieback crumbs
2 teaspoons sugar
1/2 cup pine nuts, lightly toasted

FILLING
2/3 cup milk
2/3 cup sugar
1/3 cup honey
2 1/2 cups plain whole-milk yogurt
1 1/3 cups heavy cream
2 teaspoons vanilla extract

1. PREPARE THE CRUST: Spray the tart pan with nonstick coating. Heat the butter in a medium saucepan until just melted. Add the lemon zest and set aside to cool. Add the crumbs to the butter along with the sugar and pine nuts. Stir with a fork.

2. Empty the crumb mixture into the tart pan. Press the mixture firmly into the bottom of the pan. Do not line the sides with the crumbs. Chill until ready to use.

3. MAKE THE FILLING: Place the milk, sugar, and honey in a small saucepan. Cook over low heat until the sugar is completely dissolved. Cool to tepid.

4. Empty the yogurt into a large bowl. Gradually add the milk mixture, stirring with a fork to combine. Stir in the cream, then the vanilla. Chill the yogurt base for at least 6 hours. Then pour the mixture into an ice cream maker and follow the manufacturer's directions for freezing.

5. When the ice cream holds its shape but is not too hard, spoon it into the crumb shell. Smooth the surface with an offset spatula. Bang the tart pan on the counter to remove any air pockets. Level the top of the tart with an offset spatula.

6. Place the tart on a shallow pan and freeze for 1 hour, or until the top is set. Cover the tart with plastic wrap and freeze for 6 to 8 hours before serving. (This pie can be frozen for up to 1 month before serving.)

7. SERVE THE TART: Remove the tart from the freezer and place in the refrigerator for 30 to 45 minutes to soften. Remove the plastic wrap and set the tart on top of a wide tin can. To remove the rim, push up from underneath, moving your fingers around the bottom of the pan. The rim will drop from the side. Cut the tart into wedges and serve with freshly cut nectarines or other fresh fruit.

STORAGE

Any leftover tart should be covered with plastic wrap and frozen for up to 3 days.

Of all the fruits he'd tasted there, "none please my taste as do's the pine."

GEORGE WASHINGTON'S DIARY, BARBADOS, 1751

Pineapple Zabaglione in Coconut Almond Meringue

HERE IS A REFRESHING FROZEN PIE made with fresh pineapple folded into a rum-flavored zabaglione. The filling is nestled in a tasty coconut almond meringue shell. Look for a Del Monte Gold pineapple when you make this pie.

1 9-inch Coco-Nutty Meringue shell (page 162), baked

FRUIT
2 1/2 cups coarsely chopped fresh pineapple (about 3/4 of a large pineapple) (page 36)
3 tablespoons superfine sugar
2 teaspoons fresh lemon juice

ZABAGLIONE
4 large egg yolks
1/2 cup superfine sugar
3 tablespoons dark rum
1 tablespoon fresh lemon juice
1 1/4 cups heavy cream, whipped to soft peaks

1. **START THE PINEAPPLE:** Set aside 1 1/2 cups pineapple for the zabaglione. Macerate the remaining pineapple in a medium mixing bowl with 3 tablespoons superfine sugar and 2 teaspoons lemon juice. Cover and let stand at room temperature.

2. Puree the reserved 1 1/2 cups pineapple in a food processor.

3. **MAKE THE ZABAGLIONE:** Place the egg yolks in a large mixing bowl. Set the bowl over a large pot of simmering water. Whisk the yolks while gradually adding the superfine sugar, then the rum. Whisk the mixture until it is thick and ribbony, 5 to 7 minutes. Remove the bowl from the water bath.

4. Stir the pureed pineapple and lemon juice into the zabaglione. Then with an oversize rubber spatula, fold in the whipped cream. Pour the mixture into a large, shallow pan and place in the freezer for about 1 hour. Stir the mixture 2 or 3 times while freezing.

5. When the pineapple zabaglione is almost frozen, place the macerated pineapple in a strainer and press out most of the liquid. Fold the drained fruit into the zabaglione and spoon into the pie shell, mounding the top. Freeze, uncovered, until the top of the pie has set. Then cover with plastic wrap and freeze for at least 24 hours before serving. (This pie can be frozen for up to 1 month before serving.)

STORAGE
Freeze any leftover pie covered with plastic wrap for 3 days.

Little Tarts, Pies & Turnovers

INGLE PORTION DESSERTS have an image of being special, and they are. Great care and patience goes into making them. * While scaled-down versions of pastries are more time-consuming to prepare, the advantages far outweigh the element. Of most significance, individual pastries are not portioned before serving, a quality that opens many avenues not possible when serving large pies and tarts. If the consistency of a tart filling is a bit loose, it's not a problem. Personally, I love it when my fork breaks into a crisp crust and the filling gracefully oozes onto the plate. I lap up the silky custard with a spoon. Unlike large tarts and pies, individual pastries require little thickening to hold their fillings in place.

In addition, it's a bonus to be able to devour a pastry shortly out of the oven. While most large pies and tarts require a cooling down period before they can be sliced, these individual servings can often be enjoyed almost immediately. If made with fruit, the warm juices are an asset, not a drawback. Tarts can be assembled and baked to order because most of the components are made ahead. This ensures a crisp crust every time. And when it comes to presentation, you can fuss as much as time permits. The accoutrements are not destroyed in serving, only when eaten.

Here in this chapter are some showstopping recipes as well as old favorites. Awesome Black Mission Fig and Blackberry Tarts promise to deliver raves from your guests. The nutty cornmeal pastry shell is layered with blackberry confit and swirls of chiffon filling, so pretty with wedges of pink-hued figs on top. Another exquisite dessert is the Poached Peaches and Mascarpone on Cookie Saucers. These are napped with a fresh currant sauce and vibrant-colored berries. If you were raised down South, you will welcome the sweetness of Fresh Coconut Tarts with Buttermilk Custard. Fried Apricot Pies, warm from the skillet, are every kid's delight.

With a little know-how you can transform almost any pie or tart into small or even miniature versions. Whether you choose a deep-dish pie baked in a ramekin or a "to die for" tart, remember that whoever the lucky recipient is, he or she will know it was made just for them. Check out my tips in "Making Little Pies and Tarts from Big Ones." While patience is a key ingredient here, I know you will be pleased with the rewards.

Making Little Pies and Tarts from Big Ones

One of the greatest advantages to making individual pastries is that there are so many options open to us. Rounds, squares, rectangles, diamonds, ovals, half-moons, turnovers, and bundles are but a few of the common free-form shapes you can make. Ordinary molds like round tartlet pans, little flan rings, muffin pans, ramekins, and custard cups are all readily available.

While pie dough can be used for most free-form shapes, this type of dough is too delicate for molding into tartlet pans. Cookie doughs are the best choices for these because they have a more compact, sturdy crumb. Phyllo and puff pastry should not be overlooked. These two doughs can be purchased ready made, or if time permits, try making puff pastry from scratch. It is truly a treat.

To determine how much dough to use, let the thickness of the pastry be your guide. Since most large pies and tarts use 1/8-inch thickness, a reasonable tartlet lining would be slightly less. Remember: the smaller the pan, the thinner the dough. All of the tart doughs in Chapter 1 are suitable to use. The best choices for individual free-form pies are American-style doughs like the Flaky Pie Pastry (page 98, 100), Cheddar Pastry (page 135), 1940s All-Butter Pie Pastry (page 138), Vegetable Oil Pastry (page 144), and Cream Cheese Pastry (page 157).

Most of the pie and tart fillings in this book will make eight to ten 4 1/2-inch tartlets. With the exception of pastry fillings made with uncooked fruits and berries, you can safely estimate about 1/2 cup filling for each 4 1/2-inch tartlet shell. For other pan sizes, exact filling amounts are impossible to give because there is such a broad spectrum of small baking containers. Baking times will also depend on size. Obviously, the smaller the pastry, the more quickly it will bake.

Here are some additional tips:

+ *Save leftover scraps of pastry dough for making individual tarts.*

+ *Pastry-lined tartlet pans can be stored in the freezer and used as needed.*

+ *Tartlet pans, as a rule, do not require greasing.*

+ *Choose drier fillings for free-form pastries. Save the custards for more structured shapes.*

+ *It is best to pre-cook fruit fillings for free-form pastries.*

+ *For easier handling and to prevent spillage, always bake tartlets on a shallow baking pan, never directly on the oven rack.*

+ *Cool all cooked fillings before enclosing them in pastry.*

Lining Tartlets and Other Small Pans with Pastry

THE SPECTRUM OF TARTLET PANS available makes it necessary to give more than one method for lining the pans with pastry. In addition, some doughs are more fragile than others. I have given two basic techniques. Read through them and choose the one that is best suited to your requirements, adapting it if need be.

Using Cookie-Type Doughs—Tartlet Pans with Removable Bottoms

Cookie-type doughs make superb tart crusts, but because the dough is buttery, it is difficult to roll. After baking, these shells must be handled with care because they are so fragile.

A 4^1/$_2$-inch tartlet pan will use a ball of dough made slightly larger than a golf ball (about 2 ounces). With lightly floured hands, roll each piece into a ball, then flatten it into a 2- to 3-inch disk.

METHOD 1—ROLLING PIN

✦ Place the disk between 2 sheets of lightly floured plastic wrap. Roll the dough into a 5^1/$_2$- to 6-inch circle. Remove the top piece of wrap and invert the pastry onto the tartlet pan. *Do not* remove the plastic wrap. Press the pastry gently into the pan, molding it into the bend and grooves. Remove plastic wrap, place on a shallow pan with sides, and chill for at least 5 minutes.

METHOD 2—HAND

✦ Place the disk in the center of the pan. With floured fingers, press the pastry dough against the bottom of the pan, gradually working it toward the sides. Place your forefinger at the bend and ease the dough up the sides, pushing it until it reaches the rim. Rotate the pan as you work. To even the bottom, place a sheet of plastic wrap against the dough. Using a batarde (page 457) or a smooth-bottomed glass, press against the bend and then across the bottom. Remove plastic wrap, place on a shallow pan, and chill for at least 5 minutes.

TO BAKE BLIND

✦ Preheat the oven to 375 degrees. Use a 350 degree oven for miniature tartlets. Position the oven rack in the lower third of the oven. Prick the pastry dough in several places with a fork.

✦ Cut 6-inch square pieces of aluminum foil. Butter or spray with nonstick coating a 5-inch circle on the foil. Invert the aluminum foil, buttered side down, into the tartlet pan. Mold it into the bend. Line with dried beans. For easier handling, keep the tartlet shells on the shallow pan when baking.

✦ Bake for 16 to 18 minutes. Remove the foil and beans, and continue baking for 2 minutes longer. If the aluminum foil sticks, bake the shell another 1 to 2 minutes. The crust will crisp as it cools.

Using Classic Tart Pastry—Tartlet Pans Without Removable Bottoms

Classic tart pastry (pâte brisée) is a mainstay pastry for making tartlets of all shapes and sizes. The dough is easier to roll and to shape. The double pan method suggested below ensures a well-shaped tartlet shell and eliminates the need for baking beans, but more baking tins are needed. Tartlet shells made with Classic Tart Pastry are also very fragile after baking, so handle carefully.

✦ On a lightly floured pastry cloth or a rolling surface, roll dough to slightly less than 1/8-inch thickness. Prick well with a fork. Invert one of the pans you plan to use on top of the pastry, placing it on the upper right side of the pastry. With a pastry wheel and using the pan as a guide, cut around the pan, allowing for a 1/2-inch overhang.

✦ Turn the mold right side up. Lay the cut piece of dough over the top of the mold. Prick again with a fork. Let the dough rest a few minutes.

✦ Butter the bottom of a second mold to ensure easy removal and insert it into the pastry-lined pan. Press the two together like a sandwich. Trim the edge with your fingers or a small knife.

✦ Place the double pans, inverted, on a shallow sheet pan. Continue making shells until the dough is used. Collect the leftover dough scrapes and place them on a sheet of plastic wrap. Squeeze the pieces to form a ball. Chill briefly if needed. Then re-roll pastry and shape as before. Chill the tartlets 30 minutes.

✦ Preheat the oven to 425 degrees. Position the oven rack in the lower third of the oven.

✦ Bake the tartlet shells, still inverted, for 8 to 10 minutes or until the edge of the dough starts to brown. With the tip of a paring knife, remove the top molds. Reduce the oven temperature to 375 degrees. Lightly prick the tartlet shells again and return them to the oven. Bake for 4 to 5 minutes longer, or until the shells are golden brown. Let stand about 5 minutes, then gently lift the shells from the molds and place them on a rack to cool.

Fried Apricot Pies

WHEN MY HUSBAND WAS GROWING up in Memphis, Tennessee, he used to savor the fried apricot pies his mother had waiting for him when he came home from school. Unfortunately, the recipe passed on with her many years ago.

I have discovered that the secret to making this southern snack is to use the appropriate pie dough. The pastry cannot be too fragile, or it will break apart during the frying. When trying to find just the right dough for this recipe, two fine cooks—Kimmie Durbin and Linnie Bell—from Shelby, North Carolina, came to my rescue. This mother-and-daughter team have long cooked and baked for family celebrations. Some of their family recipes date back to the Civil War.

When you make the apricot filling, soak the apricots overnight, a tip I learned from Rozanne Gold, author of *Recipes 1-2-3*. Try these warm confections. They are delicious treats from yesteryear.

DRIED APRICOT FILLING
8 ounces dried apricots
1½ cups cold water
3 to 4 tablespoons sugar
2 tablespoons unsalted butter
½ teaspoon grated lemon zest
½ teaspoon grated navel or
    Valencia orange zest

PASTRY
½ cup unsalted butter
1 large egg
3 tablespoons ice water
2½ cups sifted all-purpose flour

Vegetable oil, for frying
Confectioners' sugar, for garnish

1. **START THE APRICOTS:** Place the apricots in a medium bowl. Add the cold water and soak overnight.

2. The next day, drain the apricots, reserving ¾ cup water. Place the apricots, water, and sugar in a heavy saucepan. Cover, bring to a boil, then simmer for 40 to 45 minutes or until the apricots are soft enough to mash with a fork.

3. Using a fork, whip in the butter, lemon zest, and orange zest. Cool completely before using. (This filling will keep for several weeks. Store in an airtight glass jar and refrigerate.)

4. **MAKE THE PASTRY:** Melt the butter in a medium saucepan over low heat. Cool to tepid. Using a fork, blend in the egg and ice water.

5. Place the flour in a large mixing bowl, making a well in the center. Add the butter mixture to the well. Using the fork, draw the flour into the liquid, mixing it as best you can.

6. Lightly flour a rolling surface. Empty the dough onto the surface and with floured hands knead it 5 or 6 times, or just until smooth. Divide the dough into 8 golf ball–size pieces.

7. Roll each piece of dough into an oval measuring about 5 inches in length. Place 2 tablespoons of apricot filling on the lower half of each oval. Moisten the lower edge of the pastry with cold water. Then fold the top over to make a half-moon. Press out air pockets with your fingers before you seal the halves together.

8. Seal the edge by crimping with a fork dipped in flour, then trim with a pastry wheel. Prick the top with the fork and chill until ready to use.

9. FRY THE PIES: Heat $1/4$ inch vegetable oil in a large skillet until hot but not smoking. To test the temperature of the oil, fry a small square of bread. It should turn golden brown within a few seconds.

10. Fry the pies until golden brown on each side. Drain on a few layers of paper towels. Let cool for 10 to 15 minutes. Sprinkle the tops of the pies generously with confectioners' sugar and serve at once.

STORAGE

These pies can be well wrapped and frozen, uncooked, for up to 8 weeks. Thaw in the refrigerator overnight before frying.

VARIATION

Fried Apple Pies

Substitute Dried Apple Turnover Filling (page 390). Follow recipe as written, deleting blackberry preserves.

Sublime Chocolate Soufflé Tartlets

THESE DAINTY FLOURLESS TARTLETS will make a memorable dessert for the most elegant of dinner parties. To enhance the velvety texture and flavor, a fine-quality chocolate is a must. After baking, the tartlets are glazed with some of the unbaked batter.

At a Glance

SERVES: 6

PANS: 6 4^1/2-inch porcelain ramekins or 10-ounce ovenproof glass custard cups and shallow roasting pan

OVEN TEMP: 350 degrees

BAKING TIME: 22 to 25 minutes

DIFFICULTY: 🍫 🍫

While I like to use small ramekins for this dessert, if you don't have them, use 10-ounce ovenproof glass custard cups. They are available in most supermarkets.

BATTER
4 ounces best-quality bittersweet chocolate, coarsely chopped
2 ounces best-quality unsweetened chocolate, coarsely chopped
1 cup milk
3/4 cup sugar
1 teaspoon espresso powder
1/2 teaspoon boiling water
1/2 cup unsalted butter, softened
6 large eggs, separated
3 tablespoons Kahlúa liqueur
2 teaspoons vanilla extract
1/2 teaspoon cream of tartar

FOR DUSTING PANS
2 tablespoons sugar

1. Preheat the oven to 350 degrees. Position the oven rack in the lower third of the oven. Butter the ramekins and dust with granulated sugar. Set the ramekins in a large shallow roasting pan or a shallow ovenproof glass dish (about 2 inches deep). If necessary, use 2 pans.

2. MAKE THE BATTER: Place the chocolates, milk, and 3/4 cup sugar in a heavy saucepan. Dissolve the espresso powder in the boiling water and add it to the saucepan. Cook over low heat until the chocolate is melted and the sugar is dissolved. Use a whisk to smooth the mixture. Add the butter and stir to dissolve. Bring the mixture to a slow boil and cook until it thickens.

3. Lightly beat the egg yolks with a fork in a small bowl. Add about a third of the chocolate mixture to the yolks to temper them. Stir the yolk mixture back into the remaining chocolate, mixing well. Cook the mixture over low heat for about 2 minutes or until it becomes the consistency of a pudding. Stir constantly to prevent scorching.

4. Remove from the heat and add the Kahlúa and vanilla to the chocolate base. Remove 1/2 cup of the chocolate base and set it aside for glazing. Empty the remaining base into a large bowl and cool until tepid.

5. In a separate bowl, beat the egg whites until frothy. Add the cream of tartar and continue beating until the whites form soft peaks.

6. Using a whisk, gently stir about a quarter of the egg whites into the chocolate base to lighten the batter. Fold in the remaining whites using an oversize rubber spatula. *Do not overmix.*

7. Spoon the batter into the ramekins. Place the roasting pan with the ramekins into the oven. Make a hot-water bath by pouring about ½ inch boiling water into the roasting pan. Bake for 22 to 25 minutes, or until the tops are puffed and firm to the touch. Do not overbake.

8. Remove the roasting pan from the oven. Cool the tartlets, still in the water bath, for 15 minutes. Then remove them from the water bath and set them on a rack for about 10 minutes. Line a jelly roll pan with baking parchment. Sprinkle the paper with 1 teaspoon granulated sugar. Run a thin spatula around the edge of the ramekins and invert them onto the pan to unmold. Hit the containers hard against the pan to release the tartlets. Cool before frosting.

9. GLAZE THE TARTLETS: Using a small offset spatula, spread about 1 tablespoon of the reserved chocolate batter over the top of each tartlet. If the glaze becomes too firm, warm it for a few seconds in the microwave. Run a pastry comb over the top in a zigzag pattern or use the tines of a fork to create decorative lines. Serve on a pool of Cinnamon or Orange Crème Anglaise (page 442).

STORAGE

These tartlets can be made up to 3 days in advance. Cover with plastic wrap and refrigerate. When ready to serve, warm briefly in a 300 degree oven for 5 to 7 minutes. Freezing is not recommended.

Green Gables Bing Cherry Clafoutis

HOW FORTUNATE I WAS TO have dined at Green Gables Inn and Restaurant while vacationing at the New Jersey seaside resort of Beach Haven! One of the most delicious desserts that I could remember having in years was brought to my table. It was a clafouti. Traditionally, this is a simple dessert, native to the Limousin region of France, made with Bing cherries baked into a type of pancake batter. I spoke with Adolfo DeMartino, the owner and chef of the restaurant, and asked if he would kindly share his recipe with me. He generously consented.

Adolfo's recipe for clafouti is very different from the classic version. He bakes the cherries in a leavened cakelike batter rather than using a thin pancake mixture. The result is a sweet, delicate tart rich with tastes of hot fruit, butter, and Grand Marnier. Adolfo suggests making the clafoutis in individual porcelain tart dishes that are served warm from the oven with French vanilla ice cream. While cherries are classically used, peaches can be substituted or, in the fall, Adolfo combines pears with fresh cranberries.

This easy-to-make batter can be refrigerated for several days and conveniently baked as needed. If you don't have individual tart dishes, any small shallow ovenproof containers, such as Pyrex or French Arcoroc will do.

BATTER
2/3 cup unsalted butter
5 large egg yolks
1/2 cup sugar
1 1/2 teaspoons baking powder
1/4 cup Grand Marnier
1/2 cup heavy cream
1/2 cup milk
1 1/4 cups sifted all-purpose flour

FRUIT
1 pound Bing cherries, rinsed and
    pitted (page 22)
2 tablespoons cold unsalted butter,
    cut into thin slices (optional)

1. MAKE THE BATTER: Slowly melt the butter in the top of a double boiler or in a water bath. Keep warm.

2. Place the egg yolks in the large bowl of an electric mixer fitted with beaters or whip attachment. On medium speed, gradually add the sugar, 1 tablespoon at a time, beating until light in color. On low speed, mix in the baking powder, then slowly pour in the Grand Marnier.

3. Heat the cream and milk without stirring in a small saucepan until a skin forms on the surface.

4. While the eggs are beating, add the flour, warm butter, and hot cream in about 6 to 8 additions, starting and ending with flour. Mix until well blended.

5. Pour the batter through a fine-mesh strainer into a container, cover, and refrigerate for at least 6 hours or overnight. It will thicken as it stands.

6. ASSEMBLE THE CLAFOUTIS: Preheat the oven to 400 degrees. Position the oven rack in the lower third of the oven. Butter the tart dishes and set on a shallow baking pan.

7. Divide the cherries evenly among the containers. Spoon the batter over the cherries, about $1/2$ cup for each serving. Spread the mixture as best you can with the back of a teaspoon. Dot the top with the cold butter. Bake for 25 to 30 minutes, or until the centers are set and the tops are a rich golden brown.

8. Remove from the oven and let stand about 10 minutes to allow the fruit to cool. Top with a small scoop of French vanilla ice cream and serve at once.

STORAGE
This batter will keep for up to 4 days in the refrigerator.

Fresh Coconut Tarts with Buttermilk Custard

SINCE MY REPERTOIRE OF recipes lacked a southern coconut custard tart, I set about the not-so-easy task of finding a good one. Most of those I came across had slushy fillings made with lots of milk, and as a result had very soggy bottom crusts. I tossed them all.

At a Glance

SERVES: 8

PAN: 8 4½-inch metal tartlets

PASTRY PREP: Unbaked

OVEN TEMP: 350 degrees

BAKING TIME: 35 to 40 minutes

DIFFICULTY: 🍪 🍪

The recipe that follows was developed by a collaboration of many minds. My baking sleuth, Shirley Lynch from Greensboro, North Carolina, put me onto a sensational buttermilk coconut custard filling that was the inspiration of Candy Bernard of Philadelphia, Pennsylvania, via Greensboro. I also consulted with my housekeeper, Arlene Wilkie, who always makes hers with a bit of flour and baking powder.

A hint here and a tip there, and this is my result. These tarts scored a 10 by all who tasted them. While I prefer them with freshly grated coconut, you can use packaged if you wish. Granted, there is a lot of sugar in the filling, but don't change the amount. It's not the same without it.

½ recipe Chef's Cookie Dough for Tartlets (page 155)

FILLING
1½ cups sugar (if using sweetened flaked coconut instead of fresh, decrease sugar to 1¼ cups)
1 tablespoon all-purpose flour
¼ teaspoon baking powder
¼ teaspoon salt
3 large eggs
1 cup buttermilk
4 tablespoons unsalted butter, melted
1 teaspoon vanilla extract
1½ cups finely chopped fresh coconut
Coconut ribbons for garnish (page 58) (optional)

1. **SHAPE THE DOUGH:** With floured hands, make balls the size of golf balls, about 2 ounces each. Press a pastry ball into each pan with your fingers, working it up the side. Be sure the entire surface of the pan is covered. Lay a sheet of plastic wrap over the top of the pastry. Using a batarde (page 45) or the bottom of a glass, press into the bend in the tartlet pan to smooth the dough. Run a rolling pin over the top to level the edge.

2. Place the tartlet pans on a shallow pan and chill until ready to fill.

3. **MAKE THE FILLING:** Preheat the oven to 350 degrees. Position the oven rack in the lower third of the oven.

4. Whisk together the sugar, flour, baking powder, and salt in a small bowl.

5. Whisk the eggs in a large bowl. Add the dry ingredients, then the buttermilk, melted butter, and vanilla. Whisk just until well blended.

6. Sprinkle 2 tablespoons of chopped coconut over the bottom of each tartlet, then cover with custard mixture, slightly more than 1/3 cup per tartlet. Sprinkle the remaining coconut over the tops of the tartlets. Bake for 35 to 40 minutes, or until the pastry is golden brown and the custard begins to look golden. These tartlets are best when served still slightly warm, garnished with coconut ribbons.

STORAGE

Cover any leftover tarts loosely with aluminum foil and refrigerate for up to 4 days. Before serving, warm in a 325 degree oven for 5 to 7 minutes or just until heated through. These tarts can be frozen.

Awesome Black Mission Fig and Blackberry Tarts

THE BEST DESCRIPTION FOR these tarts came from Zach, my ten-year-old grandson, who has quite a sophisticated palate for a young boy. "These are awesome!" He wasn't alone in his opinion. Everyone who tasted them agreed.

Imagine tarts crowned with vibrant rosy figs over mounds of chiffon cream. Under the cream is a thin layer of blackberry confit resting on a crunchy nutty cornmeal tart shell. Except for the fresh fruit garnish, all of the preparation can be done a day in advance, a real advantage when you want a do-ahead dessert. If you are looking for a special company dessert, this is the perfect choice.

1 small recipe Nutty Cornmeal Crust for tartlet shells (page 154), baked

BLACKBERRY CONFIT
3 cups blackberries (2 6-ounce baskets) (see page 21)
½ cup sugar
4 teaspoons cornstarch
2 tablespoons kirschwasser
2 teaspoons fresh lemon juice

CHIFFON CREAM FILLING
½ cup sugar
2 tablespoons cornstarch
2 tablespoons unsifted all-purpose flour
¼ cup water
2 teaspoons unflavored gelatin
1½ cups milk

6 large egg yolks
2 teaspoons vanilla extract
2 to 3 tablespoons framboise liqueur or kirschwasser
3 large egg whites
1¼ cups heavy cream, whipped to soft peaks

GARNISH
8 large Black Mission figs (page 25)
¼ cup strained apricot preserves, warmed
Small mint leaves, for garnish

1. MAKE THE CONFIT: Set aside 8 blackberries of similar size for garnish. Wash and dry the remaining blackberries (page 21), then place them and the sugar in a small saucepan. Cover and cook over low heat for 5 to 7 minutes. Stir occasionally until the berries begin to release their juices.

2. Dissolve the cornstarch in the kirschwasser and stir into the blackberries, mixing until thickened. Add the lemon juice. Keep chilled while you prepare the filling.

3. MAKE THE FILLING: Combine the sugar, cornstarch, and flour.

4. Place the water in a small heatproof bowl. Sprinkle the gelatin over the top, and let stand for about 5 minutes to soften. *Do not stir.* Place the gelatin in a saucepan filled with 1/2 inch of simmering water and heat slowly for 3 to 5 minutes until the gelatin is dissolved and the liquid is clear.

5. Scald the milk in a large heavy saucepan. In a large bowl, whisk the egg yolks until light in color. Stir in the sugar mixture, whisking until blended. Add about a quarter of the hot milk into the egg yolks to warm them. Then blend in the remaining milk.

6. Pour the mixture back into the saucepan and stir constantly with a wooden spoon over low heat until it begins to thicken. Then whisk the mixture rapidly in a large figure 8 motion until it comes to a boil and is smooth. Be sure to scrape into the bend of the pot. Simmer the cream about 1 minute.

7. Remove from the heat and pour in the dissolved gelatin. Strain the cream into a large bowl. Stir in the vanilla and the liqueur. Cool the cream in an ice-water bath, stirring occasionally. *Do not overmix.* When the cream is tepid, remove from the ice water.

8. Whip the egg whites to soft peaks. Stir about a quarter of the whites into the cream to lighten the mixture. Fold in the remaining whites, then the whipped cream.

9. ASSEMBLE THE TARTS: Stir the blackberry confit with a fork to break up the larger pieces of berries. Spoon about 1 1/2 tablespoons of the confit into each baked tart shell, spreading it with the back of the spoon.

10. Fit a 16-inch pastry bag with a #828 large open star tip. Fill the bag with the cream filling. Starting at the edge of the tart shell, pipe the cream in rings, overlapping each one, until the chiffon cream is mounded in the center. (The tarts can be made a day ahead up to this point.)

11. GARNISH THE TARTS: Cut each fig into 6 wedges. Place the wedges on the cream with the points facing the center of the tart. Put a blackberry in the middle.

12. Brush the fruit lightly with the warmed apricot preserves. Just before serving, decorate with a mint leaf. After the tarts have been garnished with the fruit, they should be served within 6 hours.

STORAGE

Lightly cover with an aluminum foil tent. The ungarnished tarts will keep, refrigerated, for up to 3 days. Freezing is not recommended.

O, blackberry tart, with berries as big as your thumb, purple and black, and thick with juice, and a crust to endear them that will go to cream in your mouth, and both passing down with such a taste that will make you close your eyes and wish you might live forever in the wideness of that rich moment.

RICHARD
LLEWELLYN

Fresh Pot Pies with Puff Pastry Caps

DRIED FRUIT AND FRESH APPLES are baked in a heady syrup made from herbal tea, spices, and brandy. The baked fruits should be made at least a day in advance, as macerating will cause the juices to thicken and the flavors to intensify. Since puff pastry also benefits from resting time, baking the pastry and heating the fruit are the only chores that remain till just before serving.

At a Glance

SERVES: 6

PANS: 6 8- or 9-ounce ramekins or ovenproof glass custard cups

FRUIT PREP: Start the day before

PASTRY PREP: Unbaked

OVEN TEMP:
400 degrees for fruit
425 degrees for puff pastry

BAKING TIME:
55 to 60 minutes

DIFFICULTY: 🥟 🥟 🥟

When I want a more formal presentation, I serve these fruits in individual soufflé ramekins; however, for everyday fare, ovenproof glass custard dishes will work just fine. Top the puff pastry caps with a small scoop of ice cream or frozen yogurt. A sprig of fresh thyme inserted into the ice cream adds a nice touch.

FRUIT
2 cups water
3 chamomile tea bags
1/4 cup honey
1 3-inch cinnamon stick
1 3-inch vanilla bean, split
3 sprigs fresh thyme
8 ounces dried mixed fruit
2 tablespoons Calvados or Armagnac
2 teaspoons fresh lemon juice
4 Granny Smith apples (1 1/2 pounds)
1/3 cup granulated sugar
1/3 cup lightly packed dark brown sugar

PUFF PASTRY CAPS
1 small recipe Goof-Proof Puff Pastry (page 172)
1 large egg
1 teaspoon water
Pearl or granulated sugar, for garnish

1. START THE FRUIT: Bring the water to a boil in a medium saucepan. Remove from the heat. Steep the tea in the water for 5 minutes, then discard the bags.

2. Add the honey, cinnamon stick, vanilla bean, and thyme. Bring the liquid to a boil, then reduce the heat and simmer for about 3 minutes. Remove the vanilla bean, scrape the seeds from the pod, and return the seeds to the liquid.

3. Cut the larger pieces of dried fruits, such as the peaches and pears, to the size of the smaller ones. Add all of the dried fruit to the poaching liquid. Cover and bring to a boil, then simmer 15 to 20 minutes, or until the fruit is tender but not overcooked. Remove from the heat and add the

Calvados and lemon juice. Set aside.

4. Preheat the oven to 400 degrees. Position the oven rack in the lower third of the oven. Butter the ramekins.

5. Core and peel the apples (page 17). Cut the apples into 1/4-inch slices and divide them among the 6 ramekins. Spoon the poached fruit and juices over the apples. Sprinkle the tops with the granulated and brown sugars.

6. Cut six 6-inch pieces of aluminum foil and fold each in half, forming a square. Cover each ramekin with a sheet of the foil, molding it loosely around the top. Place the ramekins on a shallow pan and bake for 55 to 60 minutes, or until the fruit is bubbly and the apples are tender. Cool on a rack. Cover and refrigerate overnight or for up to 2 weeks.

7. SHAPE THE PASTRY: On a lightly floured surface, roll the pastry into a rectangle measuring about 16 × 12 inches. Prick the dough in several places with a fork. Using a straight-edged pastry wheel, cut six 4 1/2- to 5-inch circles (a plastic deli container lid makes a good template).

8. Line a large cookie sheet with a piece of heavy-duty aluminum foil. Tuck the ends of the foil under the pan edge to secure it, then sprinkle a few drops of water on top. Invert the circles onto the baking sheet. Using a 1 1/2-inch round cookie cutter, cut out the center of each pastry round

and reserve for another use. Cover the pan tightly with plastic wrap, and refrigerate for up to 3 days or freeze until ready to use.

9. BAKE THE PUFF PASTRY CAPS: Preheat the oven to 425 degrees. Position the oven rack to the lower third of the oven. In a small bowl, lightly beat the egg and water together with a fork. Brush the rounds lightly with the egg wash and sprinkle generously with sugar.

10. Bake the caps for 10 minutes, reduce the temperature to 375 degrees, and bake for 15 minutes longer, or until the pastry is golden brown. If the puff pastry caps were frozen, bake a few minutes longer.

11. ASSEMBLE THE RAMEKINS: Preheat the oven to 350 degrees. Position the oven rack in the lower third of the oven. Heat the fruit-filled ramekins for 15 to 20 minutes, or long enough to warm the fruit, basting once or twice. Top each dish with a puff pastry cap. Put a small scoop of ice cream or frozen yogurt in the center. Garnish with a sprig of thyme. Once assembled, this dessert should be eaten as soon as possible.

Lemon Tea Tarts Smothered with Berries

HERE WE HAVE A LEMON CURD FILLING that is lightened with a touch of whipped cream and then piled high with fresh berries. I like to use raspberries and blueberries, but you can use any combination you wish. To keep the tender crust crisp, fill these tarts to order—a simple task since everything is made ahead.

At a Glance

SERVES: 8

PANS: 8 4½-inch metal tartlets

PASTRY PREP: Baked

DIFFICULTY:

½ recipe Chef's Cookie Dough for Tartlets (page 155), baked

LEMON CURD FILLING
2 large eggs
2 large egg yolks
1 cup sugar
1 tablespoon grated lemon zest
⅓ cup fresh lemon juice
6 tablespoons unsalted butter, cut into ½-inch pieces
¼ cup heavy cream, whipped to soft peaks

TOPPING
3 cups (2 pints) raspberries (see page 37)
2 cups (1 pint) blueberries (see page 22)
3 to 4 tablespoons confectioners' sugar, for garnish
Mint leaves (optional)

1. MAKE THE LEMON CURD: Whisk the whole eggs and yolks in the top of a double boiler. Blend in all of the remaining ingredients except the whipped cream.

2. Fill the bottom of the double boiler with about 1 inch of water. Bring to a boil, then reduce the heat to simmer. Place the top of the double boiler over the water and cook the mixture for 15 to 20 minutes, stirring occasionally. The curd is done when it reaches the consistency of thick mayonnaise. Empty the mixture into a large bowl, and cover with a sheet of buttered plastic wrap, pressing it against the surface.

3. When the lemon curd is tepid, fold in the whipped cream. Place the lemon cream in a covered container and chill until ready to use.

4. ASSEMBLE THE TARTS: Spoon ¼ cup lemon cream into each tart shell. Mound about ½ cup fresh berries over the top. Strain confectioners' sugar heavily over the top and serve at once. If desired, garnish with a sprig of mint.

STORAGE
Cover any leftover lemon cream and store for up to 3 days in the refrigerator. Freezing is not recommended.

All-Fruit Mincemeat Tartlets

NOT ONLY ARE THESE FRUIT TARTS ideal to serve at buffet parties but they are also nice to give as gifts. Fill a doily-lined straw basket with tarts, wrap in cellophane, and tie with a colorful bow. Home-baked sweets are always appreciated.

2/3 block (large recipe) Goof-Proof
   Puff Pastry (page 172)
1 recipe All-Fruit Mincemeat
   (page 202)
1 large egg
1 teaspoon water
Sugar, for garnish

1. MAKE THE TARTS: Preheat the oven to 425 degrees. Position the oven rack to the upper third of the oven. Sprinkle the muffin cups with droplets of cold water.

2. Divide the puff pastry in half, then cut each piece in half again. On a lightly floured surface, working 1 piece at a time (keep the others refrigerated until using), roll the piece of dough into a 12 × 16-inch rectangle. Prick in several places with a fork. Turn the dough over. Using a dough scraper, divide the pastry into 6 squares. Repeat with the remaining 3 pieces of pastry.

3. Place a square of pastry into each muffin cup. As you pick it up, stretch the dough gently to enlarge it. Fill with mincemeat, allowing about 1 full tablespoon for each tart.

4. Lightly beat the egg and water with a fork in a small bowl. Brush the corners of the puff pastry with the egg wash. Bring opposite points of pastry to the center, pinching them together. Slightly spread the 4 openings of the pastry so that the fruit is exposed. Brush the pastry lightly with egg wash and sprinkle with a little sugar. Chill the tarts for 20 minutes.

5. Bake the tarts at 425 degrees for 10 minutes. Reduce the temperature to 375 degrees and continue baking for 10 to 12 minutes, or until the tops are golden brown.

STORAGE

Wrap any leftover tarts in aluminum foil and store in a cool place for up to 5 days. Refresh in a 325 degree oven for 3 to 5 minutes before serving. These tarts can be frozen.

At a Glance

MAKES: 2 dozen

PAN: 2 medium muffin pans

PASTRY PREP: Unbaked

STARTING OVEN TEMP:
425 degrees

BAKING TIME:
20 to 22 minutes

DIFFICULTY:

Glazed Nut Tea Tarts

A BUTTERY COOKIE CRUST HOLDS a filling made with caramelized nuts, apricot preserves, and a touch of honey. While this chewy and crunchy tart is a satisfying snack at teatime, it can easily be transformed into a more formal dessert with the addition of ice cream or whipped cream.

At a Glance

SERVES: 8

PAN: 8 4¹/₂-inch metal tartlets

PASTRY PREP: Unbaked

OVEN TEMP: 325 degrees

BAKING TIME: 20 to 25 minutes

DIFFICULTY: 🍪 🍪

¹/₂ recipe Chef's Cookie Dough for Tartlets (page 155)

FILLING
1¹/₃ cups mixed nuts (almonds, hazelnuts, walnuts)
¹/₂ cup sugar
¹/₂ cup apricot preserves
2 tablespoons honey
6 tablespoons heavy cream
1 teaspoon grated navel or Valencia orange zest

1. **SHAPE THE DOUGH:** With floured hands, make balls the size of large walnuts, about 2 ounces each. Press the pastry into each pan with your fingers, working it up the sides of the pan. Be sure the entire surface of the pan is covered. Lay a sheet of plastic wrap over the top of the pastry. Using a batarde (page 457) or the bottom of a glass, press into the bend of each tartlet pan to even the dough. Run a rolling pin over the top to level the edge.

2. Place the tartlet pans on a shallow pan and chill until ready to fill.

3. **MAKE THE FILLING:** Preheat the oven to 325 degrees. Position the oven rack in the lower third of the oven. Spread the nuts on a shallow pan and bake until lightly toasted. This will take from 8 to 12 minutes depending on the kind and size of the nut. Cool completely, then *coarsely* chop.

4. Make a caramel by placing the sugar in a heavy 12-inch skillet. Cook over low heat for 20 to 25 minutes or until the sugar melts and turns a deep amber color. The sugar crystals must be completely dissolved. Rotate the pan occasionally to circulate the syrup, but *do not stir.*

5. Have ready a buttered wooden spoon. When the caramel is done, add the chopped nuts, apricot preserves, honey, cream, and orange zest and stir with the buttered spoon. Bring the mixture to a slow boil and cook for 1 to 2 minutes or until the syrup is bubbly and thickens. If too much syrup evaporates, add 1 to 2 tablespoons more cream. Cool for 5 minutes.

6. Fill the tartlet pans with the nut filling, dividing it equally. Place the pan holding the filled tartlets into the oven and bake for 20 to 25 minutes, or until the crust is golden brown and the filling is bubbly.

7. Cool the tarts on a rack for 10 minutes. Unmold while still warm. Serve with ice cream or whipped cream.

STORAGE

Any leftover tarts should be covered with aluminum foil and refrigerated for up to 5 days. These tarts can be frozen.

Poached Peaches and Mascarpone on Cookie Saucers

DAZZLE YOUR GUESTS WITH THIS dessert. Poached peach halves, stuffed with mascarpone cream, rest on oversize cookies. Because tartlet shells are so fragile, the cookies make perfect beds to support the weight of the fruit.

At a Glance

SERVES: 8

PAN: Cookie sheet

PASTRY PREP: Baked

OVEN TEMP: 375 degrees

BAKING TIME:
15 to 18 minutes

DIFFICULTY: 🍪🍪🍪

The peaches are accented with a fresh currant sauce, Almond Crackle, and fresh berries. The best part is that all of the components are "make ahead." When assembled, this colorful pastry could compete with any of New York's finest restaurant desserts. For larger parties, this recipe can easily be doubled or tripled.

COOKIE SAUCERS
1¼ cups unsifted all-purpose flour
¼ cup strained confectioners'
   sugar
¼ teaspoon salt
½ cup cold unsalted butter, cut
   into ½-inch pieces
1 large egg yolk
1 tablespoon water
½ teaspoon vanilla extract

POACHED PEACHES
4 large Freestone peaches
1 cup water
½ cup dry white wine or
   vermouth
⅓ cup sugar
1 cinnamon stick
1 4-inch piece of vanilla bean
⅛ teaspoon cardamom
¼-inch thick slice of lemon
4 to 5 peppercorns

MASCARPONE CREAM
¾ cup (6 ounces) mascarpone
   cheese
¼ cup strained confectioners'
   sugar
¾ teaspoon vanilla extract
½ cup heavy cream, whipped to
   soft peaks

GARNISH
1 recipe Fresh Currant Sauce
   (page 445)
1 cup mixed fresh berries
   (raspberries, blackberries, and
   blueberries)
1 recipe Almond Crackle
   (page 454)

1. **MAKE THE COOKIE SAUCERS:** Preheat the oven to 375 degrees. Position the oven rack in the lower third of the oven.

2. Place the flour, confectioners' sugar, and salt in the bowl of a food processor. Pulse to blend. Add the butter and pulse 4 or 5 times, then process for 8 to 10 seconds or until the mixture forms fine crumbs.

3. Combine the egg yolk, cold water, and vanilla in a container with a spout. With the processor running, add the yolk mix-

ture through the feeder tube. Process until it just begins to form a dough.

4. Empty the mixture onto a lightly floured rolling surface and knead 6 to 8 times until smooth. Re-flour the rolling surface and roll the dough into a large sheet, 3/16-inch thick. Using a fluted 3-inch cookie cutter, cut 8 rounds of dough. Re-roll scraps of dough if needed to make all 8 saucers. Place them on an ungreased cookie sheet and prick the centers with a fork. Create a decorative edge on the saucers by pressing with the tines of a fork.

5. Bake the cookie saucers for 15 to 18 minutes, or until the edges start to brown. Let stand 5 minutes. Carefully remove from the cookie sheet and place on a rack. When the cookies are cool, store in an airtight container with sheets of waxed paper to separate the layers.

6. POACH THE PEACHES: Bring a large saucepan filled with water to a boil. To remove the skins of the peaches, make a slight X in the bottom of each peach with a paring knife. Drop the peaches into the boiling water. Check the peaches after 30 seconds. If the skins don't easily release, cook them longer, testing them frequently. The cooking time will vary according to the ripeness of the peaches, taking from 30 seconds to 3 minutes. When the peaches are ready, quickly plunge them into cold water. Cut the peaches in half; remove the pit and skin.

7. Place the water, white wine, sugar, and flavorings in a 10-inch skillet. Bring the liquid to a boil, then simmer 3 to 4 minutes to form a syrup. Add the peach halves, bring the syrup back to a boil, then cover the pan, keeping the lid askew. Simmer the peaches for 3 to 5 minutes or until fork-tender. To ensure even cooking, carefully turn the peaches halfway through. *Do not overcook.* Cool the peaches in the syrup. Place the peaches in a container and refrigerate for up to 2 weeks.

8. MAKE THE MASCARPONE CREAM: Place the mascarpone cheese in a medium bowl. Gently blend in the confectioners' sugar. Stir in the vanilla. Using a rubber spatula, slowly fold the cream into the mascarpone cheese, blending just until the mixture is smooth. *Do not overmix* or it will separate. Empty into a container, cover, and refrigerate for up to 3 days.

9. ASSEMBLE THE DESSERT: Place each cookie on an oversize dessert plate or a small dinner plate. Put about 2 tablespoons mascarpone filling in the center of each cookie. Drain the peach halves on paper towels. Top each cookie with a peach half, cut side down, over the mascarpone. Drizzle with Fresh Currant Sauce. Scatter some berries on the plate along with a few pieces of Almond Crackle. Serve at once.

Turnovers with Dried Apple and Blackberry Filling

COOKING THE DRIED APPLES FIRST not only softens them but also heightens their flavor. I especially like to use dried fruit in turnovers because the puff pastry crust will stay marvelously crisp. Of course, you can use strawberry, apricot, or other flavor jams, but use them only as accent ingredients. The preserves should enhance, not overwhelm the lovely flavor of the apples. Dried apples are available in specialty food stores and some supermarkets during the fall and winter months. Be sure to buy a commercial variety, *not* those without preservatives. The all-natural apple slices will not soften when cooked. If the apples are still in rings, cut them into quarters.

At a Glance

SERVES: 8

PAN: Large cookie sheet

FRUIT PREP: Start 12 hours ahead or day before

PASTRY PREP: Unbaked

OVEN TEMP: 400 degrees

BAKING TIME: 20 to 25 minutes

DIFFICULTY: 🥐 🥐

While puff pastry is my first choice for these turnovers, if time is of the essence, use Cream Cheese Pastry (see Variation). It's quick to make and simple to roll.

½ recipe Goof-Proof Puff Pastry (page 172)

FILLING
8 ounces dried apple slices
2 cups water
3 tablespoons sugar
¼ teaspoon ground cinnamon
⅛ teaspoon freshly grated nutmeg
2 tablespoons unsalted butter
1 teaspoon fresh lemon juice
3 to 4 tablespoons premium-quality blackberry preserves
1 large egg
1 teaspoon water

---

1. MAKE THE FILLING: Soak the apples in the water at room temperature for at least 12 hours, or preferably overnight.

2. Put the apples and 2 cups water in which they were soaking in a large, heavy saucepan. Bring the fruit to a boil, then reduce the heat and simmer for 15 to 18 minutes, or until the apples are very soft and the liquid is absorbed. It is okay if the apples become somewhat mushy.

3. Stir the sugar, cinnamon, and nutmeg into the apples and simmer the mixture for another 2 to 3 minutes. *Watch carefully to avoid scorching.* If the mixture is too dry, add a tablespoon of water or more as needed.

4. Remove from the heat and blend in the butter and lemon juice. Empty the filling into a shallow container. Cool thoroughly before using. *Note:* The filling can be made ahead and refrigerated for up to 1 month in a tightly sealed container.

5. **ASSEMBLE THE TURNOVERS:** On a lightly floured surface, roll the pastry into a long strip measuring 20 × 10 inches. When rolling the strip of dough, establish the 10-inch width first, then go for the length—it's easier. Prick the pastry well with a fork. Using a dough scraper or a straight-edged pastry wheel, trim the uneven edges. Divide the pastry into eight 5-inch squares, making 4 pieces of dough across and 2 down.

6. Mound the apple filling slightly off center, using about ¼ cup for each turnover. Then slip a slightly heaping teaspoon of preserves into the mound of apples. Lightly beat together the egg and 1 teaspoon water. Brush the edges of the pastry with the egg wash. Fold the dough over to make a triangle. With your fingertips, press around the fruit to remove air pockets.

7. Seal the edge with a fork. Using the fork, make a few steam vents in the top. Brush the tops lightly with egg wash. Chill at least 20 minutes before baking. (The turnovers can be well wrapped and frozen at this point. Do not thaw before baking. Proceed with step 8, but increase the baking time to 40 to 45 minutes.)

8. Preheat the oven to 400 degrees. Position the oven rack in the lower third of the oven. Line a large cookie sheet with heavy-duty aluminum foil. Be sure to tuck the edges of the foil under the pan so that the foil doesn't slide. Sprinkle a few drops of water on top of the foil.

9. Bake the turnovers on the foil-lined cookie sheet for 20 to 25 minutes or until golden brown. Drizzle with Vanilla Glaze (page 73) or dust with confectioners' sugar.

STORAGE
The turnovers will keep for up to 4 days in the refrigerator. Before serving, reheat in a 325 degree oven for 10 to 15 minutes.

VARIATION
Substitute 1 recipe Cream Cheese Pastry (page 157) for the puff pastry.

You will have enough dough for 12 turnovers but you will need to make 1½ times the filling recipe. Roll half the pastry at a time into a strip measuring 15 × 10 inches. Using a pastry wheel, divide the strip into six 5-inch squares. Fill as directed in recipe.

Place the turnovers on a buttered, foil-lined cookie sheet. Prick the tops 3 or 4 times with a fork, then bake at 375 degrees for 25 minutes or until golden brown.

Plum Rosettes on Shortbread

SIMPLE, PRETTY, AND OH-SO-GOOD best describes these terrific tarts. Piquant purple plums are thinly sliced and arranged in a circle on buttery shortbread. After baking, the fruit is glazed with apricot preserves. These are gorgeous to look at and a cinch to make.

At a Glance

SERVES: 10

PAN: Cookie sheet

PASTRY PREP: Unbaked

OVEN TEMP: 375 degrees

BAKING TIME:
30 to 35 minutes

DIFFICULTY:

1 large recipe Free-form Shortbread
   Tart Pastry (page 149)
1 large egg white, lightly beaten
5 to 6 Santa Rosa or Black
   Diamond plums
2 tablespoons sugar
1/2 cup apricot preserves
1 teaspoon water

1. SHAPE THE DOUGH: Roll the pastry into a sheet, 3/16 inch thick. Using a fluted 4-inch cookie cutter, cut 10 rounds of dough and place them on an ungreased cookie sheet. Brush the tops lightly with the egg white. Chill for 15 to 20 minutes.

2. Preheat the oven to 375 degrees. Position the oven rack in the lower third of the oven.

3. Wash and dry the plums (page 37). Cut the plums in half. Remove the pits and cut crosswise into 1/8-inch slices. Starting on the outside of the dough rounds, arrange the plums in overlapping slices (save the smaller slices for the center). Make concentric circles until the entire top is covered. A quicker alternative is to fan the slices. Sprinkle each with about 1 teaspoon of sugar. (The plum ro-settes can be assembled several hours ahead. Store in the refrigerator and bake when needed.)

4. Bake for 30 to 35 minutes or until the edge of the shortbread is lightly browned. While the tartlets are baking, combine the apricot preserves with the water in a small saucepan. Bring to a slow boil, then strain the preserves. When the plum rosettes are removed from the oven, gently brush the tops with the preserves. Serve while warm.

STORAGE

Cover any leftover plum rosettes with a sheet of waxed paper then aluminum foil. Refrigerate for up to 1 day. Freezing is not recommended.

Lusciously Light & Lean

I N THIS ERA OF PARING down calories and fat for a healthier lifestyle, finding a really good dessert to satisfy your sweet tooth is no easy task, especially if you want one that is free of ersatz ingredients. A fact of life is that many cake, cookie, and pastry recipes do not work when fat and sugar substitutes are used in place of the real thing. * The good news is that many pies and tarts are either naturally lower in fat or can be adapted to lighter fare. You can reduce the amount of sugar in a fruit tart, or eliminate it all together. When you want to substitute vegetable oil for butter in a pie crust, this too can be done. And if you wish to eliminate egg yolks in a cooked filling, you can—with the aid of egg substitutes.

My goal when I created the recipes in this chapter was to stay true to the guidelines for reduced fat and sugar without compromising taste or the use of wholesome ingredients. Although small amounts of butter and cream have been used, I have striven to keep them to a minimum.

Unless a very restricted diet is in order, a little fat stretched out over many portions is acceptable and not as harmful as artificial substitutes. Rousing Raspberry Chiffon Pie, an intensely fruity chiffon pie, is an example of this. The filling is lightened with a just a touch of whipped cream and a little goes a long way. Stuffed Cinnamon Apple Top-Knots have a phyllo pastry crust that is lightly brushed with a blend of butter and canola oil. Without any fat, it would be brittle and tasteless.

Whether or not you are attempting to slim down, Honey-Glazed Crustless Apple Tart makes a fabulous presentation. It features thin, overlapping slices of apples fanned into a pie plate, then inverted after baking. For comfort food, try the Deep-Dish Pear Crisp with Dried Cranberries. The tasty crumb topping, moistened with egg substitute and a bit of butter, is pleasingly crunchy and really good.

In addition to the recipes in this chapter, many in Chapter 7 can be adapted to using less fat and sugar. Cobblers, Crisps & Crumbles is another chapter to seek out. Do refer to the "Before You Begin" on the following page for information on how to make these changes. With a little know-how and a lot of discipline, a lusciously light and lean slice of pie or tart can be a reality.

Before You Begin

Here is an overview of tips and tricks for making great light and lean pies and tarts.

✦ Margarine can be substituted for butter in most recipes. Be sure to use unsalted margarine.

✦ Try blending clarified butter with canola or safflower oil. Clarified butter is more concentrated than whole (unclarified) butter and will give a more pronounced flavor.

✦ Most fresh fruits can be baked without a crust. After standing, the natural pectin in the fruit will hold it together when it is unmolded or sliced.

✦ Vegetable Oil Pastry (page 144) can be substituted for doughs made with butter and/ or vegetable shortening.

✦ To improve the flavor of pastry doughs made with vegetable oil, replace 1 to 2 tablespoons of oil with an equal amount of clarified butter. A little goes a long way.

✦ If you want to eliminate the top crust on a fresh fruit pie, tightly cover the pie with vented aluminum foil before baking. Raw fruit will not cook unless covered.

✦ Tarts commonly have only a bottom crust, which makes them good candidates for reduced-fat desserts.

✦ Pastries like cobblers, crisps, and crumbles—which have only top coverings—are also good choices when you are looking to reduce fat.

✦ Try combining small quantities of dried fruits with fresh fruit. Because their flavor is concentrated, they add character and sweetness, allowing you to reduce the sugar.

✦ Egg substitutes can be used in place of whole eggs. Although package instructions might indicate differently, allow 3 tablespoons of egg product for each whole egg.

✦ The less fat used in a filling, the looser the filling will be. This applies not only to milk products but also to low-fat cheeses, yogurts, and sour cream.

✦ If you wish to use reduced-fat ingredients, the thickening in a recipe will need to be increased.

✦ Use nonstick cooking spray for greasing pans.

✦ Recipes that use less fat will have a shorter life. Fat prevents foods from becoming too dry.

Honey-Glazed Crustless Apple Tart

HERE IS A LUSCIOUS APPLE tart made without a crust. The apples are packed into the pie plate rounded side down and baked. After I unmold the pie, I like to glaze it under the broiler. While this step is optional, the singed fruit is very appealing. Either way, this is a beautiful no-fat dessert that is bound to please those on restricted diets.

At a Glance

SERVES: 8 to 10

PAN: 9½-inch deep-dish ovenproof glass pie plate and 9½-inch ovenproof glass pie plate and shallow baking pan

OVEN TEMP: 425 degrees

BAKING TIME: 35 to 40 minutes

DIFFICULTY:

7 Golden Delicious apples (about 3 pounds)
2 teaspoons fresh lemon juice
1 cup apple cider
2 tablespoons honey
¼ cup sugar
¾ teaspoon ground cinnamon

1. PREPARE THE FRUIT: Peel and core the apples, then cut in half lengthwise (page 17). Cut apples into 3/8-inch-thick slices, cutting *across* the apple halves instead of lengthwise. Keep the apples aligned as they are sliced and line them up on a shallow pan. Drizzle the lemon juice over the apples.

2. MAKE THE TART: Preheat the oven to 425 degrees. Position the oven rack in the lower third of the oven. Spray a 10-inch deep ovenproof glass pie plate with nonstick coating.

3. Place the apple cider and honey in a small, heavy saucepan. Bring to a boil over medium heat and cook until the mixture is reduced to about ¼ cup, 12 to 15 minutes. Pour the syrup into the pie plate, spreading it as best you can.

4. Stand the sliced apples, rounded side down, snugly in the pie plate. Combine the sugar and cinnamon, and sprinkle half of the mixture over the apples. Make a second layer of apples, overlapping the slices. Sprinkle the remaining sugar mixture on top, reserving 1 teaspoon for glazing.

5. Cover the pie plate with aluminum foil, molding it tightly around the edge. Weight the apples by setting a 9-inch ovenproof glass pie plate on top of the filled 10-inch pie plate. Set the tart on a shallow pan and bake for 35 to 40 minutes, or until the juices begin to bubble.

6. Remove from the oven and place on a rack to cool. Let stand about 1 hour. Remove the excess apple liquid from the tart by pressing the 9-inch pie plate gently on the fruit. Carefully tip the plates a few times, letting the liquid drip onto a sheet pan. Reserve the juices.

7. Invert the tart onto a round, broiler-proof serving plate, such as one made by Pyrex. Sprinkle the remaining cinnamon sugar over the top. Place the tart about 6 inches from the broiler flame and broil for 4 to 5 minutes, or until the apples begin to char. Brush with the reserved apple juices 2 or 3 times while broiling. Let cool. Serve the tart slightly warm or at room temperature.

STORAGE

Cover any leftover tart with a sheet of waxed paper then aluminum foil and refrigerate for up to 5 days. Freezing is not recommended.

Stuffed Cinnamon Apple Top-Knots

THIN LAYERS OF PHYLLO encase halves of Golden Delicious apples whose cavities are filled with a heady mixture of chopped dried cherries and raisins, flavored with applejack brandy. Cinnamon sugar flavors the phyllo, and toasted almonds are added for crunch. These are baked apples with pizzazz.

At a Glance

SERVES: 8

PAN: 8 × 12 × 1 1/2-inch ovenproof glass

PASTRY PREP: Unbaked

OVEN TEMP: 375 degrees

BAKING TIME:
30 to 35 minutes

DIFFICULTY:

8 sheets phyllo pastry
2 tablespoons clarified butter (see page 52)
2 tablespoons canola oil
3 tablespoons sugar
3/4 teaspoon ground cinnamon

FILLING
4 Golden Delicious apples, peeled, cored, and halved (page 17)
2 teaspoons fresh lemon juice
1/2 cup golden raisins
1/2 cup dried cherries
2 tablespoons applejack brandy or Calvados
1/2 cup lightly packed dark brown sugar
1/4 cup toasted slivered almonds

1. MAKE THE FILLING: Place the apples in a large bowl and drizzle with lemon juice. Toss to coat and set aside.

2. Preheat the oven to 375 degrees. Position the oven rack in the lower third of the oven. Spray an 8 × 12 × 1 1/2-inch ovenproof glass baking dish with nonstick coating.

3. Place the raisins and cherries in a small bowl. Cover with boiling water and let stand 3 minutes. Drain and dry between layers of paper towels.

4. Put the dried fruit, brandy, and brown sugar in a food processor. Pulse 6 to 8 times, then process 5 seconds to coarsely chop the fruit. Add the toasted almonds and pulse 2 or 3 times to coarsely chop the nuts. *Do not overprocess.* When ready to fill the apples, mound the fruit into the cavity.

5. ASSEMBLE THE PASTRIES: Open phyllo and place on a sheet of waxed paper. Lay a strip of waxed paper over the top and cover with damp paper towels to prevent the phyllo from becoming dry (see "Working with Phyllo," page 64).

6. Combine the clarified butter and canola oil in an ovenproof glass measuring cup. Warm briefly in a microwave oven. Mix the sugar and cinnamon together and place it in a sugar shaker.

7. Working with 1 sheet of phyllo at a time, brush the edges and then the center lightly with the butter and oil mixture. Sprinkle half of the phyllo lightly with the cinnamon sugar. Fold the phyllo in half, making a 6 × 8½-inch rectangle. Brush the phyllo again with the butter and oil mixture.

8. Place the apple, stuffing side up, in the center, at a 45 degree angle to face one of the pastry points. Sprinkle the top with cinnamon sugar. Lift the 2 opposite points and bring them to the center above the apple. Then carefully gather the remaining phyllo in your hands, and press the dough against the fruit. **1**

9. Pinch the pastry at the top of the apple to fan the phyllo. With your hands cupped, gently press the pastry around the fruit a second time. It's okay if the phyllo tears a little. Place the apple in the baking dish, and repeat the process, wrapping the remaining apples with phyllo.

10. If any of the butter and oil mixture is left over, you can use it to brush the outside of the apples. Bake the apples for 30 to 35 minutes, or until golden brown. Serve warm with frozen low-fat vanilla yogurt and the juices from the bottom of the baking dish.

STORAGE

Cover any leftover apples with a sheet of waxed paper then aluminum foil and refrigerate for up to 3 days. These pastries can be frozen.

Deep-Dish Pear Crisp with Dried Cranberries

THIS PEAR CRISP IS SOMETHING different in a fruit dessert. Egg substitute in the streusel topping is a great alternative to butter when you want to lower the fat.

At a Glance

SERVES: 6 to 8

PAN: 7 × 11 × 1½-inch ovenproof glass

OVEN TEMP: 350 degrees

BAKING TIME: 45 to 50 minutes

DIFFICULTY:

TOPPING

2 tablespoons unsalted margarine, melted
3 tablespoons egg substitute
1 cup unsifted all-purpose flour
6 tablespoons sugar
1 teaspoon baking powder
½ teaspoon ground cinnamon
¼ teaspoon salt

FILLING

3 to 3½ pounds slightly underripe Red Bartlett or Anjou pears, cored, peeled, halved, and cut into 1-inch chunks (page 34) (about 7 to 8 pears)
¾ cup dried cranberries
2 teaspoons fresh lemon juice
¼ cup sugar
2 tablespoons cornstarch
½ teaspoon ground cinnamon
¼ teaspoon ground ginger
1 teaspoon grated navel or Valencia orange zest

1. MAKE THE TOPPING: Melt the butter in a large saucepan. Cool to tepid. Use a fork to mix the egg substitute into the melted fat.

2. Sift together the flour, sugar, baking powder, cinnamon, and salt. Stir the dry ingredients into the egg mixture, tossing with a fork to form crumbs. Set aside.

3. MAKE THE FILLING: Preheat the oven to 350 degrees. Position the oven rack in the lower third of the oven. Spray a 7 × 11 × 1½-inch ovenproof glass pan with nonstick coating.

4. Place the pear chunks and cranberries in the pan. Drizzle with the lemon juice. Combine the sugar, cornstarch, cinnamon, ginger, and orange zest in a small bowl. Sprinkle the mixture over the fruit.

5. Take a clump of the crumb mixture in your hand and squeeze gently to form a larger clump. Break the larger clump apart over the pears. Repeat, using all of the crumb mixture. *Do not press into the fruit.*

6. Bake for 45 to 50 minutes, or until the fruit juices are bubbling. Serve warm.

STORAGE

Cover leftover crisp with a sheet of waxed paper then aluminum foil. Refrigerate for up to 2 days. Reheat before serving. This crisp can be frozen.

Blueberry Lemon Soufflé Tartlets

THESE INDIVIDUAL CUSTARD CUPS HAVE an airy lemon filling with fresh blueberries scattered throughout. Be sure to serve the tartlets warm. When you bite into the blueberries, the juices will be bursting with flavor.

1 cup egg substitute
1¼ cups sugar
4 teaspoons cornstarch
½ teaspoon baking powder
¼ cup fresh lemon juice
1 teaspoon grated lemon zest
1 cup blueberries, washed and dried (page 22)
½ teaspoon mixed cinnamon and sugar, for top

1. Preheat the oven to 350 degrees. Position the oven rack in the lower third of the oven. Spray six 8-ounce custard cups with no-stick cooking spray.

2. Place the egg substitute in the large bowl of an electric mixer fitted with the whisk attachment. Beat until light and fluffy, about 2½ minutes.

3. Combine the sugar, cornstarch, and baking powder. Add gradually to the whipped eggs, taking about 2 minutes. Beat in the lemon juice, then the zest.

4. Pour the batter into the custard cups. Scatter the blueberries evenly over the top. Sprinkle with cinnamon and sugar. Bake for 25 to 30 minutes or until the top is set and the sides are lightly browned. Serve while still warm.

STORAGE

Leftover tarts can be stored loosely covered with aluminum foil in the refrigerator for up to 3 days. Freezing is not recommended.

At a Glance

SERVES: 6

PAN: 6 8-ounce custard cups sprayed with no-stick cooking spray

OVEN TEMP: 350 degrees

BAKING TIME: 25 to 30 minutes

DIFFICULTY:

Berry-Fruit Cream Pie

HERE IS A PARED-DOWN version of a cream filling that will satisfy most cravings for a rich dessert. Most any variety of fruits and berries can be used to cover the top. Try mixed berries, sliced kiwi, thin wedges of mango or papaya, or halved green and purple grapes. While any of these make tasty toppings, I especially like to create a colorful arrangement of several kinds.

At a Glance

SERVES: 6 to 8

PAN: 9-inch ovenproof glass

PASTRY PREP: Baked

DIFFICULTY:

I like to cool reduced-fat pastry creams before filling my baked shell. Because these less rich fillings often crack on the surface as they set, spooning a cooled filling into a shell ensures a smooth, creamy appearance. While the pie can be prepared early in the day, do not apply the glaze until you are ready to serve it, otherwise the fruit will become too soft.

1 9-inch Reduced Cholesterol Graham Cracker Crust (page 169), baked; or 9-inch Vegetable Oil Pastry crust (page 144), baked

PASTRY CREAM
1/3 cup cornstarch
3 cups 1% milk
1/2 cup sugar
2/3 cup egg substitute
4 teaspoons butter or margarine
1 1/2 teaspoons vanilla extract

FRUIT TOPPING
A variety of fresh fruits or berries (see headnote), washed and well dried
3 tablespoons all-fruit apricot preserves

1. MAKE THE PASTRY CREAM: Place the cornstarch in a medium mixing bowl. Stir in 1/2 cup of the milk. Mix until smooth. Whisk in 6 tablespoons of the sugar and the egg substitute.

2. In a large saucepan, combine the remaining 2 1/2 cups milk with the remaining 2 tablespoons sugar. Bring the milk mixture to a boil over low heat.

3. Pour about a third of the hot milk into the egg mixture and stir to temper the eggs. Then pour the egg mixture into the saucepan, blending it with the hot milk. Return the saucepan to medium-low heat, and bring the mixture to a full boil, whisking rapidly and constantly until the pastry cream is thick and smooth.

4. Remove from the heat and stir in the butter and vanilla. Spray a piece of plastic wrap with nonstick coating and lay it on top of the pastry cream to prevent a skin from forming. When cool, fill the baked pastry shell with the pastry cream. Smooth the top with the back of a tablespoon and refrigerate for at least 3 hours or until set.

5. When the pie is set, arrange the fresh fruit decoratively over the top. Just before serving, warm the preserves and brush onto the fruits and berries. If the preserves are too thick to spread, thin with a few drops of boiling water.

STORAGE
Refrigerate any leftover pie covered loosely with waxed paper then aluminum foil. Freezing is not recommended.

The cultivated blueberry is larger and sweeter than its wild cousin. According to Waverly Root, "This is just what persons gifted, or cursed, with a subtle sense of taste hold against the cultivated berry. Sweetness, they argue, is an uncomplicated taste sensation which smothers all others. What they prefer in the wild berry is a tartness which takes the edge off its sweetness and makes it more interesting, like a beauty spot on the face of a plain woman."

FOOD

Chocolate Velvet Pie with Sliced Strawberries

A CHOCOLATE CREAM PIE that's low in fat? You bet! The graham cracker crust is filled with a velvety custard that has a satisfying chocolate flavor. After filling, slice the berries lengthwise and lay them in an overlapping ring around the edge of the pie.

At a Glance

SERVES: 6 to 8

PAN: 9-inch ovenproof glass

PASTRY PREP: Baked

DIFFICULTY: 🍵

1 9-inch Reduced Cholesterol Graham Cracker Crust (page 169), baked

FILLING
4 tablespoons strained cocoa powder, preferably Dutch process
1/4 cup cornstarch
1/2 cup sugar
3 cups skim milk
2/3 cup egg substitute
4 teaspoons margarine or butter
1 1/2 teaspoons vanilla extract
1/2 pint strawberries, washed, dried, and sliced lengthwise (page 39)

1. **MAKE THE FILLING:** In a medium bowl, whisk together the cocoa, cornstarch, and 6 tablespoons of the sugar. Slowly whisk in 1/2 cup of the milk and the egg substitute. Blend until smooth.

2. In a 3-quart saucepan, over medium-low heat, combine the remaining milk and 2 tablespoons sugar and bring to a slow boil. Remove from the heat. Blend 1/4 of the hot milk into the chocolate mixture to temper it. Then pour the chocolate mixture into the saucepan with the milk.

3. Return the saucepan to the heat and bring to a slow boil while whisking vigorously. Reduce heat and simmer for 1 to 2 minutes, stirring occasionally to keep the mixture from sticking to the bottom. Be sure to reach into the bend of the saucepan.

4. Remove from the heat and add margarine and vanilla, stirring just to blend. Spray a piece of plastic wrap with nonstick coating and lay it directly on top of the pastry cream to prevent a skin from forming. When cool, fill the baked graham cracker crust with the pastry cream. Smooth the top with the back of a tablespoon. Refrigerate for at least 2 hours. Just before serving, garnish with the berries.

STORAGE
Any leftover pie should be refrigerated, loosely covered with foil, for up to 3 days. Freezing is not recommended.

Crustless Pineapple Cheese Pie

PINEAPPLE WITH CHEESE IS A dessert duo that is a sure winner every time. The pineapple adds moistness and flavor to these reduced-fat cheeses. My tasting committee couldn't believe this pie was a "healthier" dessert.

2 zwieback crackers, crushed into fine crumbs
15 ounces part-skim ricotta cheese
1 can (8 ounces) crushed pineapple in natural juice
8 ounces reduced-fat cream cheese, at room temperature
1/2 cup sugar
1/4 cup egg substitute
2 tablespoons cornstarch
1 teaspoon grated navel or Valencia orange zest
1 teaspoon grated lemon zest
1 teaspoon vanilla extract
2 large egg whites

1. Preheat the oven to 325 degrees. Position the oven rack in the lower third of the oven. Spray a 9-inch ovenproof glass pie plate with nonstick cooking spray and dust with zwieback crumbs. Invert the pan and shake out excess crumbs over the sink.

2. MAKE THE FILLING: Spread the ricotta on a linen or other smooth cloth dish towel. Fold the sides of the towel in, and roll the cheese up in the towel to remove the moisture. Let stand for 30 minutes. Remove the towel and press the cheese through a food mill or a medium-mesh strainer to remove the lumps.

3. Drain the crushed pineapple in a strainer, pressing lightly to remove the juice. Do not allow it to become too dry. Set aside.

4. In an electric mixer fitted with the paddle attachment, blend the cream cheese and sugar on medium-low speed. Mix in the egg substitute. Add the crushed pineapple, cornstarch, orange and lemon zests, and vanilla.

5. In a separate bowl, beat the egg whites until firm peaks form. Using an oversize rubber spatula, fold the whites into the pineapple-cheese mixture. Pour into the pie plate, smoothing the top with the back of a spoon.

6. Bake for 30 to 35 minutes, or just until set. Cool the pie in the oven for 1 hour with the door held ajar with a wooden spoon. Chill for 5 to 6 hours before serving.

STORAGE

Store any leftover pie in the refrigerator topped with a sheet of waxed paper and loosely covered with aluminum foil for up to 3 days. This pie can be frozen.

At a Glance

SERVES: 6 to 8

PAN: 9-inch ovenproof glass

OVEN TEMP: 325 degrees

BAKING TIME: 30 to 35 minutes

DIFFICULTY:

Stew of Summer Fruits with Phyllo Rings

HERE, INDIVIDUAL CASSEROLES ARE filled with a potpourri of summer fruits and berries. As the fruits stew in the oven, they release an exquisite ruby red lava of flavorful juice. The phyllo is cut into rings and baked separately. When you are ready to serve, top each casserole with a prebaked phyllo lid.

While the fruits and berries in this recipe were chosen for taste and color, you can use any combination you wish. Plums and dark berries contribute a glorious color, so try to include some in your mixture. If you wish to increase this recipe, allow 1 cup of cut fruit and berries for each additional serving.

PHYLLO RINGS
6 sheets of phyllo
1 tablespoon unsalted butter or
    margarine, melted
1 tablespoon canola or safflower oil

FRUIT STEW
6 cups mixed fruits and berries (I
    suggest using 2 peaches, 2 Santa
    Rosa or Black Diamond plums,
    about 1 cup raspberries, and 1
    cup blueberries)
6 tablespoons sugar, or to taste
2 to 3 teaspoons cornstarch
1½ teaspoons fresh lemon juice

1 teaspoon confectioners' sugar, for
    garnish

1. MAKE THE PHYLLO RINGS: Preheat the oven to 375 degrees. Position the oven rack in the lower third of the oven. Line a large cookie sheet with baking parchment.

2. Open the phyllo and place on a sheet of waxed paper. Lay a strip of waxed paper over the top and cover with damp paper towels to prevent the phyllo from becoming dry (see "Working with Phyllo," page 64). Combine the melted butter and vegetable oil and warm for a few seconds in a microwave oven.

3. Layer the 6 sheets of phyllo on a cutting surface, brushing each with the butter-oil mixture. Start around the edges, then brush the center. Using a 4-inch cookie cutter or other object as a guide, cut 6 phyllo circles with a sharp paring knife.

4. Place the rings of phyllo on the cookie sheet. Bake for 6 to 8 minutes, or until golden brown. Set aside until ready to use.

5. **PREPARE THE FRUIT:** Cut peaches and plums in half. Remove the pits (pages 33 and 34). Peel the peaches and dice into 1-inch cubes. Slice the unpeeled plums into ¼-inch wedges. Measure the cut peaches and plums. Wash and thoroughly dry the berries (pages 22 and 37). Add enough berries to equal 6 cups of mixed fruit.

6. **ASSEMBLE THE RAMEKINS:** Spray the baking molds with nonstick cooking spray. Place them on a shallow baking pan. Fill each ramekin with about 1 cup of the mixed fruit.

7. Combine the sugar and cornstarch in a small bowl. Sprinkle over the fruit, dividing the mixture equally among the ramekins. Sprinkle each with a little lemon juice.

8. Cut six 6-inch sheets of aluminum foil. Fold each in half to form a 6-inch square. Cover each ramekin with the foil, molding it snugly around the dish with your hands. Pierce a steam vent in each foil cover.

9. Place the ramekins in the oven and bake for 25 to 30 minutes, or until the fruit is bubbly. Let the fruit settle for about 30 minutes before serving.

10. Dust the tops of the phyllo rings with confectioners' sugar. Using a small spatula, carefully place a phyllo ring on top of each ramekin. Serve at once. *Note:* If made ahead, warm the fruit-filled ramekins before serving. Do not top with the phyllo rings until ready to serve.

STORAGE
Any leftover ramekins should be covered with a sheet of waxed paper then aluminum foil and refrigerated for up to 3 days. Freezing is not recommended.

Rousing Raspberry Chiffon Pie

CLASSIC CHIFFON PIES HAVE BEEN a popular dessert for decades, and it's no wonder. They are not too rich and are easy to digest. Here we have a raspberry puree sparked with vermouth, then bound with fluffy meringue and a touch of whipped cream. While I prefer the fruitier flavor of sweet vermouth, dry vermouth can be substituted. This is one of the most refreshing light desserts I can think of serving.

At a Glance

SERVES: 6 to 8

PAN: 9-inch ovenproof glass

PASTRY PREP: Baked

DIFFICULTY: 🥄 🥄

1 9-inch *Vegetable Oil Pastry shell (page 144), baked*

FILLING
1 (10-ounce) package frozen unsweetened raspberries
1/2 cup water
1 package unflavored gelatin
6 tablespoons granulated sugar
1/4 cup sweet vermouth
1/2 teaspoon vanilla extract
2 large egg whites
4 tablespoons superfine sugar
1/4 cup heavy cream, whipped to soft peaks (optional)

TOPPING
1 pint red raspberries
1 pint black raspberries or blackberries
1 recipe Raspberry Coulis (page 448; optional)

1. MAKE THE FILLING: Thaw the raspberries according to package directions. Discard 2 to 3 tablespoons of the watery juice. Puree the berries and remaining juice in a food processor, then pass through a fine strainer to remove the seeds. You should have 3/4 to 1 cup puree. Discard the raspberry seeds.

2. Place 1/4 cup of the water in a small bowl. Sprinkle the gelatin over the top. *Do not stir.* Let stand 5 minutes to soften.

3. Place the remaining 1/4 cup water and the granulated sugar in a small saucepan. Place over low heat until the mixture boils, stirring to dissolve the sugar if needed. Simmer the sugar syrup for 1 minute. Add the vermouth and cook just until heated. Stir in the gelatin and simmer for 1 minute, or until the gelatin is dissolved and the mixture is clear. Remove from the heat and stir in the raspberry puree and vanilla.

4. Empty the mixture into a large shallow bowl. Place in a sink filled with about 1 inch of cold water and ice cubes. Cool the raspberry mixture, stirring it occasionally with a rubber spatula. Scrape along the bottom every so often until it begins to

thicken (it could take 25 to 30 minutes).

5. Using an electric mixer, beat the egg whites on medium speed to soft peaks. Gradually add the superfine sugar, 1 tablespoon at a time. Continue to beat on medium speed for 15 seconds longer after all of the sugar has been added. *Do not overbeat.*

6. Stir about a quarter of the whites into the raspberry mixture. When smooth, fold in the remaining whites and the whipped cream.

7. ASSEMBLE THE PIE. Empty the raspberry mixture into the baked pastry shell. Chill until firm, about 4 hours.

8. Wash and thoroughly dry the berries (page 37). When ready to serve, pile mixed berries on top of the pie. Spoon the coulis over the top of each wedge.

STORAGE
Cover any leftover pie with waxed paper and a sheet of aluminum foil. Refrigerate for up to 3 days. This pie can be frozen without the fresh berries on top.

An immigrant living in Beloit, Wisconsin, wrote on November 29, 1851, to friends back in Norway: "Strawberries, raspberries and black berries thrive here. From these they make a wonderful dish combined with syrup and sugar, which is called 'pai.' I can tell you that it is something that glides easily down your throat; they also make the same sort of 'pai' out of apples or finely ground meat, with syrup added, and that is really the most superb."

THE AMERICAN HERITAGE COOKBOOK

Tangerine Meringue Pie

FOR THIS PIE, WE HAVE a snowy meringue topping covering a velvety filling made with tangerine juice. Tangerine juice has a brilliant, deep orange color and a more robust flavor than orange juice. It is also extraordinarily sweet, so less sugar is needed. The pie is light as a feather and makes a very refreshing dessert after a heavy meal.

1 9-inch *Vegetable Oil Pastry* shell
(page 144), baked

FILLING
$1/2$ cup granulated sugar
$1/3$ cup cornstarch
$1^1/2$ cups fresh tangerine juice
$1/2$ cup water
2 large eggs or 6 tablespoons egg
   substitute
$1^1/2$ teaspoons grated tangerine zest
$1/2$ teaspoon vanilla extract

MERINGUE
$1/4$ cup granulated sugar
2 tablespoons strained
   confectioners' sugar
3 large egg whites
$1/4$ teaspoon cream of tartar

1. MAKE THE FILLING: Combine $1/4$ cup of the sugar with the cornstarch in a medium saucepan. Gradually add the tangerine juice and water, whisking until smooth. Cook over medium heat, stirring constantly, until the mixture comes to a boil. Reduce the heat to low and cook for 1 minute longer, stirring occasionally.

2. Lightly beat the eggs in a medium bowl. Gradually whisk in the remaining $1/4$ cup sugar. Stir a small amount of the filling into the egg mixture to temper it. Then return the yolk mixture to the saucepan, blending the mixtures together. Be sure to reach into the bend of the pan. Cook slowly until the filling is thick, about 1 minute longer. Whisk briefly to smooth the filling, but *do not overmix.*

3. Remove the saucepan from the heat and stir in the tangerine zest and vanilla. Pour the filling into the baked pie shell.

4. MAKE THE MERINGUE: Preheat the oven to 350 degrees. Position the oven rack in the lower third of the oven.

5. Combine the sugars in a small bowl.

6. Beat the egg whites on medium speed in the large bowl of an electric mixer fitted with beaters or whip attachment, until frothy. Add the cream of tartar and increase the mixer speed to medium-high. Beat until the egg whites form firm peaks, but are not dry. Whip in the sugar mixture, 1 tablespoon at a time, taking about 1 minute. Beat the whites until thick and glossy, about 30 seconds longer.

7. With a tablespoon, drop mounds of meringue in a ring around the edge of the filling, then fill in the center. With the back of a tablespoon, spread the meringue until it completely covers the filling. Swirl the meringue with the back of the tablespoon to form peaks. To prevent weeping, be sure the meringue is sealed to the very edge of the pie crust, and that all the filling is covered.

8. Bake the pie for 15 minutes, or until lightly browned. Cool the pie on a rack away from drafts. Do not cut the pie until it is almost cool.

STORAGE

Cover any leftover pie loosely with an aluminum foil tent and refrigerate for up to 2 days. Freezing is not recommended.

Tangerines are a "kid glove fruit." They can be peeled and eaten without soiling one's Sunday best clothes.

COLONEL
G. L. DANCY

Favorite Savory Pies & Tarts

**S**AVORY PASTRIES TRULY illustrate the versatility of pies and tarts. Most everyone automatically associates pie crusts with desserts, but in reality doughs shine as well for savories as they do for sweets. The range of recipes is endless. ✳ In years past, quiche was the darling of savories. The more contemporary approach is to forget about the egg- and cream-based fillings and to pile all sorts of trendy foods

on various types of crusts. Although there is nothing new here, I am sure the popularity of these "nouvelle" pastries evolved from the diner's desire for healthier foods. This has all been for the better. And while quiches might be passé, they are still here, masquerading under the name of tarts. And the guise works.

In this chapter, you will find a mix of the old and new. Alsatian Quiche Lorraine, with its silky custard and smoky bacon filling, is a French classic that should never be tampered with. This perennial favorite will always be a menu mainstay. Corn Custard Pie with Wild Rice is a take on the traditional quiche formula, a crustless pie made with pureed sweet corn, whole corn kernels, and nutty wild rice; sparked with curry and chives and finished with melted cheddar.

Another terrific feature of savory pies and tarts is that an entire meal can be built on a crust as well as inside of one. An example of this is my current favorite: Smoky Joe's Turkey Tart. The cornmeal crust has enough variety on it to cover everyone's appetite. shredded smoked turkey breast, roasted red pepper, sautéed onion, kernels of sweet corn, and black beans, all topped with melted Monterey Jack cheese. With a green salad on the side, for brunch, lunch, or supper, that's all you need.

The Bundle of Sweet Onions and Roasted Peppers is a great complement for broiled and roasted meats. Crisp layers of phyllo enclose sweet onions sautéed until they are tender and caramelized. Flecks of roasted red pepper enliven the flavor and add a hint of color.

This chapter is only a tease when it comes to the array of savory specialties that can be made. In fact, I found it hard to turn the spout off when it came to ideas. If you enjoy crusts as much as I do, foods prepared in this manner can be transformed from the ordinary into something special.

Before You Begin

Here is an overview of tips and tricks for making great savory pies and tarts.

✦ If you wish to create your own custard tart (quiche) or to change the quantity of a recipe, the ratio is 1/2 cup milk or cream to each whole egg.

✦ If you use less than 32 percent heavy cream in a custard (quiche) filling, the filling will be watery. The less fat used, the more watery the filling will be.

✦ Either light cream or half-and-half can be used in place of heavy cream in custard (quiche) fillings. Replace the milk and heavy cream with all light cream or half-and-half in its place.

✦ Avoid overbeating the eggs in a custard filling. Too much air whipped into eggs will make the texture of the filling too spongy.

✦ To vary the type of filling in a custard (quiche) tart, substitute an equal amount of the solid ingredient that is specified in the recipe.

✦ To prevent spilling a filling, place the pan on the oven rack first, then fill it there.

✦ Crustless custard- (quiche-) style fillings must be baked in a water bath. Otherwise, they will stick to the bottom of the pan.

✦ Do not use a water bath with a two-part tart pan or with one that is very shallow without molding a sheet of heavy-duty aluminum foil around the pan.

✦ To ensure a crisp bottom crust, always fully bake (not par-bake) the pastry shell for custard (quiche) fillings. The filling will insulate the pastry and keep it from overbaking.

✦ Custard- (quiche-) style fillings are done when they puff in the center and are lightly browned. You can also test them by inserting a table knife in the center. If it comes out clean, the filling is done.

✦ The surface of a pastry shell can be sealed by brushing it with a thin layer of Dijon mustard or lightly beaten egg white. After applying, dry the surface of the crust by returning the pan to the oven for a few minutes.

✦ Fillings and pastries should be pre-cooked for open savory tarts. Both can be made ahead. Generally, when assembled, all that is needed is to heat it as a whole.

✦ Chicken, fish, meats, and vegetables must be pre-cooked before using as a stuffing or topping for savory pies and tarts.

✦ Many leftovers can be used for making filled pastries. If moistness is needed, add a little chicken stock to the filling.

✦ To prevent pre-cooked fillings on open tarts from becoming too dry, cover the top of the tart lightly with a square of aluminum foil.

✦ While leftover savory pastries can be frozen, the texture of the fillings after thawing and reheating is never quite the same.

Corn Custard Pie with Wild Rice

HERE IS A BAKED CUSTARD PIE that can be do-ahead. It is made with a puree of sweet corn, combined with whole corn kernels and wild rice. The custard has a mild curry flavor, along with a hint of fresh chives and parsley.

1½ teaspoons curry powder
2 cups cooked fresh or frozen corn kernels, preferably Country Gemtleman
1¼ cups milk
3/4 cup heavy cream
2 teaspoons sugar
1 teaspoon salt
Freshly ground black pepper
4 large eggs
1½ cups cooked wild rice
2 tablespoons minced chives
1 tablespoon chopped parsley
1/8 teaspoon freshly grated nutmeg
1 cup (3 ounces) lightly packed shredded sharp Cheddar cheese

1. Preheat the oven to 375 degrees. Position the oven rack in the lower third of the oven. Generously butter the pie plate, and set it in a larger pan, about 2½ inches deep. Have some boiling water ready in a tea kettle.

2. Sprinkle the curry powder into a small, heavy skillet. Heat over low heat until you smell the aroma of the curry roasting. Set aside.

3. Place 1 cup of the corn in a food processor. Add the milk and cream and process until the corn is pulverized. Add the curry powder, sugar, salt, and pepper. Process briefly just to blend. Empty the mixture into a large bowl.

4. Place the eggs in the food processor and process for about 15 seconds. Stir the eggs into the cream mixture with the remaining corn, wild rice, chives, parsley, and nutmeg.

5. Set both baking pans in the oven. Pour the corn filling into the pie plate. Use a spoon to distribute the corn kernels and wild rice evenly in the pan. Sprinkle the shredded cheese over the top.

6. Fill the larger pan with 1 inch of boiling water. Carefully slide the water bath and pie plate into the oven. Bake the pie for 40 to 45 minutes, or until the top is slightly puffed and golden brown. Let stand at least 15 minutes before serving. If making the pie ahead, cover it loosely with a piece of aluminum foil and warm it in a 350 degree oven for 20 to 25 minutes, or until heated through.

STORAGE
Cover any leftover tart with aluminum foil and refrigerate for up to 3 days. This pie can be frozen after baking.

At a Glance

SERVES: 6 to 8

PAN: 9½-inch deep ovenproof glass

OVEN TEMP: 375 degrees

BAKING TIME: 40 to 45 minutes

DIFFICULTY:

Deep-Dish Broccoli, Leek, and Cheddar Tart

BROCCOLI IS DELICIOUS WHEN combined with sautéed leeks, the sweetest member of the onion family. The vegetables are layered with extra-sharp Cheddar cheese, then topped with an egg custard. Although the tart can be baked in an 11-inch tart pan, I like to use a deep-dish pan because it gives me more room for the vegetables.

At a Glance

SERVES: 10 to 12

PAN: 10 × 2-inch deep tart

PASTRY PREP: Baked

OVEN TEMP: 375 degrees

BAKING TIME:
50 to 60 minutes

DIFFICULTY: 🥿 🥿

Be careful not to overcook the broccoli so that the color will stay bright green. While I prefer to use fresh broccoli, 1½ 10-ounce packages of cooked frozen chopped broccoli can be substituted. For the cheese, my preference is yellow Cheddar, as it bakes into a gorgeous golden brown top. And don't forget to use fresh savory in the filling; the herb really enhances the flavor.

1 10-inch Cheddar Pastry tart crust
   (page 135), baked
2 teaspoons Dijon mustard

FILLING
3 cups (1 to 1¼-pound bunch)
   broccoli
2 medium leeks
2 tablespoons unsalted butter
2 cups (6 ounces) lightly packed
   shredded extra-sharp yellow
   Cheddar cheese
5 large eggs
1½ cups milk
1 cup heavy cream
2 teaspoons Worcestershire sauce

1½ teaspoons chopped fresh
   savory, or ½ teaspoon crushed
   dried savory
1 teaspoon salt
Scant ¼ teaspoon cayenne
Scant ¼ teaspoon freshly grated
   nutmeg

1. Immediately after baking the tart shell, spread the mustard over the surface of the crust. Return the shell to the oven for 2 to 3 minutes to dry the coating and seal the shell.

2. PREPARE THE BROCCOLI: Trim the bottoms of the broccoli stalks. Remove any stringy fibers from the stalks with a vegetable peeler. Rinse with cold water, then cut the broccoli florets and stalks into 3/4-inch pieces. Cook in a large pot of salted, boiling water for 3 to 4 minutes or until just tender. Do not overcook.

Drain the broccoli in a colander, and immediately rinse with cold water to stop the cooking. Shake the colander to remove excess moisture. Line a shallow pan with a double thickness of paper towels. Spread the broccoli over the towels. Cover with a top layer of towels and blot dry.

3. **PREPARE THE LEEKS:** Remove the tough, dark green portion of the leeks, leaving about 2 inches of the lighter green stalk. To separate the layers and expose the leek's sandy interior, lay it on a cutting surface and cut through the leek from the top to where the white bulb begins. Turn the leek a quarter turn and repeat. Cut off the roots from the base, removing as little of the bulb as possible.

Wash the leeks under tepid, then cold water, rinsing thoroughly to remove the sand. Dry with paper towels. Cut the leeks into quarters lengthwise, then into 1/4-inch slices.

4. Preheat the oven to 375 degrees. Position the oven rack in the upper third of the oven.

5. **ASSEMBLE THE TART:** Melt the butter in a medium skillet. Add the leeks and sauté over medium-low heat until transparent, 2 to 3 minutes.

6. Spread the leeks in the bottom of the tart shell. Add the broccoli, smooth the surface, then scatter the cheese over the vegetables.

7. Place the eggs in the bowl of a food processor and process for 8 to 10 seconds. Alternatively, the eggs can be put in a large bowl and beaten with a whisk. Add the milk, cream, Worcestershire sauce, savory, salt, cayenne, and nutmeg. Pulse or whisk to blend. Empty into a 1-quart liquid measuring cup or pitcher.

8. Set the tart on an aluminum foil–lined heavy, shallow baking pan, preferably one made of dark metal (see "Pots and Pans," page 45). Pull the oven rack out and set the pan on the rack. Pour the egg mixture evenly into the tart pan. Carefully push the rack back into the oven.

9. Bake the tart for 50 to 60 minutes, or until the top is golden brown and puffy and the center of the custard is set. Place the tart on a cooling rack and let stand for 20 to 30 minutes before serving.

STORAGE

Cover any leftover tart with waxed paper then aluminum foil and refrigerate for up to 4 days.

To reheat, place on a shallow pan, cover loosely with a sheet of aluminum foil, and bake in a 350 degree oven for 20 to 30 minutes or until hot. Remove the aluminum foil during the last few minutes of baking. The length of time will depend on how large a piece is being reheated. This tart can be frozen.

Cabbage, Apple, and Onion Tart

ONE DAY, MY FRIEND Sylvia Weinstock, the perky "Grande Dame of wedding cakes," said, "Carole, you are going to have a cabbage pie in your book, aren't you?" Well, Carole hadn't really thought about it, but Sylvia sparked an idea. Cabbage is a versatile and healthy vegetable, so why not? I went to work. The pie became a tart and, according to those who tasted it, the outcome was terrific.

A sautéed mixture of shredded cabbage, tart apples, and sweet Spanish onion is spread on flaky tart pastry. The top has a diagonal lattice crust that is sprinkled with caraway seeds and a touch of coarse salt. Thank you, Sylvia, for giving me the inspiration.

1½ recipes Classic Tart Pastry (pages 102, 104), divided in half, covered with plastic wrap, and chilled

FILLING
1 (2-pound) head green or white cabbage
1 tablespoon coarse kosher salt, plus additional for garnish
2 to 3 tablespoons vegetable oil
1 large Spanish onion, cut into medium dice
1 tablespoon sugar
1 large Granny Smith apple, peeled, cored, and shredded
Salt and freshly ground black pepper to taste
1 large egg white
2 teaspoons water
½ teaspoon caraway seeds, for garnish

1. **PREPARE THE FILLING:** Discard the outer leaves of the cabbage. Cut the cabbage into quarters, then remove the core. Cut the cabbage in half again, making 8 wedges. Using a food processor fitted with the medium shredding disk, shred the cabbage using light pressure on the pusher. You should have 10 to 12 cups.

2. Place the cabbage in a large colander. Sprinkle 1 tablespoon coarse salt over the cabbage and toss with your hands to distribute. Set the colander over a large bowl and leave to drain for 30 minutes. Using your hands, squeeze the cabbage in batches to remove excess water. Place in a bowl and set aside.

3. Heat the vegetable oil in a very large skillet or sauté pan over medium-high heat. Add the onion and sugar and sauté until the onion is wilted. Blend in the cabbage and apple. Reduce the heat to low and cook for 20 to 25 minutes, or until the vegetables are very soft and

lightly browned. Stir occasionally to prevent sticking. Season with salt and pepper. Cool until tepid.

4. ASSEMBLE THE TART: Preheat the oven to 425 degrees. Position the oven rack in the lower third of the oven.

5. On a well-floured pastry cloth, roll 1 pastry disk into a 14-inch circle. Line the tart pan with the pastry. Trim excess pastry by running the rolling pin over the top. Empty the cabbage filling into the pan and smooth the surface with an offset spatula.

6. Roll the second piece of dough into a 14-inch circle. Using a pastry wheel, divide the dough into ten 1-inch strips. Make a diagonal lattice as follows: Center one of the longer strips over the filling. Place 2 shorter strips on either side, with the shortest strips toward the outer edge.

7. Rotate the tart 45 degrees. Center another longer strip over the top, weaving it over and under the first 5 strips (see page 65). Complete the weaving with the 4 remaining strips. Do not stretch the dough. Run the rolling pin over the top to trim the overhanging pastry.

8. Using a fork, lightly beat the egg white and water together in a small bowl. Brush the egg wash on each pastry strip. Sprinkle the top with the caraway seeds and coarse salt to taste.

9. Set the tart on a cookie sheet and bake for 15 minutes. Reduce the oven to 375 degrees and continue baking for 20 minutes longer or until the pastry is golden brown. Let stand for 10 to 15 minutes. Release the tart from the pan and place on a platter. Cut into wedges and serve with a dollop of sour cream or yogurt.

STORAGE

Cover any leftover tart with waxed paper then aluminum foil and refrigerate for up to 4 days.

To reheat, place a sheet of aluminum foil loosely over the top. Bake in a 350 degree oven for 10 to 15 minutes or until hot. Remove the aluminum foil during the last few minutes. The length of time needed in the oven will depend on how large a piece is being reheated. This tart can be frozen.

Chesapeake Crab Tart

MY FAVORITE SHELLFISH IS JUMBO lump crabmeat from the blue crab. To my taste it is the sweetest and most tender of all crustaceans. While it is sometimes found as far north as Nova Scotia and as far south as South America, it is most abundant in the Chesapeake Bay, in the Bahamas, and in the Gulf of Mexico.

At a Glance

SERVES: 8 to 10

PAN: 11-inch metal tart

PASTRY PREP: Baked

OVEN TEMP: 400 degrees

BAKING TIME:
30 to 35 minutes

DIFFICULTY:

Although I favor jumbo lump crabmeat, it is very costly and not practical to use in some cooked preparations. A good alternative is backfin. The morsels are also sweet, but they are smaller and therefore not quite as expensive.

This tart is one that I have made for many years. I have purposely kept the vegetables and seasonings traditional to the Chesapeake Bay area. While the tart can be made from any kind of crabmeat—fresh, pasteurized, frozen, or canned—high-quality crabmeat makes this a superior tart. At best, the life of seafood dishes is limited, so plan on eating this tart within one or two days of when it is made.

As an alternative, a poached meaty white fish like halibut or scrod can be used.

1 11-inch *Classic Tart Pastry* crust (pages 102, 104), baked
1 tablespoon Dijon mustard

FILLING
1 tablespoon unsalted butter
1/2 cup diced celery, in 1/4-inch pieces (about 2 stalks)
1/2 cup diced red bell pepper, in 1/4-inch pieces
1/4 cup chopped scallions (3 to 4 medium)
1 1/2 cups fresh crabmeat, preferably backfin, picked free of cartilage (1/2 pound)
1 cup packed shredded medium-sharp Cheddar cheese (3 ounces)
2 tablespoons minced parsley
3 large eggs
3/4 cup heavy cream
3/4 cup milk
2 teaspoons Worcestershire sauce
3/4 teaspoon salt
1/2 teaspoon Old Bay Seasoning
Scant 1/4 teaspoon freshly grated nutmeg
Scant 1/4 teaspoon cayenne

1. Coat the surface of the pastry shell with the mustard, using a small offset spatula or pastry brush. Return the shell to the oven and bake for 4 to 5 minutes or until the mustard is dry and the pastry is golden brown.

2. Turn the oven to 400 degrees. Position the oven rack in the lower third of the oven.

3. MAKE THE FILLING: Melt the butter in a medium skillet. Add the celery and red pepper. Sauté over medium heat until transparent, about 2 to 3 minutes. Stir in the scallions, then empty the vegetables into the tart shell and spread evenly over the bottom. Scatter the crabmeat, cheese, and parsley evenly over the top.

4. Place the eggs in a food processor bowl and process 8 to 10 seconds. Alternatively, put the eggs in a large bowl and beat with a whisk. Add the cream, milk, Worcestershire sauce, and seasonings. Pulse or whisk to blend.

5. Set the tart shell in a shallow baking pan lined with aluminum foil. Pull the oven rack out and set the pan on the rack. Pour the egg mixture evenly into the tart pan. Carefully push the rack back into the oven. Bake for 30 to 35 minutes, or until the surface is golden brown and puffy. Set on a rack and let stand at least 15 minutes before serving.

STORAGE

Cover any leftover tart with waxed paper then aluminum foil and refrigerate for up to 2 days.

To reheat, place a sheet of aluminum foil loosely over the top. Bake in a 350 degree oven for 10 to 20 minutes or until hot. Remove the aluminum foil during the last few minutes. The length of time needed in the oven will depend on how large a piece is being reheated. This tart can be frozen.

Eggplant Tart with Tomatoes, Greek Olives, and Feta

THE FLAVOR OF EGGPLANT IS enhanced by flame cooking and smoke. For this recipe, overlapping slices of charred eggplant are placed in a flaky pastry shell filled with sautéed sweet onions. Chopped tomatoes, black olives, and crumbled feta cheese are scattered over the top. This classic Mediterranean mix of flavors is always a welcome favorite when it comes to the table.

At a Glance

SERVES: 6 to 8

PAN: 11-inch metal tart

PASTRY PREP: Baked

OVEN TEMP: 375 degrees

BAKING TIME:
25 to 30 minutes

DIFFICULTY: 🥄

---

1 11-inch *Classic Tart Pastry* crust
(pages 102, 104), *baked*

FILLING
1 tablespoon minced garlic
3/4 teaspoon crushed dried oregano
1/2 cup extra-virgin olive oil
2 medium eggplants (about
   2 pounds total)
1 to 1 1/2 teaspoons coarse salt
1 tablespoon fresh lemon juice
1 large Spanish onion, cut into
   1/2-inch dice
1 1/2 tablespoons chopped flat-leaf
   parsley
1 1/2 tablespoons chopped fresh
   mint
4 ripe plum tomatoes, seeded and
   cut into 1/2-inch dice
16 to 18 Greek black olives, pitted
   and cut in half (about 6 ounces)
Freshly ground black pepper
4 ounces feta cheese, crumbled
A few whole mint leaves, for
   garnish

---

1. MAKE THE FILLING: Combine the garlic, oregano, and olive oil and let stand for 30 minutes.

2. Wipe the eggplant with damp paper towels. Using a large serrated knife, cut the eggplant into 1/2-inch slices. Line a shallow sheet pan with a double thickness of paper towels. Lay the sliced eggplant in a single layer on the baking pan. Sprinkle lightly with coarse salt. Place a layer of paper towels on top of the eggplant. If any slices remain, make a second layer. Lay a second pan over the first, and weight it with 2 heavy cans from your pantry. Let stand 30 minutes to extract the bitter juices.

3. Using damp paper towels, wipe the surface of the eggplant to remove excess salt. Set aside 2 tablespoons of the seasoned olive oil. Lightly brush the eggplant on both sides with the remaining oil.

4. Preheat your outdoor grill or indoor broiler. For outdoor cooking, grill the eggplant on both sides until it is charred and cooked through. *Do not burn.* If broiling, line a shallow baking pan with aluminum foil. Lay the eggplant in a single layer on the pan and broil it on both sides until charred and cooked through, about 4 to 5 minutes per side. Drizzle the eggplant with lemon juice and set aside to cool.

5. Heat the 2 tablespoons seasoned olive oil in a large, heavy skillet. Add the onion and cook over medium heat until soft and golden in color, 8 to 10 minutes. Remove from the heat and stir in half of the chopped parsley and mint. Cool for 5 to 10 minutes.

6. **ASSEMBLE THE TART:** Spread the onion evenly in the pastry shell. Arrange the eggplant in overlapping slices, making 2 concentric circles (use the smaller rounds for the inside circle). Scatter the tomatoes and black olives over the top, and season with pepper. Scatter the feta evenly. (The tart can be made up to 6 hours ahead at this point. Cover with a piece of waxed paper until ready to bake.)

7. **BAKE THE TART:** Preheat the oven to 375 degrees. Position the oven rack in the lower third of the oven. Bake the tart 25 to 30 minutes or until heated through. Sprinkle the remaining chopped parsley and mint over the top and garnish with a few whole mint leaves. Serve warm or at room temperature.

STORAGE

Cover any leftover tart with a piece of waxed paper then aluminum foil and refrigerate for up to 3 days. Reheat before serving. This tart can be frozen.

Wild Mushroom Tart with Savory Streusel

IF YOU ARE A MUSHROOM aficianado like myself, you must try this tart. It is made with fresh crimini, shiitaki, oyster mushrooms, dried porcini, and white button mushrooms. The flavor is heightened with Madeira, crème fraîche, and herbs. Most supermarkets now stock a vast selection of wild mushrooms. Other than portobellos, which are best for baking and broiling, most any combination of wild mushrooms will do.

At a Glance

SERVES: 6 to 8

PAN: Large cookie sheet

PASTRY PREP: Baked

OVEN TEMP: 375 degrees

BAKING TIME: 30 to 35 minutes

DIFFICULTY: 🍄 🍄

Make the crumbs for the savory streusel with your favorite high-quality croutons. Be sure the seasonings complement the mushroom filling. My favorite brand is Olivia's Croutons (made in Charlotte, Vermont), but many fine brands are available throughout the country. To break the croutons into coarse crumbs, put them in a plastic bag and release the air. Close the top and hit the bag a few times with a rolling pin or the bottom of a heavy pot. It works like a charm.

1 small recipe Goof-Proof Puff Pastry (page 172), shaped into an 11-inch free-form pastry shell, baked

FILLING
1 Spanish onion, diced
2 tablespoons olive oil
10 ounces button mushrooms, sliced 1/4 inch thick
8 ounces mixed wild mushrooms, sliced 1/4 inch thick

1/2 ounce dried mushrooms, reconstituted and coarsely chopped
1/4 cup Madiera or sweet sherry
1 tablespoon flour
1/2 cup chicken stock
1/4 cup crème fraîche or sour cream
1 tablespoon chopped parsley, plus additional for garnish
1 teaspoon finely chopped fresh thyme
1 teaspoon fresh lemon juice
Salt and freshly ground pepper to taste
1/4 cup grated Parmesan or Asiago cheese

SAVORY STREUSEL
1 1/2 cups fine-quality croutons, broken into coarse crumbs (see headnote)
2 tablespoons olive oil
2 tablespoons grated Parmesan or Asiago cheese

1. Preheat the oven to 375 degrees. Position the oven rack in the lower third of the oven. Line a large cookie sheet with heavy-duty aluminum foil, tucking the ends under to prevent it from sliding. Place the baked puff pastry shell on the pan.

2. MAKE THE FILLING: Sauté the onion in the olive oil in a large heavy skillet over medium heat until translucent, about 8 to 10 minutes. Remove half and set aside for the streusel topping.

3. Add the button and wild mushrooms to the remaining onion and sauté over high heat until most of the liquid has evaporated, 6 to 8 minutes.

4. Add the chopped dried mushrooms, sauté briefly, then deglaze the pan with the Madeira. When the Madeira is almost evaporated, reduce the heat to low. Sprinkle the flour over the mushrooms, stir, and cook for 2 to 3 minutes. Add the chicken stock and cook until the mixture thickens, 1 to 2 minutes.

5. Stir in the crème fraîche, then add the herbs, lemon juice, salt, and pepper. Cook for 1 to 2 minutes, stirring to combine well. Adjust the seasonings and set aside to cool to tepid. Do not fill the pastry shell until just before baking. (This filling can be made up to 2 days ahead. Reheat briefly, adding 1 to 2 tablespoons of chicken stock.)

6. ASSEMBLE THE TART: Sprinkle the grated cheese over the bottom of the baked and cooled pastry shell. Spoon the mushroom filling into the puff pastry shell and distribute it around the pan with a fork. *Do not flatten the filling.*

7. Combine the crushed croutons with the olive oil and grated cheese. Toss the reserved onion through the mixture. Sprinkle the crumb mixture over the top of the mushroom filling.

8. Bake the tart for 30 to 35 minutes, or until the streusel topping is golden brown. Garnish with chopped parsley and serve while still warm.

STORAGE

Refrigerate any leftover tart loosely covered with aluminum foil for up to 3 days.

Reheat in a 325 degree oven for 8 to 10 minutes before serving. While puff pastry is best eaten the day it is baked, the leftovers can be frozen.

Bundle of Sweet Onions and Roasted Peppers

THIS GOLDEN BROWN PACKAGE of crisp phyllo is bursting with juicy onions and roasted peppers. The vegetables make a perfect marriage with roasts and foods from an outdoor grill. Although the pastry can be assembled up to 3 days ahead, if you want the phyllo leaves to stay flaky, the dish is best if eaten within an hour or two after baking. If Vidalia onions are in season, use these sugar-sweet Georgia treats.

At a Glance

SERVES: 6 to 8

PAN: 14 × 17-inch cookie sheet

PASTRY PREP: Unbaked

OVEN TEMP: 375 degrees

BAKING TIME: 40 to 45 minutes

DIFFICULTY: 🍪

---

12 sheets of phyllo dough
$1/2$ cup clarified unsalted butter (see page 52), melted

FILLING
1 large red bell pepper
2 tablespoons olive oil
2 pounds Vidalia, Spanish, or other sweet onion, cut into $1/2$-inch dice
1 tablespoon chopped fresh savory, or 1 teaspoon dried
1 tablespoon finely chopped flat-leaf parsley
Salt and freshly ground black pepper to taste
3 tablespoons packaged seasoned bread crumbs
3 tablespoons grated Romano cheese

---

1. **MAKE THE FILLING:** Set the oven to broil and preheat. Position the oven rack about 6 inches from the heat.

2. Rinse and dry the red pepper. Cut it in half lengthwise and remove the stem and seeds. Place the pepper, cut side down, on an aluminum foil–lined pan. Broil it until the pepper is well charred. Place the charred pepper in a brown paper bag or wrap it in aluminum foil, and seal it so that it can steam. After 15 to 20 minutes, peel the skin from the pepper and cut into $1/2$-inch dice.

3. Heat the olive oil in a 12-inch skillet. Add the onions and sauté over low heat for 15 minutes or until transparent. Add the roasted pepper, savory, and parsley. Sauté for 3 to 5 minutes longer. The onions should be very soft. Season with salt and pepper, and set aside to cool.

4. ASSEMBLE THE PIE: Preheat the oven to 375 degrees. Position the oven rack in the lower third of the oven. Line a large cookie sheet with baking parchment.

5. Combine the dried bread crumbs and Romano cheese. Reserve 1 tablespoon for the top.

6. Open the phyllo and place on a sheet of waxed paper. Lay a sheet of waxed paper over the top and cover with damp paper towels to prevent the phyllo from becoming dry (see "Working with Phyllo," page 64). Warm the clarified butter.

7. Place 1 sheet of phyllo down the length of the pan. Brush lightly with clarified butter, then sprinkle with about ½ tablespoon of the crumb mixture. Lay a second sheet of phyllo in the opposite direction. Brush with butter and sprinkle with another ½ tablespoon of the crumb mixture.

8. Place the rest of the phyllo sheets in the following order: The third sheet goes in the space on the right side, between the first and second pieces. The fourth sheet goes in the space on the left side. You should have a circle of phyllo. Make 2 more layers of phyllo, using 8 more sheets. As you layer the sheets, brush each lightly with butter and sprinkle with the crumb mixture. When you are done, the circle should consist of 3 layers of phyllo.

9. Spread the onion filling in the center of the phyllo circle. Shape into a 9-inch circle. To enclose the filling, fold the phyllo leaves, 1 at time, over the filling. Lightly butter each layer and sprinkle with crumbs. When all the leaves are folded, shape the bundle into a circle and flatten it slightly. Sprinkle the top with the reserved tablespoon of crumbs.

10. Bake the bundle for 40 to 45 minutes or until golden brown. Let stand at least 10 minutes before serving.

STORAGE

Cover any leftovers with aluminum foil and refrigerate for up to 3 days. Reheat before serving. This phyllo pastry can be frozen.

Alsatian Quiche Lorraine

HOW COULD I WRITE THIS book and ignore the most renowned of all savory tarts, Quiche Lorraine. Impossible! The custard filling is flavored with diced bacon that is first blanched, then fried. Gruyère cheese gives the top of the quiche a vibrant gold and bronze color. This tart will always be a timeless favorite.

At a Glance

SERVES: 8 to 10

PAN: 11-inch metal tart

PASTRY PREP: Baked

OVEN TEMP: 375 degrees

BAKING TIME: 30 to 35 minutes

DIFFICULTY: 🖐

---

1 Classic Tart Pastry crust (pages 102, 104) baked
1 tablespoon Dijon mustard

FILLING
1/2 pound thickly sliced bacon, cut into 1-inch pieces
1 large onion, cut into 1/2-inch dice
4 large eggs
1 cup milk
1 cup heavy cream
1/2 teaspoon salt
1/4 teaspoon freshly grated nutmeg
1/8 teaspoon cayenne
1 1/2 cups shredded Gruyère cheese (5 ounces)

1. Preheat the oven to 375 degrees. Position the oven rack in the lower third of the oven. Brush the shell with the mustard. Return to the oven and bake for 1 to 2 minutes to set the the mustard.

2. Place a sheet pan in the oven to preheat.

3. MAKE THE FILLING: Place the bacon in a 3-quart saucepan. Fill the saucepan with cold water and bring to a boil. Simmer the bacon for 1 to 2 minutes, then drain it in a colander. Dry the bacon on a double thickness of paper towels.

4. Sauté the bacon over medium-low heat in a 12-inch skillet until golden brown and crisp. Drain the bacon on a double thickness of paper towels. Blot with additional paper towels.

5. Discard all but 1 tablespoon of the bacon fat (if you prefer, 1 tablespoon unsalted butter or vegetable oil can be substituted). Add the onion to the skillet and cook over medium-low heat until transparent and lightly brown. Set aside.

6. Place the eggs in the bowl of a food processor and process for 8 to 10 seconds. Alternatively, the eggs can be put in a large bowl and beaten with a whisk. Add the milk, cream, salt, nutmeg, and cayenne.

7. **ASSEMBLE THE TART:** Place the tart pan on a large sheet pan. Scatter the bacon, onion, and cheese evenly into the baked shell.

8. Pour the milk mixture into a large liquid measuring cup. Pull the oven rack out, and set the tart on the preheated sheet pan. Immediately pour the milk mixture into the tart, adding only as much liquid as the shell will hold without the mixture running over.

9. Carefully push the rack back into the oven. Bake for 30 to 35 minutes, or until the surface is golden brown and puffy. Set on a rack and let stand at least 15 minutes before serving

STORAGE

Cover any leftover tart with aluminum foil and refrigerate for up to 3 days.

To reheat, place a sheet of aluminum foil loosely over the top and bake in a 350 degree oven for 10 to 20 minutes or until hot. Remove the aluminum foil during the last few minutes. The length of time will depend on how large a piece is being reheated. This tart can be frozen.

Phyllo Spinach Pie

SPINACH PIE, A MAINSTAY OF the Greek table, has timeless appeal. I have taught this recipe to my students for many years, and its popularity has never wavered. The pie has lots of thin layers of phyllo wrapped around a tasty spinach filling. I often serve the pie for buffet dinner parties. It complements most entrées, the presentation is very appealing, and it's do-ahead. Don't bother with fresh spinach; frozen works just fine.

At a Glance

SERVES: 8 to 10

PAN: 9½-inch deep oven-proof glass pie plate

PASTRY PREP: Unbaked

OVEN TEMP: 375 degrees

BAKING TIME: 50 to 60 minutes

DIFFICULTY: 🥄🥄

---

20 sheets of phyllo dough (³/4 pound)
³/4 cup melted clarified butter (see page 52)
²/3 cup lightly toasted almonds, chopped
3 packages frozen leaf spinach, thawed
2 tablespoons olive oil
½ cup chopped scallions
1 large garlic clove, minced
1 cup loosely packed flat-leaf parsley
1 cup loosely packed fresh dill
4 ounces feta cheese
6 large eggs
8 ounces ricotta cheese
2 tablespoons grated Parmesan cheese
¼ cup milk
Salt and pepper to taste
Freshly grated nutmeg to taste

---

1. **MAKE THE FILLING:** Squeeze the spinach well in your hands to remove the water. Set aside.

2. Heat the olive oil in a small skillet. Add the scallions and garlic. Sauté on low heat until clear and transparent, about 3 minutes. Empty into a large bowl.

3. Place the parsley and dill in the bowl of a food processor. Pulse until finely chopped. Add half the spinach, the feta, and 3 eggs. Pulse 3 or 4 times or until blended. Empty the mixture into the bowl with the sautéed scallions.

4. Add the remaining spinach and 3 eggs to the food processor bowl. Process to blend, then stir into the first batch of spinach. Blend in the ricotta, Parmesan, milk, salt, pepper, and nutmeg.

5. ASSEMBLE THE PIE: Preheat the oven to 375 degrees. Butter a 9½-inch deep ovenproof glass pie plate. Open the phyllo and place on a sheet of waxed paper. Place a sheet of waxed paper over the top and cover with damp paper towels to prevent the phyllo from becoming dry (see "Working with Phyllo," page 64). Warm the clarified butter.

6. Center 1 sheet of phyllo over the pie plate, and press it in. Brush lightly with butter. Arrange the second sheet in the opposite direction and brush it with butter.

7. The remaining phyllo sheets are *not* centered in the pie plate. Each sheet is placed *off-center*, with the first half starting at the crease of the baking dish and the remaining half extended over the edge. (This will give you enough pastry to enclose the filling.)

8. Place the third sheet at the 12 o'clock position, the fourth sheet at 3 o'clock, position the fifth sheet at 6 o'clock, and the sixth sheet at 9 o'clock. Each time you put a sheet of phyllo into the plate, brush it lightly with clarified butter and sprinkle with about ½ tablespoon chopped almonds. Repeat the cycle 4 times. You have now used 18 sheets of phyllo.

9. Empty the filling into the pastry and smooth the top. Starting at 12 o'clock, take the pastry overhang and cover the filling. Continue to fold the phyllo over the filling, until all of the pastry sheets have been used. As you enclose the filling, brush each piece of phyllo with butter and sprinkle with almonds.

10. Take 1 more sheet of phyllo, fold it in half, and fit it over the top of the pie. Brush with butter. Roll the remaining sheet of pastry, and cut it into ¼-inch pieces. Scatter the shredded phyllo and remaining chopped almonds over the top. Drizzle with butter. (The pie can be made up to this point up to a day ahead.)

11. Bake the spinach pie for 50 to 60 minutes or until nicely browned. Let stand 15 to 20 minutes. Cut into wedges and serve.

STORAGE
Cover any leftover pie with aluminum foil and refrigerate for up to 3 days. Reheat before serving. This pie can be frozen.

Just when you're beginning to think pretty well of people, you run across somebody who puts sugar on sliced tomatoes.

WILL CUPPY

Swiss Chard Tart with Apricots in Rosemary Chive Crust

SWISS CHARD IS A MILD-FLAVORED, leafy green similar to spinach, but sweeter. The leaves sometimes are tinged with red, which is no surprise since the plant is cousin to the beet. The reddish variety is not as sweet as the green, but either may be used. Be sure to use the stalks. They are considered a delicacy in Europe.

At a Glance

SERVES: 6 to 8

PAN: 11-inch metal tart

PASTRY PREP: Baked

OVEN TEMP: 400 degrees

BAKING TIME: 20 to 25 minutes

DIFFICULTY:

For this tart, the Swiss chard is sautéed with onion in garlic-flavored olive oil. Shreds of prosciutto and cooked dried apricots add a wonderful salt and sweet flavor. The filling is baked with a topping of fontina cheese and pine nuts. Bring out the Chianti and enjoy!

1 11-inch Rosemary Chive Tart
    Pastry crust (page 105), baked

FILLING
3 ounces dried apricots (about 10
    medium)
1½ pounds Swiss chard
    (2 medium bunches)
1 to 2 tablespoons extra-virgin olive
    oil
1 Spanish onion, cut into ½-inch
    dice
2 teaspoons minced garlic
3 ounces prosciutto, cut into
    ¼-inch shreds
⅛ teaspoon freshly grated nutmeg
Salt and freshly ground black
    pepper to taste

2 cups shredded Italian fontina
    cheese (about 3 ounces)
3 tablespoons pine nuts

1. START THE APRICOTS:
Place the apricots in a small saucepan with enough water to cover by 1 inch. Cover the saucepan and bring to a boil. Simmer until the apricots are tender, 20 to 25 minutes. Drain, rinse with cold water, and empty onto several layers of paper towels to dry. When cool, coarsely chop. Set aside.

2. COOK THE SWISS CHARD:
Separate the stalks of Swiss chard. Trim the bottoms and rinse with tepid water to remove the sand and dirt. Fill a basin with cold water. Add the Swiss chard and swish it around in the water. Empty the dirty water, replace with fresh, and repeat the washing process. When the water remains clear, drain the Swiss chard in a colander. Pick through each stalk, discarding blemished leaves. Cut

the thick stalks from the leafy portion. Slice the stalks into 2-inch pieces. Gather the leaves into a bunch and cut across in 3 or 4 places.

3. Bring a large pot of water to a boil. Salt the water, add the stalks, and bring to a boil. Cook for 5 minutes, then add the leaves and bring the water to a boil again. Cook for about 10 minutes or until the chard is tender. Drain in a colander and immediately rinse with cold water. Squeeze the chard with your hands to remove the water. Coarsely chop on a cutting board.

4. MAKE THE FILLING: Heat the olive oil in a large, heavy skillet. Add the onion and cook over medium-low heat until soft and transparent, 8 to 10 minutes. Add the garlic, and sauté about 1 minute. Then stir in the chard and cook until heated through.

5. Remove from the heat and add the prosciutto and apricots. Season with nutmeg, salt, and pepper. Cool for 5 to 10 minutes. (The filling can be made ahead to this point. Cover with waxed paper until ready to use. Reheat to tepid before assembling the tart.)

6. ASSEMBLE THE TART: Preheat the oven to 400 degrees. Position the oven rack in the lower third of the oven.

7. Spread the filling in the baked pastry shell. Top with the shredded cheese, then the pine nuts. Bake for 20 to 25 minutes, or until the top begins to brown. Serve at once.

STORAGE

Cover any leftover tart with a sheet of waxed paper then aluminum foil and refrigerate for up to 3 days. Reheat before serving. This tart can be frozen.

Smoky Joe's Turkey Tart

OF THE MANY MEALS MY assistants, Kelly Volpe and Judie Levenberg, shared with me during the course of writing this book, this tart was their absolute favorite. The recipe sprang from my current passion for Southwestern cuisine. A free-form cornmeal pastry shell is topped with shredded smoked turkey, sweet corn, black beans, roasted peppers, and cilantro. The top is finished with melted Monterey Jack cheese. All of these wonderful flavors swirling around our taste buds made three hardworking, tired cooks very happy.

At a Glance

SERVES: 6 to 8

PAN: 14 × 17-inch cookie sheet

PASTRY PREP: Baked

OVEN TEMP: 375 degrees

BAKING TIME:
18 to 20 minutes (pastry)
20 to 25 minutes (tart)

DIFFICULTY: 🥾 🥾

When you make this tart, be sure to purchase top-quality smoked turkey breast and have it cut into ¼-inch slices. The thickness of the meat is essential because it is pulled into thin shreds with your fingertips. If you don't want to waste a whole can of black beans for the small amount used in this tart, use dried. Just soak ¼ cup dried beans overnight in cold water. The next day, cook them in fresh water until tender, about 1 hour. Or, if you're not a black bean fan, just omit them.

1 recipe Golden Cornmeal Pastry (page 150)

FILLING
1 large red bell pepper
6 ounces (2 ¼-inch-thick slices) smoked turkey
1 Spanish onion, coarsely chopped
2 tablespoons olive oil
1 teaspoon minced garlic
1 cup corn kernels (fresh or frozen)

4 teaspoons chopped cilantro
1 teaspoon coarse salt or to taste
Freshly ground black pepper
½ cup cooked black beans
1½ cups shredded Monterey Jack cheese (about 4 ounces)
1 tablespoon finely chopped flat-leaf parsley, for garnish

1. SHAPE THE PASTRY: The pastry is rolled directly on the cookie sheet. Cut a piece of 18-inch-wide heavy-duty aluminum foil, measuring about 6 inches larger than the width of the pan. Place the aluminum foil over the cookie sheet so that the ends extend over the sides. Tuck the ends under and smooth the surface.

2. Sprinkle the pan with 1 tablespoon of cornmeal, making a large circle. Place the pastry in the center of the pan. Sprinkle the top of the dough with a little flour and cover with a piece of baking parchment. Roll the

dough, preferably with a tapered rolling pin, into a 15-inch circle.

3. Fold the edge of the pastry under, making a 1-inch border. The circle should measure 13 inches. Flute the edge, and prick the center lightly with a fork. Chill for 30 minutes.

4. Preheat the oven to 375 degrees. Position the oven rack in the lower third of the oven. Bake the pastry for 18 to 20 minutes, or until lightly browned. If the center puffs up, tap it gently with the bottom of a fork to expel the air. Cool the pastry shell before filling.

5. MAKE THE FILLING: Preheat the broiler. Position the rack so that it is about 6 inches from the heat source. Wash and dry the red pepper. Cut it in half lengthwise and remove the stem, seeds, and white veins. Line a baking pan with aluminum foil and place the red pepper cut side down on the foil. Broil the pepper until it is well charred and the skin is black. Remove from the oven and wrap the aluminum foil around it; make the package airtight so that the pepper can steam. Let stand about 15 minutes. Using a paring knife, remove the skin. Dice the pepper into 1/4-inch pieces.

6. Following the grain of the meat, pull the turkey into thin shreds. Set aside.

7. In a large skillet, sauté the onion in the olive oil until transparent. Stir in the garlic and cook briefly. Add the corn, cover the skillet, and cook until the corn is almost tender. Stir in the diced red pepper and cilantro. Season to taste with salt and pepper. Remove from the heat and cool for 10 minutes. (The tart can be made ahead to this point. Just warm the vegetables and proceed from this point.)

8. ASSEMBLE THE TART: Preheat the oven to 375 degrees. Position the oven rack in the lower third of the oven.

9. Spread the sautéed vegetables over the baked pastry shell. Scatter the black beans and shredded turkey over the vegetables. Lay a square of aluminum foil loosely over the top. Bake for 20 minutes or until the filling is heated through. Remove the aluminum foil. Sprinkle the top with the Monterey Jack cheese.

10. Move the oven rack to the upper third of the oven and turn the oven setting to broil. The tart should not be too close to the heat source or it will burn. Lightly brown the cheese topping, 15 to 20 seconds. *Watch carefully.* To serve, slide the tart onto a platter with the help of a long spatula. Garnish with chopped parsley and serve while hot.

STORAGE
Cover any leftover tart with aluminum foil and refrigerate for up to 3 days. Reheat before before serving. Freezing is not recommended.

Tomato, Pesto, and Goat Cheese Galette

THE SUPERB FLAVORS IN THIS simple tart derive from quality ingredients: the freshest tomatoes of summer, fragrant fresh basil leaves, imported niçoise olives, Montrachet goat cheese, and extra-virgin olive oil. All of these luxurious ingredients are baked in a delicate puff pastry crust. I doubt that there will be a morsel left.

1 small recipe Goof-Proof Puff Pastry (page 172), shaped into a free-form 11-inch pastry shell and baked
1/3 cup pesto, homemade or fine-quality store-bought
2 tablespoons plus 1 teaspoon freshly grated Parmesan cheese
3 large, ripe summer tomatoes
4 to 5 ounces chilled goat cheese, preferably Montrachet, crumbled
1/2 cup niçoise olives, pitted
Freshly ground black pepper
1 tablespoon extra-virgin olive oil
3 to 4 tablespoons shredded fresh basil leaves (see "Chiffonade," page 458)

1. Preheat the oven to 425 degrees. Position the oven rack in the lower third of the oven. Line a large cookie sheet with heavy-duty aluminum foil, tucking the ends under to prevent it from sliding. Place the baked puff pastry shell in the center of the pan.

2. Using an offset spatula, spread the pesto over the pastry. Sprinkle 2 tablespoons of the Parmesan over the pesto.

3. Wipe the tomatoes with a damp paper towel. Core and cut into 1/4-inch slices. Starting at the outer edge of the pastry shell, arrange the tomatoes in concentric circles, overlapping each slice slightly. You should have 2 circles.

4. Crumble the goat cheese over the tomatoes. Distribute the olives on top, then sprinkle with the remaining Parmesan cheese. Grind some black pepper over the top, and drizzle with olive oil.

5. Bake the tart for 30 to 35 minutes, or until the goat cheese begins to lightly brown. Just before serving, garnish the top of the tart with the shredded basil. The tart can be served warm or at room temperature.

STORAGE
Cover any leftover tart with a piece of waxed paper then aluminum foil and refrigerate for up to 3 days. Reheat before serving. This tart can be frozen after baking.

Sauces, Toppings & Garnishes

 AUCES, TOPPINGS, AND garnishes are the finishing touches that transform the simple into the special. These accoutrements can be as predictable as a dollop of whipped cream on a slice of pie or a pool of crème anglaise next to a fruit tart. Without a doubt, such accents elevate a dessert, bringing a touch of beauty, texture, and—most important—taste to the table.

The majority of these recipes are simple to make. Crème anglaise—the English custard sauce—and the nut brittle—made with caramel—may take a bit of practice, but they are not difficult. The best part is that most of these recipes are do-ahead.

With very little effort, you can don a toque and be your own in-house pastry chef. It's a mighty good feeling when you hear those "oohs" and "ahs," and the best part is that no one will know how easy these are to prepare.

Before You Begin

Here is an overview of tips and tricks for making great sauces, toppings, and garnishes.

✦ When making a fruit or berry sauce, be sure the produce is thoroughly dried. Otherwise, the sauce will be too watery.

✦ Use a nonreactive saucepan when making a fruit or berry sauce.

✦ When a sauce contains pieces of fruit or berries, it should be mixed as little as possible to prevent the fruit from falling apart.

✦ Always remove a cooked fruit or berry sauce from a hot saucepan as soon as it is finished cooking. Since all food continues to cook off the heat, it should quickly be emptied into a cool container to prevent the fruit from becoming too soft.

✦ For more interest and visual appeal, use more than one sauce on your presentation plate. Raspberry coulis with crème anglaise is an example of this. Let them bleed into each other.

✦ When saucing a plate, choose one with a well, not a flat plate. A plate with a well frames both the sauce and the dessert being presented.

✦ To cover the well of a plate with sauce, ladle it into the center. Spread it by moving the bottom of the ladle in a circle. Then slowly tip the plate, and swirl it gently to encourage the sauce to flow to the edge of the well.

✦ When saucing the well on a plate, use only enough to conceal the china. Too much will overwhelm the pastry.

✦ Fill plastic squeeze bottles with thick sauces and use to make plate decorations. The Mango and Raspberry Coulis, Butterscotch Sauce, and Chocolate Ganache Sauce are perfect for this purpose. These containers can be purchased at beauty supply stores. Trim the tip with scissors to enlarge the opening. Make zigzag lines, dots, or both over the plate.

✦ Accent recipes should complement the primary flavor of the dessert, not overwhelm it.

✦ Crunchy garnishes should be used to complement softer fillings. Sauces and toppings can be used for both soft and crunchy fillings.

Crème Anglaise

ENGLISH CUSTARD SAUCE

CRÈME ANGLAISE, ALSO KNOWN as English custard sauce, is a foundation or parent sauce in the dessert family. It is made with beaten egg yolks, sugar, and milk (or a combination of milk and cream). With the addition of starch, the sauce becomes a pastry cream. When gelatin and whipped cream are added, it becomes a Bavarian cream; when frozen, it is transformed into ice cream. The more cream and egg yolks it contains, the smoother and creamier the ice cream will be.

MAKES: 1 cup

This sauce adapts easily to other flavors. If you take the time to make it with a vanilla bean, it reaches a much higher plateau than when made with vanilla extract (see Variations). Chocolate, cinnamon, and orange are three other flavors that especially complement the recipes in this book.

The sugar must be added to the whipped egg yolks gradually. It is best to do this with a whisk, although a hand-held mixer on low speed can be used. Too much beating creates a sauce that is too airy.

The trick to making this sauce thicken lies in cooking the ingredients to the correct temperature. If the mixture is undercooked, it will never bind. If overcooked, it will curdle. You must hit the appropriate temperature where the egg yolk proteins and milk bind.

To do this, a *heavy* 2-quart saucepan is essential—nothing smaller. Stainless steel or heavy-duty enamel is best. Without a properly insulated pot, the mixture will burn before it thickens. In addition, to ensure even cooking, the sauce must be mixed constantly and rapidly as it is heated. A wooden spoon is best for this.

The recipe that follows is quite explicit. Take the time to read it to the end, then follow the directions carefully. Once you get the knack, the prize is worth all this fuss.

4 large egg yolks
$^1/_4$ cup sugar
$^3/_4$ cup milk
$^1/_4$ cup heavy cream
1 to $1^1/_2$ teaspoons vanilla extract
1 tablespoon Grand Marnier, dark
    Jamaican rum, or other liqueur

1. Using a whisk and a large bowl, whip the egg yolks until they lighten in color. Add the sugar gradually and continue to whisk until the mixture is ribbony and becomes light in color. (A hand-held mixer can be used, but only on *low* speed.)

2. Have ready a medium bowl with a fine-mesh strainer placed over the top.

3. Scald the milk and cream in a large, heavy saucepan over low heat. Stir about a quarter of the hot milk mixture into the egg yolks to temper them. Add the yolk mixture to the remaining milk and cook over medium-low heat, mixing constantly with a wooden spoon. A light-colored foam will be present on the surface. Do not use a whisk for stirring—the sauce will become too bubbly.

4. As the mixture heats, the foam will disappear and steam will swirl over the surface. These are indications that the sauce will soon be ready. When the sauce coats the back of the spoon and reaches the consistency of heavy cream, it is done. Because this stage is difficult for some to determine, a sure way of checking this is by tipping the saucepan to see if the mixture is beginning to stick to the bottom. If so, it is done.

5. *Immediately* remove the saucepan from the heat and strain it into the bowl. This stops the cooking and ensures smoothness. If the sauce near the bottom of the pot shows any signs of curdling, discard that portion.

6. Stir the vanilla and liqueur into the sauce. Cover the bowl with plastic wrap and refrigerate to further thicken the sauce.

STORAGE
Keep in a tightly covered glass container and refrigerate for up to 3 days.

VARIATIONS
Crème Anglaise Rapide

Hats off to my good friend Sally Kofke, talented cooking instructor and microwave aficionado. On vacation in the Caribbean, she was without a heavy saucepan to prepare a crème anglaise. In typical Sally fashion, she turned to her microwave oven, and it worked!

While my preference is to make the sauce in the traditional way, if you don't own a heavy saucepan, this method will do in a pinch. Great care must be taken in your timing as the power and wattage of microwave ovens varies from unit to unit.

Follow the classic recipe above, making the following changes in the cooking procedure, beginning with step 3:

3. Place the milk and cream in a 1-quart ovenproof glass container and scald, using high power for 90 seconds or until a film forms on the surface. Stir about a quarter of the hot milk mixture into the egg yolks to temper them. Then add the yolk mixture to the remaining milk.

4. Return the mixture to the microwave oven and cook, using high power for 40 seconds. Stir, cook an additional 20 seconds, stir again, then cook for 10 to 15 seconds longer. The mixture should be the consistency of heavy cream and coat the back of a wooden spoon. *Watch carefully as overheating will cause it to curdle.* *Immediately* pour through a fine-mesh strainer into a clean bowl. Stir the vanilla and liqueur into the sauce. Cover the bowl with plastic wrap and refrigerate to thicken the sauce.

Crème Anglaise with a Vanilla Bean

Split a 3- to 4-inch piece of vanilla bean in half lengthwise. Place it in the saucepan with the milk mixture. When the liquid is scalded, turn the heat off and allow the bean to steep for 10 minutes.

Remove the vanilla bean from the liquid and scrape the tiny seeds from the pod using a paring knife. Add the seeds to the whipped egg yolks at the end of step 1. Beat until well incorporated. Proceed with the recipe, omitting the vanilla extract.

Chocolate Crème Anglaise

Chop 2 ounces of bittersweet or semisweet chocolate and add it to the milk mixture. As the mixture heats, stir to dissolve the chocolate. Increase the sugar to 1/3 cup. Proceed with the recipe as above.

Cinnamon Crème Anglaise

Combine 1/2 teaspoon ground cinnamon with the sugar. Proceed with recipe as above.

Orange Crème Anglaise

Add 1 1/2 teaspoons of grated navel or Valencia orange zest to the milk and cream. After scalding, steep, off the heat, for 15 minutes. Re-scald before proceeding with the addition of the egg yolks. Omit the vanilla extract from the recipe and use Grand Marnier, not rum, for flavoring.

Apricot Rum Sauce

1 cup *thick apricot preserves, passed through a medium-mesh strainer*
1 tablespoon *sugar*
2 teaspoons *cornstarch*
1/4 teaspoon *ground ginger*
1/2 cup *light Jamaican rum*
1/3 cup *water*
1/3 cup *fresh orange juice*
1 teaspoon *fresh lemon juice*

1. Combine the preserves with the sugar, cornstarch, and ginger in a medium, heavy saucepan. Blend well. Stir in the rum, water, and orange and lemon juices. Cook over medium-low heat, stirring with a whisk, until it comes to a slow boil. Reduce the heat and simmer for 5 minutes, stirring occasionally. Remove from the heat and let cool. The sauce will thicken as it cools. Serve at room temperature or lightly warmed.

STORAGE
Store in the refrigerator in a tightly sealed glass jar for up to 3 weeks.

MAKES: about 1 1/2 cups

Blueberry Sauce

3 cups *blueberries (1 1/2 pint basket)*
1/3 cup *sugar*
4 teaspoons *cornstarch*
1/2 cup *water*
1 teaspoon *fresh lemon juice*
2 tablespoons *crème de cassis liqueur or kirschwasser*

1. Wash and dry the blueberries (page 22).

2. Combine the sugar and cornstarch in a medium-size skillet. Blend in the water, then the blueberries and lemon juice. Mix gently to moisten the berries. Cover the pan and cook over low heat, shaking the pan frequently, until the berries reach a slow boil. Do not stir or the berries will burst. The berries are done when they are glazed and translucent.

3. Remove from the heat and drizzle the liqueur over the berries. Empty into a glass container and cool to room temperature.

STORAGE
Refrigerate this sauce stored in a covered glass jar for up to 7 days. Reheat without stirring before serving.

MAKES: 2 cups

Butterscotch Sauce

THE FLAVOR OF BUTTERSCOTCH COMPLEMENTS most fruit pies and tarts, as well as those made with nuts. If superfine sugar is unavailable, grind granulated sugar in the blender or food processor. This will keep the caramel from being grainy.

MAKES: 1 1/2 cups

3/4 cup superfine sugar
3 tablespoons water
3 tablespoons light corn syrup
1 1/2 cups plus 2 tablespoons heavy cream
6 tablespoons unsalted butter
1 1/2 teaspoons vanilla extract

1. Place the sugar, water, and corn syrup in a small, heavy saucepan. Stir gently to combine. Cover the saucepan and bring to a boil over medium-low heat. Check the sugar syrup occasionally to be sure that the sugar on the bottom of the pot has dissolved. If not, gently stir again.

2. When the syrup comes to a boil, uncover the saucepan. Reduce the heat and simmer until the mixture turns golden brown. This can take from 8 to 10 minutes or longer, depending on the weight of the pan. While the sugar syrup is boiling, *brush the side of the pot frequently with cold water* to remove small particles of sugar that may be clinging. Because the syrup burns easily, watch carefully.

3. When the syrup becomes a golden brown caramel, immediately remove it from the heat and add 1 1/2 cups heavy cream. *Be careful;* the mixture will bubble up when the cream is added. The caramel will immediately harden.

4. Return to low heat and cook, stirring constantly, until the caramel melts and the mixture is smooth. Add the butter and continue to cook for 10 to 20 minutes.

5. When the surface of the sauce has very large bubbles and the mixture thickens, remove the saucepan from the heat and place it in an ice-water bath. Stir occasionally. When the sauce is cool, beat in the remaining 2 tablespoons cream and vanilla.

STORAGE

Store in the refrigerator in a tightly sealed glass jar. This sauce will keep for 4 to 6 weeks. Reheat before serving.

Fresh Currant Sauce

TOP YOUR À LA MODE PASTRIES with this marvelous sauce. It adds a touch of elegance and complements peaches, nectarines, and pears. When preparing the sauce, leave some of the berries unstrained. It gives the sauce more character.

1/2 cup sugar
1/2 cup water
2 1/2 cups fresh red currants
    (2 6-ounce baskets)
1 teaspoon fresh lemon juice
1 to 2 tablespoons crème de cassis
    liqueur
Few drops vanilla extract

1. Bring the sugar and water to a slow boil in a medium, heavy saucepan over medium heat. When the sugar is dissolved, add the currants and lemon juice, and bring the berries to a boil. Reduce the heat, and simmer 20 to 25 minutes, or until the mixture thickens and all of the currants have popped. The cooking time depends on the thickness of your pot.

2. Remove from the heat. Reserve about a quarter of the cooked currants, and pass the remaining mixture through a fine-mesh strainer. Then stir in the reserved berries, the cassis, and vanilla. You should have about 1 cup of sauce. If not, place in a saucepan and simmer over low heat until it is reduced to 1 cup. Empty into a glass container and chill until ready to use.

STORAGE
This sauce can be stored tightly covered in the refrigerator for up to 4 weeks.

MAKES: 1 cup

Warm Fudge Sauce

THIS SAUCE IS A CHOCOLATE LOVER'S dream. It is thick and shiny, with a flavor that promises to please.

MAKES: 1 1/2 cups

4 ounces bittersweet chocolate, coarsely chopped
1 ounce unsweetened chocolate, coarsely chopped
3/4 cup heavy cream
1/2 cup sugar
1/4 cup light corn syrup
2 tablespoons unsalted butter
1 teaspoon espresso powder (optional)
1 1/2 teaspoons vanilla extract

1. Place all the ingredients in a medium, heavy saucepan. Bring to a boil over low heat.

2. Reduce the heat and simmer for 8 to 10 minutes, or until the sauce has thickened and is smooth and shiny. This sauce will thicken further as it cools.

STORAGE

Store in the refrigerator in a tightly sealed glass jar. This sauce will keep for 4 to 6 weeks. Reheat before serving.

Chocolate Ganache Sauce

GANACHE WEARS MANY HATS. It can be used as a sauce or a glaze. When slightly chilled, it can be whipped into chocolate whipped cream; and when well chilled, it can become the center of a truffle. I think this versatile preparation makes one of the best fudge sauces you'll ever taste. Be sure to use a fine-quality imported chocolate like Callebaut, Lindt, or Valrhôna. The results will be well worth it.

6 ounces fine-quality semisweet or bittersweet chocolate, chopped into 1-inch chunks
3/4 cup heavy cream
1 tablespoon light corn syrup
1 tablespoon Grand Marnier, Cointreau, or dark Jamaican rum
3/4 teaspoon vanilla extract
1/2 to 1 teaspoon hot water, if needed

1. Place the chocolate chunks in the bowl of a food processor fitted with the steel blade. Process until finely chopped.

2. Combine the cream and corn syrup in a small saucepan over low heat and heat until it comes to a gentle boil. Remove the processor cover and *immediately* pour the hot cream over the chocolate. Let stand for 1 minute so that the chocolate begins to melt. Then *pulse* 3 or 4 times and let rest 1 additional minute. Add the liqueur or rum and vanilla and *pulse* 3 or 4 more times.

3. Empty into a container. If the surface of the ganache appears oily, add the hot water and stir well. The ganache will thicken as it stands, but should remain pourable. If the sauce fails to thicken, refrigerate it for 4 to 5 minutes, taking care to not over-chill it.

STORAGE

Ganache can be left at room temperature for several hours, but should be reheated over low heat before using. It can also be made ahead and stored in the refrigerator in an airtight container for up to 2 weeks or frozen for up to 9 months.

To thaw frozen ganache, heat slowly in a double boiler or bain-marie. It is not necessary to thaw it first.

MAKES: 1 cup

Mango Coulis

1/2 cup sugar
1/2 cup water
2 ripe mangoes, peeled and cut
   into 3/4-inch cubes (page 29)
   (about 3 1/2 cups)
1 tablespoon fresh lemon juice

1. Bring the sugar and water to a slow boil in a large, heavy saucepan. Stir to dissolve. Add the mangoes, cover, and bring to a boil. Simmer about 3 minutes, or until the fruit is translucent. Strain the fruit, reserving 1/3 cup of the liquid.

2. Puree the fruit and the reserved liquid in a food processor or blender, then pass through a fine-mesh strainer. Stir in the lemon juice.

STORAGE
Refrigerate in an airtight container for up to 3 weeks.

Raspberry Coulis

2 tablespoons water
1/4 cup sugar
1 tablespoon light corn syrup
12 ounce package frozen
   unsweetened raspberries,
   thawed
1 tablespoon framboise liqueur or
   kirschwasser, or to taste
1 teaspoon fresh lemon juice

1. Place the water, sugar, and corn syrup in a heavy, medium saucepan. Cover and bring to a slow boil. When the sugar is dissolved, add the raspberries, reduce the heat, and simmer, uncovered, for 2 to 3 minutes.

2. Puree the mixture in a blender or food processor until very smooth. Using a rubber spatula, press the puree through a fine-mesh strainer, pushing as much pulp as possible through the sieve. Discard the seeds.

3. Add the framboise and lemon juice, cover, and refrigerate until 30 minutes before using.

STORAGE
Raspberry coulis can be stored in the refrigerator in a tightly covered container for up to 3 days.

Strawberry Topping

2 cups fresh strawberries, washed
  and dried (page 39)
2 to 3 tablespoons superfine sugar
1 tablespoon seedless black
  raspberry preserves
1 tablespoon fresh orange juice
1 teaspoon fresh lemon juice
1 tablespoon framboise or Grand
  Marnier liqueur

1. Cut 1 cup of the strawberries into quarters and place in a bowl. Sprinkle with the sugar and shake the bowl to distribute. Cover the bowl and macerate the berries for 30 to 40 minutes. Stir occasionally.

2. Transfer the macerated strawberries and juices to the bowl of a food processor. Add the raspberry preserves, orange juice, and lemon juice. Process until smooth.

3. Empty the puree into a heavy saucepan and bring to a slow boil. Simmer for 3 to 4 minutes. Off the heat, add the liqueur and pour the sauce into a glass bowl or container. Set aside to cool. When ready to serve, cut the remaining strawberries into thick slices and fold them into the cooled sauce.

STORAGE

Refrigerate in a covered glass jar for up to 2 days.

MAKES: 1 to 1 1/4 cups

Yogurt Topping

8 ounces plain, low-fat yogurt
2 to 3 tablespoons strained
  confectioners' sugar
1/2 teaspoon vanilla extract

1. In a small bowl, gently stir together the yogurt and confectioners' sugar.

2. Add the vanilla, cover, and refrigerate for up to 1 hour.

MAKES: 1 cup

Whipped Cream

FOR WHIPPED CREAM, it is essential that the cream, bowl, and beaters be well chilled. It's best to slightly underwhip the cream and finish it by hand with a wire whisk. Under no circumstances should the cream be whipped on high speed.

MAKES: Enough to cover a 9-inch pie or 11-inch tart

For additional information on whipping cream, refer to "About Whipped Cream" (page 60).

1 cup heavy cream, well chilled
2 tablespoons strained
  confectioners' sugar
1 teaspoon vanilla extract

1. Start whipping the cream on medium-low speed in the chilled bowl of an electric mixer, with chilled beaters. Gradually increase the speed to medium and beat until the cream begins to thicken.

2. Add the sugar and vanilla and continue whipping until the cream is thick enough to hold its shape. Use as desired or as recipe directs.

STORAGE

Cover tightly with plastic wrap and refrigerate. Whipped cream is best used within 2 to 3 hours.

VARIATIONS

Chocolate Whipped Cream

Combine 2 tablespoons of strained unsweetened cocoa powder, preferably Dutch-process, with the confectioners'

sugar and proceed with the recipe above.

Stabilized Whipped Cream

1. Place 1 tablespoon of water in a small heatproof glass dish. Sprinkle ½ teaspoon of unflavored gelatin over the top. Do not stir. Let stand for 3 to 5 minutes to soften. Set the dish in a saucepan filled with ½ inch simmering water. Heat in the water bath until the gelatin is clear and dissolved. *Cool to tepid.*

2. Follow the above recipe for whipped cream. As the cream begins to thicken, add the dissolved gelatin along with the sugar and vanilla.

Crème Chantilly

Crème Chantilly is made from the same ingredients as whipped cream, but is beaten only to soft mounds. It is not used to cover a pie or tart, but spooned over individual servings. If desired, you can flavor it with a tablespoon of your favorite liqueur. The topping can also be accented with a dusting of cinnamon or cocoa powder.

Crème Fraîche

CRÈME FRAÎCHE, WHICH IS SIMILAR to sour cream, is a thick, French-style cultured cream often used as a topping with fruit pies. It is very rich, with a 40 percent butterfat content, as compared to heavy cream, which has 32 to 36 percent butterfat. This cream can be whipped to a thicker state than heavy cream because of its richness. Although it is more readily available in local groceries than in the past, it is helpful to know how to prepare your own.

1 cup heavy cream, preferably not ultrapasteurized
1 tablespoon buttermilk

1. Heat the cream in a small saucepan until tepid. Blend in the buttermilk.

2. Empty the mixture into a clean jar and cover tightly with a lid. Shake the jar vigorously to blend the mixture well. Let stand in a warmish place until it begins to thicken, from 12 to 18 hours. The longer it stands, the sharper the flavor will be. When the desired consistency and flavor are reached, place in the refrigerator overnight, shaking the jar occasionally. As it ages, it will thicken further.

STORAGE
Refrigerate in a tightly covered container for up to 1 week.

MAKES: 1 cup

Nut Brittle

CARAMELIZED NUTS CREATE A DELIGHTFUL contrast in textures and flavors when used to garnish fruit tarts or creamy pie and tart fillings. Be sure to sprinkle them on just before serving to retain their appealing crunch.

SMALL RECIPE:
About ¹/2 cup

LARGE RECIPE:
About 1 ¹/4 cups

I recommend using skinned hazelnuts, pecans, walnuts, sliced almonds (with or without the skin), and skinned peanuts. Except for the almonds, keep the nuts whole or broken, not chopped. Using a combination of nuts is especially tasty. Try a mixture of hazelnuts and almonds or walnuts and pecans.

To make praline paste, prepare the nut brittle with hazelnuts. Whirl it in a food processor until the nuts are pulverized into a paste.

The nut brittle will keep for weeks if packaged in an airtight container and stored in a cool place. When you have the time, make up a batch to keep on hand.

SMALL	LARGE	
¹/4	³/4	cup superfine sugar
1	3	tablespoons water
¹/3	1	cup nuts

1. Butter a 15-inch sheet of heavy-duty aluminum foil. Butter a metal tablespoon to stir the nuts into the caramel. Set aside.

2. Place the sugar and water in a small, heavy saucepan. Cover the pot and cook over low heat. Before it reaches the boiling point, check the bottom of the pot to be sure all of the sugar has dissolved. If not, *gently stir the mixture, but do not stir after the boil.*

3. Uncover the pot and continue to cook the sugar syrup. Brush the side of the saucepan occasionally with a pastry brush dipped in water to remove any sugar crystals that may be clinging to the side. Cook until the syrup begins to caramelize. This can take anywhere from 10 to 30 minutes depending on the thickness of the pot and the quantity you are cooking. As the syrup changes color, to ensure even browning, tilt the pot and move it in a gentle swirling motion. *When making caramel, always use extreme caution as the syrup can cause serious burns.*

4. Add the nuts and stir quickly with the buttered spoon to coat with the caramel. Immediately spread the mixture onto the buttered aluminum foil. Let the caramelized nuts stand at room temperature until hardened. This will take only a few minutes.

5. When the caramelized nuts are hard, place them on a cutting board and coarsely chop with a chef's knife. Chop only what you need.

6. To clean the pot, immediately fill the empty saucepan with hot water. Place over low heat and simmer until the caramel dissolves. *Be careful* when you fill the pot with water as it will sizzle and steam.

STORAGE

Store the brittle in an airtight container in a cool place. Nut brittle can be kept for up to 4 to 6 months, provided it is not stored in a humid environment.

VARIATION

Candied Whole Nuts

Use candied nuts to garnish whipped cream decorations on top of cream-style pies or to embellish a dessert plate when serving individual tarts. Pick through the package and select whole nuts that are perfectly shaped.

1. Place the desired amount of nuts on a shallow pan and bake at 325 degrees until lightly toasted. Allow to cool until you are able to comfortably handle them.

2. Have ready a buttered sheet of aluminum foil and a buttered fork.

3. Make the small or large recipe of caramel above, depending on the number of nuts you wish to candy. It is better to have too much than too little.

4. When the caramel becomes a light golden brown, remove it from the heat. Using the buttered fork, immediately dip one or two nuts at a time into the caramel, turning them to coat the entire surface. Lift the fork, letting the caramel drip through and place the candied nut top side up onto the buttered foil. Repeat dipping nuts, reheating the caramel over low heat as needed. The nuts will harden as they cool.

STORAGE

Store in an airtight container in a cool place for up to 6 months.

Almond Crackle

USE TO GARNISH FROZEN DESSERTS, cream-style pies, and tarts.

MAKES: 1 to 1¼ cups

1 large egg white
3 tablespoons granulated sugar
1 cup sliced almonds

1. Preheat the oven to 300 degrees. Position the oven rack in the lower third of the oven.

2. Place the egg white on a large, shallow baking pan with sides. Sprinkle with 1 tablespoon of the sugar and beat lightly with a fork to combine.

3. Add the almonds and stir with a fork until all of the nuts are coated. Spread in a shallow layer, separating the larger clusters. Sprinkle with the remaining sugar.

4. Bake the nuts, turning them every so often, for 20 to 25 minutes or until glazed and lightly browned.

STORAGE

Store in an airtight container and refrigerate for up to 4 weeks.

Chocolate Curls and Shavings

CHOCOLATE CURLS AND SHAVINGS CAN be made from bittersweet, semi-sweet, milk, or white chocolate. The more fat the chocolate contains, the quicker it will soften and the more carefully it must be handled.

Use block chocolate or 1-ounce squares such as Baker's or Nestlé's for semisweet and dark chocolate decorations. Block white and milk chocolates are usually stocked only in stores that specialize in cake decorating or candy making. Do not attempt to make curls or shavings from thin chocolate bars.

TO SOFTEN DARK CHOCO-LATE: Set a chunk of dark chocolate on a paper towel and place it in a microwave oven. Using the *defrost* setting, warm the chocolate for 15 to 20 seconds; turn it over and repeat. You may need to repeat the warming process an additional time to soften the chocolate, depending on its size and freshness.

TO SOFTEN WHITE OR MILK CHOCOLATES: Follow the directions for softening dark chocolate, reducing the warming time. White chocolate will take less time than milk chocolate, and both must be checked frequently as they soften quickly.

TO MAKE CURLS: Hold the chocolate with a piece of paper towel to prevent the warmth of your hand from melting it. Scrape a vegetable peeler along the chocolate, peeling off curls. If the chocolate doesn't curl, it needs additional warming.

TO MAKE SHAVINGS: Place the chocolate on a very clean cutting board. Using a chef's knife, cut thin shavings from the side of the chocolate chunk. Keep rotating the chocolate as you cut, using all of the exposed sides for your shavings. If the center of the chocolate is too hard, it needs additional warming.

STORAGE

Store in a flat, aluminum foil container with a lid. Seal well and keep in a cool place. Darker chocolate can be kept for up to 6 weeks, milk chocolate for up to 3 weeks, and white chocolate for 1 week to 10 days.

Candied Citrus Zest

USE AS A GARNISH FOR cream-style citrus pies or tarts. To retain the crunchiness of the candied zest, decorate the dessert just before serving.

MAKES: Enough to garnish a 9-inch pie or 11-inch tart

¹/₂ cup water
Zest of 2 lemons or limes, or
  1 navel or Valencia orange, cut
  in tiny slivers
2 tablespoons plus 2 teaspoons
  sugar

1. Bring the water to a boil in a small saucepan over medium heat. Add the citrus slivers and blanch for 4 to 5 minutes. Remove from heat and strain, reserving ¹/₄ cup of the liquid. Return the reserved liquid to the saucepan, add 2 tablespoons of sugar, and bring to a boil. Reduce the heat and simmer for 5 minutes. Add the zest to the syrup and simmer for 5 minutes or until glazed and transparent.

2. Using a fork, remove the citrus slivers from the syrup and place on several layers of paper towels to dry, separating them as best you can. Sprinkle them with the remaining 2 teaspoons of sugar, tossing them lightly to coat on all sides.

3. Spread the sugared slivers in a single layer and allow to dry, at room temperature, for several hours or overnight.

STORAGE
Place in an airtight container and refrigerate for up to 4 weeks.

GLOSSARY OF TERMS

ACIDULATED WATER Water to which an acid, usually lemon, lime, or orange juice, has been added. Used for dipping or sprinkling on cut fruits to prevent them from discoloring once exposed to air. Use five parts water to one part citrus juice.

AERATE Synonymous with *sift.* To add air and remove lumps from ingredients.

À LA MODE Originally meant the style in which a dish was served. In America, this phrase has come to mean a dessert topped with ice cream. From the French phrase for "in the manner of."

ALMOND PASTE Made from finely ground almonds, confectioners' sugar, egg white, and glucose or corn syrup. Slightly grainy in texture and not quite as sweet as marzipan, it is used both in pastry fillings and for decorating. Almond paste will turn hard and brittle if it is not tightly wrapped and stored in the refrigerator, where it can keep for up to 6 months. To make it pliable after refrigeration, warm it for 3 to 5 seconds in a microwave oven.

AMARETTI Traditionally, almond macaroons from Italy. Generally wrapped in pairs in paper, they are delicious plain, dipped in sweet wine, or ground and used in pastry crusts and fillings.

ARROWROOT An expensive, high-quality thickener made from the tropical arrowroot tuber. Can be used in desserts and toppings, replacing cornstarch. It has a neutral flavor, becomes clear when cooked, and does not become chalky when undercooked. Always mix with a cold liquid before adding it to a hot mixture.

BAIN-MARIE See *water bath.*

BAKE BLIND To bake a pastry shell before it is filled. See "Baking Blind," page ooo.

BAKING NUGGETS Also known as pie weights. Used for weighting down a pie crust when blind baking to prevent shrinkage.

BAKING PARCHMENT Also known as parchment paper. Nonstick, greaseproof paper used to line baking pans and for making pastry cones for decorating. Available in rolls and sheets in better supermarkets and cookware shops.

BAKING OR PIZZA STONE A flat stone that is preheated and used for browning of bottom crusts.

BARQUETTE From the French for "little boat." A little, oval-shaped tartlet, either sweet or savory.

BATARDE Round, flat-bottomed kitchen tool traditionally used for pounding meat. Because of its weight and shape, it is an excellent tool for smoothing and leveling pastry doughs and crumb crusts when shaping. Also known as a *batticarne.*

BAVARIAN CREAM Rich custard fortified with whipped cream, flavoring, and gelatin. Known in French as *Bavarois.*

BENCH, DOUGH, OR PASTRY SCRAPER A large, flat piece of metal with a handle, used to clean rolling surfaces and for handling pastry; see page ooo.

BETTY Classic American baked dessert of layered fruit, sugar, and buttered bread crumbs.

BIND To add a thickening agent or ingredient to a hot liquid and cause it to thicken.

BISCOTTI Italian biscuit or cookie that is twice baked. Comes in a wide variety of flavors, many with nuts. Delicious plain, or can be ground and used in pastry crusts or fillings.

BLANCH Technique of briefly plunging fruits, nuts, or vegetables into boiling water to loosen skins for peeling or to heighten color and flavor. After the plunging, foods must immediately be cooled down with cold water to stop the cooking process.

BOIL To cook until bubbling (212 degrees): (a) slow boil—to bring to a boil over low heat to avoid scorching. A few bubbles will appear on the surface. (b) rapid boil—to bring to a boil over high heat. Many bubbles will appear on the surface.

BREAK DOWN The separation of butterfat from milk solids, which results in a curdled appearance.

BRITTLE Candy made from nuts coated with a caramelized sugar syrup. See Nut Brittle (page 452).

BROWNED BUTTER Also known as *beurre noisette*. Butter cooked over low heat until it reaches the color of hazelnuts.

BUCKLE Deep-dish fruit dessert where fresh fruit is layered over cake batter and baked. The batter bubbles up between the fruit slices, forming a crust that is crisp and sweet.

BUTTERSCOTCH Flavor derived from a combination of brown sugar and butter.

CANDY THERMOMETER See page 43.

CARAMELIZE To cook sugar slowly until it turns to liquid and the color changes to medium or dark amber (310 to 350 degrees). The resulting syrup is known as caramel or burnt sugar.

CHALAZAE The two thick strands of egg white that are attached to the yolk, which harden when cooked. The fresher the egg, the more prominent the chalazae will be. Can be removed with fingertips before

cooking (optional); this step is sometimes referred to as "defeathering."

CHANTILLY CREAM Heavy cream whipped to soft mounds, sweetened, and often flavored with vanilla or liqueur. See page 000 for recipe.

CHIBOUST CREAM Pastry cream flavored with vanilla and lightened with stiffly beaten egg whites.

CHIFFON Creamy filling for pies and tarts, made lighter with the addition of beaten egg whites and stabilized with gelatin.

CHIFFONADE Stacked, rolled flat greens, cut into thin, ribbonlike strips. A technique commonly used with green leafy vegetables or leafy herbs, such as basil.

CLAFOUTI French variant on a fruit tart featuring fruit baked in a pancakelike batter and served warm.

CLARIFIED BUTTER See page 52.

COAT A SPOON Used as a test to check the readiness of cooked custards. A film will adhere to the back of a spoon dipped into the mixture. A separation should remain when a line is drawn through the film with your finger.

COBBLER American baked fruit dessert, usually but not always, with a biscuit-type topping.

CONCENTRIC CIRCLES Circles of gradually increasing or de-

creasing size, arranged around a common center.

CORNER To thoroughly remove dough or filling from a pan using a spatula or rubber scraper.

COULIS A sauce used as a garnish for desserts, made from pureed fruit. See page 448 for recipes.

COUPLER Two-piece device, made of plastic, used to attach a pastry tip to a pastry bag. Its screw-on design allows for changing pastry tips without emptying the bag. See page 74.

CREAM To beat solid fats, such as butter, alone or with other ingredients, like sugar, until well blended. Creaming will produce a smooth texture, increased volume, and a lightened color.

CRÈME ANGLAISE Also called English custard sauce. An egg custard sauce used as a base for many desserts preparations including pastry cream (crème pâtissière), Bavarian cream, and ice cream. Also used as an accompaniment for cakes, pies, tarts, and fruit desserts. Can be served warm or cold. See page 440 for recipe.

CRÈME FRAÎCHE A high-fat, cultured French cream that is sometimes whipped. Similar in thickness to sour cream, with a characteristic tangy taste, see page 000.

CRIMP To seal or pinch together. Usually done to seal the top and bottom crust of a pastry. Also used for single-crust pastries to form a decorative, raised edge to prevent the filling from spilling over. May be done with the fingers, a fork, or with a pastry crimper (see page 66) See also "Sealing the Edge," page 92, for decorative sealing.

CRISP A deep-dish, baked fruit dessert that is topped with a sweet streusel-like, or crumb, topping.

CROUSTADE An edible container to hold a sweet or savory filling, often made of baked pastry.

CRUMBLE Baked fruit dessert, similar to a crisp, topped with a crumbly mixture, usually made with uncooked oats, flour, butter, nuts, and spices.

CRYSTALLIZATION The forming of crystals as sugar melts, usually created from undissolved granules. Commonly occurs around the side of a saucepan. Covering the pot and/or brushing down its side with a wet pastry brush will dissolve the crystals. The addition of honey, cream of tartar, or corn syrup can inhibit crystallization.

CURDLE The separation of liquid from solid, or curds from whey, in overheated dairy or egg-based sauces made without starch or when an acid has been introduced to a dairy product.

CUT IN To blend fats into dry ingredients with 2 knives or a pastry blender, forming small particles of fat-coated flour.

DOCK To pierce pastry dough at regular intervals with a docker (see page 175) or a fork to cut the gluten strands. Keeps air bubbles in the dough from forming during baking and helps to retain the shape of the pastry.

DOUBLE BOILER A double, or nested, pot. The bottom is filled with a water level low enough so that the top portion does not touch the water underneath. Used to prevent the scorching of foods that are heat sensitive and/or require long cooking.

EGG WASH Glaze made from whole egg, white, or yolk, used for pastry doughs. See page 72.

EMULSIFY Slowly, often drop by drop, joining fat and water-based ingredients to one another while stirring rapidly to form a suspension.

FEUILLETAGE French word for the making of puff pastry.

FEUILLETÉE The folding over of leaves of dough when making puff pastry.

FLAKY Term to describe the texture of pastry that has dried into layers of delicate, thin, flat pieces.

FLAN RING See page 63.

FLUTE To create a decorative or ornamental edge on pie pastry by shaping the dough with thumb and fingers. See "Sealing the Edge," page 92, and "Making Decorative Edges," page 66.

FOLD IN Combining two substances to maintain air and/or volume.

FRAISAGE To combine fat and flour into a pastry dough by smearing the mixture on a flat surface with the heel of the hand. A classic French technique; see page 69.

FRANGIPANE A thick, egg-based, nut custard or cream, traditionally made from almonds. In fruit tarts, used as a base to keep bottom crusts crisp, or as a protective topping.

FROTHY Showing a surface of light, foamy bubbles.

GALETTE A flat, usually round, pastry base for sweet or savory toppings.

GANACHE A blend of chocolate, usually bittersweet or semisweet, and heavy cream often used for glazing, whipping, or for making truffles. Its consistency can be varied by adjusting ingredient amounts and the temperature at which it is used. See recipe, page 447.

GLAZE A thin covering to shield a baked pastry shell, to finish the top of a tart filling, or to cover the top of a cake. See also pages 72.

GLUTEN The elastic mesh that forms when two proteins in wheat flour, gliadin and glutenin, come in contact with liquid. These proteins are the only ones strong enough to form the gumlike gluten web that traps air when doughs are made.

GRUNT A type of cobbler, topped with a biscuit-type topping and steamed in a covered kettle.

HULL To remove the calyx or cap from strawberries.

ITALIAN MERINGUE A meringue made by beating egg whites until firm, then beating in a hot sugar syrup.

JALOUSIE A puff pastry filled with a fruit preserve with horizontal slits down the center at 1-inch intervals, like a "jalousie" or venetian blind.

LATTICE An openwork top dough used to cover a pie or tart. Made of dough strips arranged in a crisscross or woven pattern. See "Making Lattice Crusts," page 64.

LEAVENING The addition of a gaseous element, such as baking powder or baking soda, to a batter or dough to make baked goods rise.

LEKVAR An intensely flavored, concentrated fruit preserve, Hungarian in origin, traditionally made from prunes or apricots.

LIAISON To bind or thicken one substance with another. The thickening agent can be a starch, egg yolks, and/or heavy cream.

LIGHTEN To add a light substance, such as beaten egg whites or whipped cream, to a thick mixture to decrease its density.

MACERATE To soften or draw out liquid by soaking in liqueur or sprinkling with sugar; usually applies to fresh and dried fruit.

MEAL Coarse-textured ground grain, such as oats or corn.

MERINGUE A mixture formed by adding sugar to whipped egg whites, then beating until it holds its shape. See pages 54, 115–117.

MOUSSE A smooth, airy, rich mixture containing cream and/or eggs that can be used as a filling for pies and tarts.

NONREACTIVE Refers to metal cooking equipment (can be bowls, skillets, or saucepans) with a cooking surface that does not interact with acidic foods, salty foods, or eggs. To avoid pitting, discoloration of food, and a metallic flavor, Do not use these ingredients with cookware having an interior surface made of aluminum, copper, or iron.

NOUGATINE Nut brittle made with hazelnuts and almonds and caramelized sugar syrup. Often used crushed in fillings for pies or tarts.

PANDOWDY Related to cobblers and grunts. Sweetened fruit is topped with a biscuitlike topping and baked. Partway through baking, the crust is broken and pushed into the fruit to absorb the juices.

PARCHMENT PAPER See *Baking Parchment*.

PASTRY CREAM (CRÈME PÂTISSIÈRE) A rich, cooked custard made with eggs, sugar, milk and/or cream, thickened with starch. Commonly used as a filling for tarts, eclairs, cakes, and napoleons.

PÂTE BRISÉE Classic European-style, general purpose pastry; it is more durable than American-style flaky pie pastry.

PÂTE FEUILLETÉE Classic puff pastry. Created by making a series of folds with a water and flour-based dough wrapped around a thick layer of butter. The dough can be rolled and folded up to 6 times, spreading the butter thinner and thinner. When baked, steam forms between the layers, producing thin, crisp leaves of pastry.

PÂTE SABLÉ Sweet, rich, short dough used for tarts and tartlets. *Sable* means "sand," which refers to its delicate and crumbly texture.

PÂTE SUCRÉE Rich, sweet, cookielike pastry dough used for tarts, tartlets, and other pastries.

PÂTISSÈRIE French term for the art of making pastry, as well as the name for shops where pastries are sold.

PEAK STAGE A condition, usually of beaten egg whites or whipped cream, in which the whipped substance holds a peak of varying degrees of firmness.

PEARL SUGAR Also known as decorating or coarse sugar, its grains are 4 to 6 times larger than granulated and is used for decorative purposes.

PECTIN Naturally occurring gelling substance found in some fruits.

PHYLLO DOUGH Also known as Fillo, ready-made, paper-thin sheets of dough used widely in Greece and the Middle East as pastry for both sweet and savory dishes. See "Working with Phyllo," page 64.

PIE WEIGHTS See *Baking Nuggets*.

PLUMP Process of softening dried fruits by immersion in hot water or by steaming.

PRALINE A hardened candy made of caramelized sugar and nuts, usually almonds or hazelnuts. Often ground or made into a paste for use in pie and tart fillings. Not to be confused with the famous pecan praline candy from Louisiana. See "Praline Paste," page 452.

PUFF PASTRY See *Pâte Feuilletée*.

QUICHE A savory pie made with a base of eggs, cream, and milk.

RIBBONY A very thick stage of a beaten mixture, commonly egg yolks and sugar. When poured from a height, the substance falls in overlapping, ribbonlike waves that hold their shape for a few seconds.

SCALD To heat slowly without stirring to just under the boiling point until bubbles appear around the edge of the saucepan and a thin film forms over the surface.

SCORE To press slight indentations with the side of your hand across a disk of dough in a tic-tac-toe pattern.

SHORT Term to describe pastry with a high ratio of fat to flour. Short doughs are rich, crumbly, and tender.

SIFT To strain or sieve through a mesh screen to remove lumps and to aerate and/or combine dry ingredients.

SLUMP A type of cobbler, similar to a grunt, but baked instead of steamed. May have both a top and bottom biscuit-type crust.

SLURRY Used as a quick thickening remedy for loose fillings or sauces. A paste made from cornstarch or flour, added to a fluid mixture. The starch is first combined with a small amount of liquid and rapidly whisked in to allow for smoother incorporation.

STABILIZE To fortify a delicate substance, such as beaten egg whites or whipped cream, with an ingredient like gelatin to strengthen it.

STREUSEL From the German word for "sprinkle," a crumbly mixture of butter, flour, sugar, spices, and often nuts used to top fruit desserts and coffeecakes.

SWISS MERINGUE A combination of egg whites and sugar heated over water to dissolve the sugar, then whipped until cool, shiny, and stiff.

TEMPER To modify one substance with another to adjust temperature for smooth blending. See page 53.

TENDER A term used to describe baked pastry that has a fine-grained, melt-in-the-mouth texture.

TEPID Moderately or slightly warm in temperature.

WATER BATH Also known as a bain-marie. A container filled with a mixture, placed into a larger container of water, to slowly and gently adjust its temperature. Used with simmering water to heat or ice water to chill. Also used for oven cookery when baking custards, cheesecakes, or other delicate dishes.

WEEPING The beadlike tears of moisture that form when egg whites have been either improperly beaten or under- or overbaked, cooled in a draft, or not properly sealed to a filling. They will also form during humid weather or when a meringue topping is sealed with an airtight covering, such as plastic wrap.

ZEST The colored, outer skin of citrus fruit that contains the flavorful oils. Also erroneously known as the rind (which also contains the bitter white pith).

BIBLIOGRAPHY

BOOKS

Adams, Charlotte. *The Four Seasons Cookbook*. New York: Ridge Press, 1971.

American Family Cookbook. New York: Broadway Books, 1950.

Appelbaum, Diana Karter. *Thanksgiving*. New York: Facts on File, 1984.

Bayou Cuisine. Indianola, Miss.: St. Stephens Episcopal Church, 1970.

Beard, James, Milton Glaser, Burton Wolf, Barbara Poses Kafke, Helen S. Witty, and Associates of the Good Cooking School, eds. *Cooks' Catalogue*. New York: Harper & Row, 1975.

Belden, Louise Conway. *The Festive Tradition*. New York: W. W. Norton, 1983.

Betty Crocker's Picture Cookbook. New York: McGraw-Hill, 1950.

Bianchine, Francesco, Francesco Corbetta, and Marilena Pistoia. *The Complete Book of Fruits and Vegetables*. New York: Crown Publishers, 1973

Bliss, Mrs. *The Practical Cookbook*. Philadelphia: Lippincott, Grambo & Co., 1850.

Bloom, Carole. *The International Dictionary of Desserts, Pastries, and Confections*. New York: Hearst Books, 1995.

Braker, Flo. *The Simple Art of Perfect Baking*. New York: William Morrow, 1985.

Bridge, Fred, and Jean F. Tibbetts. *The Well-Tooled Kitchen*. New York: William Morrow, 1991.

Buying Guide for Fresh Fruits, Vegetables, Herbs and Nuts. Castle & Cooke, 1990.

Campbell, Susan. *Cook's Tools*. New York: William Morrow, 1980.

Casella, Dolores. *A World of Baking*. New York: David White, 1968.

Chalmers, Irena. *The Great Food Almanac*. San Francisco: Collins Publishers, 1994.

Child, Julia, Simone Beck, and Louisette Bertholle. *Mastering the Art of French Cooking*, Vol. 1. New York: Alfred A. Knopf, 1961.

Child, Julia, and Simone Beck. *Mastering the Art of French Cooking*, Vol. 2. New York: Alfred A. Knopf, 1973.

Claiborne, Craig. *Southern Cooking*. New York: Times Books, 1987.

———. *The New York Times Cookbook*. New York: Harper & Row, 1961.

Committee of Amish women. *Amish Cooking*. Scottsdale, Pa.: Herald Press, 1980.

Committee of Ladies of the Society of Faithful Workers. *Faithful Workers' Cook Book*. Port Chester, N.Y.: St. Peter's Church, 1895.

Cunningham, Marion. *The Fannie Farmer Baking Book*. New York: Alfred A. Knopf, 1984.

Davidson, Alan. *On Fasting & Feasting*. London: MacDonald Orbis, 1988.

———. *Fruit, a Connoisseur's Guide & Cookbook*. New York: Simon & Schuster, 1991.

De Gouy, Louis P. *The Pie Book*. New York: Dover Publications, 1949.

Dodge, Jim. *The American Baker*. New York: Simon & Schuster, 1987.

———. *Baking with Jim Dodge*. New York: Simon & Schuster, 1991.

Dull, Mrs. S. R. *Southern Cooking*. New York: Grosset & Dunlap, 1997.

Dupree, Nathalie. *New Southern Cooking*. New York: Alfred A. Knopf, 1986.

Dutton, Margit Stoll. *The German Pastry Bakebook*, Radnor, Pa.: Chilton, 1977.

Editors of *American Heritage* magazine. *American Heritage Cookbook*. New York: American Heritage Publishing, 1964.

Egerton March, ed. *Since Eve Ate Apples*. Portland, Oreg.: Tsunami Press, 1994.

Elliot, Rose. *Book of Savoury Flans and Pies*. London: Fontana Paperbacks, 1984.

Fance, W. J. *The Student's Technology of Breadmaking and Flour Confectionery*. London: Routledge and Kegan Paul, 1960.

Farmer, Fannie Merritt. *The Fannie Farmer Cookbook*. Revised by Marion Cunningham. New York: Alfred A. Knopf, 1979.

———. *The Boston Cooking School Cookbook*. Little, Brown & Co., 1909.

Farm Journal's Best Ever Pies. Garden City, N.Y.: Doubleday, 1981.

Farm Journal's Complete Pie Cookbook. New York: Doubleday, 1965.

Feuer, Janice. *Fruit-sweet and Sugar-free*. Rochester, Vt.: Healing Arts Press, 1993.

Field, Michael. *Cooking Adventures with Michael Field: Pies, Tarts, and Chou Puffs*. New York: Nelson Doubleday, 1971.

Fine, Diane. *Perfect Pies*. New York: William Morrow, 1985.

Fisher, M. F. K. *The Art of Eating*. New York: Collier, 1990.

Foods of the World. New York: Time-Life Books, 1968.

Frazier, Greg, and Beverly Frazier. *Aphrodisiac Cookery*. San Francisco: Troubador Press, 1970.

Friberg, Bo. *The Professional Pastry Chef*. New York: Van Nostrand Reinhold, 1990.

Furnas, C. C., and S. M. Furnas. *Man, Bread & Destiny*. Great Britain: Cassell, 1938.

Grabhorn, Robert. *Commonplace Book of Cookery*. San Francisco: North Point Press, 1985.

Graves, Eleanor. *Great Dinners from Life*. New York: Time-Life Books, 1969.

Hale, William Harlan, and editors of Horizon Magazine. *The Horizon Cookbook: Illustrated History of Eating and Drinking Through the Ages*. New York: American Heritage Publishing, 1968.

Heatter, Maida. *Book of Great Desserts*. New York: Alfred A. Knopf, 1965.

Henderson, Mary F. *Practical Cooking and Dinner Giving*. New York: Harper Brothers, 1877.

Herbst, Sharon Tyler. *Food Lover's Companion*. New York: Barron's Educational Series, 1990.

Heritage Academy of Columbus, Mississippi. *Grand Heritage*. Memphis, Tenn.: Wimmer Brothers Books, 1983.

Hibben, Sheila. *American Regional Cookery*. Boston: Little Brown, 1946.

Hill, Lois. *Great Pies*. New York City: Weathervane Books, 1991.

Hooker, Richard J., ed. *A Colonial Plantation Cookbook, The Receipt Book of Harriott Pinckney Horry*. 1770. Columbia, S.C.: University of South Carolina Press, 1984.

How to Make a Pie: The Cook's Illustrated Library. Brookline, Mass.: Boston Common Press, 1996.

Jones, Evan. *American Food*. New York: Vintage Books, 1981.

Kuper, Jessica, ed. *Anthropologists' Cookbook*. New York: Universe Books, 1977.

Larousse Gastronomique. London: Hamlyn Publishing Group, 1961.

Leopold, Allison Kyle. *Victorian Sweets*. New York: Clarkson Potter, 1992.

Livingston, A. D., and Helen Livingston. *Edible Plants and Animals*. New York: Facts on File, 1993.

Luchetti, Emily. *Stars Desserts*. New York: HarperCollins, 1991.

Lundberg, Donald E., and Lendal H. Kotschevar. *Understanding Cooking*. Holyoke, Mass.: Marcus Printing Co., 1965.

Makay, Ian, ed. *Food for Thought*. Freedom, Calif.: Bay Publishing, 1995.

Malgieri, Nick. *Perfect Pastry*. New York: Macmillan, 1989.

———. *How to Bake*. New York: HarperCollins, 1995.

Margen, Sheldon, and the editors of the University of California at Berkeley *Wellness Letter*. *The Wellness Encyclopedia of Food and Nutrition*. New York: Rebus, 1992.

Mariani, John. *Dictionary of American Food & Drink*. New Haven, Conn.: Ticknor & Fields, 1983.

McBride, Mary Margaret. *Harvest of American Cooking*. New York: Putnam, 1957.

McCulloch-Williams, Martha. *Dishes & Beverages of the Old South*. Knoxville: University of Tennessee Press, 1988.

McCully, Helen. *Nobody Ever Tells You These Things*. New York: Holt, Rhinehart & Winston, 1967.

McGee, Harold. *On Food and Cooking*. New York: Scribners, 1984.

———. *The Curious Cook*. New York: Collier Books, 1990.

McNair, James. *James McNair's Pie Cookbook*. San Francisco: Rockpile Press, 1989.

Medrich, Alice. *Cocolat*. New York: Warner, 1990.

Mrs. Gillette's Cookbook. Akron, Ohio: Saalfield Publishing Co., 1908.

Mrs. Seely's Cookbook: Antique American Cookbooks. Birmingham, Ala.: Oxmoor House, 1984.

Naftalin, Rose. *Grandma Rose's Book of Sinfully Delicious Cakes, Cookies, Pies, Cheesecakes, Cake Rolls & Pastries*. New York: Random House, 1975.

Napolitano, Pete. *Produce Pete's Farmacopeia*. New York: Hearst Books, 1994.

National Council of Negro Women. *Black Family Reunion Cookbook*. Memphis, Tenn.: Tradery House, 1991.

Neal, Bill. *Biscuits, Spoonbread & Sweet Potato Pie*. New York: Alfred A. Knopf, 1990.

New York Herald Tribune Home Institute. *America's Cookbook*. 1940.

Panati, Charles. *Extraordinary Origins of Everyday Things*. New York: Harper & Row, 1987.

Paston-Williams, Sara. *The Art of Dining*. London: Perry N. Abrams, Inc., 1993.

Peck, Paula. *The Art of Fine Baking*. New York: Simon & Schuster, 1961.

Penner, Lucille Recht. *The Colonial Cookbook*. New York: Hastings House, 1976.

Pepin, Jacques. *La Technique*. New York: Times Book Co., 1976.

Perfect Fruit Pies. Pownal, Vt.: Storey Communications, 1992.

Pies & Pastries. Alexandria, Va.: Time-Life Books, 1981.

Pies & Tarts. Williams-Sonoma Kitchen Library. San Francisco: Time-Life Books, 1992.

Purdy, Susan. *As Easy as Pie*. New York: Collier Books, 1984.

Radecka, Helena. *The Fruit & Nut Book*. New York: McGraw-Hill, 1984.

Reynolds, Cuyler. *The Banquet Book*. New York: G. P. Putnam & Sons, 1902.

Ritter, Irene. *The Cobbler Crusade*. Tucson, Ariz.: Fisher Books, 1992.

Robbins, Maria Polushkin, ed. *Cook's Quotation Book*. New York: Penguin Books, 1983.

Rombauer, Irma, and Marion Becker. *The Joy of Cooking*. New York: Bobbs-Merrill, 1975.

Root, Waverly. *Food*. New York: Simon & Schuster, 1980.

Roux, Michel. *Michel Roux's Finest Desserts*. New York: Rizzoli, 1995.

Roux, Michel, and Albert Roux. *Patisserie*. New York: Prentice-Hall, 1986.

Rubin, Maury. *Book of Tarts*. New York: William Morrow, 1995.

Sax, Richard. *Classic Home Desserts*. Shelburne, Vt.: Chapters Publishing, 1994.

Seranne, Ann. *The Complete Book of Home Baking*. New York: Doubleday, 1950.

Shand, P. Morton. *A Book of Food*. New York: Alfred A. Knopf, 1928.

Silverton, Nancy. *Desserts*. New York: Harper & Row, 1986.

Simon, Andre L., and Robin Howe. *Dictionary of Gastronomy*. London: Rainbird Reference Books, 1970.

Southern Cook Book. Culinary Arts Press, 1939.

Soyer, Alexis. *The Pantropheon, or A History of Food and It's Preparation in Ancient Times.* 1853. New York/London: Paddington Press, 1977.

Stewart, Martha. *Pies & Tarts.* New York: Clarkson Potter, 1985.

Strause, Monroe Boston. *Pie Marches On.* New York: Ahrens Publishing, 1939.

Sultan, William J. *Practical Baking.* Westport, Conn.: Avi Publishing, 1986.

Thomas, Gertrude I. *Foods of Our Forefathers.* 3 vols. F. A. Davis, Philadelphia, 1941.

Toussaint-Samat, Maguelonne. *A History of Food,* trans. by Anthea Bell. Cambridge, Mass.: Blackwell Publishers, 1992.

Unrivaled Dixie. Atlanta, Ga.: L. A. Clarkson & Co.

Walheim, Lance, and Robert L. Stebbins. *Western Fruit, Berries & Nuts.* Tucson, Ariz.: HP Books, 1981.

Walter, Carole. *Great Cakes.* New York: Ballantine, 1991; Clarkson Potter/Publishers, 1998.

Warren, Mildred Evans. *The Art of Southern Cooking.* New York: Gramercy Publishing, 1981.

White, Martha. *Southern Sampler.* Nashville, Tenn.: Rutledge Hill Press, 1989.

Wilkerson, Arnold, with Patricia Henley and Michael Deraney. *Little Pie Company of the Big Apple, Pies and Other Dessert Favorites.* New York: HarperCollins, 1993.

Willan, Anne. *Look & Cook: Perfect Pies & Tarts.* New York: Dorling Kindersley, 1994.

Worth, Helen. *Damn Yankee in a Southern Kitchen.* Richmond Westover Pub. Co., 1972.

Yockelson, Lisa. *Country Pies.* New York: Harper & Row, 1988.

Zimmerman, L., and Peggy Mellody. *Cobblers, Crumbles, and Crisps.* New York: Clarkson Potter, 1991.

ARTICLES

Anderson, Pam. "Mix and Match Fruit Cobblers." *Cook's Illustrated,* August 1996.

Boyle, Tish. "The Perfect Pie." *Chocolatier,* November 1996.

Corriber, Shirley. "The Secrets of Tender, Flaky Pie Crust." *Fine Cooking,* October/November 1996.

Cullen, Peggy. "Summer Pies." *Food & Wine,* August 1994.

Dodge, Jim. "Cobblers and Grunts Showcase Summer Fruits." *Fine Cooking,* August/September 1994.

Willan, Anne. "Turning out a classic Tarte Tatin." *Fine Cooking,* October/November 1994.

MAIL ORDER SOURCES

GENERAL

BRIDGE KITCHENWARE
214 East 52nd Street
New York, NY 10022
800-274-3435

Complete line of domestic and imported cook- and bakeware, extensive selection of tart and tartlet pans, flan rings, assorted decorating equipment, baking accessories, and baking parchment (packaged in sheets) sold in bulk. Popular supplier to chefs and restaurants. Catalog available.

BROADWAY PANHANDLER
477 Broome Street
New York, NY 10013
212-966-3434

Varied line of domestic and imported cook- and bakeware, baking accessories, giftware, linens, and serving pieces. No catalog available.

CHEF'S CATALOG
3215 Commercial Avenue
Northbrook, IL 60062
800-338-3232

Mail order catalog. "Professional Restaurant Equipment for the Home Chef."

COOKTIQUE
9 Railroad Avenue
Tenafly, NJ 07670
201-568-7990

Varied line of domestic and imported cook- and bakeware, baking accessories and boutique giftware. Quality rolling pins. No catalog available.

COOKWARE & MORE
110 Broad Street
P.O. Box 2170
Flemington, NJ 08822
800-272-2170

Discount source for upscale cookware, Kaiser and Chicago Metallic bakeware, and Wüsthof knives. Brochure available.

J. B. PRINCE AND COMPANY
29 West 38th Street
New York, NY 10018
212-302-8611

Sells primarily to the professional trade. Complete line of imported and domestic bakeware, tart and tartlet pans, flan rings, extensive selection of baking accessories and decorating equipment. Catalog available.

LA CUISINE
323 Cameron Street
Alexandria, VA 22314
800-521-1176

Extensive line of high-quality bakeware, maple pastry boards, rolling pins, imported wooden spoons and spatulas, baking accessories, and decorating equipment. Catalog available.

NEW YORK CAKE & BAKING DISTRIBUTORS
56 West 22nd Street
New York, NY 10010
212-675-2253

Extensive line of decorating equipment and specialty baking pans, cookie and canapé cutters, pie boxes, and cardboard cake rounds. Also stocks bulk chocolate. Catalog available.

SUR LE TABLE
1765 Sixth Avenue South
Seattle, WA 98134
800-243-0852

Upscale kitchen shop with a complete line of specialty baking pans and accessories, rolling pins, decorating equipment, cookware, candy-making supplies, kitchen gadgets, small appliances, and gift items. Catalog available.

SWEET CELEBRATIONS (FORMERLY MAID OF SCANDINAVIA)
7009 Washington Avenue South
Edina, MN 55439
888-328-6722

Everything imaginable in decorating equipment. Cake boxes and other packaging materials for baked goods. Catalog available.

WILLIAMS-SONOMA
Mail Order Department
P.O. Box 7456
San Francisco, CA 94120-7456
800-541-2233

"A Catalog for Cooks." Upscale catalog features "cutting edge" culinary equipment, baking accessories, and giftware. Good source for Nielsen-Massey vanilla extract and premium chocolate for baking. Many items are available only through the catalog.

ZABARS
249 West 80th Street
New York, NY 10024
212-496-1234 or 800-697-6301

Varied line of domestic and imported cook and bakeware. Good prices on small kitchen appliances. Known for their selection of specialty food items. Catalog available.

PIE BIRDS

CLAY CITY POTTERY
Box 305
Clay City, IN 47841
800-776-2596

CHUCK MYERS
Cupboard Classics
Box 373
Deer Trail, CO 80105
303-769-4326
Brochure available.

LOUISE'S OLD THINGS
163 West Main Street
Kutztown, PA 19530
610-683-8370

SALMON FALLS STONEWARE
Box 452
Dover, NH 03820
800-621-2030

SPECIALTY INGREDIENTS

DEAN & DELUCA
560 Broadway
New York, NY 10012
800-221-7714

Premium specialty food items, White Lily flour, bulk chocolate, high-quality extracts, premium dried fruits. Limited line of fine baking equipment. Catalog available.

MAISON GLASS, INC.
P.O. Box 317-H
Scarsdale, NY 10583
800-822-5564

Source for professional-quality praline paste, premium dried fruits and nuts, chocolate covered coffee beans, bulk chocolate. Catalog available.

ROWE-MANSE EMPORIUM
1065 Bloomfield Avenue
Clifton, NJ 07012
800-633-3100

High-quality specialty foods, candies, and good source for nesselrode fruit.

TAFTSVILLE COUNTRY STORE
Taftsville, VT
802-457-1135
Catalog 800-854-0013

Granulated maple sugar, pure Vermont maple syrup.

FLOURS

ARROWHEAD MILLS
Box 866
Hereford, TX 79045
806-364-0730

Distributes an extensive line of grain and specialty flours, including whole wheat pastry flour.

WHITE LILY FLOUR COMPANY
Box 871
Knoxville, TN 37901
423-546-5511

Producers of high-quality flours. Renowned for soft wheat pastry and biscuit flour.

KING ARTHUR FLOUR COMPANY
The Baker's Catalogue
P.O. Box 876
Norwich, VT 05055
800-827-6836

Manufacturer of high-quality flours, specializing in bread flour and equipment. Catalog lists a variety of baking ingredients, specialty baking pans, utensils, and accessories.

APPLIANCE REPAIRS AND PARTS

CUISINART
P.O. Box 2160
East Windsor, NJ 08520
800-726-9499

CULINARY PARTS UNLIMITED
80 Berry Drive
Pacheco, CA 94553
800-543-7549

Replacement parts for more than 20 of the most popular brands of appliances.

KITCHENAID
701 Main Street
St Joseph, MI 49085
800-541-6390

EQUIVALENTS AND SUBSTITUTIONS

AMOUNT AND INGREDIENT	EQUIVALENT
1 cup sifted cake flour	1 cup less 2 tablespoons sifted all-purpose flour
1 cup sifted all-purpose flour	1 cup plus 2 tablespoons sifted cake flour
1 ounce unsweetened chocolate	3 tablespoons cocoa plus 1 tablespoon vegetable oil or shortening
1 cup buttermilk	1 cup plain or low-fat yogurt
1 cup plain or low-fat yogurt	1 cup buttermilk
1 cup whole milk	1/2 cup evarporated milk mixed with 1/2 cup water
1 tablespoon cornstarch	2 tablespoons flour or 1 tablespoon arrowroot
1 tablespoon arrowroot	2 tablespoons flour
1 tablespoon tapioca	1 tablespoon cornstarch
1 tablespoon tapioca	2 tablespoons flour
1 tablespoon flour	1 1/2 teaspoons tapioca
1 tablespoon potato starch (potato flour)	2 tablespoons flour
1 teaspoon double-acting baking powder	1/4 teaspoon baking soda plus 5/8 teaspoon cream of tartar
1 teaspoon single-acting baking powder	1/2 teaspoon cream of tartar plus 1/4 teaspoon baking soda plus 1/4 teaspoon cornstarch
1 teaspoon baking soda	2 teaspoons double-acting baking powder
2 egg yolks	1 whole egg
1 cup light brown sugar	1/2 cup granulated sugar plus 1/2 cup dark brown sugar
1 cup granulated sugar	1 cup firmly packed light or dark brown sugar
1 cup granulated sugar	1 cup superfine sugar
1 cup granulated sugar	3/4 cup maple syrup
3/4 cup maple syrup	1 cup granulated sugar
1 cup honey	1 1/4 cups granulated sugar plus 1/4 cup liquid
1 teaspoon sugar	1/8 teaspoon noncaloric sweetener
1 cup molasses	1/2 cup sugar plus 1/4 cup liquid
1 cup dark corn syrup	3/4 cup light corn syrup plus 1/4 cup light molasses
1 cup butter	1 cup vegetable shortening less 1 tablespoon (plus additional liquid as needed for crusts)
1 cup butter	1 cup less 3 to 4 tablespoons lard
1 cup butter	1 cup margarine
1 cup butter	1 cup less 3 to 4 tablespoons vegetable oil
1/4 ounce (1 envelope) gelatin	4 sheets gelatin (4×9 inches)

SOLID OR STICK MEASURING CHART BY WEIGHT

Applies to butter and/or other solid fats

4 sticks = 16 ounces = 32 tablespoons = 2 cups = 1 pound = 454 grams
2 sticks = 8 ounces = 16 tablespoons = 1 cup = 1/2 pound = 227 grams
1 1/2 sticks = 6 ounces = 12 tablespoons = 3/4 cup = 3/8 pound = 169 grams
1 1/3 sticks = 5 1/3 ounces = 10 2/3 tablespoons = 2/3 cup = 1/3 pound = 151 grams
1 stick = 4 ounces = 8 tablespoons = 1/2 cup = 1/4 pound = 113 grams
3/4 stick = 3 ounces = 6 tablespoons = 3/8 cup = 3/16 pound = 84 grams
2/3 stick = 2 2/3 ounces = 5 1/2 tablespoons = 1/3 cup = 1/6 pound = 76 grams
1/2 stick = 2 ounces = 4 tablespoons = 1/4 cup = 1/8 pound = 56 grams
1/4 stick = 1 ounce = 2 tablespoons = 1/8 cup = 1/6 pound = 28 grams

DRY MEASURING CHART
BY VOLUME For raw fruits and vegetables (rounded off)

4 pecks = 1 bushel
1 peck = 8 quarts
1 quart = 4 cups = 2 pounds = 908 grams
1 pint = 2 cups = 16 ounces = 454 grams
2,000 grams = 2 kilograms
1,000 grams = 1 kilogram
500 grams = 1/2 kilogram

DRY MEASURING CHART
BY VOLUME For dry ingredients

16 tablespoons = 1 cup = 8 ounces
14 tablespoons = 7/8 cup = 7 ounces
12 tablespoons = 3/4 cup = 6 ounces
10 2/3 tablespoons = 2/3 cup = 5 1/3 ounces
8 tablespoons = 1/2 cup = 4 ounces
5 1/3 tablespoons = 1/3 cup = 2 2/3 ounces
4 tablespoons = 1/4 cup = 2 ounces
2 tablespoons = 1/8 cup = 1 ounce
1 tablespoon = 3 teaspoons = 1/2 ounce
1/2 tablespoon = 1 1/2 teaspoons = 1/4 ounce
1/3 tablespoon = 1 teaspoon
Pinch or dash = the amount held between two fingers

METRIC EQUIVALENTS OF MEASURES BY WEIGHT (rounded off)

2 3/16 pounds = 1 kilogram
2 pounds = 32 ounces = 908 grams
1 pound = 16 ounces = 454 grams
1/2 pound = 8 ounces = 227 grams
1/4 pound = 4 ounces = 113 grams
1/8 pound = 2 ounces = 57 grams
1 ounce = 28 grams
1/2 ounce = 14 grams
1/4 ounce = 7 grams

FLUID MEASURING CHART
BY VOLUME (rounded off)

1 gallon = 4 quarts = 4 liters
1/2 gallon = 2 quarts = 2 liters
1 quart = 4 cups = 1,000 milliliters (1 liter)
1 pint = 2 cups = 500 milliliters (1/2 liter)
1/2 pint = 1 cup = 250 milliliters (1/4 liter)
1 quart = 32 ounces = .946 milliliter
1 fifth = 25 ounces = .739 milliliter
2 cups = 16 ounces = .473 milliliter
1 cup = 8 ounces = .236 milliliter
1/2 cup = 4 ounces = .118 milliliter (1 gill)
1/4 cup = 2 ounces = .059 milliliter
1 jigger = 1 1/2 ounces = .045 milliliter = 3 tablespoons
2 tablespoons = 1 ounce = .030 milliliter
1 tablespoon = 1/2 ounce = .015 milliliter
Dash = a few drops

INDEX

ACIDULATED WATER, 457
aerate (sift), 457
Alexandrou, Catherine, Tart of
    Blood Oranges, Rhubarb,
    and Dried Fruit, 204
All-Fruit Mincemeat
    Jalousie, 202
    Tartlets, 385
All-Nut Pastry Shell, 163;
    freezing, 78
all-purpose flour, bleached, 3;
    unbleached, 4
Almond(s)
    Amaretti Cookies with (nut
        crumb crust), 167
    Biscotti with (nut crumb
        crust), 167
    Butter Cookies with (nut
        crumb crust), 166
    Coco-Nutty Meringue Shell,
        162
    Crackle, 454
    Lemon Cookies with (nut
        crumb crust), 167
    Nut Pastry, 151
    Nut Pastry, Cheese-Layered
        Tart Cherry Pie in, 196
    Nut Pastry, Flourless
        Macaroon Tart in, 308
    oven toasting, 56–57
    paste, 457
    skillet toasting, 57
    skinning, 57
    Toasted, Vanilla Wafers with
        (nut crumb crust), 166
    Zwieback with (nut crumb
        crust), 166
Alsatian Quiche Lorraine, 428
Amaretti, 457

Cookies with Almonds or
    Hazelnuts (nut crumb
    crust), 167
Tutti-Frutti Tart, 362
American pie and tart, early
    lore, ("coffin," "trap," etc.),
    103
American-style rolling pins, 87
angled flute, decorative edge for
    pie crust, 66
Apple(s), 17–19
    Appleberry Pie, Crimson, 180
    Cabbage, and Onion Tart, 418
    choosing, 17
    Crisp, Maple Pecan, 328
    Crunch Pie with Dried
        Fruits, Sour Cream, 244
    Dried, and Blackberry Filling,
        Turnovers with, 390;
        variation, with Cream
        Cheese Pastry, 391
    history of, 17
    peeling and coring, 19
    Pie (lesson 1), 106–7; tips for,
        110–11
    Pie, Old-Fashioned
        American, 108
    Pies, Fried, 373
    Pot Pies, Fresh, with Puff
        Pastry Caps, 382
    -Pumpkin Chiffon Pie in a
        Chocolate Crumb Crust,
        300
    season available, 17
    storing and handling, 18–19
    Tart, Big Easy, 178
    Tart, Crustless, Honey-
        Glazed, 396
    Tart, A Simple (lesson 3), 121
    Tarte Tatin, 228
    Top-Knots, Stuffed
        Cinnamon, 398
    varieties of (Baldwin, Granny
        Smith, Stayman, etc.), 17–18
    Walnut Tart in Sweet Tart
        Pastry, 182

Appleberry Pie, Crimson, 180
Apricot(s), 19–20
    Cherry Pie with Almond
        Crunch Topping, Roy's, 186
    choosing, 20
    freezing, 20
    glaze for tarts, 73
    history of, 19–20
    and Pear Strudel Pie, 216
    Pie, Fresh, with Apricot Rum
        Sauce, 184
    Pies, Fried, 372; variation,
        Fried Apple, 373
    and Prune Crackle Tart, 224
    Rum Sauce, 443
    season available, 19
    storing and handling, 20
    Swiss Chard Tart with, in
        Rosemary Chive Crust, 432
arrowroot, 5, 457
Autumn
    Fruit Crumble with Oatmeal
        Crunch Topping, 332;
        variation, Prune Plum, 333
    Pear and Grape Pie in
        Cheddar Pastry, 218

**BAIN-MARIE (WATER
    BATHS)**, 47, 61–62, 461
baking. *See also* techniques and
    procedures
    blind, 70, 91, 94, 95–96; puff
        pastry shell, 174; for tartlets,
        370
    chocolate, 12
    equipment (flan ring, pans,
        pie plates, etc.) for making
        pies and tarts, 42

nuggets, 457
pans, 47, 62–63. *See also* pans
par-baked or fully baked, 95
parchment, 457
powder, 5
soda, 6
stone (pizza stone), 457
Banana(s), 20–21
    choosing, 21
    Cream Pie with Pecan Brittle, 246
    freezing, 21
    history of, 20–21
    Lemon Tart, Glazed, Steven Santoro's, 188
    season available, 20
    storing and handling, 21
barquette (tartlet), 157
basic recipes. *See* The Primer
basic techniques. *See* techniques and procedures
batarde (meat pounder), 40, 457
Bavarian(s), 276–77, 457
    cream and mousse-type fillings, freezing and thawing, 77–78
    Lemon Tart, Sorbet Frosted, 350
    -style, Java Eggnog Pie, 288
    -style, Snappy Mango Madness, 294
beating eggs, 53; egg whites, 53–54
bench, dough, or pastry scraper, 43, 457
Berry(ies). *See also* Name of Berry
    Crisp, Three, with Butter-Nut Crumb Topping, 339
    Fresh, Fluted Cream Cheese Flan with, 258
    -Fruit Cream Pie, 402
    and fruit glossary, 17–40. *See also* Name of Berry or Fruit
    Lemon Tea Tarts Smothered with, 385
    and Peaches with Patchwork Linzer Crust, 208
bibliography, 462–65

Biscotti, 457
    with Almonds or Hazelnuts (nut crumb crust), 167
Biscuit
    Dough, Sweet Cream, 140
    freezing, 78
    Topping, Quilted, Strawberry Fig Cobbler with, 340
bitter (unsweetened) chocolate, 11–12; bittersweet, 12
Black
    and Blue Mango Pie, 190
    Bottom Cream Pie, 278
    Forest Cherry Tart, 280
    Mission Fig and Blackberry Tart, Awesome, 380
    Pepper Wine Pastry, 143; Fresh Tart Cherry Pie in, 194
Blackberry(ies), 21–22. *See also* Berry(ies)
    Black and Blue Mango Pie, 190
    and Black Mission Fig Tart, Awesome, 380
    choosing, 21
    Cobbler, Double-Crust, 330
    and Dried Apple Filling, Turnovers with, 390
    freezing, 21
    history of, 21
    Mango Tart with, 200
    season available, 21
    storing and handling, 21
blanching, 457
bleached all-purpose flour, 3
blind-baking. *See* baking blind
Blood Oranges, Rhubarb, and Dried Fruit, Catherine Alexandrou's Tart of, 204
blooming and dissolving gelatin, 60–61
Blueberry(ies), 22. *See also* Berry(ies)
    Black and Blue Mango Pie, 190
    choosing, 22
    Crumb Pie with Warm Blueberry Sauce, 192
    freezing, 22

history of, 22
    Lemon Soufflé Tartlets, 401
    and Peach Cobbler, 337
    Sauce, 443
    season available, 22
    storing and handling, 22
    Tart, Walnut-Topped, 238
boiling, 457–58
brandies, for flavoring, 14
break down (of butterfat), 458
brittle (candy), 458
Broccoli, Leek, and Cheddar Tart, Deep-Dish, 416
brown sugar, 6; handling, 50; measuring, 50–51
browned butter, 52, 458
browning bottom crust, 73–74
brushes, pastry and goosefeather, 47
buckle (deep-dish dessert), 458
Butter, 8. *See also* fats
    All-, Pie Pastry, 1940s, 138
    browned, 52, 458
    clarifying, 52
    Cookies with Pecans, Walnuts, or Almonds (nut crumb crust), 166
    -Crumb Topping, Dutch Peach Pie with, 206
    measuring, 51
    -Nut Crumb Topping, Three Berry Crisp with, 339
    Pastry, Press-On, 158
Buttermilk, 11; Custard, Fresh Coconut Tarts with, 378
Butterscotch, 458; Sauce, 444

CABBAGE, Apple, and Onion Tart, 418
Caffe White Chocolate Tart, 284
cake flour, 3, 4

Candied
  Citrus Rind, 456
  Peel, Lemon Cream Tart
    with, 262
  Whole Nuts, 453
cantaloupe. *See also* Melon
  choosing, 30–31
  Melon and Mascarpone Tart
    in Chocolate Crumb Crust,
    266
caramel, tips for, 303
caramelizing, 303, 458
Caramelized Walnut Tart, 310
caraway seeds, 15
Cashew Cluster, Colossal, 306
chalazae, 458
Chantilly Cream, 458; Crème
  Chantilly, 450
Cheddar
  Broccoli, and Leek Tart,
    Deep-Dish, 416
  Pastry, 135; Autumn Pear and
    Grape Pie in, 218
Cheese, 9. *See also* Cheddar;
    Cream Cheese; Goat
    Cheese; Marscapone
  about (many), 9
  as a fat for pastry dough, 9
  -Layered Tart Cherry Pie in
    Almond Nut Pastry, 196
  Pineapple Pie, Crustless, 405
Chef's Cookie Dough for
    Tartlets, 155
Cherry(ies), 22–23
  Apricot Pie with Almond
    Crunch Topping, Roy's, 186
  Bing, Green Gables Clafoutis,
    376
  choosing, 22–23
  freezing, 23
  history of, 22
  pitting, 23
  season available, 22
  storing and handling, 23
  Tart, Black Forest, 280
  Tart, Cheese-Layered, Pie in
    Almond Nut Pastry, 196
  Tart, Fresh Pie, in Black
    Pepper Wine Pastry, 194
Chesapeake Crab Tart, 420

Chess Pie, Lemon, Anne
    Semmes', 248
chiboust cream, 458
Chiffon(s), 458
  about, 276–77
  Pie, Lemon, 290
  Pie, Pumpkin-Apple, in a
    Chocolate Crumb Crust,
    300
  Pie, Raspberry, Rousing, 408
chiffonade, 458
chilling shaped pastry before
    baking, 94
Choco-Nouga Chew Chew
    Tart, 348
Chocolate, 11–13
  baking, 12
  bitter, 11–12
  bittersweet, 12
  Black Bottom Cream Pie,
    278
  Candy Tart, Devilish, 252
  Chip Cookie Pie, Main
    Attraction, 320
  chips, 12
  Choco-Nouga Chew Chew
    Tart, 348
  chopping, 55
  cocoa beans, 11
  cocoa butter, 11
  cocoa powder, unsweetened,
    12–13; Dutch-process, 13;
    straining, 50
  conching, 11
  Cream Pie in a Nutty
    Cornmeal Crust, 254
  Crème Anglaise, 442
  Crumb Crust, 168
  Crumb Crust, Melon and
    Mascarpone Tart in, 266
  Crumb Crust, Pumpkin-
    Apple Chiffon Pie in a, 300
  -Crusted Raspberry Soufflé
    Pie, 358
  Curls and Shavings, 455
  Fudge-Nut Tart, Prickly, 304
  Fudge Sauce, Warm, 446
  Fudge Walnut Sundae Pie,
    357
  Ganache Sauce, 447

handling (chopping, melting),
    55–56
  milk, 12
  Mississippi Mud Pie with
    Fudge Candy Icing, 312
  Pecan Mousse Tart, 282
  Pecan Pie, 315
  Ripple Ricotta Tart, 272
  semisweet, 12
  Soufflé Tartlets, 374
  storing, 13
  Tart Pastry, 148
  unsweetened (bitter), 11–12
  Velvet Pie with Sliced
    Strawberries, 404
  white, 12
  White, Caffe Tart, 284
chopping
  chocolate, 55
  nuts, 57
Cinnamon
  Apple Top-Knots, Stuffed, 398
  Crème Anglaise, 442
  Crumbs (topping) and Plums
    Tart, 268
Citrus. *See also* Lemons; Limes:
    Oranges; Tangerines
  fruits, handling (juicing,
    supreming, zesting), 59
  Pie, Shaker, in a Cookie
    Crust, 250
  Rind, Candied, 456
  Zest Flaky Pie Pastry II,
    101
Clafouti(s), 458; Green Gables
    Bing Cherry, 376
clarified butter, 52, 458;
    microwave method for, 52;
    stovetop method, 52
classic tart pastry, 85
Classic Tart Pastry I (Pâte
    Brisée), 102; Pastry II, 104;
    variation, Rosemary Chive,
    105
  double pan method for, 71
  for tartlet pans without
    removable bottoms, 371
Cobbler(s), 324–26, 458. *See also*
    Crisps; Crumbles
  about, 327

Blackberry, Double-Crust, 330
Double-Crust Lattice Top for, 337
Peach, Peachy, 336; variation, Peach and Blueberry, 337
Pear, Double-Header, 342
Pear 'n' Plum, 338
Short Pastry Dough for, 139
Strawberry Fig, with Quilted Biscuit Topping, 340; variation, Strawberry Cobbler, 341
Coco-Nutty Meringue Shell, 162
cocoa
  beans, 11. *See also* Chocolate
  butter, 11
  powder, unsweetened, 12–13; Dutch-process, 13; straining, 50
Coconut, 23
  Almond Meringue, Pineapple Zabaglione in, 366
  choosing, 23
  Coco Nutty Meringue Shell, 162
  Cream Pie, Toasted, The "Real" Tavern, 286
  Crust, Meringue-Topped Coconut Pie in, 256
  freezing, 23
  history of, 23
  Pie, Meringue-Topped, in Coconut Crust, 256
  removing meat of, 23
  season available, 23
  shredding, toasting, etc., 58
  storing and handling, 23
  Tarts with Buttermilk Custard, Fresh, 378
  Toasted, Pie Pastry, 136
coffee and espresso flavorings, 14
"coffins," early American pie, 103
cold water bath, 62
confectioners' sugar, 6–7; straining, 50
convection ovens for making pies and tarts, 48

conventional ovens for making pies and tarts, 48
cooked fillings (pie) with baked pastry shells, tips for, 116–17
Cookie(s)
  Crumb and Nut Crusts (many), 166–67. *See also* Nut Crumb Crusts
  Crust, Shaker Citrus Pie in a, 250
  Dough for Tartlets, Chef's, 155
  Saucers, Poached Peaches and Mascarpone on, 388
  sheet, 47
  -style dough, rolling and shaping, for pies and tarts, 69
  -style dough, for tartlet pans (with removable bottoms), 70, 370–71
  -style pastry, shaping and baking free-form, 71–72
cooking equipment for making pies and tarts, 42
cordials (liqueurs), brandies, liquor and wine for flavoring, 14
Corn Custard Pie with Wild Rice, 415
corn syrup, 7–8
corner (dough), 458
Cornmeal, 4
  Crust, Nutty, 154
  Pastry, Golden, 150; variation, Cornmeal Pepper, 150
cornstarch, 5
cottage cheese, for flaky crust, 9
Coulis, 458
  Mango, 448
  Raspberry, 448
coupler, 458
Crab Tart, Chesapeake, 420
Cranberries, 24
  choosing, 24
  Dried, Deep-Dish, Pear Crisp with, 400
  freezing, 24
  history of, 24
  season available, 24
  storing and handling, 24

cream(s)
  for cream and custard fillings, 11
  and custards, about, 242–43; for garnishing and decorating, 74
  of tartar, 6
Cream Chantilly, 458; Crème Chantilly, 450
Cream Cheese
  Flan, Fluted, with Fresh Berries, 258
  Pastry, 157
  for pastry dough, 9
Cream Pie
  Banana, with Pecan Brittle, 246
  Berry-Fruit, 402
  Black Bottom, 278
  Chocolate, in a Nutty Cornmeal Crust, 254
  Toasted Coconut, The "Real" Tavern, 286
Cream Tart, Lemon, with Candied Peel, 262
creaming (beating solid fats), 458
Crème
  Anglaise (English Custard Sauce), 440, 458; variations, Chocolate, 442; Cinnamon, 442; Crème Anglaise Rapide, 441; Orange, 442; with Vanilla Bean, 442
  Chantilly, 450
  Fraîche, 11, 451, 458
  patissière (pastry cream), 124–25, 460
crimp (pastry), 458–59
crimped edge for tart crust, 67
crimper, pastry, 48
Crimson Appleberry Pie, 180
Crisp(s), 324–26. *See also* Cobblers; Crumbles
  about, 327, 459
  Maple Pecan Apple, 328
  Pear, Deep-Dish, with Dried Cranberries, 400
  Three Berry, with Butter-Nut Crumb Topping, 339

crosshatch, decorative edge for
pie crust, 67
croustade, 459
Crumb Crust (Crusted), 165
Chocolate, 168
Chocolate, Melon and
Mascarpone Tart in a, 266
Chocolate, Pumpkin-Apple
Chiffon Pie in a, 300
Chocolate, Raspberry Soufflé
Pie in a, 358
freezing, 78
Master, 164; additions to,
166–67. See also Nut Crumb
Crusts (many)
Reduced-Cholesterol Graham
Cracker, 169
Crumb Pie, Blueberry, with
Warm Blueberry Sauce,
192
Crumb Topping
Butter-, Dutch Peach Pie
with, 206
Butter-Nut, Three Berry
Crisp with, 339
Blueberry Crumb Pie with
Warm Blueberry Sauce, 192
Cinnamon Crumbs and
Plums Tart, 268
Crumbles, 324–26. See also
Cobblers; Crisps
about, 327, 459
Autumn Fruit, with Oatmeal
Crunch Topping, 332;
variation, Prune Plum, 333
Gooseberry, 334
Crust(s). See also Pastry
All-Nut Pastry Shell, 163
Amaretti Cookies with
Almonds or Hazelnuts, 167
Biscotti with Almonds or
Hazelnuts, 167
bottom, browning, 73–74, 79
Butter Cookies with Pecans,
Walnuts, or Almonds, 166
Chocolate Crumb, 168
Coco-Nutty Meringue Shell,
162
crumb, about, 165

Crunchy Shells (many),
159–69
decorative edges for, 66–67
Double-, Blackberry Cobbler,
330
dough for. See dough
Ginger Snaps with Pecans,
166
Graham Crackers with
Pecans or Walnuts, 166
Krispie Meringue, 159;
variation, Krispie Pistachio,
159
lattice, diagonal, traditional,
or unwoven, 64–66
Lemon Cookies with
Walnuts, Pecans, or
Almonds, 167
Master Crumb, 164
Meringue Shell, 160;
variation, Petite Shells,
160
Nut Crumb (many), 166–67
par-baked or fully baked?
95
Reduced-Cholesterol Graham
Cracker, 169
top, for double-crust pie, 92;
sealing, 92; steam vents for,
93
Vanilla Wafers with Toasted
Almonds, 166
Zwieback with Almonds or
Hazelnuts, 166
Crustless. See also Cobblers;
Crisps; Crumbles
Apple Tart, Honey-Glazed,
396
Chocolate Soufflé Tartlets,
374
Fluted Cream Cheese Flan
with Fresh Berries, 258
Mississippi Mud Pie with
Fudge Candy Icing, 312
Pineapple Cheese Pie, 405
crystallization, 459
cultured dairy products, for
pies and tarts (buttermilk,
crème fraîche, sour cream,
yogurt), 11

curdle, 459
Curls and Shavings, Chocolate,
455
Currant(s), 24–25
choosing, 24–25
freezing, 24
history of, 24
Sauce, Fresh, 445
season available, 24
storing and handling, 25
Custard(s)
Buttermilk, Fresh Coconut
Tarts with, 378
and creams, about, 242–43
cups for pies and tarts, 47
Pie, Corn, with Wild Rice,
415
Sauce, English (Crème
Anglaise), 440; variations,
Chocolate, 442; Cinnamon,
442; Crème Anglaise
Rapide, 441; Orange, 442;
with Vanilla Bean, 442
cut in (shortening), 459
cutting and serving pies and
tarts, 75–76
cutting wheels, pastry, 48

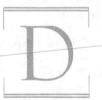

DAIRY PRODUCTS, cultured,
for pies and tarts
buttermilk, 11
crème fraîche, 11
sour cream, 11
yogurt, 11
Danish Nut Dough for Tartlets,
156
decorating pies and tarts.
See garnishing and
decorating
decorative edges for pie
crusts, 66–67; for tart
crusts, 67

Deep-Dish
    Broccoli, Leek, and Cheddar
        Tart, 416
    Pear Crisp with Dried
        Cranberries, 400
Devilish Chocolate Candy Tart,
    252
dock (pastry dough), 459;
    docker, 44
double boiler, 459
Double-Crust
    Blackberry Cobbler, 330
    Lattice Top for Cobblers, 337
    pie, top crust for, 92; sealing,
        92; steam vents for, 93
Double-Header Pear Cobbler,
    342
double pan method for classic
    tart pastry, 71, 371
dough(s), 85–89. See also Pastry
    defined, 85
    differences between classic
        tart and flaky pie, 85
    hand vs. food processor for,
        86
    overworking, 86
    rolling and shaping, 86–88;
        rolling pins for, 87; rolling
        surface, 87–88
Dried Fruit(s)
    for baking, 16
    Blood Oranges, and Rhubarb
        Tart, Catherine
        Alexandrou's, 204
    handling (cutting, macerating,
        plumping), 58–59
    Pot Pies, Fresh, with Puff
        Pastry Caps, 382
    Sour Cream Apple Crunch
        Pie with, 244
dry and liquid measures for
    pies and tarts, 42
Dutch Peach Pie with Butter-
    Crumb Topping, 206
Dutch-process cocoa, 13

EDGES, decorative, for crusts,
    66–67
egg(s). See also Meringues
    beating, 53
    handling, 9–10, 52–54
    for pies and tarts, 9–10; egg
        substitutes, 10
    separating, 53, 276
    storing, 10
    tempering, 53, 276
    wash, 459; for pastry dough
        glaze, 72; as sealer, 72, 96
    whites, 9, 53–54; beaten,
        stages of, 54; for meringues,
        54
    yolks, 9–10
Eggnog Pie, Java, 288
Eggplant Tart with Tomatoes,
    Greek Olives, and Feta, 422
electric mixers for making pies
    and tarts, 45
emulsifying, 459
Enriched Pastry Cream, 127
equipment for making pies and
    tarts, 41–48. See also
    garnishing and decorating;
    name of equipment
    bain-marie, 47
    baking, 42
    bench, dough, or pastry
        scraper, 43
    brushes (pastry), goosefeather
        and pastry, 47
    cookie sheet, 47
    cooking, 42
    decorating equipment (pastry
        bags and tips), 48
    for dry and liquid measures,
        42
    electric mixer, 45
    food processor, 44
    for garnishing, 42
    graters, 44
    kitchen scales, 42
    for measuring ingredients,
        41–42
    for mixing and shaping, 41–42
    ovens, convection,
        conventional, and
        microwave, 48
    pastry blender, 43
    pastry cloth and rolling pin
        cover, 43
    pastry crimper, 48
    pastry cutting wheels, 48
    pastry docker, 44
    pie plates, 45–46; standard
        sizes, list, 46
    pots and pans, 45
    ramekins and custard cups,
        47
    rolling pins and surfaces,
        43–44
    for serving, 42
    shallow baking pan, 47
    sifters, 44
    spatulas, offset and rubber, 47
    strainers, 44
    tart and tartlet pans, 46–47;
        standard sizes, list, 46
    thermometers, 43
    whisks, balloon and sauce, 47
equivalents and substitutions,
    468–69
espresso and coffee flavorings,
    14
extracts, flavored (almond,
    lemon, orange, etc.), 14

FANNING FRUIT, 183
fat(s), 8–9. See also name of fat
    butter, 8, 51
    clarifying butter, 52
    cream cheese (for pastry
        dough), 9

fat (*cont.*)
  handling, 51–52
  hydrogenated vegetable
    shortening, 8
  lard, 8–9
  "low-fat," 9
  margarine, 8
  measuring, 51–52
  plastic, 51
  temperature of, 51–52
  vegetable oils, 9
feuilletage, 459
feuilletée, 459
Fig(s), 25
  Black Mission, and Black-
    berry Tart, Awesome, 380
  choosing, 25
  freezing, 25
  history of, 25
  season available, 25
  storing and handling, 25
  Strawberry Cobbler with
    Quilted Biscuit Topping,
    340; variation, Strawberry
    Cobbler, 341
fillings, changing pies to tarts
  and visa versa, 63
flaky, 459; pie pastry, 85. *See also*
  Pastry
Flaky Pie Pastry I, 98; II, 100;
  variations, Citrus Zest, 101;
  Sesame, 101
Flan
  Cream Cheese, Fluted, with
    Fresh Berries, 258
  ring, 46, 63
flavoring and spirits, 13–14
  coffee and espresso, 14
  flavored extracts (almond,
    lemon, orange, etc.), 14
  liqueurs (cordials), brandies,
    liquor and wine, 14
flour(s), meals, and starches,
  2–5; handling, 49–50
  arrowroot, 5
  bleached all-purpose flour, 3
  cake flour, 3, 4
  cornmeal, 4
  cornstarch, 5
  and food processor, 50

instant flour, 4
pastry flour, 4; whole-grain
  (whole wheat), 4
potato flour (potato starch), 5
protein in, 3
rolled oats (oatmeal), 5
self-rising flour, 4
sifting and straining
  (aerating), 50
tapioca, 5; flour, 5
unbleached all-purpose flour,
  3, 4
Flourless Macaroon Tart in
  Almond Nut Pastry, 308
flute, angled, 66; pointed, 71
folding and lightening
  ingredients (mixing
  techniques), 61
food processor, 44
  for chopping nuts, 57
  and flour, 50
  for pastry dough, 86
Ford's, Terry, Green Tomato
  Pie, 198
forked decorative edge for pie
  crust, 67
fraisage, 69, 459
Frangipane, 459
  Plum Tart, Italian, 222; varia-
    tion, Nectarine Tart, 223
Free-Form
  puff pastry, shaping a round,
    175
  Shortbread Tart Pastry, 149
  tart shells, shaping and
    baking, 71–72
  tarts, baking, 62
freezing (frozen) pies, tarts,
  cobblers. *See also* Frozen
  Pies and Tarts
  Bavarian cream and mousse-
    type fillings, 77–78
  fruit pies and tarts, 77
  fruits (unsweetened) for
    baking, 16. *See also* Name of
    Fruit
  meringue shells, 78
  pastry doughs, 78; shaped
    and rolled, 78; unshaped,
    78

pre-baked pastries, 77
thawing, 77
unbaked pastries, 78
wrapping pastries for, 77
French Fruit Tart with Pastry
  Cream, 126; (lesson 4),
  124–25; tips for, 128–29
French-style rolling pins, 87
Fried Apricot Pies, 372;
  variation, Fried Apple, 373
frozen fruits. *See* freezing; Name
  of Fruit
Frozen Pies and Tarts, 344–66
  about, 344–47
  Choco-Nouga Chew Chew
    Tart, 348
  Chocolate-Crusted Raspberry
    Soufflé Pie, 358
  Fudge Walnut Sundae Pie, 357
  Honey Yogurt Tart with Pine
    Nut Crust, 364
  Key Lime Pie with a Twist,
    352
  Krispie Meringue Crust for,
    159
  Pineapple Zabaglione in
    Coconut Almond
    Meringue, 366
  Pistachio 'n Peach Ice Cream
    Pie in Krispie Meringue,
    354
  Sorbet-Frosted Lemon
    Bavarian Tart, 350
  Strawberry Ice Cream Pie,
    Triple, 360
  Tutti-Frutti Amaretti Tart, 362
Fruit(s), *See also* Name of Fruit
  All-, Mincemeat Tartlets, 385
  and berry glossary, 17–40
  canned, 16
  citrus, handling (juicing,
    supreming, zesting), 59. *See
    also* Citrus Fruit,
  Crumble, Autumn, with
    Oatmeal Crunch Topping,
    332; variation, Prune Plum,
    333
  dried, 16. *See also* Dried Fruit
  fanning, 183
  frozen, 16; unsweetened, 16

Pies and Tarts, 176–239; about, 176–77
pies, tips for, 110–11
Summer, Stew of, with Phyllo Rings, 406
Tart, French, with Pastry Cream, 126;(lesson 4), 124–25; tips for, 128–29
tarts, Almond Nut Pastry for, 151
tarts, Open (lesson 3, A Simple Pear), 118–19; tips for, 122–23
tarts with pastry cream, 124–25
testing for moisture (suitability for pies and tarts), 20
Viennese Linzer Tart, Fruity, 236
Fruity Viennese Linzer Tart, 236
Fudge. *See also* Chocolate
Candy Icing, Mississippi Mud Pie with, 312
-Nut Tart, Prickly, 304
Sauce, Warm, 446
Walnut Sundae Pie, 357
fully baked or par-baked crusts for blind-baked shells, 95

GALETTE, 459
Nectarine, 211
Tomato, Pesto, and Goat Cheese, 436
Ganache, 459; Chocolate Sauce, 447
Garnish(es), 452–56. *See also* Sauces and Toppings
Almond Crackle, 454
Candied Citrus Rind, 456
Chocolate Curls and Shavings, 455

Nut Brittle, 452; variation, Candied Whole Nuts, 453
garnishing and decorating pies and tarts, 74–75
equipment for, (decorating comb, pastry bag, tips, etc.), 42, 48
pastry bag, for, 48, 74
spacing a design, 75
squeeze bottle for, 75
gelatin, plain unflavored, 16; blooming and dissolving, 60–61; as stabilizer, 60
Ginger Snaps with Pecans (nut crumb crust), 166
"at a glance" boxes, explained, 76
glass ovenproof pie plates, 45; advantages of, 45
Glazed
Banana Lemon Tart, Steven Santoro's, 188
Nut Tea Tarts, 386
glazes, 459; and sealers (apricot, eggs, jelly, milk and cream, preserves), 72–73
glossary, fruit and berry, 17–40. *See also* Name of Fruit or Berry
gluten, 459
Goat Cheese, Tomato, and Pesto Galette, 436
Goof-Proof Puff Pastry, 172
Gooseberry(ies), 25–26
choosing, 26
Crumble, 334
freezing, 26
history of, 25–26
season available, 25
storing and handling, 26
goosefeather and pastry brushes, 47
Graham Cracker(s)
Crust, Reduced-Cholesterol, 169
with Pecans or Walnuts (nut crumb crust), 166
granulated sugar, 6; measuring, 50

Grape(s), 26–27
freezing, 27
history of, 26
and Pear Pie, Autumn, in Cheddar Pastry, 218
Pie, Creamy Green, 260
season available, 26
storing and handling, 27
varieties, 26–27
graters, equipment for making pies and tarts, 44
Green Gables Bing Cherry Clafoutis, 376
Green Tomato Pie, Terry Ford's, 198
grunt (cobbler), 460

HALL OF FAME RASPBERRY STREUSEL TART, 270
hand mixing for pastry dough, 86
Hazelnuts (filberts)
Amaretti Cookies with (nut crumb crust), 167
Biscotti with (nut crumb crust), 167
oven toasting, 57
skinning toasted, 57
Zwieback with (nut crumb crust), 166
herbs (fresh and dried), 15
high-gluten flour, 142
Honey, 7
-Glazed Crustless Apple Tart, 396
Yogurt Tart with Pine Nut Crust, Frozen, 364
honeydew. *See also* Melons
choosing, 31
Melon and Mascarpone Tart in Chocolate Crumb Crust, 266

hot water bath (bain-maries), 61–62; for oven, 62; for stove, 62
hydrogenated vegetable shortening, 8; measuring, 51

ICE CREAM PIE. *See also* Frozen Pies and Tarts
  Fudge Walnut Sundae, 357
  Pistachio 'n Peach, in Krispie Meringue, 354
  Triple Strawberry, 360
ingredients for pies and tarts, 2–16. *See also* name of ingredient
  canned and frozen fruit, 16
  chocolate, 11–13; handling, 55–56
  citrus fruits, handling, 59
  coconut, toasting, shredding, etc., 58
  dried fruits, 16; handling, 58–59
  eggs, 9–10; handling, 52–54; meringues, making, 54
  fats, 8–9; handling, 51
  flavoring and spirits, 13–14
  flour and other dry ingredients, handling, 49–50
  flours, meals, and starches, 2–4; instant, 4
  gelatin, 16, 60–61
  leavening and stabilizers, 5–6
  lightening and folding, 61
  liquids, 10–11; measuring, 54
  non-wheat flours and meals, 4–5
  nuts, chopping, toasting, etc., 56–58
  nuts and seeds, 15
  phyllo, working with, 64

seasonings, spices, and herbs, 14–15
sugar and other sweeteners, 6–8
sugars and thick syrups, handling, 50–51
whipped cream, about, 60
instant flour, 4
Italian
  Frangipane Plum Tart, 222; variation, Nectarine Tart, 223
  meringue, 460

JALOUSIE (PUFF PASTRY), 460
jams and preserves, 8
Java Eggnog Pie, 288
jellies and preserves as sealers and glazes, 73
juicing citrus fruits, 59
juicy fillings, running over, 72

KEY LIME(S), 28–29. *See also* lime
  choosing, 29
  history of, 28
  Pie, 264
  Pie with a Twist, 352
kitchen scales, 42
kiwifruit (Chinese gooseberries)
  choosing, 27
  history of, 27

season available, 27
storing and handling, 27
Krispie Meringue
  Crust, 159; variation, Krispie Pistachio, 159
  Pistachio 'n Peach Ice Cream Pie in, 354

LARD, 8–9
Lattice
  Crust, Strawberry Rhubarb Pie with, 234
  crusts, 460; making diagonal, traditional, or unwoven, 64–66
  Top, Double-Crust, for Cobblers, 337
leavening, 5–6, 460
  baking powder, 5
  baking soda, 6
  cream of tartar, 6
Leek, Broccoli, and Cheddar Tart, Deep-Dish, 416
lekvar, 460
Lemon(s), 28. *See also* Citrus
  Banana Tart, Glazed, Steven Santoro's, 188
  Bavarian Tart, Sorbet-Frosted, 350
  Chess Pie, Anne Semmes', 248
  Chiffon Pie, 290
  choosing, 28
  Cookies with Walnuts, Pecans, or Almonds (nut crumb crust), 167
  Cream Tart with Candied Peel, 262
  freezing (juice and zest), 28
  history of, 28
  juicing and zesting, 28

Meringue Pie, 114
Meringue Pie (lesson 2),
    112–13; tips for, 116–17
season available, 28
Soufflé Tartlets, Blueberry,
    401
storing and handling, 28
Tea Tarts Smothered with
    Berries, 384
lessons
    Apple Pie, Old-Fashioned
        American, 108
    French Fruit Tart with Pastry
        Cream, 126
    Lemon Meringue Pie, 114
    Pear Tart, A Simple, 120
liaison (bind or thicken), 460
Light and Lean Pies and Tarts,
    393–410
    about, 393–94; tips and tricks,
        395
    Berry-Fruit Cream Pie, 402
    Blueberry Lemon Soufflé
        Tartlets, 401
    Chocolate Velvet Pie with
        Sliced Strawberries, 404
    Crustless Pineapple Cheese
        Pie, 405
    Honey-Glazed Crustless
        Apple Tart, 396
    Pear Crisp, Deep-Dish, with
        Dried Cranberries, 400
    Raspberry Chiffon Pie,
        Rousing, 408
    Stew of Summer Fruits with
        Phyllo Rings, 406
    Stuffed Cinnamon Apple
        Top-Knots, 398
    Tangerine Meringue Pie, 410
lighten (with egg whites or
    cream), 460
lightening and folding
    ingredients, 61
lime(s), 28–29. See also Key Lime
    freezing (juice and zest), 29
    history of, 28
    season available, 28
    storing and handling, 29
    varieties of, 29

lining
    pie plate with pastry, 91
    tart pan with pastry,
        93–94
    tartlet and other little pans,
        70
Linzer
    Crust, Peaches and Berries
        with, Patchwork, 208
    Tart, Fruity Viennese, 236
liqueurs (cordials), brandies,
    liquor and wine for
    flavoring, 14
liquid and dry measures, 42
liquid(s) for pie and tart dough,
    10–11
    cream, 11
    cultured dairy products
        (buttermilk, crème fraîche,
        sour cream, yogurt), 11
    milk, 10–11
    water, 10
Little Tarts, Pies and Turnovers,
    367–92
    about, 367–68
    All-Fruit Mincemeat Tartlets,
        385
    Black Mission Fig and
        Blackberry Tarts,
        Awesome, 380
    Chocolate Soufflé Tartlets,
        Sublime, 374
    Coconut Tarts, Fresh, with
        Buttermilk Custard, 378
    Fried Apricot Pies, 372
    Glazed Nut Tea Tarts, 386
    Green Gables Bing Cherry
        Clafoutis, 376
    Lemon Tea Tarts Smothered
        with Berries, 384
    making little from big, 369
    pans for tartlets, 370–71
    Plum Rosettes on Shortbread,
        392
    Poached Peaches and
        Mascarpone on Cookie
        Saucers, 388
    Pot Pies, Fresh, with Puff
        Pastry Caps (dried fruit
        and apples), 382

Turnovers with Dried Apple
    and Blackberry Filling, 390
"low-fat" fats, 9

MACADAMIA RUM SOUFFLÉ
    TART, 292
Macaroon Tart, Flourless, in
    Almond Nut Pastry, 308
macerating (softening fruit), 58,
    460
Main Attraction Chocolate
    Chip Cookie Pie, 320
Mango(es), 29–30
    "cheeks," about removing, 30
    choosing, 29
    Coulis, 448
    freezing, 30
    history of, 29
    Madness, Snappy, 294
    Pie, Black and Blue, 190
    season available, 29
    storing and handling, 30
    Tart with Blackberries, 200
    varieties of, 29–30; Tommy
        Atkins, most popular, 30
Maple Pecan Apple Crisp, 328
maple sugar, 7; maple syrup, 7
Marcia's Pumpkin Pie in
    Sinfully Rich Pecan Pastry,
    318
margarine, 8. See also fats
    measuring, 51
    temperature of, 51
Mascarpone
    and Melon Tart in Chocolate
        Crumb Crust, 266
    and Poached Peaches on
        Cookie Saucers, 388
Master Crumb Crust, 164; Nut
    Crumb variations (many),
    166–67. See also Nut Crumb
    Crust

meals. *See also* flours, meals, and
    starches
    cornmeal, 4
measures (measuring)
    butter or margarine, 51
    dry ingredients, 42, 49–50
    equipment for making pies
        and tarts, 41
    liquids, 42, 54
    nuts, 58
    sugars (brown, white), 50–51
    syrups, 51
    vegetable shortening and oils,
        51–52
Melon(s) (cantaloupe and
        honeydew), 30
    choosing, 30
    history of, 30
    and Mascarpone Tart in
        Chocolate Crumb Crust,
        266
    season available, 30
    storing and handling, 31
melting
    chocolate in liquids, 56
    dark chocolate (bittersweet,
        semisweet, unsweetened),
        55–56; in double boiler, 55;
        in microwave, 56; in oven,
        56; in water bath, 55;
        milk and white chocolate,
        56
Meringue(s), 460
    Crust, Krispie, 159; variation,
        Krispie Pistachio, 159
    egg whites for, 54
    for garnishing and decorating,
        74
    for Lemon Meringue Pie
        (lesson 2), 115
    making, 54
    Shell, 160; variation, Petite
        Shells, 160
    Shell, Coco-Nutty, 162
    sugars (confectioner' and
        superfine) for, 116–17
    Tangerine, Pie, 410
    -Topped Coconut Pie in
        Coconut Crust, 256
    toppings, tips for, 116–17

"weep-proof," 115
    whipping, 113;
metal pie plates, 45–46
microwave
    for clarifying butter, 52
    for dissolving gelatin, 61
    for melting chocolate, 56
    ovens, 48
Middle Eastern Nut Swirl,
        Orange-Scented, 322
milk
    chocolate, 12
    and cream as glaze for pies
        and tarts, 72
    for pastry dough, 10–11
Mincemeat
    All-Fruit Jalousie, 202
    Tartlets, All Fruit, 385
Mississippi Mud Pie with
        Fudge Candy Icing, 312
mixers, electric, for making pies
        and tarts, 44. *See also* food
        processor
mixing and shaping equipment
        for making pies and tarts,
        41
à la mode, 457
molasses, 7
Mousse(s), 276–77, 460
    Tart, Chocolate Pecan, 282
    -type fillings, thawing, 77–78
Mud Pie, Mississippi, with
        Fudge Candy Icing, 312
Mushroom, Wild, Tart with
        Savory Streusel, 424

NECTARINE(S), 31–32
    choosing, 31
    freezing, 32
    Galette, 211
    history of, 31
    pitting, 32

season available, 31
    storing and handling, 31
    Tart, 223
Nesselrode Pie, New York, 296
1940s All-Butter Pie Pastry, 138
non-wheat flours and meals,
        4–5. *See also* wheat flours
    arrowroot, 5
    cornmeal, 4
    cornstarch, 5
    potato flour (potato starch), 5
    rolled oats (oatmeal), 5
    tapioca, 5; tapioca flour, 5
nonreactive (metal), 460
nonstick cooking spray, 62
notched edge for tart crust, 67
nougatine, 460
Nut(s), 56–58. *See also* Name of
        Nut (Hazelnuts, Pine Nuts,
        Pecans, etc.)
    Brittle, 452; variation,
        Candied Whole Nuts, 453
    chopping, 57; food processor
        for, 57
    Dough, Danish, for Tartlets,
        156
    -Flavored Pastry, 145
    -Fudge Tart, Prickly, 304
    measuring, 58
    nougatine (nut brittle), 460
    Nutty Cornmeal Crust, 154
    oven toasting (almonds,
        hazelnuts, walnuts, etc.),
        56–57
    Pastry, Almond, 151
    Pastry, Pine Nut, 152
    and seeds for baking, 15
    skillet toasting (almonds, pine
        nuts), 57
    skinning (almonds, hazelnuts,
        pistachios), 57
    Swirl, Orange-Scented
        Middle Eastern, 322
    Tea Tarts, Glazed, 386
Nut Crumb Crust, 166–67
    Amaretti Cookies with
        Almonds or Hazelnuts,
        167
    Biscotti with Almonds or
        Hazelnuts, 167

Butter Cookies with Pecans, Walnuts, or Almonds, 166
Ginger Snaps with Pecans, 166
Graham Crackers with Pecans or Walnuts, 166
Lemon Cookies with Walnuts, Pecans, or Almonds, 167
Vanilla Wafers with Toasted Almonds, 166
Zwieback with Almonds or Hazelnuts, 166
Nutty Cornmeal Crust, 154
Chocolate Cream Pie in a, 254
Southern Peach Pie in, 212

OATMEAL (ROLLED OATS), 5
Oatmeal Crunch Topping, Autumn Fruit Compote with, 332
oils and vegetable shortenings, measuring, 51
Olive Oil Pastry, Savory, 145
Onion(s)
Cabbage, and Apple Tart, 418
Sweet, and Roasted Peppers, Bundle of, 426
open fruit tarts (lesson 3), 118–19; tips for, 122–23
Orange(s), 32. See also Citrus
Blood, Rhubarb, and Dried Fruit Tart, Catherine Alexandrou's, 204
choosing, 32
Crème Anglaise, 442
freezing (juice and zest), 32
history of, 32
and Risotto Tart, Sweet, 274
-Scented Middle Eastern Nut Swirl, 322

season available, 32
storing and handling, 32
order sources, 466–67
ornamental pastry cutouts, 68–69
ovenproof glass pie plates, 45; advantages of, 45. See also pans
ovens, convection, conventional, microwave, 48
overworking pastry dough, 86

PAIR OF PEARS TART, 214
pan(s)
baking, shallow, 47
cookie sheet, 47
custard cups, Pyrex, 47
lining with pastry, 70, 91, 93–94
pie, and ovenproof glass pie plates, 45–46, 62–63; standard sizes, list, 46. See also Pies
pie plates, lining with pastry, 91
preparing for baking, 62
ramekins, 47
specialty, 63
tart, 46; tartlet, 47; standard sizes, list, 46. See also Tarts and Tartlets
pandowdy (cobbler), 460
papayas, 32–33
choosing, 33
history of, 32–33
season available, 32
storing and handling, 33
par-baked crusts (for blind-baked pie or tart shell), 95
parchment paper, 457
Pastry, 84–129, 132–58. See also Cookie(-style) Dough;

Crusts; Phyllo Dough; Puff Pastry; Savory Pies and Tarts; Tart Pastry; Sweet Tart Pastry
about doughs 85–87; classic tart, 85; flaky, 85
about tips for making, 97, 134
Almond Nut Pastry, 151
bag for decorating, 48, 74; tips for, 48
baking blind, 70, 91, 94, 95–96; puff pastry shell, 174; tartlets, 370
Cheddar Pastry, 135
cheese for, 9
Chef's Cookie Dough, for Tartlets, 155
chilling shaped, before baking, 94
Chocolate Tart Pastry, 148
Classic Tart Pastry I (Pâte Brisée), 102; Pastry II, 104; variation, Rosemary Chive, 105
cloth and rolling pin cover for, 90
Coconut Pie Pastry, Toasted, 136
cookie-style, rolling and shaping, 69–70; techniques for, 69–70
Cornmeal Pastry, Golden, 150; variation, Cornmeal Pepper, 150
cream cheese and cottage cheese for, 9
Cream Cheese Pastry, 157
cream, fruit tarts with, 124–25
cutouts, ornamental for, 68–69
Danish Nut Dough for Tartlets, 156
docking, 459
equipment, 41–48. See also equipment for making pies and tarts
Flaky Pie I, 98
Flaky Pie II, 100; variations, Citrus Zest, 101; Sesame, 101

Pastry (cont.)
    fraisage for, 69
    Free-Form Shortbread Tart
        Pastry, 149
    for free-form tart shells, 71–72
    freezing rolled and shaped,
        78; unshaped, 78
    hand vs. food processor for,
        86
    individual, converting from
        big ones, 369
    individual (little pies, tarts,
        turnovers), 367–69;
    ingredients for, 2–16. See also
        ingredients for pies and
        tarts
    lining pie plate with, 91
    lining tart pan with, 93–94
    lining tartlet pans with, 70
    liquids for, 10–11
    milk for binding and
        brushing on top, 10
    1940's All-Butter Pie Pastry, 138
    Nutty Cornmeal Crust, 154
    overworking, 86
    Pecan Pastry, Sinfully Rich,
        141
    phyllo, 461; tips for working
        with, 64
    Pine Nut Pastry, 152
    pre-baked, freezing and re-
        heating, 77
    Press-On Butter Pastry, 158
    primer (lessons), 84–105
    problem solving, list, 79
    puff (pâte feuilletée), about,
        170; tips for, 171
    rolling, 86; rolling pins for,
        87; and shaping, 88–89; tips
        for, 89
    salt and pepper in, 14–15
    sealers and glazes for, 72–73,
        96
    shell, baking blind, 95
    shells, baked, with cooked
        fillings, tips for, 116–17
    Short Pastry, for Cobblers, 139
    substituting one for another,
        147

Super Tender Pie Pastry, 137
Sweet Cream Biscuit Dough,
    140
Sweet Tart Pastry (Pâte
    Sucrée), 146
    in tartlet pans with
        removable bottoms, 70;
        without removable
        bottoms, 71, 371
techniques and procedures
    for, 49–79. See also
        techniques and procedures
thawing, pre-baked, 77; rolled
    and shaped, 78; unbaked,
    78
unbaked, freezing and
    baking, 78
Vegetable Oil Pastry, 144–45;
    variations, Nut-Flavored,
    Savory Olive Oil, Whole
    Wheat, 145
water for binding, 10
Whole Wheat Pastry, 142, 145
Wine Pastry, 143; variation,
    Black Pepper, 143
Pastry Cream (crème patissière),
    460
    French fruit tarts with,
        (lesson 4), 124–25; tips for,
        128–29
    French Fruit Tart with, 126;
        Enriched, 127
Pâte Brisée (tart pastry), 460
    Classic Tart Pastry I, 102;
        Pastry II, 104; variation,
        Rosemary Chive, 105
    for tartlet pans without
        removable bottoms, 371
Pâte Feuilletée (Puff Pastry),
    about, 170, 460; tips for, 171
pâte sablé, 460
Pâte Sucrée (Sweet Tart Pastry),
    146, 460
pâtissière, 460
Peach(es), 33–34
    and Berries with Patchwork
        Linzer Crust, 208
    choosing, 33–34

Cobbler, Peachy, 336;
    variation, Peach and
    Blueberry, 337
freestone, peeling and pitting,
    34
freezing, 34
history of, 33
Pie, Dutch, with Butter-
    Crumb Topping, 206
Pie, Southern, in Nutty
    Cornmeal Crust, 212
'n Pistachio Ice Cream Pie in
    Krispie Meringue, 354
Poached, and Mascarpone on
    Cookie Saucers, 388
season available, 33
storing and handling, 34
peak stage (beaten egg whites),
    460
Peanutty Tart, Sam's Favorite,
    298
Pear(s), 34
    and Apricot Strudel Pie, 216
    choosing, 34
    Cobbler, Double-Header, 342
    Crisp with Dried
        Cranberries, Deep-Dish,
        400
    and Grape Pie, Autumn, in
        Cheddar Pastry, 218
    history of, 34–35
    Pair of, Tart, 214
    peeling and coring, 35
    'n' Plum Cobbler, 338
    season available, 34
    storing and handling, 35
    Tart, A Simple (lesson 3), 120;
        variation, Apple Tart, 121
    Tarte Tatin, 230
    varieties of, 35
pearl sugar, 7, 461
Pecan(s)
    Apple Maple Crisp, 328
    Brittle, Banana Cream Pie
        with, 246
    Butter Cookies with (nut
        crumb crust), 166
    Chocolate Mousse Tart, 282
    Chocolate Pie, 315

Ginger Snaps with (nut crumb crust), 166
Graham Crackers with (nut crumb crust), 166
Lemon Cookies with (nut crumb crust), 167
oven toasting, 57
Pastry, Sinfully Rich, 141
Pie, Southern, 314; variation, Chocolate Pecan, 315
Pumpkin Pie in Sinfully Rich Pastry, Marcia's, 318
pectin, 461
pepper, use in pastry, 14–15
Peppers, Roasted, and Sweet Onions, Bundle of, 426
Pesto, Tomato, and Goat Cheese Galette, 436
Petite Shells, 160
Phyllo
    Bundle of Sweet Onions and Roasted Peppers, 426
    dough, 461; tips for working with, 64
    Orange-Scented Middle Eastern Nut Swirl, 322
    Pear and Apricot Strudel Pie, 216
    Rings, Stew of Summer Fruits with, 406
    Spinach Pie, 430
    Stuffed Cinnamon Apple Top-Knots, 398
Pie(s) See also Cobblers; Garnishes; kind of pie (Chocolate, Frozen; Fruit, etc.); Pastry; Sauces; Savory Pies and Tarts; Tarts and Tartlets; Toppings
    about tips for, 303
    baking blind, 91, 94–96
    birds, about using, 239
    browning bottom crust of, 73–74
    chilling before baking, 94
    cutting and serving, 75–76
    equipment, 41–42. See also equipment for making pies and tarts
    freezing, 77–78

garnishing and decorating, 42, 74–75
ingredients for, 2–16. See also ingredients for pies and tarts; name of ingredient
lessons for making, 108, 114. See also Apple; Lemon Meringue
lining (plates), with pastry, 91
little. See Little Pies, Tarts and Turnovers.
measuring, 41
mixing and shaping, 41
pans and plates, 45–46, 62–63; standard sizes, list, 46
reheating, 76
sealers for, 96
serving, 42
storing, 76
to tarts, changing, 63
and tarts, difference between, 85
techniques and procedures for, 49–79. See also techniques and procedures
Pine Nut (pignola)
    Crust, Frozen Honey Yogurt Tart with, 364
    oven toasting, 57
    Pastry, 152
    skillet toasting, 57
Pineapple, 36–37
    Cheese Pie, Crustless, 405
    choosing, 36
    history of, 36
    peeling and coring, 36
    Pie, Tropical, 220
    season available, 36
    storing and handling, 36–37
    Zabaglione in Coconut Almond Meringue, 366
Pistachio(s)
    Crust, Krispie, 159
    'n Peach Ice Cream Pie in Krispie Meringue, 354
    skinning, 57
Plum(s), 37
    choosing, 37
    and Cinnamon Crumbs Tart, 268

history of, 37
'n Pear Cobbler, 338
Rosettes on Shortbread, 392
season available, 37
storing and handling, 37
Tart, Italian Frangipane, 222; variation, Nectarine Tart, 223
varieties of, 37
plumping (dried fruit), 58, 461
Poached Peaches and Mascarpone on Cookie Saucers, 388
pointed flute, for pie crust, 67; for tart shells, 71
poppy seeds, 15
Pot Pies, Fresh, with Puff Pastry Caps (apples and dried fruit), 382
potato flour (potato starch), 5
pots and pans, for making pies and tarts, 45–47
praline, 461
preparing pans for baking, 62
preserves and jams, 8
preserves and jellies as sealers and glazes, 73
Press-On Butter Pastry, 158; freezing, 78
Prickly Fudge-Nut Tart, 304
The Primer (basic techniques), for pastry, pies, and tarts, 82–129. See also Pastry; Pies; Tarts;
procedures for baking. See techniques and procedures
Prune
    and Apricot Crackle Tart, 224
    Plum Crumble, 333
Puff Pastry (pâte feuilletée), about, 170; tips for, 171
    Goof-Proof, 172
    shaping a round free-form, 175
    shell, blind-baking, 174
Pumpkin
    -Apple Chiffon Pie in a Chocolate Crumb Crust, 300

Pumpkin (*cont.*)
  Pie in Sinfully Rich Pecan
    Pastry, Marcia's, 318
Pyrex pans, 45; glass custard
  cups, 47

QUICHE, 461; Lorraine,
  Alsatian, 428

RAMEKINS AND CUSTARD
  CUPS, for pies and tarts, 47
Raspberry(ies), 38. *See also*
    Berry(ies)
  Chiffon Pie, Rousing, 408
  Chocolate-Crusted Soufflé
    Pie, 358
  choosing, 38
  Coulis, 448
  freezing, 38
  history of, 38
  Fruity Viennese Linzer Tart,
    236
  Pie, Summer, with Wine
    Pastry, 226
  Puree, Tart of Strawberries
    in, 232
  season available, 37
  storing and handling, 38
  Streusel Tart, Hall of Fame,
    270
Recipe Roundup (tips for)
  fruit pies, 110–11
  fruit tart with pastry cream,
    128–29

meringue and cooked filling
  pies and tarts, 116–17
open fruit tarts, 122–23
Reduced-Cholesterol Graham
  Cracker Crust, 169
reheating pies, tarts, cobblers,
  76–77
releasing tart from pan, 75
removable bottom tart pans, 70
  cookie-style dough for, 370
Rhubarb, 38–39
  Blood Oranges, and Dried
    Fruit Tart, Catherine
    Alexandrou's, 204
  choosing, 38
  freezing, 39
  history of, 38
  season available, 38
  storing and handling, 39
  Strawberry Pie with Lattice
    Crust, 234
ribbony (beaten mixture), 461
Ricotta Chocolate Ripple Tart,
  272
Risotto and Orange Tart, Sweet,
  274
rolled oats (oatmeal), 5
rolled and shaped pastry
  doughs, 78
rolling pin(s), 43
  American and French, 87
  array of, 43; specialty, 43
  cover "stocking" and pastry
    cloth, 43, 90
rolling and shaping
  cookie-style dough, 69;
    techniques for, 69–70
  pastry, tips for, 88–89
  pies and tarts, equipment for,
    41
rolling surface for pastry, 43,
  87–88
Rosemary Chive
  Crust, Swiss Chard Tart with
    Apricots in, 432
  Tart Pastry, 105
Roy's Apricot Cherry Pie with
  Almond Crunch Topping,
  186
Rum Soufflé Tart, Macadamia,
  292

SALT AND PEPPER FOR
  BAKING, 14–15
Sam's Favorite Peanutty Tart,
  298
Santoro, Steven, Glazed Banana
  Lemon Tart, 188
Sauce(s), 437–51. *See also*
    Garnishes; Toppings
  about, 437–48; tips and tricks,
    439
  Apricot Rum Sauce, 443
  Blueberry Sauce, 443
  Butterscotch Sauce, 444
  Chocolate Ganache Sauce,
    447
  Crème Anglaise, 440;
    variations, Chocolate, 442;
    Cinnamon, 442; Crème
    Anglaise Rapide, 441;
    Orange, 442; with Vanilla
    Bean, 442
  Crème Fraîche, 451
  Currant Sauce, Fresh, 445
  Fudge Sauce, Warm, 446
  Mango Coulis, 448
  Raspberry Coulis, 448
  Strawberry Topping, 449
  Whipped Cream, 450;
    variations, Chocolate
    Whipped Cream, 450;
    Crème Chantilly, 450;
    Stabilized Whipped
    Cream, 450
  Yogurt Topping, 449
Savory Pies and Tarts, 412–36
  about tips and tricks for, 414
  Alsatian Quiche Lorraine,
    428
  Bundle of Sweet Onions and
    Roasted Peppers, 426
  Cabbage, Apple, and Onion
    Tart, 418
  Chesapeake Crab Tart, 420

Corn Custard Pie with Wild Rice, 415
Deep-Dish Broccoli, Leek, and Cheddar Tart, 416
Eggplant Tart with Tomatoes, Greek Olives, and Feta, 422
herbs and spices for, 14 15
Phyllo Spinach Pie, 430
salt and pepper for, 14–15
seeds (caraway, poppy, sesame) for, 15
Smoky Joe's Turkey Tart, 434
Swiss Chard Tart with Apricots in Rosemary Chive Crust, 432
Tomato, Pesto, and Goat Cheese Galette, 436
Wild Mushroom Tart with Savory Streusel, 424
scald (heating slowly), 461
scalloped decorative edges for pie crust, 67; for free-form tart shells, 72
score (press indentation), 461
Scottish shortbread (pastry), 149
sealers
  cookie crumbs, 96
  egg wash, 72, 96
  eggs, 9
  and glazes (apricot, jelly, preserves, etc.), 72–73, 96
  protective coatings for pies and tarts, 96
seasonings (salt and pepper), spices, and herbs, 14–15
seeds and nuts for baking, 15. See also Name of Seed or Nut
self-rising flour, 4
semisweet (bittersweet) chocolate, 12
Semmes, Anne, Lemon Chess Pie, 248
separating eggs, 53
serving pies and tarts, 75–76; equipment for, 42
Sesame Flaky Pie Pastry II, 101
sesame seeds, 15
Shaker Citrus Pie in a Cookie Crust, 250

shallow baking pan, for making pies and tarts, 47
shaping equipment for making pies and tarts, 41
shaping pastry. See rolling and shaping
shell. See Crust; Pastry; Pies; Tarts and Tartlets
Short Pastry, 461; Dough for Cobblers, 139
Shortbread
  Plum Rosettes on, 392
  Tart Pastry, Free-Form, 149
shortening, hydrogenated vegetable, 8
shredding coconut, 58; coconut ribbons, 58
sift (strain or sieve), 461
sifters, 44
sifting and straining dry ingredients, 50
Sinfully Rich Pecan Pastry, 141
skinning toasted nuts (almonds, hazelnuts, pistachios), 57
slump (cobbler), 461
slurry (quick thickener), 461
Smoky Joe's Turkey Tart, 434
Sorbet-Frosted Lemon Bavarian Tart, 350
Soufflé
  Pie, Chocolate-Crusted Raspberry, 358
  Tart, Macadamia Rum, 292
  Tartlets, Blueberry Lemon, 401
  Tartlets, Chocolate, Sublime, 374
Sour Cream 11; Apple Crunch Pie with Dried Fruits, 244
Southern
  Peach Pie in Nutty Cornmeal Crust, 212
  Pecan Pie, 314; variation, Chocolate Pecan, 315
spatulas, offset and rubber, 47
specialty equipment. See also equipment for making pies and tarts
  pans, 63

rolling pins (marble, patterned, Teflon coated, etc.), 43
spices (cinnamon, nutmeg, etc.), 15
Spinach Pie, Phyllo, 430
squeeze bottle, for decorating, 75
stabilize (fortify), 461
stabilizer, gelatin for fillings, 60–61
standard pie and tart pans, 46
starches. See also flours, meals, and starches
  arrowroot, 5
  cornstarch, 5
  potato, 5
  tapioca, 5
steam vents for double-crust pie, 93
Stew of Summer Fruits with Phyllo Rings, 406
storing pies, tarts, cobblers, 76
strainers, for making pies and tarts, 44
Strawberry(ies), 39
  Chocolate Velvet Pie with, 404
  choosing, 39
  Cobbler, 340
  Fig Cobbler with Quilted Biscuit Topping, 340; variation, Strawberry Cobbler, 341
  history of, 39
  Ice Cream Pie, Triple, 360
  Rhubarb Pie with Lattice Crust, 234
  season available, 39
  storing and handling, 39
  Tart of, in Raspberry Puree, 232
  Topping, 449
Streusel, 461
  Savory, Wild Mushroom Tart with, 424
  Tart, Raspberry, Hall of Fame, 270
Strudel Pie, Pear and Apricot, 216

Stuffed Cinnamon Apple Top-
     Knots, 398
substituting doughs, 147
substitutions and equivalents,
     table of, 468–69
sugars, 6–7, 50–51. *See also*
     sweeteners
  brown, 6
  confectioners', 6–7
  granulated, 6
  measuring, 50–51
  pearl, 7
  substitutes, 50
  superfine, 6
Summer
  Fruits, Stew of, with Phyllo
     Rings, 406
  Raspberry Pie with Wine
     Pastry, 226
Sundae Pie, Fudge Walnut, 357
superfine sugar, 6
supreming citrus fruit, 59
Sweet Cream Biscuit Dough,
     140; freezing, 78
Sweet Potato Pie, Smashing, 316
sweet potatoes or yams? 317
Sweet Tart Pastry (Pâte Sucrée),
     146
  Apple Walnut Tart in, 182
sweeteners, 7–8. *See also* sugar
  corn syrup, 7–8
  honey, 7
  jams and preserves, 8
  maple sugar, 7; maple syrup,
     7
  measuring thick syrups, 51
  molasses, 7
Swiss Chard Tart with Apricots
     in Rosemary Chive Crust,
     432
Swiss meringue, 461
syrups, thick (honey, molasses,
     etc.), measuring, 51

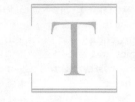

TANGERINE(S), 40. *See also*
     Citrus
  choosing, 40
  freezing (juice and zest), 40
  history of, 40
  Meringue Pie, 410
  season available, 40
  storing and handling, 40
tapioca, 5; flour, 5
Tart(s) and Tartlets. *See also*
     Garnishes; kind of tart
     (Chocolate, Frozen, Fruit,
     etc.); Pastry; Pies; Sauces;
     Savory Pies and Tarts;
     Toppings
  about tips for, 303
  baking blind, 70, 91, 94–96,
     370
  browning bottom crust of,
     73–74
  chilling before baking, 94
  cookie-type dough for, 70
  cutting and serving, 75–76
  equipment, 41–42. *See also*
     equipment for making pies
     and tarts; name of
     equipment
  freezing, 77–78
  garnishing 42; and decorating,
     74–75
  ingredients for, 2–16. *See also*
     ingredients for pies and
     tarts; name of ingredient
  lessons for making, 120, 126.
     See also French Fruit Tarts
     with Pastry Cream; Pear
     Tart
  lining pans for, 70, 93–94
  little. *See* Little Pies, Tarts,
     and Turnovers
  making big ones from little
     ones, 369
  mixing and shaping, 41

  pans, 46–47, 62–63; standard
     sizes, *list*, 46; with and
     without removable
     bottoms, 70–71
  pastry (pâte brisée) for tartlet
     pans without removable
     bottoms, 370–71
  to pies, changing, 63
  and pies, difference between,
     85
  reheating, 76
  releasing from its pan, 75
  serving, 42
  shells, shaping and baking
     free-form, 71–72
  storing, 76
  sweet tart pastry (pâte
     sucrée) for, 146, 460
  techniques and procedures
     for, 49–79. *See also*
     techniques and procedures
Tarte Tatin, Pear, 230
Tavern Toasted Coconut Cream
     Pie, The "Real," 286
techniques and procedures for,
     pies and tarts, 49–79. *See
     also* equipment for making
     pies and tarts
  for bain-maries (water baths),
     61–62
  browning bottom crust, 73
  chocolate, chopping and
     melting, 55–56
  citrus fruit, juicing,
     supreming, and zesting, 59
  coconut, shredding, toasting,
     58
  for decorative pie crust edges,
     66–67
  dried fruits, "plumping," 58
  eggs, 52–54; beating, 53;
     separating, 53; tempering,
     53
  fats, 51–52. *See also* butter;
     margarine; vegetable
     shortening and oil
  flour and other dry
     ingredients, 49–50
  fraisage, 69
  gelatin, 60

glazes, 72
for keeping juice from
running out, 72
for lattice crusts, 64–66
lightening and folding, 61
for lining, shaping and
baking tart and tartlet pans,
70–72
liquids, measuring, 54
making meringues, 54
nuts, 57–58
for ornamental pastry
cutouts, 68–69
phyllo, working with, 64
for rolling and shaping
cookie-style doughs, 69
sealers, 72
sugars and thick syrups, 50;
measuring, 50–51
whipped cream, 60
tempering eggs, 53; egg yolks,
276, 461
tender (pastry), 461
Tender Pie Pastry, Super, 137
thawing frozen (pastry)
Bavarian cream and mousse-
type fillings, 77–78
pastry dough, 78
pies and tarts, 77
pre-baked pastry, 77
unbaked pastries, 78
thermometers, candy and oven,
43
Three Berry Crisp with Butter-
Nut Crumb Topping, 339
Toasted
Coconut Cream Pie, The
"Real" Tavern, 286
Coconut Pie Pastry, 130
toasting coconut, 58; nuts, 56–57
Tomato(es)
Eggplant Tart with, Greek
Olives and Feta, 422
Green, Pie, Terry Ford's, 198
Pesto, and Goat Cheese
Galette, 436
tools for pastry and pie
making, 47–48. See also
equipment for making pies
and tarts; name of tool

top crust for double-crust pie,
92; sealing, 92; steam vents
for, 93
Toppings. See also Garnishes;
Sauces
Almond Crunch, Roy's
Apricot Cherry Pie with,
186
Butter-Crumb, Dutch Peach
Pie with, 206
Butter-Nut Crumb, Three
Berry Crisp with, 339
Cinnamon Crumb for Plum
Tart, 268
Oatmeal Crunch, Autumn
Fruit Crumble with, 332
Quilted Biscuit, Strawberry
Fig Cobbler with, 340
Strawberry, 449
Yogurt, 449
"trap," early American pie, 103
Tropical Pineapple Pie, 220
Turkey Tart, Smoky Joe's, 434
Turnovers with Dried Apple
and Blackberry Filling, 390;
variation, with Cream
Cheese Pastry, 391
Tutti-Frutti Amaretti Tart, 362

UNBAKED PASTRIES, freezing
and baking, 78
unbleached all-purpose flour, 3,
4
unremovable bottoms, tarts
pans with, 71, 371
unshaped pastry doughs, 78
unsweetened
(bitter) chocolate, 11–12
cocoa powder, 12–13; Dutch-
process, 13

VANILLA
as flavoring, 13–14
glaze, 73
Wafers with Toasted
Almonds (nut crumb
crust), 166
vegetable
oils, 9
shortening, hydrogenated, 8
shortenings and oils,
measuring, 51
Vegetable Oil Pastry, 144–45;
variation, Nut-Flavored,
145; Savory Olive Oil, 145;
Whole Wheat, with
Vegetable Oil, 145
freezing, 78
Viennese Linzer Tart, Fruity, 236

WALNUT(S)
Apple Tart in Sweet Tart
Pastry, 182
Butter Cookies with (nut
crumb crust), 166
Fudge Sundae Pie, 357
Graham Crackers with (nut
crumb crust), 166
Lemon Cookies with (nut
crumb crust), 167
oven toasting, 57
Tart, Caramelized, 310
-Topped Blueberry Tart, 238
water baths, hot and cold
(bain-maries), 61–62, 461
water, for pastry dough, 10

"weep-proof," meringue, 115
weeping (egg whites), 461
wheat flours, 3–4. *See also* non-
    wheat flours and meals
  bleached all-purpose, 3
  cake, 4
  instant, 4
  pastry, 4
  self-rising, 4
  unbleached all-purpoe, 4
  whole-grain (whole wheat)
    pastry, 4
Whipped Cream, 450;
    variations, Chocolate
    Whipped Cream, 450;
    Crème Chantilly, 450;
    Stabilized Whipped
    Cream, 450
  for garnishing and decorating,
    74
  tips for, 60
whisks, balloon and sauce, 47
White Chocolate, 12; Caffe Tart,
    284
white sugar, handling, 50;
    measuring, 50
whole-grain (whole wheat)
    pastry flour, 4

Whole Wheat Pastry, 142; with
    Vegetable Oil, 145
Wild Mushroom Tart with
    Savory Streusel, 424
Wild Rice, Corn Custard Pie
    with, 415
wine for flavoring, 14
Wine Pastry, 143; variation,
    Black Pepper, 143
  Summer Raspberry Pie with,
    226
wrapping pastries for freezing,
    77

YAMS OR SWEET POTATOES?,
    317
Yogurt, 11
  Honey Tart with Pine Nut
    Crust, Frozen, 364
  Topping, 449

ZABAGLIONE, Pineapple, in
    Coconut Almond
    Meringue, 366
zesting citrus fruit, 59, 461. *See
    also* Name of Citrus Fruit
Zwieback with Almonds or
    Hazelnuts (nut crumb
    crust), 166

ABOUT THE AUTHOR

CAROLE WALTER studied patisserie and the culinary arts with notable chefs in the United States, France, Austria, Italy, and Denmark. Her book *Great Cakes* won the Best Baking and Dessert Book award from the James Beard Foundation in 1992.